THE NATIONAL UNDER\

COMMERCIAL PROPERTY COVERAGE GUIDE, 6TH EDITION

This newest edition of the *Commercial Property Coverage Guide* delivers everything professionals have come to expect from the powerful guide, including the insights, analysis, and forms needed to be certain that your decisions are based on current language, laws, and interpretations.

Commercial Property Coverage Guide, 6th Edition, includes expert coverage analyses of ISO and AAIS commercial property forms and also addresses MSO commercial property programs as well as certain provisions commonly offered by individual insurance carriers.

In addition, the book you hold in your hands has been fully revised with new content added, including:

- Expert analysis of new endorsements

- Guidance on the MSO commercial property program

- New case law

- Coverage of currently relevant, real-life scenarios

- Discussion of coverage gaps and how they can be filled

- Information on the Terrorism Risk Insurance Program Reauthorization Act of 2015

The new, 6th edition includes up-to-date, multi-jurisdictional legal decisions on the most debated provisions of the commercial property form.

Commercial Property Coverage Guide, 6th Edition is the only resource that enables you to:

- Confidently interpret key aspects of the most recently published ISO commercial property form CP 00 10 10 12, in the context of prior forms and case law

- Access policies *and* analyses of MSO and AAIS commercial property programs

- Quickly develop expertise on current hot topics and real-life coverage application issues

- Follow today's most significant legal developments related to the commercial property insurance form

Finally, you also benefit from expert insights into commercial property developments and issues related to Chinese drywall, green building concepts, marijuana manufacturing and distribution, and income disruption insurance.

For customer service questions or to place additional orders, please call 1-800-543-0874.

Coverage Guides Also Available:

- Businessowners Policy

- Business Interruption

- Condominium Insurance

- Construction Defects Coverage Guide

- Commercial Auto Program

- Commercial General Liability

- Critical Issues in CGL

- Directors and Officers Liability

- Employment Practices Liability

- Guide to Captives and Alternative Risk Financing

- Homeowners

- Insurance Claims: A Comprehensive Guide

- Mold Claims Coverage Guide

- Personal Auto

- Personal Umbrella

- Workers Compensation

6th Edition

Commercial Property Coverage Guide

Commercial Lines Series

George E. Krauss, D.Ed., CPCU, CLU, ChFC, ARM
Donald S. Malecki, CPCU
Susan L. Massmann, CPCU

The National Underwriter Company

Copyright © 2013, 2015 by
THE NATIONAL UNDERWRITER COMPANY
4157 Olympic Blvd.
Suite 225
Erlanger, KY 41018

Sixth Edition, March 2015

International Standard Book Number: 978-1-941627-47-1
Library of Congress Control Number: 2015933884

Printed in the United States of America

ABOUT THE NATIONAL UNDERWRITER COMPANY

For over 110 years, The National Underwriter Company has been the first in line with the targeted tax, insurance, and financial planning information you need to make critical business decisions. Boasting nearly a century of expert experience, our reputable Editors are dedicated to putting accurate and relevant information right at your fingertips. With *Tax Facts*, *Tools & Techniques*, *National Underwriter Advanced Markets*, *Field Guide*, *FC&S®*, *FC&S Legal* and other resources available in print, eBook, CD, and online, you can be assured that as the industry evolves National Underwriter will be at the forefront with the thorough and easy-to-use resources you rely on for success.

The National Underwriter Company
Update Service Notification

This National Underwriter Company publication is regularly updated to include coverage of developments and changes that affect the content. If you did not purchase this publication directly from The National Underwriter Company and you want to receive these important updates sent on a 30-day review basis and billed separately, please contact us at (800) 543-0874. Or you can mail your request with your name, company, address, and the title of the book to:

The National Underwriter Company
4157 Olympic Boulevard
Suite 225
Erlanger, KY 41018

If you purchased this publication from The National Underwriter Company directly, you have already been registered for the update service.

National Underwriter Company
Contact Information

To order any National Underwriter Company title, please

- call 1-800-543-0874, 8-6 ET Monday – Thursday and 8 to 5 ET Friday

- online bookstore at www.nationalunderwriter.com, or

- mail to The National Underwriter Company, Orders Department, 4157 Olympic Blvd., Ste. 225, Erlanger, KY 41018

About the Authors

Authors

Dr. George E. Krauss, CPCU, CLU, ChFC, ARM is President of The Magellan Group, Inc., a risk management and consulting firm located in Pittsburgh, Pennsylvania.

Dr. Krauss holds a B.S.B.A. from Robert Morris University in Pittsburgh, Pennsylvania, and a M.Ed. and D.Ed. in adult education from The Pennsylvania State University in State College, Pennsylvania. His insurance career includes a wide range of positions at both agencies and companies with experience in the sales, marketing, underwriting, and claim fields.

Dr. Krauss holds the professional designations of Chartered Property Casualty Underwriter (CPCU) and the Associate in Risk Management (ARM) from The Institutes and Chartered Life Underwriter (CLU) and the Chartered Financial Consultant (ChFC) designations from The American College. He is a former board member of the Pittsburgh Chapter of the Society of Financial Service Professionals (SFSP), former board member of the Pittsburgh Life Underwriters Association (NAIFA), past president of the Allegheny Chapter CPCU Society, and former National Governor of the East Central Region of the CPCU Society.

In addition to his academic background, Dr. Krauss is an active member of the insurance educational community. He is a frequent instructor at various colleges and insurance education associations. He has also acted as an expert witness and consultant in over 300 legal cases involving various aspects of insurance agent, broker, and insurance company practices as well as policy interpretation. He has authored numerous insurance reference manuals including *Homeowners Analysis*, *Personal Auto Analysis*, *Dwelling Policy and Personal Umbrella Policy*, and the *Businessowners Policy Coverage Guide*. In addition, his property and casualty, life, accident and health, and public adjusting study manuals are among the most widely used sources of producer and adjuster licensing preparation in Pennsylvania.

Donald S. Malecki, CPCU was a principal of Malecki, Deimling, Nielander & Associates, LLC, an insurance, risk, and management consulting firm in Erlanger, Kentucky. He was also president of Malecki Communications Company, the publisher of *Malecki on Insurance*, a monthly newsletter on commercial insurance subjects. He earned his bachelor of science degree, with a major in business and an emphasis on insurance, from Syracuse University. He was also awarded the Korean service medal.

Don was an author and co-author of eleven books, including the *CGL Coverage Guide*, published by the National Underwriter Company, and three textbooks that were used in the American Institute's Chartered Property Casualty Underwriter curriculum.

Don passed away on December 12, 2014.

Don was a recognized insurance and risk management expert who spent over fifty years in the business as a writer, consultant, and expert witness. Don began his career as a fire underwriter and later as a supervising casualty underwriter. He began his writing career when he joined the staff of *FC&S*®, a publication of the National Underwriter Company, in 1966. Don left the National Underwriter Company in 1984 to start his own consulting practice, a practice in which he contributed his every working hour toward understanding the insurance business and sharing that understanding and knowledge with all those seeking his guidance. Don was a recognized expert witness who was called upon numerous times over his career to testify in courts around the country as to the history and meaning of insurance policy language. He was past president of the Cincinnati Chapter of Chartered Property Casualty Underwriters and a member of the Society of Risk Management Consultants.

Author/Editor

Susan L. Massmann, CPCU, is an editor of *FC&S*®, specializing in commercial property and business income coverage. She has been with the National Underwriter Company since 1997.

Ms. Massmann has written for various books and publications, including *The Tools & Techniques of Risk Management and Insurance, Claims* magazine, and *National Underwriter Property & Casualty* newsweekly. She manages the electronic *FC&S*® *Online* and edited a number of publications, including the *Condominium Insurance Coverage Guide* and previous editions of the *Commercial Property Coverage Guide*.

Before joining the National Underwriter Company, she was a paralegal and worked for a court research firm. She is a graduate of Evangel University.

Table of Contents

Introduction

The Building and Personal Property Coverage Form, CP 00 10

A business—from the one person office or store to the highly complex global manufacturing or industrial giant—has property exposures that need to be addressed from the overall risk management perspective. These exposures include owned or leased real property, business equipment, processed or unprocessed inventory, property of others such as commercial bailments or employees' and customers' property, and the stream of income generated by the business. These exposures must be analyzed and appropriately protected through various risk management and loss mitigation techniques.

The foundation of a solid risk management program for these items is a property insurance program that transfers the economic consequence of loss or damage to an insurance company. Smaller commercial businesses usually arrange coverage on a businessowners policy, a packaged set of insurance coverages for the insured's liability, property, and auto exposures. This set of coverages is the topic of *Businessowners Policy Coverage Guide*, another National Underwriter Company title in the Coverage Guides series. Larger concerns will use separate general liability, commercial property, business auto policies, and other specialized coverages such as directors and officers (D&O) and employment practices liability (EPL), tailored to work together.

ISO Building and Personal Property Coverage Form, CP 00 10

The standard contract for insuring building and personal property exposures of commercial insureds is the Insurance Services Office (ISO) Building and Personal Property Coverage Form (BPP), CP 00 10. Introduced by ISO in 1985 as part of the development of simplified language insurance policies, the form has undergone many revisions. To date, there have been nine editions (also sometimes referred to as versions) of the building and personal property coverage form. The form edition date is the last two sets of digits in the form number. For example, the first edition of the policy was issued as the CP 00 10 07 88 edition, meaning it was released for use in July 1988. It currently exists—where approved—as the CP 00 10 10 12 version;

1

it is this edition of the form that is the basis of this book. A historical tracing of the edition dates is relevant because insurance litigation frequently involves loss under previous forms. The following is a listing of all editions released since 1988:

CP 00 10 07 88

CP 00 10 10 90

CP 00 10 10 91

CP 00 10 06 95

CP 00 10 02 00

CP 00 10 10 00

CP 00 10 04 02

CP 00 10 06 07

CP 00 10 10 12

Not all insurance companies employ the standard ISO BPP Form. Some insurers use ISO forms; others add, delete, or modify policy provisions for competitive or other business reasons. The American Association of Insurance Services (AAIS) offers its own commercial property policy, which is similar to the ISO policy but varies in several respects. This form's differences from the ISO policy are discussed in Chapter 14. The Mutual Service Office (MSO) also provides a commercial property program, which is discussed in Chapter 15.

This book's analysis puts the form into context with the rest of the ISO commercial property program and all its basic forms and permutations. In that vein, it is important to keep in mind that a form is a document that commonly includes the insuring agreement, the property covered and not covered, certain extensions, limitations, exclusions, and some conditions. A form in and of itself is not a policy. To have a complete property policy requires the declarations page, the form, the causes of loss form (discussed in Chapters 3 and 4), common policy conditions and commercial property conditions (both of which are discussed in Chapter 5). In addition to the BPP coverage form, this book treats the commercial property program's optional coverages, builders risk and business income coverage forms and options, and the other coverage forms comprising the ISO commercial property program.

The Building and Personal Property Coverage Form, as mentioned, is one building block in the ISO commercial property program. Also, the commercial property program is one part of the protection available for commercial insureds. Property coverage usually must be combined with general liability, crime, fidelity, inland marine, workers compensation, and automobile coverages in order to adequately protect the interests of commercial insureds.

Property Coverage Forms

Virtually all types of commercial businesses are eligible for the Building and Personal Property Coverage Form (BPP). Specialized versions of property coverage forms exist for use with condominium and builders risk exposures. Other coverages, such as legal liability, value reporting, mortgageholders errors and omissions, tobacco sales warehouses, and leasehold interest are available through separate forms. The policy's basic coverage may be modified in many ways through the use of various endorsements that add, remove, or change in some way the terms of the unendorsed policy.

The BPP Form, as mentioned, is not self-contained; it is part of ISO's modular format for a seamless combination with a policy declarations form, an appropriate causes of loss form (basic, broad, or special), two conditions forms (commercial property and common policy), and any appropriate endorsements to form a *coverage part*. A commercial property coverage part may be used as a monoline policy covering property only or combined with other commercial lines coverages (e.g., general liability and commercial auto) to form a commercial package policy.

ISO Rules

The rules for the BPP are in the ISO Commercial Lines Manual (CLM) at Division Five—Fire and Allied Lines. A review of some of the basic rules is helpful in putting the form's use into context. These are the ISO rules, which are often supplemented by the underwriting manuals or guidelines of individual insurance companies.

ISO rules allow policies to be written for a specific term, up to three years—for one year, two years, or three years—or on a continuous basis. A policy may be renewed by renewal certificate or by use of the Commercial Property Coverage Part Renewal Endorsement, CP DS 02. When a renewal certificate is used, it must conform in every aspect to current rules, rates, and forms at the time of renewal.

The Common Policy Conditions Form, IL 00 17, is used with all policies. This form contains six conditions that must be incorporated into any policy written and that apply to all the policy's coverages. Most of these common policy conditions are restatements of provisions of the standard fire policy, which meet the statutory requirements of the states for writing property insurance. The conditions included in IL 00 17 are cancellation, changes, examination of your books and records, inspections and surveys, premiums, and transfer of rights and duties.

Commercial Property Conditions Form, CP 00 90, is also attached to all policies, except when Mortgageholder's Errors and Omissions Coverage Form, CP 00 70, is the only form applicable to commercial property coverage. CP 00 90 contains the following provisions: concealment, misrepresentation, or fraud; control of property; more than one coverage applying to loss; legal action against the company; liberalization; no benefit to bailee; other insurance; policy period; coverage territory; and subrogation.

Interstate accounts may be written on the same policy. One policy may be written to cover locations in more than one state. The coverage may be property or business income and may cover on either a specific or blanket basis. Such a policy is subject to the rules of the state in which the insured's largest-valued location or headquarters is located or where the insurance is negotiated.

Where contributing insurance is an issue—coverage is divided between two or more insurers on a percentage basis—Contributing Insurance endorsement, CP 99 20, may be attached. This endorsement provides that the insurance company's liability on any loss will not exceed its percentage of total coverage. If there are two policies covering a piece of property, one with a limit of $70,000 and the other with a limit of $30,000 ($100,000 total coverage), the first insurer would be liable for only 70 percent of the total of any loss.

ISO rules also call for protective services or devices to be required. Where this is the case, the policy must be endorsed to require that the company be notified if the devices or services are discontinued or out of service using the Protective Safeguards endorsement, IL 04 15. The endorsement can include automatic sprinkler systems, automatic fire alarms, security services, and security contracts. The Burglary and Robbery Protective Safeguards endorsement, CP 12 11, may also be required.

Underwriting Property Risks

Insurance practitioners use a mnemonic to express the four major areas evaluated when underwriting a risk: COPE. This refers to type of *construction* (what the building is made of), *occupancy* (how the insured uses the building), *protection* (fire protection, such as sprinklers or proximity to fire department service), and *exposure* (such as construction of nearby buildings and how those buildings are used). Together, these indicate the acceptance or nonacceptance of a building risk.

ISO identifies seven different types of construction: frame, joisted masonry, noncombustible, masonry noncombustible, modified fire resistive, fire resistive, and mixed. In addition to the construction of the building itself, the underwriter also looks at the floors, roofs, and partitions. The area of the building and any unprotected openings are also considered.

The use of firewalls between portions of a building can greatly reduce the rate for property insurance. The area between firewalls is a fire division. Fire divisions prevent the spread of fire from one section of a building to another. The lack of fire walls can have an adverse effect on the rate charged. For example, a shopping mall had been a one-story structure with two-story anchor stores at each of the corners. The one-story portion was divided by firewalls into several fire divisions, in effect creating several small exposure units. A remodeling project added a second story over the one-story section. The firewalls were not extended up and through the new second story. The mall went from being several small fire divisions to being one big fire division. Even though the mall was equipped with a sprinkler system and was masonry noncombustible construction, the rate for property insurance increased substantially.

Occupancy refers to the use of the structure. A building that houses fireworks will likely pay a higher rate for property insurance than the office building next door.

Protection refers to the kind and quality of protection, both public and private, available to a structure. Private protection ranges from fire extinguishers and sprinkler systems to a private fire department. Only the biggest of companies (such as huge manufacturers) have their own fire departments.

Towns and cities receive a protection class code based upon several factors: the firefighting equipment, the training of the firefighters, the mix of full-time and volunteer firefighters, and the local water supply. Class codes range from one to ten, with one being the best and ten being a risk with no responding fire department within five miles. Classes two through five require all full-time firefighters. Classes six, seven, and eight can be a mix of full-time and volunteer. Class nine is typically all volunteer, and class ten may not have any fire department at all. One issue that many older cities are facing is the downgrading of their fire protection classes, due mainly to the aging of their infrastructure, specifically the water supply apparatus. As the cities get older, many are experiencing a drop in water pressure. Combine the lower water pressure with more and taller buildings, and a problem arises in the efficacy of the fire fighting.

Exposure refers to external exposure of the building. In other words, what is next to the insured structure? In the previous example, the office building next to the fireworks warehouse may pay a higher rate than a comparable office building in an office park elsewhere in the same city. The office building faces a greater chance of loss from fire at the fireworks warehouse.

The National Underwriter Company Coverage Guides

This work is one of a number of books published by The National Underwriter Company reviewing and analyzing individual insurance forms. Other titles in the Coverage Guide series include *Personal Auto, Homeowners, Personal Umbrella, CGL, Business Auto, Businessowners, Directors and Officers Liability, Employment Practices Liability, Workers Compensation,* and *Cyber Liability.* Although business income, also referred to as time element coverage, is discussed as a part of the commercial property program in this book in Chapter 7, a new comprehensive treatment of this critical coverage can be found in *Business Income Coverage Guide.* Additional forms and issues are treated in the *FC&S Bulletins* and *FC&S Online.*

Chapter 1

The Insuring Agreement: Covered and Not Covered Property

Section A. Coverage

Apart from the policy's declarations page, which identifies who is covered (named insured), the insurer providing the coverage, the agent of record, the period of coverage, the nature of covered property, and the covered causes of loss (perils), the first place one looks in determining coverage is the insuring agreement. It is the insuring agreement that is discussed first when determining coverage under an insurance policy. Known also as the broad grant of coverage, the insuring agreement is where the insurer pledges, in broad terms, not only the nature of the loss to be covered—direct physical loss or damage—but also the statement that coverage is to apply to certain covered property from any covered causes of loss. What needs to be addressed, following analysis of the insuring agreement, is the nature of covered property and, of course, the property not covered. Once that has been established, it is important to discuss the meaning of "direct physical loss or damage" and the causes of loss or damage covered and not covered.

What Is Direct Physical Loss or Damage?

For as long as the insuring agreement of property policies has applied to direct physical loss or damage it seems that defining what this phrase means would not be difficult. The problem, of course, is that the meaning of *direct physical loss or damage* is not often sought in a vacuum but, instead, dependent on the facts of each event. In a vacuum, the contractual obligation to pay for direct physical loss or damage to covered property means that the policy responds to loss or damage directly caused by an insured peril (or covered caused of loss).

Directly caused means there is a causal relationship between the event immediately responsible for the loss or damage (an insured event such as fire, theft, vandalism, or windstorm) and the damage done to property that is included within the policy meaning of *covered property* (building, structure, or business personal property). For example, high winds in a thunderstorm blow shingles off a roof—that damage is directly caused. Contrast that to the same storm knocking out power to the building, allowing refrigerated chemicals to spoil. That damage—to the chemicals— is consequential. The cause of the loss was not the wind but the heating of the chemicals. If loss or damage is not direct, then it is consequential; it is the distinction between the two that dictates whether damage to property is covered. (There are endorsements and coverages for some consequential losses—see Chapter 13, Commercial Property Endorsements.)

While the meaning of *direct physical loss or damage* in a vacuum may be helpful, when coverage is not disputed and in making one's argument for or against coverage, much, as mentioned, will hinge on the facts. In that vein, this insuring agreement can be very troublesome.

Physical loss is not synonymous with damage or physical damage. Too often, when reference is made to this insuring agreement, physical loss is not mentioned as if it does not exist. It does exist, and it is different from physical damage. A case that appears to clarify this matter is *Manpower, Inc. v. Insurance Co. of the State of Pennsylvania*, No. 08C0085, 2009 WL 3738099 (E.D. Wisc. Nov. 3, 2009), which involved a dispute over a partial collapse of an office building in Paris, France. The question in dispute was whether the named insured suffered a loss within the meaning of the policy, which covered "all risk of direct physical loss of or damage to covered property." The named insured argued that the collapse rendered its property physically inaccessible and therefore resulted in a direct physical loss. The insurer contended that the named insured did not sustain a covered loss because the collapse did not physically damage, move, or alter the property in any way.

The court rejected the insurer's argument that a peril must physically damage property in order to cause a covered loss. The policy covered physical losses in addition to physical damage, explained the court, and if a physical loss could not occur without physical damage, then the policy would contain surplus language. The court said that a contract must, where possible, be interpreted so as to give reasonable meaning to each provision without rendering any portion superfluous. Thus, the court added that *direct physical loss* must mean something other than *direct physical damage*. Indeed, the court said that if "direct physical loss required physical damage, the policy would not cover theft, since one can steal property without physically damaging it; and ISOP did not contend that the policy did not cover theft."

Interestingly, *Ward General Ins. Services, Inc. v. Employers Fire Ins. Co.*, 114 Cal. App. 4th 548 (Cal. Ct. App. 2003) involved loss of stored computer data not accompanied by loss or destruction of the storage medium—a loss not covered by the policy. The court gratuitously explored the meaning of *direct physical loss* versus *damage to covered property* without reference to direct physical damage, even though this was not raised by the named insured.

Specifically, the court explained that in considering the phrase *direct physical loss or damage to covered property*, it wondered if this phrase should be interpreted to mean that coverage is afforded both for "damage to covered property" and for "damage to covered property, whether the damage is physical or nonphysical, direct or indirect." The court stated that it did not adopt this interpretation because it constituted a strained and clumsy meaning—not an ordinary and popular meaning.

The court went on to say that most readers expect the first adjective in a series of nouns or phrases to modify each noun or phrase in the following series, unless another adjective appears. The court offered the following example: If a writer were to say, "The orphanage relies on donors in the community to supply the children with used shirts, pants, dresses and shoes, the reader expects the adjective 'used' to modify each element in the series of nouns, 'shirts,' 'pants,' 'dresses,' and 'shoes.' The reader does not expect the writer to have meant that donors supply 'used shirts,' but supply 'new' articles of other types of clothing." Thus, the court concluded, "We construe the words 'direct physical' to modify both 'loss of' and 'damage to.'"

Courts have ruled on a variety of losses that do not meet the criteria for being considered direct physical loss or damage. In *Source Food Technology, Inc. v. U.S. Fidelity and Guar. Co.*, 465 F.3d 834 (8th Cir. 2006), the court held that there was no direct physical loss to property when a U.S. embargo on Canadian beef due to mad cow disease prevented an insured from receiving beef products needed for its business. The particular beef for the insured's shipment was not contaminated.

In *Port Authority of New York and New Jersey v. Affiliated FM Ins. Co*, 311 F.3d 226 (3d Cir. 2002), plaintiffs argued that asbestos contamination and expenses incurred due to the abatement of asbestos-containing materials constituted physical damage to structures.

The lower court determined that physical loss or damage could be found only if the imminent threat of the release of asbestos existed, or if an actual release occurred and resulted in contamination that resulted in eliminating or destroying the property's function. Just the presence of asbestos was not enough for coverage to apply.

The appeals court said that "unless asbestos in a building was of such quantity and condition as to make the structure unusable, the expense of correcting the situation was not within the scope of a first party insurance policy covering 'physical loss or damage.'"

Caused by versus Resulting from

The words *caused by* refer to the proximate cause. The textbook definition is "the unbroken chain of events from the cause to the result." A legal definition of *proximate cause*, taken from *Black's Law Dictionary*, Fifth Edition, is "that which, in a natural and continuous sequence, unbroken by any efficient intervening cause, produces injury, and without which the result would not have occurred." A simplified example is when lightning strikes a building, which causes a fire, the fire in turn produces smoke damage, with further damage occurring when the sprinklers are activated. Here, the cause that set the result into motion was lightning. As long as the proximate cause of loss is a covered cause, the resulting loss should be covered. Sometimes there can be two causes converging on covered property, one of which is covered and other not covered. In such a case, it is the efficient proximate or predominate cause that dictates whether coverage applies.

The words *resulting from* refer to ensuing loss. If, for example, a policy excludes direct physical loss or damage by mold, and mold is created following defective construction (also excluded) that allows water to seep through the walls, there is no coverage. Simply stated, damage resulting from a covered cause would be covered by a resulting loss provision, whereas damage resulting from an excluded covered cause remains excluded. Where reference to *resulting loss* can get complicated is when an exclusion makes an exception to an ensuing loss not otherwise excluded. There are a number of such ensuing loss clauses in the causes of loss forms. This is a complex subject in part because of the number of disputes and litigation this subject has generated over the years, particularly in relation to builders risk policies. Also, policy provisions dealing with ensuing loss can vary and so, too, can the issues and results.

Section A.1. Covered Property

The BPP form covers an insured's property exposures; there is no liability coverage under the policy. Even what appears to be a type of liability coverage—coverage for the property of others in the insured's possession—is first-party property coverage. It is not the insured's liability for damage to property of others that is covered under the policy, but property coverage for a specific class of property—property of others on the insured premises. This excludes any coverage for loss of use claims arising out of loss or damage to property of customers, employees, or invitees.

The following three types of property are included under the BPP form:

1.   building

2.   the named insured's (your) business personal property

3.   personal property of others, in certain circumstances

Coverage must be selected on the policy declarations page. A limit must also be shown in the declarations for that type of property to be covered; for example, the insured may carry $1,000,000 in building limits, $200,000 in business personal property limits, and $20,000 for property of others. The policy can be written to cover only buildings or only contents (business personal property); property of others coverage must also be separately stated on the declarations except when the property is leased under contract.

This section of the policy (A. Coverage) contains a provision (A.1) that describes covered property and another section (A.2) that describes property not covered. In policy terms, *covered property* means the type of property described in Section A.1., and limited in A.2., Property Not Covered, if a limit of insurance is shown in the declarations for that type of property.

Section A.1.a. Building Coverage

The BPP form covers the buildings and structures shown in the declarations. For that reason, careful underwriting requires more than a street address to describe an insured's premises. An appropriate statement might be "The premises at 500 Main St., the principle building, two maintenance sheds, a processing pool (pools are structures), and a garage."

A tenet of insurance contract interpretation is that words and phrases in insurance policies are governed by their common dictionary definition unless otherwise specifically defined within the policy. The BPP form contains only three defined terms: *fungus*, *stock*, and *pollutants*. Therefore, these terms have the meaning that is specifically given to them in the form; all other terms will be given a common usage meaning. In the absence of a policy definition, if there is a common usage meaning that is more favorable to the insured than the meaning put forth by the insurer, the insured will be allowed the more favorable definition.

Building means the building or structure described in the declarations. (It is important to keep in mind here that in some of the policy provisions, the word *building* does not also include structure.) As neither *building* nor *structure* is further defined in the policy, a common meaning will be implied. Inasmuch as the building or structure must be described in the declarations, not much argument can arise regarding what is a building or structure in terms of policy interpretation. The building or structure described in the declarations is the covered item of property. The issue is when there might be multiple buildings at one address; all need to be described separately in the declarations.

However, the term *structure* is broader than the term *building*, and some items that might not readily suggest themselves as buildings could be named in the declarations, thereby affording coverage. These items might include, among others, swimming pools, garages, solar arrays, wind turbines, or semi-permanent items such as a wooden stage floor covered by a tent that is used for events at a private club. The important point is that such items be listed in the declarations. Failure to list all structures for which coverage is desired will result in no insurance recovery on loss to undeclared structures.

Some confusion can arise regarding the meaning of the phrase "covered property at the premises described in the declarations." Must the covered property be described, or just the premises? The Supreme Court of Montana tackled similar language in *Park Place Apartments, L.L.C. v. Farmers Mut. Ins. Co.*, 247 P.3d 236 (Mont. 2010).

Following a heavy snowfall, Park Place Apartments' carport collapsed and buried numerous vehicles. Farmers Mutual denied the claim, stating that the carport was not listed separately on the declarations page of the policy. Park Place argued that, under the plain language of the policy, all buildings and structures at the address listed on the declarations page were covered property at the premises.

The declarations page provided space for listing locations, building numbers, and descriptions of the buildings. Park Place asserted that "the insured premises are defined as the property address, and that in any case, the limit of insurance for the apartment building included the carport."

The court said the insurer's flawed logic stated that "the phrase means that coverage is limited to the *buildings and structures described in the Declarations*, as opposed to buildings and structures *at the premises described in the Declarations*." The court stated that the insurer seemed to ignore "at the premises" in the definition of "covered property."

The court held that the insured's interpretation—all buildings and structures at the described premises are covered—was more reasonable and that the insurer's interpretation could lead to an ambiguity.

Nonfunctioning Water Tower as Covered Property?

An insured hotel suffered extensive fire damage. On top of the hotel was a nonfunctional water tower valued at about $40,000. The insurance company adjuster believed the cost of the water tower should not be included in the insurance settlement because it was not functional and therefore had no value. The agent believed that the insurer should pay the $40,000 cost to replace it because (1) there could have been an alternate use for the tower; (2) the tower was a part of the building and did have a value even though at the time it was nonfunctional (and could have been considered decorative); and (3) when a company insures a structure, it insures the complete structure whether a portion of it is functional or not. The issue is how the tower should be adjusted.

The Building and Personal Property form does not refer anywhere to functional or nonfunctional property. It refers only to covered and not covered property. Covered property includes the building. The water tower, being attached to the building as either a fixture or permanently attached machinery and equipment, qualifies as covered property. If a coinsurance requirement is shown in the policy declarations, and if the insured has met the coinsurance requirement for insuring to value, the building, including the water tower, is covered to the full limit of the policy. If the insured has not met the coinsurance requirement, the penalty will apply, lowering the amount available to cover the loss and capping recovery.

An attempt to deny coverage for the tower due to its present nonfunctional state is analogous to denying coverage for an unused second story of a building. It would not be correct to reduce the value of a building due to the nonuse of a portion of that building. It is just as incorrect to reduce coverage for the loss due to whether the building structure is functional. The tower should be included in the insurance recovery. How to value the water tower in the event of loss should have been determined at the time of underwriting the account.

The use of the singular (building or structure) rather than the plural (buildings or structures) does not mean that the policy cannot be used to cover more than one building or structure. Using the singular construction avoids confusion after policy inception in the event the insured builds additional buildings or structures that were not on the premises at the time of the original policy. The phrase *buildings or structures* might be interpreted (or misinterpreted) by insureds (and courts) as implying that *all* buildings and structures on the insured premises are covered, regardless of the qualifying language, "described in the Declarations."

Building coverage is not limited to realty. The Building and Personal Property form also provides coverage for the following five other types of property under the building portion:

1. **Completed additions.** The policy covers the new portion if the insured has added onto the described building. This provision offers automatic coverage for new additions during the term of the policy; however, it can also raise a coinsurance issue if the overall amount of insurance is not adjusted to account for the increased values. The insured should be counseled to report additions to buildings that affect the value.

2. **Fixtures, including outdoor fixtures.** The policy also covers fixtures under the building limit. *Merriam-Webster's Dictionary* defines *fixtures* as "something that is fixed or attached (as to a building) as a permanent appendage or as a structural part <a plumbing *fixture*>." *Merriam-Webster's* also provides another meaning: "an item of movable property so incorporated into real property that it may be regarded as legally a part of it." For example, a light mounted into a brick wall on a patio is a fixture; a table lamp on a pool side table attached to the wall only by its electric cord is not a fixture. A hot tub built into a hotel suite such that its removal would destroy the bathroom is a fixture. Were it not for the fact that underground pipes, flues, or drains are not covered property, an underground sprinkler system would also fall into this category of a permanently installed fixture.

    In determining whether an object is a fixture and thus realty, a trade fixture and thus personal property, or simply personal property, the courts generally rely on some version of what the court in *Wayne County v. Britton*, 563 N.W.2d 674 (Mich. 1997) referred to as the *Morris* test (*Morris v. Alexander*, 175 N.W.264 [Mich. 1919]): that is, "property is a fixture if (1) it is annexed to the realty, whether the annexation is actual or constructive; (2) its adaptation or application to the realty being used is appropriate; and (3) there is an intention to make the property a permanent accession to the realty." Constructive annexation to realty means that removal of the personal property would leave the personal property so unfit for use that it would be unable to be used elsewhere.

    In *Mouser v. Caterpillar, Inc.*, 336 F.3d 656 (8th Cir. 2003), the court held that a rubber mixer in the Caterpillar plant was a fixture because it met all three elements of the *Sears* (*Sears, Roebuck & Co. v. Seven Palms Motor Inn, Inc.*, 530 S.W.2d

695 [Mo. 1975]) test, which includes the following criteria: "annexation to the realty, adaption to the use to which the realty is devoted, and intent of the annexor that the object become a permanent accession to the freehold." The court noted that Missouri adopted the constructive annexation doctrine, which states that "a particular article, although not permanently attached to the land, 'may be so adapted to the use to which the land is put that it may be considered an integral part of the land and constructively annexed thereto.'" Applied to the mixer in an industrial setting, the court said, the doctrine is sometimes called the integrated industrial plant rule. Under this rule, the court found that the rubber mixer and its stop pin mechanism were integral to the plant's rubber mixing system and that the way the mixer had been incorporated into the plant's operations satisfied the intent and adaptation requirements, so they were fixtures and part of the real property.

Lawn Tent as a Fixture?

A country club has a tent that it uses for outdoor events such as receptions and dances. This tent has permanent solid flooring to which the tent is attached. The tent is dismantled each year during the winter and stored.

The tent was damaged by fire, a covered cause of loss. The insurance agent maintained that it is a fixture, and as such is covered under building coverage. The adjuster saw it otherwise, arguing that the tent is business personal property, and, as such covered under the contents coverage.

The tent is not a fixture. It is a structure. Not all structures are fixtures. It is not affixed to the building or to the realty and therefore is not covered under building coverage unless it is listed in the policy declarations as a covered structure. The tent is business personal property and is covered under the contents section.

---

3. **Permanently installed machinery and equipment.** The BPP form's building coverage also applies to permanently installed machinery and equipment. This could include drive-on scales, pulleys, hydraulic lift systems, and similar property. The form does not define *permanently installed*, but *install* commonly means "to set up for use or service," and *permanently* means "continuing or enduring without fundamental or marked change; stable."

An item does not have to become a part of the structure of the building for it to be considered permanently installed. This may become important when contents coverage limits have been depleted or exhausted, but building coverage limits have not. One such case where the contents coverage limits were inadequate and attention turned to seeking coverage under the building limit is *Amery Realty Co. Inc. v. Finger Lakes Fire and Cas. Co.*, 947 N.Y.S.2d 630 (2012). The named insured owned a building that was damaged by fire. The second floor of the building contained apartments, and the first floor contained two spaces for retail stores and a self-service Laundromat owned and operated by the named insured and open to the public. At the time of the fire, the limit on the building was $829,000 and the contents limit was $50,000. With the laundry equipment valued at $60,723 and the insurer offering its contents limit of $50,000, the named insured disputed such settlement, which led to litigation. Included as part of the insurance on the building was "permanent fixtures, machinery and equipment forming a part of or pertaining to the services of the building or its premises." Coverage on business personal property, on the other hand, included "furniture and fixtures...machinery and equipment not servicing the building... [and] all other business personal property owned by...and used in the...business."

In support of its position that the laundry equipment was insured under Coverage A, buildings, the named insured submitted an affidavit opining that because the laundry equipment was hard-wired into the utilities systems of the building, it was part of the "structural integrity of the laundry walls" and, therefore, constituted fixtures forming a part of, and pertaining to the services of, the building. The insurer, on the other hand, produced expert evidence from an independent adjuster that the laundry equipment neither formed a part of, nor pertained to, service of the building. According to the court, the remaining evidence of the insurer supported the finding that the laundry equipment was property used by the named insured solely in the business of the Laundromat and was not used by the named insured in its capacity as a landlord to service the apartments. Coverage, therefore, applied under the contents limit, which was inadequate.

Similarly, in *The Prytania Park Hotel Limited v. General Star Indemnity Co.*, 179 F.3d 169 (5th Cir. 1999), the court, applying Louisiana law, said that by law "custom-made armoires, night stands, entertainment centers, chests of drawers, desks, wall mirrors, and luggage racks, which were screwed or bolted to hotel walls, were articles of 'furniture,' not fixtures for purposes of property policy that covered only actual cash value of furniture and fixtures as business personal property, but covered full replacement value of permanently installed fixtures."

The insured must be careful in declaring values for limit-setting purposes. If the insured makes a claim for permanently installed machinery and equipment, all permanently installed machinery and equipment must then be considered for coinsurance purposes. Carrying an adequate limit on the building but not on business personal property might lead to serious coinsurance penalties in the event of a loss.

Note that permanently installed machinery or equipment could be covered under building coverage or the business personal property coverage, whichever is more favorable to the insured.

4. **Personal property used to maintain the building.** Personal property that the insured owns and uses to service or maintain the building or structure or its premises is covered under the building coverage section. Because of the use of the word *including* in the lead-in to the section, the policy contains a nonexclusive list, by way of example, of such equipment: fire extinguishing equipment; outdoor furniture; floor coverings; and appliances used for refrigerating, ventilating, cooking, dishwashing, or laundering. This category might include many other types of personal property, such as a golf cart used to carry items around the premises, lawn mowers, or snow blowers. The list is illustrative, not comprehensive.

5. **Additions under construction or alteration and repairs to the building or structure.** In-progress construction, alteration, and repairs are covered if no other insurance covers the property, such as a builder's risk form. These items, as well as materials, equipment, supplies, and temporary structures within 100 feet of the described premises used for making additions, alterations, or repairs to the building or structure are also covered under the building section of the policy. This section would provide coverage for building supplies, tools, and the like involved in the project, but it would not cover new construction.

The BPP form's other insurance provision provides for a pro rata or excess payment of loss if other insurance exists. Other insurance cooperation does not apply to additions, alterations, or repairs in progress. Other insurance in this special case rules out coverage of this property entirely under this form. This points out the distinction between the commercial property policy's incidental coverage for smaller repairs or new construction projects and the more appropriate builder's risk insurance for new building and major construction.

While the BPP form does not state that materials, supplies, and equipment must be owned by the insured, the insured must have an insurable interest in order for these items to be covered under the insured's policy. If a contractor working for the insured leaves a backhoe on the premises with the keys in the ignition and it is stolen, the insured's commercial property policy will not respond, as the insured has no insurable interest in the property. If, however, the backhoe was leased to the insured and the insured was legally liable for it, the insured would have an insurable interest and coverage applies.

Section A.1.b. Your Business Personal Property

In addition to building property, the BPP form also covers the insured's business personal property. Business personal property is enumerated in this policy and, in addition to these specified types of property, includes "all other personal property owned by you and used in your business." This broad characterization of property allows for a wide interpretation of what is covered under the contents portion of the policy.

The BPP form covers business personal property that is located in or on the building or structure described in the declarations or in the open (or in a vehicle) within 100 feet of the building or structure or within 100 feet of the premises described in the declarations, whichever distance is greater. *In the open* includes property in bales or otherwise stored in the open, as well as that stored in open sheds. Reference to *structure* was added with the 2012 revisions, presumably to encompass, to the extent coverage otherwise applies, to a structure that is not a building.

Meaning of *Premises*

The BPP form covers business personal property including property in the open within 100 feet of the premises. *Premises* is not restricted to the building but includes the grounds, parking lot, and so on that are part of the property on which the building is located, extending to the perimeters of the property.

Thus, coverage applies to property temporarily stored within 100 feet of the premises on, for instance, an adjoining vacant lot awaiting movement onto the insured's property. In the absence of a more restrictive definition in the policy itself, the dictionary definition of *premises* is "a tract of land with the buildings thereon" or "a building or part of a building, usually with its appurtenances (as grounds)," applies. But grounds should not be thought of so broadly as to include any amount of acreage on which a building might be situated. The grounds are those that pertain to the service of the building.

Inasmuch as the term *premises* is a broader term than *building*, coverage for property off the insured's premises is provided as long as the property is located within 100 feet of the premises. For example, the insured's business personal property in a car parked across the street from the insured's business is covered as long as the car is parked within 100 feet of the insured's premises.

One of the potential problems with the footage limitation is when the BPP form is issued to a tenant of a building consisting of multiple occupancies and the tenant's premises is described as a suite or room. If the suite or room is on the upper floors of the building, the 100-foot radius for coverage of property might be inadequate, as opposed to when the tenant's premises is described as a certain building number or address. In light of this possible limitation confronting some tenants, the policy was amended so that coverage is extended 100 feet from the building or structure or within 100 feet of the premises described in the declarations, whichever of the two is the greater of the distances.

The 2012 revision still would not have been of any benefit to the business in *Evergreen Nat. Indem. Co. v. Tan It All, Inc.*, 111 S.W.3d 669 (Tex. Ct. App. 2003). Tanning equipment was stolen from a Tan It All (TIA) truck, while parked in the common area of the shopping center designated by the landlord. At the time of the theft, the truck was parked 280 feet from the front entrance of the salon (Suite C-5) where the premises was described as a street address and a suite number. TIA contended that the policy covered business personal property within 100 feet of any portion of the shopping center. The court ruled in favor of the insurer. In doing so, the court stated that had the parties intended to encompass the entire shopping center, they would not have inserted "Suite C-5" into the description of covered property.

Meaning of *Property in the Open*

As mentioned earlier, *property in the open* includes property in bales, or otherwise stored in the open, as well as in open sheds. Does this mean that property within containers would be considered as property in the open or does it mean that it is only the containers that are in the open? One would think that if the property describes and places a value on the contents of what is within one or more containers, those contents would be considered covered property. But are such contents considered to be in the open?

Although not directly impacting on the kind of commercial property policy discussed here, a court decision that can have an influence on loss of property while in the open, that is worth noting, is *QBE Specialty Insurance Co. v. FSI, Ind.*, No. 3:09cv435, 2011 WL 1655591 (W.D. N.C. May 2, 2011). After the insurer issued a commercial lines policy, thieves broke into the named insured's premises and stole an intermodal shipping container filled with computer monitors. The monitors were never recovered, but the container was found. The named insured made a claim under its policy for theft of the container's contents.

The issue before the court was whether the commercial property coverage provision of the commercial lines policy extended coverage for loss of the contents stored on the named insured's premises. The form on which the applicable provision was written read in part: "We will pay those sums that you become legally obligated to pay as damages because of direct physical loss or damage, including loss of use to Covered Property caused by accident and arising out of any Covered Causes of Loss."

The term *covered property* was defined in the form as "tangible property of others in your care, custody or control that is described in the declarations or on the coverage schedule." Reference was made to "personal property of others in the open" on the policy's declarations page. "Personal property of others in the open" was also listed under the description of property in the coverage schedule.

The insurer's key argument was that cargo contained inside the shipping containers stored on the grounds of the named insured's property was not covered because it was not in the open. The insurer contended that the cargo was not in the open because it was inside shipping containers. The insured pointed out, in response, that references to *in the open* in the policy were words of inclusion, and terms of inclusion must be broadly read in favor of coverage.

Because the phrase *in the open* was not defined in the policy, the court stated that it should be given its ordinary meaning. Referring to the *Merriam-Webster's Dictionary*, the term *open* in relevant part is defined as "having no enclosing or confining barrier; accessible on all or nearly all sides" and also as "completely free from concealment; exposed to general view or knowledge." Such definition, the court said, was also consistent with the definitions found in case law cited by the insurer. When the phrase *in the open* was applied to the undisputed facts of this case, the court said, it was readily apparent that the policy provided no coverage or duty to defend.

One of the 2012 revisions, which is discussed in Chapter 2, concerns a new extension applicable to property in storage units in the open.

This extension is said to possibly be necessary in those cases where an insurer has not previously viewed property in a storage unit as being property in the open.

Covered Business Personal Property

With one exception, coverage regarding business personal property is divided into two categories. The first category is the named insured's business personal property, and the second consists of personal property of others. The exception is that included within the business personal property of the named insured is leased personal property only when the named insured has a contractual responsibility to insure such personal property. For example, if the named insured leases office equipment and the written lease agreement requires that the named insured maintain certain insurance on that equipment against its direct physical loss or damage, that property comes within the category of the named insured's business personal property. If there is no requirement to obtain insurance on that leased property, or the personal property is not leased, the coverage is subject to the second category, referred to as personal property of others coverage.

Both of these kinds of personal property belonging to others are considered to be bailments. *Bailment* means that someone has temporary possession of another's personal property for a specific purpose. An example is the business owner who leases photocopiers. In this example, the owner of the property is the bailor and the one who has temporary possession is the bailee. Bailments can be for the sole benefit of the bailor or bailee but are often for the mutual benefit of both parties, which is what the leasing of photocopiers would be since the bailor is receiving a charge for the lease of equipment and the bailee is obtaining a use interest.

Although no separate limit must be declared for leased personal property, the named insured has to make certain that the value of that property is included with the value of other personal property of the named insured in order to avoid any co-insurance penalty. Whether loss adjustment on leased personal property is on an actual cash value or replacement cost basis will depend on what valuation has been chosen by the named insured for its business personal property. Otherwise, when Leased Property endorsement, CP 14 60, is issued, the agreed value shown in the endorsement applies but is still subject to any applicable co-insurance requirement.

The classes of business personal property covered by the BPP form are outlined in the following paragraphs. In cases where not all of the coverages listed are needed, the insured may use Your Business Personal Property – Separation of Coverage Form, CP 19 10, and assign individual limits for each category of business personal property. By assigning individual limits for certain categories, the insured is, in effect, excluding categories that are not assigned a value.

1. **Furniture and fixtures.** Coverage for fixtures appears both under the building and business personal property sections of the BPP form. If the insured has purchased both coverages, fixtures are covered under either. The insured is free to call for coverage under whichever of the two coverages—building or property—yields the greater advantage under the following circumstances:

    a. if the business personal property is not insured for the same causes of loss as the building;

    b. if the business personal property is subject to a different coinsurance requirement; or

    c. if the limits under one or the other coverages are exhausted.

    Fixtures that are tenants' improvements and betterments (meaning affixed to the realty and considered the landlord's property) are not included in this item in the tenant's policy. Rather, the tenant's use interest is covered under item number 6.

Modular Office System as Fixture

An insured business that carried only building coverage (not contents) suffered a loss due to a hurricane. The business had a modular office system that was custom designed and installed. The agent argued that those panels that were mounted on the building's walls are fixtures and therefore covered under the commercial property building coverage. The adjuster countered that they can be removed and relocated to other areas as they are furniture and are not covered.

The panels require a wall-mounting kit. In order to move the wall-mounted panels, the insured would have to call an installer because the insured could not move the panels himself.

The issue is whether these panels can be covered as building items or whether the insured would have to have contents coverage in order to recover for their damage.

The panels are fixtures. The term *fixture* is not further defined in the policy, leaving its interpretation to common lay meaning. A common usage dictionary defines *fixture* as "something that is fixed or attached (as to a building) as a permanent appendage or as a structural part." The term is further defined as "an item of movable property so incorporated into real property that it may be regarded as legally a part of it." *Permanent* does not mean that the item has to be so attached to the property that it can never be removed. It means "continuing or enduring" and "stable." The issue must be decided on whether the insured business could take the panels if the building sold. If the panels can be removed, they are not covered; if not, they are. Free-standing panels, not installed in any way into the building, are not fixtures and could only be covered under contents coverage.

2. **Machinery and equipment.** Building coverage includes permanently installed machinery and equipment; business personal property coverage protects any machinery or equipment of the insured regardless of the state of installment. Permanently installed machinery or equipment could be covered under business personal property or building coverage, whichever is more favorable to the insured.

3. **Stock.** The BPP form covers the insured business's stock. *Stock* is one of three defined terms in the policy, so any meaning the term may otherwise have is replaced by this specific definition. The policy's definition of *stock* is "merchandise held in storage or for sale, raw materials and in-process or finished goods, including supplies used in their packing or shipping."

The fact that *stock* is a defined term does not mean its meaning will not ever be disputed. In fact, that term was the center of controversy in the *CSS Publishing Co. v. Am. Economy Ins. Co.*, 740 N.E.2d 341 (Oh. App. 2000). Following a fire that destroyed some publisher's books, the insurer was willing to pay the loss as personal property of others since the books belonged to the authors, subject to a $40,000 limit. The named insured, on the other hand, maintained that the books were covered as stock under business personal property, subject to a limit of $2,795,000. The insurer disagreed, arguing that before the books could be considered stock, ownership was a criterion. The appeals court disagreed, stating that the issue of ownership is not addressed in the policy with regard to these items.

One of the property not covered provisions (clause q) contains a list of certain property that is not covered while outside of buildings. The list includes trees, shrubs, and plants. A coverage extension provides limited coverage for trees, shrubs, and plants (*see* Chapter 2). Provision q accepts stock of trees, shrubs, and plants from the property not covered list. As a result of the 2012 revisions, what is not excepted are trees, shrubs, or plants that are stock or are a part of a vegetated roof. Therefore, an insured's stock of outdoor trees, shrubs, and plants is treated as any other stock and is not subject to the coverage limitations imposed by the outdoor property coverage extension. The limited coverage for trees and shrubs provided under the coverage extensions does not apply to trees and shrubs as stock—full business personal property limits are available.

Reference to the undefined term, *vegetated roof*, is discussed later with reference to property not covered and with the exception for lawns, trees, shrubs, and plants, which are a part of a vegetated roof. The term *vegetated roof* was first introduced with the green trend in building construction.

The issue of whether goods sold but not delivered are treated as the insured's business personal property or as the property of others is determined by the bill of sale provisions and the Uniform Commercial Code. After ownership is established, the amount of coverage available and the value of the property must be determined. If treated as the insured's business personal property, the policy's valuation provision states that stock sold but not delivered is valued at the selling price less discounts and expenses the insured otherwise would have incurred. For example, ABC Widget normally sells its product for $5 each. In a contract with XYZ for 10,000 widgets, ABC offers such a large quantity at $4 each. If a fire destroys those widgets while still at ABC, ABC's insurance policy will value them at $4 each—the normal selling price less the offered discount.

If considered the property of others, the limit for property of others is available. If this coverage has not been purchased, $2,500 of coverage is available under a coverage extension if a coinsurance provision of at least 80 percent or a value reporting symbol is shown in the declarations (see Chapter 2, Coverage Extensions).

4. **All other personal property owned by you and used in your business.** This broad statement means that personal property—of any kind—is covered property under the BPP form, subject to the requirements that it be owned by the insured and used in the insured's business. There is no requirement that the property be used exclusively in the insured's business. For example, an

MP3 player used in both the insured's home and office would be covered as personal property used in the insured's business.

5. **Labor, materials, or services furnished or arranged by the insured on personal property of others.** This represents the value of the insured's business processes or operations where loss involves property of others that the insured has performed service or processes upon. For example, the insured business is a computer repair shop. A fire occurs and damages a customer's computer that was in for repairs. The business's commercial property policy will cover the cost of the computer plus the value of the materials and labor he put into it prior to the fire. If the business receives $30 an hour for labor and has expended $50 in parts and two hours labor to repair the computer, the policy will pay $110. The policy will also make payment to the customer for the value of the computer.

6. **Use interest as tenant in improvements and betterments.** When a tenant makes a permanent addition to a leased building, the improvements usually become part of the building and the property of the landlord. A new store front, installed by the tenant with the expectation of attracting more customers, is a good example. The tenant, of course, has the right to use the improvement for the term of the lease but cannot undo the improvement and betterment upon moving out.

Where there is insured damage to the improvements before the lease expires, the insured/tenant has lost no property that belongs to him; the improvements belong to the landlord. What the tenant has lost is the use of the property, and it is the right of use for the term of the lease that creates the tenant's insurable interest in the improvements. It is the possible loss of use of the improvements in which the tenant has invested that represents the tenant's exposure.

Is Improvements and Betterments Coverage Dependent on Term of Lease?

A building suffered lightning damage to a central air conditioning unit. The insured is a tenant and not the building owner. The insured paid for the air conditioning unit five years ago.

The insured carries contents insurance, which includes the use interest in improvements and betterments. The insurance company initially declined the claim, stating that the units were part of the building and, as there was no building coverage, there could be no recovery. The agent argued that the unit was an improvement and betterment. The company agreed with this and agreed that the cause of loss was a covered cause of loss.

The claim was then denied on the basis that the tenant had no insurable interest in the improvement and betterment because the lease is an annual renewable lease. Nothing in the lease addresses ownership of improvements and betterments. The lease was first executed a decade ago and renews automatically unless one party notifies the other within a certain time prior to the end of the annual period. The insurance company based its position on the fact that when any lease renews, all improvements and betterments belong to the building owner, and a tenant has only an insurable interest for the period of the lease, in this case one year.

Improvements and betterments coverage would be severely impinged upon under this interpretation. It would limit coverage for improvements and betterments made by the tenant to a one year lease term, when in actuality, the building in question has been continuously leased for ten years.

It is the insured's use interest in improvements and betterments that is covered; further, an improvement and betterment is specifically stated to be a fixture made a part of the building the insured occupies but does not own and that was acquired or made at the insured's expense but cannot be legally removed. The definition of *improvements and betterments* does not tie coverage to the lease term. If there is a fixture that qualifies as an improvement and betterment and the insured's use interest is damaged, there is coverage. In this case, the insured acquired a fixture at his expense that was made a part of the building the insured occupies but does not own and that he cannot legally remove. His use interest in that fixture is damaged and therefore coverage applies.

The phrase *improvements and betterments* implies a substantial alteration, addition, or change to real property that enhances its value. The BPP states that improvements and betterments are "fixtures, alterations, installations, or additions: (a) Made a part of the building or structure you occupy but you do not own; and (b) You acquired or made at your expense but cannot legally remove." Coverage is automatic if the insured has an improvements and betterments exposure since business personal property is said to consist of, among other things, the named insured's use interest as tenant in improvements and betterments.

Questions have arisen as to whether under given circumstances particular work paid for by the tenant falls within its meaning. An example is the issue of whether repairs made on the building by the tenant constitute improvements and betterments. A court ruled "no" in *Modern Music Shop v. Concordia Fire Ins. Co. of Milwaukee*, 226 N.Y.S. 630 (1927). The case provides some guidance, though it involved an older form that referred simply to "the insured's interest in improvements and betterments." The court said, "These words imply and mean a substantial or fairly substantial alteration, addition, or change to the premises used and occupied by the insured, rising above and beyond and amounting to something more than a simple or minor repair."

In *U.S. Fire Ins. Co. v. Martin*, 282 S.E.2d 2 (Va. 1981), the Virginia Supreme Court decided that air conditioners the insured tenant had repaired but not installed were not within the meaning of improvements and betterments. The court reasoned that the tenant had not made the original expenditures for the air conditioners, that the expenditures were not later acquired by the tenant, and the expenses put out by the tenant were for repair only; therefore, there was no coverage under the terms of the policy.

The current policy provision and the decisions in these two cases demonstrate that an improvement must substantially alter the building. A maintenance or repair task, such as painting the building or installing new locks on doors, is not an improvement in the insurance meaning of the word. Tenants often agree to maintain the building or to undertake repairs via lease provision or do these things voluntarily. Such expense should not be viewed as an improvement and betterment.

There is a distinction between *improvements* and *trade fixtures*. The latter are installed by the tenant, often in such a way that they become a part of the building, but—either by express provision in the lease or by established custom—the vacating tenant removes them. Trade fixtures retain the character of personal property. Taking a store as an example, a new front installed by the tenant is an improvement, but counters, no matter how firmly attached to the building, are usually trade fixtures.

The BPP form sets out three methods (under section E.7.e. Loss Conditions, Valuation; *see* Chapter 5) for determining recovery when improvements are damaged by an insured peril:

1. If the insured makes the repairs at his expense and is not reimbursed by the landlord, the BPP form covers the

improvements at actual cash value just as though the insured owned them. The policy requires that repairs be made promptly but does not define *promptly*.

A court has held that the amount recoverable by the tenant for improvements is reduced by any amount that the tenant is reimbursed by the owner for the cost of the improvements. In *Atlanta Eye Care, Inc. v. Aetna Cas. and Sur. Co.*, 364 S.E.2d 634 (Ga. App. 1988), the insured was covered under a Businessowners policy for improvements and betterments. The insured made improvements costing $19,000 to the leased property. The lease agreement, however, provided that the owner would reimburse the tenant $8,000, and this was done. After the property suffered a loss, the insurer paid all but $8,000 of the tenant's claim for improvements and betterments. Ruling in the insurer's favor, the court found that the coverage was correctly limited to those improvements for which the tenant had not been reimbursed.

2. If someone else (usually the landlord) repairs the improvements at his expense for the insured's use, the policy owes nothing. In this situation, the insured has suffered no loss. Where the insured has suffered temporary loss of business because of the damage to the improvements, the loss should be covered by business income coverage if the insured has arranged such protection.

3. If the improvements are not repaired or replaced promptly, the insured tenant recovers a proportion of the original cost of the damaged improvements. The insurer determines the proportionate value by multiplying the original cost of the improvements by the number of days from the loss or damage to the expiration of the lease. Then this amount is divided by the number of days from the installation of improvements to the expiration of the lease. If the insured's lease contains a renewal option, the expiration of the renewal option period becomes the expiration date for use in determining the amount recoverable. The lease option provision does not require that the tenant give notice to the owner, either verbally or in writing, of intent to exercise the option.

The third situation is the one that most often presents difficulties. If neither the insured nor the landlord repairs or replaces the improvements promptly—and there is no definition of the word *promptly*—the policy pays an amount generally referred to as the unamortized portion of the investment. An example of recovery under this situation is a tenant who has invested $10,000 in improvements at the beginning of a ten year lease. In effect, the tenant has bought the use of these improvements for ten years for $10,000. A fire destroys the improvements after five years, and the tenant loses half of the investment. If the improvements are not replaced, the third provision sets up the machinery for recovery of that lost half. Of course, when this third provision takes effect is open to question due to the lack of a time schedule. Does promptly mean sixty days, ninety days, six months, or more probably, depending on the particular circumstances surrounding the loss and its aftermath? If the damaged property is not repaired, there is nothing against which to measure *promptly*. The insured's loss of use is measured from time of loss.

When the insured or the landlord does not promptly repair or replace the damaged improvements, the basis for recovery under the policy is the original cost of the improvements. Depreciation makes no difference. Neither does whether those improvements would cost more or less to replace at the time of loss than they actually cost to install matter. Actual cost of installation is the insured's investment and that investment is what was lost—wholly or partially—if the improvements are destroyed and not restored.

Suppose an insured spent $10,000 on improvements at the beginning of November 2007 under a lease running to the end of 2021. At the beginning of February 2008, the improvements are destroyed and not replaced. Under the formula for recovery in CP 00 10, the $10,000 is multiplied by 167 months, as that is the amount of time from the loss to the expiration of the lease. The resulting amount, $1,670,000, is divided by 170 or the amount of time from the installation of the improvements to the expiration of the lease. The recovery is $9,823.53.

The original cost may be greater than the actual cash value of the improvements. If the insured must tear out a portion of the building in making the alterations or improvements, the original investment is the cost of the improvements plus the amount spent getting ready for them. An example is that the insured tenant spends $10,000 for improvements. But before these improvements could be made the tenant had to spend an additional $4,000 to remove the building front and inside wall. The total investment in improvements is $14,000. A fire totally destroys the improvements. If the tenant chooses to replace the improvements, she will not have to redo the demolition work. The commercial property policy thus ignores the $4,000 that she originally spent, and her recovery is the actual cash value of the improvements—replacement cost less depreciation, which might be more or less than $10,000.

On the other hand, if the tenant does not replace the improvements, the policy bases recovery on the total original cost—$14,000, the cost of the demolition work plus the original cost of the improvements. The policy still bases recovery on the provisions as set forth in the form in the event of a month-to-month lease. However, the tenant has very little enforceable time of tenancy. If the tenant replaces the improvements, she will recover their actual cash value just as if under a lease with a long time to run. But if she does not replace them, her recovery will be very little since the fraction arrived at by the procedure for the third situation will reflect only a small portion of the cost of the improvements.

Such was the situation presented to the New Hampshire Supreme Court in *Magulas v. Travelers Ins. Co.*, 327 A.2d 608 (N.H. 1974). The insured had a two-year verbal lease, but he knew that as a tenant-at-will his legally enforceable tenancy was limited to thirty days. The owner told him that the building, which he leased to use as a restaurant, might be demolished but that it would not be demolished for at least two years. The insured relied on the likelihood of staying in the building for two years and made improvements of $20,000. Two months after the restaurant opened it suffered a fire loss, and the owner refused to rebuild. The insurer argued that the insured's interest in the improvements and betterments was limited to his legally enforceable right to have thirty days' notice before tenancy could be terminated. The court found that the insured's insurable interest in the improvements and betterments was not so limited, stating: "[The insured] expected to use the improvements for two years and should recover on the basis of that expectation despite the fact that his legally enforceable rental term was limited to thirty days."

However, if the insured has an option to purchase, his insurable interest in improvements and betterments is still bound by the unexpired term of the lease. Once the option to purchase is exercised, the improvements and betterments are transformed into building property in which the insured has an absolute interest, not merely a use interest.

A.1.c. Personal Property of Others

The final category of covered property in the BPP form—also a bailment—is property of others in the named insured's care, custody, or control. The same conditions, and 2012 revisions, as to location of such property apply here with respect to the insured's own business personal property: the property must be in or on the building or structure described in the declarations or in the open (or in a vehicle) within 100 feet of the building or structure or with 100 feet of the premises described in the declarations, whichever distance is greater.

Contrast coverage for property in the insured's care, custody, or control under the BPP form and the Commercial General Liability (CGL) coverage form. The CGL coverage form contains an exclusion of property that is in the insured's care, custody, or control. In order for coverage to attach for property of others under the BPP, property must be in the insured's care, custody, or control. This illustrates a difference in the nature of the policies. The CGL coverage form does not cover property, per se. It covers the insured's legal liability for damage. The BPP form covers direct property damage to covered property, including property of others in the insured's care, regardless of legal liability.

The BPP form automatically provides $2,500 of additional insurance for the property of others by means of a coverage extension (see Chapter 2). The purchase of additional and specific personal property of others coverage is appropriate when the insured needs coverage of values in excess of $2,500. For example, the insured has charge of $10,000 worth of personal property of others at his business. The policy provides coverage for the first $2,500 as an extension of business personal property (assuming 80 percent coinsurance is listed on the declarations). The insured should purchase an additional $7,500 of coverage under personal property of others. The BPP form provides no coverage for the property of others, other than the $2,500 extension, unless the agent activates the coverage by the appropriate entry on the declarations page.

If the replacement cost optional coverage is shown as applicable in the declarations, replacement cost also applies to business personal property of others.

Any loss to property of others is adjusted for the account of the owner of the property. What this means is that in the event of a covered loss, payment by the insurer is made to the property owner, not the named insured. Also, coverage is made without having to prove any fault on the named insured's behalf.

Section A.2. Property Not Covered

The BPP form lists seventeen categories of property not covered. With the exception of land, water, and contraband, property not covered items can be insured either by the Additional Covered Property endorsement (CP 14 10) to this policy, by a separate inland marine policy, or by some other type of policy specifically designed to cover that property. Property items listed as not covered generally require specialized underwriting (accounts, currency, securities, bridges, piers, and wharves) or are not covered due to their low susceptibility to loss (building's foundation, underground pipes, flues, and drains). In addition, the elimination of these property items as covered property also reduces the amount of insurance needed to comply with the policy's coinsurance requirement. Note that although most of the property not covered items may be insured under the BPP's Additional Covered Property endorsement, individual underwriters have the discretion to accept or not accept certain types of property as covered items.

a.   **Accounts, bills, currency, food stamps, or other evidences of debt, money, notes, or securities.** This category of property not covered can be insured under the Additional Covered Property endorsement to the BPP, or more commonly, it is insured under a Commercial Crime Policy. Note that in previous versions of the BPP, deeds were included on this list but have been dropped; therefore the cost of reproducing a deed lost by a covered event is recoverable. The form also specifically includes coverage for lottery tickets held for sale (stock) by stating that lottery tickets held for sale are not securities.

b.   **Animals.** Although animals are listed as property not covered under the BPP, limited coverage is provided if the animals belong to others that the insured boards (kennel) or if the animals are owned as stock while inside a building (pet/animal distributor). Animals owned by the insured for display (zoo, wild life park), raised for slaughter (livestock) or personally owned exotic animals, are examples of property not covered. Coverage for these types of exposures can be insured under the Additional Covered Property endorsement to the BPP, the Commercial Farm Policy's Livestock Form, or through an Animal Mortality Policy.

c. **Automobiles held for sale.** Automobiles held for sale are commonly insured under a commercial auto policy using the Auto Dealers Coverage Form. Non-auto dealer operations such as auto repair shops, parking lot operators, and similar non-auto dealership businesses can insure their exposures through the Commercial Auto Policy using the Business Auto Coverage Form or Commercial General Liability Policy with the appropriate garagekeepers coverage endorsements. Although coverage for automobiles held for sale may be insured under the Additional Covered Property endorsement to the BPP, coverage is limited to the BPP's policy perils with physical damage limited to within 100 feet of the insured premises. Due to these endorsement limitations, most insureds who own automobiles for sale commonly use the more specialized Commercial Auto Policy arrangement.

d. **Bridges, roadways, walks, patios, or other paved surfaces.** These property items are not covered due to their low susceptibility to loss. Of these items, bridges, especially ones that transverse a ravine or a stream or provide sole access to the insured's property, present a unique exposure from both a property loss and possible business income perspective. Coverage for bridges and any of the other cited property items can be insured under the Additional Covered Property endorsement to the BPP or by an inland marine policy.

e. **Contraband, or property in the course of illegal transportation or trade.** Contraband is any property that is unlawful to produce or possess. Examples of contraband would include counterfeit merchandise and smuggled goods.

f. **Cost of excavations, grading, backfilling, or filling.** These activities are generally conducted in conjunction with losses related to structural damage to a building. For example, if a building's foundation is damaged, a natural consequence in the repair process would be the excavating, grading, and backfilling of ground on or near the foundation walls. Since these types of property items (foundations/structures below the lowest basement floor) are not covered (see Property Not Covered g.), activities that are generally conducted in conjunction with foundation and structure losses are also not covered. Coverage for these activities may be added to the BPP by the Additional Covered Property endorsement. Although this provision appears rather straightforward, it has been the center of disputes as illustrated in the following examples.

May the Exclusion of Excavation Costs Be Applied to Debris Removal?

An insured suffered a total fire loss to his business insured on a commercial property form. The debris from the destroyed building fell into the foundation and heaped-up above ground level. The insurer stated that it was not responsible for removing the debris from within the foundation walls and that its only responsibility was to pay for removal of debris above ground level and to fill any remaining hole with dirt to level the surface. The company relied upon provision 2.f. under property not covered: "Covered property does not include...the cost of excavations, grading, backfilling or filling."

The insurer was mistaken in applying the exclusion of coverage for the cost of excavation to the debris removal provision. They are two distinct things. The policy does promise to pay the cost to "remove debris of covered property caused by...a covered cause of loss." The fire was the covered cause of loss, and the resulting debris of the covered property is what must be removed from within the foundation walls. Nothing in the additional coverage limits what debris will be removed.

The cost of excavation exclusion, on the other hand, is found within a list of items that are either uninsurable, such as contraband, or should be insured elsewhere, such as automobiles held for sale. Further, "the cost of excavations" appears within the list of other items commonly associated with new construction, such as grading, backfilling, or filling.

The debris removal additional coverage provision contains only one exclusion: the cost to extract pollutants from land or water or to remove, restore, or replace polluted land or water. Therefore, debris removal from within the foundation walls is covered.

Excavation of Broken Water Pipe Covered?

An insured's building suffered water damage from a broken underground water pipe. The damaged pipe led from the water main in the street to the insured's building. The broken pipe had to be dug up to be repaired in order to avoid continued water damage to the building. The insurance company authorized payment for the water damage to the building but refused to pay the cost of digging up the water pipe to repair it, citing the policy provision stating that the cost of excavations, grading, backfilling, or filling is property not covered. Thus, the insurer reasoned that the cost of excavating the pipe to repair it was not covered.

The BPP says that covered property does not include the cost of excavation. The building is covered property, so its insured value does not include the cost of excavation. Excavation is a service that goes into the cost of constructing a building if the building is set in the ground. It is part of the cost of the building, as is the cost of painting it or the cost of cleaning up the construction debris once the building is finished.

The form drafters wanted to cover most costs involved in replacing a building destroyed by a covered cause of loss, but they did not want to cover the portion of the building's cost attributable to excavation. To use policy language to exclude the cost of digging up a broken water pipe is unwarranted. By excavating, the insured is preventing further water damage to his building.

One of the insured's duties in the event of the loss as set out in the form is to "take all reasonable steps to protect the Covered Property from further damage by a Covered Cause of Loss." The form asks the insured to keep records of expenses incurred in arranging emergency repairs "for consideration in the settlement of the claim." Repairing a broken water pipe that causes water damage to an insured building is the type of emergency repair that the form contemplates.

g. **Foundations of buildings, structures, machinery, or boilers,** if such foundations are below the lowest basement floor or the surface of the ground, if there is no basement. Like other property items that have a low susceptibility to loss, foundations of buildings, structures, machinery, or boilers are similarly categorized as property not covered if such foundations are below the surface of the ground, if there is no basement. In other words, building foundations, structures, machinery, or boilers are covered if they are above the basement or above the surface of the ground. Foundations of buildings, structures, machinery, or boilers below ground are property not covered and may be insured under the Additional Covered Property endorsement to the BPP or a specialized inland marine policy.

Foundations as Property Not Covered

Included under the property not covered section of the BPP are "foundations of buildings, structures, machinery or boilers if their foundations are below: (1) the lowest basement floor; or (2) the surface of the ground, if there is no basement." Some adjusters have said that because of the use of "*their* foundations" instead of "*the* foundations," machinery on a foundation with a top surface below ground level is not covered. If "the" had been used, then coverage would be effective as to machinery but not as to the foundation.

This is incorrect. Only foundations are the subject of the provision A.2.g regarding foundations as property not covered. The reference goes back to the word *foundation*. Foundations of buildings, structures, machinery, or boilers are not covered property if the foundation is below the lowest basement floor or the surface of the ground, if there is no basement. The use of the word "their" rather than "the" does not affect coverage for the building, structure, machinery, or boiler. Those remain items of covered property and are not included in the scope of property not covered.

h.   **Land, including the land on which the property is located, water, growing crops, or lawns**. This provision makes clear that the ground upon which the insured property is located is not covered. Although land may have a fair market value for resale purposes, land itself is not covered property and is generally uninsurable. Water, such as water in a lake on the insured's property, is also not covered. Some losses involving water might involve an on-premises leak in a water pipe that causes a sudden rise in the insured's water bill. While most losses of this type will be of amounts so small that they would never reach litigation, an argument can be made that the excess over the normal water bill is covered. Also included in this category of property not covered are growing crops and lawns Note that in the 2012 revisions, an exception for lawns that are a part of a vegetated roof was introduced. As a result of this revision, lawns that are part of vegetated roofs are viewed as part of the building and subject to all of the covered causes of loss (discussed in Chapters 3 and 4) and the limit of insurance. This category of property is not eligible for coverage under the Additional Covered Property endorsement to the BPP although crops may be insured by specialty insurance carriers under a crop insurance policy.

i.   **Personal property while airborne or waterborne.** There is no coverage for items of the insured while in transit on air or water. Generally some form of cargo insurance is the appropriate insurance mechanism for this exposure. For example, delivery of property by helicopter (equipment for installation) or by drone (personal property for delivery) would not be covered. Coverage for these activities may be added to the BPP by the Additional Covered Property endorsement by the purchase of cargo insurance (for property being transported), an installation floater (for equipment being installed), or through specialty insurance (for property being transported by drone).

j.   **Bulkheads, pilings, piers, wharves, or docks.** These property items, like other property items that have a low susceptibility to loss (such as foundations below ground level, paved surfaces, and roadways) are similarly categorized as property not covered.

Bulkheads are structural safety devices. Cited in this category, the policy is referring to a sea, lake, or river wall that is used to reduce costal soil erosion. Pilings are poles that are driven into soil to help support a pier or similar water structure. Piers are structures that are generally constructed onto pilings to form a bridge or walkway. Wharves are structures on a shore or river bank where ships may dock to load and unload cargo. Similarly, a dock is a structure or group of structures used to load or unload cargo. All of these items relate to marine property exposures and may be added to the BPP by the Additional Covered Property endorsement or insured under specialized marine property policies.

k. **Property more specifically described in another coverage form.** Some property items covered under the BPP may be insured under a specific policy. This is generally due to the insured's need for broader coverage. For example, the BPP form covers equipment and machinery. Boiler equipment would fall under this category. If, however, the insured has an equipment breakdown policy where the boiler equipment is specifically described (listed in the declarations), the item is covered only for any excess amount of loss (whether collectible or not) over the amount of the more specific insurance. Large commercial insureds often have separate policies on boiler machinery, electronic data processing equipment, fine arts, and other types of property.

l. **Retaining walls, unless the retaining wall is part of a building.** A retaining wall is a structure designed to restrain soil from cascading down a sloped property. These types of structures are commonly used for the landscaping of terrain but may also be a structural part of a building. For example, if a retaining wall is used exclusively for landscaping, it would not be covered property. If, however, the retaining wall was used to support a part of the building, the retaining wall would fall within the coverage of the BPP. Retaining walls that are not part of a building may be added to the BPP by the Additional Covered Property endorsement or insured through an inland marine policy.

m. **Underground pipes, flues, or drains.** These property items, like other property items that have a low susceptibility to loss, are similarly categorized as property not covered. The defining characteristic precluding coverage is if these property items are underground. In one case, an apartment building owner brought an action against its insurer to recover for loss caused by leaking underground water pipes. The court in *General Acc. Ins. Co. v. Unity/Waterford-Fair Oaks, Ltd.*, 288 F.3d 651 (5th Cir. 2002) held that coverage did not apply for the cost of repairing the pipes, which had rusted through, even though the policy's exclusion for damage caused by rust or corrosion contained an exception for rusted or corroded property itself. Pipes and drains were not covered property. As with other categories of property not covered, underground pipes, flues, and drains can be added to the BPP by the Additional Covered Property endorsement or insured through an inland marine policy.

Outdoor Sprinkler System as Underground Pipes

The insured had a sprinkler system in the yard, which had pipes underground. The sprinkler heads extended about a quarter of an inch above ground. A windstorm toppled a concrete-footed light pole, which, as it fell, uprooted the sprinkler pipes, damaging the sprinkler system. The insurer denied coverage for damage to the sprinkler system, as underground pipes are specifically property not covered. The insured argued that the loss should be covered as a permanently installed fixture or equipment or as personal property used to maintain the premises.

The BPP provides only partial coverage for the sprinkler system. There is no coverage for the sprinkler system as permanently installed fixtures or equipment. That coverage is under the building or structure coverage and does not extend to items that are not part of the building or structure. If the underground system extended from the building's plumbing it would ordinarily qualify as "building, including permanently installed fixtures." However, the policy specifies that underground pipes are property not covered.

The insured's argument that the sprinkler system is personal property used to maintain the premises appears to have merit; however, because a fixture to the realty normally cannot be removed without damage to the realty, the sprinkler system would be seen as real, not personal, property. Even if considered personal property, the exclusion of underground pipes prevails. Any damage to the underground pipes is not covered; however, any damage to sprinkler heads or connecting pipes above ground would be covered.

---

n.   **Electronic data;** and

o.   **Cost to Replace or Restore.** Prior to the 04 02 edition of the commercial property policy, the form did not specifically address data itself. Rather, the cost to reproduce the data was addressed. The following is the previous property not covered provision in the CP 00 10 regarding data:

n.   The cost to research, replace or restore the information on valuable papers and records, including those which exist on electronic or magnetic media, except as provided in the Coverage Extensions.

Previous editions of the CP 00 10 lumped electronic data in with other types of valuable papers and records. With insureds having more and more of their information in electronic format, a better way was needed to cover such data.

The CP 00 10 04 02 deleted the former provision that addressed just the cost of reproduction as property not covered and replaced that provision with the following two provisions under property not covered:

n.   Electronic data, except as provided under the Additional Coverage—Electronic Data. Electronic data means information, facts or computer programs stored as or on, created or used on, or transmitted to or from computer software (including systems and applications software), on hard or floppy disks, CD-ROMs, tapes, drives, cells, data processing devices or any other repositories of computer software which are used with electronically controlled equipment. The term computer programs, referred to in the foregoing description of electronic data, means a set of related electronic instructions which direct the operations and functions of a computer or device connected to it, which enable the computer or device to receive, process, store, retrieve or send data. This paragraph n., does not apply to your "stock" of prepackaged software;

o.   The cost to replace or restore the information on valuable papers and records, including those which exist as electronic data. Valuable papers and records include but are not limited to proprietary information, books of account, deeds, manuscripts, abstracts, drawings and card index systems. Refer to the Coverage Extension for Valuable Papers And Records (Other Than Electronic Data) for limited coverage for valuable papers and records other than those which exist as electronic data.

These two provisions take the property not covered considerably further than previous editions of the form. Provision n. specifies that the policy does not cover any types of electronic data, regardless of where it exists. The definition was expanded to include the data and any systems or applications software. The policy does, however, make an exception for the insured's stock of prepackaged software (necessary for the insured who is a software dealer). Also, with the 2012 revisions, this provision does not apply to electronic data that is integrated in and operates or controls the building's elevator, lighting, heating, ventilation, air conditioning, or security system. This change also affects the time element forms. In light of this revision, the limitation under additional coverages, discussed in Chapter 2, is unnecessary and, therefore, has been deleted.

Provision o. then removes coverage for the cost of replacing or restoring data. There is, however, an additional coverage that provides up to $2,500 to restore or replace electronic data, which is addressed in Chapter 3.

Insureds with significant electronic data exposures beyond the reach of the limited coverage of the BPP may add the Additional Covered Property endorsement or insure the exposure through an electronic data processing policy or a similar specialized policy.

p. **Vehicles or self-propelled machines.** This category removes coverage for vehicles (specifically including aircraft and watercraft) that are licensed for use on public roads or that are operated principally away from the insured premises. These types of vehicles and self-propelled machines are commonly insured under a commercial auto, aircraft, or watercraft policy. By exception, property not covered makes an exception (thus providing coverage) for the following:

1. vehicles that the insured manufactures, processes (including vehicles used to service the premises), or warehouses (including autos);

2. vehicles held for sale (other than autos);

3. rowboats and canoes out of water at the insured premises; and

4. trailers, but only to the extent they are covered in the coverage extension for nonowned detached trailers.

    Exception 4 is a change in the BPP form that was first written into the 2000 edition and carried forward. There is a coverage extension for trailers that the insured does not own but uses in his business. Thus, exception 4 applies only to the extent of the coverage extension. For more on this coverage extension, see Chapter 2.

    As with other categories of property not covered, vehicles and self-propelled machines may be added to the BPP by the

Additional Covered Property endorsement; a specific commercial auto, aircraft, or watercraft policy; or through some other specialized inland marine policy.

q.   **Property while outside of buildings.** The following two types of property are not covered while outside of buildings:

1.   Grain, hay, straw, or other crops; and

2.   Fences, radio or television antennas, including satellite dishes, and their lead-in wiring, masts, towers, trees, shrubs, or plants. Specifically excepted by the 2012 revisions are trees, shrubs or plants that are stock or are part of a vegetated roof, and as otherwise provided in the coverage extensions.

The BPP form picks up limited coverage ($1,000) for such property under the coverage extensions section (see Chapter 2).

Outdoor signs coverage was revised in the 2007 edition of the policy. Outdoor signs (other than signs attached to buildings) were previously included in property not covered provision q except to the extent covered under the outdoor property coverage extension. ISO revised the property not covered and outdoor property coverage extension sections to remove reference to signs. Coverage for detached outdoor signs is subject to the applicable causes of loss form and to a special provision in the limits of insurance condition. The limit of insurance for attached outdoor signs is increased from $1,000 to $2,500 per sign in any one occurrence. The limit of insurance for detached outdoor signs is increased from $1,000 per occurrence (in total) to $2,500 per sign in any one occurrence. Further, coverage for detached outdoor signs is broadened to include all causes of loss otherwise covered under the applicable causes of loss form.

Outdoor property not covered (grain, hay, straw, and crops) and/ or limited by the policy coverage extension (such as fences, radio/TV antennas, and satellite dishes) can be added to the BPP by the Additional Covered Property endorsement or insured through a separate crop policy or an inland marine policy.

Chapter 2

Additional Coverages, Coverage Extensions, and Optional Coverages

Additional Coverages

Section 4 of the Building and Personal Property (BPP) form deals with additional coverages. The expenses covered under the additional coverages here all result from a direct loss. While not directly attributable to the insured peril, they are nevertheless attendant expenses necessary to return the insured to a preloss state and for which insurance coverage has been designed to respond. Examples are when a covered loss leaves debris behind that must be removed, undamaged property must be moved to be protected against further loss, or building codes create increased rebuilding costs. The BPP form provides six additional coverages:

- Debris Removal

- Preservation of Property

- Fire Department Service Charge

- Pollutant Clean-up and Removal

- Increased Cost of Construction

- Electronic Data

Section 4. Additional Coverages

4.a. Debris Removal

After damage to covered property by an insured peril, often a significant expense to the insured is the expense to remove debris. Since this expense is not a direct result of the peril (consequential, indirect damage), it does not meet the requirement of direct physical damage in the insuring agreement. However, the additional coverage for debris removal provides money for the insured to remove debris.

43

The CP 00 10 02 00 edition of the BPP form introduced a rewritten provision with a much expanded description of how debris removal coverage works and what it pays. It pays the insured's expense to remove debris of covered property that result from a covered peril occurring during the policy period. Also, with the 2012 revisions, coverage is extended to apply to other debris on the described premises, provided such debris is created by a covered cause of loss occurring during the policy period. The expenses must be reported to the insurer within 180 days of the date of loss.

Debris removal expense is within the limit of liability, except in two situations where the policy may include an additional $25,000 debris removal coverage. In any situation, the most the insurer will pay in any loss for both covered loss and debris removal is the policy limit for that type of property (i.e., building or contents), plus $25,000. (These additional limits were increased from $10,000 with the 2012 revisions.)

The form caps the amount of debris removal coverage at 25 percent of the total loss (amount of loss payable plus deductible). Added with the 2012 revisions is a limit of $5,000 for the removal of other property, when no covered property has sustained direct physical loss or damage, provided the removal is otherwise covered under this part of the policy. An example would be a windstorm or other covered peril, that damages a neighboring property causing debris to fall onto the insured's property. In this example, up to $5,000 would be payable to the insured to remove that debris.

The form contains the following example to illustrate: assume a limit of insurance of $90,000 with a deductible of $500. Further assume a loss of $50,000, for a loss payable amount of $49,500 (the damage, $50,000, less the deductible of $500). Debris removal expense is $10,000. The total debris removal expense of $10,000 is recoverable because $10,000 is 20 percent of $50,000, which is less than 25 percent of the loss payable ($49,500 plus the $500 deductible). The insured would recover $59,500 ($49,500 for the loss less the deductible plus $10,000 for debris removal expense). In this example, any amount of debris expense over $12,500 would not be covered.

There are cases when the basic debris removal coverage, as described in the previous paragraphs, is not adequate. The sum of the direct damage plus debris removal might be greater than the form limit, or the amount of debris removal might exceed 25 percent of the total loss. In that case the policy provides an additional flat amount of $25,000 for debris removal. Here is another example under this scenario: assume everything is the same as the earlier example, except the fire loss is now more serious—$80,000 direct damage, with $40,000 in debris removal expenses. The insurer's payment for the direct damage is $79,500 ($80,000 – $500). Even though the initial calculation of debris removal is $20,000 (25 percent of $80,000), the policy will pay only $10,500. That brings the insurer's total payment for direct and indirect damage to the limit of liability, $90,000. In other words, the sum of the loss payable ($79,500) and the basic debris removal amount payable ($10,500) cannot exceed the limit of insurance ($90,000). Then, the additional amount of $25,000 is payable for debris removal because the debris removal expense ($40,000) exceeds 25 percent of the loss payable plus the deductible ($40,000 is 50 percent of $80,000) and because the sum of the loss payable and debris removal expense ($79,500 + $40,000 = $119,500) would exceed the ($90,000) limit of insurance The additional amount of debris removal expense, therefore, is $25,000, the maximum payable under paragraph (4). The total debris removal expense payable, therefore, is $35,500, leaving $4,500 of debris removal expense uncovered. Extra debris removal coverage can be arranged using the Debris Removal Additional Insurance endorsement, CP 04 15.

The method for calculating debris removal charges was put to the test in *Strowig Properties, Inc. v. American States Ins. Co.*, 80 P.3d 72 (Kan. App. 2003). Following a strong windstorm that destroyed a theater owned by Strowig, American States paid the $139,000 policy limit plus $25,000 for debris removal. (The insured's policy was issued before the 2012 changes increased the limit to $25,000, so the limit was increased by endorsement.) Strowig claimed it was owed $34,974 (25 percent of the policy limit) more for debris removal.

The insured argued that, because the coverage was under the heading of "Additional Coverages," the amount payable was in addition to the basic coverage and that the coverage was not included in the limit of insurance in the declarations. Although Strowig had been paid the flat limit that applies when the total of actual debris removal expense plus the amount payable for direct physical loss or damage exceeds the limit of insurance on covered property that sustained the loss or damage, it claimed it was also owed 25 percent of the sum of the deductible plus the amount payable for direct physical loss or damage to the covered property.

The court pointed to the policy provision stating that the debris removal additional coverage does not increase the limit of insurance. Strowig urged the court to find the provision ambiguous, saying it was unclear what the debris removal limit actually was. The court, however, said that "because American States did use clear and explicit language to alert the insured to the limits of coverage, Strowig's assertion that the limits of insurance include additional coverage for debris removal is an unreasonable interpretation."

Debris removal expense is payable if the insured reports the expense in writing to the insurer within 180 days of the physical loss. Former policy editions provided 180 days from the date of the loss or from the end of the policy period, whichever was earlier. The current provision states expense must be reported within 180 days of the date of the loss.

If the insured chooses not to replace the building, the $10,000 flat amount for debris removal is payable. The form does not require that the building be repaired or replaced before this coverage is available. The policy states that if the sum of the direct physical loss and debris removal expense exceeds the limit of insurance or if the debris removal expense exceeds 25 percent, then an additional $10,000 for each location in one occurrence is available. Neither this additional coverage nor the loss payment conditions require the insured to repair or replace the building. However, if the insured chooses not to replace the building, loss settlement reverts to actual cash value.

Debris removal coverage specifically does not pay to extract pollutants from land or water. Nor does it cover the expense to remove, restore, or replace polluted land or water.

As a result of the 2012 commercial property revisions, the following are also not covered:

1. costs to remove debris of the named insured's property not insured under this policy or property in the named insured's possession that is not considered to be covered property

2. costs to remove debris consisting of property owned by or leased to the landlord of the building where the named insured's described premises are located unless the named insured has a contractual responsibility to insure such property and it is insured under this policy

3. costs to remove any property that is property not covered (see Chapter 1), including property referred to under the outdoor property coverage extension

4. costs to remove property of others that would not be considered covered property under this policy

5. costs to remove deposits of mud or earth from the grounds of the described premises

These 2012 changes dealing with debris removal not only affect the BBP form, but also the Condominium Association Coverage Form, CP 00 17; Condominium Commercial Unit-Owners Coverage Form,

CP 00 18; Builder's Risk Coverage Form, CP 00 20; and Standard Property Policy, CP 00 99. The Tobacco Sale Warehouse Coverage Form, CP 00 80, is affected only by the increase in the additional limit for this debris removal.

Debris Removal Coverage and the Coinsurance Provision

This example illustrates operation of the debris removal provision where the insured does not carry an adequate amount of insurance to meet the coinsurance requirement. A building insured on form CP 00 10 suffered both direct damage and debris removal expense. However the property was underinsured, thus resulting in a coinsurance penalty. The issue is whether the same coinsurance penalty is applied to debris removal payment as to the direct damage payment. The appropriate result is that it is not. An indirect penalty already applies when property is underinsured. The debris removal clause provides up to 25 percent of the amount paid for direct loss, not 25 percent of the amount insured. With the coinsurance penalty applied to the direct loss settlement, the amount payable for debris removal is 25 percent of an already penalized amount.

4.b. Preservation of Property

Additional coverage b. is preservation of property. If the insured must move property to another location off described premises in order to preserve it from loss or damage, the BPP provides protection against direct physical loss while in the process of being moved and for up to thirty days while it is temporarily stored at another location. The property need not be moved just for protection of property after a covered loss (e.g., after the roof has blown off and contents need to be protected from exposure), but in order to protect the property from damage by a covered loss at all. For example, if fire in a neighboring building causes the insured to move office furniture or equipment to protect it from burning, that property is covered while being moved or stored for up to thirty days. Because the word *any* is used rather than stating that the property is covered for the same perils covered by whichever causes of loss form the insured has, this preservation of property coverage is very broad. For an insured who must move any undamaged property, the policy provides protection for that property against loss or damage from perils such as flood, war, and nuclear hazard, which are normally excluded. In the previous example, assume the insured moves equipment to preserve it from fire in the neighboring building and that the insured's building also burned. The insured moves his property to a warehouse for safekeeping after the fire. Unfortunately the warehouse floods, ruining the property. The BPP will pay for the flood damage—generally excluded—under this additional coverage.

4.c. Fire Department Service Charge

Sometimes an insured must agree upfront in a contract to pay for a fire department's service, or a local ordinance may call for such payment. Fire department service charge is an additional coverage that will pay up to $1,000 when the fire department is called to respond to a covered cause of loss and liability for the charges was assumed prior to the loss or is required by local ordinance.

ISO revised the June 2007 edition to provide a mechanism for easily adjusting fire department service charge coverage if the insured needs a larger limit. The provision was changed with the phrase "unless a higher limit is shown in the Declarations," allowing the insured to schedule the necessary amount of economic protection.

With the 2012 revisions, ISO clarified this coverage to make the basic limit of $1,000, or higher selected limit, apply to each premises described in the declarations. The applicable limit, furthermore, is the maximum, regardless of the number of responding fire departments, units, or type of services provided. This change not only affects the BBP form but also Condominium Coverage Form, CP 00 17; Condominium Commercial Unit-Owners Coverage Form, CP 00 18; Builder's Risk Coverage Form, CP 00 20; Tobacco Sales Warehouses Coverage Form, CP 0080; and Standard Property Policy, CP 00 99.

This coverage in the BPP form differs from similar coverage in the homeowners policy. The homeowners policy does not cover this expense if the covered property is located within the limits of the city, municipality, or protection district that furnishes the protection. The BPP form does not restrict where the property may be located. Also, the BPP pays this expense if required by local ordinance. The homeowners policy does not mention this at all.

The fire department service charge additional coverage limit is payable in addition to the policy's limit of insurance and is not subject to a deductible.

Fire Department Service Charge Coverage

In rural areas, town fire departments often have contracts with smaller towns, villages, or townships to provide service. The question may arise about the provision in the additional coverage that ties payment for fire department service charges to the insured's liability assumed by contract or agreement. In most cases, the only contract is between the local governments and not between the individual property owner and a government entity. The insured has coverage under such circumstances. No formal contract is required for coverage since an agreement will suffice. According to *Webster's Ninth New Collegiate Dictionary*, an *agreement* is "an arrangement as to a course of action." Simply by being located in the town, the insured has made an agreement to abide by local ordinances, regulations, and arrangements for payment of services. The insurance policy does not specify who the parties to the agreement must be. If all property owners of a particular town must pay for services passed down to them for services provided by an out-of-town fire department, coverage applies.

4.d. Pollutant Clean-up and Removal

Pollutant clean-up and removal, the fourth additional coverage, provides an annual aggregate amount of $10,000 for expenses associated with cleanup or removal of pollutants that result from covered losses. The additional coverage covers land and water at the insured location. It responds if a covered peril causes the discharge, dispersal, seepage, migration, release, or escape of pollutants.

It is important to note that the provision applies to removal of pollutants from land and water only. The court in *Commerce Center Partnership v. Cincinnati Ins. Co.*, No. 265147, 2006 WL 1236745 (Mich. App. May 9, 2006) also had to remind an insured that the pollutant must result from a covered cause of loss.

The basement of the insured's building suffered water damage and black mold, which allegedly originated from a break in a city water main. Cincinnati Insurance denied coverage for the claim, stating that the water damage exclusion applied. The insured argued that the pollutant clean-up and removal provision should provide coverage for the removal of the mold.

The court held that the underlying cause of loss—water damage—was not covered, so the cleanup of the resulting black mold was not covered by the provision.

The concept of an annual aggregate is unusual in property insurance, generally associated with liability insurance. What this means is that the coverage for pollutant cleanup is limited to $10,000 *each year*. For example, an insured gas station suffers vandalism in January, which is the start of the annual policy term. As a result, some petroleum products are spread on the grass around the station. The cost to clean up the ground is $8,000. Note that only cleanup of ground or water is available under this additional coverage—this is not the same as coverage available in the exception to the pollution exclusion, which applies to covered property. If another covered pollutant event occurs before the end of the year, the insured would have $2,000 of coverage remaining for pollutant cleanup. The limit is refreshed to $10,000 at the start of the next annual period.

The policy does not cover the cost of tests to monitor or assess the existence or effects of pollutants. However, it does cover such costs if the testing occurs during the course of the pollutant removal.

Insureds may increase the $10,000 additional coverage for pollutant cleanup and removal to a higher amount, generally in the $25,000 to $50,000 range, subject to underwriting approval. Higher limits and broader coverage for pollution cleanup may be secured through on-site cleanup coverage as part of environmental impairment policy or through a specialized policy.

4.e. Increased Cost of Construction

Often after a loss an insured must make repairs to damaged buildings or structures to meet current building or zoning laws. An example would be an older warehouse that has knob and tube wiring; local building code now requires the building's owner to rewire with Romex (circuit breakers). The cost for this upgrade was not covered by the BPP, unless specifically endorsed, until additional coverage e. was introduced in the CP 00 10 10 00. The CP 00 10 10 00 edition added increased cost of construction as the fifth additional coverage. It provides up to $10,000—above the coverage limit—for increased costs associated with enforcement of building or zoning laws.

In its explanatory comments, ISO stated that the purpose of this coverage is "to respond in some measure to the situation where a building code requires some upgrades but not major construction changes." Of course the insured may still need coverage beyond the $10,000 amount, which can be arranged via endorsement. Note that this coverage applies only to buildings for which the insured has purchased the replacement cost optional coverage.

The increased cost of construction additional coverage responds to expense necessary for compliance with minimum standards of an ordinance or law in repairing or rebuilding damaged property. The phrase "minimum standards of" was added with the 2012 revisions in place of the words "enforcement of." The law must regulate construction or land use at the described premises and must be in force at the time of the loss. If a law required compliance prior to the loss and the insured did not comply, coverage does not apply. For example, if an insured failed to install a fire escape as required by ordinance or law, and a subsequent fire occurs, the insurer is not obligated to pay the $10,000 increase in cost of construction.

As with the debris removal additional coverage, this coverage does not apply to costs for pollutant removal. While it has never covered the costs associated with pollution testing, detoxifying, or cleanup, as of the rollout of CP 00 10 04 02, cost associated with the presence of mold is excluded.

The previous language read as follows:

Under this Additional Coverage, we will not pay:

any costs associated with the enforcement of an ordinance or law which requires any insured or others to test for, monitor, clean up, remove, contain, treat, detoxify or neutralize, or in any way respond to, or assess the effects of "pollutants".

An example is a convenience store that sells gasoline. After a fire damages a substantial part of the convenience store, the local ordinance will not permit the owner to rebuild until he certifies that no gasoline is leaking from the tanks. The cost of that certification is not covered by the BPP.

The 2012 version states:

Under this Additional Coverage, we will not pay for:

(a) The enforcement of or compliance with any ordinance or law which requires demolition, repair, replacement, recon-struction, remodeling or remediation of property due to con-tamination by "pollutants" or due to the presence, growth, proliferation, spread or any activity of "fungus," wet or dry rot or bacteria; or

(b) Any costs associated with the enforcement of or compliance with an ordinance or law which requires any insured or others to test for, monitor, clean up, remove, contain, treat, detoxify or neutralize, or in any way respond to, or assess the effects of "pollutants," "fungus," wet or dry rot or bacteria.

The effect is that the form not only excludes payment for the tank testing, it also excludes payment for any government-ordered mold removal.

The limit for this additional coverage is the lesser of 5 percent of the limit of insurance on the building or $10,000. If the policy provides blanket coverage on several buildings, this coverage is limited to the lesser of $10,000 or 5 percent times the value of the damaged building as of the time of loss times the applicable coinsurance percentage.

The additional coverage for increased cost of construction has its own conditions. It does not pay for the increased cost until the insured actually replaces the damaged property. It also does not pay unless the repairs or replacement are made as soon as reasonably possible, not to exceed two years (this period may be extended with the cooperation of the insurer). The insured may replace at the described premises or any other premises. However, if he chooses to replace at another premises, the policy pays only the amount it would have paid at the old premises for the increased construction costs. If the insured must relocate due to the dictates of a law, the policy pays increased costs at the new location.

This additional coverage is not subject to the ordinance or law exclusion to the extent they may conflict.

Higher limits for increases in cost of construction due to compliance with building ordinances or laws costs can be purchased under the Ordinance or Law Coverage endorsement, CP 04 05.

4.f. Electronic Data

The CP 00 10 04 02 edition introduced the additional coverage for electronic data. This provides an aggregate annual amount of $2,500 for destruction or corruption of electronic data unless a higher amount is shown in the declarations. Reference to the word *aggregate* means that the limit is the maximum payable, during the policy period, regardless of the number of occurrences of loss or damage. Electronic data, by specific reference, has the same meaning as in the property not covered section, thereby mirroring the provisions—electronic data is eliminated as covered property under the form and then brought back in as an additional coverage, subject to limits and limitations.

The destruction or corruption must be due to a covered cause of loss. Coverage provisions depend upon which causes of loss form is attached.

As mentioned in Chapter 1, electronic data is not considered to be a type of covered property. Specifically excepted, however, is electronic data integrated in and that operates and controls the building's elevator, lighting, heating, ventilation, air conditioning, or security system. In light of that coverage exception, the CP 00 10 10 12 edition, dealing with electronic data, does not apply under this additional coverages section. This edition, dealing with additional coverages, also does not apply to stock of prepackaged software because this kind of property does not fall within the category of electronic data considered not to be covered.

Under the special form (discussed in Chapter 4), the data is covered only against damage from the specified causes of loss as set out and the peril of collapse. If the insured has chosen the broad form perils (discussed in Chapter 3), electronic data is covered for the broad form perils and for collapse. However, if the insured has purchased extra causes of loss (such as flood or earthquake), those purchased causes do not apply to electronic data.

An important addition under this section is coverage for damage done by a virus to the data. The policy says a *virus* is "designed to damage or destroy any part of the system or disrupt its normal operation." The virus may be introduced by almost anyone from almost anywhere. However, the policy excludes damage manipulation by employees, including leased and temporary employees. It also excludes viruses introduced by or manipulation by anyone the named insured hires to work on the computer system (e.g., a repair technician or IT consultant).

Insureds commonly have substantial electronic data, e-commerce, and computer hardware exposures that are susceptible to unique losses that are generally limited or excluded under the BPP. These exposures can be handled by increasing coverage for destruction or corruption of electronic data by a declaration entry, by adding the Electronic Commerce (E-Commerce) endorsement, CP 04 30, for businesses conducting e-commerce, or by purchasing a separate electronic data processing policy.

Section 5. Coverage Extensions

Following the additional coverages is section 5, Coverage Extensions. The coverage extensions operate to allow the insured to extend coverage to certain property or property in certain situations if either of two conditions are met: a coinsurance percentage of 80 percent or a value reporting period symbol is shown on the declarations page. The coverage extensions are as follows:

- Newly Acquired or Constructed Property

- Personal Effects and Property of Others

- Valuable Papers and Records (Other Than Electronic Data)

- Property Off-premises

- Outdoor Property

- Non-owned Detached Trailers

- Business Personal Property Temporarily in Portable Storage Units

Except where specified otherwise, coverage extensions apply to property located in or on the described building or in the open or in a vehicle within one-hundred feet of the described premises. Unlike the additional coverages, the coverage extensions are additional insurance, which represent increased limits of liability.

5.a. Newly Acquired or Constructed Property

The first coverage extension addresses newly constructed or acquired property of the same type already covered. The first part of this coverage extension addresses newly acquired or constructed building property and the second addresses newly acquired business personal property.

If the insured is building a new building on the described premises, this coverage extension covers that building during construction. (Note that the BPP covers additions to existing buildings under building coverage).

The policy also covers buildings at a different location that the insured acquires. Coverage for these buildings is subject to the following two conditions:

1.   They must be intended for similar use as the described building; or

2.   They must be intended for use as a warehouse.

The policy provides up to $250,000 coverage per covered building under the coverage extension. This $250,000 coverage extension amount is available even if the insured carries less insurance on the declared building. For example, the insured's present building is insured for $100,000; however, a new building under construction on the same premises is, or will be, worth $500,000. If this building under construction suffers covered damage, the insured may collect up to $250,000, the limit of this coverage extension, and is not limited to the $100,000 carried on the existing building. This is a per building amount. It applies to a new building under construction on the described premises. It also applies to a building that the insured acquires at another location—as long as he intends to put that building to use in a similar manner as the existing building or intends to use it as a warehouse. The $250,000 coverage extension can be increased by adding the Newly Acquired or Constructed Property – Increase Limit endorsement, CP 04 25, to the BPP.

Part 2 of the newly acquired or constructed property coverage extension was extensively revised in the CP 00 10 10 00 edition; most of those revisions carry forth into the current edition. If the insured already carries coverage on business personal property, this extension gives the insured up to $100,000 coverage at a newly acquired location, regardless of the stated policy limit for business personal property. This extension does not, however, apply to business personal property at fairs, exhibitions, and trade shows.

While the CP 00 10 06 95 edition of the form promised coverage for business personal property at any location the insured acquires other than fairs or exhibitions, the CP 00 10 10 00 edition added clarifying language stating that coverage for newly acquired business personal property was divided into these three categories:

1.   Business personal property, including newly acquired business personal property, at any location (with the exception of fairs, exhibitions, and trade shows)

2.   Business personal property in newly constructed or acquired buildings at the described location

3.   Newly acquired business personal property at the described location

In the CP 00 10 10 12 edition, the third category was deleted with the explanation that when significant changes in volume and value of business personal property occur at described premises, it would be more appropriate to handle these changes by way of endorsement or through the use of a value reporting form. In other words, this coverage extension continues to provide a $100,000 limit of insurance if the business personal property is located at a newly acquired location; however, it eliminates the $100,000 coverage extension if newly acquired business personal property is received at the described premises (e.g., large inventory delivery). This makes good sense, particularly in light of the fact that the business personal property in the third category has nothing to do with newly acquired property. This not only affects the BBP form, but also Condominium Association Coverage Form, CP 00 17; Condominium Commercial Unit-Owners Coverage Form, CP 00 18; Standard Property Policy, CP 00 99; and Condominium Commercial Unit-Owners Changes – Standard Property Policy, CP 17 98.

The extension for newly acquired business personal property does not cover the following:

1.   Business personal property of others upon which the insured is working

2.   Business personal property of others that the insured has temporarily in his possession while manufacturing or wholesaling

The coverage extension to newly acquired buildings and business personal property operates for thirty days. The thirty-day period begins when the insured acquires or begins to build new property. It ends after thirty days, at policy expiration, or when the insured reports the values to the insurer, whichever is earliest. The additional premium due for the additional property is calculated from the date the construction begins or the insured acquires the property.

The temporary nature of the provision was discussed in *S. Kornreich & Sons, Inc. v. Genesis Ins. Co.*, 65 Cal. Rptr. 2d 418 (1997). The insureds purchased an apartment complex and asked the carrier to add it to the commercial property coverage. The carrier asked for additional information on the property for underwriting purposes. No coverage was bound for the acquired property, and fire damaged the apartment complex. Coverage for the damage was denied.

The insureds stated that the newly acquired property provision should grant them permanent coverage for the apartment complex because the newly acquired property was similar to the original properties covered by the policy and because values were reported within ninety days of the acquisition.

The court, though, concluded that the provision "for newly acquired buildings is merely a method of providing temporary coverage while the insured obtains permanent coverage, either through endorsement, a separate policy, or another insurer." The temporary coverage had expired prior to the loss, so no coverage was available for the loss.

Newly Acquired Location

Property insured under the BPP was damaged by a tornado. In addition to damage at the premises listed on the declarations page, the insured made a claim for property on premises it had rented at a second location. This location, used as a warehouse, had been rented within thirty days prior to the loss. As of the date of loss, the location had not been added to the policy. The question is whether the location qualifies for coverage as a newly acquired location.

One argument is that *acquired* means "to buy" and does not include renting property. The issue is if *to acquire* includes an element of control or must be ownership. Absent a specific policy definition of the word, the insured is entitled to the most favorable common dictionary meaning. "To come into possession of" does not necessarily connote ownership; it is broad enough to encompass other forms of possession, such as renting, leasing, or borrowing. Additionally, the policy uses the word *acquired* rather than *purchased* or some other term meaning "obtaining title." As acquiring is a broader term than purchasing, it is appropriate to include means of obtaining property other than acquiring ownership through purchase.

This additional premises is afforded coverage under the newly acquired property provision to rented locations, provided the insured is legally responsible for damages. Coverage would not extend to the building on the premises absent a legal obligation of the insured.

5.b. Personal Effects and Property of Others

The second coverage extension provides up to $2,500 for damage to property of others. As mentioned in Chapter 1, if the property of others is leased and requires insurance, it is included as business personal property of the named insured. If it is not leased, its value needs to be declared or the most that would be covered is the extension discussed here. The first part of the extension provides coverage for personal effects belonging to the named insured and officers, directors, partners, employees, members, or managers of the insured. Recognizing the increased use of the limited liability company formation, members and managers were added to the CP 00 10 10 02 edition. All perils of the policy apply to this personal effects and property of others coverage extension except theft. Property coverage beyond this limited coverage extension for personal effects belonging to the named insured and officers, directors, partners, employees, members, or managers of the insured is commonly provided under their respective homeowners policies.

The other part of this extension covers property of others that is in the care, custody, or control of the insured. The $2,500 limit represents goodwill coverage and is insufficient for an insured who regularly takes in property of others for servicing or processing. Theft under this coverage extension is covered for this second class of others' property. Property coverage beyond this limited coverage extension for property of others may be secured through a declarations entry for personal property of others, a separate Legal Liability Policy, or a specialized bailees coverage form.

The first part of this coverage extension provides much narrower coverage than the second. The policy limits coverage for employees, officers, directors, partners, members, or managers to their personal effects. A standard desktop dictionary says that *personal effects* are "privately owned items (as clothing and toilet articles) normally worn or carried on that person."

5.c. Valuable Papers and Records
(Other Than Electronic Data)

When a covered peril destroys valuable papers and records at a described location, several separate items must be taken into consideration, such as:

1.   the cost of blank paper, film, disks, or other storage media

2.   the cost of actually transcribing or copying such papers and records from available duplicates

3.   the cost of research and other expenses in reconstructing the records if no duplicates exist

The third item, the expense of research involved in recompiling data, is the subject of coverage extension 5.c. The insured may apply up to $2,500 for such research costs following destruction of valuable papers and records by an insured peril. Without this extension, the BPP covers only the first two items, new stock and transcription. This extension does not cover the expense associated with data stored electronically. That is addressed by the additional coverage for electronic data.

As well as adding a new additional coverage for electronic data, the CP 00 10 04 02 edition revised the coverage extension for valuable papers and records other than electronic data. This extension of $2,500 was revised to cover all valuable papers and records other than electronic data. As with the additional coverage for electronic data, an insured with the special causes of loss form is limited to the specified causes of loss for this coverage. Collapse is added for insureds with broad form perils.

The $2,500 limit applies on a per-location basis. Coverage includes cost of blank material on which records are reproduced and labor to do the job. However, those costs are not subject to the $2,500 limit and instead are within the limit applying to business personal property.

Higher limits for valuable papers and records may be secured through a declarations entry or through the purchase of a separate inland marine policy.

5.d. Property Off-premises

The BPP form provides $10,000 coverage for property located away from the described premises. The policy lists these three places where it covers such property:

1.   at a location the insured does not own, lease, or operate

2.   at a leased storage location if the insured entered into the lease after the effective date of the policy

3.   at any fair, trade show, or exhibition

The coverage provided by number 3 was introduced in the CP 00 10 10 00 edition. Previous editions specifically eliminated property at fairs, trade shows, and exhibitions from this extension. This is not in-transit coverage as property is not covered off-premises while in a vehicle. Further, the extension does not apply to property (samples, usually) in the control of any of the insured's salespersons unless the salesperson has the property at a fair, trade show, or exhibition. Stock off-premises is also covered under this extension. The policy defines *stock* as "merchandise held in storage or for sale, raw materials, or in-process or finished goods, including supplies used in their packing or shipping."

Considering that the named insured's business personal property is addressed in more than one coverage extension can present a problem, particularly when there is a disparity in the limits. For example, business personal property under the extension dealing with newly acquired property offers a limit of $100,000, whereas the limit dealing with the property off-premises extension is $10,000.

A case where both coverage extensions were involved in a dispute is *On-Site Fasteners and Construction Supplies, Inc. v. Mapfre Ins. Co. of Florida*, 82 So.3d 1001 (Fla. App. 2011). The named insured, a construction supply business, had two locations in Florida: Orange Park and St. Augustine. The commercial property policy issued by the insurer excluded theft of property at the Orange Park location but included coverage at the other location. This policy covered various provisions for extending coverage for up to thirty days for newly acquired property and property off-premises. The named insured entered into an agreement to lease another warehouse facility in the same business park in which its Orange Park premises was located. Although the named insured was to take possession on a certain date, it obtained permission to take occupancy two weeks earlier to accommodate a large shipment of inventory. The shipment was stored in the newly leased warehouse; two weeks later, approximately $19,000 of inventory was stolen during a burglary. The insurer denied coverage because it occurred as a result of theft.

In support of its motion, the named insured argued that it was entitled to coverage pursuant to the newly acquired property extension, which applied to "business personal property, including such property that you newly acquire, at any location you acquire other than at fairs, trade shows or exhibitions." The named insured also argued that the theft exclusion applied only at the Orange Park address listed on the declarations, that the loss did not occur at that location, and nothing either in the policy or in the declarations indicated that the exclusion applied to newly acquired property stored in a different location. Given the ambiguity, the named insured maintained that the provisions should be read favorably to it.

The insurer, on the other hand, argued that the property off-premises provision applied, subject to a limit of $10,000, because the theft exclusion for the Orange Park location applied to the newly-leased premises located in the same business park as the Orange Park premises. Although the trial court found coverage for the named insured, it erred by applying the incorrect policy provision.

In affirming the trial court's denial of the insurer's motion for summary judgment and reversing the trial court's order to the extent it relied on the incorrect provision, the court of appeal held that the off-premises provision applied to temporary storage situations, such as those involving property that had been located in a site described in the policy, but moved offsite for storage, or where covered property was transported to a fair, trade show, or exhibition. In this case, however, the stolen property, the court said, was not "away from the described premises." Rather, it was in a shipment of new inventory housed in the newly-leased warehouse. The newly acquired property section of the policy, the court said, provided for a less transient situation than that contemplated by the off-premises provision.

The court stated that while the appropriate provision of the newly acquired property section covering the loss was poorly drafted, it provided coverage for business personal property located at a newly acquired location as long as it was not at a fair, trade show, or exhibition—it was not a temporary situation covered by the off-premises provision. In addition, the court said, it covers business personal property that is newly acquired.

Insureds with property exposures beyond the reach of the limited property off-premises coverage extension may cover this exposure with an inland marine policy.

Meaning of *Locations You Own, Lease, or Operate*

A commercial property insured went to a customer's location to answer a service call. While at the customer's shop, a piece of equipment the insured brought with him fell off a ledge and was damaged to the amount of $2,900. The claim was denied under this provision stating the insured was operating at this location while making the service call. At issue is if the property off-premises coverage extension applies to the damaged equipment.

> The BPP form's property off-premises provision allows the extension of coverage (up to $10,000) to apply to covered property that is temporarily at a location that the insured does not own, lease, or operate. Performing a service call at a customer's premises is not equivalent to a location that the insured operates. The phrase *own, lease, or operate* denotes a control feature absent here. Coming onto a customer's premises to perform services does not turn control of that location over to the person coming in. The word *operate* must be viewed in relation to the other words in the provision and interpreted in that context. Therefore, the equipment is covered for up to $10,000 under coverage extension 5.d.

5.e. Outdoor Property

The BPP form lists as property not covered a variety of outdoor property that may sometimes be found around a commercial enterprise. This extension restores coverage for direct damage and debris removal for loss to the following types of outdoor property (which are not covered under the basic BPP): outdoor fences, radio and television antennas (including satellite dishes), and trees, shrubs, and plants (other than trees, shrubs, or plants that are stock or a part of a vegetated roof).

Prior to the CP 00 10 06 07 edition, detached signs were eliminated from coverage in the property not covered section and limited coverage was brought back in here. ISO revised the property not covered and outdoor property coverage extension sections to remove reference to detached signs. Coverage for outdoor signs is thereby subject to the applicable causes of loss form and to a special provision in the limits of insurance condition. The limits of insurance condition are revised to increase coverage on outdoor signs from $1,000 per sign to $2,500 per sign in any one occurrence. Although outdoor signs are subject to the policy's applicable causes of loss form, its low dollar limitation commonly requires securing a higher dollar amount through an endorsement to the BPP or through a separate inland marine policy.

This outdoor property extension applies only if loss is caused by fire, lightning, explosion, riot or civil commotion, or aircraft. The total amount available for direct damage and debris removal is $1,000 per occurrence, regardless of the types or number of items lost or damaged in that occurrence, subject to a $250 maximum for any one tree, shrub, or plant. Trees, shrubs, or plants that are stock or are part of a vegetated roof are not included in this coverage extension as they are not included in the property not covered section.

New with the CP 00 10 10 12 edition is coverage for the expense of removing—from the described premises—the debris of trees, shrubs, and plants that are the property of others, except in the situation where the named insured is a tenant and the property is owned by the landlord of the described premises. This expense, in other words, would apply if the property belonged to a neighbor. This 2012 revision affects Debris Removal Additional Insurance, CP 04 15; and Outdoor Trees, Shrubs and Plants, CP 14 30.

Endorsements covering outdoor property that may be added to the BPP include Outdoor Trees, Shrubs and Plants, CP 14 30; Outdoor Signs, CP 14 40; and Radio and Television Antennas, CP 14 50. More specialized endorsements for these and other types of outdoor property are available through various inland marine policies.

5.f. Non-owned Detached Trailers

The CP 00 10 10 00 edition of the BPP form added this sixth coverage extension. ISO explains the addition by stating, "Many insureds have goods delivered by truck and may be held responsible by the trucking company for damage to or theft of detached trailers left on the insured's premises for unloading and retrieval. In addition, insureds who rent detached trailers from others for storage purposes may be held responsible for damage to or theft of the trailers." The BPP form provides no automatic coverage for such trailers. ISO introduced this coverage extension to provide limited coverage on non-owned detached trailers.

The policy provides $5,000 of coverage (with larger amounts available) for non-owned trailers that the insured has on its premises. This additional coverage is excess over any other applicable insurance, whether or not it is collectible.

In order to qualify for this coverage, the non-owned trailer must meet the following three requirements:

1. It must be used in the insured's business.

2. It must be in the insured's care, custody, or control at the described premises.

3. The insured must have a contractual obligation to pay for damage to the trailer.

Coverage does not apply while the trailer is attached to a motor vehicle or while it is being hitched or unhitched. There is also no coverage if the trailer becomes accidentally unhitched from a motor vehicle. Trailers that are attached to a motor vehicle are covered under the Business Auto Policy.

Insureds with non-owned detached trailer exposures beyond the limited $5,000 coverage extension may increase coverage by a declarations entry or by purchasing an inland marine policy.

5.g. Business Personal Property Temporarily in Portable Storage Units

New with the CP 00 10 10 12 edition of the BPP form is an extension providing a ninety-day coverage period for business personal property temporarily stored in a portable storage unit (including a detached trailer unit) located within one-hundred feet of the described premises, subject to a sublimit of $10,000, regardless of the number of storage units. A higher limit can be entered in the declarations page. This 2012 revision affects the BBP form; Condominium Association Coverage Form, CP 00 17; Condominium Commercial Unit-Owners Coverage Form, CP 00 18; and Standard Property Policy, CP 00 99.

If the applicable covered causes of loss form is subject to any limitation or exclusion dealing with loss or damage from sand, dust, sleet, snow, ice, or rain to the property in a structure, such limitation also applies to the property in such portable storage units.

As mentioned, the time limit for otherwise covered business personal property is ninety days after it has been placed in the unit. This extension, however, does not apply if the storage unit has been in use at the described premises for more than ninety consecutive days even if the business personal property has been stored there for ninety or fewer days as of the time of loss or damage. The storage unit, or container, in other words, must be of a transient nature and not fixed.

The basic limit of $10,000, which may be increased, is considered part of, and not in addition to, the applicable limit of insurance on the insured's business personal property. Thus, payment under this extension will not increase the applicable limit of insurance of the insured's business personal property.

This extension does not apply to loss or damage not otherwise covered under this the BPP form or any endorsement, and does not apply to loss or damage to the storage unit itself.

As a matter of background information, ISO stated, with reference to this new extension that the BPP form covers listed types of business personal property, while in or on the covered building, or in the open within one-hundred feet of the described premises, or in a vehicle within one-hundred feet of the described premises, unless otherwise specified.

Also, the language addressing business personal property in the open or in a vehicle does not expressly handle situations where business personal property is located outside of the covered building in a storage unit.

The addition of the term *structure* might be another way to have handled this situation. The problem is that the term *structure* may relate more to something that is fixed at a location, which is unlike a portable container that is mobile in nature.

According to ISO, this extension represents a broadening of coverage unless an insurer has previously treated property in a storage unit as property in the open. In this case, it would be limitation in light of the sublimit. Property within a container at the described premises should be covered to the extent coverage applies to property in the open within the permitted distance. But not all insurers necessarily will follow that line of reasoning. In fact, one of the cases that may have prompted ISO to introduce this extension is *QBE Specialty Insurance Co. v. FSI, Ind.* 2011 WL 1655591, No. 3:09cv435 (W.D. N.C. May 2, 2011), which was discussed in Chapter 1 relating to the meaning of *property in the open*.

Higher limits for business personal property temporarily in portable storage units may be secured through a declarations entry or through the purchase of a separate inland marine policy.

Optional Coverages

The BPP form offers the insured four optional coverages that are so frequently used as to be available in the basic policy. As these are built into the form, no extra endorsements are required. The optional coverages may be activated on the policy declarations if appropriate or desired. They are contained in section G. of the policy and include the following:

- Agreed Value

- Inflation Guard

- Replacement Cost

- Extension of Replacement Cost to Personal Property of Others

Section G.1. Agreed Value

When the insured selects agreed value, this coverage provides for a predetermined amount to be paid in the event of a total loss to the described property. If the insured does not desire this option for the entire policy period, he may choose when to make this option effective and when to terminate it. This allows the BPP form to be integrated more seamlessly into the insured's business where there may be seasonal differences in inventory or value.

When the insured chooses this option, the coinsurance condition does not apply. However the rules state the insured must carry an amount equal to 80 percent of the building's value or 90 percent for risks written on a blanket basis. Property written on a reporting basis is not eligible for agreed value, nor are builders risk policies. The insured must complete the Statement of Values endorsement, CP 16 15. Replacement cost values are used if the insured has purchased replacement cost coverage.

If the building is insured on an agreed value basis for $200,000 and is a total loss, the insurer would simply write the insured a check for $200,000. The insured may also choose to cover some or all contents on this basis.

In *Society of St. Vincent De Paul in Archdiocese of Detroit v. Mt. Hawley Ins. Co,,* 49 F.Supp 2d 1011 (E.D. Mich. 1999), the court ruled that the agreed value provision affects the amount of insurance the insured is entitled to recover, not the amount of the loss.

The insured argued that the agreed value was the amount of the loss, and that amount should be paid under the policy. The court said that the agreed value clause provides the advantage to the insured that it is adequately insuring the property. The clause, the court said, "clarifies the maximum amount of insurance dollars that will be paid for a covered loss; it does not address how that covered loss is to be valued."

The court also distinguished the agreed value provision from a valued policy, stating, "The policy at issue here does not provide that, in the event of total loss, the insurer must pay the insured the 'Agreed Value' of the destroyed property."

Section G.2. Inflation Guard

As a protection against the effects of inflation, the insured may choose the inflation guard optional coverage to automatically increase limits for designated property, either completed buildings or personal property, by a predetermined annual percentage. Inflation guard may be used on policies written on either a specific or blanket basis. If there is a midterm loss, the limit of liability is increased on a pro rata basis, from either the effective date of the policy or the effective date of the last change in the limit.

The current edition of the BPP form contains the following example of how this coverage works:

If: The applicable limit of insurance is $100,000

The annual percentage increase is 8 percent

The number of days since the beginning of the policy year (or last policy change) is 146

The amount of increase is $100,000 x .08 x 146/365, which equals $3,200

Section G.3. Replacement Cost

The insured may purchase replacement cost coverage on various property, such as

1. buildings and permanent machinery, fixtures, and equipment that are covered with the building.

2. business personal property including furniture, fixtures, machinery, and equipment.

3. merchandise and stock if the including stock option is shown as applicable in the declarations.

4. tenants improvements and betterments. The specific provision states that for the purposes of replacement cost coverage tenants improvements and betterments are not considered the property of others. Since these items become the property of the landlord, some confusion existed in the past about how to treat them in the event of a loss. This wording makes it clear that a tenant who has purchased this coverage will receive replacement cost coverage for the improvements he has made to a building.

5. personal property of others if the extension of replacement cost to personal property of others is shown as applicable in the declarations (discussed later).

The policy specifies the following types of property as not eligible for replacement cost coverage:

1. personal property of others

2. contents of a residence

3.   works of art, antiques, or rare articles, including etchings, pictures, statuary, marbles, bronzes, porcelains, and bric-a-brac

4.   stock unless the insured includes stock on the declarations

Replacement cost coverage operates by the insured making a claim for the actual cash value (ACV) of damaged property at the time of loss and requesting replacement cost settlement within 180 days. By first making an ACV claim, the insured gets some insurance payment and may engage a contractor to start work. The insured must make repairs or replacement as soon as reasonably possible; the insurer does not make a replacement cost settlement until repairs or replacements are completed.

The optional coverage adds the following two conditions regarding paying replacement cost for tenant improvements and betterments:

1.   If the insured does not replace the improvements or does not replace them as soon as reasonably possible after loss, loss adjustment reverts to the valuation condition (See Chapter 5).

2.   If someone else, such as the landlord, pays to repair or replace the improvements, the policy pays nothing.

The BPP pays the least of the following:

1.   the limit of liability applicable to the damaged property

2.   the cost to replace the property for the same use, with material of comparable material and quality

3.   the amount the insured actually spends

Provision 2 was changed in the CP 00 10 10 00 edition. The wording *on the same premises* was removed because it caused confusion and could be interpreted to mean that the policy required the insured to rebuild on the same location to receive replacement cost, which is not a requirement. The revision added the following wording that clearly allows the insured to rebuild at a new location: "If a building is rebuilt at a new premises, the cost described in e.(2) above is limited to the cost which would have been incurred if the building had been rebuilt at the original premises." For example, if the building cost $300,000 to replace at its current location but the insured chooses to rebuild at a different location where it will cost $350,000, he will receive only $300,000 from the insurer.

Provision f., the last provision of this optional coverage, precludes coverage having to do with the increased cost attributable to the enforcement of any ordinance or law regulating the construction, use, or repair of any property. This provision was changed with the 2012 revisions. The wording *or compliance with* was added so that no coverage applies for any increased cost attributable to enforcement of or compliance with any ordinance or law. The addition was made necessary because building code enforcement comes about through the permit process. Compliance, on the other hand, is something that building owners and managers have a duty to know and to comply with in light of the existence of building codes promulgated by statute or regulatory authority.

A key element for recovering under replacement cost insurance is that payment will not be made on a replacement cost basis until the lost or damaged property is actually repaired or replaced, a fact reiterated in *Fitzhugh 25 Partners, L.P. v. KILN Syndicate KLN 501*, 261 S.W.3d 861 (Tex. App. – Dallas 2008).

The insured carried replacement cost coverage on an apartment complex, which was damaged by fire. The insurer paid Fitzhugh the actual cash value for the loss. The apartments were eventually demolished, and their lots remained empty.

Fitzhugh later purchased an interest in an urban commercial office park and notified the insurer that the apartment complex was being replaced by another commercial building—the office park in which he had bought an interest. He claimed he was owed additional recovery based on the replacement cost provision of the apartment complex's policy.

While the court agreed with Fitzhugh that the apartment buildings did not have to be replaced with identical buildings at the same site, it disagreed that this gave Fitzhugh free reign to use the replacement cost recovery for whatever he wanted. The new buildings are required to be devoted to the same use as the damaged ones. By not replacing the apartment complex with something functionally similar, Fitzhugh did not meet the provision's requirements.

Replacement by Substitution

An insured building was heavily damaged by fire, and the insured found another suitable building, which, after remodeling, would become a replacement for the damaged one. The insurance company agreed to pay the cost of the acquisition but not the cost of improvements. The values of the two sites were generally equivalent, as were the outbuildings. Thus, the transaction represented an even trade from that standpoint. So, in essence, what the insured was requesting of the insurer was to allow him to spend the dollars improving the substitute site that would have been spent in repairing the original. Yet, the insurer balked at the transaction.

When an insured chooses the optional replacement cost coverage, the Business and Personal Property Coverage Form stipulates three limits. It agrees to pay the least of the following:

1. the limit of insurance applicable to the lost or damaged property

2. the cost to replace the lost or damaged property with other property of comparable material and quality and used for the same purpose

3. the amount the named insured actually spends that is necessary to repair or replace the lost or damaged property

The third limitation opens the promise to replacement at any site. Consequently, if the third category expenditure is both less than the coverage limit and less or even equal to the price of repairs at the original site, then the conditions of the policy are met and the insured may make the move.

The word *necessary* might seem to be a curious entry in the third limitation. Since it is not defined in the policy, that judgment is left to the insured, which is appropriate. The first limitation protects the insurer. It limits the insurer's payment to no more than the applicable limit stated in the contract. Whether the insured elects to repair the damage to the existing structure or move off site, the insurer's possible maximum loss is not affected.

Replacement Cost and Reconditioned Property

This scenario examines the meaning of *comparable material and quality*.

A commercial property insured elected the replacement cost option. Lightning destroyed the insured's computerized phone system to the extent it could not be repaired and had to be replaced. The insurer located a used reconditioned phone system of the same make and model as the damaged system and offered to purchase and install it. The insurer believed that this option met the policy obligation since the policy states that the insurer has the option to pay the cost of repairing or replacing the lost or damaged property.

The BPP form states that the value of covered property (the phone system) will be determined at replacement cost without deduction for depreciation. A reconditioned phone system is a used phone system and, as such, is depreciated. The policy promises the insured that losses to covered property will be adjusted on a replacement cost basis, so the insured is entitled to a new phone system.

Replacement Cost and New Location

What happens if the replacement cost of a building is less than its actual cash value (ACV), as possible when real estate values decline rapidly?

The insured owned a building that was destroyed. The ACV of the building was $190,000, but the insured had it covered for replacement cost at $300,000. Rather than replacing the building at the same location, the insured bought another building at another location. The new building was one-third larger than the destroyed building, yet it cost less. It cost $230,000, and the insured put $20,000 into it to make it usable for a total of $250,000. Since the building is one-third larger than the old building the insurer wanted to pay only 75 percent of the cost of the new building, or $187,500. This figure was less than the ACV on the old building. The insurer claimed that the extra square footage in the new building was a betterment for which the insurer should not pay. Should the insured have been paid full replacement cost, actual cash value, or the value of the new building prorated for the number of square feet in the destroyed building?

This is one of the few examples of a replacement cost settlement on a commercial property loss paying less than an actual cash value settlement. Situations such as this illustrate why the insured is given the chance to choose an actual cash value settlement even though the replacement cost option is in force.

Under paragraph e. of the replacement cost option, the insurer states that it will pay the least of three replacement costs: (1) the limit of the policy; (2) the cost to replace the property with property of comparable material and quality for the same use; or (3) the actual amount spent to replace the property at any location.

In this case, the third option applies and must be used. Since the replacement property was one-third larger than the original property, the cost of actually replacing the destroyed property's square footage is 75 percent of the cost of the new property (i.e., 100 sq. ft. × 1.333 = 133 sq. ft.; but 100 sq. ft. = 75 percent of 133 sq. ft., because 133 × .75 = 100). Since the new property cost less per square foot to construct than the old property, the insured receives a lower settlement at replacement cost than if he had chosen the actual cash value valuation.

Section G.4. Extension of Replacement Cost to Personal Property of Others

The option for the insured to extend replacement cost coverage to the property of others was introduced with the CP 00 10 10 00 edition.

When the insured chooses this option, it deletes the reference to property of others as not being covered under the replacement cost option.

If an item of personal property of others is subject to a written contractual obligation governing the insured's liability for that item, the policy covers loss or damage to such property only at the amount for which the insured is liable under the contract.

For example, insureds commonly lease large high speed copiers, computer systems, and other high priced personal property of others. Generally those lease agreements require the insured/lessee to replace the leased property if it is damaged. This extension deletes the reference to property of others as not being covered under the replacement cost option and pays the lesser of the property's replacement cost or the limit of insurance.

Chapter 3

Covered Causes of Loss— Named Perils Forms

Chapters 1 and 2 described and analyzed what is—and is not—covered property for purposes of the Building and Personal Property Coverage form. The damage-causing events and incidents that the policy is meant to protect against—the *perils* covered—are determined by the insured's selection of a causes of loss form that enumerates and defines these covered and excluded perils. One of three causes of loss form is attached to the building and personal property coverage form to make a policy, along with endorsements and conditions forms. The options are the *basic form* (named perils), the *broad form* (named perils still, but the number of perils expanded), and the *special form* (any peril not otherwise excluded), also referred to as *open perils* or in older nomenclature, *all risks* (the term *all risks* went out of favor in the 1980s as the term caused policy interpretation problems with judicial decisions vitiating exclusions where the insurer promised *all risks* coverage).

The perils covered by the BPP and several other of the insuring forms comprising the commercial property program depend upon the insured's choice of one of the three causes of loss forms. The basic and broad causes of loss forms are treated in this chapter; Chapter 4 deals with the special causes of loss form.

The basic form covers eleven basic perils, and the broad form adds three perils and one additional coverage—collapse. Under previous commercial property programs, insureds had to purchase separate coverage for the glass in their buildings using form CP 00 15. That form is no longer in use. ISO simplified the underwriting process and the policy by writing coverage on glass under the BPP form and subject to the perils applicable to other property.

CP 10 10—Causes of Loss – Basic Form

This form provides named perils coverage and is the most limited of the causes of loss forms. Only those perils specifically included in the form are covered, and loss or damage must be directly caused by the peril. The covered perils under the basic form are fire, lightning, explosion, windstorm and hail, smoke, aircraft or vehicles, riot or civil commotion, vandalism, sprinkler leakage, sinkhole collapse, and volcanic action.

Fire. The named peril forms do not limit the peril of fire; however, courts have long held that fire means a *hostile* fire, one that has left its intended confines. Hostile fires are contrasted to the *friendly fire* doctrine. The friendly fire doctrine provides that loss by friendly fires is not insured and that a friendly fire is one that the insured intentionally kindles and that remains in the place it was intended to be. A hostile fire is one that is either not confined to the place intended or one not started intentionally. A minority of courts have expanded the idea of hostile fire to include those that they characterize as excessive, as when a thermostat or other part of a furnace malfunctions and damages either the heating device itself or some other property through extreme heat.

In *Engle v. Redwood County Farmers Mut. Ins. Co*, 281 N.W.2d 331 (Minn. 1979), the Minnesota Supreme Court ruled that a fire may be hostile even if it burns at its usual rate if it burns for a greater length of time than intended.

The insured constructed a hog barn on his farm, which was heated by a furnace that blew hot air into the barn via a fan. The insured found fifteen of the hogs in the barn dead. The deaths were caused by loss of oxygen due to increased temperature. The furnace shorted out, rendering the thermostat inoperable.

The fire inside the furnace burned and produced heat at its normal rate. The fire itself did not cause any damage to barn and was confined to the furnace. The insurer denied coverage for the loss, stating that it was the result of a friendly fire rather than a hostile fire.

While the insured argued that a fire burning at its usual rate would not be considered excessive, the court said, "A fire which causes damage by burning for a greater length of time than intended is no less uncontrolled merely because it continues to burn at its usual rate."

The thermostat caused the furnace to burn until the temperature in the barn reached 120°, past the preset temperature of 75°. The court said that under those circumstances, the fire would not be considered controlled.

The distinction between friendly and hostile fires applies only to insureds that have purchased named perils coverage. On a special causes of loss form, the doctrine of friendly fire does not apply; coverage is not restricted to named perils but responds to damage unless a specific exclusion applies.

Lightning. As with the peril of fire, the policy does not limit lightning. From the earliest insuring forms lightning has been an accepted corollary of the fire peril. Lightning is naturally generated electricity from the atmosphere (e.g., lightning strike during a thunderstorm) as opposed to artificially generated electricity (e.g., electricity produced by a power station). This distinction (naturally generated electricity vs. artificially generated electricity) is important when losses involve damage to electronic components. For example, if lightning strikes a building causing a surge in voltage that damages property with electronic components, coverage applies under the lightning peril. However, if a power surge from an electric generating station damages electronic components, coverage is excluded. The exclusion for damage to electronic components caused by artificially generated electricity is reviewed further in Chapter 4. Note that in any case, a following fire loss that originates from a lightning strike or from a manmade electrical surge is covered.

Explosion. The policy does not define *explosion*, so it is subject to broad interpretation. The dictionary defines *explosion* as "the act of exploding," "to burst forth with sudden violence or noise from internal energy," "to undergo a rapid reaction with the production of noise, heat and violent expansion," or "to burst violently as a result of pressure from within."

Because the policy does not define *explosion*, courts have sometimes been asked to do so, often stating what does not constitute an explosion. For instance, in *Living Challenge, Inc. v. Foremost Ins. Group*, No. A09-2062, 2010 WL 3119454 (Minn. App. Aug. 10, 2010), the court ruled that the breaking of a shower valve that resulted from water freezing in pipes would not be considered an explosion. Likewise, in *Schmieder v. State Farm Fire & Cas. Co.*, 339 So.2d 390 (La. App. 1976), the court found that a concrete roof falling due to improper reinforcement of the roof and failure to furnish adequate support was not an explosion, even if the roof cracking makes a loud noise similar to one accompanying an explosion.

Coverage is provided for damage caused by an explosion caused by gases or fuels (e.g., natural gas or fuel oil) within a furnace or any fired vessel or within the flues or passages through which the gases of combustion pass. The BPP's causes of loss forms were designed to cover this type of explosion. If, however, loss or damage was caused by a rupture, bursting, or operation of pressure relief devices (such as when a valve from a steam boiler ruptures), no coverage would apply. This type of exposure is not covered under any of the BPP's causes of loss forms. Steam boilers and similar equipment pose a greater exposure than explosion caused by natural gas, oil, or coal. Consequently, steam explosions are not covered under the BPP's explosion peril. Likewise, rupture or bursting due to expansion or swelling of the contents of any building or structure caused by, or resulting from, water is also excluded. For example, if a storage container expands and ruptures due to an accumulation of water, no coverage would apply under the explosion peril.

Coverage for these kinds of exposures can be secured under an Equipment Breakdown Cause of Loss endorsement, CP 10 46, or under a separate equipment breakdown protection policy.

Is a Gunshot an Explosion?

The insured is a gun shop covered on a BPP with the Causes of Loss – Basic form, CP 10 10. While the store owner was cleaning a gun it accidentally discharged, causing a large hole in one of the interior walls. Although the agent argued that this constituted an explosion, the insurer denied the claim.

The policy does not define *explosion*. In the policy's description of the explosion peril, it does, however, include explosion of gases or fuel in a furnace. It also excludes rupture of pressure relief devices. It does not specifically exclude gunshot from the definition of *explosion*. A definition of *explosion* is "a large-scale, rapid, and spectacular expansion, outbreak, or upheaval." That is what happened, and the damage to the shop's wall is covered. The important point is that the form does not say it must be the covered property that explodes; it is damage by explosion that is covered.

Exhibit 3-1

Causes of Loss – Basic Form Perils		
Fire	Smoke	Sprinkler Leakage
Lightning	Aircraft or Vehicles	Sinkhole Collapse
Explosion	Riot or Civil Commotion	Volcanic Action
Windstorm or Hail	Vandalism	

Windstorm or Hail. The policy's coverage for damage by windstorm or hail is limited by three provisions that state coverage does not include the following:

1. frost or cold weather

2. ice (other than hail), snow, or sleet, whether driven by wind or not

3. loss or damage to the interior or a building or structure (or the property inside) caused by rain, snow, sand, or dust, whether

driven by wind or not. In order for such a loss to be covered the building or structure must first sustain wind or hail damage to the roof or walls through which the rain, snow, sand, or dust enters.

Direct Loss from Windstorm

A subject of coverage argument and litigation has been determining the meaning of direct physical loss caused by or resulting from windstorm. Another topic of significant interest following the hurricane season of 2005, which included hurricanes Katrina, Rita, and Wilma, and the hurricane season of 2012 that included hurricane Sandy, is the relationship between windstorm coverage and flood insurance and what can be covered as wind damage and what is excluded as flood damage. Forms do not define *windstorm*, so courts are often asked to do so within the circumstances of a particular case. In *Koory v. Western Cas. and Surety Co.*, 737 P.2d 388 (Ariz. 1987), the Arizona Supreme Court said, "A windstorm is a wind of sufficient force to proximately cause damage to the ordinary condition of the thing insured."

A majority of courts agree that the wind does not need to be the only cause of loss for a loss to be directly related to windstorm. For example, assume damage is not by wind knocking over a covered shed but from a board picked up by the wind hitting the shed. The rule is that the windstorm must be the proximate cause or the efficient proximate cause of the loss. The minority of courts have followed the rule that any contributing cause to the damage must itself not be excluded by the policy.

Many courts have followed the rule that a direct loss from windstorm occurs when it is shown that the force or strength of the wind caused the damage. Some jurisdictions require that the winds be tumultuous and have the nature of a storm. Courts have also addressed the issue of whether there is direct loss from windstorm when the wind-damaged property was in poor physical condition. Generally, these courts have held that there is covered loss if the windstorm was the proximate cause.

The first part of the exclusionary language reaffirms the policy intent that damage by frost or cold weather is not equivalent to damage by windstorm or hail. However, a windstorm during the winter months that causes damage that is not equivalent to damage by cold weather (e.g., freezing) would be covered.

The policy states that before windstorm or hail damage to the interior of a building is covered, the exterior must suffer damage from wind or hail. Once wind or hail damages the exterior of the building, the policy covers the interior for damage caused by rain, snow, sand, or dust entering the structure. A common type of claim reached by this exclusion is water damage to walls, ceilings, or personal property that occurs during a windstorm but for which there is no apparent source. Sometimes this type of damage results from seepage around window casings or eaves that are of adequate soundness for ordinary weather but not for extraordinary wind events. The argument has been made that absent some kind of damage, temporary though it may be, water would not have seeped through the window or ceiling.

Added with the 2012 ISO revisions precluding coverage with regard to hail is loss or damage to lawns, trees, shrubs, or plants that are part of a vegetated roof.

Is a Tarp a Roof?

A business insured under the BPP with the basic causes of loss form contracted to have the roof changed from a flat rolled roof to a metal gable roof. This required the contractor to cut the roof edges to install a new sill plate on the exterior block walls so the new roof trusses could be properly secured. At the end of each day, the contractor covered the edge of the roof with tarps. During construction a windstorm ripped the tarps off the roof and allowed water to enter the building causing damage to contents.

The claim was denied based on the policy language that requires a building to first sustain wind or hail damage to its roof or walls before the policy covers water damage to contents. The insurer argued that the tarps used to cover the roof were not part of the roof or walls. Because the structure did not sustain damage, there was no coverage for the water damage to the contents.

The basic causes of loss form qualifies the windstorm or hail peril with language that eliminates coverage for loss or damage to the interior of a building or its contents unless the building first sustains damage to its roof or walls through which the rain enters. A standard dictionary defines *roof* as "the cover of a building"; "material used for a roof"; and "something suggesting a roof: as a canopy of leaves and branches." Absent a specific policy definition, the insurance contract is broadly interpreted in favor of coverage. In this case the tarp was acting as a substitute for the actual roof and was, in fact, the roof at the time of the incident.

In *Homestead Fire Ins. Co. v De Witt*, 245 P.2d 92 (Okla. 1952), the court ruled that a canvas covering was a roof, A construction company was building an addition to a school. In order to join the new and old sections, an opening was left in the roof of the old building. The construction company covered the opening with canvas to protect the old building. A sudden windstorm arose, ripped off the canvas, and rain damaged the interior.

Even though this case preceded the policies of today, it contained similar language that required roof damage before the insurer would cover water damage to the interior or its contents. The court ruled that because the contractors "evidently considered [as] adequate" the canvas that had been placed on the opening, this "brought it within the provisions of the windstorm clause, since except for the action of the wind, the opening was adequately closed." The canvas was a roof. This case has been cited numerous times over the years and has not been overturned.

However, a California appeals court saw things differently in *Diep v. California Fair Plan Ass'n.*, 15 Cal.App.4th 1205 (1993). The court said: "While 'roof' has many different meanings (e.g., roof of the mouth), dictionary definitions are consistent with respect to that which people usually expect to find on top of a building...a roof is commonly considered to be a permanent part of the structure it covers. Roof is not an ambiguous or vague word...the parties to the insurance contract could not have originally intended the result the plaintiff seeks here."

Windstorm or hail is one of three causes of loss that may be removed from coverage by the Windstorm or Hail Exclusion endorsement, CP 10 54. Insurers doing business in areas such as the South Atlantic or Gulf coast often refuse to write wind coverage or write it subject to high rates and large deductibles. One such ISO endorsement is Windstorm or Hail Percentage Deductible, CP 03 21. The form offers three percentages—1, 2 or 5 percent—which apply separately to the covered property. Endorsement CP 03 20, the Multiple Deductible form, offers multiple fixed deductibles for causes of loss not limited to windstorm or hail. In other areas windstorm coverage is available through a catastrophe pool or similar facility administered by a governmental entity.

Smoke. The term *smoke*, like *fire*, is undefined in the policy. Many courts have followed a definition similar to this one from *Webster's Tenth New Collegiate Dictionary*: "the gaseous products of burning carbonaceous materials especially of organic origin made visible by the presence of small particles of carbon."

At one time, smoke damage referred only to sudden and accidental smoke from the faulty operation of a heating or cooking unit at the insured premises. Damage resulting from smoke from a fireplace was excluded.

The current property forms cover sudden and accidental smoke damage from almost any source except for agricultural smudging (i.e., the use of smudge pots to produce a smoky fire for protecting certain crops from frost and insects) and industrial operations (i.e., smoke damage from a neighboring industrial plant). The BPP excludes smoke damage from these sources because such operations represent constant or constantly recurring exposures. Damage is certain to occur, so there is no insurable risk; there is a certainty of loss.

Courts usually apply a definition of *smoke* that requires a visible product of combustion. However, in *Henri's Food Products Co. v. Home Ins. Co.*, 474 F. Supp. 889 (E.D. Wisc. 1979), the court held that the insured was covered for smoke damage when the outside of bottles of salad dressing stored in a warehouse were contaminated by the vaporization of agricultural chemicals also stored in the warehouse. The court did not discuss its reasoning in any depth, stating simply that it relied on *Words and Phrases* and *Webster's Third New International Dictionary*. Perhaps the court relied on the inclusion of *vapor* among the dictionary definitions.

A court in another case disagreed with the Wisconsin court's opinion. In *K & Lee Corp. v. Scottsdale Ins. Co.*, 769 F. Supp. 870 (D.C. Pa.1991), the court held, "An unabridged comprehensive dictionary lists every conceivable usage of words, including those that are arcane, archaic, and obscure. While smoke may result from some chemical reactions, the common usage of the term refers to the products of combustion and, more importantly, to matter that is visible."

The term *industrial operations* raises another interpretation issue. A Georgia appeals court said that the term did not to apply to what the court described as a small neighborhood bakery in *Georgia Farm Bureau Mut. Ins. Co. v. Washington*, 243 S.E.2d 639 (Ga. App. 1978). The insured was a dress shop owner whose merchandise was damaged by smoke that escaped from the faulty exhaust vent of the nearby bakery. The trial court held for the insured, and the court of appeals affirmed with little comment. The trial court held that exclusions and exceptions must be taken more strongly against the insurer and that a layman's reasonable reading of words in an insurance contract—in their plain, ordinary, and popular sense—prevails.

Other than the reference to agricultural smudging or industrial operations, the named perils forms cover smoke damage from any other source *as long as the damage is sudden and accidental*. There are no other qualifications or limitations with respect to this peril. Thus, even when smoke originates away from the insured premises—at an adjacent building or even at a more distant location—smoke damage is covered.

Aircraft or Vehicles. The aircraft or vehicles cause of loss covers damage done to covered property by physical contact with an aircraft or vehicle. By specific statement this also includes damage done by a spacecraft or a self-propelled missile. It also covers damage from objects that fall from an aircraft or are thrown up by a vehicle although this would not include damage to covered property thrown *from* a vehicle, as by a vandal. The loss must be caused by an object being thrown up from a vehicle, as by running over the object.

There are many instances in which a vehicle can cause damage without coming into actual contact with the damaged property. From time to time, insureds report losses of the following nature: a truck pulling away from a building to which, unknown to the driver, a chain was attached; a vehicle hitting another object and propelling it into the side of a building; or a vehicle shearing off a water hydrant with resultant severe water damage to property in a nearby building. Due to the peril's requirement of physical contact between the property and the vehicle, these claims are often denied.

However, courts have found coverage under the vehicle peril in situations where, for example, a boom fell off a crane and damaged an insured building. The court in *H.R. Weissberg Corp. v. New York Underwriters Ins. Co.*, 272 A.2d 366 (Md. App. 1971) stated that "to exclude this loss because contact was only with the boom would be similar to excluding loss caused if a tractor-trailer loaded with piling jackknifed and the projecting piling, but not the trailer, damaged a building. The difference is simply one of degree." The implication is that, in some instances, damage without actual physical contact by the vehicle could be covered even where the policy states that coverage applies only in cases of physical contact.

On the other hand, the court in *Backer v. Newark Ins. Co.*, 305 N.Y.S.2d 858 (1969) held that no actual physical contact occurred where a truck pulled a cable through a doorway. A boiler on the cable damaged the building. The damage occurred when a barrel that supported a beam or upright to a beam was dislodged, causing the roof to sag eight to ten inches. The insured argued that the term *vehicle* included every accessory piece of equipment attached to the vehicle. The court found the term was not ambiguous and refused to apply the insured's definition to the construction of the policy.

Perhaps the difference in interpretation between this case and the one in the previous paragraph was the nature of the equipment that caused the damage. Whereas a crane cannot be effectively operated without a boom, so that the boom is an integral part of the machine, a cable is more remotely related to the day-to-day operation of a truck. The question of relatedness to the vehicle is one of degree.

The form further states that damage by vehicles owned by the named insured or by vehicles operated in the course of the named insured's business is excluded.

Riot or Civil Commotion. The common definition of *riot*, although it may vary slightly among cases and commentators, can be stated as, "Any tumultuous disturbance of the public peace by three or more persons mutually assisting one another in execution of a common purpose by the unlawful use of force and violence resulting in property damage of any kind." *Black's Law Dictionary* defines *riot* in a much longer passage, but with the same meaning that a riot is a public disturbance of more than one person.

Generally, the courts have not found coverage where the damage was done stealthily or secretly, meaning that a riot must be a public event. An example is *Providence Washington Ins. Co. v. Lynn*, 492 F.2d 979 (1st Cir.1974). In this case three inmates of the maximum security section of the Adult Correctional Institution (ACI), Cranston, Rhode Island, set fire to the facility by pushing a burning mop through a tiled roof. The resulting conflagration caused physical damage to the building exceeding $300,000. They performed the act in secret and intended it to stay that way but were caught. The legal argument by the institution was that a felony like arson is a "tumultuous event offending the peace and dignity of the state" and that the consequences flowing from the arson, rather than the act of setting the fire itself, established a riot.

These consequences included evacuation and transport of displaced prisoners, increased security, excitement and activity occasioned by a major fire, and the presumed fear and confusion caused by a blaze in a prison, particularly among those prisoners who were in lockup when the fire broke out. The court did not agree, stating that a clear doctrine of the common law that a stealthy act of destruction is not transformed into an act of riot because upon later discovery of the damage there is a public disturbance.

The meaning of *civil commotion* is more obscure than that of *riot* and has received less attention from the courts. Some authorities doubt that it is possible to conceive of a case in which a loss would be paid as a civil commotion but would not be covered under a policy or endorsement referring only to riot. In *Hartford Fire Ins. Co. v. War Eagle Coal Co.*, 295 F. 663 (4th Cir. 1924), the War Eagle Coal Company was insured on a property form that excluded loss or damage by civil commotion. The United Mine Workers had been organizing in West Virginia, violence had erupted, and the governor declared martial law. The evidence showed conclusively that a conspiracy of five men blew up the mine property as part of union activity. The insured proved that although there had been disturbances in the area, there had been no disorder at the mine or disturbances until the explosion and fire. The explosions and fire were started secretively at one in the morning. The insurer denied coverage, but the trial court held for the insured and the court of appeals affirmed.

The court quoted the following definition of *civil commotion* from the legal commentary in *Corpus Juris*: "An uprising among a mass of people which occasions a serious or prolonged disturbance and an infraction of civil order, not attaining the status of war or an armed insurrection. A civil commotion requires the wild or irregular action of many persons assembled together." The court said that since a serious issue of fact had been raised as to whether the property damage was a consequence of the civil commotion in the general area or was due to the independent initiative of the conspirators it would affirm the lower court's decision.

The policy specifies two events that do constitute a riot or civil commotion: (1) acts of striking employees occupying the described premises, and (2) looting at the time and place of a riot or civil commotion. Although a property takeover and subsequent damage caused by striking employees is a seldom occurrence today, looting at the time and place of a riot or civil commotion is more common and may result in substantial theft of property and property damage initiated by the looters to gain entrance into various businesses. Examples of riot and civil commotion losses include the Watts' riots in Los Angeles in 1965 (property damage of $40 million), the South Central Los Angeles riots in 1992 (property damage of $1 billion), and most recently the Ferguson, Missouri, riots in 2014.

Vandalism. *Vandalism* is the willful and malicious damage to or destruction of covered property. In earlier editions of the BPP the peril was called vandalism and malicious mischief. Malicious mischief is no longer part of the name of this peril although the definition remains the same as that of vandalism or malicious mischief in earlier forms—willful and malicious damage to or destruction of the insured property. Dropping the term *malicious mischief* has no effect on coverage and simplified the contract language.

Courts have emphasized that there must be an element of intent, malice, or even reckless disregard for the rights of others for an act to be considered vandalism. For example, in *Woodcliff Lake Bd. of Educ. v. Zurich American Ins. Co.*, No. L-3124-11, 2013 WL 4081012 (N.J. Super. Aug. 14, 2013), the court ruled that the improper handling of asbestos by workers and its spread to parts of a building was not vandalism. The court stated, "There is no evidence of any trespasser coming into the Middle School property to wreak havoc with asbestos." Without intent, the act could not be viewed as vandalism.

Remodeling as Vandalism

A building owner discovered that a tenant, who had a lease agreement for two units, renovated the rental space without the landlord's consent as directed by a condition in the lease. The renovations were discovered from a complaint to the building inspector due to discard of debris. The landlord was cited for renovation without proper permits having been secured and directed to fix the problem by tearing it out.

The landlord made a claim under the vandalism and malicious mischief coverage of his Building and Personal Property Coverage form, CP 00 10, with a Causes of Loss – Broad Form, CP 10 20.

The vandalism peril requires a malicious and willful act. While the remodeling was willful, unless there was malicious intent to cause damage, it would not be considered vandalism. The tenant may have violated the terms of the lease, but that is a legal determination that is not addressed by the policy.

The CP 10 10 10 00 edition revised vandalism coverage in the named peril forms in regard to building glass. Previous editions excluded glass breakage caused by vandalism. An insured was required to purchase the broad form perils, which added glass breakage as an additional coverage, or to purchase the Glass Coverage Form, CP 00 15. Now both named peril forms cover glass breakage from any of the named perils, treat glass as part of the building, and include glass coverage within the limit of liability for the building.

Building damage caused by the break-in or exit of burglars is covered, but other loss caused by or resulting from theft is excluded. Burglary, theft, and other crime coverages are addressed by specialized insurance policies.

Under earlier forms of commercial property insurance, vandalism and malicious mischief coverage was optional. Under the current program, the insured may choose to exclude this coverage via endorsement CP 10 55, Vandalism Exclusion.

Vandalism is one of six causes of loss (sprinkler leakage, glass breakage, water, vandalism, theft, and attempted theft) for which there is no coverage if the building where the loss occurs has been vacant for more than sixty consecutive days prior to loss or damage. See Chapter 5 for a review of the vacancy condition and how it applies to the six cited causes of loss.

Sprinkler Leakage. Under earlier commercial property forms, an insured had to purchase this coverage separately, if desired. It is now automatically part of the policy, and the insured may choose to exclude it via endorsement CP 10 56, Sprinkler Leakage Exclusion. Coverage is for leakage or discharge from an automatic sprinkler system, including the collapse of the system's tank, if there is one.

Automatic sprinkler system is a defined term within the context of the sprinkler leakage cause of loss. It refers to an automatic fire protective or extinguishing system. The definition includes sprinklers, nozzles, ducts, pipes, valves, fittings, tanks, pumps, and private fire protection mains. It also includes nonautomatic systems, hydrants, standpipes, and outlets supplied from an automatic system.

If the insured's building is covered property, this cause of loss also pays to repair or replace damaged parts of the system. The policy does not specify what must cause the damage to the system. It states only that repair or replacement of damaged parts to the sprinkler system will be made if the damage is a result of sprinkler leakage or is directly caused by freezing. Therefore, damage to the system itself might be from an uncovered cause of loss, but if sprinkler damage results, the sprinkler damage is covered and any damaged parts to the system itself will also be replaced or repaired.

The policy also covers the cost of tearing out and replacing part of the structure in order to repair the system if there has been sprinkler damage that necessitates such tearing out or replacement.

Sprinkler leakage is one of six causes of loss (also glass breakage, water, vandalism, theft, and attempted theft) for which there is no coverage if the building where the loss occurs has been vacant for more than sixty consecutive days prior to loss or damage.

Sinkhole Collapse. Coverage for sinkhole collapse was previously available only by endorsement and only in certain regions of the country where sinkholes occur with some frequency. The provision defines *sinkhole* for coverage purposes as "loss or damage caused by the sudden sinking or collapse of land into underground empty spaces created by the action of water on limestone or dolomite." The source of the water that creates the sinkhole is immaterial.

Sinkhole Collapse under the Building and Personal Property Coverage Form

The insured building was covered by the BPP form with basic causes of loss. The building had a system of pipes that diverted water runoff from the roof into a retention basin. One of those pipes broke, and the water coming out of it eroded the underlying limestone. A sinkhole was created and part of the building slipped into that sinkhole.

The claim was denied, citing the exclusion for collapse into man-made underground cavities.

The form defines *sinkhole collapse* as the sudden sinking or collapse of land into underground empty spaces. The space is one created by the action of water on limestone or dolomite. The source of the water is not material to the definition. Collapse into underground "man-made cavities" is outside the definition of sinkhole collapse. Thus collapse into a mine shaft or other man-made holes would not be covered.

A standard dictionary defines *man-made* as "manufactured, created, or constructed by man." Those three very active verbs in the definition preclude the notion that a thing can be man-made by accident. An accidental water spill that causes a building to collapse into a sinkhole is covered. Again, the source of the water does not matter.

This sinkhole collapse definition limits coverage to loss or damage caused by the sudden (not gradual) sinking or collapse of land into underground empty spaces created by the action of water on limestone or dolomite. So, if an insured building, or part of it, falls into a collapsed sinkhole, coverage would apply to the building. However, if a sinkhole merely collapsed with no damage to the building, as in an open area on the insured premises, there would be no coverage. An example of a notable sinkhole collapse claim was the collapse of part of the floor at the National Corvette Museum in Bowling Green, Kentucky, in 2014. The display floor collapsed into a sinkhole along with eight vintage Corvette automobiles. Damage to repair the building alone was $3.2 million.

In addition, coverage does not apply to the settlement of earth caused by voids created by underground mining. These are man-made underground cavities and, as such, are excluded. Coverage for this type of exposure may be secured through mine subsidence insurance.

Volcanic Action. Volcanic action coverage was also previously available only on an optional basis by endorsement. This peril is now part of the causes of loss forms and covers damage from the above-ground effects of a volcanic eruption: Volcanic action coverage was at one time available only on an optional basis by endorsement. After the Mt. St. Helen's volcanic eruption in the state of Washington in 1980, the peril became part of the causes of loss forms. The volcanic action peril covers damage from the above-ground effects of a volcanic eruption: (a) airborne blast and shock waves; (b) ash, dust, particulate matter; and (c) lava flow. It does not include the removal cost of volcanic ash or dust that has not physically damaged insured property. The earth movement exclusion precludes coverage for damage from the seismic effects of a volcanic eruption. This cause of loss is clarified with the 2012 revisions by stating that all volcanic eruptions concerning (a), (b), and (c) occurring within a seven-day period (168 hours) constitute a single occurrence.

CP 10 20—Broad Form Causes of Loss

In addition to the eleven named perils of the basic causes of loss form, the Causes of Loss – Broad Form, CP 10 20, adds coverage for falling objects; weight of snow, ice, or sleet; and water damage. It also provides two additional coverages—collapse and limited coverage for fungus, wet and dry rot, and bacteria.

Exhibit 3-2

Causes of Loss – Broad Form Perils The Basic Form Causes of Loss Plus:		
Falling Objects	Weight of Snow, Ice, Sleet	Water Damage

Falling Objects. Falling objects covers damage by falling objects to buildings or structures and the inside of buildings or property within buildings if the falling object first damages the roof or an outside wall. Damage by a dropped or falling object within a building, such as a chandelier falling on the table below it or a heavy object accidentally dropped on a piece of furniture, does not come within the scope of this peril.

Falling objects coverage also does not apply to personal property in the open. However, as the aircraft/vehicles cause of loss provides coverage for damage by objects falling from aircraft, if an object falling from an airplane damages personal property in the open, that damage is covered.

Weight of Snow, Ice, or Sleet. The weight of snow, ice, or sleet peril applies to all covered property other than personal property outside of buildings or structures and, as newly introduced with the 2012 revisions, loss or damage to lawns, trees, shrubs, or plants that are part of a vegetated roof. Earlier editions of CP 10 20 did not cover damage to gutters and downspouts. That language has been removed, thus providing coverage for gutters and downspouts from the weight of snow, ice, or sleet.

Reimbursement for Expenses to Prevent Further Loss

A nursing home is insured on a CP 00 10 with CP 10 20 attached. It was hit by a huge snow storm. Due to the weight of ice and snow the roof was sagging, leaking, and causing worry that a collapse was impending. The management of the nursing home had holes cut in the ceilings to allow water and snow to drop in, relieving the pressure. The roof was already damaged and this was done to prevent further damage—or even a major collapse—to the roof.

The nursing home also hired a contractor to clear the ice and snow from the roof, and, based on the policy's requirement that the insured mitigate further loss or damage, submitted a claim for this expense. The insurer refused to reimburse the insured for this action, the adjuster citing the policy language that such expenses should be submitted *for consideration* in the payment of the claim. For the part of the loss that the insurer agreed to pay the figure was considerably less than any estimate the insured has received.

The policy obligates the insured to mitigate further loss and agrees to pay the insured for any expenses incurred in that mitigation. The policy says that the insured should submit receipts for that work for consideration in the payment of the claim. That does not mean the insurer will consider whether or not to pay it. The money spent here is just one more item to be included in overall payment of the claim.

The roof could not be repaired without removal of the snow. Again, that also makes the snow removal payable under the policy. It is analogous to removal of a fallen tree from the roof. The roof cannot be repaired until the tree is removed. Likewise, the insured's roof could not be repaired until the snow was removed.

Suppose there were no damage to the roof prior to the decision to act to relieve the pressure of the weight of ice and snow? Would the policy respond to repair the roof? The policy provides for the payment of expense involved in mitigating against *further* loss to covered property, but without initial damage to the property, this clause in not technically invoked. The preservation of property additional coverage pays for damage to property while being moved or stored temporarily to preserve it from covered loss, but that is not the case here either. Contacting the insurer's loss protection professionals for guidance in the situation would be beneficial.

Water Damage. This provision covers damage done by the accidental discharge or leakage of water or steam when any part of a system or appliance containing water or steam breaks or cracks. The CP 10 20 10 00 edition added an enumeration, carried forward into subsequent editions, of the systems covered: plumbing, heating, air conditioning, or other. Water damage coverage does not encompass leakage or discharge from an automatic sprinkler system, which is the subject of coverage under a separate cause of loss. Nor does it cover discharge from a sump, regardless of what causes the discharge. The form excludes overflow due to sump pump failure or the inability of the sump pump to keep up with the amount of water. Damage caused by the discharge of water or waterborne materials from a sewer, drain, or sump that is not related to flood is available under the Discharge from Sewer, Drain or Sump endorsement, CP 10 38. ISO added a provision to the CP 10 20 10 00 edition of the form that also excludes coverage for damage done by water that comes out of roof drains, gutters, downspouts, or similar fixtures or equipment. In its materials ISO stated that this change to the policy represented no change in coverage, but it might be argued that it represented a narrowing of coverage. What happens when a roof drain gets clogged and cannot properly remove water from a roof? Under previous forms, the resulting damage would have been covered.

The peril also covers the cost of tearing out and replacing part of the building or structure to repair damage to the system or appliance if the building is covered property. For example, if the accidental discharge was from the sudden rupturing of a pipe in the insured's fire sprinkler system and the system's pipes are within the insured's walls, the cost of tearing out and repairing the walls is covered. The defect that caused the loss or damage is not covered. That would eliminate coverage for the broken pipe itself unless the damage to the pipe was by another covered cause of loss.

The form specifies that it does not cover damage from repeated leakage occurring over a period of at least fourteen days. Added with the CP 10 20 04 02 edition were mold-inducing hazards as falling under this exception to the water damage cause of loss. Water damage does not include "repeated seepage or leakage of water, or the presence or condensation of humidity, moisture or vapor" that occurs over fourteen days or more.

There is no coverage for plumbing rupture caused by freezing unless the insured maintains heat in the building or structure or has drained the heating equipment and shut off its water supply. Earlier versions of commercial property forms imposed these last conditions on coverage for freezing losses only when the building was vacant or unoccupied.

Broad form CP 10 20 makes no such distinction, imposing the conditions with respect to freezing losses regardless of the building's status. Coverage for water damage does not apply after the building has been vacant for sixty days prior to loss or damage.

Although the water damage peril provides coverage for accidental discharge type claims, other types of water damage claims including damage from flooding, surface water, waves, mudslides or mudflows, sewer back-up, sump-pump failure, and foundation seepage are excluded. See Chapter 4 for a review of the water damage exclusion.

Costs to Repair Leak Even If Building Is Undamaged

A pipe burst under the concrete slab of a building insured under the BPP with the CP 10 20 attached. This break in the pipe caused a loss of water into the ground under the building. The insurer denied the insured's request for coverage for the cost of tearing out and replacing the concrete slab so the broken pipe could be fixed. The denial stated that the policy did not cover this loss because the escaping water ran into the ground and did not damage covered property.

The policy does, however, cover the costs of tearing out and replacing the slab. The wording of the water damage peril does not require damage to covered property by water before such costs are covered. What it requires is that the damaged system be contained in covered property. In this case, the pipe is part of the system contained within the covered building.

The building coverage insuring agreement also states that the insurer will pay for direct physical damage to covered property caused by or resulting from a covered cause of loss. Destruction of the covered property (the slab) resulted from the covered peril of accidental discharge. Digging up the slab was made necessary by the covered peril. An argument can also be made that the insured was damaged by the increase in his water bill caused by the leaking system.

Exclusions That Apply to Both Named Perils Causes of Loss Forms

Section B of the basic and broad causes of loss forms contains the applicable exclusions. Section B contains three subsections. Subsection 1 is identical in both forms, with the following exclusions: ordinance or law, earth movement, governmental action, nuclear hazard, utility services, war and military action, and water.

Exhibit 3-3

Basic and Broad Form Exclusions Exclusions Subject to the Concurrent Causation Provision:		
Ordinance or Law	Nuclear Hazard	Water
Earth Movement	Utility Services	Fungus, Wet Rot, Dry Rot and Bacteria
Governmental Action	War and Military Action	
Basic and Broad Form Exclusions Exclusions Not Subject to the Concurrent Causation Provision:		
Artificially Generated Electrical, Magnetic, or Electromagnetic Energy	Explosion or Steam Boilers	Mechanical Breakdown
	Neglect	

The lead-in language applies concurrent causation language to section B exclusions. The concurrent causation doctrine, which arose as a legal concept in the mid-1980s, holds that if two independent causes of loss converge on covered property, one of which is excluded and the other covered, the entire loss is considered to be covered. An example is loss caused by flooding or earth movement, and some other peril not excluded by the policy, such as negligence of a third party in bulldozing a slope.

One of the earlier and perhaps seminal cases fostering this concept is *Safeco Ins. Co. v. Guyton*, 692 F.2d 551 (Ct. App. Cal. 1982). Damage caused by flood waters was held to be covered under an all risks homeowners policy, despite its flood exclusion, because the flooding was caused by a third party's negligent maintenance of flood control structures. Not all states adopted the concurrent causation doctrine, but its development prompted Insurance Services Office (ISO) and insurers filing independent policies to alter property forms in an attempt to avoid recovery in concurrent causation situations. (As discussed in Chapter 4, however, a 2012 revision is earmarked to also exclude loss by earth movement whether caused naturally or man-made.) Where the concurrent causation doctrine has been accepted coverage would apply. Under the revised concurrent causation lead-in language, the damage would be appropriately excluded as intended.

A more recent case purportedly following the concurrent causation doctrine is *Davidson Hotel Co. v. St. Paul Fire and Marine Ins. Co.*, 136 F.Supp.2d 901 (W.D. Tenn. 2001). This loss involved water leaking from a rusted water heater that dripped into a duct in an electrical room, which in turn caused a sprinkler malfunction, which in turn caused extensive water damage. The insurer cited several exclusions: rust or corrosion, electrical disturbance, and water. The court, treating each exclusion in turn, said that Tennessee followed the "concurrent causation doctrine, which allows for recovery where the loss is essentially caused by an insured peril with the contribution of an excluded peril merely as part of the chain of events leading to the loss." Because the court found that the dripping water was the peril insured against and proximate cause of the loss, it did not matter that the other excluded perils—rust and electrical disturbance—contributed to the loss. A provision at the end of the Subsection B.1 exclusions states that the exclusions apply "whether or not the loss event results in wide-spread damage or affects a substantial area." ISO said that it added this language "for the purpose of making this point explicit." What probably generated this additional language are cases where the courts have held that the earth movement or subsidence exclusions, for example, were meant to apply solely to protect insurers from disasters that affect wide swaths of people and not to bar the application of the exclusions to damage by man-made work that causes earth movement or subsidence.

Ordinance or Law. This exclusion, which was modified with the 2012 revisions, eliminates payment for losses arising out of the enforcement of, or compliance with, building laws or ordinances, including those that may require the demolition of damaged structures that increase the cost of repairing or rebuilding damaged property. For example, a city's building code may require that any building undergoing substantial renovation or repair after a major loss must be equipped with facilities for handicapped access, or the building code might dictate additional safety features that were not part of the original building. Additionally, the law may require that a building not in conformance with current building codes that is damaged to more than 50 percent of its value may not be repaired but must be demolished and rebuilt. For example, if an insured building were determined to be a 60 percent loss, it could not be rebuilt, and the undamaged portion would have to be demolished. As demolition after loss is not a covered cause of loss, there is no coverage for the cost of demolishing the undamaged portion and removing debris. The addition of the words "or compliance with," is necessary because building owners and managers have a duty to comply with codes and to eliminate any argument that the exclusion applies solely to enforcement of such codes. This change also complements subpart (b) of this exclusion, which specifically refers to compliance with an ordinance or law.

The ordinance or law exclusion excludes insurance payment under these forms for the cost of compliance with these requirements. However, the BPP provides $10,000 of coverage for the increased costs of construction incurred due to the enforcement of a building law (*see* Chapter 2). The insured may also purchase additional coverage via endorsement CP 04 05, Ordinance or Law Coverage. (*see* Chapter 9).

Earth Movement. Both named perils causes of loss forms exclude all types of earth movement—such as earthquake, landslide, or mine subsidence—other than sinkhole collapse. In light of the 2012 revisions, earthquake tremors and aftershocks are also excluded. The basic and broad causes of loss forms specifically include sinkhole collapse as a specified peril. The policy covers ensuing fire or explosion damage.

Until the 2012 ISO revisions, the term *earth movement* applied only to naturally occurring phenomena of a catastrophic nature (e.g., landslide or earthquake). For example, damage to an insured building done by the earth shifting as a result of seismic tremors was readily excluded under the BPP with the basic or broad causes of loss form attached. As discussed more fully in Chapter 4, however, courts generally held that man-made earth movement losses were covered, despite some argument by insurers to the contrary.

The earth movement exclusion also eliminates coverage for loss caused by volcanic eruption, explosion, or effusion. However, the policy does cover fire damage occurring as a result of these events. The policy also covers loss attributable to volcanic action—the above-ground effects of volcanic eruption, an insured cause of loss under the basic and broad forms.

To ensure that the earth movement exclusion is not solely limited to natural causes, the 2012 revisions adds another statement to the effect that this exclusion applies regardless of whether any of the listed earth movements is caused by an act of nature or "is otherwise caused." Whether the added words are the right choice to encompass man-made losses is something that only time will tell. Insureds may add coverage for earth movement related exposures such as earthquake through the Earthquake and Volcanic Eruption endorsements, CP 10 40 and CP 10 45, or for mine subsidence through a separate mine subsidence policy.

Governmental Action. The policy does not cover seizure or destruction of covered property as an act of governmental authority. An example of an act of governmental authority is if the police break down a door or damage walls in executing a search warrant, which was the case in *Alton v. Manufacturers and Merchants Mut. Ins. Co.*, 624 N.E.2d 545 (Mass. 1993). Police damaged a building in executing various warrants to search for cocaine, currency, records, receipts, and implements used in administering and preparing controlled substances. In the course of executing the warrants, police caused over $17,000 in damage. The insured owned the building but did not occupy it. The insured argued that the search warrants did not constitute an order of governmental authority. The court, though, ruled that the warrants did in effect "command" the police to search the building, which is considered an order of governmental authority.

The exclusion does make an exception for the destruction of property when ordered to prevent the more general spread of fire if the fire itself would be a covered cause of loss (e.g., if fire authorities burn down a building to create a fire break to prevent the spread of a wildfire).

Damage by Police Action

A health clinic covered under the BPP suffered damage when a man who was trying to evade capture by the police ran into the clinic and took hostages. Eventually he was forced to surrender by the police, who used tear gas and gunfire. In the process of capturing the fugitive, damage was done to both the building and personal property of the health clinic.

The insurance company denied coverage under the governmental action exclusion, which eliminates coverage for loss or damage caused directly or indirectly by seizure or destruction of property by order of governmental authority.

Before examining the exclusion, the existence of a covered peril under form CP 10 20 must be addressed. The one that might apply is explosion; exploding tear gas canisters and bullets contributed to the damage. Smoke damage may be another.

Once a named peril that covers the damage is found, an analysis of the application of the exclusion for seizure or destruction of property by order of governmental authority is necessary. The aim of the exclusion is to eliminate coverage for the intentional destruction of property by governmental authority because of some hazard that the property presents, such as when the government orders the destruction of vegetables that are infected with the Mediterranean fruit fly or a building burned down to create a firebreak. The type of loss occasioned by this scenario seems to be outside of the scope of the exclusion.

In this case, the destruction done by the police was incidental to the capture of the fugitive. Bullets that damaged equipment were intended to control the fugitive—they were not fired because the equipment posed any danger to people or property. One would not expect the police officer in charge to state that he ordered the destruction of property. For these reasons, the insured might have coverage under the policy. However, a New Jersey court ruled that damage done to an apartment by the police in conducting a duly authorized search was properly excluded under the governmental authority exclusion, so such damage could also be excluded.

Nuclear Hazard. The nuclear hazard exclusion eliminates coverage of loss by nuclear reaction, radiation, or radioactive contamination, regardless of the cause. The policy does pay for any ensuing fire loss. Radioactive contamination coverage may be purchased with form CP 10 37, Radioactive Contamination.

Utility Services. This exclusion was revised in the September 2007 edition of the form. It now applies both to the failure of power or other utility service (e.g., water, communication, or gas) to the insured premises that originates away from those premises and that originates on premises if on-premises failure involves equipment used to supply the utility services to the described premises from a source away from the premises. For example, a power plant's turbine suffers mechanical breakdown, which results in a shutdown of services or a power outage. That power outage results in food spoilage in the refrigerator at an insured's premises. The BPP does not cover the food spoilage. The exclusion operates regardless of the failure's cause—even if the failure is brought about by a covered cause of loss.

The exclusion addresses situations such as a brown out or rolling outage, stating that "failure of any utility service includes lack of sufficient capacity and reduction in supply." Loss or damage caused by a surge of power is excluded as well if the surge would not have occurred except for the event that caused the power failure, a change added with the September 2007 edition.

If failure or surge of power or other utility service results in a covered cause of loss, that damage is covered. For example, if heat interruption causes pipes to freeze and rupture, and the broad causes of loss form applies, there is coverage.

If, on the other hand, a lightning strike away from the insured premises knocks out the electrical power at the premises, consequential property damage on the premises is not covered. Two examples of such losses are spoilage of refrigerated products or of property-in-process depending on continuous heat or cooling. Though lightning is a covered cause of loss, the underlying agreement is to pay for direct physical loss caused by a covered cause of loss. Lightning that strikes off premises and runs in on a line to cause lightning damage directly on premises is covered under *these provisions*.

The exclusion provides a description of communication services, which include, but are not limited to, Internet-related services and electronic, satellite, and cellular networks.

Insureds may add coverage for physical damage to covered property stemming from interruption in utility service on or away from the described premises through the Utility Services – Direct Damage endorsement, CP 04 17. Companion time element coverage is available through the Utility Services – Time Element endorsement, CP 15 45.

War and Military Action. This exclusion applies to three related causes of loss: war (including undeclared or civil war); warlike action by any governmental military force; and acts of insurrection, rebellion, revolution, or usurped power.

Following the terrorist attack on the World Trade Center in 2001, the President of the United States stated that "this is war"; that he had declared war on terrorism; and that the nation is at war. It also is not unusual today to hear news commentators, in particular, say that terrorism is war. This, however, does not mean that a state of war exists for purposes of applying the war exclusion, particularly in relation to terrorists activities where the war exclusion does not specifically encompass terrorists activities. Generally speaking, the term *war*, however described or defined, requires as a necessary element the exertion of force, violence, or struggle, between two nations or politically organized governmental bodies. The September 11, 2001, act of terrorism was at the hands of a group known as al-Qaeda led by the now deceased Osama bin Laden. This organization has no capital city or standing army. It is recognized as a network of terrorists, not a nation, state, or even a quasi-governmental body, as that term is used. This distinction between *war* and *terrorism* is important, from an insurance perspective, because it should rule out the application of war exclusions in property and liability policies that do not specifically refer to terrorism. Terrorism is currently subject to a different exclusion that can be purchased out of the policy, depending on the exposure. Two important cases addressing the war exclusion are discussed in the following paragraphs.

In *Pan American World Airways, Inc. v. Aetna Casualty & Surety Co.*, 505 F.2d 989 (2d Cir. 1974), members of a political activist group from Jordan hijacked an aircraft over London and destroyed the aircraft on the ground while in Egypt. The court said the resulting loss to the aircraft was not due to war within the meaning of the term as used in the exclusionary clauses of the all risks policies covering the aircraft. The court reasoned that since the activist group had never claimed to be a state, it could not be acting on behalf of any of the states in which it existed when the plane was hijacked, especially since those states uniformly and publicly opposed hijacking. The hijackers were agents of a radical political group and not a sovereign government. The court concluded that although war can exist between sovereign states, a guerrilla group or radical political group must have at least some incidence of sovereignty before its activities can properly be defined as war.

In a similar case, *Holiday Inns Inc. v. Aetna Ins. Co.*, 571 F. Supp. 1460 (S.D.N.Y. 1983), a court ruled against the war risks exclusion for a claim brought by an insured hotel in Beirut, Lebanon. The hotel suffered shelling damage during hostilities. The insurer argued that the conflict in Lebanon involved three clearly defined independent entities, each having the attributes of sovereignty or, at the least, quasi-sovereignty, and that the war exclusion could be applied to deny coverage. The court focused on the faction occupying the hotel at the time of the fighting and concluded that it was not a sovereign entity. The court further stated that even if the group possessed the necessary sovereignty, it was not fighting with another sovereign government at the time of the damage, and therefore, the war exclusion clause could not be invoked by the insurer.

Water. In 2008, ISO introduced the Water Exclusion Endorsement, CP 10 32, following the litigation that ensued in light of Hurricane Katrina in 2005. As the BPP was issued, this endorsement was automatically added to replace the water exclusion clause, which is found on all three causes of loss forms. With the 2012 revisions, the three causes of loss forms now include the language that was contained in the CP 10 32 endorsement.

In comparing the replaced exclusion with the exclusionary endorsement CP 10 32 (which has been withdrawn), one will notice some broadening features of the exclusion, which is comprised of five categories of exclusions, followed by two paragraphs of explanatory notes.

The first category of exclusions deal with flood, surface water, waves (including tidal wave and tsunami), tides, tidal water, overflow of any body of water, or spray from any of these, all whether or not driven by wind (including storm surge). References to tsunami and storm surge are new with the 2012 revisions. Considering the destructive nature of a tsunami, such as the one that took place in Japan in March 2011 following an earthquake of 8.9 magnitude, one can understand the addition of tsunamis to this exclusion.

Surface water has traditionally been excluded when it occurs naturally. The fact that *surface water* is not defined, however, will hinge on the facts.

In *M and M Corp. of South Carolina v. Auto-Owners Ins. Co.*, 701 S.E.2d 33 (S.C. 2010), the court stated that surface water is waters of a casual and vagrant character, which ooze through the soil or diffuse or squander themselves over the surface, following no definite course. They are waters that, though customarily and naturally flowing in a known direction and course, have nevertheless no banks or channels in the soil and include waters that are diffused over the surface of the ground and are derived from rains and melting snow.

The second part of this exclusion states that mudslide or mudflow are excluded.

Part three of the exclusion—water that backs up or overflows or is otherwise discharged from a sewer, drain, sump, sump pump, or related equipment—became considerably more restrictive with the addition of the words *overflows* and *sump* in the 1995 edition. Previous editions did not address the issue of overflow. And by not specifically excluding water coming from a sump, it was left up to interpretation as to whether a sump is a sewer or drain or part of the plumbing system. Not all insurers adopted ISO's wording in this instance and continue to treat water coming from a sump as an overflow of the plumbing system.

New with the 2012 revision is the addition of the phrases and terms *or otherwise discharged*, *sump pump*, and *or related equipment*. Part four of the exclusion eliminates coverage for water that seeps through underground portions of a building (hydrostatic water pressure) and for water that seeps through other openings, such as doors and windows.

The fifth part, new with the 2012 revision, applies to loss or damage from waterborne material carried or otherwise moved by any of the water referred to in parts (1), (3), or (4), or material carried or otherwise moved by mudslide or mudflow.

New to this exclusion is the statement that the foregoing exclusion applies regardless of whether any of the aforementioned in parts (1) through (5) is caused by an act of nature or is otherwise caused (i.e., man-made). To clarify this exclusion's application, ISO offers the following example of a situation intended not to be covered. It is, namely, where a dam, levee, seawall or other boundary, or containment system fails, in whole or in part, for any reason, to contain the water.

However, what continues to remain unchanged is coverage for loss resulting from the listed five parts in fire or explosion, or sprinkler leakage, if the latter is an otherwise covered cause of loss.

Although the water damage exclusion is far reaching, the BBP form can be endorsed to cover certain water damage claims under the Discharge from Sewer, Drain or Sump (not Flood Related) Endorsement (CP 10 38) or cover specific flood damage under the Flood Coverage Endorsement (CP 10 65).

Fungus, Wet Rot, Dry Rot, and Bacteria. Mold damage and insurance coverage for mold-related expenses became a frequently disputed and litigated issue in the 1990s. Subsequently, insurers attempted to limit exposure to mold-related claims and have clarified the situation by redrafting insurance policies.

To clarify the policy's position on covering mold damage, a fungus, wet rot, dry rot, and bacteria exclusion was added to causes of loss forms in the 2002 editions. In addition, a definition of *fungus* was added to the policy's definitions in both the causes of loss forms and the Building and Personal Property coverage form: "Fungus means any type or form of fungus, including mold or mildew, and any mycotoxins, spores, scents or by-products produced or released by fungi."

The fungus exclusion eliminates coverage for mold or fungus losses except in two situations—fire and lightning—or as falls under the additional limited coverage for fungus, wet rot, dry rot, and bacteria.

The exclusion covers the presence, growth, proliferation, spread, or any activity of fungus, wet or dry rot, or bacteria. The exclusion does not apply in the following situations:

1. when the fungus results from fire or lightning (this addresses the most common claims-related event—mold growing from water used to put out fire)

2. to the extent coverage is provided under the additional coverage—limited coverage for fungus, wet rot, dry rot, and bacteria

Subsection B.2. Exclusions

Subsection B.2. of each of the causes of loss forms contains several more exclusions. Unlike the subsection B.1. exclusions, these do not contain the concurrent causation language. The basic form has six exclusions in this part, while the broad form has four because two of the six perils excluded by the basic form are covered perils in the broad form (sprinkler leakage and water damage).

Both forms exclude loss or damage from artificially generated electrical, magnetic, or electromagnetic energy that damages, disturbs, disrupts, or otherwise interferes with electrical or electronic wires, devices, appliances, systems, or networks, or such devices, systems, networks, appliances using satellite or cellular technology. Included in the description of electrical, magnetic, or electromagnetic energy is electric current and arcing, electrical charge produced or conducted by a magnetic field, electromagnetic energy pulse, microwaves, and electromagnetic waves. The list is not an exhaustive one.

ISO changed the language in this exclusion in the 2007 edition. In its explanatory materials, ISO said, "We are updating this exclusion by explicitly incorporating various terms that reflect current understanding of technology with respect to power sources and associated systems, such as electromagnetic energy (including electromagnetic pulse or waves) and microwaves, and the various risks presented by them." The main objective of the exclusion is to address power surges.

Both cover loss or damage from an ensuing fire. For example, if a power surge causes a piece of office equipment to short, damaging the piece of equipment and causing a fire damaging other property, the fire damage is covered but damage to the piece of equipment caused by the surge is not. Fire damage to the equipment is covered.

Both forms also exclude loss from explosion of steam boilers, steam pipes, steam engines, and steam turbines. If such an explosion causes a fire or combustion explosion, that damage is covered. This exclusion emphasizes the special nature of the exposure presented by boilers, heavy machinery, and equipment of that kind. Equipment breakdown coverage is a specialized coverage necessary for insureds with boiler and machinery exposures.

Both forms also exclude mechanical breakdown but will pay for any loss that results from a covered peril. Again, as in the other exclusions in B.2., this exclusion is not subject to the concurrent causation language. Therefore if mechanical breakdown leads to otherwise covered damage, there is coverage. For example, an air conditioning unit suffers a mechanical breakdown and causes the unit to catch fire, burning down the building. The loss to the building could not be denied based on the mechanical breakdown exclusion. The only excludable damage would be the damage to the air conditioner directly caused by the mechanical breakdown. All resultant damage would be covered. However, if the air conditioner were consumed in the fire, that would also be covered.

Application of the Mechanical Breakdown Exclusion

A retail business with the basic causes of loss form had a failure in a solenoid switch in the furnace, causing a small fire. The claim was denied citing the exclusion that reads, "We will not pay for loss or damage caused by or resulting from mechanical breakdown" because it was the mechanical breakdown of the solenoid switch that caused the loss.

The mechanical breakdown exclusion's purpose is to prevent the insurer from paying for a maintenance claim. If the insured had found that the solenoid switch was defective, he could not turn to his property insurer and expect payment for a new switch.

The only part of this claim that should be denied is the mechanically unsound solenoid switch itself. The policy does not respond to damage caused by mechanical breakdown. The resultant fire damage is covered. Damage to the solenoid is properly excluded as mechanical breakdown, but the fire damage claim that followed is payable because it resulted from a covered cause of loss.

Special Exclusions

The final exclusion section of both forms excludes certain losses where the following coverage forms are made a part of the policy: business income and extra expense, leasehold interest, and legal liability. These exclusions are treated in the chapters in this book dealing with those forms.

Additional Coverages

The basic causes of loss form adds one additional coverage, limited coverage for fungus, wet rot, dry rot and bacteria. The broad form adds two, limited coverage for fungus and collapse.

Collapse

In the early 1980s collapse was moved out of the perils section of the policy and set aside as an additional coverage. One reason is that collapse is not a cause of loss but rather the result of a covered cause of loss. Another reason was based largely on the doctrine of concurrent causation and numerous court decisions that liberalized the meaning of *collapse*. Briefly, the doctrine of concurrent causation, which was brought about by some California court decisions and has more impact with special causes of loss, holds that when two independent causes of loss converge on covered property, one that is excluded and the other is covered, the entire loss is considered to be covered. One such case is *Safeco Ins. Co. of American v. Guyton*, 692 F.2d 551 (9th Cir.1982). A flood (excluded) was determined to have been caused by a negligently construction flood control wall (not excluded) and, in light of the negligent work, was held to be covered.

Prior to 1990, only a minority of jurisdictions adopted the view that a collapse occurs when there is a serious impairment to the soundness of a building or a portion of a building. This viewpoint does not limit collapse to a complete falling down or reduction to rubble. This became the majority viewpoint.

For example, in *Royal Indem. Co. v. Grunberg*, 553 N.Y.S.2d 527 (1990), the court stated, "In the view of a numerical majority of American jurisdictions, a substantial impairment of the structural integrity of a building is said to be a collapse." This language has become the test of whether an insurable collapse loss has occurred. The building is not required to fall into rubble to be considered a collapse; instead, if the building is in imminent danger of collapsing, coverage is triggered.

Because of this court decision and others, ISO significantly changed the collapse additional coverage. It now includes a definition of what collapse is and is not. A collapse is "an abrupt falling down or caving in." This falling down or caving in may be of a building or any part of a building. The result must be that the building or part thereof cannot be occupied as intended.

The broad form, unlike the special form, covers a building against collapse caused by perils listed. Note that, while the Building and Personal Property Coverage Form applies to both buildings and structures, collapse coverage applies only to buildings or to a part thereof. Structures are not covered.

In addition to coverage for the perils of the policy, the form lists the following as covered causes of collapse:

- hidden decay, unless the presence of such damage is known to the insured prior to the loss

- hidden insect or vermin damage, unless the presence of such damage is known to the insured prior to the loss

- weight of people or personal property

- weight of rain that collects on a roof

- use of defective materials or methods in the construction, remodeling, or renovation of a building if the abrupt collapse occurs during the course of such work. If the collapse occurs after the construction, remodeling, or renovation has been completed, it must be caused in part by a cause of loss listed, even when the use of defective materials or methods contribute to such collapse.

"What is hidden decay?" is a question that is not easily answered because it is no where defined in the policy provisions. The insurers' perspective, for the most part, is that decay is limited to rot or decomposition of organic material. The fact that *decay* is not a defined word in the policy means that when there is a dispute to its meaning, insureds should be given the benefit of the doubt, if there is doubt, of course. An especially informative case on this subject that might be influential in jurisdictions recognizing, in particular, the concept of reasonable expectations is *Stamm Theatres, Inc. v. Hartford Cas. Ins. Co.*, 113 Cal. Rptr.2d 300 (2001).

The named insured, the owner of a theater built in 1948, notified its insurer under a commercial property policy that ceiling plaster was falling and cracking. An engineer hired by the insurer found the building to be in a state of imminent collapse. The roof was supported by wooden trusses that were cracked. The named insured's structural engineer attributed the failure of the trusses to the increased load created by a partial reroofing, to repeated cycles of elevated temperatures over the years that degraded the strength of the truss members, and the presence of knots in the bottom chords of the trusses. The primary degradation, however, was said to be due to temperature differences. Although the insurer conceded that the roof of the theater had collapsed, it denied coverage anyway because of the failure of the trusses.

The parties asked the court for a ruling on the meaning of the term *hidden decay*. The court decided that *decay* was synonymous with the words *rot* and *decomposition*. *Rot* and *decomposition*, in turn, are the destruction of organic matter as a result of bacteria, fungus, insects, vermin, or like action. In ruling for the insurer, the trial court reiterated that *decay* meant the destruction of organic matter by rot or decomposition and concluded "the reaction of the wooden roof trusses at the theater to heat and the moisture in the air that existed from the time of construction onward was a wear and tear factor and not a catastrophe of the type that the policy was intended to cover."

On appeal, the named insured argued that the policy term *decay* is broadly synonymous with deterioration, connoting a decline in strength or soundness. The named insured also contended that if ambiguity arises from the narrower meaning of *decay*, as rot or decomposition, the named insured claimed that the ambiguity should be resolved against the insurer.

The appeals court stated that the named insured's argument had merit. One of the dictionaries referred to, which the court said gave the more general definition first, was *Merriman-Webster's Collegiate*, which defined the noun *decay* as:

> 1:   gradual decline in strength, soundness, or prosperity or in degree of excellence or perfection 2: a wasting or wearing away: RUIN 3 obsolete: DESTRUCTION, DEATH 4 a: ROT; specifically: aerobic decomposition of proteins chiefly by bacteria b: product of decay 5: a decline in health or vigor 6: decrease in quantity, activity or force: as a: spontaneous decrease in the number of radioactive atoms in radioactive material b:spontaneous disintegration (as of an atom or particle)

In the final analysis, the appeals court stated that if the insurer did not intend to create a reasonable expectation of coverage for collapse due to natural decline, it could have used a term other than *decay*. The exclusion for wear and tear, the court added, also did not impose or imply a restriction on the coverage for collapse caused by hidden decay. The wear and tear exclusion, the court added, was immediately followed by an exclusion for damage caused by "rust, corrosion, fungus, decay, deterioration, hidden or latent defect or in any quality in property that causes it to damage or destroy itself." The court added that the meaning of the statement in the collapse coverage provisions that "[c]ollapse does not include settling, cracking, shrinkage, bulging or expansion" was not immediately clear. In fact, the court said, it would be difficult to imagine a building collapsing without any of these symptoms appearing. The only reasonable interpretation of this language, the court added, was that mere settling, cracking, shrinkage, bulging, or expansion was not enough, there must also be imminent or actual collapse of the structure.

It makes sense that even if a jurisdiction does not recognize the concept of reasonable expectations, the meaning of *latent decay* should encompass more than simply rot and decomposition, particularly since the term is not defined in the causes of loss forms but is defined broadly in some dictionaries, which are commonly referred to by any laypersons seeking the meaning of words or terms.

If listed as covered property, the following are covered against loss or damage by collapse of a building insured under the policy: outdoor radio or television antennas (including satellite dishes) and their lead-in wiring, masts, or towers; awnings, gutters, and downspouts; yard fixtures; outdoor swimming pools; fences; piers, wharves, and docks; beach or diving platforms or appurtenances; retaining walls; and walks, roadways, and other paved surfaces.

The policy covers personal property if it "abruptly falls down or caves in"—even if it is not the result of a building collapse. However, the collapse of the personal property must be caused by one of the listed causes of collapse, be inside a building, and not be one of the items listed as covered against collapse (e.g., antennas or gutters).

The form states that collapse of personal property does not include settling, cracking, shrinkage, bulging, or expansion. Any payments for collapse are included within the limit of liability for the covered property.

The following are not considered *collapse* under the BPP:

1. a building that is only in danger of falling down or caving in

2. a part of a building that is still standing, even if it has separated from the rest of the building

3. any building, or part thereof, that is still standing, even if it shows evidence of cracking, bulging, sagging, bending, leaning, settling, shrinkage, or explosion

Limited Coverage for Fungus, Wet Rot, Dry Rot, and Bacteria

In addition to revising the exclusionary language related to mold, ISO added an additional coverage to the 2002 causes of loss forms. Under this additional coverage, the BPP provides a limited amount of coverage ($15,000) for the cleanup of fungus, wet or dry rot, or bacteria. If the fungus results from fire or lightning, the policy limit applies. If it results from any of the specified causes of loss, the $15,000 applies. The $15,000 is also available for fungus that results from a flood if the policy contains the Flood Coverage endorsement. In light of the 2012 revisions, however, this additional coverage does not to apply to lawns, trees, shrubs, or plants that are a part of a vegetated roof.

As a reminder, the policy defines the specified causes of loss as follows:

2. "Specified Causes of Loss" means the following: Fire; lightning; explosion; windstorm or hail; smoke; aircraft or vehicles; riot

or civil commotion; vandalism; leakage from fire extinguishing equipment; sinkhole collapse; volcanic action; falling objects; weight of snow, ice or sleet; water damage.

a.   Sinkhole collapse means the sudden sinking or collapse of land into underground empty spaces created by the action of water on limestone or dolomite. This cause of loss does not include:

(1)   The cost of filling sinkholes; or

(2)   Sinking or collapse of land into manmade underground cavities.

b.   Falling objects does not include loss or damage to:

(1)   Personal property in the open; or

(2)   The interior of a building or structure, or property inside a building or structure, unless the roof or an outside wall of the building or structure is first damaged by a falling object.

c.   Water damage means accidental discharge or leakage of water or steam as the direct result of the breaking apart or cracking of a plumbing, heating, air conditioning or other system or appliance (other than a sump system including its related equipment and parts), that is located on the described premises and contains water or steam.

The additional coverage provides coverage for the following three things:

1.   direct damage done by fungus to the covered property

2.   the cost to tear out and replace any part of the covered property in order to get at the fungus

3.   testing after either of the first two are complete if there is reason to believe that fungus is still present.

Chapter 4

Special Causes of Loss Form (CP 10 30)

The Causes of Loss – Special Form, CP 10 30, provides insurance protection for "direct physical loss, unless the loss is excluded in the exclusions section," which means the insured does not have to make a claim stating a specific cause of loss, but rather, all losses are covered unless a policy exclusion applies. This is referred to as open perils coverage, offering the insured the broadest possible protection. The special form includes a number of important additional perils in comparison to the broad form, CP 10 20, including, but not limited to, the theft of property, interior water damage caused by melting snow and ice, damage caused by friendly fire, and damage caused by the accidental discharge of molten materials.

At one time the special form was referred to as the all risks form. However, a line of court cases held that a policy touting all risks coverage should provide just that—coverage against all risks of loss, regardless of any exclusions or limitations; that it is reasonable for the insured to expect coverage against any and all exposures, based on the policy language pledging to cover all risks. To counter this expectation, ISO adopted phrasing that eliminated the all risks phrasing. These revised policies have been called open perils forms to distinguish them from named perils forms. In the commercial property program, open perils coverage is designated as the Causes of Loss – Special form, CP 10 30. The last version of the CP 10 30 to use the word all in the perils section was the 01 83 edition when ISO was still using nonsimplified versions of commercial property forms. In October of 1983 (still in the nonsimplified versions), the word was dropped. That form insured against "risk of physical loss," instead of "all risks of physical loss." The wording "risks of direct physical loss unless the loss is excluded or limited in this policy" was adopted in the first readable version in November 1985. With the 2012 ISO revision, it is again revised with the elimination of the words "risks of." Whether the reference in property policies has been to "all risks" or "risks of," both were intended to mean coverage for direct physical loss or damage to all perils or causes of loss. When applied to property loss exposures, however, another meaning of risk—chance of loss—refers to the possibility of direct physical loss or damage, which exists whether any property damage ever occurs or not. Taken in this light, and reading a policy or form literally, one might be somewhat confused when the policy's insuring agreement is stated to cover direct physical loss or damage, not from an actual covered cause, but from the chance (risk) of physical loss or damage. It is a non sequitur. There is either physical loss or damage or there is not. To say that coverage also applies to the chance of direct physical loss or damage is extending coverage a bit too far.

Yet, the courts have not seen it that way. One such case is *Ocean Winds Council of Co-Owners v. Auto-Owners Ins. Co.*, 565 S.E. 2d 306 (S.C. 2002). In this case, which was also cited with approval in *Buczek v. Continental Cas. Co.*, 378 F.3d 284 (3d Cir. 2004), the policy covered risks of direct physical loss involving collapse of a building or any part of a building. The owner had alleged that its buildings had suffered substantial structure impairment from hidden decay as a result of water infiltration and termite damage, although the buildings had not yet fallen to the ground. The court rejected the contention that actual collapse was required and held that imminent collapse was the most reasonable construction of the policy covering "risks of direct physical loss involving collapse." The policy, therefore, required only proof of imminent collapse for coverage to apply. With this latest change, ISO refers to yet another case, *401 Fourth Street, Inc. v. Investors Ins. Group*, 879 A.2d 166 (Penn. 2005), for making the revision. The Pennsylvania Supreme Court stated, in part, with respect to collapse coverage:

> We conclude that the policy language [risks of direct physical loss involving collapse of a building or any part of a building] provides coverage that extends beyond the situation where in which an insured's building falls to the ground, even in light of the traditional interpretation of the term "collapse." It covers not only loss for a collapse, but also the *risk* of loss *involving* a collapse. To interpret this broad policy language to be limited to only the falling down of the building, even under existing case law, would be to give too narrow an interpretation to the broad language drafted by the insurer.

According to ISO, this change in policy language is intended to reinforce the intent, even though the policy language addressed by the court in this case did not appear in the standard ISO coverage forms and *collapse* was defined to address abrupt collapse.

The special causes of loss form's insuring agreement is not defined by a listing of named or specified causes of loss insured by the policy. Instead, the form states that when *special* is shown in the declarations, the covered causes of loss are "Direct Physical Loss, unless the loss is excluded in the Exclusions section or limited in the Limitations section." Therefore, the scope of covered perils is not defined by what is listed as a covered peril but by what is excluded under the otherwise broad coverage of the policy.

A maxim of insurance policy interpretation is that coverage grants are interpreted as broadly as reasonably possible in favor of the insured and that exclusions are read as narrowly as reasonably possible in favor of the insured. This adage provides an advantage to the insured in proof-of-loss situations. While it is the insured's obligation to prove a loss falls under the coverage of a named peril, it is the insurer's obligation to prove the applicability of exclusions. Open perils coverage generally creates a situation where a loss may be assumed to be covered unless the insurer can show the applicability of policy exclusion.

Similarities to Named Perils Forms

The first set of exclusions in the special causes of loss form (clauses B.1.a. to B.1.h.) is identical to those found in the basic and broad named perils forms: ordinance or law, earth movement, governmental action, nuclear hazard, utility services, war, and water. See Chapter 3 for a discussion of these exclusions pertinent to all causes of loss forms. The lead-in language applies concurrent causation language developed to avoid covering losses where a nonexcluded peril operates in conjunction with an excluded peril to cause damage. The concurrent causation theory is first described in Chapter 3 and again in this chapter.

Like the other two forms, the special form gives back coverage for losses from fire, glass breakage, and volcanic action caused by a volcanic eruption. Coverage for volcanic action is provided in the basic and broad forms as a named peril; in the special form it is an exception to the earth movement exclusion.

Heavy Construction and the Earth Movement Exclusion

During the time a dwelling was covered against special causes of loss, the named insureds reported that nearby blasting activities caused structural damage to their home and personal property. The claim was denied under the earth movement exclusion.

While the earth movement exclusion might have seemed to apply to exclude coverage, generally the exclusion was found to apply only to earth tremors caused by natural forces. Most courts would have likely agreed with the opinion expressed in *Fayad v. Clarendon Nat. Ins. Co.*, 899 So.2d 1082 (Fla. 2005), wherein the earth movement exclusion applied to earthquake, including land shock waves or tremors before, during, or after a volcanic eruption; landslide; mine subsidence; mudflow; earth sinking, rising, or shifting. The examples of earth movement listed in the exclusion (earthquake; landslide; mine subsidence; earth sinking, rising, or shifting; and volcanic eruption) provided support for the notion that natural causes were the subject of the exclusion. The court, in upholding coverage despite the earth movement exclusion, stated that "absent specific language in the policy to the contrary, earth movement exclusion is limited to damage caused by natural phenomena.

Apparently insurers finally got the message that if they wanted to also exclude manmade activities that produce damage, the policy must say so. This is undoubtedly the rationale for the 2012 ISO change that states that the earth movement exclusion applies regardless of whether any of the named causes "is caused by an act of nature or is otherwise caused." Whether the phrase *is otherwise caused* is clear enough to those who purchase insurance to mean manmade earth movement remains to be seen.

Fortuity Doctrine

Before discussing the various causes of loss that are excluded with reference to the special causes of loss forms (or open perils form), it is important to first introduce the subject of fortuity because it is a cause that is not specifically listed but can nevertheless preclude coverage. Fortuity and accident are synonymous terms. If it is determined that an insured either expected or intended the specific loss in question to occur, the loss would be considered nonfortuitous and not covered.

The cases that consider fortuity are legion. In the article, "Fortuity: The Unnamed Exclusion," by Stephen A. Cozen and Richard C. Bennett, published in *The Forum* (20, No. 2, [Winter 1985]), the authors state, "Despite the age of the fortuity doctrine and its relatively universal acceptance by the courts…there are few cases which hold that a particular loss is, indeed, nonfortuitous and, therefore, excluded from coverage for that reason."

A case illustrating the application of the fortuity doctrine is *40 Gardenville, LLC v. Travelers Property Cas. of America*, 387 F.Supp. 2d 205 (W.D. N.Y. 2005), in which the court stated, "As applied, the fortuity doctrine prevents insurers from having to pay for losses arising from undisclosed events that existed prior to coverage, as well as events caused by the manifestation during the policy period of inherent defects in the insured property that existed prior to coverage."

One case where insurers on policies covering against "all risks" of direct physical loss or damage were not entitled to rely on nonfortuity and known loss affirmative defenses is *Wal-Mart Stores, Inc. v. U.S. Fidelity and Guar. Co.*, 816 N.Y.S.2d 17 (2006). The insured (store) brought an action under its property policy to recover lost business income, expenses incurred in reducing the loss of business income, and expenses incurred in adjusting the claim. The court held that (1) a genuine issue of material fact existed as to whether the insured's closing of its store was necessitated by the physical damage to the store caused by a rockslide, and (2) the insurers were not entitled to rely on nonfortuity and known loss affirmative defenses. According to the court, the rockslide, which caused damage to the insured's store, while a known risk at the time the policies took effect, was not "substantially certain to occur."

Many courts have held, and continue to hold, that absent some exclusion or exception, all risk policies, now referred to as special causes of loss forms, cover losses attributable to the insured's own negligence. See, for example, *Ingersoll Mill. Mach. Co. v. M/V Bodena*, 829 F.2d 293 (2d Cir. 1987).

Like the named perils form, the open perils form adds a provision that the described exclusions apply regardless of how widespread a loss is.

Open Perils Exclusions—Section B.2.

Exclusion provisions B.2.a. through B.2.m, the second set of exclusions, have traditionally been called the all risks or open perils exclusions. Some eliminate coverage for events that are historically uninsurable, such as wear and tear or mechanical breakdown—occurrences that happen over time with some certainty, contrasted to sudden and accidental occurrences. Others exclude loss more appropriately handled by specialized coverage such as the boiler explosion or employee dishonesty exclusions (which can be covered by equipment breakdown and fidelity coverage). Still others exclude exposures that, as a matter of underwriting policy either due to the enormous potential economic consequences of the event or because of the morale hazard, the drafters of the BPP decided against covering. Examples of such exposures include the release of pollutants or the voluntary entrustment of property (again, specialized coverage forms have been developed to handle some of these exposures).

Artificially Generated Electrical, Magnetic, or Electromagnetic Energy. As in the named perils forms, the special form also excludes damage to electrical devices, appliances, systems, networks—including those that use cellular or satellite technology—or wires caused by artificially generated electrical, magnetic, or electromagnetic energy. This exclusion applies to any manmade electrical current, so a lightning strike on a building that damages electrical devices would not be subject to this exclusion. Any ensuing fire damage resulting from artificially generated electrical, magnetic, or electromagnetic energy is covered.

Delay; Loss of Use; Loss of Market. This exclusion emphasizes the BPP's intent to cover direct and not consequential loss. Delay and loss of use or market are indirect losses that are the result of a covered loss, such as a restaurant losing customers with the attendant loss of revenue while rebuilding after a fire, or retail customers finding other places to shop while repairs are performed and not returning. The insured may purchase business income and extra expense insurance to cover some of this exposure.

Smoke, Vapor, or Gas from Agricultural Smudging or Industrial Operations. This is the same exclusion that appears in the named perils forms under the peril of smoke. The form does not pay for this type of damage because such operations represent constant or constantly recurring exposures. Damage is certain to occur, so there is no risk but a certainty of loss given time.

Section 2.d.(1) to (7) Exclusions

Several exclusions of a similar nature are grouped together in section 2.d. of the special causes of loss form, listed as 2.d. (1) through 2.d. (7). These are causes of loss that are generally uninsurable, in that, given time, the event will occur. A component will wear out or an inherent defect will eventually reveal itself as damage.

In this regard, the special form excludes loss or damage caused by the following:

1. wear and tear;

2. rust, or other corrosion, decay, deterioration, or a hidden or latent defect, or any quality in property that causes it to damage or destroy itself;

3. smog;

4. settling, cracking, shrinking, or expansion;

5. nesting or infestation, or discharge or release of waste products or secretions of birds, insects, rodents, or other animals;

6. mechanical breakdown, including rupture or bursting caused by centrifugal force, though resulting elevator collision is covered;

7. with respect to personal property, marring or scratching, dampness or dryness of atmosphere, and changes in or extremes of temperature.

If any of these excluded events causes resulting damage from building glass breakage or from one of the specified causes of loss listed in definitions section F of the form (specified causes of loss, listed in the next paragraph), that resulting loss is covered. For example, if mechanical breakdown in a piece of machinery causes a fire that destroys the machinery and damages the building, the resulting fire damage to both the machinery and building is covered, excluding any damage to the machinery that was directly caused by the mechanical breakdown.

Although the special form utilizes an open perils approach to determine if coverage applies to most categories of covered property, it utilizes a specific perils approach for losses to animals, fragile articles, and to builders' machinery, tools, and equipment. The *specified causes of loss* applicable to these categories of property include fire; lightning; explosion; windstorm or hail; smoke; aircraft or vehicles; riot or civil commotion; vandalism; leakage from fire extinguishing equipment; sinkhole collapse; volcanic action; falling objects; weight of snow, ice, or sleet; water damage; or building glass breakage.

Unlike the broad form, which defines most of its covered perils, the special form provides a list of covered specified perils, only defining the perils of sinkhole collapse, falling objects, and water damage. The lack of definitions of the listed specified perils under the special form may result in a broadening of coverage over the broad form due to their lack of specificity. In other words, an insured may argue that coverage applies since the peril involved in the loss is not defined, making it ambiguous, and as such, coverage should apply.

The form defines the specified causes of loss for the following perils:

a.   *Sinkhole collapse* means the sudden sinking or collapse of land into underground empty spaces created by the action of water on limestone or dolomite. This cause of loss does not include:

   (1)   The cost of filling sinkholes; or

   (2)   Sinking or collapse of land into mine shafts or other man-made underground cavities.

b.   *Falling objects* does not include loss or damage to:

   (1)   Personal property in the open; or

   (2)   The interior of a building or structure, or property inside a building or structure, unless the roof or an outside wall of the building or structure is first damaged by a falling object.

With the 2012 revisions, ISO has broadened coverage for loss by water damage, as a specified cause of loss, to include accidental discharge or leakage of water or waterborne materials as the direct result of the breaking apart or cracking of certain off-premises systems due to wear and tear. Getting a better perspective of what is intended to be covered that was not covered prior to the 2012 revisions requires looking at the specific definition of water damage, particularly the second part of the definition. *Water damage* is defined to mean the following:

(1)   Accidental discharge or leakage of water or steam as the direct result of the breaking apart or cracking of a plumbing, heating, air conditioning or other system or appliance (other than a sump system including its related equipment and parts), that is located on the described premises and contains water or steam; and

(2)   Accidental discharge or leakage of water or waterborne material as the direct result of the breaking apart or cracking of a water or sewer pipe that is located off the described premises and is part of a municipal potable water supply system or municipal sanitary sewer system, if the breakage or cracking is caused by wear and tear.

But water damage does not include loss or damage otherwise excluded under the terms of the Water Exclusion. Therefore, for example, there is no coverage under this policy in the situation in which discharge or leakage of water results from the breaking apart or cracking of a pipe which was caused by or related to weather-induced flooding, even if wear and tear contributed to the breakage or cracking. As another example, and also in accordance with the terms of the Water Exclusion, there is no coverage for loss or damage caused by or related to weather-induced flooding which follows or is exacerbated by pipe breakage or cracking attributable to wear and tear.

To the extent that accidental discharge or leakage of water falls within the criteria set forth in c.(1) or c.(2) of this definition of "specified causes of loss," such water is not subject to the provisions of the Water Exclusion which preclude coverage for surface water or water under the surface of the ground.

The second part of the definition of water damage is a welcomed addition. For example, a large water main below the intersection of a city in Kentucky broke because of wear and tear. The break occurred during the early hours of the morning and went unnoticed for a few hours. As a result of that break, the flooding of surrounding buildings resulted in the interruption of business, not only from public authorities that closed off the use of those streets, but also because of the inability of the businesses to function properly. With coverage for water systems limited to the described premises, the businesses found themselves without insurance coverage. Adding to this bad news was the fact that through sovereign immunity, suing the city for both physical damage to the businesses and loss of business income as a consequence was virtually futile. With this latest revision, coverage appears more of a probability than it once was.

The purpose for the lengthy definition and explanation of water damage is to make clear that no coverage is intended for losses otherwise excluded under the form's water exclusion.

Wear and Tear, Cracking and Shrinking, and Mechanical Breakdown

Some of the excluded items in the list found in B.2.d.—the so-called wear and tear exclusions—deserve further analysis.

Applying the wear and tear exclusion can be confusing. For example, a rusted-out pipe inside a wall bursts and causes water to leak into an office. The initial reaction might be to deny the claim based on the wear and tear exclusion, as the loss was caused by the wear and tear on the pipe. However, the only property that is not covered is the pipe itself; the damage done by the water as well as the cost to repair the damage to the wall necessary to remove and replace the leaking pipe is covered.

The purpose of the wear and tear exclusion (sometimes referred to as the maintenance exclusion) is to avoid payment for things that the insured should maintain as a matter of course. In the previous example, if the insured had discovered the rusted pipe before it actually burst, he could not look to his insurance policy to replace the pipe. The wear and tear exclusion precludes insurance recovery for normal maintenance. However, once wear and tear causes a covered loss, that loss is covered.

Damage to Shower Stall and the Wear and Tear Exclusion

The insured is an apartment complex insured on a BPP form with special causes of loss. One of the tenants was a very large individual. This tenant stepped into the shower enclosure and, due to his excessive weight, cracked the floor area of the shower. There was immediate and direct damage to the apartment below. The crack required replacement of the shower/tub unit, as well as cleanup of the damage.

The insured entered a claim for replacement of the shower unit and repair of the ceiling in the apartment below. The carrier extended coverage for the ceiling damage but denied coverage of the shower enclosure due to the wear and tear exclusion, although the shower unit was relatively new.

> The damage to the ceiling and shower unit are covered. The wear and tear exclusion does not apply. The wear and tear exclusion is one of a number of exclusions in the special causes of loss form that eliminate coverage for what are essentially nonfortuitous losses—losses that are certain to happen and as such are not appropriate subjects for insurance coverage. If something is used long enough it will wear out. This is not an insurable event. However, a sudden and accidental breaking of a new shower unit by a very large individual is not wear and tear but is direct damage.

Corrosion took on special significance with the class action suits of homeowners brought about by the manufacture, distribution, sale, and installation of Chinese-manufactured drywall. This drywall was used to replace damage following hurricanes that struck Florida and Louisiana. Although the policies differed, they were common in that they covered for direct physical loss or damage and excluded rust, corrosion, pollution, and other causes. One of these cases was *In re Chinese Manufactured Drywall Products Liability Litigation*, 759 F.Supp.2d 822 (E.D. La. 2010).

Insofar as the corrosion exclusion was concerned, the plaintiffs cited *Trus Joist Macmillan v. Neeb Kearney & Co., Inc.*, No. Civ. A 99-2964, 2000 WL 306654 (E.D. La. March 23, 2000) to demonstrate that the corrosion exclusion applied only to naturally occurring corrosion and not to the rapidly occurring, unnatural corrosion in the present cases. The court, however, disagreed, stating that under "the plain, ordinary and generally prevailing meaning," (and according to *Merriam-Webster's Dictionary*), corrosion is defined as "the action, process, or effect of corroding" and a "product of corroding."

It would appear that both rust and corrosion have a temporal aspect, meaning that neither comes about rapidly. In fact, what is excluded is meant to clarify nonfortuity or, in other words, with the right conditions, losses that are likely to eventually come about. As far as the Chinese drywall cases are concerned, however, corrosion did not appear to have a temporal aspect. In fact, another case where corrosion was held not to have a temporal meaning is *Gilbane Building Co. v. Altman Co.*, No. 04AP-664, 2005 WL 534906 (Ohio App. March 8, 2005) After a certain kind of muriatic acid was applied to concrete floors for purposes of etching, it was observed that there was some discoloration of the stainless steel door hardware, switch plates and copper piping in the rooms where the etching took place. When the insurer denied coverage, litigation ensued.

The insured maintained that while the parties stipulated that the loss was due to rust and corrosion, the court should apply the commonsense and ordinary understanding of the terms *rust* and *corrosion* and conclude that "a fast-acting, acid-based chemical reaction," which caused the rust and corrosion in this case, was not the type of rust and corrosion intended to be excluded. In ruling for the insurer, however, the court held that the rust and corrosion exclusion applied because the policy did not qualify this exclusion to cover only gradual-forming rust and corrosion or fast forming rust and corrosion. Interestingly, an exception to the rust and corrosion exclusion is loss caused by specified causes of loss. With one of these specified causes being smoke, the insured argued that muriatic acid vapor is considered smoke and, thus, pursuant to this exception rust and corrosion loss was covered. The insured, in support of this argument, cited a case concerning an issue of fact as to whether the resulting damage was caused by smoke or acid vapor because the experts used the terms interchangeably. In *Gilbane*, however, it was undisputed that rust and corrosion was caused by an acid vapor and, as such, was not included in the list of specified causes of loss. The exception to the rust and corrosion exclusion therefore was held to be inapplicable.

Like the other causes of loss forms, the special form also has mechanical breakdown exclusion. However, the CP 10 30 has a clarifying provision that the exclusion does not apply to any resulting loss or damage caused by elevator collision.

Mechanical breakdown is another area that has caused confusion. When a piece of machinery breaks down, ensuing loss from a covered peril is covered. However, claims have been denied for such loss, citing the mechanical breakdown exclusion. The purpose of this exclusion is the same as that for the wear and tear exclusionary provision. If a piece of machinery just stops working, the insured may not look to his insurer to repair it. However if that machine breaks down and causes a covered loss, that loss should be paid.

Mechanical Breakdown Exclusion and Concurrent Causation

Air conditioning units on a church insured under a BPP form with the special causes of loss form were damaged by freezing. The insurer-engaged engineer reported that there were two causes of loss: (1) failure of the pump-down solenoid, which allowed the compressors to run during freezing conditions, eventually resulting in the freezing of the circulating chilled water system and destruction of the system; and (2) a control rod did not close on the louver vent economizer system, which allowed the very cold outside air into the church. The engineer concluded that the failure of the system was due to the mechanical failure of these devices. The insurer denied the loss, stating that the concurrent causation language in the policy removed coverage for any damage resulting from mechanical breakdown.

Analysis discloses the loss is not appropriately denied in its entirety for several reasons. First, the concurrent causation language of the CP 10 30 does not apply to the mechanical breakdown exclusion. The lead-in language to section B. Exclusions, clause 2.—where the mechanical breakdown exclusion is located—reads, "We will not pay for loss or damage caused by or resulting from any of the following." This is not concurrent causation language; in fact, this was the original lead-in to both B. sections 1 and 2, which was changed because of the development of the concurrent causation doctrine.

Because the concurrent causation language does not apply to this set of exclusions, if mechanical breakdown causes damage not otherwise excluded to something other than the item that actually broke down, any subsequent damage is covered. In this case, the loss to the air conditioning system was not caused by mechanical breakdown but was due to freezing resulting from the mechanical breakdown. The failure of the solenoid may have set the stage, but it did not cause the loss. Freezing did.

By way of example of how the mechanical breakdown exclusion works, apply these facts to a peril other than freezing. Suppose that the breakdown of the solenoid caused heat to build up and the entire building burned down rather than damaging just the components of the air conditioning system. The loss would not be denied for the fire damage due to the mechanical breakdown of the solenoid.

Dampness or Dryness of Atmosphere and Changes in or Extremes of Temperature

Two of the exclusions that appear to be obscure but nonetheless are troublesome at times are (7) (a) dampness or dryness of atmosphere, and (7) (b) changes in or extremes of temperature. These two exclusions involve losses to personal property resulting in condensation, water damage, mold, fungus, warping, and freezing, among others.

One of the more problematic aspects of these exclusions has to do with the meaning of *atmosphere*, as it appears with reference to the exclusion dealing with dampness or dryness. The question is whether *atmosphere* refers to the outside of a building or structure, inside, or both. The exclusion of the property policy is not the only source of controversy. Reference to atmosphere has also been a problem having to do with the earlier pollution exclusions of commercial liability policies.

One of the court decisions, relating to the exclusion of dampness or dryness of the atmosphere that is recommended reading, is *Blaine Const. Corp. v. Insurance Company of North America*, 171 F.3d 343 (6th Cir. 1999).

A construction contractor filed a claim with its insurer under a builder's risk policy written on a special causes of loss basis and claiming coverage for the cost of replacing ceiling insulation ruined by water that had condensed within the insulation cavity. The water condensed after a subcontractor had failed to install a vapor barrier properly. Two of several reasons the insurer denied coverage was based on the exclusion of dampness or dryness of atmosphere and extremes or changes in temperature.

One of several arguments was over the meaning of *dampness of atmosphere*. The court said that the insured must demonstrate the inapplicability of this exclusion and do more than show that *dampness of atmosphere* could mean outdoor humidity. The court, instead, said that the insured would have to prove that "dampness of the atmosphere could not mean indoor humidity." The damage done in this case, the court said, was covered only if the latter was a reasonable interpretation. If the insured could reasonably contend that *dampness of the atmosphere* meant only outdoor humidity, it would win. If all the insured could do, however, is to reasonably contend that *dampness of the atmosphere* also means outdoor humidity, it could not win.

The court rejected the insurer's affirmative defense based on the faulty workmanship exclusion but upheld a defense under dampness of atmosphere, and an appeal and cross-appeal was taken. The court of appeals held that the loss was within the ensuing loss exception to the faulty workmanship exclusion, under Tennessee law, and that the phrase *dampness of atmosphere* was ambiguous and, thus, construed in favor of the insured.

One of the interesting opinions expressed in this case that insurer's may wish to ponder is the following:

If INA had wanted to exclude dampness or dryness generally, the layman might think, there would have been no need to use the word "atmosphere" at all. The insurance company could simply have described the excluded peril as "dampness or dryness." By adding a word that would not have been necessary if the company had not intended to refer to the "atmosphere," in the most commonly used sense, and by speaking in the next breath of "extremes or changes in temperature," INA ran the risk, it seems to us, of being taken to mean that it was simply talking about weather conditions—the extreme heat and humidity of Florida, e.g., or the sub-zero temperatures of Alaska.

Other Exclusions

Explosion of Steam Boilers, Steam Pipes, Steam Engines, or Steam Turbines. This exclusion applies to steam equipment that the insured owns, leases, or operates. Ensuing loss from fire or combustion explosion is covered. Again, as in the basic and broad causes of loss forms, this exclusion reiterates the fact that boiler equipment and industrial type machinery is beyond the scope of the policy and is more appropriately covered by an equipment breakdown policy.

Continuous or Repeated Seepage or Leakage of Water. An exclusion of damage from continuous or repeated seepage or leakage of water over a period of fourteen days or more modifies coverage for plumbing discharge under special form coverage, just as it does the named cause of loss of water damage in the broad form. Some have argued that the fourteen-day period should begin when the insured first discovers the leakage, but it is damage caused by the undiscovered leak that the policy specifically excludes. The fourteen-day period begins with the onset of the leakage and not when the insured discovers the leak or damage. Also excluded is damage from the presence or condensation of humidity, moisture, or vapor.

In *General Star Indem. Co. v. Sherry Brooke Revocable Trust*, 243 F.Supp. 2d 605 (W.D. Tex. 2001), the court was asked to determine if damage from leaking pipes was covered by a commercial property policy. The insured owned apartment complexes that suffered damage attributable to plumbing leaks. The insurer denied the claim based on the continuous or repeated seepage or leakage of water exclusion. The insured argued that the fourteen-day time period mentioned in the exclusion suggested it was a notice exclusion, meaning that the fourteen-day time period begins when the leak or damage was discovered. The court, though, found this interpretation of the exclusion unreasonable and that the leaks had gone on for months before being repaired, or maybe longer. The court found in favor of the insurer.

Repeated Seepage or Leakage

The floors in an insured building were becoming soft. Investigation in the crawl space under the floor disclosed a leak in a hot water pipe, which caused moisture damage to the floor above. The damage was calculated at $123,000. The claim was denied due to the special causes of loss form's exclusion of repeated seepage or leakage over a period of more than fourteen days. The insured could not hear or see the water leak and had no way of knowing what was going on under the floor. The insured disputed application of the exclusion, stating that the fourteen-day period should begin at the discovery of the leak or damage and not from the date of the beginning of the occurrence.

The exclusion is appropriately applied. This type of loss is the type meant to be excluded by the policy's repeated seepage or leakage exclusion. The fact that the insured could not easily make himself aware of the impending damage does not make it any less a nonfortuitous loss or bring it outside of the clear language of the exclusion.

Water, Other Liquids, Powder, or Molten Material. The policy does not cover damage by water, other liquids, powder, or molten material if, due to freezing, they leak or flow from plumbing, heating, air conditioning, or other equipment, except fire protective systems. The exclusion applies unless the insured does his best to maintain heat in the building or structure or drains the equipment and shuts off the supply if the heat is not maintained. If the insured meets these conditions, the exclusion does not apply. The form does not exclude all damage by water, other liquids, powder, or molten material. It excludes only damage by these items if caused by freezing, and only then if the insured has not maintained heat or drained and shut off the system. This reinforces the necessary maintenance concept.

Dishonest or Criminal Acts. This exclusion eliminates coverage for dishonest or criminal acts committed by the named insured, partners, employees, directors, trustees, or authorized representatives of the named insured, or anyone to whom the named insured entrusts covered property. The CP 10 30 10 00 edition added members, officers, and managers in order to recognize the limited liability company form of organization. This exclusion applies whether the person commits the act alone or in collusion with others and regardless of whether the act occurs during working hours.

In light of the 2012 revisions, this exclusion is restructured so that it applies differently between those who have a role in the named insured's business and those who do not serve in a fiduciary capacity. Thus, no coverage applies for loss or damage caused by or resulting from dishonest or criminal acts, including theft by the named insured, any of its partners, members, officers, managers, employees—which includes temporary employees and leased workers—directors, trustees, or authorized representatives. This exclusion applies whether these people are acting alone or in collusion.

The exclusion also applies to theft by any person to whom the named insured entrusts the property for any purpose, whether these persons are acting alone or in collusion with any other party.

While this exclusion applies to theft, it specifically does not exclude loss from acts of destruction committed by employees, temporary employees, leased workers, and authorized representatives. Therefore, while the form does not cover an employee or any one of the other persons stealing office equipment, if an employee or other persons damages or destroys a photocopying machine as an act of revenge, the policy will respond.

A court applied the exclusion to arson committed by a shareholder and corporate officer in *Minnesota Bond Ltd. v. St. Paul Mercury Ins. Co.*, 706 P.2d 942 (Or. 1985). A partner with a 50 percent interest set the building on fire, hoping to collect the insurance so she could pay a debt. The trial court originally refused to apply the exclusion to this case and held that the "context of a 'willful or dishonest act' is described by the remainder of the language in the exclusion, which speaks to unexplained or mysterious disappearance of property or the voluntary parting with titled possession of property as a result of a fraudulent scheme. This Court concludes that this exclusion is inapplicable to the factual situation."

The Supreme Court of Oregon overturned that decision without any discussion of the coinsured's position. In its reversal, the court said, "Although it may have been unwise for this insured to purchase a policy with such a far-reaching exclusion as contained in exclusion No. 4, nevertheless that decision was made by the plaintiff corporation when it chose to insure its property under this policy. The exclusion is clear and unambiguous and fully applicable to this loss. There is no coverage for this loss under the policy."

This case involved individuals who have such control over the corporation that their acts essentially constitute the acts of the corporation; where a regular employee (not an officer, director, or partner) commits an act of arson, the policy would respond.

In another case of arson—*One Suzie-Q Corp. v. Secura Ins. Co.*, 198 F. Supp.2d 1105 (E.D. Mo. 2002)—the court ruled that the exception for acts of destruction by the insured's employee did not apply to a store manager who burned the insured store. While the manager was an employee of the corporation, he was also a corporate officer and someone to whom the property was entrusted. Thus, the dishonesty exclusion applied to the loss.

Although coverage for dishonest criminal acts by the named insured, partners, employees, directors, trustees, authorized representatives of the named insured, or anyone to whom the named insured entrusts is excluded, coverage does apply if the dishonest criminal act is perpetrated by other individuals. An example would be a customer or burglar who steals merchandise or inventory from the business premises. Theft coverage is one of the most important coverage expansions over the broad form.

Voluntary Parting with Property (Trick or Device). This provision eliminates coverage where the insured has been tricked out of property; for example, voluntarily turning over a car for a test drive, and the prospective customer absconds with it. This exclusion applies if the insured or anyone to whom the property has been entrusted has been induced to part voluntarily with the property by fraudulent scheme, trick, device, or false pretense. This exclusion reiterates the intent of the form to provide coverage for direct loss to property and not fidelity or theft coverage (which is available under the crime insurance program).

In the typical trick or device loss, the insured is defrauded. An example of such a scheme would be where a customer pays for an item with a bad check or stolen credit card and obtains possession of the property. The insured cannot look to the BPP form for coverage in such situations.

Rain, Snow, Ice, or Sleet Damage to Personal Property in the Open. The form covers personal property in the described building or structure or in the open (or in a vehicle) within one-hundred feet of the building or within one-hundred feet of the premises described in the declarations, whichever distance is greater. The policy also covers personal property temporarily off premises at certain locations (*see* Chapter 2). The exclusion modifies this coverage and is another example of a nonfortuitous loss. Personal property left out in the open in rain, snow, ice, or sleet will be damaged. Risk management techniques other than insurance are more appropriate to this exposure (for example, bringing it inside).

Collapse. The grant of collapse coverage (limited by its terms) coexists with a broad exclusion of collapse. That is, collapse is excluded, except to the extent that coverage is provided under the terms of the additional coverage. Under the additional coverage, coverage is provided for an abrupt falling down or caving in, subject to the terms of that additional coverage. ISO most recently revised the exclusion in the CP 10 30 06 07 to describe various conditions affecting property, to reinforce the relationship between the exclusion (broad) and the coverage grant (which builds back limited coverage). ISO also revised the exclusion to specify that it does not apply to *specified causes of loss* (defined in the form as various named perils), building glass breakage, weight of rain that collects on a roof, and weight of people or personal property. Previously, this exception was conveyed under the additional coverage for collapse by way of stating that the criteria defining a covered collapse do not limit coverage otherwise provided for the aforementioned perils. In other words, there is coverage for loss or damage by the aforementioned perils, whether the loss or damage involves collapse, subject to any other applicable policy provisions.

Discharge, Dispersal, Seepage, Migration, Release, or Escape of Pollutants. The pollution exclusion originally read "release, discharge, or dispersal of pollutants or contaminants." This phrasing was replaced by an exclusion that removed coverage for loss or damage caused by or resulting from the release, discharge, or dispersal of pollutants unless the release, discharge, or dispersal is itself caused by any of the specified causes of loss. Resulting loss or damage by the specified causes of loss was covered.

The policy was revised again in 1990 with a modification by adding the words *seepage*, *migration*, and *escape* of pollutants as well, thus giving stronger emphasis to the exclusion of nonsudden pollution losses. This change was in accord with changes made in the Building and Personal

Property Coverage form (CP 00 10 10 90). This phrasing has been carried forward. The effect of the exclusion is to limit pollutant cleanup and removal coverage in the commercial property program to those sudden and accidental occurrences brought on by the specified causes of loss—the broad form perils.

CP 10 30 10 00 added an exception. The exclusion does not apply to damage to glass done by chemicals that are applied to the glass. This is part of the simplification of glass coverage. Damage done by chemicals was covered by the old glass form. Since that form has been removed, the policy now provides the coverage by means of this exception to the exclusion.

An interesting case dealing with the pollution exclusion and the exception of specified causes of loss dealing with vehicles is *Cincinnati Ins. Co. v. German St. Vincent*, 54 S.W. 3d 661 (Mo. Ct. App. 2001). The insurer maintained that its property policy did not provide coverage for damage to the interior of a building caused by a floor scraper's removal of old vinyl flooring that contained asbestos. The court of appeal held that friable asbestos was a pollutant, within the meaning of the pollution exclusion, and that the scraper was a *vehicle* and, therefore, a specified causes of loss and was an exception to the pollution exclusion. The court said that the policy covered the damage since it was ambiguous. This case is unusual because asbestos is not commonly considered to be a pollutant and that is the reason some insurers add an asbestos exclusion endorsement to their policies.

Neglect. The CP 10 30 10 00 edition added the exclusion for neglect. By eliminating coverage for damage caused by the insured's neglect to protect property post-loss against further damage, the insured's responsibility to protect his property from further loss at the time of the initial loss is emphasized.

Concurrent Causation Exclusions

The special form contains a third set of exclusions (designated 3.a., b., and c.) that preclude coverage under the doctrine of concurrent causation. Concurrent causation is a legal doctrine developed in case law to find coverage despite common property policy exclusions, such as earth movement or flooding. For example, a third-party contractor is negligent in the preparation of the soil prior to the construction of an office building. After the building is completed and occupied, it suffers earth movement damage. While earth movement is excluded, using the doctrine of concurrent causation the building owner could claim that the loss was caused by the negligence of the contractor that prepared the soil. Without these exclusions, the claim would be payable under the special causes of loss form because third-party negligence is not an excluded peril.

A case in which the court applied the concurrent causation doctrine is *Davidson Hotel Co. v. St. Paul Fire and Marine Co.*, 136 F.Supp. 2d 901 (W.D. Tenn. 2001). The insured's hotel, the Hotel Deauville, suffered damage when water infiltrated a duct in the electrical room, resulting in an electrical disturbance that activated the sprinkler system. Water damage ensued, and the fire department was called to the scene. The water was able to travel freely from the eleventh floor to the ninth floor duct because workmen had left a hole in the floor. Davidson submitted a claim with St. Paul, and the claim was denied. Since several factors were involved in the loss, the parties argued over whether Tennessee followed the efficient proximate cause doctrine or the concurrent causation doctrine.

The court concluded that Tennessee was a concurrent causation state. St. Paul argued that the loss resulted from corrosion in a water heater, which was excluded by the policy, as well as water flowing from the water heater. The court noted that the rust exclusion contained an exception for rust or corrosion for damage caused by another nonexcluded peril. The court also found that the water exclusion did not apply. St. Paul asserted that the faulty workmanship exclusion applied due to the hole left in the floor by workers. Again, the court pointed out that this exclusion contained the same exception as the rust exclusion, and that the water flowing from the water heater was not an excluded peril. The court ruled that "a substantial and proximate cause of the loss in this case was the water which flowed onto the bus duct. Therefore, the covered peril of water, despite other factors leading to the loss which might have been excluded, renders St. Paul liable on this policy under Tennessee law's application of the concurrent causation doctrine."

To avoid otherwise unintended insurance recovery in concurrent causation situations, ISO included concurrent causation lead-in language ("such loss is excluded regardless of any other cause or event") to a number of exclusions and added this concurrent causation exclusion with three subparts. These include loss or damage caused by weather conditions; acts or decisions (or failure to act) of individuals and groups; and faulty, inadequate, or defective planning, design, defective materials, or maintenance.

They do not defeat coverage for a covered cause of loss that happens to involve damage by the excluded cause of loss. For example, a building suffers flood damage because of negligent maintenance of a dam. The flood damage is excluded under the surface water exclusion, and the concurrent causation exclusion operates to defeat coverage for a claim of negligent maintenance. If the building also suffers vandalism as a result of the flood, that vandalism is covered because the policy does not exclude vandalism.

There is no coverage for ensuing losses caused by one of the three special exclusions if the ensuing losses fall under one of the excluded risks. Thus, there would be no coverage if faulty construction (one of the special exclusions) caused natural subsurface water damage to the foundation.

Weather Conditions Exclusion

The weather conditions exclusion applies only if weather conditions contribute in any way with a cause or event excluded in exclusion section 1 (ordinance or law, earth movement, nuclear hazard, utility services, war and military action, and water). Assume heavy rain causes a landslide, which in turn damages an insured structure. The policy excludes earth movement, and the claim should be denied. However, at court the insured argues that it was not earth movement that caused the damage to the house, but instead, the cause of damage was the rainfall (a weather condition). Prior to the adoption of the concurrent causation exclusions this argument sometimes prevailed. ISO adopted the concurrent causation exclusions to retain the original intent to not cover damage by earth movement or the other excluded causes of loss, regardless of what caused the earth to move, subject to the caveat regarding natural versus manmade earth movement, discussed prior.

Acts or Decisions and Faulty Planning Exclusions

The second of the concurrent causation exclusions eliminates as a cause of loss the acts or decisions, including the failure to act or decide, by persons, groups, or governmental bodies. For example, governmental officials fail to act in a crisis and allow a dam to overflow and damage insured property. Under a seminal concurrent causation case, the court allowed the nonexcluded peril of negligent decision-making to override the policy's flood exclusion and found coverage under these same facts. The current version of the BPP form eliminates this possibility.

Part c. of these exclusions eliminates coverage where the cause of loss is inadequate, faulty, or defective planning, zoning, development, surveying, siting, design, specifications, workmanship, repair, construction, renovation, remodeling, grading, compaction, maintenance, or materials used in repair, construction, renovation, or remodeling.

All three parts of the exclusion are subject to the provision that if loss or damage by a covered cause of loss results from one of these excluded perils; coverage applies to the resulting loss or damage. For example, if faulty workmanship in the electrical system of a building results in fire, the resulting fire loss is covered. Or, if earth movement causes a fire, the fire damage is covered. Or, if the failure of the fire officials to act in creating firebreaks causes a building to burn, the fire damage is covered.

Loss or Damage to Products

Some years ago, in what is still a commonly cited case, a manufacturer brought an action against its insurer seeking coverage under its all risks property policy for destruction of cream-style corn being canned. Despite its efforts through testing, the manufacturer was unable to determine the cause of the loss and elected to destroy all of the suspected corn processed at that particular plant because of the possibility that it was spoiled and unfit for human consumption. When the claim was submitted for over $6 million, one of the insurers on the risk agreed that the loss was covered, but the others denied coverage. They maintained that the cream-style corn at that plant was of the same quality as in previous years and that the method of testing had changed. These insurers, therefore, asserted that had the named insured used prior testing methods, it might have been able to isolate the spoiled product and salvage and sell the remainder.

These insurers also maintained that this loss was not fortuitous for a number of reasons. The policy contained an exclusion for the cost of restoring faulty workmanship, material, construction, or design. In addition, they pointed to another exclusion of loss or damage to inherent vice or change in flavor, color, or texture, unless caused directly by a peril not otherwise excluded. Interestingly, however, these insurers were unable to show the inapplicability of these exclusions in that they could neither prove what workmanship was faulty nor that the loss even resulted from faulty workmanship. The inherent vice exclusion was also held to be inapplicable. The court, therefore, in *Pillsbury Co. v. Underwriters at Lloyd's, London*, 705 F. Supp. 1396 (D. Minn. 1989), ruled that coverage applied.

Perhaps it was the growing number of losses involving property processing errors that caught the attention of ISO because it introduced a clarifying new exclusion in the special causes of loss form with the 06 07 edition related to production errors. Some examples of errors in production are introduction of foreign matter, addition of a wrong ingredient or element, or wrong measure of a particular element. An error in the production process is a business risk; it is not a peril intended to be insured under property insurance. In certain circumstances, some claims may involve errors in production and allege that the need to destroy a now useless product constitutes physical loss or damage to that product, thereby asserting a broad and nontraditional interpretation of the concept of physical damage under an insurance contract.

To avoid this result, ISO inserted Additional Exclusion 5, which applies only to the specified property and is entitled Loss or Damage to Products:

> We will not pay for loss or damage to any merchandise, goods or other product caused by or resulting from error or omission by any person or entity (including those having possession under an arrangement where work or a portion of the work is outsourced) in any stage of the development, production or use of the product, including planning, testing, processing, packaging, installation, maintenance or repair. This exclusion applies to any effect that compromises the form, substance or quality of the product. But if such error or omission results in a Covered Cause of Loss, we will pay for the loss or damage caused by that Covered Cause of Loss.

This exclusion is not limited solely to edible (fit to eat) products, even though a number of cases involving contaminated and genetically-modified foods have occurred over the years. (*See*, for example, Marc S. Mayerson, "Insurance Recovery For Losses from Contaminated or Genetically Modified Foods," *Tort Trial & Insurance Practice Law Journal*, American Bar Assn., Vol. 39, No. 3, Spring 2004, p. 837.)

According to ISO, one example of error in production is the introduction of foreign matter. Although brought as a liability claim, rather than a property claim, one is reminded of *Shade Foods, Inc. v. Innovative Product Sales & Marketing, Inc.*, 93 Cal. Rptr. 2d 364 (2000). A wholesale manufacturer of nut clusters brought an action against an almond processor after wood contamination was found in the almonds. In upholding liability, the court ruled that wood contamination of almonds, which required their destruction, was physical loss of stock within qualifying language of first party coverage and that evidence was sufficient to support an award for loss of profits to the processor. The circumstances involving this case presumably would be subject to the loss or damage to product exclusion in a property policy given that it also precludes coverage for an arrangement where work or a portion thereof is outsourced.

While quality control may help to reduce the chances of loss, accidents are still likely to happen. One case where safety in the workplace, rather than quality control, took on more significance is *Interstate Gourmet Coffee Roasters, Inc. v. SEACO Ins. Co.*, 794 N.E.2d 607 (Mass. Ct. App. 2003). The named insured was a coffee roasting plant. During the process, one of the employees caught his fingers in a grinding machine. The severed parts of the employee's hand entered the machinery, resulting in the contamination of, and consequent destruction of, approximately 16,064 pounds of blended coffee beans. There was no dispute that the contamination of the coffee constituted a covered property loss. The dispute, instead, was over the costs of lost coffee and cleanup, which amounted to almost $70,000 that was considered by the court to be covered. The latest ISO exclusion applies only with the special causes of loss form. This means that the insured need only show that loss occurred and that it was fortuitous. On the other hand, the insurer's burden, when coverage is written on a special causes of loss basis, is to show that an exclusion precludes coverage. If it turns out, for example, that the insurer cannot show that error or omission was the cause of loss, such as in the *Pillsbury* case involving cream-style corn, this type of an exclusion would not apply.

The fact that some ISO forms refer to "negligent act, error or omission" while the Product Errors exclusion refers only to "error or omission" may cause some attorneys representing insureds to seize upon this difference to seek coverage based on an ambiguity.

In the final analysis, it remains to be seen how effective this exclusion will be, but undoubtedly it is aimed at the growing number of incidences involving damages due to product errors and the complexity at which products are being produced today and may be produced in the future.

Special Exclusions

The final exclusion section of the commercial property policy excludes various losses on business income and extra expense, leasehold interest, and legal liability coverage forms. These exclusions are treated in the chapters in this book dealing with those forms.

Limitations

Under this section (C), the form (1) clarifies that it does not cover loss or damage to certain types of property; (2) places dollar limits on certain types of property; and (3) limits coverage on other types to the specified causes of loss.

Steam Boilers, Steam Pipes, Steam Engines, or Steam Turbines. The policy does not cover these items for damage that results from a condition or event inside the equipment. As mentioned earlier, ensuing loss from fire or combustion explosion is covered.

Steam Boilers—Condition or Event Inside

Property covered under a special causes of loss form suffered the following loss: water was seen coming out an unoccupied building, and the fire department was notified. They turned off the water and asked the power company to turn off the power. The management company was notified a few days later, and on inspection, found the boilers had frozen and were damaged.

Loss did not result from any condition or event inside the equipment, as contractually required. The event that caused the damage was the power company turning off the power, something outside the equipment and not reached by the exclusion. The limitation in the policy concerns loss caused by a condition or event inside the equipment.

The limitations in Part C must be read in context. The limitations apply to items that should be separately insured and to losses that are foreseeable and therefore uninsurable. For example, if the boilers were damaged due to lime buildup, the loss could have been prevented through proper maintenance and is therefore not covered. The freezing loss was outside the insured's control and is covered.

Hot Water Boilers or Other Water Heating Equipment. As with the steam equipment previously discussed, the special form does not cover these items for damage caused by or resulting from any condition or event inside the equipment other than an explosion. Therefore, explosion damage, regardless of whether the explosion is caused by an internal condition or event, is covered.

Collectively, loss to steam boilers, steam pipes, hot water boilers, and similar steam and hydronic systems may be insured under an equipment breakdown protection coverage form.

Building Interiors and Personal Property in a Building. The special form addresses the applicability of coverage to a building interior and personal property in a building in two scenarios. First, the building interior and personal property in the building are not covered for damage caused by rain, snow, sleet, ice, sand, or dust unless the building first sustains damage by an insured peril to its roof or walls through which the rain, snow, sleet, ice, sand, or dust enters. In other words, there must be exterior damage caused by an insured peril to the building to trigger interior damage. A common example would be a severe windstorm that tears off a portion of a roof exposing a building's interior.

The second scenario affirmatively provides coverage for water damage to a building's interior and its personal property without the requirement of exterior building damage. This commonly results from the freeze/thaw cycle that occurs after a heavy snow storm. In these cases, ice dams and the ensuing melting water migrate into the building's interior causing property damage. This second scenario illustrates the importance of one of the many additional special form coverage advantages provided in comparison to the previously reviewed broad form.

Water Damage and Boarded-Up Windows

A building covered by a special causes of loss form suffered rain damage to an unoccupied second floor. The second story windows were boarded up with plywood to prevent water from entering through any broken panes. Extremely heavy storms accompanied by heavy winds and wind-driven rain knocked the plywood boarding loose, resulting in water penetrating the window openings and damaging the insured's business personal property stored on the second floor.

The insured was denied coverage under the limitation on water damage that requires the building must first suffer damage to its roof or walls by a covered cause of loss through which the rain enters. In supporting the denial, the adjuster compared the boarding being blown in to that of a windowpane being blown open. The adjuster stated that coverage would not apply in this similar situation unless the windowpane would be blown out or damaged.

According to *Merriam-Webster's Dictionary*, a window is the opening in a wall; covered by a material, typically glass (the glass is called a windowpane). The windows, including the boarding, are part of the wall, and the material covering the openings does not have to be glass. Wind is a covered cause of loss, and it damaged the wall by blowing out the window covering, triggering coverage for the damage to the insured's interior business personal property. The loss is covered.

Building Materials. The policy excludes theft of building materials and supplies that are not attached to the building or structure. For example, no coverage applies if the insured has building supplies that are to be used to make repairs to a building or structure if they are stolen from the premises. Alternatively, if an insured operated a building supply business and had building materials and supplies on its premises, coverage would apply. Note that businesses that make repairs to their buildings or structures can cover the theft of building materials used in construction under a Builders Risk Policy.

Missing Property. The policy does not pay for missing property if the loss can be documented only by an inventory shortage or if there is no physical evidence to show what happened to the property.

Missing Property—No Physical Evidence

A hospital insured under the special causes of loss form submitted a claim for a scientific video monitor used in the intensive care unit. Hospital officials claimed that the monitor was stolen. The claim was denied based on the following exclusion: "We will not pay for loss or damage to…property that is missing, but there is no physical evidence to show what happened to it, such as a shortage disclosed on taking inventory."

Limitation of coverage 1.e. does not require visible signs of forcible entry, which is a requirement for coverage under the peril of burglary in the crime policy. This limitation refers instead to the loss of property that could not be recognized except by reference to written records. For example, if the hospital had a storage room filled with hundreds of monitors and one were stolen, that theft probably could not be recognized by physical evidence alone. The physical absence of one monitor out of hundreds could not be seen without counting the monitors and comparing the total to a known number.

In this case, the absence of the monitor could be immediately noticed by anyone familiar with the room. It is physically missing and the hospital does not have to rely on an inventory to know that it is gone. The purpose of the limitation of the coverage in question is to prevent claiming theft when the loss might, in fact, be due to poor record keeping. The limitation is not intended to exclude theft, which might be thought of as the disappearance of property from a specific place during a specific time period.

Transferred Property. There is no coverage for property transferred to an off-premises person or place on the basis of unauthorized instructions. This is similar to the trick or device exclusion and eliminates what is more appropriately covered under crime or fidelity policies.

Lawns, Trees, Shrubs, or Plants That Are Part of a Vegetated Roof. These types of plants and vegetation are not covered for dampness or dryness of atmosphere or of soil supporting the vegetation, changes in or extremes of temperature, disease, frost or hail, or rain, snow, ice, or sleet.

Property Limited to Specified Causes of Loss. Although the special form utilizes an open perils approach to determine if coverage applies to most categories of covered property, it utilizes a specified perils approach for losses to animals, fragile articles, and to a builders' machinery, tools, and equipment. The specified perils include fire; lightning; explosion; windstorm or hail; smoke; aircraft or vehicles; riot or civil commotion; vandalism; leakage from fire extinguishing equipment; sinkhole collapse; volcanic action; falling objects; weight of snow, ice, or sleet; or water damage or by building glass breakage.

Animals. The policy covers animals only if they are killed or if they must be destroyed by a specified peril or by building glass breakage.

Fragile Articles. The policy covers fragile articles such as statuary, marbles, chinaware, and porcelains damaged by a specified peril or by building glass breakage. By exception, glass and containers of property held for resale are not subject to this limitation. For example a retail business selling glass or containers held for resale would be afforded the broader special form coverage.

Builders' Machinery, Tools, and Equipment. The policy covers the insured's tools and equipment that are owned or entrusted to the insured for the specified perils or by building glass breakage if away from the premises. In the event the loss occurs on the premises, the tools and equipment are covered for the broader special form perils.

Marble Slab as Fragile Article

An insured covered by a special causes of loss form had a marble slab resting on a platform. The platform collapsed and the marble slab broke into pieces. The insurer denied the claim due to the limitation that eliminates coverage for breakage of fragile articles such as glassware, statuary, marbles, chinaware, and porcelains unless damage is caused by one of the defined specified causes of loss. The issue is whether the limitation's specific reference to marbles places the marble slab in the fragile articles category and precludes coverage for this loss.

The loss to the unrefined marble slab does not fall under the scope of the fragile articles limitation. The operative word in the provision is *fragile*, and the items listed in the exclusion are examples, not definitions. Although a delicate piece of marble artwork is a fragile article, a large block of marble is outside the limitation. Many things (such as concrete blocks or bricks) may be breakable given sufficient force. However, they would hardly be considered fragile articles.

Special Theft Limits. The following items are subject to a special limit for any one occurrence of theft. The special limit shown for each category is the total limit for loss or damage to all property in that category, no matter the number of items involved. A 2012 revision clarifies that since an insurer may be willing to increase the following limits, the following limits apply unless a higher limit is shown in the declarations:

a. $2,500 for furs, fur garments, and garments trimmed with fur.

b. $2,500 for jewelry, watches, watch movements, jewels, pearls, precious and semiprecious stones, bullion, gold, silver, platinum, and other precious alloys or metals. This limit does not apply to jewelry and watches worth $100 or less per item.

c. $2,500 for patterns, dies, molds, and forms.

d. $250 for stamps, tickets, including lottery tickets held for sale, and letters of credit.

Cost to repair any system from which any liquid or molten material escapes. The final policy limitation precludes coverage for the cost to repair any system from which any liquid or molten material escapes. Fire extinguishing equipment is covered for discharges or for loss caused by freezing.

Additional Coverages and Limitation

As does the broad causes of loss form, the special causes of loss form provides two additional coverages: collapse and limited coverage for fungus, wet rot, dry rot, and bacteria.

These additional coverages are exactly the same in both forms. For a complete discussion, see Chapter 3.

Additional Coverage Extensions

Form CP 10 30 provides three additional coverage extensions: property in transit; water damage, other liquids, powder, or molten material damage; and glass.

The form allows the insured to extend coverage on business personal property in transit more than 100 feet from the described premises. The extension does not apply to property in the care of the insured's salespersons. The property must be located in or on a vehicle that the named insured owns, leases, or operates within the coverage territory.

The policy covers property in transit for the following perils: fire; lightning; explosion; windstorm or hail; riot or civil commotion; vandalism;

vehicle collision, upset, or overturn (but not contact with the roadbed); and theft of an entire bale, case, or package. Theft is covered only in the case of forced entry into a securely locked body or compartment of the vehicle. The insured must show visible marks of the forced entry.

The limit of liability for this additional coverage extension is $5,000. This amount is in addition to the limit of liability.

Property in Transit

An insured plumber's tools were stolen from his van while parked on his home driveway. The tools were valued at more than $2,000. A claim was made for $1,000 under the property in transit additional coverage extension. The claim was denied.

Property in transit coverage is not designed for the insured's tools and business property; this coverage is intended for the insured's goods while being shipped or delivered to another location. The coverage applies to personal property of the insured in transit more than one-hundred feet from described premises, while in or on a motor vehicle. Damage must be by one of the described perils. Loss caused by theft is covered only where theft is of an entire bale, case, or package. The vehicle or compartment must be locked and there must be visible marks of forced entry.

Therefore, tools left loose in the vehicle do not qualify. If all the tools were contained in a case, and that case was stolen by someone leaving visible marks of forced entry, coverage would apply. If the tools were not packaged or in a case, there would be no coverage.

The second additional coverage extension applies in case of a covered loss due to water, other liquids, powder, or molten material. The insurer agrees to pay the cost to tear out and replace any part of the building in order to repair the appliance or system from which the material escaped. Unlike the broad form, which was reviewed in the previous chapter, the special form extends coverage to damage that results from the escape of molten material. This expansion of coverage over the broad form is important for foundries and similar manufacturing businesses that may utilize molten metal processes in their operation.

The third additional extension is glass, which was added in the 2000 edition. In the event the insured suffers a loss to building glass, this coverage extension pays for temporary plates or other coverings if the repair is delayed. The limit of insurance provided by this extension is included in the limit of liability.

Chapter 5

Conditions

Commercial Property General Conditions

The Common Policy Conditions form, IL 00 17, of the ISO commercial property program contains six conditions that must be incorporated into any policy written and that apply to all the policy's coverages. Most of these common policy conditions are restatements of provisions, modified in varying degree, that have been standard features of property provisions since the advent of the standard fire policy. The Common Policy Conditions form has not been revised nearly as often as the Building and Personal Property Coverage Form and the causes of loss forms. The two editions that have been released are the IL 00 17 11 85 and IL 00 17 11 98.

Cancellation

The cancellation provision gives the named insured the ability to cancel the policy at any time by notifying the insurer. The notification may be that the insured's copy of the policy is returned or a lost policy release is signed. Because the insured requests the cancellation, the return premium is calculated at rates less than pro rata.

The insurer may also cancel the policy at any time with appropriate written notice mailed to the insured. Cancellation for nonpayment requires a ten day notice; for any other reason, thirty days must be provided. When the insurer cancels, the return premium is figured on a pro rata basis. Jurisdictions may have different statutory requirements regarding form and timing for insurance policy cancellations. These requirements are tracked in *FC&S Cancellation and Nonrenewal*, an annual compendium published by The National Underwriter Company.

The policy calls for cancellation notices to be to or from the *first named insured* (the person or entity whose name appears first on the policy).

Changes

This condition stipulates that any changes in the terms of the policy can be made only by endorsement issued by the insurer. Any change requests by the insured must be by the first named insured.

Examination of Your Books and Records

This condition gives the insurer the right to audit books and records of the insured relating to the policy. The examination or audit may be made during the policy period or any time within three years after the policy period ends. The condition does not allow the insurer to go randomly through the insured's records. Rather, the insurer may examine only the records that relate to the policy. Such related records may involve finances, safety, inventory, and so on.

Inspection and Surveys

The first part of this condition (D.1.a through c) gives the insurer the right to conduct inspections, surveys, and reports, and to make recommendations. These may be part of the underwriting process or may involve the insurance company's loss control or safety programs. They might relate to risk management, insurability, or conditions on the premises.

The second part of the condition (D.2.) makes clear that the insurer is not accepting liability related to these inspections, surveys, and reports. This acts as a disclaimer of liability so that liability for conditions existing in the insured's operations that may or may not be discovered or disclosed in an insurer's inspection cannot be passed on to the insurance company. Inspections, surveys, or reports the insurer performs do not act as a guarantee.

The forms states:

> We are not obligated to make any inspections, surveys, reports or recommendations and any such actions we do undertake relate only to insurability and the premiums to be charged. We do not make safety inspections. We do not undertake to perform the duty of any person or organization to provide for the health or safety of workers or the public. And we do not warrant that conditions:
>
> a.   Are safe or healthful; or
>
> b.   Comply with laws, regulations, codes or standards.

This condition makes the point that an insurance inspection for underwriting or other purposes is not meant as a warranty from the insurer that the insured's operations are safe or healthful. Nor does it warrant that the insured is in compliance with legal requirements that may pertain to those operations.

Another part of the condition brings any rating, advisory, or similar organization—such as Insurance Services Office (ISO) or American

Association of Insurance Services (AAIS)—who may make inspections or reports under the liability disclaimer.

The inspection and surveys condition was called into play in the 1977 litigation involving a fire at the Beverly Hills Supper Club in Kentucky that killed 165 people. The property insurer had recently inspected the building. Based on this inspection, some plaintiffs' attorneys attempted to hold the insurer and ISO liable for the deaths and injuries sustained in the fire. The courts, however, did not allow the suit to go forward. (The cause of the fire was eventually determined to be due to faulty aluminum wiring.)

The potential liability of insurers for engineering and safety inspections services first became a real concern in 1964 following the Illinois Supreme Court decision in *Nelson v. Union Wire Rope Corp.*, 199 N.E.2d 769 (Ill. 1964). The court held that a workers compensation insurer was liable in tort for having failed to detect a dangerous condition in the course of its inspection of a material hoist. The court did not maintain that the insurer had a duty to perform an inspection. Rather, the court held that after having done so, the insurer was liable for its negligence in that regard.

As a matter of interest, the first standard general liability policy provisions contained an inspection and audit condition, which read: "The company shall be permitted to inspect the insured premises, operations and elevators." The wording remained unchanged through the 1943, 1947, and 1955 policy changes. However, after the *Nelson* case, this condition was amended in 1966 (and has remained unchanged to date) with the explanation by the National Bureau of Casualty Underwriters (NBCU) that a modification was necessary in light of recent court decisions.

In its written memorandum of changes, the NBCU stated that the modified condition indicates that "the company has the right but no obligation to inspect the insured's property and operations and that neither the existence nor the exercise of the right to inspect shall constitute an undertaking to determine or warrant that the property or operations are safe. In light of many new laws affecting business premises, inspections by insurers have taken on even greater importance, including the increased risk of claims against the insurers, themselves."

Premiums

This condition specifies that the first named insured is responsible for paying the policy premium. It also calls for any return premiums to be sent to the first named insured.

Transfer of Rights and Duties under This Policy

There is a tendency to confuse this condition with the commercial property condition I., Transfer of Rights of Recovery Against Others To Us. A distinction here is that condition I mentions the word *recovery*, which deals with subrogation. Condition F of the common policy conditions deals with assignment of rights. The named insured, for example, a small auto parts store that sells the business and agrees to transfer the rights of the policy, and perhaps the property coverages as well, to the purchaser, will be precluded from doing so because of this condition.

An insurance policy is a personal contract because it protects people, not liability or the property. Insurers, therefore, are interested in knowing who these people are who claim to have an insurable interest and desire insurance. Insurance company underwriters have a right to evaluate the personal characteristics of those persons seeking insurance, and this can only be done when the identity of that person is known to the underwriter.

Condition F simply seeks to prevent insureds from transferring their policy rights to another entity, which was not the subject of underwriting scrutiny. It should be pointed out, however, that this condition does not preclude transferring the right of recovering sums payable on behalf of the insured. In some cases involving liability, for example, when an insurer refuses to pay damages on behalf of its insured, the party bringing the suit against the insured may take an assignment of rights, meaning it obtains the rights to collect sums due to the insured. There is no transfer of rights under the policy, however, only as to who collects proceeds due the insured. This can also involve a property loss but is more common with liability claims.

If this condition did not exist, the seller of property arguably could transfer the insurance coverage to the purchaser, to the insurer's detriment, and that is precisely what this condition attempts to prevent. Given the different purposes for both conditions—commercial property condition 1 and common policy condition F—both are of equal value and do not conflict with one another. Part of the confusion is that one must read the whole condition, and not part of its title, and then come to the conclusion of ambiguity. A second bit of advice here is that the entire provision must be read. Once that is done, one will note differences, not similarities, between these two conditions.

The final comment about this common policy condition F is that it requires the insurer's written consent in order to transfer the insured's rights and duties under the policy to another person. The only time the written consent of the insurer is not needed is upon the death of a named insured. When a named insured dies, his rights and duties are transferred to the named insured's legal representative. In such cases, the legal representative exercises the deceased insured's rights and duties while acting as legal representative. Until a legal representative is appointed, rights and duties of the deceased insured with respect to the deceased insured's property pass to anyone having proper temporary custody of that property. Such individuals might include a spouse, a partner, or a corporate officer.

Commercial Property Policy Conditions

In addition to the common policy conditions, the Commercial Property Policy Conditions form is attached to form a commercial property policy. The current edition of this form is the CP 00 90 07 88, meaning that these conditions have had no revisions since July 1988. The following conditions comprise this form:

1. Concealment, Misrepresentation, or Fraud

2. Control of Property

3. Insurance under Two or More Coverages

4. Legal Action against Us (the insurer)

5. Liberalization

6. No Benefit to Bailee

7. Other Insurance

8. Policy Period, Coverage Territory

9. Transfer of Rights of Recovery against Others to Us

Concealment, Misrepresentation, or Fraud

This condition voids coverage if, at any time pre- or post-loss, the named insured commits a fraudulent act relating to the policy. Misrepresenting the use or occupancy of the building—representing the property as a pharmacy when in reality it is an illegal methamphetamine lab, for example—or misrepresenting the value of destroyed equipment to boost insurance recovery is fraud. Such an act before or after loss voids coverage. *Void* does not mean that the policy is canceled or suspended, but that a contract between the insurer and insured never existed. In other words, a bargain was never struck due to the misrepresentation or fraud of the party.

The policy is also void if the named insured or any other insured intentionally conceals or misrepresents a material fact about the coverage, the covered property, a claim under the policy, or the named insured's interest in the property.

Fraud of *any* type by the named insured related to the policy voids coverage. Concealing or misrepresenting *material facts* by the named insured or any other insured also voids coverage.

The phrase *any other insured* does not void the policy only for the person committing the misrepresentation or concealment. It is possible that the act of any insured could void the policy as to all other insureds, including the named insured. A number of courts have interpreted the language *the insured* under the concealment, fraud, or neglect provisions of the standard fire policy as applying only to the individual insured guilty of the fraud, giving coverage to other innocent insureds. However other court decisions have interpreted language similar to the ISO *any other insured* phrase in certain fire policies as unambiguously precluding coverage to innocent, as well as guilty, insureds. In *Employers Mut. Cas. Co. v. Tavernaro*, 4 F. Supp.2d 868 (E.D. Mo.1998), the Tavernaros owned a business covered on a businessowners policy (with the same wording as the BPP form). Mr. Tavernaro set the building on fire and Mrs. Tavernaro attempted to collect the insurance proceeds as an *innocent coinsured*. The court concluded that "the language clearly precludes recovery by either party in this case."

Note that although the standard fire policy cited has been phased out of everyday use, most of its policy provisions have been incorporated into today's modern property policy forms.

Control of Property

A building owner permitted a tenant to do some extensive internal improvements to better suit the tenant's operations. The work, however, was so poorly performed that it actually caused extensive damages to the owner's property requiring a substantial amount of money to rectify. When the owner submitted the claim to its property insurer, coverage was denied on the basis of faulty, inadequate or defective workmanship, construction, repair or renovation of any part of the property at the described premises.

In another case, a property owner was forced to bring an action against its property insurer to recover the costs incurred in correcting the separation of a brick veneer wall, constructed some years ago. The insurer had denied coverage based on the negligent work exclusion.

Are the insurers right or wrong in denying these claims? Insurers sometimes deny such claims for at least two reasons. First, even though not the fault of the policy's named insured, physical loss or damage is considered not to be covered because the exclusions are viewed as being applicable regardless of who causes the loss. In other words, the property provisions are not viewed as several as they are with respect to a liability policy, where coverages apply separately against each insured against whom claim is made or suit is brought. A second reason is that the chances of recouping the payment of loss by way of subrogation show little or no promise.

The answer as to whether these claims should be paid actually depends not only on what the policy, as a whole, says, but also what any applicable laws of the jurisdiction have to say in relation to policy wording. Some property policies specifically contain a severability of interests provision (or separation of insureds condition) that has the same effect as the separation of insureds condition contained in a standard commercial general liability policy. Similar provisions in other policies may require closer examination.

Take, for example, the ISO Common Policy Conditions, CP 00 90, which must be issued in conjunction with commercial property coverage forms. Condition B, Control of Property, states, "Any act or neglect of any person other than you beyond your direction or control will not affect this insurance." Property Form CP-100 of the American Association of Insurance Services also contains a condition entitled Control of Property, which states, "The Commercial Property Coverage is not affected by any act or neglect beyond your control."

Taking these provisions on their face, with reference to the two previously discussed loss scenarios, there should be no basis for an insurer's denying the claims based on faulty or negligent work, unless, of course, the named insureds had some direction or control over the work as it was being performed. These conditions, in effect, serve the same purpose as the separation of insured condition of the commercial liability form.

Another point to consider is that there is no time limitation relating to when the faulty work was actually performed. Property insurance, similar in some ways to liability insurance, provides coverage at the time of physical loss or damage to the covered property and not when the faulty work was actually performed. So, the fact the work has been performed on the covered property years prior to the physical loss or damage should be of no relevance.

Tracing the History

Early insurance history points out not only the need for a control provision but also another one dealing with divisibility. The latter basically made clear that if, for example, the named insured owns and covers two buildings on one policy and coverage is breached at one location because of a vacancy or unoccupancy, coverage remains unaffected at the other location. It was recommended in the early 1900s that fire policies be endorsed so as to be considered both divisible and several, as if separate policies were issued on each building or its contents or both.

In *The Agents Key to Fire Insurance* (New York, Spectator Company, 1922)—a publication written to assist insurance agents—it was recommended that fire policies be amended with a provision stating: "This insurance shall not be invalidated by the act or neglect of any other occupant within the described premises, providing such act or neglect is not within the knowledge and control of the insured." The reason given for this recommendation was that some authorities, at the time, held that a breach of a policy condition by any tenant of a building adversely affected all insurance coverages applicable to the covered building.

When the special multiperil package policies were introduced in 1960 for the better-than-average-risks, they automatically included a no control clause that consisted of what is referred to today as the control condition, plus the divisibility clause. Interestingly, both the 1966 and 1973 editions of the no control provision were more limited in scope than the control condition of current ISO forms because they dealt with owners and occupants of buildings. The no control portion of these package policy conditions stated that the insurance would not be prejudiced by any act or neglect of the owner of any building if the insured is not the owner, or by any act or neglect of any occupant (other than the insured) of any building when such act or neglect of the owner or occupant is not within the control of the insured.

The wording *no control* apparently gave way to *control of property* in the early 1980s. The Special Risk Property Form, CF 00 13, carrying an edition date of January 1983, for example, contained both a control of property and a divisible contract clause, which read as follows:

2.   Control of Property: This insurance shall not be prejudiced by any act or neglect of any person (other than the named insured), when such act or neglect is not within the control of the named insured.

3.   Divisible Contract Clause: If this policy covers two or more buildings, the breach of any condition of the policy in any one or more

of the buildings covered or containing the property covered shall not prejudice the right to cover for loss occurring in any building covered or containing the property, where at the time of loss, a breach of condition does not exist.

The divisible contract clause has since been eliminated with its provision forming the second part of the control of property condition of current ISO forms, which reads: "The breach of any condition of the Coverage Part at any one or more locations will not affect coverage at any location where, at the time of loss or damage, the breach of condition does not exist."

If the current ISO control of property condition were to read like it did in the 1920s when it had to be specifically included in fire policies, insurers would have a better argument for denying claims such as the ones mentioned earlier. Earlier provisions applied only for the act or neglect of any other occupant of the described premises, providing such act or neglect was not within the knowledge or control of this insured. Under current standard forms, however, the control of property condition states that any act or neglect of *any person* beyond the direction and control of the named insured will not affect the insurance. This latter provision, furthermore, does not place a time limit on when that act or neglect must take place.

In the final analysis, if property policies are going to defeat the expectation that the insured has coverage for losses beyond its control, there needs to be specific wording to convey that intent and to defeat what will otherwise be an expectation of coverage.

Insurance under Two or More Coverages

In the event that more than one of the policy's coverages applies to a loss, this condition prevents double payment. It limits the amount of payment to the actual amount of loss or damage. For example, a piece of business equipment might be covered under both the building and contents section of the BPP. The insured cannot recover under both. However, if the amount of coverage left under one section is insufficient to pay the entire loss, it could be paid under either or both sections, up to the actual amount of loss or damage.

Legal Action against Us

An insured must first fully comply with all the policy terms in order to bring suit against the insurer. The insured must bring the suit within two years following the loss or damage (not two years after a formal denial of the claim). Earlier policies that incorporated the standard fire policy language gave the insured one year in which to bring suit.

Liberalization

The policy states that if the insurer liberalizes the policy (i.e., broadens or adds coverage) without any corresponding premium increase, the revisions automatically apply to the insured's unrevised policy. This provision applies to any liberalization adopted by the insurer during the policy term or forty-five days prior to the inception date. For example, the policy provides $250,000 for a newly acquired or constructed building. If an insurer changes its policy to provide $300,000, without increasing the premium, all existing policyholders receive the $300,000 coverage immediately. In other words, the insured does not have to physically receive the policy renewal or endorsement for the broadened coverage to apply.

No Benefit to Bailee

The policy is intended to protect the insured's property; there is no insurance under the policy for the benefit of others to whom insured property may be entrusted. If the insured owns a clothing store and sends some of the clothing out to be dry cleaned, the dry cleaner is responsible for the clothing while it is in his care. If the clothing is damaged while at the dry cleaner, the dry cleaner cannot look to the clothing owner's policy for coverage. While the insurer may eventually settle with its own insured, it would still retain the right to enter into subrogation proceedings against the dry cleaner to recover the insurer's payment and would make no payment to the insured or the bailee for the benefit of the bailee.

Other Insurance

While this condition does not prohibit an insured from carrying more than one property policy—and, in fact, states that the insured may have other insurance subject to the same plan, terms, conditions, and provisions—it spells out how a loss is handled in such a situation.

If the insured has more than one policy that covers the same plan, terms, conditions, and provisions, then any loss will be split pro rata by limits. For example, the XYZ Company headquarters is insured for $1 million with two policies covering the same plan, terms, conditions, and provisions. ABC Insurance has a policy for $750,000; DEF Indemnity has a policy for $250,000. If the XYZ building suffers a $400,000 fire loss, the payments would be split as follows: ABC—$300,000; DEF—$100,000. The insured would be responsible for two deductibles under this scenario.

The second part of this condition makes the policy excess over any other policy that does not cover the same plan, terms, conditions, and provisions. The policy is excess even if the insured cannot collect from the other insurer.

Policy Period, Coverage Territory

The policy covers losses that commence during the policy period, which is shown on the declarations page of the policy. The loss must also commence within the coverage territory—the United States (including territories and possessions), Puerto Rico, or Canada. The coverage territory also includes property that is being transported between points within the coverage territory. For example, coverage would apply to property being transported by motor vehicle between California and Alaska but not between California and Mexico.

Insureds doing business outside the policy territory may secure limited property coverage under the Business Personal Property Limited International Coverage, CP 04 32, and/or Property in Process of Manufacture by Others Limited International Coverage, CP 04 33. In addition, limited time element coverage may be secured under the Business Income from Dependent Properties Limited International Coverage, CP 15 01. Insureds with more robust foreign property exposures beyond the limited coverages of the previously cited endorsement would be better served with a more comprehensive foreign package policy.

Transfer of Rights of Recovery against Others to Us

This condition defines the insurer's subrogation rights when it makes a payment under the policy. To expedite the claim process, many times an insurer will pay its insured for property that was damaged by someone else. This condition allows the insurer to pursue the responsible party to recover the amount it paid to the insured.

The subrogation condition also preserves the rights of the insurer when it comes to third parties such as a bailor or mortgagee. The insurer is first in line to get money back from the responsible party (at least for the amount it paid).

At any time *prior to a loss* an insured may waive, in writing, possible recovery rights against anyone. However, once a loss has occurred the insured may waive those rights against only another insured, a business that the insured owns or controls (or owns or controls the insured), or a tenant of the insured. Even though the policy permits an insured to waive its recovery rights prior to a loss, it is a good idea to check to see if a given state still requires an endorsement dealing with such waivers, since some states makes these requirements.

Other Relevant Provisions of the Building and Personal Property Coverage Form

While not designated as conditions, there are several provisions in the Building and Personal Property Coverage Form that operate as conditions.

Limits of Insurance

The policy states that the most it will pay for loss or damage in any one occurrence is the limit of liability shown on the declarations page. Unlike commercial general liability policies, the commercial property policy is not subject to annual aggregate limits (meaning that once the limit is exhausted during the policy period, it is gone); instead, the policy's limits are per occurrence. For example, if the insured's building is insured for $100,000 and suffers fire damage in the first month of the policy period of $75,000, full policy limits of $100,000 are available for windstorm that may occur in the eleventh month.

The section provides $2,500 coverage for outdoor signs—whether attached to buildings or not. The amount is per sign in any one occurrence.

The limits section indicates that the amounts of insurance applicable to fire department service charge, pollutant cleanup and removal, increased cost of construction, and electronic data are in addition to the declared policy limits.

The limits section concludes by putting the additional coverage of preservation of property within the policy limits. Debris removal was included here, as well in previous editions, but the debris removal additional coverage now describes the maximum payable under that coverage (see Chapter 2).

Higher dollar amounts for these policy limitations are generally secured through a declarations entry or through the purchase of a separate policy.

Deductible

One deductible applies per loss occurrence, that is, not per insured peril or each item of building or personal property damaged. A loss may involve both fire and windstorm damage—only one deductible applies; or, the loss may involve damage to (1) the insured's building; (2) a structure on the premises; and (3) items of personal property—again, one deductible applies.

By policy provision, the amount of loss is first reduced (if required) by the coinsurance condition or the agreed value option coverage. If this adjusted amount of loss is less than the deductible, the insurer pays nothing on the claim. If the adjusted amount of loss exceeds the deductible, the deductible is subtracted from the adjusted amount of loss and that is the amount the insured recovers, subject to the applicable policy limits.

The deductible condition explains the application of the deductible when the occurrence involves loss to more than one item of covered property and separate limits apply to those items. For example, a building on the property has a $60,000 limit and another has a value of $80,000. Both are damaged in the same occurrence, building #1 with damage totaling $60,110, and loss to building #2 is $90,000. The losses to each building are not combined in determining the application of the deductible, but the deductible is applied only once per occurrence (see the following example from the policy).

Deductible	$250
Limit of Insurance—Building #1	$60,000
Limit of Insurance—Building #2	$80,000
Loss to Building #1	$60,100
Loss to Building #2	$90,000

The amount of loss to building #1 ($60,100) is less than the sum of the limit of insurance applicable to building #1, plus the deductible ($60,250). The deductible is subtracted from the amount of loss in calculating the loss payable for building #1 ($60,100 - $250) for a loss payable on building #1 of $59,850.

Because the deductible applies only once per occurrence, it is not subtracted in determining the loss payable for building #2. The loss payable for building #2 is its limit of insurance ($80,000). The insured still has an uninsured loss in the amount of $10,000 (because the loss was $90,000 and the limits are $80,000) and a deductible is not applied to building #2.

In policy example number 2, the deductible and limits are the same as in example number 1.

Loss to Building #1 (Exceeds Limit of Insurance plus Deductible)	$70,000
Loss to building #2 (Exceeds Limit of Insurance plus Deductible)	$90,000
Loss Payable – Building #1 (Limit of Insurance)	$60,000
Loss Payable – Building #2 (Limit of Insurance)	$80,000
Total amount of loss payable	$140,000

How to Apply Deductible

The insured property is a hotel located on the coast of North Carolina. The hotel is insured on a CP 00 10 with special causes of loss form, CP 10 30. The amount of building coverage is $6,905,000 with a deductible of $353,193. In order to get the insurance, the hotel owners had to agree to a manuscripted change in the form. It excludes hail damage to some types of outdoor property, such as exterior paint, landscaping, and parking lots.

When Hurricane Floyd hit the Carolinas, this hotel suffered severe damage. The amount of the loss is $5 million; out of that $5 million, $1.3 million is uncovered damage to exterior property. Of the remaining $3.7 million, only about $800,000 is damage to covered property.

The difficulty is the application of the deductible. The adjuster says that it applies to the amount of the covered loss. Thus, the deductible of $353,193 applies to the $800,000 that is payable, leaving an amount payable of $446,807.

The policy says the deductible applies "in any one occurrence of loss or damage (herein referred to as loss)." This is not otherwise qualified by "covered loss" or "the amount of loss covered by this policy." The deductible in a commercial property policy applies to the total amount of the loss as respects the insured—not to the limit of liability or special sublimits of liability.

The deductible is applied to the total amount of the loss, $5 million, leaving $4,646,807 as the amount of loss. However, that amount is further limited by the exclusion of damage to certain types of exterior property. Thus, the $1.3 million in uncovered hail damage is taken from that, leaving a final amount of $3,346,807.

Even if the insurer prevails at appraisal and is correct that only $800,000 is payable under the policy, the deductible still applies to the amount of the loss—$5 million. If the insurer prevails in appraisal and the amount payable is reduced to $800,000, the insurer will still owe the full $800,000: amount of loss ($5 million); less the deductible ($353,193) for an initial amount payable of $4,646,807; less the $1.3 million in uncovered hail damage (leaving $3,346,807); less $2,546,807 that the insurer claims is not covered (leaving a total amount payable of $800,000). No further deductions would be taken.

For example, a standard limitation in the CP 10 30 is $2,500 for the theft of patterns, dies, molds, and forms. A thief breaks into a machine shop covered by a CP 00 10 and CP 10 30. The deductible is $1,000.

> The thief takes $4,000 worth of patterns, dies, molds and forms. The $1,000 deductible first applies to the loss, leaving $3,000 payable. However, that amount is further limited to $2,500 by the above provision. This insured is owed $2,500 by his insurer. If the deductible of $1,000 were applied to the sublimit of $2,500, the insured could collect only $1,500. If this were the case, the policy would never pay its full limits.

Loss Conditions

In addition to the common policy conditions and the commercial property conditions, the BPP contains a set of loss conditions that operate in case of a loss.

Abandonment and Appraisal

Abandonment. The first loss condition is abandonment. The insured may not simply abandon damaged property to the insurance company. The insurer has the right to the salvage value of property for which it makes total payment but cannot be compelled to take damaged or destroyed property.

Appraisal. The second loss condition, appraisal, provides a method to settle differences between insured and insurer regarding the valuation of damaged property or the amount of the loss. In this event each party selects its own appraiser. Then the two appraisers select an umpire. If the appraisers cannot agree on an umpire they may request that the umpire be chosen by a judge of a court having jurisdiction. The appraisers then separately value the property and set the value of the loss. If the appraisers are unable to agree the matter goes to the umpire. A decision to which any two agree (either both appraisers or an appraiser and the umpire) is binding on both parties. The condition states that each party must pay its own appraiser. The costs of the umpire and of the appraisal process are shared equally.

Some confusion can arise over the term *amount of loss*. Is this just the monetary value of the loss, or does this phrase also apply to the scope or cause of loss?

In *Wells v. American States Preferred Ins. Co.*, 919 S.W.2d 679 (Ct. App. Tex. 1996), the question was whether a plumbing leak or another event caused or did not cause damage to the foundation. The court found that the appraisal section did not authorize the appraisers to make that type of causation determination. However, in *State Farm Lloyds v. Johnson*, 290 S.W.3d 886 (Tex. 2009), a hail storm damaged the named insured's roof. A dispute arose as to whether the appraisal was appropriate to determine which portions of the roof needed to be replaced under the policy.

The Supreme Court of Texas held that the appraisal was the appropriate process not only for determining which portions of the roof were damaged, but also whether undamaged portions of the roof would need to be replaced in order to fix the damage caused by the event.

The condition ends with these words: "If there is an appraisal, we will still retain our right to deny the claim." The inclusion of this statement helps the insurer avoid the implication that by participating in the appraisal process there is an implied agreement to pay the claim. It also prevents the insured from claiming that entering the appraisal process keeps the insurer from denying the claim later. Appraisal applies to the value of property, not whether the loss is covered.

Appraisal of a Loss

A commercial property insured suffered a major fire loss. The insured first hired a public adjuster, submitted a proof of loss, and awaited the insurer's decision. When the insured and the insurer could not agree on the amount of the loss, the dispute was submitted to appraisal.

The appraisers reached a decision favorable to the insured. At that point the insurer decided that it wanted to readjust the claim, but that is contractually impermissible. Once a claim goes through the appraisal process and an amount is set, the insurer no longer has the options it had. The language clearly says that the decision of any two of the three (appraisers and umpire) is binding on all parties.

An insured must submit a proof of loss so that the insurer may investigate the claim. That was already done in this case. The policy says that the insurer will pay a loss within thirty days after receiving the proof of loss and an appraisal award has been made. In this case, the appraisal award was made. The insurer cannot now decide to settle the claim in a different manner.

Appraisal Clause and Disinterested Appraisers

The insurer and insured disputed resolution of a fire loss claim. There was no dispute as to the cause of the fire loss, and the insured prepared a building estimate. The dispute was over the extent and valuation of the loss.

The insured instituted the appraisal process under the policy and submitted the name of a disinterested builder and asked the insurer to do likewise. The insurer selected the original builder with whom the insured could not agree about the amount of damages.

The appraisal clause states that "each party will choose a competent appraiser." If these two cannot reach an agreement, they select an umpire. Having one of the original parties to the dispute chosen as an appraiser seems to build a barrier in the appraisal process, but the policy requires only that the appraiser must be competent; it does not require that each party select a disinterested appraiser.

The hope is that because the appraisers are competent professionals who are one step removed from the dispute, they will reach an agreement despite a certain natural bias in favor of their employer. If they cannot, the policy offers a mechanism for them to choose an umpire who decides which of the appraisers is right. If they cannot agree on an umpire, the policy provides for a court to select the umpire. These contingencies for involving an umpire are based in part on the recognition that the appraisers chosen by the parties might not be completely unbiased.

The Insured's Duties in the Event of Loss

The policy lists eight things an insured must do in the event of loss or damage under the policy. It also specifies the right of the insurer to examine the insured under oath without any other insured being present. The policy specifies that the insured must do the following:

1. Notify the police if a law was broken. The police notification requirement promotes several important objectives. First, it encourages the insured to inventory stolen or damaged items soon after the loss has occurred. This promotes claims accuracy. Second, it minimizes fraudulent theft claims by requiring the named insured to make a police report. Third, notification gives police an opportunity to investigate the loss, thereby increasing the possibility of apprehending the criminals and/or recovering stolen property. Fourth, the reporting of theft losses promotes certain socio-economic goals by permitting law enforcement the opportunity to focus their efforts on such crimes and their effects on the community.

2. Send the insurance company a notice of loss that includes a description of the property. The condition begins with the word *give* not *send*, so presumably notice to the insured's agent of loss by telephone is sufficient to fulfill this condition. The provision does not specify that the description must be in writing, but it must be given promptly. Prompt notice is not defined in the policy, but it is widely held to mean timely notice or as soon as practicable. For example, an insured may not know a loss has

occurred or that it is covered. In these cases, coverage will still apply as long as the insured's delay has not affected the insurer's ability to investigate the claim. The primary purpose of this condition is to ensure that the insurer's rights will not be prejudiced by the insured's actions or inactions (e.g., late notice or failing to cooperate). Claims involving late notice must be carefully reviewed.

3. Provide a description of how, when, and where the loss or damage took place. This must be done as soon as possible.

4. Protect the covered property from any further damage and keep track of costs for emergency and temporary repairs to do so. This includes separating damaged from undamaged property if feasible. The insured must document expenses incurred in preserving the property from further loss. Such documentation is necessary for consideration in the settlement of the claim. These expenses are subject to the limit of insurance. "For consideration in the settlement of a claim" does not mean that the insurance company can consider whether to reimburse the insured for expense to protect covered property from further damage; consideration here can be taken in the contract context of consideration, meaning "due consideration" in a pecuniary sense.

    The insured must protect the covered property from any further damage, not just damage from a covered peril. However, the insurer is not liable for subsequent loss or damage resulting from any uncovered cause of loss.

5. Compile an inventory of damaged and undamaged property if the insurer so requests.

6. Allow the insurer to inspect the property, including the insured's books and records. The insurer may also take samples of damaged and undamaged property. Comparing these types of property helps in the investigation of a loss.

7. Submit a signed, sworn proof of loss, if requested. This provision requires the named insured to send a signed, sworn proof of loss statement containing the information the insurer requests to investigate the claim. Commonly, the insurance company adjuster assists the named insured in completing the inventory and/or worksheets needed to determine the amount of claim. At that time, the named insured usually signs the proof of loss. If the insurer forwards a formal written demand for a proof of

loss, it may be an indication that the insurer believes that the claim is suspicious. Since the proof of loss is a sworn statement, information provided on it that later proves to be false may serve to invalidate the policy on the basis of material misrepresentation.

8.   Generally cooperate with the insurance company. Cooperation includes submitting to questions under oath. It also includes allowing the insurer to examine the insured's books and records. Any insured answering such questions in writing must sign his answers.

The form states that the insurer may examine the insured under oath (a term that courts have held encompasses both oral and written examination). The insurer may examine insureds separately and out of the presence of other insureds. In *USF&G v. Hill*, 722 S.W.2d 609 (Mo. App. 1986), the court found the insurer's right to examine insureds separately had to be made explicit in the policy or the insurer had no such right. This language was added to the form.

In one case, the insured's property was damaged by fire. In the aftermath, the insured took steps over a period of time to protect the property from further damage before the damage was remedied, and substantial expenses were incurred. At issue was whether those expenses were covered under the policy. Specifically, in *American Commercial Finance Corp. v. Seneca Ins. Co.*, 850 N.E.2d 1114 (Mass. App. Ct. 2006), pipes burst on the insured property, and the sprinklers became inoperable as a result. Then a fire broke out. The insured hired a private security service for several months thereafter to not only protect the property from vandalism but also to protect it from further fire damage since the sprinklers were inoperable. The policy condition over which the dispute concerned was similar to number 4 in the previously discussed list of the insured's duties in the event of a loss.

The amount of the expenses incurred was $79,350.50, which, when added to the amount paid by the insurer to the insured for damage to the covered building, did not exceed the limits of insurance. The loss condition of the insured's policy required the following duties after a loss occurs:

> Take all reasonable steps to protect the Covered Property from further damage, and to keep a record of your expenses necessary to protect the Covered Property, for consideration in the settlement of the claim. This will not increase the Limit of Insurance. However, we will not pay for any subsequent loss or damage resulting from a cause of loss that is not a Covered

> Cause of Loss. Also, if feasible, set the damaged property aside and in the best possible order for examination.

Under Limits of Insurance, the policy stated:

> The most we will pay for loss or damage for any one occurrence is the applicable Limit of Insurance shown in the Declarations ... The limits applicable to the Coverage Extension and the Fire Department Service Charge and Pollution Clean Up and Removal Additional Coverages are In addition to the Limits of Insurance.

The insurer maintained that the policy language relied upon was preceded by the heading, "Duties [of the insured] In the Event of Loss or Damage" and was located within the part of the policy dealing with loss conditions. The insurer, in other words, argued that with the language was located in an area of the policy involving conditions and did not deal with coverage.

The court disagreed and held that if such amounts were not to be paid, there would be no need to state that such amounts could only be paid if, in doing so, the limits of insurance would not be exceeded.

The court also stated that the insurer's argument that the record of expenses was merely for consideration in a settlement did not explain how the concept of consideration would make any sense if the reasonable amount of such expenses were not to be compensated. An additional argument of the insurer, that the purpose of requiring the insured to keep a record of its expenses was to enable it to prove to the insurer that the insured took steps to protect the property, was, from the court's perspective, far-fetched. The court added that the insured could prove what steps it took by evidence far more direct than showing how much such efforts could cost.

The loss condition of ISO forms is identical to the provision of the Seneca Insurance Company policy. As a matter of interest to some, perhaps, the reference in this condition with regard to keeping a record of expenses was first introduced in ISO forms with the 1988 edition. However, at that time, the provision read as follows: "Also keep a record of your expenses for emergency and temporary repairs." This particular sentence was amended in 1995 to what it currently reads with the deletion of the reference to "emergency and temporary repairs."

Accompanying this change in 1995 was an addition to the reference that it would not increase the limit of insurance, as follows: "However, we will not pay for any subsequent loss or damage resulting from a cause of loss that is not a Covered Cause of Loss. Also, if feasible, set the damaged property aside and in the best possible order for examination."

When this loss condition was amended in 1995, ISO stated that the insured must keep records of all expenses incurred to protect the property and not solely the expenses relating to temporary or emergency repairs. The document also stated that the expenses incurred to protect the property from further damage—following a covered cause of loss—will be considered in the settlement of the claim.

It is uncertain whether the insurer in *American Commercial Finance Corp.* had this kind of ISO document at the time of the claim because it might have avoided the dispute entirely. If this provision had not been amended in 1995 and had applied to the policy, the insurer in the case might have had a stronger argument because the expenses were not incurred for temporary or emergency repairs.

In the final analysis, however, whether coverage will apply is going to hinge on the facts. In *American Commercial Finance Corp.*, the court noted that another case, *Klein's Moving and Storage, Inc. v. Westport Ins. Corp.*, 766 N.Y.S. 2d 496 (2003) involved identical language but did not hold for coverage. The language was interpreted in *Klein's* as not requiring the insurer to pay the cost of moving goods out of a warehouse for the purpose of repainting the premises that had been damaged by fire and not for the purpose of further loss from damage. This same court did, however, cite two additional cases where coverage applied: *Royal Indem. Co. v. Grunberg*, 553 N.Y.S.2d 527 (1990), *and Benjamin Shapiro Realty Co. v. Agricultural Ins. Co.*, 731 N.Y.S. 2d 453 (2001). Both cases involved costs incurred in preventing much greater loss where the insureds had a contractual duty to take all reasonable steps to protect the covered property from further damaged by a covered cause of loss.

Loss Payment

After a covered loss, the insurer has four settlement options; the policy specifically gives the insurer the selection of which option to employ. Settlement will be effected using one of the following options:

1. **Pay the value of the property**. Prior editions of the BPP did not define the word *value*, but the CP 00 10 10 00 edition added a paragraph in the provision stating that the insurer will determine the value of the damaged property or the cost to repair or replace in accordance with the valuation condition(e.g., actual cash value or replacement cost).

2. **The cost to repair or replace the damaged property.** The policy reiterates the ordinance or law exclusion by specifically eliminating insurance recovery for any extra costs due to the operation of building or zoning laws.

3. **The insurer may take the property at an agreed or an appraised value.**

4. **The insurer may actually repair, rebuild, or replace the property with that of "like kind and quality."** This option also excludes any extra costs due to the operation of building laws.

Most property claims are finalized with a cash settlement although insurers may choose to pay the cost to repair or replace the damaged property, take the property at an agreed price for salvage value, or repair, rebuild, or replace the property with like and quality.

The insurer is required within thirty days of receipt of the sworn proof of loss to advise the insured which option it chooses. Whichever option is chosen, the insurer will not pay the insured more than the insured's financial interest in the property.

Property of others is also subject to the same four options. The insurer deals directly with the owner of the property in the insured's stead. Again, the insurer owes the owner of the property no more than his financial interest in it.

Sometimes the owners of damaged property may bring suit against the insured. The insurer promises to defend such suits at its own expense.

Once the insurer receives the signed, sworn proof of loss and reaches an agreement with the insured regarding the value of the property, the loss will be paid within thirty days. Reaching an agreement on the value includes the award of an appraisal.

ISO added a loss payment condition to address exposures related to party walls in the CP 00 10 06 07 edition. A *party wall* is generally defined as a wall that divides two adjoining properties and in which each of the owners shares the rights. Ownership of a party wall may or may not be shared; there are numerous legal variations including tenancy in common and unilateral ownership with easement rights. A coverage issue may arise when one owner of a party wall refuses or is unable to repair his side of a party wall following loss or damage.

The policy was revised to identify the exposure and convey loss adjusting procedures for it. In this provision, loss payment relating to a party wall reflects the insured's partial interest in that wall. However, if the owner of the adjoining building elects not to repair or replace that building (and the building insured under this insurance is being repaired or replaced), this insurance will pay the full value of the party wall, subject to all other policy provisions.

Actual Cash Value Defined

Actual cash value (ACV) has three meanings in actual usage:

1. **Fair market value,** which is usually described as the price a willing buyer would pay to buy property from a willing seller in a free market.

2. **Replacement cost less depreciation**, which is generally accepted to mean the cost to replace property at the time of the loss minus its physical depreciation.

3. **The broad evidence rule,** which involves a judicious application of either one or two to the unique circumstance of the claim, whichever is more favorable to the insured.

State laws vary considerably on the definition. In California, an appeals court decided that ACV means fair market value in *Cheeks v. California Fair Plan Assn.*, 61 Cal. App. 4th 423 (1998). The court admonished insurers: "If it [the insurer] wants to determine actual cash value on the basis of replacement cost less depreciation, all it has to do is say so in the policy." Courts in Pennsylvania have taken the opposite view that ACV means replacement cost, such as in *Judge v. Celina Mut. Ins. Co.* 449 A.2d 658 (Pa. Super. 1982).

Fair market value, replacement cost, and *depreciation* are all fairly common and have commonly accepted meanings. They have been used over and over in establishing the value of damaged property.

The broad evidence rule, on the other hand, tries to bring other factors into consideration. *McAnarney v. Newark Fire Ins. Co.*, 247 N.Y. 176 (1928) is a leading case on this question. The case involved the fire destruction of an old brewery that could not be used because of the National Prohibition Act. The building apparently had no other economic use, and the owner advertised it for sale, unsuccessfully, for a fraction of the amount of insurance carried. In striking a compromise between the insured and the insurer, the court said: "Where insured buildings have been destroyed, the trier of fact may, and should, call to its aid in order to effectuate complete indemnity, every fact and circumstance which would logically tend to the formation of a correct estimate of the loss. It may consider original cost and cost of reproduction; the opinions upon value given by qualified witnesses; declarations against interest which may have been made by the insured; the gainful uses to which the buildings may have been put; as well as any other reasonable factor tending to throw light on the subject." In so reasoning, the court decided on a value between replacement cost less depreciation and the market value of the building.

The most important point regarding the broad evidence rule was quoted in *McAnarney*. The court said that "every fact and circumstance which would logically tend to the formation of a correct estimate of the loss," including the economic value of the property, should be considered in determining the actual cash value.

To mitigate the ambiguity in determining the actual cash value of property at the time of loss as reviewed previously, some insuring forms provide a definition of actual cash value. For example, in Pennsylvania an ISO change endorsement defines *actual cash value* as follows:

> Actual cash value is calculated as the amount it would cost to repair or replace Covered Property, at the time of loss or damage, with material of like kind or quality, subject to deterioration, depreciation, and obsolescence. Actual cash value applies to valuation of Covered Property regardless of whether that property has sustained a partial or total loss or damage.

> The actual cash value of the loss or damage property may be significantly less than its replacement cost.

Valuing Business Personal Property

Valuing business personal property may be less difficult because the value of the contents is not tied to the value of the land as with a building. The problem with using replacement cost less depreciation is that business personal property is often diverse, is acquired over a period of time, and depreciates at various rates. Often receipts are unavailable. Market value is also not a reliable guide. Few businesses would want their fairly new office furniture replaced with similar furniture that had been rented to others.

Another problem for businesses is the value of stocks of merchandise and raw materials. These items usually do not suffer depreciation. In such a case the proper measure of recovery is the cost of replacing them at the current market value, less any salvage value. Merchandise that has become shopworn and has deteriorated in value should be subject to depreciation. The measure of recovery might be more or less than the original cost; however, the standard of recovery is the cost to the insured not the price at which it is expected to sell. Rules in most states permit use of a market value or selling price clause that converts, for some insureds such as manufacturers and retailers, finished stock from actual cash value to selling price less discounts and unincurred expenses. Form CP 99 30, Manufacturer's Selling Price (Finished Stock Only), provides for valuation based on selling price, less any applicable discounts and expenses, for all completed stock (not just finished stock that is sold but not delivered, as in the building and personal property coverage form).

Recovered Property

This condition provides a method for loss readjustment in case stolen property is recovered. If either party recovers any property after loss settlement, prompt notice must be given to the other party. The insured has the option to return the amount of claim payment in return for the original item. The insurer cannot require the insured to return payment and take back recovered property. Recovery expenses and necessary repairs to the property are borne by the insurance company up to the applicable limit.

Vacancy

The vacancy provision contains two parts. The first defines *building* for both an owner-occupant and a tenant as meant in the vacancy provision. The second describes the manner in which losses to vacant buildings are handled.

The form defines *building* for a tenant as that portion rented or leased to the insured. The tenant's portion is vacant when it does not contain enough business personal property to conduct customary operations, which would mean its normal business.

When the policy is issued to the owner or general lessee rather than a tenant, the policy says that a building is vacant if the insured does not rent at least 31 percent of the floor space to others or if the insured does not use at least 31 percent of the floor space for his own operations.

Under prior editions, a building with the furniture and fixtures of a business—but from which the stock had been removed—would be considered vacant since customary operations are not possible without stock. In post-2000 editions, a building containing fixtures, fittings, and business personal property would still be considered vacant if it were being underutilized. The vacancy provision could be an issue for insureds where a storefront operation is the only going concern in a multiple story building. Despite the going concern on the first floor, if less than 31 percent of the building is unrented or not used for customary operations, the building is considered vacant and the provisions related to vacant property are applicable.

Prior to 1995, only buildings under construction were exempt from the vacancy provision. The 1995 version added buildings under renovation. The times when the Building and Personal Property Coverage Form applies—by coverage extension—to a building under construction are rare and are limited by the provisions of the form (thirty days). An existing structure, on the other hand, can be subject to renovation at any time with no requirement of notice to the insurance company since it will not be considered vacant. However, the insured must be careful of a coinsurance problem if much value is added prior to notifying the insurer.

The second part of the vacancy condition describes how losses are handled when the building has been vacant for more than sixty consecutive days, or longer, if so endorsed. There is no coverage for damage from vandalism, building glass breakage, water damage, theft or attempted theft, or sprinkler leakage, unless steps have been taken to protect the system against freezing. The policy covers loss from a covered peril in a vacant building at a reduction of 15 percent in what it otherwise would pay.

Questions can arise as to when the sixty-day time period begins. For instance, in *West Bend Mut. Ins. Co. v. New Packing Co Inc.*, No. 1-11-1507, 2012 IL App (1st) 111507-U (Ill. App. Nov. 30, 2012), the insureds purchased a warehouse that had been vacant for more than sixty days. Shortly after adding the warehouse to its policy, the warehouse was vandalized, causing damage to the building. West Bend invoked the vacancy clause, but New Packing argued that the warehouse had been added to the policy only a few weeks before the vandalism occurred, so the building should not be considered vacant under its ownership—the sixty-day period should not begin tolling until the effective date of the endorsement adding the warehouse to the policy. The court disagreed with New Packing, stating that "the vacancy provision defines the vacancy period retrospectively, whereby the days of vacancy are calculated by looking back from the date of loss, rather than prospectively by looking forward from the effective date of coverage."

Valuation

The policy covers loss to covered property at actual cash value unless some other valuation method (such as replacement cost) has been arranged. The policy does, however, provide four exceptions. Valuable papers and records were at one time a fifth exception, but the CP 00 10 04 02 edition's treatment of electronic data and valuable papers and records necessitated its removal from this section. The exceptions are as follows:

1. If the insured meets the coinsurance requirement, the policy covers any loss under $2,500 at replacement cost. However, the following building items are still subject to ACV adjustment: awnings, floor coverings, appliances, outdoor equipment, and furniture. Replacement cost does not include any extra cost due to the operation of building laws.

2. Stock sold but not delivered is valued at selling price less any applicable discounts and normally incurred expenses. For example, if the insured sells widgets at $100 each and offers a discount of 2 percent if paid within ten days, entire amount due within thirty days, with $10 in shipping expense, the recovery on the $100 item might be $88 ($100 selling price less 2 percent discount minus shipping fee of $10). Trade and business practice, along with examination of books and records, determines actual valuation.

3. The policy provides for replacement of damaged glass with safety glass if required by law.

4. Tenants improvements and betterments are adjusted at ACV if repairs are made promptly. If the insured does not make repairs promptly to improvements and betterments, the insurer offers a proportional settlement via the following formula: the original cost of the improvement times the number of days from the loss to the lease's expiration or the expiration of the renewal option period, if applicable. The amount computed is then divided by the number of days from the installation of the improvement to the expiration of the lease or the expiration of the renewal option period. The inclusion of renewal option periods addresses the long standing question of whether such periods should be considered during loss settlement calculations to provide a better restitution for an insured's use interest in a damaged improvement.

    Assume a tenant holds a one-year lease for a commercial building that expires on July 31. The lease contains a one-year renewal option. On March 3, the tenant installs paneling costing $1,500. A fire occurs on June 2 that causes damage so extensive that the insured closes the business permanently. Had no loss occurred, the tenant would have stayed in business and exercised the renewal option.

    Without taking the renewal option period into consideration, the insured stands to receive a $600 payment for the improvement ($1,500 × 60/150 = $600; where 60 equals the days from loss to

lease expiration and 150 equals the days from improvement installation to lease expiration). When the renewal option period (365
days) is included in the calculation, the result of the proportional
loss settlement is $1,238—[$1,500 × (60 + 365/150 + 365)] =
$1,238—a significant difference.

These formulas come into play only if the insured does not make
the repairs promptly, thus disqualifying him from actual cash
value recovery. The insured receives nothing from the insurer if
someone other than the tenant (the landlord, for instance) repairs
damaged improvements.

Valuation and Selling Price

A load of nonalcoholic beer was damaged when the load shifted
during transit. The insured's customer made a claim against the insured
for replacement of the shipment, and a dispute over the value of the
beer ensued.

Even though the buyer of the beer was to pay $4,300 for it,
replacement cost for the damaged goods to the insured was $10,260. It
is standard practice in that industry to reduce the price on one product
and increase prices on other products in order to maintain (or increase)
profit margins.

The insurer took the position that it would pay the smaller of the
replacement cost or actual cash value at the time of the loss. At the time
of the loss, the value was the selling price, $4,300.

However, because the insured sold the beer for less than it cost does
not reduce the value to that amount. What needs to be established is the
ACV of the beer. The insured needs to demonstrate that this practice
of selling certain items for less than their cost is a standard business
practice in this industry.

Additional Conditions

The BPP (under the respective coverage forms) contains two additional
conditions: coinsurance and mortgageholders.

Coinsurance. Coinsurance is widely misunderstood among insurance
buyers, and it is not until after a significant loss that insureds learn
about its importance in price-making and why they are often penalized
for maintaining inadequate limits. The principle of coinsurance says
that in exchange for a reduced rate the insured must agree to maintain a

specified relationship between property values and amount of insurance (e.g., 80 percent). For example, a building with a value of $1,000,000 must be insured for at least $800,000. If the insured agrees to carry this amount ($800,000) of coverage, the rate charged may be fifty cents per thousand dollars of coverage; however, if the insured chooses to carry only $500,000, that rate might increase to seventy-five cents or a dollar. Insureds who carry higher limits of insurance receive a lower rate per thousand of coverage.

The purchase and continued maintenance of a limit of insurance that complies with the coinsurance requirement of a policy is necessary to avoid a coinsurance penalty at time of claim. The following illustrates the coinsurance formula with examples of loss scenarios of both adequate and inadequate limits of insurance and applicable penalties using the previously cited amounts with a $1,000 deductible.

Coinsurance Formula

$$\frac{\text{Limit of insurance}}{\text{Value of property} \times \text{Coinsurance percentage}} \times \text{Loss} = \text{Covered} - \text{Deductible}$$

Adequate Example $\dfrac{\$800,000}{\$800,000} \times \$100,000 = \$100,000 - \$1,000$

Inadequate Example $\dfrac{\$500,000}{\$800,000} \times \$100,000 = \$62,500 - \$1,000$

The policy form further illustrates the mechanics of the coinsurance. Provision, including its application when property is written on a blanket basis (one limit of insurance covering more than one property). It also examines the ramifications of a coinsurance penalty.

To minimize the application of a coinsurance penalty, it is quite common to insure multiple properties on a blanket basis incorporating the agreed value option.

Since 1986, every version of the coinsurance provision found in the CP 00 10 applies the deductible after the calculation of the coinsurance penalty. The wording in the 2000 policy was rearranged to emphasize this point. Prior to 1986, the forms applied the deductible prior to the calculation of the coinsurance penalty, a manner more advantageous to the insured.

The following is an example of the interaction between the deductible and the coinsurance clause: two insureds each have a $50,000 loss under policies with a $250 deductible. Insured A is in compliance with the coinsurance requirement and recovers $49,750 ($50,000 minus $250). Insured B is underinsured and must accept 25 percent of the loss as a coinsurer. Insured B will collect $37,500 (75 percent of $50,000) less the $250 deductible for a net recovery of $37,250. Had insured B been covered under a pre-1986 form, he would have collected $37,316 (75 percent of $49,750). Subtracting the deductible before calculating the coinsurance penalty makes a difference of $66 for the insured.

One case where the insureds learned the hard way about the principle of coinsurance is *Wetmore v. Unigard Ins. Co.*, 107 P.3d 123 (Wash. App. 2005). The issue on appeal was whether Majestic Inn (insureds), insured by Unigard (insurer) were entitled to the full policy limits for a fire loss rather than a reduced amount calculated on the basis of the policy's coinsurance provision.

The property policy issued to the insureds covered the hotel and its contents for a limit of $1,750,000, subject to a 90 percent coinsurance provision, described later. When fire damaged the property, the market value, on a cash basis, was only $950,000, according to an appraisal performed after the fire. The insureds elected to make a claim on an actual cash value basis for $949,000, which took into consideration a $1,000 deductible. Thereafter, the insureds made a claim for the replacement cost for the $776,000 difference between the policy limit of $1,725,000 and the $949,000 that the insurer paid for the actual cash value loss. The insurer, however, disputed this amount noting that the coinsurance provision applied because the replacement cost bid for the building was $3,577,700 and the insurance at the time of loss was $1,725,000. Because 90 percent of the replacement cost bid—$3,219,930— was the total amount of insurance that the insureds should have carried on the property, the insurer claimed the amount of the replacement cost payment should be reduced accordingly. The trial court granted the insurer's summary judgment motion and the insureds appealed.

On appeal, the insureds argued that the application of the coinsurance provision for replacement cost was determined using the actual cash value of the insured property, not its replacement cost. The court disagreed and proceeded to explain step-by-step the application of the coinsurance provision:

1.   Coinsurance

     If a coinsurance percentage is shown in the Declarations, the fol-
     lowing [value] condition applies.

     a.   We will not pay the full amount of any loss if the value of
          Covered Property at the time of loss times the Coinsurance

percentage shown for it in the Declarations is greater than the Limit of Insurance for the property.

The court stated here that a 90 percent coinsurance provision appearing in the policy declarations satisfied the first condition of this coinsurance provision. The court then stated that it was necessary to refer to the valuation provision, which stated:

> We will determine the value of covered property in the event of loss or damage as follows:
>
> a.   At actual cash value as of the time of loss or damage...
>
> There was no dispute in this case that this provision governed the valuation of covered property when a claim for actual cash value is made. But that did not end the court's inquiry because an actual cash value claim was not at issue. The Insurer had already paid such a claim in this case. One other condition, the court said, that bore on the question to be decided was found under OPTIONAL COVERAGES:

3.   Replacement Cost

> a.   Replacement Cost (without deduction for depreciation) replaces Actual Cash Value in the Loss Condition, Valuation, of this Coverage Form.

The court explained that the plain words of these provisions, when read together, made clear that the value of the property covered by the policy was a condition to the amount to be paid. It also said that an insured's exercise of the right to elect the type of claim made affects the pertinent value. Specifically, the court stated that an insured has two claim options: (1) actual cash value instead of replacement cost, or (2) actual cash value in addition to replacement cost. Reading these provisions together and giving full effect to each, the court concluded that replacement cost valuation applied to the insured's second claim, the only claim that the insurer contested. Neither the policy language nor logic supported the view that this replacement cost claim was to be determined on an actual cash value basis, the court added.

Once replacement cost is chosen, the court explained, and replacement cost replaces actual cash value in the valuation section of the policy, the coinsurance provision must apply to the replacement cost coverage. The coinsurance provision did not apply to the initial ACV claim, the court said, because the policy limit exceeded 90 percent of the ACV. With a replacement cost estimate of $3,577,700, the insurer informed the insureds that they were subject to a 53 percent coinsurance penalty. (The 90 percent figure of $3,219,930 represented the amount of insurance the insureds were required to maintain in order to avoid the penalty. Dividing that amount by the amount they actually insured the hotel building for, $1,725,000, resulted in the 53 percent coinsurance penalty.) This was a bitter pill to swallow, but something that many insureds are required to do when failing to obtain appraisals on a periodic basis. Simply relying on an inflation guard provision does not always do justice, particularly if the value on which the inflation guard is based is too low or inaccurate.

Mortgageholders

This condition spells out the rights and duties of any mortgagees or trustees (here referred to as mortgageholders) that are named on the declarations. In the event of a claim, any listed mortgageholder receives payment for losses as interests may appear. However, the insured must be in compliance with all coverage terms. Even if foreclosure proceedings or similar actions have begun on a building that suffers a loss, a mortgageholder may collect a loss payment.

Further, even if the insurer denies a claim to the insured due to the insured's actions or lack of compliance with the terms for coverage, the mortgageholder may still collect. The mortgageholder must pay any premium due and submit the appropriate proof of loss. Additionally, a mortgageholder must notify the insurance company of any known change in ownership, occupancy, or increase of hazard. When these conditions are satisfied, all terms of the form become applicable to the mortgageholder.

If partial claim payment is made to a mortgageholder and not to an insured, the insurance company inherits a proportion of the mortgageholder's rights under the mortgage based on the extent of claim payment, and the mortgageholder retains subrogation rights and may attempt to recover the full amount of the claim.

The insurance company may, at its option, pay the mortgageholder the full amount of the principal and interest on the mortgage in exchange for transfer of the mortgage to the insurance company. In this case, the insured continues mortgage payments, but to the insurance company instead of the original mortgageholder.

If the insurer cancels the policy, it must send written notice to the mortgageholder thirty days before the effective date of cancellation. If the cancellation is due to nonpayment of premium by the insured, then notice to the mortgageholder is only ten days. In the event of nonrenewal, the insurer must also send a ten-day notice to the mortgageholder.

Loss during Foreclosure

A large warehouse was insured for over $1 million. The mortgageholder foreclosed on the property. Shortly after the foreclosure a fire caused nearly $700,000 in damage to the warehouse. The agent wondered about the insurer's obligation to the mortgageholder.

The amount of the loss does not determine the insurer's obligation to the mortgageholder; the amount of debt still owed on the property does. That amount is the mortgageholder's insurable interest.

The insurer's obligation to the named insured owner is the value of the loss limited to the former owner's insurable interest. If the owner of the building has complied with all the policy conditions, the insurer owes the loss to the named insured and the mortgageholder as their interests may appear.

Chapter 6

Builders Risk

Buildings under construction are not eligible for coverage under the Building and Personal Property Coverage Form, which forms the basis for a commercial property policy. Due to the unique exposures faced by a building under construction, such as the increased risk of fire, collapse, theft, and vandalism, different rates and forms must be used. The Builders Risk Coverage Form, CP 00 20, is combined with one of the causes of loss forms to cover buildings under construction. It can also be used to cover additions and alterations, foundations, temporary structures, materials and supplies owned by the insured, and on a limited basis, building materials and supplies of others.

As with the BPP and causes of loss forms, the Builders Risk Coverage Form has been revised by Insurance Services Office (ISO) from time to time. The builders risk editions are as follows (the date is the last four digits of the form number):

- CP 00 20 07 88

- CP 00 20 10 90

- CP 00 20 10 91

- CP 00 20 06 95

- CP 00 20 02 00

- CP 00 20 10 00

- CP 00 20 04 02

- CP 00 20 06 07

- CP 00 20 10 12

ISO Eligibility and Rules

Buildings in the course of construction are eligible for the builders risk coverage form. The rules recognize that even some buildings that, once occupied, are not eligible for the BPP form because use occupancy may still be covered on the CP 00 20 while under construction. ISO includes three examples in the rules of such exposures: boarding or rooming houses of one to four units, farm properties, and dwellings. The rules state that "the following are some examples of risks which are eligible during the course of construction but which may not be eligible when occupied," so the list is not comprehensive.

Builders risk coverage is written for a minimum one-year term to cover a new building or structure under construction or an existing structure undergoing additions, alterations, or repairs. The rules state that policy inception should begin no later than the date that construction starts above the level of the lowest basement floor, or, if there is no basement, the date construction begins. The rules permit pro rata cancellation when construction is completed whether insurance on the completed structure is rewritten with the same company or companies. If the policy is cancelled before the structure is completed, the general cancellation provisions found in the common policy conditions apply.

Blanket insurance covering more than one building or structure is subject to the rating rules for such coverage. Blanket coverage is useful for housing projects and other large risks with several units being erected at the same time.

A builders risk policy is written for the completed value of the insured building. This is known as the completed value approach of insuring buildings under construction. Under this method, the insured amount should include the value of all permanent fixtures and decorations that will become part of the building. The rules include the following warnings: "Contract price does not necessarily equal the full value at completion" and, "Failure to maintain the proper limit of insurance may cause the insured to share proportionately in a loss." The rates contemplate the fact that the insurer does not face the total amount of exposure for the entire policy term.

While not described as a coinsurance penalty, the builders risk form does penalize the insured in the event of a loss when the limit of liability is inadequate. The need for adequate insurance provision calls for a reduction in loss payment by the percentage the customer is underinsured. If the building has a completed value of $200,000 but is insured for only $100,000, any loss payment will be reduced by 50 percent. The provision says, "We will not pay a greater share of any loss than the proportion that the Limit of Insurance bears to the value on the date of completion."

The builders risk insured with more than one location may choose to cover all locations on a blanket basis. The countrywide rules contain a formula for calculating the blanket average rate.

As an alternative to the completed value approach, an insured may choose to insure a building under construction on a reporting form basis. This method is reviewed later in this chapter.

Value of the Building on the Completion Date

The Builders Risk Coverage form, CP 00 20, contains what amounts to a 100 percent coinsurance clause based on the value of the building on its completion date, but it is not always clear what comprises the completed building's value. More specifically, assume construction of a building that has a great deal of asphalt blacktop and a sizable volume of poured concrete in the footings and base slabs. The insured might not feel that these items should be included in the amount of insurance although they are included in the contract price of the building.

The following is an example of why these items need to be insured. Keep in mind that these items will be excluded upon completion.

Builders risk coverage applies to the building described in the policy declarations while in the course of construction. It does not contain the exclusion of foundations below the lowest basement (or, lacking a basement, below the surface of the ground) found in the Building and Personal Property Coverage Form. In fact, the Builders Risk Coverage Form explicitly states that it covers foundations in this provision: "(1) Covered Property…Building Under Construction, meaning the building or structure described in the declarations while in the course of construction, including: (a) Foundations; (b) The following property… (3) Your building materials and supplies used for construction; provided such property is intended to be permanently located in or on the building…or within 100 feet of its premises."

Unlike with a completed structure, there is a time during the course of construction when the footings and slabs the insured would like to exclude are exposed to loss. Fire or wind could destroy the forms before the concrete is poured and cause a legitimate builders risk loss. If construction has not yet begun—and insurance should be in place before construction begins—the insured and the underwriter might agree to write an endorsement eliminating coverage for foundations, materials, and supplies connected with them in exchange for an appropriate reduction in the amount of insurance. If construction is beyond the foundation stage, the insured has had the protection of the insurance while it was needed and there would be no justification for eliminating foundation values from the completed building value.

The same can be said for the asphalt blacktop. The builders risk form affords coverage for building materials and supplies used in construction, provided the materials are to remain permanently in or on the building or structure described in the declarations or within one-hundred feet of its premises. Perhaps the reason insureds generally decline this type of coverage is that the risk of damage or loss to the materials seems low. Instead, insureds often prefer to carry the risk themselves. Again, if the underwriter agrees, the value of the blacktopping might be removed from the completed value of the building in a preconstruction agreement if the insured is willing to accept an endorsement excluding coverage of materials and supplies used in that operation.

Covered Property

The Builders Risk Coverage Form covers direct loss or damage to covered property. The list of covered property is short compared to the list of covered property in the Building and Personal Property Coverage Form because the property covered by the commercial property policy is being put to its intended use while a builders risk policy covers property under construction. *Building under construction* is defined under A.1. Covered Property as meaning "the building or structure described in the Declarations while in the course of construction." Foundations are included. The form also covers fixtures and machinery, equipment used to service the building, and the insured's building materials and supplies used for construction. The insured must intend that these items be permanently located in or on the building or within one-hundred feet of the premises. It is important to keep in mind that a building is a structure but not all structures are buildings. This is important because the ISO causes of loss forms make a distinction between buildings and structures. Referring to Causes of Loss – Special Form, CP 10 30, for example, one will note that when it comes to additional coverage for collapse, coverage applies only to buildings and not to structures.

The form also does not define the phrase *in the course of construction*; therefore common usage applies. According to *Webster's New International Dictionary*, *construction* is "the act of putting together to form a complete integrated object: fabrication."

However, in *Patton v. Aetna Ins. Co.*, 595 F. Supp. 533 (N.D. Miss. 1984), the court expanded the meaning. The court ruled that the term includes activities related to, but prior to commencement of, construction. The case concerned a builders risk policy issued to cover a building scheduled for renovation. A fire destroyed a large portion of the building.

At the time of the fire only preparatory work towards the renovation had been done. This included removing the furnace and lattice work, unhooking the gas and plumbing lines, and engaging in discussions with contractors regarding the lowering of the building. The court determined that since the insured and the insuring company understood that renovation of the house was intended, it was reasonable to interpret *construction* to mean alterations of any type, whether additions or removals. As a result, the activities of the insured were considered construction and covered under the provisions of the builders risk policy.

There is no coverage for business personal property. Nor is there any coverage for the property of others. The builders risk form does, however, provide an additional coverage in the amount of $5,000 for material and supplies owned by others.

Temporary structures built on the premises are covered property if there is no other insurance on them. Such structures include cribbing, scaffolding, and construction forms. If a contractor should have purchased contractors' equipment coverage but failed to do so, the contractor may still be able to obtain coverage on loss or damage to equipment by maintaining that it is a temporary structure. Conversely, an insurer could deny coverage on some temporary structures maintaining that they should have been covered by a contractors' equipment floater. This is more likely to be a problem with larger construction projects than those that would be covered by the ISO Builders Risk Coverage Form.

Property Not Covered

As with the property covered section, the property not covered section is also rather short as compared to the BPP form. Again, much of the property indicated as not covered under the BPP form is property that would be present only at a business already in operation. The form specifically excludes land and water. It also excludes lawns, trees, shrubs, and plants; radio or television antennas, including lead-in wiring, masts, or towers; and detached signs. Coverage may be bought back via endorsement.

The builders risk form excludes land and water. Based on the 2012 revisions, an exception concerns lawns that are a part of a vegetated roof. As a result of this revision such property is viewed as part of the building subject, of course, to all of the covered causes of loss discussed in Chapters 3 and 4. It is important to keep in mind that the value of land becomes important in construction during the excavation process.

Covered Causes of Loss

The Builders Risk Coverage Form is combined with one of the causes of loss forms: CP 10 10, CP 10 20, or CP 10 30. For a discussion of these forms, see Chapters 3 and 4.

Additional Coverages

The form provides four additional coverages: debris removal, preservation of property, fire department service charge, and pollutant cleanup and removal. These coverages are identical to those contained in the Building and Personal Property Coverage Form, CP 00 10. In that regard both debris removal and fire department service charge provisions are affected by the 2012 revisions. (See Chapter 2.)

Coverage Extensions

The builders risk form provides two coverage extensions: building supplies and materials of others and sod, trees, shrubs, and plants.

Building Supplies and Materials of Others

The first extension pays up to $5,000 per location for material and supplies owned by others. The insured may purchase a higher amount by making an entry on the policy declarations. This is an additional amount of insurance and applies at each described premises. These losses are settled for the account of the property owner. This coverage extension applies when the property of others is in the insured's care, custody, or control and is located in or on the described building or within one-hundred feet of the premises.

In order for this extension to apply, the insured must intend to make the property a permanent part of the building (e.g., air conditioning or heating equipment), thus precluding coverage for the builder's machinery and equipment used in the construction. The builders risk coverage form was released in 1986 with no separate item of coverage for builders machinery, tools, and equipment as found in previous versions. According to explanatory information from ISO, the provision was deleted because broader coverage is available to builders and contractors through inland marine policies.

However, the current edition provides limited coverage for builders machinery, tools, and equipment when Special Causes of Loss form, CP 10 30, is attached to the builders risk coverage form. The property must be owned by or entrusted to the insured. Found in the limitations section of the CP 10 30, it provides coverage against the specified causes of loss to builders' machinery, tools, and equipment.

Sod, Trees, Shrubs, and Plants

Sod, trees, shrubs, and plants are not covered under the builders risk policy. However, coverage extension b provides limited coverage for these items. It covers sod, trees, shrubs, and plants for the perils of fire, lightning, explosion, riot or civil commotion, and aircraft. Coverage is limited to $1,000 per occurrence, regardless of the type or number of items lost, with a limit of $250 for any one tree, shrub, or plant.

Newly added to this extension with the 2012 revisions is coverage for the expense in removing from the described premises the debris of trees, shrubs, and plants that are the property of others, except in the situation where the policy named insured is a tenant and such property is owned by the landlord of the described premises.

Limits of Insurance

The limits of insurance as shown on the declarations page apply to covered property on a per occurrence basis. A sublimit of $2,500 applies per outdoor sign per occurrence.

The amounts payable under the coverage extensions—building supplies and materials of others and sod, trees, shrubs, and plants—apply in addition to the limit of liability. Likewise, two additional coverages are outside the limit of liability: fire department service charge and pollutant cleanup and removal (see Chapter 2).

The amounts payable under the other two additional coverages, debris removal and preservation of property, are included in the limit of liability. The debris removal provision contains the same $25,000 extra amount payable under certain conditions as in the Building and Personal Property Coverage Form (see Chapter 2).

Deductible

The deductible applies after any deduction required by the additional condition—need for adequate insurance (discussed later in this chapter).

Loss Conditions

The following builders risk loss conditions are exactly the same as those found in the BPP form: abandonment, appraisal, duties in the event of loss or damage, and recovered property.

The 2000 edition added wording to the loss payment condition. It specifies that the insurer determines the value of covered property in accordance with the applicable terms of the valuation condition. The only valuation method used is actual cash value (ACV). Remember that the policy does not define *actual cash value*.

The Builders Risk Coverage Form was revised in the 06 07 edition identically to the BPP form as regards party walls. A *party wall* is generally defined as a wall that divides two adjoining properties and in which each of the owners shares the rights. Ownership of a party wall may or may not be shared; there are numerous legal variations including tenancy in common and unilateral ownership with easement rights. A coverage issue may arise when one owner of a party wall refuses or is unable to repair his side of a party wall following loss or damage. The 06 07 edition revised the builders risk form to identify the exposure and convey loss adjusting procedures for it. Provisions were added under loss payment relating to a party wall reflecting the insured's partial interest in that wall. However, if the owner of the adjoining building elects not to repair or replace that building (and the building insured under this insurance is being repaired or replaced), this insurance will pay the full value of the party wall, subject to all other policy provisions.

The vacancy loss condition, found in the BPP form, is not present in the builders risk form because any building under construction is usually vacant. The rates for builders risk contemplate this increase in exposure.

Additional Conditions

The builders risk form contains four additional conditions: mortgageholders, need for adequate insurance, restriction of additional coverage—collapse, and when coverage ceases.

Mortgageholders. This condition is the same as that found in BPP form.

Need for adequate insurance. This additional condition resembles the coinsurance condition of the BPP form and operates in the same fashion. It serves to penalize the insured in the event of a loss if the building is not insured to 100 percent of its completed value. The policy calls for a reduction in loss payment by the percentage the customer is underinsured. If the building has a completed value of $200,000, but is insured only for $100,000, any loss payment will be reduced by 50 percent.

Restriction of collapse coverage. The broad and special causes of loss forms include collapse of a building as an additional coverage.

One of the covered causes of collapse is use of defective material or methods in construction, remodeling, or renovation if the collapse occurs during the course of the construction, remodeling, or renovation. The builders risk form eliminates this covered cause of collapse. Thus, the builders risk form provides no coverage for collapse caused by the use of defective material or methods.

When coverage ceases. The builders risk form states that coverage ceases when one of the following first occurs:

a.   the policy expires or is cancelled;

b.   the property is accepted by the purchaser;

c.   the named insured's interest in the property ceases;

d.   the named insured abandons the construction with no intention to complete it;

e.   unless the insurer specifies otherwise in writing:

   (1)   ninety days after construction is complete; or

   (2)   sixty days after any building described in the declarations is:

      (a)   occupied in whole or in part; or

      (b)   put to its intended use.

Builders risk rates do not contemplate the increased exposures of occupied premises. However, the policy does not define *occupied*. Courts have often held that a building or structure is not considered occupied until it is ready or put to its intended use. This definition of *occupied*, then, becomes synonymous with a building being put to its intended use. The builders risk form has employed the current policy language since 1985, subject to some revisions over the years.

In *Indian Harbor Ins. Co. v. Assurance Co. of America*, No. CA 08-146 ML, (D. Ct. R.I. May 21, 2000), the court found that builders risk coverage was terminated when the insured procured commercial property coverage on the property.

Previous editions of the builders risk form covered property in transit for $5,000 if subject to the special causes of loss form, CP 10 30. The previous edition of form CP 10 30 covered only this property for

$1,000. This additional coverage has been removed from the builders risk form because the CP 10 30 now provides this coverage in the amount of $5,000.

Builders Risk Coverage Options

The builders risk form provides six optional endorsements to modify the basic form. They include building renovations; builders' risk reporting form; separate or subcontractor's interests; collapse during construction; theft of building materials, fixtures, machinery, equipment; and building materials and supplies of others.

Building Renovations

When renovations are made to existing buildings, builders risk coverage can be amended to exclude the value of existing realty. This endorsement, Builders Risk Renovations, CP 11 13, changes the definition of *covered property*. Instead of insuring the building under construction, this endorsement covers renovations under construction. It provides coverage only for the value of building improvements, alterations, or repairs under construction. Unlike the CP 00 20, the CP 11 13 does not cover foundations. It does cover fixtures, equipment used to service the building, and building materials. These items must be intended for use in the building or within one-hundred feet of the premises. This endorsement adds the value of buildings or structures existing prior to construction of the improvements, alterations, or repairs to property not covered.

This endorsement also modifies the need for adequate insurance condition. This condition acts like a 100 percent coinsurance clause in that it requires insurance in the full amount of the completed value of the structure. Since a completed structure already exists, that condition becomes impractical. Instead, form CP 11 13 requires the insured to carry 100 percent of the value of the improvements, alterations, or repairs at the described premises. When using this endorsement, the when coverage ceases condition does not apply.

Builders Risk Reporting Form

As an alternative to the completed value approach that was reviewed earlier in this chapter, the insured may choose to report monthly values of the building under construction using endorsement CP 11 05, Builders Risk Reporting Form. The form requires the insured to choose a date when values will be reported each month. This choice must be made within thirty days of coverage inception.

If the insured does not make the required reports on form CP 11 05, the policy lists two different penalties. Being late with a report relegates loss adjustment to the last reported value. If the insured does not file any reports, the building is valued at ACV as of the inception date.

Endorsement CP 11 05 removes the need for adequate insurance condition. However, losses will still be adjusted by the proportion of values last reported to the ACV of the property at the time of loss. Total loss payment is limited to the limit of liability, even if the reported values exceed that amount.

Because the values at risk change, the premium changes as well. The initial premium is based on the ACV of the property at policy inception. Subsequently the insurer makes adjustments based on the reported values.

Although available for use, the Builders Risk Reporting Form is seldom used due to the additional work involved in completing monthly reports along with the additional burden of assuring accurate values are reported in a timely fashion.

Separate or Subcontractors Interest

The insured may choose to exclude the interests of other contractors or subcontractors by endorsement CP 11 14, Builders Risk – Separate or Sub-Contractor's Exclusion. This endorsement adds the value of the installation that the contractor makes at the described location to the definition of property not covered. Such value includes labor, materials, and supplies. The endorsement also removes such an installation from the requirements under the need for adequate insurance condition.

Endorsement CP 11 15, Builders Risk – Separate or Sub-Contractors Coverage, covers the interests of other contractors or subcontractors. It does the opposite of CP 11 14. It adds labor, materials, and supplies to the definition of *covered property* and specifies that the installation described is the only item to which the need for adequate insurance condition applies. It must be kept in mind that covering the interests of contractors does not mean they are named insureds or additional insureds. If the labor, materials, or supplies cause a loss of or to a project, the insurer of the builders risk form can exercise its right of subrogation against the contractor(s) who caused the loss or damage.

Collapse During Construction

If the insured chooses broad or special causes of loss, the builders risk form removes coverage for collapse during construction. Endorsement

CP 11 20, Builders Risk – Collapse during Construction, restores this coverage for an additional premium. The rates for this coverage are published in the multistate pages of the Commercial Lines Manual. However, if the policy covers an architect, engineer, or building trade contractor as an insured or additional insured, the rate is increased five times. In custom and practice, architects and engineers do not commonly seek additional insured coverage under builders risk policies. What these professionals seek, instead, are waivers of subrogation. A problem is that a growing number of insurers not only will not permit additional insured coverage but also reserve their rights of subrogation against these professionals.

Theft of Building Materials, Fixtures, Machinery, Equipment

Endorsement CP 11 21, Builders Risk – Theft of Building Materials, Fixtures, Machinery, Equipment, provides theft and attempted theft coverage for building materials, fixtures, machinery, and equipment that are intended to become a permanent part of the building if they are located within 100 feet of the building. The amount of insurance shown on this endorsement is separate from the amount of coverage shown on the declarations as applicable to the building. The minimum deductible for this form is $1,000 and applies separately from the deductible under the builders risk policy. In order for coverage to apply, a watchman must be on duty during the hours when no construction is being conducted. If no watchman is on duty, there is no coverage.

Theft or attempted theft, as covered under this endorsement, does not include dishonest or criminal acts by the named insured or any of the named insured's partner employees, directors, trustees, or authorized representatives. Newly added with the 2012 revision are members, officers, and managers, along with temporary employees and leased workers. Dishonest or criminal acts by any contractors or subcontractors or their respective employees, including temporary employees and leased workers (both of which are added with the 2012 revision) are also not included, as well as acts committed by any person to whom the property is entrusted for any purpose.

This exclusion applies whether the dishonest or criminal act is committed by someone acting alone or in collusion with any other party, or whether the dishonest or criminal act occurs during the insured's normal hours of operation.

Theft or attempted theft also does not include voluntary parting with any property by the named insured or anyone else to whom the property is entrusted if induced to do so by any fraudulent scheme, trick, device, or false pretense; or property that is missing, where the only evidence of loss or damage is a shortage disclosed on taking inventory, or other instances where there is no physical evidence to indicate what happened to the property.

Building Materials and Supplies of Others

For an additional premium, the insured may choose to increase the coverage provided for these items. The basic amount is $5,000. The increase is indicated on the declarations page.

Need for Builders Risk on Renovations to Existing Building

The question arises of when, if at any time, would a builders risk policy need to be written in conjunction with a commercial property form on an existing building undergoing remodeling or renovation? This is a question that needs careful consideration for the following reasons.

If an ISO Builders Risk Coverage Form is purchased, and Builders Risk Renovations endorsement, CP 11 13, is added, the form specifically states that covered property does not include the value of buildings or structures existing prior to construction of the improvements, alterations, or repairs. Sometimes it is possible to have the existing property added to the builders risk.

If the Building and Personal Property Coverage Form is relied on for coverage instead of by a separate builders risk and renovations endorsement, there is coverage even when the building has been vacant for more than sixty consecutive days. The reason is that the BPP form, CP 00 10, states that buildings under construction or renovation are not considered vacant. This means that if there is loss by vandalism, water, or theft, coverage remains intact without limitation. This is unlike some commercial property forms that do not make an exception for vacant buildings under renovation. When there is a loss in these cases, arguments over coverage are virtually guaranteed.

Who Can Be Covered

According to the ISO CLM manual dealing with builders risk coverage options, the Interests Insured section states that the policy may be written to cover the following:

(1) The interest of the building owner;

(2) The interest of the contractor; or

(3) The owner or contractor jointly as their interest may appear.

What is confusing about this eligibility rule is, as mentioned earlier, that covering one's interest in property does not mean that such a person is a named insured or additional insured. It simply means that such person's insurable interests are covered to the extent coverage otherwise applies.

The fact that the owner who purchases the policy will likely be the named insured begs the question of whether a contractor also can be a named insured when the policy is written jointly. It is a question that cannot be answered since it will depend on what an insurer decides to do.

Limited Usage

Form CP 00 20 is ideally suited for the smaller construction projects where it is unnecessary to add contractors of all tiers as named insureds.

Many builders risk forms today are written as inland marine policies because of the loss potential having to do with materials, equipment, and other property while in transit and also at other locations awaiting transit to the construction site. The ISO Builders Risk Coverage Form is not an inland marine form. Coverage of the ISO form is meant to be site specific.

Also, to the extent collapse coverage applies, it applies only to a building and not to a structure. Whenever a structure is the subject of insurance, one must make sure that wherever the word *building* appears within the builders risk coverage form the word *structure* also should be added.

Despite the foregoing, the builders risk form has its advantages for small risks. One such advantage is that unless the insurer specifies otherwise, coverage ends ninety days after construction is complete or sixty days after any building is occupied in whole or in part or put to its intended use. This gives the named insured ample time to get the coverage transferred to a permanent coverage form to avoid any gap. Many inland marine builders risk policies terminate coverage when the construction has been substantially completed (i.e., ready for its intended occupancy) or occupied in whole or in part.

Chapter 7

Business Income Coverage Forms

Business income insurance, also referred to as business interruption or time element, and in older nomenclature, use and occupancy coverage, protects the business income of the insured, the money that would be earned absent the (covered) event. It is commonly purchased as an important complement to the BPP coverage form. The purpose of business income insurance is to replace what the business would have financially received had no loss occurred during the period of business interruption. Loss of net income, the prime source of money for continuing operating expenses, as well as profit, if any, is the subject of coverage. Business income forms cover the net income plus continuing normal operating expenses that businesses would have earned had no covered direct property damage loss occurred.

The purpose of this chapter is to discuss coverage under the Insurance Services Office (ISO) business income forms, as they form part of the commercial property protection program. Aspects of business income coverage are complex. A much more comprehensive treatment of the subject can be found in *Business Income Coverage Guide*, also published by the National Underwriter Company.

There are three ISO forms available to cover an insured's business income and extra expense exposures. The edition date is current with the Building and Personal Property Coverage Form—10 12.

- Business Income (And Extra Expense) Coverage Form, CP 00 30

- Business Income (Without Extra Expense) Coverage Form, CP 00 32

- Extra Expense Coverage Form, CP 00 50

Like other forms in the commercial property program, there have been various edition dates for the ISO business income forms. In large, the various edition dates are the same as the edition dates for revisions in the Building and Personal Property Coverage Form and the causes of loss forms.

Coverage for Business Income

Visualizing a profit and loss statement is helpful in understanding business income insurance. In a mercantile operation, for example, the retailer's operating expenses and profit are derived from resale at a markup of goods purchased. The merchant buys goods from a manufacturer or wholesaler for sale to the consumer. The dollar difference between sales income and cost of goods purchased provides funds for operating expenses and profit—the basis of insurable interest under business income coverage. Similarly, a manufacturing operation derives its income from the increase in value of materials that it converts into its product.

ISO rules for business income coverage define a *mercantile or non-manufacturing risk* as "one in which the business consists principally of the sale or storage of merchandise, or the furnishing or rendering of a service." Some businesses provide services with little or no sale of merchandise. Examples include banks, bowling alleys, laundries, and legal or accounting firms. In these businesses, cost of goods or raw materials purchased is minimal, consisting mainly of consumable supplies, so nearly all of the income from the sale of the services is used to pay expenses and provide a profit.

According to ISO rules, a manufacturing risk is "one in which the operation consists principally of changing raw stock into finished stock by aging, assembling, converting or seasoning through the use of hand or machinery processes or the application of mechanical, electrical, thermal or chemical energy. Property including grain elevators, grain storage buildings, grain tanks and/or equipment for drying grain is a manufacturing risk." A specific rule provision states that "building service machinery or the use of machinery for packing and shipping or minor repairing or altering incidental to a predominantly mercantile or non-manufacturing risk does not require the occupancy to be classified as a manufacturing risk."

Since the subject for business income insurance is the income of the business, it is fundamental to this type of insurance that there be earnings and that earnings continue to be possible. If a business is idle and likely to remain that way for a long time, there are neither present nor prospective earnings and no need for business income coverage. But the mere fact that a business is not operating does not necessarily eliminate the need for this coverage. If a business is definitely scheduled to resume operations but the property is damaged or destroyed by an insured peril, there will be a loss of income and, hence, a business income exposure. The exposure commences on the date operations were scheduled to resume. A seasonal business, such as an ice cream shop in a vacation area, is one example of this situation.

Similarly, insurance can be written for a business operator whose premises are under construction. Loss to an uncompleted building postpones the date of occupancy, and any loss of earnings from the date business operations should have begun can be insured.

With respect to loss of income coverage because of loss or damage to personal property in the open or in a vehicle, the distance within which such property can be situated is similar to the 2012 revisions dealing with the Building and Personal Property Coverage Form, CP 00 10. Thus, if the named insured occupies the building, the personal property must be within one-hundred feet of the described premises. If, however, the named insured occupies only part of a building, the named insured premises is defined to mean not only the portion of the building the named insured rents, leases, or occupies, but also for purposes of personal property in the open or in a vehicle, the area within one-hundred feet of the building or within one-hundred feet of the premises described in the declarations, whichever distance is greater. Also, any area within the building or at the described premises if that area services or is used to gain access to the portion the building the named insured rents, leases, or occupies. This 2012 revision also applies to the Business Income (Without Extra Expense) Coverage Form, CP 00 32.

Coverage can properly be written for businesses whose earnings are sufficient to meet all or part of the operating expenses but not sufficient to show a profit. Some businesses, although currently unable to produce a profit, still have a substantial exposure in the form of continuing expenses if a suspension of business occurs. Coverage is to the extent that those expenses were being earned prior to loss. But, for businesses not operating at a profit, close underwriting scrutiny is necessary. In addition, the amount collectible will be reduced by the normal net loss.

When Coverage Applies

Another consideration of business income insurance is that recovery applies only for the time required to repair or replace damaged property with the exercise of due diligence and dispatch, or as required in the business income coverage form, "with reasonable speed," so that normal operations can be resumed. This criterion is the yardstick that measures the amount of loss to be paid. The restoration period applies for the time required to rebuild or repair the buildings and equipment, replace the merchandise or raw materials, and, for a manufacturing establishment, bring unfinished products to the same point of manufacture that had been reached at the time of the covered loss or triggering event.

Within this standard of reasonable speed, the actual time required to rebuild or replace can vary considerably, depending upon conditions at the time of loss. For example, weather, availability of materials, labor, and transportation can and often do affect the time needed to restore the property. Considering all the variables involved, chances are that even the most reasonable and well intentioned estimators will not be in exact agreement as to the day or perhaps even to the week when the business could be resumed.

The thrust of the provision is two-pronged. It puts the insured on notice that any unreasonable delay in construction will affect the amount of insurance recovery, thereby eliciting the insured's cooperation and giving the insurance company an avenue to escape the consequences of unreasonable delays in the restoration. But, the insurer also has an incentive to adjust the property and business income claims promptly, enabling the insured to proceed with restoration, as delay in claim settlement extends the time given the insured to restore operations and increases the amount of the loss.

Extra Expense

Some businesses must make every effort to continue operating no matter how serious the damage and regardless of the cost. A prime example is the *New Orleans Times-Picayune* and its efforts to resume publishing immediately in the days after Hurricane Katrina in 2005. Other examples are dairies, insurance agencies, and banks. For such risks, the principal need is extra expense insurance.

These types of businesses also may not be able to avoid a temporary suspension following severe damage. To avoid long-term loss of customers they will spend substantial amounts of money to get back into operation. Other businesses have some operations that must go on and others that could be suspended. One example is a newspaper and printing firm in which the newspaper publication must continue but job printing can be interrupted. For such an operation, a combination of business income and extra expense insurance is needed.

Extended Loss after Operations Resume

A common complaint about recovery under older forms of business income coverage was that the full loss to the business was limited to the time required to restore the property. For example, a popular restaurant in a remote location, if damaged and forced to close, would need regular business income insurance to cover the loss during reconstruction, but it would undoubtedly suffer an additional loss beyond that time until its clientele was fully reestablished. Losses occurring during the lag between physical reopening and the time when business was operating at the level it was before the loss occurred were not covered under the standard business interruption forms. To insure such losses under business income policies, an optional endorsement was used, extending the period of indemnity to include this lag. Under the current ISO business income coverage, this feature is built into the form with the 2012 revision, the thirty-day limit is increased to sixty days, and the option to increase the number of days of coverage as needed is available.

Blanket Coverage

When an insured has interdependent operations in two or more separately rated buildings or at more than one location and a loss at one location will curtail business at other locations, blanket business income insurance is ordinarily recommended.

Blanket coverage may also be arranged when the separate locations are independent of one another, but the principal advantage here, if any, is cost. If the average rate results in lower overall costs than would be the case with each location covered separately, then blanketing might be advised. Otherwise, the necessity of adjusting any loss on the basis of the business being done at all covered locations (for coinsurance purposes) may offset any blanketing advantage.

Incidentally, blanket business income insurance should not be confused with business income from dependent properties coverage. Blanket insurance covers two or more separately rated units of the insured's own operations. Income from dependent property insurance covers the loss that the insured will suffer if the operation of a key supplier, customer, or leader property on which the insured's operations are dependent is shut down by an insured peril.

ISO Simplified Business Income Program

As previously noted, there are three basic ISO forms available for use in covering an insured's business income and extra expense exposures: Business Income (And Extra Expense) Coverage Form, CP 00 30, which covers both business income and extra expense; Business Income (Without Extra Expense) Coverage Form, CP 00 32, which limits coverage only to business income; and Extra Expense Coverage Form, CP 00 50, which limits coverage only to extra expenses. Insureds choose a coverage form based upon their individual needs. For example, a manufacturing business would generally have a need for both business income and extra expense coverage while a service-related business may elect the narrower and lower premium coverage of extra expense coverage.

In addition to the choice of which form best meets a business's needs, the Business Income (And Extra Expense) and Business Income (Without Extra Expense) Coverage forms provide the insured a choice of selecting one or more optional limits of insurance as shown in the declarations. These optional limits of insurance cover the following:

- **Business income including rental value.** For example, under this option, business income and rental value would apply to the insured's owned multi-tenant building that housed the insured's retail business and other tenants. In the event of a loss, coverage would apply to the insured's loss of business income from the retail store as well as the insured's loss of rental income from the tenants.

- **Business income other than rental income.** This option would apply only to the insured's business income loss but not to rental income from tenants. A business with no rental income may choose this option;

- **Rental only.** This option would cover only rental value. An insured that owns a building and rents out space to tenants as their landlord commonly would purchase rental only coverage.

The definition of *business income* under the forms is (a) the net income (net profit or loss before income taxes) that would have been earned or incurred, and (b) continuing normal operating expenses incurred, including payroll. For manufacturing risks, net income includes the net sales value of production.

The use of a two-item definition of business income has created a problem of interpretation in cases where a business operates at a loss. A court ruled that the two items—net income and continuing normal operating expenses—are separate, unrelated items of covered business income and that a negative net income should not be used to offset continuing expenses. For instance, in *Continental Ins. Co. v. DNE Corp.*, 834 S.W.2d 930 (Tenn. 1992), the court found that adding DNE's net income to its continuing expenses yielded a negative number so there was no business income recovery.

Three elements included in the Section A coverage provision are required for coverage to apply: (1) a necessary suspension of business operations during the period of restoration, (2) a direct physical loss of or damage to property at the described premises caused by or resulting from a covered cause of loss, and (3) an actual loss of business income.

Pre-2000 forms did not define *necessary suspension*. As some insurers' policies still use previous editions or independently filed forms containing variations, a look at litigation surrounding this definition is helpful. Courts are divided on the meaning. For instance, in *American States Ins. Co. v. Creative Walking, Inc.*, 16 F. Supp.2d 1062 (E.D. Mo. 1998), the court found that *necessary suspension* meant a complete cessation of business operations. Creative Walking suffered direct physical damage due to a water main break, leaving its premises untenantable. It moved to a temporary facility a few weeks later and made the temporary facility its new headquarters. Creative Walking submitted a business income and extra expense claim to the insurer stating that it suffered a business slowdown for about eighteen weeks following the loss. The court said, "If the insured is able to continue its business operations at a temporary facility, it has not suffered 'necessary suspension' of its operations." Therefore, Creative Walking was entitled only to compensation for the two-week period before moving to the new location and the expenses incurred in relocating.

Similar rulings were made in these cases: *Keetch v. Mutual of Enumclaw Ins. Co.*, 831 P.2d 784 (Wash. Ct. App. 1992) (motel experienced only a partial interruption of business, not enough to trigger coverage, due to eruption of Mt. St. Helens burying it in six inches of volcanic ash); *Quality Oilfield Products, Inc. v. Michigan Mutual Ins. Co.*, 971 S.W.2d 635 (Tex. App. 1998) (slowdown of business following burglary of design information, computer disks, process orders, and other key operational materials did not constitute the necessary interruption of business required for coverage to apply); and *The Home Indemnity Co. v. Hyplains Beef. L.C.*, 893 F. Supp. 987 (D. Kan. 1995) (failure of computer system resulting in less efficiency and a slowdown in operations at a cattle slaughter and processing company did not qualify as a necessary suspension of operations).

However, a court has found that companies can recover expenses for mitigating damages. In *American Medical Imaging Corp. v. St. Paul Fire and Marine Ins. Co.*, 949 F.2d 690 (3d Cir. 1991), the court ruled that a business that set up temporary offices with a reduced phone capacity suffered a necessary or potential suspension of operations. Following a fire that caused smoke and water damage, American Medical Imaging relocated to an alternate site for six weeks while its facilities were unusable. The company relied on fewer telephone lines at the temporary location and claimed that it lost nearly $1 million and incurred extra expenses. The court said that American Medical was entitled to coverage because it acted promptly to mitigate the damages and that its operations had been suspended.

To clarify the issue the 2000 business income/extra expense form added a definition of *suspension*:

a.   The slowdown or cessation of your business activities; or

b.   That a part or all of the described premises is rendered untenantable, if coverage for Business Income including "Rental Value" or
"Rental Value" apples.

This resolved the contract interpretation argument over whether a
slowdown of business activities is sufficient to trigger coverage, and not
complete cessation.

The first required element for coverage also specifies that the
suspension of business operations occur during the period of restoration.
Period of restoration is a defined policy term. The period includes a time
deductible, with coverage beginning seventy-two hours after the time of
direct physical loss for business income insurance. The time deductible
does not apply to extra expense coverage, and that recovery is available
immediately after the time of direct loss. The period ends on the date
when the property at the described premises should be rebuilt, replaced,
or repaired with similar quality and reasonable speed or when the business
resumes at a new permanent location, whichever is earlier. The period is
not terminated by the policy expiration date, meaning that business income
coverage may extend past the policy term. Note that the seventy-two-hour
time deductible applicable to business income can be eliminated with
the Business Income Changes – Beginning of the Period of Restoration,
endorsement, CP 15 56.

Courts have been asked to determine when the period of restoration
actually ends, such as in *Lava Trading, Inc. v. Hartford Fire Ins. Co.*,
365 F.Supp. 2d 434 (S.D. N.Y. 2005). The insured's offices were destroyed
as a result of the September 11, 2001, terrorist attack of the World Trade
Center. The company had a backup facility that was not damaged by the
attack but was also not operational until October 11, 2001, and company
officials did not believe they would be back to where they were before the
attack until November 2001.

Hartford determined that operations had been suspended from
September 11 through October 31, 2001. Lava, however, claimed that
because Hartford did not pay the claim by December 2001, it had to obtain
financing to continue its operations and that the business was not fully
restored until October 2002.

The court identified two questions that needed to be answered. First,
what constitutes property at the described premises, the replacement
of which dictates the ending of the period of restoration? The court
concluded that "the 'period of restoration' ends when the property in
Lava's 83rd floor offices (and not the entire World Trade Center complex

or the One World Trade Center building) should have been repaired, rebuilt or replaced with reasonable speed and similar quality."

The second question was whether this trigger for the end of the period of restoration had happened. Hartford argued that the period of restoration should have ended when Lava relocated. Lava, though, contended that the period should have ended when the entire World Trade Center building was rebuilt, and since it could not be rebuilt in twelve months, the period of restoration should be the maximum twelve months permitted by the policy.

The court did not agree that the described premises meant the World Trade Center complex but applied to the insured's offices within the complex, which could be relocated. The court stated that the period of restoration did not end when operations resumed, but that the period looks to when the premises should be repaired, replaced, or rebuilt—not the time necessary to resume functionally equivalent operations. So, the court ruled that Harford's calculations were correct for when the period of restoration ended.

The second element required for coverage is that the loss must result from direct physical damage to or loss of property at premises described in the declarations resulting from a covered cause of loss. Causes of loss will vary depending upon which of the three causes of loss forms is selected by the insured. As in the Building and Personal Property Coverage Form, *direct physical damage and loss* is not defined.

Courts have upheld that physical damage is necessary for business income coverage to apply. For example, a North Carolina appeals court held that inability to access a business did not trigger business income coverage when no physical damage occurred in *Harry's Cadillac-Pontiac-GMC Truck Co. v. Motors Ins. Corp.*, 486 S.E.2d 249 (N.C. Ct. App. 1997). When a snowstorm struck, Harry's car dealership could not be reached for a week. The court said that business income insurance "does not cover all business interruption losses, but only those losses requiring repair, rebuilding, or replacement."

Likewise, the court in *St. Paul Mercury Ins. Co. v. Magnolia Lady, Inc.*, No. 2:97CV-153-B-B, 1999 WL 33537191 (N.D. Miss. Nov. 4, 1999) decided that loss of earnings could not be reimbursed if the insured location suffered no direct physical loss or damage. A barge collided with a bridge near a casino-hotel owned by Magnolia Lady. State authorities closed the bridge for three weeks following the collision, which Magnolia Lady argued caused a dramatic decrease in business. Because the casino-hotel remained accessible and suffered no damage, the court said no coverage was available.

Actual loss of business income is the third requirement for a business income loss. If there is no loss of business income, coverage is not triggered. The Tennessee Supreme Court affirmed this element in *Continental Ins. Co. v. DNE Corp.*, 834 S.W.2d 930 (Tenn. 1992). DNE owned a plant that had been operating at a loss when it was damaged by a tornado. During the period of restoration, DNE paid continuing operating expenses as defined by its business income coverage. The insurance promised recovery only if a loss of actual business income was sustained, which is the net income that would have been earned had business not been interrupted plus continuing operating expenses. The addition of DNE's net income and continuing expenses yielded a negative number, and the court found that there was no coverage.

Does a Bomb Threat Trigger Business Income Coverage?

A bomb threat necessitated the evacuation of insured premises, effectively shutting down operations. The insured questioned whether the shutdown was covered under its business income policy.

Business income coverage under the standard business income coverage form is triggered by a suspension of operations "caused by direct physical loss" of or damage to property at the premises described in the declarations. Absent physical damage there is no coverage for suspension of operations caused by threats. A bomb threat does not trigger business income coverage.

Extra Expense

Extra expense is not a defined term in the policy definitions section, but the term is given a specific policy meaning for coverage purposes in section A: "necessary expenses you [the insured] incur during the period of restoration that you would not have incurred if there had been no direct physical loss or damage to property caused by or resulting from a covered cause of loss." Most frequently the kinds of expenses for which coverage is afforded are rental of a temporary office or store, computer or communications rental equipment, and items of that kind.

The policy provides coverage for two categories of extra expenses:

1. Extra expense to avoid or minimize the suspension of business and to continue operations at the insured premises or at replacement premises or temporary locations. Relocation expenses and costs to equip and operate a replacement or temporary location are included. The costs to rent, move, and set up a temporary

facility or obtain temporary or replacement equipment would be paid by this portion of the policy.

2.   Extra expense incurred to minimize suspension of business if operations cannot be continued. The hiring of additional workers or paying existing employees overtime in order to reopen the business would be covered here.

The form also provides coverage for extra expenses necessary to repair or replace property but only to the extent the amount of loss otherwise payable is reduced.

While the policy offers an explanation of what constitutes an extra expense, confusion sometimes arises regarding specific expenditures and whether they should be covered. The court in *Midwest Regional Allergy, Asthma, Arthritis & Osteoporosis Center, P.C. v. Cincinnati Ins. Co.,* No. 12-03351-CV-SW-DGK, 2013 WL 4400823 (W.D. Mo. Aug. 15, 2013), was asked to determine if certain relocation and repair costs fell under extra expense coverage.

Midwest Regional's clinic was struck and destroyed by a tornado that devastated Joplin, Missouri, on May 22, 2011. Prior to the tornado, part of Midwest Regional's operations included diagnostics and treatments such as x-rays, MRIs, bone density scans, laboratory analysis, and infusion therapy. Significant income was realized from MRI imaging and laboratory services. The MRI machine was damaged by the tornado, and all other equipment was destroyed.

Midwest Regional operated from a temporary location while waiting for construction to be completed on its permanent new location. Midwest Regional was unable to function at its full capacity at the temporary location. When the permanent location was ready, the insured paid to repair the MRI, for installation of the MRI, and for a new x-ray machine, bone density scanner, laboratory analysis equipment, infusion equipment, and specialty chairs. The costs were necessary to bring the practice back to its pre-tornado operations.

Cincinnati Insurance paid the limits of the building and personal property coverages, as well as the business income losses and some extra expenses, but denied the insured's claim for the expense of repairing and installing the MRI and other equipment. The insured argued that these expenses were incurred during the period of restoration to minimize the slowdown of business and to continue business activities. The insurer countered that the expenses were subject to the primary coverage under the covered property portion of the policy.

The court ruled that the insured was correct, stating, "The contested expenditures here are clearly 'Extra Expenses' as the phrase is defined in the Policy. Plaintiffs repaired and replaced the MRI machine and other laboratory equipment in order to continue the business in which they were engaged at the Premises prior to the tornado." Thus, the court concluded that the insured could recover under the extra expense provision even if the expenses were insured under the covered property portion of the policy. The court said that the insurer made a compelling case that the equipment was covered under the property portion of the policy, but there was nothing in the extra expense portion of the policy stating that the expenses were not covered there. At best, there was an ambiguity, which would also be construed in favor of the insured.

Covered Causes of Loss

As with the BPP form, insurance protection can be arranged on three levels: basic, broad, and special. The forms used are the same used with the BPP form and are the starting point in triggering a business income claim. These causes of loss forms are the topics of Chapters 3 and 4.

Exclusions and Limitations

Each of the covered causes of loss forms also contains a section of special exclusions applicable to the business income coverage and extra expense coverage forms only.

Business income and extra expense losses caused directly or indirectly by power or other utility service failure that do not result in a covered cause of loss are excluded. For example, a storm causes a power outage to an insured premises, and the lights and cash register will not operate. Business income coverage is not triggered because there is no physical damage to the property.

The utility service exclusion was substantially revised in the 06 07 editions of the business income forms. The existing utility services exclusion for time element applies to the failure of power or other utility service supplied to the described premises if the failure occurs outside of a covered building. In the 06 07 edition, reference to power and other utilities was expanded to make explicit mention of water and communication services, which are common services and currently addressed in optional coverage endorsements.

The pre-06 07 exclusion precluded coverage for failure that occurs away from the described premises, whereas the revised exclusion focuses on events that involve an off-premises supplier and embraces certain events originating on-premises as well. Often, occurrences of utility service failure involve equipment failure. Equipment used or supplied by an off-premises utility service provider may be located at the site of the utility company's facility (away from the insured premises) and (in the case of such things as transmission lines and cables) at various sites in the area being supplied, including the insured premises.

ISO revised the exclusion to address utility failure that originates at the described premises when such failure involves equipment used to provide utility service supplied by an off-premises provider. This revision is consistent with the focus of the exclusion previously described with respect to precluding coverage for utility failure related to an off-premises provider. The revised exclusion applies to all coverage forms and eliminates the distinction between the property damage and time element versions of the exclusion. The exclusion applies to utility failure that originates at the described premises when such failure involves equipment used to provide utility service supplied by an off-premises provider. The aforementioned statement is relevant to the covered building since the time element exclusion already includes failure originating on the described premises outside a covered building. There was also a broadening of coverage, in that on-premises failure is limited to situations where the failure involves equipment used to supply utility service from an off-premises source.

A provision added in the 06 07 edition makes it explicit that the exclusion encompasses power surge related to the power failure event and that communication services include electronic network access and internet service.

Losses that arise from direct physical loss or damage to radio or television antennas and their lead-in wiring, masts, or towers are also not covered. However, this exclusion may be eliminated with the purchase of endorsement CP 15 50, Radio or Television Antennas – Business Income or Extra Expense.

Another exclusion prohibits business income coverage for any loss caused by or resulting from damage or destruction of finished stock or the time required to reproduce such stock. *Finished stock* is defined as "stock you have manufactured, including whiskey and alcoholic beverages being aged, but not manufactured stock held for sale at any retail outlet insured on the form." This exclusion does not apply to extra expense coverage.

Interference at the insured premises by strikers or others with rebuilding or replacing the property or with the resumption or continuance of business is specifically excluded as well. Because the reference is to delay by interference at the premises, an increase of loss caused by a strike elsewhere—such as one affecting material suppliers, transportation lines, or the availability of workers to do the restoration—is covered.

Suspension, lapse, or cancellation of any license, lease, or contract not directly caused by the suspension of operations is also excluded. Extra expenses incurred beyond the period of restoration due to suspension, lapse, or cancellation of any license, lease, or contract are not covered, either. Any other consequential losses are also excluded (see the discussion in Chapter 1 for the distinction between direct and consequential losses).

Who Pays for Accounting Documentation?

Loss adjustment may involve an insurance company request that the insured provide accounting documentation to support the claim. To comply with the request the insured might incur professional services costs from an accountant to accumulate the data and provide the report to the company.

There is nothing in the wording of the business income portion of the policy that obligates the insurance company to pay the insured's accounting cost to determine the extent of the business income loss. The policy promises to pay for "the actual loss of Business Income you sustain due to the necessary suspension of your 'operations' during the 'period of restoration.'" *Business income* is defined in the policy to mean "a. Net Income (Net Profit or Loss before income taxes) that would have been earned or incurred; and b. Continuing normal operating expenses incurred, including payroll." The accountant's fee is neither net income nor continuing normal operating expenses.

However, the form also provides extra expense coverage. *Extra expense* is defined as "necessary expenses you incur during the 'period of restoration' that you would not have incurred if there had been no direct physical loss." The accounting fees in question would not have been incurred had there been no loss. The policy also requires that the extra expense be incurred to "avoid or minimize the suspension of business and to continue 'operations.'" It is fair to assume that the insurance company would not have paid the business income loss if the insured had not submitted the requested accounting information. The insured's business also would have continued to be suspended or operated at reduced income if the insured had not been paid for the business income loss.

Therefore, it seems reasonable to conclude that accounting fees incurred at the request of the insurance company are an insured extra expense as intended under the policy.

Additional Limitation

Forms CP 00 30 and CP 00 32 contain an additional limitation for interruption of computer operations. This limitation points out the specialized exposures computer operations and data present. Specific computer and electronic data coverage has evolved to protect against the economic effects of these types of loss.

If a suspension of operations is caused by destruction or corruption of electronic data or any loss or damage to electronic data, coverage for business income does not apply. If action is taken to avoid or minimize a suspension of operations caused by the destruction or corruption of electronic data or any loss or damage to electronic data, coverage for extra expense does not apply.

Electronic data is defined as "information, facts or computer programs stored as or on, created or used on, or transmitted to or from computer software (including systems and applications software), on hard or floppy disks, CD-ROMS, tapes, drives, cells, data processing devices or any other repositories of computer software which are used with electronically controlled equipment."

There is an exception to this limitation, a modest give-back of coverage. The interruption of computer operations limitation does not apply to losses covered under the interruption of computer operations additional coverage, which is discussed subsequently in this chapter.

Also, with the 2012 revisions, this additional limitation does not apply when loss or damage to electronic data involves only electronic data that is integrated in and operates or controls a building's elevator, lighting, heating, ventilation, air conditioning, or security system.

Additional Coverages

There are four additional coverages on form CP 00 30: civil authority, alterations and new buildings, extended business income, and interruption of computer operations. Form CP 00 32 contains additional coverage for expenses to reduce loss, civil authority, and alterations and new buildings. These additional coverages extend the basic business income coverage without increase in the limit of insurance unless noted otherwise.

Civil Authority

Additional coverage for civil authority extends the business income and extra expense coverage to include loss caused by action of civil authority that prohibits access to the described premises "due to direct physical loss of or damage to property, other than at the described premises, caused by or resulting from any covered cause of loss." If, for instance, a fire at a building down the block from the insured location causes the police to close the street for a week for inspections and debris removal, coverage will apply. Coverage for business income begins seventy-two hours after action by civil authorities, immediately after civil action for extra expense. The coverage applies for up to three consecutive weeks from the date of the action, and, for extra expense, when business income coverage ends.

The pre-2000 ISO business income and independently filed policies have slightly different civil authority additional coverage language, requiring damage to adjacent property, rather than the "damage to property, other than at described premises" phrasing later adopted in the CP 00 30 04 02 and CP 00 32 04 02. Under the "adjacent property" wording, courts have held that damage to adjacent property must occur to trigger business income coverage.

In *Syufy Enterprises v. The Home Ins. Co.*, 1995 WL 129229, No. 94-0756 FMS, (N.D. Cal. March 21, 1995), the court said that a company that closed during an officially imposed curfew period did not experience a business income loss. Syufy Enterprises owned and operated several theaters in Los Angeles, San Francisco, and Las Vegas. Civil authorities in those cities imposed dusk-to-dawn curfews following rioting and looting. Access was not denied to the theaters by authorities, no property next door to or across the street from the theaters was damaged, and no property located within two blocks of the theaters was damaged as a direct result of the riots. Syufy contended that any property damage within the curfew zones should have been sufficient to elicit business income coverage. The court, though, maintained that "Syufy opted to close its theaters as a direct result of the city-wide curfews, not as a result of adjacent property damage." Because there was no riot-induced damage within close proximity to Syufy's theaters and because the theaters were voluntarily closed, there was no coverage.

Language in the current edition, though, is broader than the more specific language requiring a covered loss involving property adjacent to the insured premises, as upheld in the *Syufy* opinion. With the current form, the property damage producing the action of civil authority need not be in the insured's immediate vicinity. For example, loss from a fire or explosion in a chemical plant located several miles from the insured's premises that forces evacuation of a large area around the plant would be covered by the current form but not by the policy language in *Syufy*.

This issue was revisited again with the 06 07 editions, clarifying coverage issues that arose after the September 11, 2001, terrorist attacks on the World Trade Center and the Pentagon. In its explanation of changes ISO stated, "Historically, this Additional Coverage, in general, provided coverage in cases where there was a prohibitive action of civil authority due to damage by a covered peril in close proximity to the insured premises. However, in more recent times, situations have arisen where civil authority actions are taken in response to an event taking place far from the insured premises."

ISO revised the civil authority additional coverage so that it applies if the insured premises are not more than one mile from the damaged property and the action of civil authority is taken in response to dangerous physical conditions resulting from the damage or continuation of the covered cause of loss that caused the damage, or the action is taken to enable a civil authority to have unimpeded access to the damaged property. This settles the issue for the type of business income losses that occurred on 9-11.

The use of a radius of one mile to circumscribe civil authority coverage is from a technical (though not historical) perspective, a reduction in coverage—that is, a narrowing of the circumstances under which this coverage may be triggered. A companion rule filing addresses use of optional endorsement CP 15 32, Civil Authority Change(s), to modify the radius. Civil authority coverage is broadened, in that the basic coverage period is increased from three weeks to four weeks. The current option to further increase the coverage period (under endorsement CP 15 32) will remain in effect.

Additionally, the civil authority coverage period is extended in these coverage forms from three weeks to four.

As always, direct physical loss is required in order for business income coverage to apply when loss of income is caused by acts of civil authority, as was exhibited in *Dickie Brennan & Co., Inc. v. Lexington Ins. Co.*, 636 F. 3d 683 (5th Cir. 2011).

The mayor of New Orleans issued a mandatory evacuation order due to the approach of Hurricane Gustav. No damage had been reported, but high lake and marsh tides were anticipated due to tidal surge. Flooding, hurricane winds, and intense thunderstorms were also possible.

The Brennans operated restaurants in New Orleans at the time the evacuation was ordered. They suffered loss of income because they were unable to operate during the evacuation. New Orleans experienced only minor damage from Gustav, so Lexington denied the insured's business income claim.

The insured contended that because Gustav caused damage in the Caribbean that the nexus was met for the requirement of "damage to property, other than that at the described premises." Lexington stated that there must be a causal relationship between the prior damage, and the civil authority action must be near the insured premises to satisfy the link. (The policy did not contain the current ISO language requiring a one-mile radius.)

The court said that the evacuation order "did not mention the earlier property damage in the Caribbean. It lists possible future storm surge, high winds, and flooding based on Gustav's predicted path as reasons for evacuation." There was no damage in Louisiana when the order was issued. The court was not persuaded that the insureds had demonstrated a nexus between the prior property damage and the evacuation order, and thus there was no coverage for the business interruption loss.

Airports Closed by Order of Civil Authority

The terrorist attacks on September 11, 2001, created some business income loss scenarios that had not been addressed before. In the wake of the attacks, and for the first time in the nation's history, the federal government shut down all airports in the country. Even as the airports reopened, many people were fearful of flying and stayed away from airports and the businesses located in them. Were these businesses eligible for business income coverage?

ISO's policy has a time deductible of seventy-two hours. If the airports reopened by September 14, that deductible would not have been met to allow coverage to take effect. However, Reagan National Airport remained closed longer than other airports, so businesses located there may have been eligible for coverage.

The closures met the policy's requirements of direct physical loss or damage to property other than at the described premises—the World Trade Center towers and the Pentagon—and that access was prohibited by civil authority. The reduced traffic after the airports reopened, though, would not meet the criterion that access was denied by civil authority. Courts have held that complete cessation of business is necessary for the civil authority additional coverage to kick in. A mere fall off of business is not sufficient to trigger this coverage.

Businesses dependent on airlines for deliveries or other aspects of their operations would also find no coverage in a standard business income policy. Likewise, businesses, such as hotels and travel agencies, that saw a drastic drop in clients and profits after the attacks would find it difficult to recover their losses under standard business income policies. Without direct physical loss or damage to their premises or nearby property, and if an order of civil authority did not specifically deny access to their premises, they do not meet the requirements for business income coverage to apply.

Alterations and New Buildings

Additional coverage for alterations and new buildings extends the business income coverage to cover loss of business income sustained due to direct physical loss or damage at the described premises by any covered cause of loss to the following:

1. new buildings or structures, whether complete or under construction;

2. alterations or additions to existing buildings or structures; and

3. machinery, equipment, supplies, or building materials located on or within 100 feet of the described premises and used in the construction, alterations, or additions, or incidental to the occupancy of the new buildings.

Note that the distance where personal property in number 3 can be located does not conform to the 2012 revision describing how far within the building or described premises personal property can be located. The probable reason is that occupancy of new construction generally terminates coverage unless an extension is added by endorsement.

If the covered damage delays the start of operations, the period of restoration for which loss is payable begins on the date that operations would have begun except for occurrence of the loss.

To illustrate, suppose that an insured is expanding its suite of offices in order to house two additional practitioners and that the new offices are scheduled to be operational on January 1. On December 15, there is a small fire and the offices cannot be occupied until February 1. Any extra expense the insured undertakes to speed up the repairs is covered under the basic insuring agreement. The expenses associated with the additional coverage start on January 1, the date when the offices would have been available, and applies to expenses such as the cost of acquiring temporary office space for the two new persons during the delay.

Extended Business Income

This coverage pays for additional loss of business income that exists after damaged property, other than finished stock, is actually repaired and operations are resumed. It provides business income recovery until the business can be restored, with reasonable speed, to the condition that existed before the loss occurred. Loss caused by unfavorable business conditions is not covered.

Extended business income is designed to enable the insured to recapture market position following completion of repairs and resumption of operations. For example, a retailer that endured a long closure for repairs may not see its customers return right away. It may need to entice customers back from other stores or wait for new customers to be found. The loss of income during this period is covered by extended business income.

The basic coverage applies for up to sixty consecutive days after resumption of operations. In form CP 00 30, though, another provision states that a longer extended period of indemnity can be provided by inserting a higher number in the space provided on the declarations. That number of days then replaces the customary sixty-day extension.

Interruption of Computer Operations

While the forms contain a limitation for interruption of computer operations, this additional coverage gives back a small amount of business income coverage for losses arising from certain types of computer interruptions. Coverage is extended, subject to the provisions of the additional coverage, when the suspension of operations caused by an interruption in computer operations results from a covered cause of loss.

For instance, up to $2,500 of business income coverage may be available if a hacker tampers with a company's network and causes it to crash, temporarily interrupting business operations. Depending on which form is used, the covered causes of loss are subject to the following:

1. For the special form, the additional coverage is limited to the specified causes of loss as defined and collapse.

2. In the broad form, the additional coverage applies to collapse.

3. If an endorsement adds a covered cause of loss, the additional covered cause of loss does not apply to the coverage provided under this additional coverage.

4.   This additional coverage applies if the covered causes of loss include a virus, harmful code, or similar instruction introduced into or enacted on a computer system, electronic data, or a network to which it is connected, designed to damage, destroy, or disrupt any part of the system or its operation. No coverage is extended, though, if an employee, including a temporary or leased employee, manipulates the insured's computer system or electronic data. Coverage also does not apply to manipulation of computer systems or electronic data by another entity that inspects, designs, installs, maintains, repairs, or replaces the system and is retained by the insured.

The amount of additional coverage is limited to $2,500 for all loss sustained and expense incurred during any one policy year. The limit applies no matter how many interruptions occur or the number of insured premises or computer systems involved. The additional coverage does not extend beyond the period of restoration. The limit for this additional coverage is separate from the policy limit. Since it may be possible to increase this limit, the 2012 revision adds that $2,500 is the limit unless a higher limit is shown in the declarations.

Subject to all the provisions of the interruption of computer operations additional coverage, the named insured may extend the insurance that applies to both business income and extra expense to apply to a suspension of operations, as those terms are defined, caused by an interruption in computer operations due to destruction or corruption of electronic data from a covered cause of loss. However, with the 2012 revision, this additional coverage is said not to apply when the Additional Limitation—Interruption of Computer Operations does not apply, based on Paragraph A.4.d. As has been mentioned, Paragraph A.4.d. states that the additional limitation does not apply when loss or damage to electronic data involves the building's elevator, lighting, heating, ventilation, air conditioning, or security system.

Expense to Reduce Loss

Unlike the full extra expense coverage of form CP 00 30, coverage under this item of form CP 00 32 is limited to payment of expenses incurred to reduce the business income loss that would otherwise be payable under the coverage. Recovery is restricted to no more than the amount by which the business income loss is reduced by incurring the added expenses.

Restaurant Closed Due to Robbery

A small restaurant was robbed at 9:30 PM on a Saturday night. Everyone was locked in a cooler by the robbers while they emptied the cash drawer and smashed the computer that operates the cash register and customer order system. Because the computer was down, the restaurant remained closed Saturday night and did not open again until its normal opening time of 11:00 AM Monday morning. The computer had been fixed by this time. The insured carried a Business Income Coverage form (Without Extra Expense) with the extended business income option and a Special Causes of Loss form. The insurance company paid the business income loss for the balance of Saturday night and Sunday but denied the extended business income option for the decrease in business the insured suffered during the week following the robbery. Business was down by one-third that week.

In the insurance company's adjustment, the decrease in business during the week following the robbery was due to patrons' fear of bodily injury and was not caused by the time required to repair the physical damage to the computer. The insurer maintained that the short-term closing was not long enough to cause the loss of customer base intended to be covered by the extended business income option.

In this scenario, all of the elements required for a covered extended business income loss are present. Business was suspended because of direct physical loss or damage to the computer ordering system. The loss was caused by a covered cause of loss. The insurance company adjustment supports this by paying the business income loss suffered from Saturday night until Monday morning. An additional loss of business income began on the date the property was repaired and operations were resumed and ended at the end of the week when the insured's operations were restored to the condition that would have existed if no direct physical loss or damage occurred.

The motives of the customers who stayed away from the restaurant are not relevant. All that is required is a covered loss and a decrease in business during the time period allowed by the policy.

Coverage Extension

Both forms provide a coverage extension for newly acquired locations (except fairs or exhibitions) if 50 percent or higher coinsurance is shown in the declarations for the business income coverage. The extension's limit is separate from the policy's limit. It is not subject to the coinsurance clause.

The limit paid under the extension for both business income and extra expense is $100,000 per location. Since a higher limit may be available, ISO added the phrase, with its 2012 revisions, that the designated limit applies "unless a higher limit is shown in the Declarations." The coverage begins when a new location is acquired or construction is begun and ends when the first of the following occurs: (a) the policy expires, (b) thirty days elapse after date of acquisition or start of construction, or (c) values for the location are reported to the insurer. Additional premium is charged for the new location from the date of acquisition.

This coverage parallels coverage provided for buildings and personal property and is useful as a temporary form of automatic coverage for newly acquired or constructed locations until permanent coverage can be arranged. But for locations acquired just before policy expiration, perhaps after renewal coverage has been ordered without knowledge of the new location, the coverage will expire with the policy. There is no provision for carrying the coverage over to the new policy for the remainder of the thirty days or until the location is recognized and values reported.

Application of Negligent Work Exclusion

A motel's power lines were cut by a sewer subcontractor while doing work on the premises. The insurer denied an ensuing business income loss claim stating that the damage was caused by negligent work of the sewer contractor and the policy does not provide coverage for this loss.

However, business income coverage is triggered by suspension of the insured's operations caused by "direct physical loss of or damage to property at the premises described in the declarations." The direct loss or damage to property on the insured's premises is the damage to the power lines. Therefore, absent a validly applied exclusion, this loss is covered. Damage to property on the insured's premises caused a suspension of operations.

Limits of Insurance

The limits of insurance section provides that payment of loss in any one occurrence is limited to the applicable limit of insurance shown in the declarations, except that the limit applicable to the interruption of computer operations and the coverage extension for newly acquired locations are separate from the limit of insurance.

The clause also provides that payments under certain additional coverages do not increase the applicable limit of insurance. The limit is not increased by payments under additional coverages for alterations and new buildings, civil authority, extra expense, and extended business income for business income coverage; nor for payment under alterations and new buildings and civil authority for extra expense coverage.

Loss Conditions

The loss conditions section of forms CP 00 30 and CP 00 32 are similar to those of the Building and Personal Property Coverage Form.

The section on appraisal stipulates that either party may make a written demand for appraisal if they disagree on the amount of the loss or net income and operating expenses. Each party selects an appraiser, who in turn selects an umpire. Each appraiser states the amount of the loss or net income and operating expenses. If the appraisers do not agree on the amount, they submit the differences to the umpire. A decision agreed by any two will be binding. Each party pays for its appraiser and split the cost of the appraisal and the umpire. Submitting to an appraisal does not negate the insurer's right to deny the claim.

The section on duties in the event of loss of business income lists the following requirements of the insured:

1. Notify the police if a law may have been broken.

2. Give the insurer prompt notice of the loss or damage, including a description of the property.

3. Give a description of how, when, and where the damage or loss occurred.

4. Keep a record of expenses and take all reasonable steps to protect the property from further damage. Also, the damaged property should be set aside if possible.

5. Permit the insurer to inspect the property; examine and make copies of books and records; and take samples of damaged and undamaged property for testing, inspection, and analysis.

6. Send a signed, sworn proof of loss within sixty days of the insurer's request.

7. Cooperate with the insurer in the investigation and settlement of the claim.

8. Resume operations as quickly as possible if the business is to continue.

The policy further states that the insurer may examine any insured under oath, while not in the presence of other insureds, and that the answers must be signed.

Note that each of the previously cited loss conditions are explained in depth in Chapter 5.

Loss Determination

The condition for loss determination explains how business income loss and extra expense payments are determined. This section reads as follows:

a. The amount of business income loss will be determined based on:

   (1) The net income of the business before the direct physical loss or damage occurred;

   (2) The likely net income of the business if no physical loss or damage had occurred, but not including any Net Income of the business that would likely have been earned as a result of an increase in the volume of business due to favorable conditions caused by the impact of the Covered Cause of Loss on customers or other businesses.

Therefore, for example, if a lumber yard was put into a cessation-of-business condition in a hurricane-wrecked area and, but for the damage to the business, would have been able to serve the rebuilding needs of the entire area, that presumed increase in net income would not be a factor in adjusting the business income loss of the lumber yard.

   (3) The operating expenses, including payroll expenses, necessary to resume "operations" with the same quality of service that existed just before the direct physical loss or damage; and

   (4) Other relevant sources of information, including:

      (a) Your financial records and accounting procedures;

      (b) Bills, invoices, and other vouchers; and

      (c) Deeds, liens, or contracts.

b. The amount of extra expense will be determined based on:

   (1) All expenses that exceed the normal operating expenses that would have been incurred by "operations" during the "period of restoration" if no direct physical loss or

damage had occurred. We will deduct from the total of such expenses:

(a)   The salvage value that remains of any property bought for temporary use during the "period of restoration," once "operations" are resumed; and

(b)   Any extra expense that is paid for by other insurance, except for insurance that is written subject to the same plan, terms, conditions, and provisions as this insurance; and

(2)   Necessary expenses that reduce the business income loss that otherwise would have been incurred.

Part b. is on form CP 00 30 only.

Resuming operations in whole or in part by using damaged or undamaged property at the described premises or elsewhere reduces the business income amount of loss determined in this section. Damaged or undamaged property includes stock and merchandise. For extra expense losses, the amount is reduced to the extent operations return to normal, thus discontinuing the need to incur extra expense. If operations are not resumed as quickly as possible, recovery will be based on the amount of time necessary to restore operations as quickly as possible.

Other Loss Conditions

Other loss conditions include loss payment and resumption of operations. The loss payment provision states that loss will be paid within thirty days after the insurer receives the sworn proof of loss, provided the insured has complied with all terms of the coverage and agreement has been reached on the amount of the loss or an appraisal award has been made.

The resumption of operations clause provides that the insurer will reduce the amount of business income loss, other than extra expense, to the extent the insured can resume operations in whole or part by using damaged or undamaged property including merchandise or stock at the insured premises or elsewhere, and extra expense loss to the extent the insured can return operations to normal and discontinue such extra expense. If the insured does not resume operations or does not resume operations as quickly as possible, CP 00 30 will pay based on the length of time it would have taken to resume operations as quickly as possible.

The resumption of operations clause on CP 00 32, Business Income Coverage Form (Without Extra Expense), reads the same as that on CP 00 30, except that reference to extra expense is deleted.

Coinsurance

Like the BBP coverage form, the Business Income Coverage Form includes a coinsurance condition; however, there are two main differences.

First, under the Business Income Form the insured can choose a coinsurance percentage ranging from 50 to 125 percent rather than the standard 80 percent coinsurance percentage found in the BBP form. The insured, generally in conjunction with its accountant and insurance producer, uses a business income worksheet in determining the estimated maximum loss, the proper coinsurance percentage, and limit of insurance. Like coinsurance in the BPP form, the premium rates charged by the insurer decrease as the coinsurance percentage increases. Note that insureds may choose to insure their business income exposures on a less cumbersome method by using the maximum period of indemnity, the monthly limit of indemnity, the extended period of indemnity, or the agreed value option. Each of these options is reviewed later in this chapter.

The second major difference involves the coinsurance basis, which is the dollar amount multiplied by the coinsurance percentage in determining if a penalty applies at time of loss. In the Business Income Coverage Form, the coinsurance percentage is applied against the sum of the net income (net profit or loss before income taxes), and operating expenses, including payroll expenses, that would have been earned or incurred (had no loss occurred) by the insured's operations at the described premises for the twelve months following the inception or last previous anniversary date of the policy—whichever is later. Conversely, in the BBP form, the coinsurance percentage is applied against the property value (either replacement cost or actual cash value) at time of loss.

The coinsurance condition applies if a coinsurance percentage is inserted on the declarations page. The application of the coinsurance clause in forms CP 00 30 and CP 00 32 bases the coinsurance measurement on the twelve months following inception or last previous anniversary of the policy, whichever is later. This is advantageous to insureds as they are required to anticipate values only for the current policy year and insure accordingly.

Business growth during the policy year, not anticipated when the initial insurable values were estimated, can cause underinsurance if the amount of insurance is not increased appropriately after the accelerated growth has become apparent.

The coinsurance clause is based on the sum of net income (net profit or loss before income taxes) and all operating expenses, including payroll expenses, that would have been earned by the operations at the insured premises for the twelve months of the current policy term had no loss occurred.

The clause includes a list of expenses that are deducted from the total of all operating expenses, including prepaid freight; returns and allowances; discounts; bad debts; collection expenses; cost of raw stock and factory supplies consumed, including transportation charges; cost of merchandise sold, including transportation charges; cost of other supplies consumed, including transportation charges; cost of services purchased from outsiders, not employees, to resell that do not continue under contract; power, heat, and refrigeration expenses that do not continue under contract, all ordinary payroll expenses or the amount of payroll expenses excluded; and special deductions for mining properties.

To illustrate business income coinsurance, assume an insured has net income and operating expenses for the twelve months following policy inception of $400,000, a coinsurance percentage of 50 percent, a limit of insurance of $200,000, and a business income loss of $80,000. In this example, the insured would be have complied with the coinsurance requirement by carrying an insurance limit of $200,000, which is the coinsurance requirement of 50 percent of the insured's business income cost basis of $400,000. Any business income loss up to the $200,000 limit of insurance is paid in full.

Using the same facts but changing the limit of insurance to $150,000, the insured would not have complied with the coinsurance requirement because the $150,000 amount would have been less than the 50 percent coinsurance required of $200,000. In this case, the insured would collect only 75 percent ($150,000 ÷ $200,000) of the amount of the loss. Note that in either case, any loss in excess of the limit of insurance is borne by the insured.

The following chart illustrates the coinsurance formula with examples of loss scenarios of both adequate and inadequate limits of insurance.

Coinsurance Formula

$$\frac{\text{Limit of insurance}}{\text{BI} + \text{operating expenses} \times \text{Coinsurance percentage}} \times \text{Loss} = \text{Covered}$$

Adequate Example	$\dfrac{\$200,000}{\$200,000}$	× $80,000	=	$80,000
Inadequate Example	$\dfrac{\$150,000}{\$200,000}$	× $80,000	=	$60,000

In the adequate example, the insured complied with the 50 percent coinsurance requirement by carrying a limit of insurance of $200,000 and is paid in full for the $80,000 business income loss. In the inadequate example, the insured failed to comply with the 50 percent coinsurance requirement by carrying a limit of insurance of $150,000 and is penalized. The coinsurance penalty is calculated by dividing the $150,000 limit of insurance carried by the $200,000 amount required, resulting in an underinsurance penalty and a payment of 75 percent of the amount of the loss, or $60,000. These illustrations are also cited in the policy form, which is included in the back of this book.

The insured's coinsurance basis and the accompanying limit of insurance can be reduced based upon the insured's individual needs and circumstances. For example, the insured can choose to limit payroll expenses by using the Payroll Limitation or Exclusion endorsement, CP 15 10, or limit power, heat, and refrigeration expenses by using the Power, Heat, and Refrigeration Deduction endorsement, CP 15 11. Both will result in a lower business income insurance limit and a lower premium cost.

Note that the coinsurance provision is applicable only to business income coverage. It does not apply to extra expense coverage.

Optional Coverages

Forms CP 00 30 and CP 00 32 include four optional coverages activated by appropriate entries on the commercial property declarations page. Their use is an alternative to coinsurance.

The first three options—maximum period of indemnity, monthly limit of indemnity, and agreed value—are mutually exclusive—any one of them, but only one, may be applied to any one item of business income coverage. The fourth option, extended period of indemnity, may be used alone or with options two or three but not with option one.

Maximum Period of Indemnity

The first optional coverage is called maximum period of indemnity. This option is most advantageous to businesses that are not likely to suffer an interruption longer than four months. When this option is selected the coinsurance provision is deleted and a provision substituted stating that the most the insurer will pay for loss of business income is the smaller of the amount of loss sustained during the 120 days immediately following the direct physical loss or damage, or the limit of insurance shown in the declarations.

Monthly Limit of Indemnity

The second optional coverage is monthly limit of indemnity. This option deletes the coinsurance provision and substitutes a monthly limit of insurance, which can be either one-third, one-fourth, or one-sixth of the total limit of insurance shown in the declarations. To activate this option, the appropriate fraction is entered in the space provided on the declarations page.

Optional coverage two includes an example on the form itself of how the fractional limit for each thirty days of loss applies to an actual situation. In the example, the limit of insurance is $120,000 and the monthly limit is one-fourth; the most the insurer will pay for loss in each period of thirty consecutive days is $30,000. If the actual loss for the first thirty days is $40,000, the second thirty days is $20,000, and the third thirty-day period is $30,000, then the insurer will pay $30,000 for the first period, $20,000 for the second period, and $30,000 for the last period.

Unlike the maximum period of indemnity option, which applies to the first 120 days immediately following the loss, coverage with the monthly limit of indemnity option applies for the entire period that it takes to resume operations (and, under the extended business income additional coverage of the basic form, thirty days beyond). The only limitations are the actual stated limit of insurance and that the coverage for loss of business income shall not exceed the indicated fraction of the total limit for each thirty consecutive days after the beginning date of the loss. So, with a one-fourth monthly limit, if the actual loss in any of the thirty-day periods is less than one-fourth of the limit of insurance, loss extending beyond the 120 days could be covered (again subject to the one-fourth monthly limit) until the limit of insurance is exhausted.

The example cited applies only to loss of business income and does not illustrate the way the insurance applies to extra expense, which is not subject to the fractional monthly limit. With a loss involving only extra expense, the entire coverage limit can be applied to extra expenses incurred to maintain or quickly restore production, regardless of when they are incurred.

This option is best suited for small businesses that can easily predict what net profits and continuing expenses will be. For instance, a seasonal business like a family-run miniature golf course may operate from April to September, with July being its best month. If net profits and continuing expenses for July are expected to be $10,000, then that amount is set as the monthly limit. The insured would estimate the duration of a shutdown and choose the one-third, one-fourth, or one-sixth monthly limit.

If this business chose one-sixth, then the amount of insurance purchased would be $60,000, or six times the monthly limit of $10,000.

Agreed Value

The third optional coverage, agreed value, provides the means for suspending the coinsurance provision on a year-to-year basis. Businesses that are in a growth mode or anticipate growth or increased sales would benefit from this option.

This optional provision is activated by entering the amount of the agreed value in the appropriate space on the declarations page and by attaching a completed Business Income Report/Worksheet form, CP 15 15, showing actual business income values for a twelve-month period already completed and estimated values for the twelve months after inception of the agreed value provision. The agreed value must equal or be more than the appropriate coinsurance percentage times the coming year's estimated values. As long as at least this amount of insurance is carried, the application of the coinsurance provision is suspended for the twelve months covered by the report, unless the policy expires before the end of that time.

If less insurance is carried than the agreed value, the insured's recovery of loss is reduced in proportion to the deficiency, regardless of whether the amount of insurance carried is adequate to satisfy the coinsurance provision. Thus, in a time of declining business in which the initial current policy year estimate proves to be too high, the insured may wish to reduce the amount of insurance to reflect the reduced business. Under the agreed value option the insured must complete a new worksheet with the revised estimate and change the agreed value amount shown in the policy before reducing the amount of insurance. Otherwise, the reduced amount of insurance will be insufficient to provide for complete recovery of loss.

When the business income coverage is divided among two or more policies, the total amount of the agreed value is shown in the space for agreed value on the declarations, rather than each insurer's individual portion of the total. The sum of the limits of insurance for all of the individual policies of the insured (or business income coverage parts) sharing the coverage should equal the agreed value.

Form CP 15 15 carries a statement certifying that the report is a true and correct report of values as required under the policy for the periods indicated and that the agreed value for the period of coverage is the stated dollar amount based on the stated coinsurance percentage. The statement must be signed by a company official. The business income report/work sheet becomes a part of the policy provisions, so an understatement of values, when there is evidence of deliberate intent, could be viewed as material misrepresentation. The insurance would be entirely voided rather than the amount of recovery being reduced. In the absence of such evidence, though, there is no penalty for understating values.

The agreed value optional coverage is not to be used with policies having the following forms attached: Business Income from Dependent Properties—Broad Form, CP 15 08; Business Income from Dependent Properties—Limited Form, CP 15 09; and Business Income Premium Adjustment endorsement, CP 15 20.

Extended Period of Indemnity

The fourth optional coverage, extended period of indemnity, is used to extend the period of coverage under the extended business income additional coverage from the sixty days provided in the basic form to any of seven longer options up to 360 days. Businesses such as hotels or restaurants in competitive locations that require a longer period of time to recapture customers following a shutdown may choose to extend the period of indemnity using this option. Thirty-day increments are available up to 180 days, then ninety-day increments up to 360 days.

This extension option is activated by inserting the appropriate number of days in the space provided on the declarations page. A separate endorsement is not necessary.

Extra Expense Insurance

Contrasted with Business Income Coverage

What will be the insured's most pressing need if a fire or other disaster interrupts normal business operations? If normal relations with customers are interrupted for a time, what will be the effect on the insured's operations over the long term? Does the insured deal in services of a type that can be readily transferred to a new location so that the prospect of an interruption of significant duration need not even be contemplated? The answers to these issues provide the strongest guide in determining whether business income coverage or extra expense insurance is the primary need.

Most insureds that anticipate a temporary suspension of operations will also anticipate only a temporary suspension of the flow of customers. It is even possible that, in the case of retailers, the interest generated by fire sales and by a gala reopening of remodeled premises can have a beneficial effect on the business. Firms that are able to anticipate that the customer flow will resume in step with the resumption of operations are those that, in general, market their goods or services broadly to a wide and general market. Such firms are most in need of funds to replace the income that the business would have generated and that it will need to meet the unavoidable financial obligations that continue during a business shutdown. They need business income coverage.

Other firms, especially those dealing in services, may face a permanent loss of customers if the service is interrupted for any significant length of time. Banks and newspapers are frequently cited as examples of businesses that cannot tell their customers to go elsewhere for a month or two and expect them to return. Far more numerous are firms that expect brief interruptions because their operations are readily transportable to a temporary location. For example, firms that offer professional services and depend more on persons than on facilities can more easily operate from temporary locations. Firms in this category primarily need extra expense insurance. As long as they have a source of funds to support the extraordinary expenses of staying in business, they should not experience a drop in income from the business.

Insured May Need Both

Having determined that the primary need is for either business income coverage or extra expense insurance, the insured that chooses the latter should also give careful consideration to the extent of the business income exposure and perhaps arrange some coverage for that exposure also. The same process is not required of the insured that purchases business income coverage with extra expense because that form automatically provides extra expense insurance. Since the loss of income from interruption of operations is not covered by the extra expense insurance, the insured may want to purchase business income coverage to apply to those operations.

Because some business income forms have extra expense insurance built in, consideration might be given to using those forms in lieu of the extra expense form. In most cases, however, the insured who has a need only for extra expense insurance will find it both more economical and more convenient to choose the extra expense form. For example, an enterprise might have an exposure of $200,000 per month in terms of business income coverage, but $50,000 per month in terms of extra expense. If by an emergency expenditure of $50,000 the insured can avoid the $200,000 loss of business income, then the purchase of extra expense insurance (instead of business income coverage) is clearly the proper choice. Such a decision requires adoption of a recovery plan that provides a blueprint for an immediate resumption of operations.

Extra Expense Coverage Form, CP 00 50

The current edition of the extra expense coverage form is CP 00 50 10 12, corresponding to the other form editions in the ISO commercial property program. (The preceding edition was 06 07. When this former edition was replaced, a number of changes were made to the form, all of which are identical to those applying to the Business Income forms CP 00 30 and CP 00 32, and discussed therein.) The coverage agreement of the extra expense form is to pay to the insured "the actual and necessary extra expense you sustain due to direct physical loss of or damage to property at premises described in the declarations." Described premises include the area within 100 feet of the site at which described premises are located. The loss or damage must be caused by or result from any covered cause of loss, which will depend upon the causes of loss form selected by the insured.

Extra expense is defined as "necessary expenses you incur during the period of restoration that you would not have incurred if there had been no direct physical loss or damage to property." This is a broad definition allowing the insured flexibility in getting the business back into operation, subject only to the requirement that the extra expense be necessary. Renting equivalent office space to restore operations would qualify; renting larger office space with plans to expand business would not.

The period of restoration begins with the date of covered direct physical loss or damage and ends when the property should be repaired if reasonable speed is applied to getting the property back to its preloss condition or when business is resumed at a new permanent location.

The term limit of the policy has no bearing on this period of time; that is, the expiration of the policy will not end the time for restoration of the property. On the other hand, the operation of any building or zoning law or ordinance that interferes with repairs or reconstruction will not extend the time when extra expense coverage is payable. Likewise, any environmental protection ordinance that regulates the prevention or cleanup of pollution damage does not increase the period of restoration. The period of restoration remains based on that period of time during which repairs should be accomplished.

Insureds who have a building ordinances exposure are able to obtain an increased period of restoration via endorsement CP 15 31, Ordinance or Law – Increased Period of Restoration. The endorsement allows for the operation of laws affecting construction, repairs, or demolition as legitimate factors in the computation of restoration time. This endorsement does not extend the period of restoration as regards the operation of environmental protection laws, though.

Interference by strikers or others at the site of repairs or reconstruction that causes a delay in the resumption of operations is excluded from consideration in the period of restoration as well. This is stipulated in the causes of loss forms and is one of several special exclusions that are applicable to extra expense insurance. See the causes of loss section later in this analysis.

The coverage agreement also applies to money spent to minimize the suspension if it cannot be avoided and to facilitate the repair or restoration of property to the extent that the latter reduces the amount that would otherwise have been necessary to spend. For example, the cost of air shipment of a vital part is covered as a legitimate extra expense if air shipment will reduce the period of restoration and save payment of other expenses that would otherwise be at least equal to the cost of air shipment.

However, restoring the damaged property is secondary to the central concern of the coverage. The major extra expenses that the policy insures are those involved with keeping the insured enterprise in operation at the described premises or getting it moved and operating at a new location.

Causes of Loss

Whether property damage at the insured premises triggers extra expense coverage depends upon whether the triggering peril is covered. This is determined by the causes of loss form that is a necessary part of the policy.

In addition to setting up the perils and the applicable exclusions, the causes of loss forms all contain one set of exclusions that specifically apply to extra expense insurance. The exclusions are essentially the same as those for business income discussed earlier, with a few exceptions. For example, the exclusion for finished stock does not apply to extra expense coverage.

There is also no coverage for extra expense associated with the termination of any license, lease, or contract beyond the period of restoration. Just as there is no coverage for any other consequential loss with the business income coverage, the same is true for extra expense coverage. If, for example, an advertising agency insured is prevented from soliciting a new account because a fire destroys the layout on the day before a scheduled presentation, the consequential loss exclusion rules out coverage under the extra expense form.

Additional Limitation—Interruption of Computer Operations

The extra expense coverage form contains an additional limitation for interruption of computer operations that is similar to that discussed in the business income section, without reference to limitation for business income coverage, of course. Note that the business income form provides a base limit of $2,500 for interruptions of computer operations unless a higher limit is indicated in the declarations. Insureds with substantial computer operations would generally find broader and more robust coverage under a separate electronic data processing policy with specific business income coverage.

Coverage Extension and Additions

If the insured acquires a new location during the term of the policy, the extra expense form automatically provides limited coverage at the new location. The added coverage is in addition to the coverage at the locations described in the declarations. This automatic insurance expires thirty days from the date of acquisition of the property or on the date the acquisition is reported to the insurance company, whichever occurs first. Expiration of the policy terminates the coverage as well.

The form addresses four other areas of exposure under the additional coverages section.

Alterations and new buildings. One of the additional coverages relates to alterations and new buildings on the described premises. Coverage for these eventualities might be inferred from the basic insuring agreement, which covers extra expense losses caused by physical damage to insured property at described locations (including personal property in the open or in vehicles within one-hundred feet of the described locations). Additions and new construction are distinguished in terms of additional coverage because the time frame for the extra expense loss is different. If an already existing structure is damaged, extra expense insurance runs from the date of damage through the time the damage should be repaired. If a new structure or an alteration is damaged, extra expense insurance begins to run on the date that the new property would have been operational if no loss had occurred.

Civil authority. Additional coverage also applies when damage by an insured peril occurs away from the insured's premises and civil authorities seal off the area or otherwise prohibit the insured's access to the described premises. Firefighters cordoning off a city block during and after a fire on neighboring property is an example of an interruption by civil authority during which extra expense insurance applies. There is coverage for up to three weeks of such blocked access.

This additional coverage responds only to blockades imposed by civil authority. Extra expense insurance does not provide for coverage if access to the insured's premises is reduced or cut off by some other means—as when weather conditions or heavy construction activity near the insured's premises discourages customers or clients. Likewise, blockage by civil authorities in the face of an uninsured cause of loss, such as flood, does not activate this additional coverage. The changes to this form track the civil authority clause of the business income form, discussed in this chapter.

While the form contains a limitation for the interruption of computer operations, it also includes an additional coverage for interruption of computer operations. Again, it is similar to the provision found on the business income forms, with variations depending on the causes of loss form chosen, as previously indicated. The coverage applies to the destruction or corruption of electronic data due to a covered cause of loss. For example, a customer may send an email with an attachment containing a virus. If the attachment is opened and infects essential operating files, which then causes a suspension of business activities, the extra expense incurred to clean up the network and return to normal operations will be covered. If, however, an employee or contractor working for the company hacks into the system and manipulates electronic data, no coverage for extra expense is available.

Limits

The system of recovery under extra expense insurance requires careful attention. There is a limit set out in the declarations that specifies the most that the insurance company will pay on an extra expense loss. However, the declarations also specify percentages of the policy limit that are recoverable in thirty day intervals. A 40-80-100 arrangement is the most common. With this, the insured may not recover more than 40 percent of the policy limit when the recovery period is thirty days or less; 80 percent when the recovery period is over thirty but less than sixty days; and 100 percent of the limit only when the recovery period exceeds sixty days.

As an example, the extra expense form itself contains a limit on loss payment provision that shows what happens when proven expenses do not line up favorably with the selected limits. The insured in the form's example recovers only $80,000 on a $90,000 loss even thought the policy limit is $100,000. The insured cannot recover $10,000 of proven expenses. The time for recovery—the period of restoration—is forty-five days, and the insured had a 40-80-100 arrangement. Thus, the most the insured could recover for a restoration period of sixty days or less was 80 percent of the $100,000 limit, even though extra expenses had amounted to $90,000.

The insured has the option—and the challenge—of selecting the number of thirty day intervals and the percentages of the overall limit that will become available at each limit. Endorsement CP 15 07, Expanded Limits on Loss Payment, is used when four or more recovery intervals are contemplated. The 40-80-100 arrangement commonly shown on the declarations page can often be altered on the page itself.

The most foolproof arrangement is to have 100 percent of the coverage available during the first thirty days. The time of recovery could extend beyond thirty days, in which case the full amount of the policy is still available. Even a one-day period of restoration is sufficient to bring the total policy limit into play. However, this arrangement is also significantly more expensive. The cost of the coverage decreases as the limit is spread through longer intervals into the policy term. An insured who could realistically expect a very slow recovery and a gradual payout of extra expenses might choose a 300-day recovery with 10 percent of the policy limit becoming available every thirty days. The premium would be relatively inexpensive, but few insureds are in a position to take advantage of that extended arrangement. Only a careful examination of maximum expenses during the first thirty-day interval, maximum expenses during the second thirty-day interval, and maximum time of restoration can guide the insured in determining the firm's individual and special requirements.

Other Insurance

In the Commercial Property Conditions form, CP 00 90, extra expense insurance holds itself as excess to recovery of the same expenses that the insured receives from another source unless the other source "is written subject to the same plan, terms, conditions and provisions as this insurance." As mentioned earlier, many insureds may need both business income coverage and extra expense insurance although business income coverage has some extra expense insurance built in.

An examination of the business income forms reveals close parallels between the coverage of those forms and the plan, terms, conditions, and provisions of the extra expense form. The parallels are sufficient to call into question the interoperation of the two forms. In that context, it is important to know that the drafters of the extra expense insurance form express the opinion (according to ISO explanatory material) that the coverage of the extra expense form is excess to the extra expense recovery of the business income coverage form.

Other Exposures

Although the following exposures are not addressed in ISO's program, they may be contained in independently filed or manuscripted policies and should be considered when embarking on the management of business income and extra expense exposures.

Ingress and Egress

Ingress refers to access or entrance to one's premises. In turn, *egress* means the freedom to exit or leave those premises. Some situations may prevent business owners, customers, or both from coming or going. A tornado, for instance, may make roads to a business impassable because of fallen trees, thus blocking access to the business. The case previously discussed where heavy snow blocked access to an auto dealership, and the court held there was no physical damage and thus no trigger for business income coverage, is an example of an ingress and egress exposure. Because no direct physical damage or loss to property occurs, ISO business income and extra expense coverages will not address these losses.

Manuscript and company-specific policies may add an ingress/egress clause to provide coverage. The court found coverage under such a provision in *Fountain Powerboat Industries v. Reliance Ins. Co.*, 119 F. Supp.2d 552 (E.D. N.C. 2000). Fountain Powerboat could not reach its manufacturing facility and headquarters because the sole road approaching them was inaccessible after Hurricane Floyd dumped heavy rainfall in the area. Reliance paid claims for physical damage to the premises but denied business income coverage, arguing that the physical losses to the insured property were not the cause of the business income losses. The court, though, stated that the clause clearly provided coverage even though no direct physical damage or loss had occurred.

Flood

Commercial property policies generally exclude the peril of flood. National Flood Insurance Plan (NFIP) forms do not include provisions for business income or extra expense, so a gap could exist even if direct flood damage to a property is covered by an NFIP-based policy. The greatest losses to businesses as a result of flood are not usually property damage but lost income because the premises is shut down for flood cleanup and extra expenses incurred from operating at a temporary site.

Absence of Profits

Calculating a business income loss for a company that is operating at a net loss is particularly important for certain types of companies. Start-up companies, which may not have established a predictable earnings flow, and high-tech companies, which may rely on grant money and stockholders equity during their developmental stages, are two examples of companies that may be operating at planned net losses at the time of a covered loss.

Consider a high-tech company that raised operational money through a public offering. This company's business plan includes operating in the red for five years. It will take the company that much time to develop a product from research it has licensed, work out the bugs, take the product to market, and begin to earn income from it. During this time, the money raised through the public offering is funding operations. If business is suspended by a loss for six months in the middle of the five-year plan, it continues to draw on stockholders equity in order to stay alive. But it will not make any progress in its business plan during the interruption, causing it to fall short of plan and, possibly, fail.

In addition, a high-tech company may be especially exposed to a high level of continuing expenses because it needs to keep its technical employees on the payroll during the down time. The standard business income coverage form would not adequately cover these continuing expenses because the loss calculation combines the net profit or loss with the continuing expenses. If the net loss is $200,000 a month and continuing expenses are $250,000 a month, the insured would be able to collect only $50,000 a month, well short of the $250,000 necessary to cover continuing expenses. In severe cases, no business income recovery would be possible.

A method to handle this situation is with a valued business income coverage form.

This form is appropriate in the situation described because it pays a set amount for each period of business suspension as specified in the policy declarations. The time period could be twenty-four hours, one week, or one month.

Because the limit is established prior to the loss, there is no need to perform a lengthy calculation to establish the amount of loss after it occurs. This means that the issue of a net loss or net profit is addressed prior to the insurance being purchased. There also is no coinsurance clause.

Professionals are cautious of using the valued form of coverage for several reasons, including the following:

1.   fear that the form promotes a moral hazard;

2.   the possibility of miscalculating the limit and not purchasing sufficient coverage; and

3.   possible settlement problems if only a partial interruption triggers the coverage.

Careful underwriting of a company's business plan is necessary to counter the possibility of promoting a moral hazard. The form should be used as a tool to craft coverage that is suited to companies in their developmental stages, and careful review of the company's business plan is necessary. It should not be used just because a company is operating at a net loss.

Insureds assume the burden of setting the limit of coverage. Even though this method does not rely on the insured's internal financial data when adjusting the loss, it does require careful preparation of a business income worksheet by the insured when the coverage is underwritten. Special attention must be given to the amount of anticipated continuing expenses, as well as any extra expense that might be incurred. The insured must realize that the limit established for each unit of recovery (day, week, or month) is the maximum amount recoverable during each recovery unit.

In addition to the per unit limit, the form also lists a maximum amount recoverable. As an example, a form may provide for a loss payment of up to $5,000 per day with a maximum payable of $900,000. This means that the insured could recover up to $5,000 per day for a total of 180 days. However, if less than $5,000 a day is paid during a partial suspension, the $900,000 cap still applies.

Companies with seasonal swings, or companies that are directly affected by outside economic factors, also need to take special care in developing the limit of insurance. Since there are maximum limits payable per unit and per loss, it is important that the limit accurately reflect seasonal and economic upswings.

In the event of a partial suspension of business, the form pays a percentage of the per unit limit. It is important for companies to understand that the amount paid each day will be decreased proportionately when a partial shutdown occurs. This percentage is equal to the value of lost production or income divided by its normal value prior to the loss. The formula for a partial suspension is as follows:

Lost Production × Working Day Limit = Partial Loss Payment

The partial loss formula would be triggered when only a portion of the business is suspended because of a loss. It also comes into play as a company begins to resume operations after a total suspension.

The premium charged for a valued form could be higher than for a standard business income form. However, in certain situations the benefit would greatly outweigh the possibly higher premium. It is a useful tool in designing coverage that is suited to a particular type of insured.

Chapter 8

Leasehold Interest Coverage Form, CP 00 60

A building tenant may have a favorable lease; however, if property at the location suffers damage, the tenant may lose the advantage of that favorable lease (the leasehold interest). This coverage form refers to *property* and not to *covered property*. Thus, the damage leading to insurance recovery may be to the building owned by someone else or to the insured's property located in the rented location. Leasehold interest insurance protects the tenant from this possibility. A building owner, on the other hand, would look to his business income coverage to pay his rental income in case of covered loss to the property.

The Leasehold Interest Coverage Form has not been revised as often as other forms in the ISO commercial property program. The current edition of the leasehold interest coverage form is CP 00 60 06 95. It also exists as the CP 00 60 07 88 and CP 00 60 10 91.

What Is Insured—Types of Leasehold Interest

The form defines four types of leasehold interest: tenants lease interest, bonus payments, improvements and betterments, and prepaid rent.

Tenants lease interest may take one of two forms:

1. The tenant occupies the premises under a favorable lease. This means that the insured holds a lease on premises that is under the market price of comparable premises. For example, the premises may be rent-controlled or, because of the terms of a long-term lease entered into years previously, comparable premises rent in the current market for substantially more. The leasehold interest is the difference between the actual rental value of the premises and the rent payable for the unexpired term of the lease. To illustrate, the insured has a lease with three years remaining at $250 per month. The current market price of comparable premises is $400 per month. A complete fire loss to the building causes the lease to be terminated. The insured would collect $5,400 ($400 actual rental value

227

minus favorable lease amount, $250, equaling $150 × 36 months of the unexpired term of the lease).

2. The tenant has a valuable lease and sublets the premises at a higher rental. The leasehold interest is the profit the tenant-insured receives through subleasing for the unexpired term of the sublease.

Bonus payments. For the second type of leasehold interest, an insured may pay an upfront bonus to obtain a favorable lease. If the bonus is nonrefundable, the monthly leasehold interest on such cash bonus is the original cost of the bonus divided by the number of months remaining in the lease at the time the bonus was paid. For example, if the bonus paid at the inception of the lease is $5,000 and the lease is for three years, the monthly leasehold interest is $138.89 ($5,000 divided by 36). A bonus does not include rent, whether or not prepaid, or security.

Improvements and betterments. If a tenant makes improvements to the premises, the unamortized portion of payments for those improvements represents a leasehold interest. The monthly leasehold interest in the improvements and betterments is the original cost of the improvements and betterments divided by the number of months remaining in the lease at the time of installation. If the installation of the improvements and betterments increases the rental value of the premises, the monthly leasehold interest is the increase in rental value divided by the number of months remaining in the lease at the time of installation.

For example, an insured currently leases his retail outlet for $1,000 per month. In the third month of the lease, he adds improvements and betterments to the store that result in an increase in the rental value of $6,000 per year. This insured's increase in monthly leasehold interest would be calculated by dividing $6,000 by nine months, or $666.

Prepaid rent. The fourth and final type of leasehold interest is prepaid rent. If the insured has prepaid rent and it is not refundable, the unamortized portion is insured. However, this does not include the customary rent due at any rental period (monthly or otherwise).

Causes of Loss, Exclusions, and Limitations

For these items, the leasehold interest form refers to the appropriate causes of loss form. In order for leasehold interest to be payable, property at the insured premises must suffer direct damage by a covered cause of loss.

Each of the basic, broad, and special causes of loss forms contains an identical special exclusions section regarding the leasehold interest coverage form with two provisions:

1.   The building ordinance or law exclusion does not apply to claims for leasehold interest. Therefore, if zoning prohibits rebuilding, the leasehold interest loss is covered.

2.   There is no coverage if the insured cancels the lease; if there is a suspension, lapse, or cancellation of any license that causes the cancellation of the lease (liquor sales licenses, for example); or from any other consequential loss.

Thus leasehold interest applies if a lease is cancelled due to the operation of building laws, as long as a covered cause of loss causes the physical damage to the building. However, other consequential loss is not covered.

Terms in a Lease

Terms in a lease can have an appreciable effect on insurance and warrant close attention when advising an insured on proper coverage. Any questions should be addressed with a leasing professional. For example, an insured with a lease that is totally silent on both continuing rents and cancellation of the lease may have a problem. If damage to property at the described premises from a covered cause of loss leads the insured to cancel his lease, there is no coverage. A special exclusion in the causes of loss form is used with the leasehold interest coverage form to prevent coverage where the insured cancels the lease ("we will not pay for any loss caused by: (a) your canceling the lease").

Therefore, the insured cannot cancel the lease and turn to the policy for recovery. A lease that is silent on the matter of cancellation can prove troublesome to the tenant for many reasons, particularly where the tenant has a lease on untenable premises with no contractual provision to protect him. Again, the advice of a leasing professional should be sought.

In short, the leasehold interest coverage form will not respond where the insured cancels the lease. Where the lease is favorable, the insured will not want it cancelled and should be further protected with business income and extra expense coverages to maintain business income in the event the leased premises are unusable for some period.

Limits of Insurance

In two clauses, the policy describes separate limits of insurance for tenants lease interest and for bonus payments, improvements and betterments, and prepaid rent.

Tenants lease interest. The most the insurer will pay because of the cancellation of a lease is the net leasehold interest. The ISO rules state this amount as the present value of the gross leasehold interest (difference between monthly rental value and actual rent payable for the unexpired term of the lease of the insured's premises) as of the policy inception date. This amount decreases automatically each month. The amount of net leasehold interest at any time is the gross leasehold interest multiplied by the leasehold interest factor for the remaining months of the lease. For any period of less than a month a proportionate factor is used. The leasehold interest coverage policy always contains a table of leasehold interest factors.

Alternately, the net leasehold interest is the amount that placed elsewhere at the assumed rate of interest would be equivalent to the insured's receiving the gross leasehold interest for each month of the unexpired term of the lease.

Bonus payments, improvements and betterments, and prepaid rent. The most the insurer will pay because of the cancellation of a lease is the net leasehold interest. A proportionate share of the monthly leasehold interest applies to periods of less than a month. After cancellation, if the landlord allows the tenant to stay under a new lease or other arrangement, the insurance covers the difference in rent between the cancelled lease and the rent under the new arrangement.

Loss Conditions

The loss conditions of the leasehold interest form are similar to those in the BPP form. However, because the leasehold interest form does not cover tangible property, the provisions are modified to eliminate property abandonment, the inventory requirement, recovered property, and valuation.

Loss payment. Covered loss is paid within thirty days after receipt of the sworn proof of loss if the insured has complied with the terms of the leasehold interest coverage part and an agreement has been reached on the amount of loss or an appraisal award made.

Vacancy. The first portion of the vacancy clause specifies that it applies only to the area actually leased to the insured. The insured's suite or unit is vacant "when it does not contain enough business personal property to conduct customary operations." A building under construction is not considered vacant. Vacancy and customary operations are discussed in Chapter 5.

If the insured subleases the premises to someone else, the vacancy clause applies somewhat differently. If the sublet building has been vacant for more than sixty consecutive days before the loss, there is no coverage for leasehold interest loss caused by vandalism, sprinkler leakage (by freeze rupture in spite of the insured having protected the system against freezing), building glass breakage, water damage, theft, or attempted theft. Any other covered loss is paid with a reduction of 15 percent. If there is no sublease agreement at the time of loss, the policy will not pay any leasehold interest loss.

Cancellation

The leasehold interest form contains an additional condition relating to cancellation. This cancellation provision supersedes the cancellation clause of the common policy conditions form.

The difference between the two cancellation provisions is in the method provided for computing return premium. Because the amount of leasehold interest decreases steadily from inception to expiration, the daily earned premium is greatest early in the policy term. Cancellation must be computed based on the higher average net leasehold interest between inception and the date of cancellation, rather than the lower average leasehold interest for the full original term of the policy, the basis of the original premium. Only the difference between original premium and the earned premium for this higher average amount of insurance is returnable. As in the common policy conditions, the refund may be more favorable if the insurer, rather than the insured, cancels.

The ISO Commercial Lines Manual sets out the steps for premium determination and computation of earned premium at cancellation.

Leasehold Interest Schedule, CP 19 60

Along with leasehold interest form CP 00 60, a Leasehold Interest Schedule, CP 19 60, applies. This form shows the necessary information about the lease and the way the amount of leasehold interest insurance is developed. The schedule includes spaces to enter the inception and expiration dates of the lease, the number of months remaining at inception of the policy, and the percentage of interest that applies.

The schedule also shows the amount of gross leasehold interest, monthly leasehold interest, net leasehold interest at policy inception, and premium.

Leasehold Interest Factors

A table of leasehold interest factors used in determining the tenant's net leasehold interest is attached to each leasehold interest policy. Form CP 00 60 states that the tenant's net leasehold interest is the amount that, placed at the applicable interest rate, would provide the insured with the equivalent of the gross leasehold interest for each month of the unexpired lease term. ISO provides a series of endorsements (CP 60 05 through CP 60 15) for interest rates ranging from 5 to 15 percent.

The appropriate form, reflecting the current level of interest rates, is selected. The interest rate should be selected carefully in consultation between agent and insured. If interest rates change dramatically during the course of the policy, a rewrite should be considered. If for example, form CP 60 10, showing a 10 percent interest rate is selected, 10 percent is also entered in the interest space on form CP 19 60. The table shows interest factors for months numbered from 1 to 400. These factors are used to compute the amount of net leasehold interest coverage for tenant's lease interest at inception, throughout the policy term, for cancellation, or to determine the amount of loss payable under the policy if the lease is cancelled due to a covered cause of loss.

Although the previous analysis of leasehold interest illustrates its importance in a business's risk management program, leasehold interest insurance is seldom purchased. Many insureds either fail to fully realize the exposure and/or assume the consequences as a self-insured. In any event, leasehold insurance offers an insured the ability to cover a favorable lease arrangement.

Chapter 9

Mortgageholders Errors and Omissions Coverage Form, CP 00 70

Mortgageholders (banks, mortgage companies, credit unions, and other mortgage lenders) have insurance in place on property under mortgage to them in the event of loss or damage, generally in the event the borrower has not complied with mortgage terms to keep appropriate insurance coverage on the property.

The current Mortgageholders Errors and Omissions Coverage Form is CP 00 70 10 12 and covers a lending institution or other mortgage servicing agency against losses arising out of the failure to have proper insurance in force to protect the mortgaged property as a result of error or accidental omission. Such a lack of insurance is usually the result of a mistake in the mortgagee's office procedure. A policy might be entered incorrectly into the mortgagee's data systems or misfiled, for example, and subsequently expire without being renewed. If a fire destroys the property and the mortgagor is unable to continue payments, the institution holding the mortgage would have nothing but ruins upon which to foreclose.

Mortgageholders errors and omissions insurance covers lenders against both direct damage and legal liability losses that may arise out of error or accidental omission in its customary mortgage-handling procedures. It offers four coverage agreements: A and B deal with property coverage, while C and D describe liability coverage. The form itself lists the applicable causes of loss under the provisions for each individual coverage so that no separate causes of loss form needs to be attached.

The Commercial Lines Manual specifies that the Commercial Property Conditions form, CP 00 90, is not to be used with form CP 00 70. Instead, the form itself includes a modified version of those commercial property conditions that apply in addition to the common policy conditions of form IL 00 17. The rules specify that no causes of loss form is attached; rather, each coverage agreement is subject to a different set of perils.

The declarations page indicates the estimated number of mortgages that the insured will own or service during the policy period. The policy is to cover one named insured only and may not be endorsed to the names of servicing agents or other interests.

The Four Coverage Agreements

The four coverages in this form are as follows:

1. Coverage A—Mortgageholder's Interest

2. Coverage B—Property Owned or Held in Trust

3. Coverage C—Mortgageholder's Liability

4. Coverage D—Real Estate Tax Liability

Coverage A—Mortgageholder's Interest

Coverage A promises to pay for loss of the insured's mortgageholders interest. The form defines this interest as the insured's "interest, as mortgageholder, in real or personal property, including your interest in any legal fiduciary capacity." It protects the insured against loss arising from errors and accidental omissions by the insured or a representative in requiring, procuring, or maintaining valid insurance to protect its interest.

Covered property for coverage A may be real property (such as a building where business is conducted) or personal property secured in connection with that real property. Such personal property might include the contents of a business purchased as a going concern; for example, an existing dry cleaner with all the attendant machinery. Coverage A applies during and after the named insured's foreclosure. It also applies to property sold under an agreement whereby the named insured retains title (such as a conditional sales agreement).

Coverage A lists property not covered as accounts, bills, currency, deeds, evidences of debt, money, notes, or securities. The form specifies that food stamps are evidences of debt (and excluded) and that lottery tickets held for sale are not securities (and not excluded). The form also states that land (including the land where the property is located), water, growing crops, or lawns are not covered property. In light of the 2012 revisions, an exception applies to lawns that are part of vegetated roofs.

Another kind of property not covered is electronic data, as defined in the form. A 2012 revision, however, makes an exception for electronic data that is integrated in and operates or controls the building's elevator, light, heating, ventilation, air conditioning, or security system. What must consistently be kept in mind is the reference to *building*, which does not include a structure, a significant difference explained earlier in this book.

Covered causes of loss under coverage A are those that the named insured customarily requires mortgagors to insure. This may range from named perils to unspecified risk of physical loss (special form or open perils). What is customarily required by the mortgageholder is the rule of thumb. In the event of a dispute over what the named insured customarily requires its customers to insure, the Common Policy Conditions, IL 00 17, contains the examination of your books and records provision. By allowing the insurer to examine the mortgageholder's records, what it customarily requires can be readily ascertained.

The form specifies that the causes of loss do not include losses insured under mortgage loan guarantee insurance—insurance that protects the mortgageholder in the event that the mortgagor defaults (often called private mortgage insurance or PMI)—or under title, life, health, or accident insurance policies.

Coverage A extends to losses arising from mortgages owned by others and serviced by the named insured, as if the named insured owned the mortgageholder's interest. This servicing by the named insured must be done through a written contract. Losses are payable jointly to the named insured and the mortgageholder.

Coverage B—Property Owned or Held in Trust

While coverage A protects the insured against loss to property on which it has loaned money, coverage B protects the insured against loss to property it actually owns or in which it has a fiduciary interest.

Coverage B pays for loss to covered property if the loss is not otherwise insured. The absence of insurance must be due to error or accidental omission in the named insured's customary procedure in procuring valid insurance payable to the named insured as owner or trustee. If an insured buys both coverage A and coverage B, recovery under both coverages may be possible. For example, coverage A includes real property "during and after your foreclosure." Since coverage B covers property owned by the insured, a property that has been foreclosed on would fall under both coverages, allowing the insured to collect any remaining balance under B if the limits under A prove inadequate.

However, the limits of coverage A and B cannot be combined to collect an amount greater than the insured's loss.

The list of property not covered is identical to that under Coverage A.

While the covered causes of loss under Coverage A are quite broad (whatever the named insured normally requires its customers to purchase), the perils under Coverage B are limited to fire, lightning, explosion, windstorm or hail, smoke, aircraft or vehicles, riot or civil commotion, sinkhole collapse, and volcanic action. With another 2012 revision, loss or damage from hail to lawns, trees, shrubs, or plants that are part of a vegetated roof is not covered. Also, a 2012 clarification is made with reference to volcanic action. With respect to coverage for volcanic action, as set forth in (a) airborne volcanic blast or shock waves; (b) ash, dust, or particulate matter; or (c) lava flow, all eruptions that occur within any 168-hour period will be considered as a single occurrence. For a further discussion of these perils, see Chapter 3.

Vandalism and sprinkler leakage are not covered under Coverage B, presumably because the insured lender often actually owns vacant property, and these perils become much more of a risk to the insurer.

The additional conditions in form CP 00 70 state that Coverage B protection ends on the earlier of (1) ninety days after the date that the insured acquires the property or the insured's fiduciary interest begins, or (2) the day that other insurance is obtained.

Coverage C—Mortgageholder's Liability

In some cases, a mortgageholder may decide to purchase insurance on a mortgaged property instead of having the customer purchase it. For those instances, the insured lending institution needs Coverage C.

Like the previous coverages, this protects the lender from damages due to errors or omissions in obtaining insurance. However, this time the insurance is purchased for the benefit of the mortgagor. Coverage C is similar to Coverage A in that the perils covered are those that the lender normally requires its customers to purchase. There are exclusions, including losses insured under mortgage guarantee insurance policies or programs or title, life, health, or accident insurance policies. Collapse coverage is limited.

If the insured, in its capacity as a mortgageholder, mortgage fiduciary, or mortgage servicing agency, has agreed with the mortgagor to procure and maintain insurance against loss, thereby relieving the mortgagor of those responsibilities, and then fails to obtain such insurance, Coverage C will pay the legal obligations that subsequently may befall. The duty to defend is also included under Coverage C although this duty ends when the Coverage C limit is used up in settlements or judgments.

In addition to the limits of liability shown, Coverage C provides supplemental payments for the following:

1. All expenses of the insurer

2. Cost of bonds

3. Expenses incurred by the insured at the request of the insurer, including loss of earnings of up to $100 per day

4. Costs taxed against the insured in the suit

5. Pre- and post-judgment interest

Coverage C extends to additional insureds, such as the named insured's partners, executive officers, trustees, directors, managers, and stockholders. They are covered only in their capacity as such. Newly acquired organizations (other than partnerships, joint ventures, or limited liability companies) are automatically insured. Coverage for newly acquired organizations is limited to ninety days from the date of acquisition. The policy specifies that it does not apply to errors and omissions that occurred before the insured acquired the organization.

Coverage D—Real Estate Tax Liability

Some mortgages are set up so that the lending institution pays the real estate taxes on the property. This arrangement may be for the convenience of the borrower, who then makes monthly payments toward the tax, rather than two large payments per year. Or, it may be that the lender has some concerns about payment of the taxes and it may take the responsibility itself. With the proliferation of home mortgages now available with little money as a down payment, lenders routinely require that they collect and pay the real estate taxes via an escrow account until the owner's equity in the home reaches 20 percent.

Problems can arise in such an arrangement if the lender does not pay the taxes. In such a case, the property owner may suffer damages. These damages are insured by Coverage D. The policy limits the amount payable to not more than 15 percent of the limit of insurance for damages in connection with any single mortgage. Explanatory information from ISO states that this limit is expressed as a percentage rather than a dollar amount in order to reflect that property values, upon which real estate taxes are based, usually affect the amount of insurance selected by the mortgagee and thus the revised computation will be more accurately tied to the mortgagee's insurance needs. The 15 percent limit also corresponds to the requirements for real estate tax errors and omissions liability coverage of the Federal National Mortgage Association (Fannie Mae).

Exclusions

The following exclusions apply to all coverages under form CP 00 70: the enforcement of or (in light of the 2012 revisions) the compliance with any ordinance or law; earth movement; governmental action; nuclear hazard; utility services; war; water damage; fungus, wet or dry rot, and bacteria. These exclusions apply "regardless of any other cause or event that contributes concurrently or in any sequence to the loss" (the concurrent causation wording).

One of the 2012 changes affecting earth movement is that earthquake also includes tremors and aftershocks. Another revision, perhaps more significant, is that the earth movement exclusion, which encompasses earthquake, landslide, mine subsidence, earth sinking, and volcanic eruption, applies whether caused by an act of nature or is otherwise caused. The phrase "or is otherwise caused" precludes coverage for man-made events.

The exclusion dealing with water has been broadened and reworded with the 2012 revisions. Since the exclusion is identical to the one in the special causes of loss form, this exclusion is explained in Chapter 3. The coverage form excludes damage from the "discharge, dispersal, seepage, migration, release or escape of 'pollutants,'" without the concurrent causation wording. However, if the lender customarily requires its customers to insure the property under the Causes of Loss – Special form, CP 10 30, pollution losses caused by one of the specified causes of loss defined in the policy are covered. Following the language that has been added to other forms in the commercial property program, *pollutants* are defined as "any solid, liquid, gaseous or thermal irritant or contaminant, including smoke, vapor, soot, fumes, acids, alkalis, chemicals and waste." Waste includes materials to be recycled, reconditioned, or reclaimed.

Losses caused by artificially generated electrical, magnetic, or electromagnetic energy are excluded but resulting fire loss is covered. Also excluded is any event that occurs thirty or more days after a lender knows that an error or omission may have occurred.

Newly added with the 2012 revisions is an exclusion for loss or damage to lawns, trees, shrubs, or plants that are part of a vegetated roof, caused by or resulting from (1) dampness or dryness of the atmosphere; (2) changes in or extremes of temperature; (3) disease; (4) frost or hail; or (5) rain, snow, ice, or sleet.

The policy excludes loss or damage caused by or resulting from the insured's failure to obtain, maintain, or process title insurance, mortgage guarantee, life, or health or accident insurance.

The neglect exclusion removes coverage if the insured does not use reasonable means to protect property from further loss.

A set of exclusions that was introduced to avoid coverage under the concurrent causation doctrine corresponds to exclusions already found in the CP 10 30. Excluded as part of this group are loss or damage caused by or resulting from collapse (except as modified by the additional coverage for collapse); weather conditions; acts or decisions (and the failure to act or decide) of individuals or groups; and faulty, inadequate, or defective (1) planning, zoning, development, surveying, siting; (2) design, specifications, workmanship, repair, construction, renovation, remodeling, grading, compaction; (3) materials used in repair, construction, renovation, or remodeling; or (4) maintenance—in regard to any property, whether on or off the described premises. However, if loss or damage by a covered cause of loss results from one these excluded events, coverage applies to the resulting loss or damage. This same exclusion is treated in more detail in Chapter 4.

The 06 07 edition introduced a production errors exclusion. Some examples of errors in production are introduction of foreign matter, addition of a wrong ingredient or element, and wrong measure of a particular element. An error in the production process is a business risk; it is not a peril intended to be insured under fire/allied lines property insurance. In certain circumstances, some claims may involve errors in production and allege that the need to destroy a now-useless product constitutes physical loss or damage to that product, thereby asserting a broad and nontraditional interpretation of the concept of physical damage under an insurance contract.

ISO added the following provision to address errors in production, shown in the context of CP 10 30, the Causes of Loss - Special Form:

B. Exclusions

   5. Additional Exclusion

      The following provisions apply only to the specified property.

Loss Or Damage To Products

We will not pay for loss or damage to any merchandise, goods or other product caused by or resulting from error or omission by any person or entity (including those having possession under an arrangement where work or a portion of the work is outsourced) in any stage of the development, production or use of the product, including planning, testing, processing, packaging, installation, maintenance or repair. This exclusion applies to any effect that compromises the form, substance or quality of the product. But if such error or omission results in a Covered Cause of Loss, we will pay for the loss or damage caused by that Covered Cause of Loss.

The impact is that coverage intent is reinforced, with an explicit provision, in light of sporadic claims being asserted in contradiction of intent. With respect to individual insurers, impact may vary based on past claims and loss settlement history.

Limits of Insurance

In the event of a covered loss, the most the insurer will pay is the amount shown on the policy declarations, subject to certain limitations. Under Coverage A—Mortgageholder's Interest, or Coverage B—Property Owned or Held in Trust, limit of insurance is the least of the following:

1. The amount that would have been payable by the borrower's property insurance if no error or accidental omission in its pro-curement or maintenance by the lender had occurred. The mort-gageholders E&O policy reduces this payment by the amount of any other insurance payable to the lender.

2. The amount that would have been payable under policies that the lender should have obtained but failed to do so.

3. The amount of the lender's mortgageholder's interest.

For Coverage C—Mortgageholder's Liability, the insurer's limit of liability is shown on the declarations page. For Coverage D—Real Estate Tax Liability, the insurer's limit of liability is 15 percent of the amount of insurance as shown on the declarations page. This limit applies on a per mortgage basis.

Additional Coverage—Collapse

Collapse coverage applies under CP 00 70 for covered property. The coverage is for an *abrupt* collapse, which the form describes as "an abrupt falling down or caving in of a building or any part of a building with the result that the building or part of the building cannot be occupied for its intended purpose."

Collapse is covered if due to hidden decay; hidden insect or vermin damage; use of defective materials or methods in construction, remodeling, or renovation if the collapse occurs during construction, remodeling, or renovation; use of defective materials or methods in construction, remodeling, or renovation if the collapse occurs after the construction, remodeling, or renovation, but only if caused by hidden decay or hidden insect or vermin damage, a specified cause of loss, breakage of building glass, weight of people or personal property, or weight of rain that collects on a roof.

As in the Building and Personal Property Coverage Form, the 2000 edition added a caveat to the hidden decay and insect damage causes. Such decay or damage is not a covered cause of collapse if the existence of the decay or damage is known to an insured prior to a collapse. Under previous wording, an insured may have known about the damage, but if it was hidden, the BPP form would cover resulting collapse.

The coverage does not apply to buildings or parts of buildings that are in danger of falling down; a part of a building that is standing; or a building that is standing or any part of a building that is standing even if it shows evidence of sagging, bending, cracking, bulging, leaning, expansion, shrinkage, or settling.

As with other causes of loss forms, personal property must be located inside a building to be covered for collapse. The collapse must be due to one of the covered causes of collapse.

Additional Coverage—Limited Coverage for Fungus, Wet Rot, Dry Rot, and Bacteria

This additional coverage was introduced in the CP 00 70 04 02, at the same time mold and fungus treatment was revised in other parts of the commercial property program.

This coverage applies when fungus (a defined term) or rot or bacteria is the result of a specified cause of loss other than fire or lightning or is caused by flood, provided the flood coverage endorsement applies.

The coverage applies to the following:

1. Direct physical loss or damage caused by fungus, wet or dry rot, or bacteria, including the cost of removal

2. The cost to tear out and replace any part of the building or other property as needed to gain access to the damaged area

3. The cost of testing performed after removal, repair, replacement, or restoration, provided there is a reason to believe that fungus, wet or dry rot, or bacteria is present

This coverage is limited to $15,000 in an annual period for all loss or occurrences. With respect to particular occurrences that result in fungus, wet or dry rot, or bacteria, the insurer will not pay more than $15,000 even if the fungus continues to be present or recurs in a later policy period.

Another clause makes clear that this is an additional coverage but does not increase the overall limit of insurance. For example, if fungus and other covered damage exceed the limit, no more than the limits will be paid (not the limit plus $15,000).

Added with the 2012 revisions is an exclusion for lawns, trees, shrubs, or plants that are a part of a vegetated roof.

Additional Conditions

Form CP 00 70 contains one additional condition that applies only to coverage A, four additional conditions that apply to coverage B, and two additional conditions that apply to coverages C and D.

The insurer may, in concert with other insurers on the risk, pay the lender the full outstanding amount of any mortgage, even if that amount is greater than the amount of the loss. Then, the insured lender must assign the mortgage and all other securities pertaining to it to the insurance company.

In the event of loss or damage under coverage B, the insurer reserves the choice of four options:

1. Pay the value of lost or damaged property

2. Pay the cost of repairing or replacing the lost or damaged property

3. Take all or any part of the property at an agreed or appraised value

4. Repair, rebuild, or replace the property with other property of like kind and quality

In any case, the policy restricts the insured's recovery to its financial interest in the covered property. Furthermore, the value of lost or damaged property is determined at actual cash value as of the time of loss or damage.

If either the insured or insurer recovers lost property, it must notify the other party. The option of whether the insured takes back the property remains with the insured. If the insured chooses to take the property back, the amount of the claim must be repaid to the insurer. The insurer, on the other hand, agrees to pay recovery expenses and to pay for repairs to the property (up to the limit of liability).

As mentioned under the discussion of coverage B, the protection ends on the earlier of (1) ninety days after the date the insured acquires the property or the insured's fiduciary interest begins, or (2) the day that other insurance is obtained.

Coverages C and D (mortgageholders liability and real estate tax liability) contain two additional conditions: bankruptcy and separation of insureds. Even if the insured declares bankruptcy, the insurer is still obligated under Coverages C and D. The separation condition clarifies that the policy applies separately to each insured except for the limits of liability.

Conditions Applicable to All Coverages

The following conditions apply to the entire policy, though some apply differently to different portions:

1. **Abandonment.** As with other property policies, no property may be abandoned to the insurer.

2. **Appraisal (Coverages A and B Only).** As with other property policies, the mortgageholders E&O form sets up a procedure for settling differences regarding the value of a loss. If the parties cannot agree, each hires its own appraiser, and the two appraisers then hire an umpire. After reviewing the facts, the decision of any two of the three is binding on all parties.

3. **Duties in the Event of Loss.** Because this form covers both property and liability, different conditions exist for the different coverages. In the event of a loss under the property coverages (A and B), the insured must do the following:

   a. Notify the police in the event of a crime

   b. Give prompt notice to the insurer

c.   Protect the property from further damage and keep a record of expenses in connection with this activity (Although anything spent by the insured in this regard does not increase the limit of liability, the insurer will not pay for subsequent losses from perils not covered. The insured must also separate the damaged and undamaged property for inspection by the insurer.)

d.   Provide the insurer with inventories of both the damaged and undamaged property

e.   Allow the insurer to examine books and records and permit the insurer to take samples of damaged and undamaged property for testing and analysis

f.   Submit a signed, sworn proof of loss within sixty days of request by the insurer

g.   Cooperate with the insurer

The policy gives the insurer the right to examine any insured under oath about the claim "while not in the presence of any other insured." Courts have held that the term *examine* encompasses both oral and written questioning, and the right to isolate the insured from others was made clear after a Missouri court ruled that the insurer had no such right without an explicit provision. (See *U.S Fidelity & Guar. Co. v. Hill*, 722 S.W.2d 609 [Mo. App. 1986].)

In the event of a claim under coverages C or D, the insured must do the following:

a.   Give the insurer prompt notice of the claim or suit

b.   Send the insurer copies of all correspondence and other papers in connection with the claim

c.   Authorize the insurer to obtain any necessary information

d.   Cooperate with the insurer

e.   Assist the insurer in enforcing its right of subrogation

f.   Give a signed statement of facts regarding the claim

The insured may not make any payment or assume any obligation without the consent of the insurer.

4. **Insurance under Two or More Coverages.** It is possible that more than one of the form's coverages may apply. In this case, the insurer still pays no more than the actual amount of the loss.

5. **Legal Action against Us.** Under coverages A and B, no one may bring a suit against the insurer unless all terms of the policy have been met. No suit may be brought later than two years after the insured discovers the error or omission.

   As with Coverages A and B, under Coverages C and D no one may bring a suit against the insurer unless all terms of the policy have been met. Also, the policy prohibits anyone from joining the insurer in a suit against the insured.

   After an agreed settlement or actual trial resulting in a judgment against the insured, suit may be brought to recover the amount due. The form defines an agreed settlement as a settlement and release of liability signed by all parties.

6. **Liberalization.** If within the forty-five days prior to the policy's inception the insurer adopts a policy provision that broadens coverage without an additional premium that provision automatically applies.

7. **Loss Payment.** Once the insured submits a proof of loss and the parties reach an agreement or an award is made in arbitration as to the amount of the loss, the insurer will pay the loss within thirty days.

8. **Other Insurance.** The policy shares pro rata with other insurance containing the same plan, terms, conditions, and provisions. However, it is excess over any other type of insurance—whether or not the insured can collect on the other policy.

9. **Policy Period, Coverage Territory.** Coverage under the mortgageholders coverage form is occurrence-based. Coverage applies to loss or damage, claims, or suits (including arbitration proceedings) arising from an event that "occurs during the policy period shown in the

Declarations." Therefore, even if an error or accidental omission happens outside the policy period, this coverage applies as long as the loss or damage occurs within the policy period.

This form specifies the territory by limiting the location of the mortgaged property to the United States, its territories and possessions, and Puerto Rico.

10. **Transfer of Rights of Recovery against Others to Us.** The insured transfers any rights to recover from another under all coverages to the insurer, to the extent of the insurer's payment. In addition, the insured must do nothing to impair the insurer's rights.

   Under coverages A and B, the insured may—prior to any loss—waive his rights against another party if the waiver is in writing. The insured may make a post-loss waiver against any of the following:

   a.   Someone else covered by the policy

   b.   A firm that owns or controls the insured

   c.   A firm that the insured owns or controls

   d.   The insured's tenant

11. **Vacancy.** The insurance does not cover damage to buildings that have been vacant for more than sixty days prior to the loss. It also does not cover suits arising out of such buildings. Under the policy, a vacant building is one where at least 31 percent of its square footage is not rented and used by the tenant to conduct normal operations or where at least 31 percent of the square footage is not used by the building owner.

12. **Your Duties.** In addition to the specific duties after a loss, the insured has other, ongoing duties. This condition requires the insured to make every reasonable effort to procure and maintain valid insurance (either a valid policy or other evidence of insurance) on the mortgaged property. In the case of Coverage D, the insured must make prompt payment of real estate taxes on behalf of the mortgagor.

Definitions

The policy concludes with the definitions of six terms. *Fungus*, *pollutants*, *specified causes of loss*, and *suit* are defined the same as in the BPP form.

Mortgageholder's interest is what the policy protects—the lienholder's (named insured's) interest in mortgaged property. *Valid insurance* refers to what must be missing in order for the mortgageholders E&O policy to be activated.

Chapter 10

Tobacco Sales Warehouses Coverage Form, CP 00 80

The Tobacco Sales Warehouses Coverage form, CP 00 80, is an annual reporting form that covers direct physical loss of or damage to tobacco in sales warehouses. The tobacco warehouse and any other business personal property must still be covered on the BPP form, CP 00 10. The form is revised occasionally as are other forms in the commercial property program. The edition history includes the following:

- CP 00 80 07 88

- CP 00 80 10 90

- CP 00 80 10 91

- CP 00 80 06 95

- CP 00 80 02 00

- CP 00 80 10 00

- CP 00 80 06 07

- CP 00 80 10 12

Because tobacco is stored in a warehouse only long enough to be sold at auction and shipped, the policy term is different from other property policies. The coverage applies only at the described premises and begins at 12:01 A.M. of the fifteenth day before the opening of the regular auction season. It ends at 12:01 A.M. of the fifteenth day following the official closing date of the regular auction season. The length of the auction season varies according to local custom.

The Tobacco Sales Warehouses Coverage Form requires the insured to report tobacco sales at each location and to pay premium on the amount of sales reported. These reports must be filed within thirty days of the close of the auction season. Reports may be in any format provided they are in writing.

Covered Property

Tobacco in the described warehouse is the only type of property covered by this form. The tobacco may be "leaf, loose, scrap and stem." It may either be the tobacco of others of which the insured has care, custody, or control (a bailment situation) or it may be tobacco that the insured has purchased and is holding for resale. The tobacco is covered for whatever causes of loss the insured chooses (basic, broad, or special).

The form specifies the following types of property as not covered:

a.   Growing crops or water

b.   Tobacco insured elsewhere that is more specifically described

c.   Tobacco outside buildings or structures

d.   Tobacco while waterborne

e.   Contraband or property in the course of illegal transportation or trade

Additional Coverages

The form provides additional coverages for debris removal, preservation of property, fire department service charge, and pollutant cleanup and removal. These are the same as the additional coverages in the BPP form.

A rare conflict could theoretically arise under the additional coverage of preservation of property. For example, a fire occurs at a tobacco warehouse located next to a river. The insured must move the undamaged tobacco away in order to protect it. If the insured moves the tobacco onto a boat and it becomes damaged while on the boat, a possible conflict exists because the definition of covered property excludes tobacco that is waterborne. The additional coverage of preservation of property provides thirty-day coverage for any direct physical loss or damage to the tobacco while it is being moved or stored at another location. Whether this would include the tobacco being temporarily stored on the boat might give rise to a coverage dispute.

A more plausible scenario might be that the no-coverage status for tobacco outside of buildings and structures might give rise to a conflict with the preservation of property additional coverage. Say, for example, the insured removes tobacco from a burning warehouse and temporarily stores it under tarps. Rain subsequently damages the tobacco before it can be moved inside. Close cooperation with the insurer's loss teams in such a case would be desirable.

Coverage Extension

As in the BPP form, the Tobacco Sales Warehouses Coverage Form provides $10,000 coverage for property off premises.

Exclusions and Limitations

These are described on the appropriate causes of loss form.

Additional Conditions

Although this section is near the end of the form, some of the previous provisions make reference to its terms, hence its discussion here.

Reports of Value: The form is a reporting form. The policy requires a report within thirty days of the close of the auction season that contains the total weight in pounds of the tobacco that the insured sold or resold during the season and the total price per pound.

Premium Adjustment: The insurer bases the final premium for the policy on the information contained in these reports and charges additional premium or makes a refund.

Need for Full Reports: While not labeled a coinsurance penalty, the policy operates to penalize the insured in the event the report does not equal 100 percent of the values at risk. In this case, the reported value is divided by the actual value at risk. That figure is then multiplied by the amount of the loss to arrive at a final payment.

For newly acquired locations (those acquired after the last report of values), the values at all locations are divided by the values at risk at all locations (including the new locations) and then multiplied by the amount of the loss to arrive at a final payment.

Deductible

The deductible condition is the same as that in the BPP form with one exception. The policy applies the deductible after any deduction calculated under the "need for full reports."

Loss Conditions

The loss conditions of form CP 00 80 are the same as in the BPP form, except for the valuation clause. Damaged tobacco is valued at the average price for similar grades and types. The average is based on the sale price on the day of the loss, two days prior to the loss, and two days following the loss.

The prices are those at the warehouse nearest to where the loss occurs. Total sales are divided by total number of pounds sold to arrive at an average price. The final price is determined by subtracting any unearned warehouse charges, unearned auction fees, and unpaid government taxes from the coverage price.

Definitions

The only word defined is *pollutants*. It is the same definition as in the BPP form: "any solid, liquid, gaseous or thermal irritant or contaminant, including smoke, vapor, soot, fumes, acids, alkalis, chemicals and waste. Waste includes materials to be recycled, reconditioned or reclaimed."

Chapter 11

Condominium Association Coverage Form, CP 00 17, and Commercial Condominium Unit-Owners Coverage Form, CP 00 18

Condominium Association Coverage Form, CP 00 17

A condominium association consists of a group of individual condominium unit-owners and their undivided ownership interest in the building(s) in which the units are situated. The condominium association is managed by a condominium board (made up of unit-owners) that sets forth the insurance responsibilities of both the association and its unit-owners. Since condominium association agreements differ and applicable state laws may apply, it is important to review the association agreement. This is particularly important in coordinating coverage between the association and its unit-owners on such things as building fixtures, built-in appliances, and improvements and betterments that may be insured under the association's or the unit-owners' coverage.

Condominiums are typically occupied by their owners as a residence under a Homeowners HO 00 06, Condominium Unit-owners Policy, with the building (being owned in common by all unit-owners) insured on a master policy. For property owned by condominium associations (such as buildings, clubhouses, and pools), ISO has form CP 00 The Condominium Association Coverage Form editions history is as follows:

- CP 00 17 07 88

- CP 00 17 10 90

- CP 00 17 10 91

- CP 00 17 06 95

- CP 00 17 02 00

- CP 00 17 10 00

- CP 00 17 04 02

- CP 00 17 06 07

- CP 00 17 10 12

Form CP 00 17 is similar to CP 00 10 in most respects. It has been modified to better fit the needs of the condominium association. This discussion centers on those differences.

Covered Property

Like the Building and Personal Property Coverage Form, CP 00 10, the Condominium Association Coverage Form covers items such as the building, structures (which was added to this and other coverage forms in 2010), completed additions, and permanently installed equipment. The BPP form covers appliances used for refrigerating, ventilating, cooking, dishwashing, or laundering. The condominium association form limits coverage to those items not contained within individual units. This places the responsibility for insuring such items on the unit-owner—the person who actually owns the equipment—but would provide coverage for association-provided facilities.

Form CP 00 17 adds a sixth class of covered property consisting of certain items within individual units if the condominium association agreement or bylaws require the association to insure such property. This property consists of the following:

1. Fixtures, improvements, and alterations that are a part of the building or structure

2. Appliances, such as those used for refrigerating, ventilating, cooking, dishwashing, laundering, security, or housekeeping

The important wording here is "if the condominium association agreement or bylaws requires." As indicated earlier, when writing coverage for a condominium association, it is always important to review the association agreement and the bylaws to be certain about whose responsibility it is to insure various items.

Carpeting in Condominiums

Inexperienced adjusters may have problems adjusting losses to carpeting, wallpaper, and paint inside a condominium unit under form CP 00 17. Conventional wisdom is that if the condo master deed and bylaws require the association to insure, for example, all units, common elements, and limited common elements, the CP 00 17 would pick up coverage for carpet, wallpaper, and paint. Although association agreements vary, typically limited common elements are outside of the building but serve only one unit. These include porches, sidewalks leading to the door, and areas between privacy fences.

In many losses, the damage is confined to a single unit and it is necessary to replace vinyl or carpet and padding because of the buckling of the subflooring. Confusion occurs in trying to determine which policy covers the damage.

The HO 00 06, Condominium Unit-owners Policy, contains a statement making it excess over any recoverable insurance held by the association. The CP 00 17 is specific that it is primary and not contributing. There is some question regarding the interaction with the HO-6 in the case of a large deductible on the CP 00 17. Specifically, if the damage is under the amount of the deductible on the CP 00 17, would the HO-6 become primary?

At one time condo unit-owners were considered to have purchased air space, and everything from bare walls out was considered the owner's responsibility to insure. Now the condo association master policy may cover individual unit owners' fixtures, improvements, and alterations that are part of the building structure as long as the association agreement requires it. Improvements and alterations that are part of the building include, but are not limited to, paint, wallpaper, lighting fixtures, and counters. Appliances, such as dishwashers, are also covered.

Coverage for carpeting follows the same logic. If wall-to-wall carpeting is included in the mortgage, it is part of the realty and thus falls under the improvements and alterations that are part of the building structure. If not so designated, then generally where carpet is laid over an unfinished floor it is considered part of the building and would be covered as such. If the carpet is laid over a finished floor, and its removal would not materially damage the floor, courts have generally considered it contents. Coverage would therefore be found under the HO-6.

> If the unit-owner receives no payment from the association policy because the loss is under the deductible, then the unit owner's coverage becomes primary. The purpose is to prevent double payment for a loss, not to prevent payment for a claim.

The coverage for business personal property is more limited on the condo association form than on the BPP form. Like the CP 00 10, the CP 00 17 covers the following:

1.   The insured's interest in the labor, materials, or services that the condo association furnishes or arranges on personal property of others

2.   Leased personal property that, via contract, is the insured association's responsibility to insure

3.   Personal property of others in the condo association's care, custody, or control, which must be located in or on the building or structure described in the declarations or in the open (or in a vehicle) within 100 feet of the described premises

The unique provision of the CP 00 17 is that, in addition to covering the personal property owned by the association, it also covers personal property owned indivisibly by all unit-owners (such as pool furniture). The form specifies that property belonging to a unit-owner is not covered.

The property not covered section, which includes certain exceptions, is the same as in form CP 00 10.

Other Provisions

As with the CP 00 10, the CP 00 17 covers the property for whatever causes of loss form is attached. The CP 00 17 provides the same additional coverages: debris removal, which is revised extensively with the 2012 revisions; preservation of property; fire department service charge, also revised in 2012; pollutant cleanup and removal; increased cost of construction; and electronic data (see Chapter 2). CP 00 17 also provides the same extensions of coverage, including 2012 revisions, as the CP 00 10: newly acquired or constructed property, personal effects and property of others, valuable papers and records (other than electronic data), property off-premises, outdoor property, nonowned detached trailers, and a 2012 addition covering business personal property temporarily in portable storage units (see Chapter 2). The limits of insurance provision also reads the same in both forms (see Chapter 6).

The loss conditions are the same in both forms with three exceptions. Often, a condominium association appoints an insurance trustee to handle claims with its insurer. If that is the case, then the insurer agrees to pay the trustee.

The second difference addresses the issue of a unit-owner's insurance. If a unit-owner has insurance on property that is also covered by the association policy, the association policy is primary and does not contribute with the unit-owner's policy. The unit-owner's policy then becomes excess coverage.

The final difference is that the insurer agrees upfront to waive any subrogation rights against any unit-owner. In other commercial property forms, it is a simple matter for a building owner to waive subrogation rights against a tenant after a loss. The condo association form requires such a waiver.

The Condominium Association Coverage Form has the same two additional conditions as does the BPP form: coinsurance and mortgageholders.

The final two sections contain identical optional coverages: agreed value, inflation guard, replacement cost, and replacement cost for personal property of others (see Chapter 2.); and a definition of *pollutants*: "any solid, liquid, gaseous or thermal irritant or contaminant, including smoke, vapor, soot, fumes, acids, alkalis, chemicals and waste. Waste includes materials to be recycled, reconditioned or reclaimed."

Commercial Condominium Unit-Owners Coverage Form, CP 00 18

Although most condominiums are residential type with unit-owners being insured under the Homeowners HO 00 06 policy, condominiums may also include commercial establishments with coverage provided under the Commercial Condominium Unit-Owners Coverage Form, CP 00 18. The current edition is CP 00 18 10 12, and the edition history is the same as the Condominium Association Coverage Form outlined in the previous section. The form is available for business or professional firms that own commercial condominium units. The form closely follows the BPP form, CP 00 10, but is modified to fit the needs of commercial condominium unit-owners. In addition, ISO has provided an optional endorsement, form CP 04 18, offering loss assessment coverage and miscellaneous real property coverage.

The following is a discussion of the current form, with differences from the previous form and the CP 00 10 noted.

Property

The first difference between the CP 00 10 and the CP 00 18 is that the condominium unit-owners form has no provision to cover any building or structure property other than coverage on building or structure fixtures, improvements, and alterations owned by the unit-owner. It begins with "your business personal property."

Property not covered includes fixtures, improvements, and alterations that are a part of the building, and appliances "such as those used for refrigerating, ventilating, cooking, dishwashing, laundering, security, or housekeeping," when the condominium association agreement requires that such property be insured by the association. Note that this provision is an absolute exclusion—unlike the provision of form HO 00 06 (covering owner-occupied condos used as a residence) where the unit-owners coverage is excess over the association coverage in the same situation—and it applies even when the association insurance is not properly written and does not, in fact, provide the coverage required by the agreement.

A potential problem here is that business personal property includes "property located in or on the building or structure described in the Declarations." However, item (2) of the kind of property covered lists "[f]urniture, improvements and alterations making up a part of the building and owned by you." No reference is made to those kinds of property on or within a structure, a term newly added with the 2012 revisions. Whether this is intentional or an omission is uncertain. Whatever the case may be, this affects not only the covered property section but also property contained within a unit that is required to be insured by the condominium association.

Additional Coverages and Coverage Extensions

The unit-owners form offers these additional coverages, just as does the BPP form, including the 2012 revisions: debris removal, preservation of property, fire department service charge, pollutant cleanup and removal, and electronic data. The similar coverage extensions are newly acquired property, personal effects and property of others, valuable papers and records (other than electronic data), property off-premises, outdoor property, nonowned detached trailers, and business personal property temporarily in portable storage units.

Limits and Deductible

The limits of insurance and deductible provisions of the CP 00 18 are the same as in the BPP form.

Loss Conditions

The loss conditions of form CP 00 18 duplicate those in the CP 00 10 with one addition, condominium association insurance. The unit-owner's policy is excess of such other insurance. It is not intended to contribute with the other policy.

Other Provisions

Finally, these provisions of the CP 00 18 are identical to those in the CP 00 10: the coinsurance additional condition and the optional coverages of agreed value, inflation guard, replacement cost, and replacement cost for the property of others.

The terms *pollutants* and *stock* are defined terms in the unit-owners coverage form as they are in the BPP form.

Chapter 12

Legal Liability Coverage Form, CP 00 40

There are situations where something different than direct property damage coverage, such as that found in the BPP form, is called for. Businesses may have leased machinery and equipment that the lease calls on the business to insure or perhaps leases real property for all or part of its operations. Similarly, a business may have property of others in its care, custody, and control for servicing. These exposures can be insured under the BPP form with coverage triggered on a direct no fault basis, or alternatively, under the Legal Liability Coverage Form, CP 00 40, with coverage triggered on a legal liability basis. Due to this difference, the legal liability coverage will have a lower premium structure.

The Legal Liability Coverage Form, CP 00 40, is part of the commercial property program, although it is actually a liability coverage and closer in format to the Commercial General Liability (CGL) policy. The reason the Legal Liability Coverage Form is part of the property coverage program is because the actual loss, for which the insured is legally liable, must be from a covered cause (peril).

The Legal Liability Coverage Form edition history includes the following:

- CP 00 40 07 88

- CP 00 40 10 90

- CP 00 40 06 95

- CP 00 40 10 00

- CP 00 40 04 02

- CP 00 40 06 07

- CP 00 40 10 12

The form covers the insured's legal liability for loss or damage to real and personal property of others. The property must be in the insured's care, custody, or control, and the damage must be caused by a covered causes of loss. It also covers loss of use of the property and provides defense coverage. The loss to covered property must be caused by accident, thus eliminating coverage for intentional damage brought about by the insured. The loss must be caused by an insured peril, as indicated on the appropriate causes of loss form.

Coverage can be applied to commercial property—mercantile or manufacturing, building or contents—in the care, custody, or control of the insured. However, ISO rules say that form CP 00 40 cannot be used for a contractor while working on a building. A contractor needs a Commercial General Liability (CGL) policy. However, such a policy still excludes damage to work performed. The CGL covers the contractor for damage done to a part of the building not directly being worked on.

Manual rules state that the policy declarations (Legal Liability Coverage Schedule form, CP DS 05) must include a precise description of the insured's business operations, location, and the property of others for which the insured may be legally liable. In actual practice, it is most often written for the tenant of a commercial building, where the tenant is—by lease terms—responsible for damage to the building.

Legal liability coverage may be written under a separate policy or included as a separate item in the same policy with property coverages.

The declarations page must indicate a definite description of the insured's business operation and location, a description of the property of others for which the insured may be legally liable, and separate limits of liability that apply for this coverage on or in each building.

The amount of insurance is usually based on replacement cost of the property, though consideration should also be given to the fact that coverage contemplates protection for the insured's liability as respects loss of use as well as damage or destruction of the property itself. Thus, the lessee of a building that has a replacement cost of $100,000 and earns $2,000 per month in rental fees might purchase legal liability insurance with a limit of $112,000—replacement cost plus rent for a maximum of six months of reconstruction. Obviously, a good deal of speculation and investigation is involved in the final selection of the amount of coverage. What are the chances of the building being totally destroyed, what are the prospects for speedy reconstruction, what does the lease have to say about continuation of rent payments while the building is shut down, and so on?

Tenants of multi-occupant buildings purchase legal liability coverage (in the CGL policy) on *that part of the building* in their care, custody, or control. Coverage for their liability as respects the remainder of the building is properly the subject of general liability insurance—with attention to the matter of adequate property damage limits.

Many times the named insured under the form may be required to add different entities as additional insureds under the policy. Such entities may include someone buying the building under a land contract; co-owners of the premises, with respect to their liability as such; and mortgagees, assignees, or receivers. The ISO rules state that most may be added without an extra premium charge. However, adding the following additional insureds requires a surcharge of 25 percent: (1) general lessees, managers, or operators of premises in policies covering tenants or lessees of such premises; and (2) employees other than executive officers or partners in policies covering their employers. A general lessee of a multi-tenant building cannot purchase a policy and include the interests of each of the tenants as additional insureds. However, each of the tenants can purchase a policy in which the interest of the general lessee is covered as an additional insured.

The following may not be added as additional insureds at any time: (1) contractors or subcontractors in policies covering tenants or lessees of premises; and (2) tenants, lessees, concessionaires, or exhibitors, in policies covering general lessees, managers, or operators of premises.

Coverage

The insuring agreement of form CP 00 40 requires the insurer to "pay those sums that the insured becomes legally obligated to pay as damages because of direct physical loss or damage, including loss of use, to covered property caused by accident and arising out of any covered cause of loss."

The form describes covered property as "tangible property of others in your care, custody or control and described in the declarations." With one exception, there is no coverage for electronic data under the legal liability coverage form. With the 2012 revisions, covered property includes electronic data that is integrated in and operates or controls the building's elevator, light, heating, ventilation, air conditioning, or security system. The form's definitions of *electronic data* and *computer programs* are the same as in the BPP form.

The phrase *legally obligated* is used in the insuring agreement to emphasize that the insurance is in no way direct coverage. The policy does not cover damage to the property; it covers the insured's responsibility following damage as imposed by law. Naturally, the insurer will use whatever legal defenses are available to the insured in resisting the assessment of responsibility. The policy reserves the insurer's right to investigate and settle any claim or suit.

The second aspect of legal liability coverage is that the insurer has the right and duty to defend any suit seeking damages and will bear the cost of defending a suit against the insured. A suit includes an arbitration proceeding. Payment of legal expenses is in addition to the limit set forth in the policy.

The insurer agrees to pay the cost of defense attorneys and court costs. The amount payable for these expenses are limited only by the provision that the insurer's obligation to defend ends when the insurer has paid the limit in payment of judgments or settlements. In other words, the insurer must pay whatever the insured's legal expenses are (even if they exceed the policy limit) until a judgment or settlement is reached and the amount of the limit has been paid out in the judgment or settlement.

The form also agrees to make the following supplemental payments in addition to the limit of liability:

1. All expenses that the insurer incurs

2. The cost of bonds to release attachments

3. All reasonable expenses incurred by the insured at the insurer's request, including actual loss of earnings up to $250 a day because of time off work

4. All costs taxed against the insured in the suit

5. Prejudgment interest awarded against the insured

6. All interest on the full amount of any judgment that accrues after entry of the judgment

Coverage Extensions—Additional Insureds and Newly Acquired Organizations

If the named insured is a partnership or corporation, partners, executive officers, trustees, directors, and stockholders are additional insureds while acting within the scope of their duties, as are the managers of a limited liability company. Other employees may be named as additional insureds by endorsement, subject to an additional premium charge equal to 25 percent of the policy premium. Coverage under this extension does not increase the limit of insurance.

If the policy is appropriately endorsed, it is permissible (with two exceptions) to include others as insureds. The exceptions are a policy issued to a tenant or lessee may not also cover the insurable interest of a contractor or subcontractor, and a policy issued to a general lessee (one who leases an entire premises and sublets to others) or manager may not include the interest of a tenant, concessionaire, or exhibitor.

The form covers newly acquired organizations within the applicable limit of insurance for legal liability arising out of direct physical loss that occurs after the insured acquires or forms the organization. An insured includes any organization (other than a partnership, joint venture, or limited liability company) that the insured newly acquires or forms and over which the insured maintains ownership or majority interest, provided there is no other insurance available to that organization. This extension of coverage runs for ninety days after the acquisition or formation of the organization, unless the policy expires first.

Newly Acquired Property

Form CP 00 40 allows for limited automatic coverage for property (building and personal) that comes under the insured's care, custody, or control during the policy period. In order for a building to be covered by this provision, it must be intended for similar use to the one described in the declarations or for warehouse use. Coverage under the extension ends at the earliest of policy expiration; thirty days after the insured acquires care, custody, or control; or the insured reports values to the insurer. Additional premium is charged and payments under the newly acquired property extension are in addition to the limits of insurance.

Coverage for a total loss of all newly acquired covered buildings arising out of one accident is limited to $250,000 at each building. The building limit can be increased by adding endorsement CP 04 25.

Newly acquired personal property must be either at a location owned by or in the care, custody, or control of the insured at the time of loss. There is no provision for adding newly acquired property that is in the insured's care, custody, or control at fairs or exhibitions. Total coverage for loss to this personal property resulting from one accident is $100,000 at each building. Endorsement CP 04 25 cannot be used to increase this limit.

Causes of Loss and Exclusions

Under the form any of the three causes of loss forms used with the commercial property program may be employed (basic, broad, or special). (See Chapter 3 for a discussion of the basic and broad causes of loss, including the 2012 changes, and Chapter 4 dealing with the special causes of loss form.) The Causes of Loss – Special form, CP 10 30, however, may not be attached when coverage is written for personal property of others in the insured's care, custody, or control or warehouse risks involving personal property. Presumably these ineligible risks involve *business personal property* of others. However, the rules do not specify that limitation.

Since most if not all of the perils covered (extended coverage, vandalism and malicious mischief, or the open perils of form CP 10 30) typically involve either fortuitous events or acts of others, insureds sometimes question the logic of including these perils in their legal liability protection. Some would argue that the likelihood of their becoming legally involved seems remote. Nevertheless, the chance is there and it is just as expensive to defend a groundless suit as any other kind. The cost of defense and coverage, contrasted with the normally very slight expense of adding these perils, is usually enough to balance the decision. And the extended coverage perils of smoke, vehicle damage, and explosion are clearly valid items for inclusion in the legal liability contract.

Both the basic and broad causes of loss forms exclude damage from a vehicle owned or operated by the named insured in the course of business. Employees are outside the scope of the exclusion except with respect to vehicles owned by the insured.

In relation to legal liability coverage, all three causes of loss forms contain a contractual liability exclusion. This exclusion provides that the insurer will not "defend any claim or 'suit', or pay damages that [the insured is] legally liable to pay, solely by reason of [the insured's] assumption of liability in a contract or agreement."

Loss Conditions

Since the CP 00 40 covers liability, the loss conditions read more like those of the CGL than those of a commercial property policy. The form imposes the following conditions on the insured in the event of a loss:

1. Duties

    a. Notify the insurer of how and when the accident occurred and the names of any possible witnesses;

    b. Provide the insurer with prompt notice of any claim or suit;

    c.   Send copies of any demands, summons, or other legal papers to the insurer;

    d.   Authorize the insurer to obtain any necessary information;

    e.   Cooperate with the insurer;

    f.   Assist the insurer in the enforcement of its subrogation rights; and

    g.   The insured may not, except at its own expense, make any settlement or offer any payment.

2.   Legal Action Against the Insurer—no one may join the insurer in a suit against the insured and no one may sue the insurer under this form until all terms have been met.

3.   Other Insurance—this policy responds pro rata with other like insurance.

4.   Subrogation—the insured must do nothing to impair the insurer's subrogation rights. If the insurer requests, the insured must bring suit to help enforce those rights.

Additional Conditions

The following four conditions apply in addition to the commercial property conditions:

1.   Amendment of commercial property conditions: the only commercial property conditions that apply to the legal liability form are:

    a.   Condition A, Concealment, Misrepresentation or Fraud;

    b.   Condition C, Insurance Under Two or More Coverages; and

    c.   Condition E, Liberalization.

2.   Bankruptcy of the insured does not relieve the insurer of its obligations.

3.   Policy period, coverage territory: the policy period is shown on the declarations page, and the territory is the United States, Canada, and Puerto Rico.

4.   Separation of insureds: the insurance applies separately to all insureds, except for the limits of liability.

Chapter 13

Commercial Property Endorsements

ISO offers many endorsements to tailor the commercial property program to the needs of the insured. This chapter alphabetically lists and explains many of the endorsements that are available to add, delete, or modify coverage under the BPP form, as well as business income and builders risk coverage forms.

Additional Building Property, CP 14 15

Business personal property items that are owned but not permanently installed may be designated as building items on this endorsement. See Chapter 1 for a discussion of issues related to business personal property coverage under the building section of the form.

Additional Covered Property, CP 14 10

The insured may purchase coverage for certain excluded items of both building and personal property on this endorsement. Coverage applies only to those items scheduled and only at the premises designated. This endorsement adds coverage for certain building items, generally at the building rate (unless special class rates apply). The following may be added to building coverage: cost of excavations, grading, backfilling, or filling; certain foundations; underground pipes, flues, or drains; bulkheads, pilings, piers, wharves, or docks; fences; freestanding retaining walls; bridges, roadways, walks, patios, or other paved surfaces.

ISO Commercial Lines Manual (CLM) Rule 30 allows for vehicles or self-propelled machines (including aircraft and watercraft) and animals to be covered (and that the BPP form otherwise excludes).

For vehicles to be covered, they must be licensed for road use and operated principally away from the described premises. The insured may not manufacture, process, warehouse, or hold any of these vehicles for sale. The endorsement also adds coverage for animals.

The endorsement adds only these items as covered property under the CP 00 10. That form limits personal property coverage to that property on or within 100 feet of the described premises. The coverage is for physical damage only and is not as broad as coverage under the comprehensive coverage of a commercial auto policy or an open perils inland marine policy.

Additional Exclusions, CP 10 50

This endorsement can be used with any of the causes of loss forms (basic, broad, or special) and contains a schedule of premises and buildings where a windstorm or hail, vandalism, or sprinkler leakage exclusion is added. If loss or damage for another covered cause of loss results, that loss is covered.

Additional Insured – Building Owner, CP 12 19

Endorsement CP 12 19 enables adding the building owner as an additional named insured under a tenant's building coverage. If there is any source of confusion here, it will be with the endorsement's title and explanation. Note that the title of this endorsement is Additional Insured – Building Owner. However, the actual endorsement itself states that "[t]he building owner identified in this endorsement is a Named Insured." It may not mean anything insofar as this endorsement is concerned, but there are significant differences between a named insured and an additional insured, particularly with reference to liability insurance.

Additional Locations – Special Coinsurance Provisions, CP 13 20

Some insureds may want to make use of multiple location average rating, but their personal property values at each location do not fluctuate enough to warrant use of value reporting form CP 13 10. Endorsement CP 13 20 extends business personal property coverage to include personal property at all reported, acquired, and incidental locations. It does not cover property at fairs or exhibitions.

CLM Rule 35 says that the following types of property are eligible for this endorsement:

1. Merchandise and stock (raw, in process, or finished) that the insured owns;

2. All business personal property that the insured owns;

3. Personal property owned by others in the care, custody, or control of the insured.

The CLM also specifies that property subject to the following rating schedules is ineligible for this endorsement:

1.   Petroleum Properties Schedule;

2.   Petrochemical Plants Schedule;

3.   Public Utility Electric Generating Stations Schedule;

4.   Public Utility Natural Gas Pumping Stations Schedule; and

5.   Rating Plan for Highly Protected or Superior Risks.

The endorsement applies a coinsurance percentage (at least 90 percent is required) to an overall limit of insurance. The overall limit is the sum of the total values from each individual location, including any reported, acquired, and incidental locations. It is shown in the declarations or on the Reported – Acquired – Incidental Locations Schedule, CP DS 04. The average rate and premium are derived from the overall limit. It is not a blanket limit; however, each location possesses its own individual limit. A sample loss settlement is included on the endorsement to clarify the use of the overall limit.

Additional Property Not Covered, CP 14 20

The insured may choose to exclude items of building or business personal property by scheduling them on this endorsement. The underwriter may not write the risk without excluding certain items of property or that the insured is willing to exclude certain items to get a lower insurance cost. CLM Rules 30 and 31 describe the types of property that may be excluded:

Building items that may be excluded include the following:

a.   Awnings or canopies of fabric or slat construction, including their supports;

b.   Brick, metal, stone, or concrete chimneys or stacks that are not part of a building; or metal smokestacks;

c.   Crop silos;

d.   Swimming pools, diving towers, or platforms;

e.   Waterwheels, windmills, wind pumps, or their towers;

f.   The value of improvements, alterations or repairs (including labor, materials, and supplies) being performed by a named individual or organization; (This includes existing real property that will be demolished or permanently removed in the course of making the improvements, alterations, or repairs) and

g.   Any other type of property for which more specific property damage coverage is available.

Business personal property items that may be excluded include the following:

a.   Personal Property contained in safes or vaults;

b.   Contents of crop silos;

c.   Glass that is not part of a building or structure;

d.   Metals in ingots, pigs, billets, or scraps;

e.   Ores, gravels, clay, or sand;

f.   Property of others;

g.   Property stored in open yards;

h.   Signs inside the premises;

i.   Vending machines or their contents;

j.   Any other type of property for which more specific property damage coverage is available;

k.   The following types of property contained within a condominium unit and covered under CP 00 18 whether owned by the Condominium Association or by the unit-owner, unless the Condominium Association Agreement requires the Condominium Association to insure this property:

(1) Fixtures, improvements, and alterations that are part of the building; and

(2) Appliances.

Agricultural Products Storage, CP 13 30

Insureds who store grain (such as grain elevator operators) may cover it with endorsement CP 13 30. This endorsement covers grain or grain products on the premises and part of stock at a manufacturing, warehousing, processing, or finishing plant. Rice, flaxseed, beans, soybeans, seeds, or seed grain are also eligible.

This endorsement amends the property not covered provision of the property coverage forms pertaining to grain, hay, straw, or other crops outside of buildings. If such property is harvested and not in storage, it is covered under CP 13 30.

This form does not cover agricultural products stored at fairs or exhibitions or in transit; nor does it cover storage or elevator charges or unpaid customs duties on agricultural products.

In case of loss to covered property in terminal grain elevator plants, payment is made jointly to the named insured and anyone else with an established interest in the property. Such interest may be established by ownership, having a pledge for property, or holding or having a pledge for warehouse receipts. For losses to property stored at other locations, all liens, storage tickets, and warehouse receipts must be satisfied and released before payment occurs.

The endorsement values damaged or destroyed agricultural products at the market value of the covered property less any unincurred expenses such as commissions, loading and unloading charges, and freight. Loss to other commodities (those commodities for which market value is inappropriate) is figured at actual cash value of the property as of the time and place of the loss.

Alcoholic Beverages Tax Exclusion, CP 99 10

This endorsement has two purposes:

1. It excludes the value of taxes and custom duties paid on alcoholic beverages if the beverages suffer damage from a cause of loss other than theft. These taxes and custom duties are refundable under law when the beverages are damaged by a cause of loss other than theft.

2. When theft is a covered peril (as it is only under the special causes of loss form, CP 10 30), endorsement CP 99 10 includes the value of taxes and custom duties in the loss valuation. The insured cannot receive government reimbursement for such costs in the case of theft and therefore needs insurance protection.

A special theft limit may be scheduled at each covered location under business personal property, stock only, or personal property of others.

The Distilled Spirits and Wines Market Value endorsement, CP 99 05, also excludes the value of taxes and duties, so endorsement CP 99 10 does not need to be added for that purpose when endorsement CP 99 05 applies. However, if the insured has theft coverage under the special causes of loss form, endorsement CP 99 10 may be used in conjunction with CP 99 05. The addition of both endorsements allows for valuation at market value with different limits for theft versus causes of loss other than theft.

Brands And Labels, CP 04 01

When an insurer takes the salvage of damaged property, an attempt to sell the salvaged property is made in order to recoup some of its payment. Such a situation, however, might place the insurer in direct competition with its customer, since the customer is still trying to sell new, undamaged merchandise of the same kind.

The brands and labels endorsement provides the original manufacturer with two options in this situation:

1.   He may stamp such merchandise as salvage material.

2.   The insured may remove the brands or labels if doing so does not damage the merchandise.

The endorsement provides that the insurer will cover such expenses within the limit of liability that applies to the covered property.

Broken Or Cracked Glass Exclusion Form, CP 10 52

Endorsement CP 10 52 identifies, at policy inception, any broken or cracked glass on the insured premises. It clarifies that no coverage applies for damage caused by or resulting from the existing cracks. It also eliminates coverage for damage done by the extension of these cracks. The insured may identify the existing damage either via a diagram of the glass or by a written description of the damage.

Builders Risk – Theft Of Building Materials, Fixtures, Machinery, Equipment, CP 11 21

This endorsement was revised with the 2012 changes to track with the changes made to exclusion 2.(h) of the Causes of Loss – Special Form, CP 10 30. Thus, if coverage is purchased, subject to this endorsement, the exclusion dealing with theft or attempted theft precludes coverage for dishonest or criminal acts. The pre-2012 endorsement applied only to the named insured, its partners, directors, trustees, or authorized representatives. With the 2012 revision, loss also is not covered if caused by members, officers, managers, temporary employees, or leased workers. Dishonest or criminal acts by contractors and subcontractors continue to be excluded, except that this part of the exclusion has been broadened to include temporary employees and leased workers. The third part of this exclusion is clarified by precluding loss by any person to whom the property is entrusted for any purpose.

This exclusion has also been amended with the 2012 revision to clarify that it applies whether the dishonest or criminal act is committed while acting alone or in collusion with others, or the act occurs during the named insured's normal hours of operation.

The only exception to this exclusion is for acts of destruction by the named insured's employees, leased workers, temporary employees, or authorized representatives.

Building Glass – Tenant's Policy, CP 14 70

The Glass Coverage Form, CP 00 15, was withdrawn in 2000 when that edition of the BPP form was updated to include building glass. Prior to its withdrawal, the form was sometimes used when a tenant was contractually required to provide coverage for glass that is part of the building, but the tenant's policy did not insure the building itself. An entry on the declarations could limit building coverage to building glass. With the 2007 edition, ISO introduced endorsement CP 14 70 to enable coverage of building glass under a tenant's policy that does not otherwise cover the building.

The policy to which this endorsement is attached (the underlying policy) contains a deductible clause that is applicable to all insured property unless otherwise specified. Generally, it is the policy declarations that state the applicable deductible. Since CP 14 70 may be used instead of a declarations entry for coverage of building glass under a tenant's policy, a line item is added with the 2012 revision for the deductible amount in the schedule of this endorsement, to the extend a deductible otherwise applies. If none applies, the endorsement schedule can be left blank.

Burglary And Robbery Protective Safeguards, CP 12 11

The Burglary and Robbery Protective Safeguards endorsement identifies safeguards that protect the insured's property from burglary and robbery. According to rating procedures in the CLM, such devices warrant rate credits.

The endorsement refers to four different types of systems:

1. BR-1: Automatic Burglary Alarm, protecting the entire building, that signals to:

    (a) An outside central station or

    (b) A police station.

2. BR-2: Automatic Burglary Alarm, protecting the entire building, that has a loud sounding gong or siren on the outside of the building.

3. BR-3: Security Service, with a recording system or watch clock, making hourly rounds covering the entire building, when the premises are not in actual operation.

4. BR-4: The protective safeguard described in the schedule.

Previous versions of the endorsement required the insured to notify the insurer immediately in the event of any malfunction of the protective systems (burglar alarms, gongs, security services) at the premises. That requirement no longer appears. Rather, the requirement is that the insured must maintain the protective devices and/or services listed in the schedule.

The insured must also give notice of any failure to maintain such systems. If the insured does not make the notification or does not maintain the systems in working order, the theft coverage is suspended.

Business Income Changes – Beginning Of The Period Of Restoration, CP 15 56

Chapter 7 addresses changes made in the 06 07 policy edition to civil authority coverage in the underlying business income policy. The changes include use of a one-mile radius as one of the qualifications to trigger civil authority coverage and a basic coverage period of four weeks. ISO revised endorsement CP 15 56 because it referred to a three-week coverage period for civil authority coverage. The endorsement amends the definition of *period of restoration* to eliminate the seventy-two-hour time deductible. An option for a twenty-four-hour time deductible was also added. That option was previously contained in endorsement CP 15 55, Business Income Changes - Time Period, which has been withdrawn.

Business Income Changes – Educational Institutions, CP 15 25

Education institutions (such as schools, colleges, and camps) have unique business income loss exposures that differentiate them from traditional manufacturing, retail, or rental business operations. For example, if a fire damages a residential building that houses college students shortly before the beginning of the start of the school term, the educational institution may not be able to secure adequate housing. The end result could be a substantial loss of tuition, especially if students choose to transfer to another college. This endorsement amends the period of restoration to the earlier of (1) the day before the opening of the next school term following the date when the property should, with all reasonable speed and quality, be repaired or rebuilt, or (2) the date when the school term resumes at a new permanent location. If the actual date repairs are completed is sixty days or less before the start of the scheduled opening of the school term, the endorsement provides extended business income coverage for actual loss of business income sustained during the school term following the date of repair. This endorsement can be written on limited or broad form coverage. Limited coverage includes tuition and fees, including fees from room, board, laboratories, and similar sources. Broad form coverage includes, in addition to the previous fees, income from bookstores, athletic events, activity related to research grants, and business activities other than those that generate tuition, and related fees from students.

Business Income From Dependent Properties – Broad Form, CP 15 08

Dependent properties must be identified in the schedule and are divided into the following categories: contributing locations, recipient locations, manufacturing locations, and leader locations. An unscheduled dependent location deductible may also be applied to a small portion of the limit. These unscheduled or miscellaneous locations encompass business entities or organizations that become contributing, recipient, leader, or manufacturing locations in mid-policy term with respect to the insured's operations.

Miscellaneous locations coverage recognizes other situations as well, such as where certain entities or organizations do not represent a significant dependency or are temporary. In the 2007 revision, ISO added language to the description of miscellaneous locations to make it clear that highways and other transportation conduits are not considered miscellaneous locations. ISO also added references to the business income's policy limit in the 2007 revision. The 2012 revision added an option for covering secondary dependencies focused on contributing and recipient locations. This option is more fully discussed in this chapter regarding CP 15 01 – Business Income from Dependent Properties – Limited International Coverage.

Business Income From Dependent Properties – Limited Form, CP 15 09

The difference between this endorsement and the broad form, CP 15 08, is primarily with the limits of insurance. The schedule of the limited endorsement contains a section in which to place the applicable limit. This endorsement also states that the limits of insurance shown in the schedule are separate from any business income limit of insurance in the policy applicable when direct physical loss or damage occurs at the named insured's premises. The broad form, on the other hand, states that the provisions of the business income coverage form concerning direct physical loss or damage at the described premises, including the limit of insurance, will apply separately to each dependent property described in the schedule.

Business Income From Dependent Properties – Limited International Coverage, CP 15 01

This form is used to obtain coverage for loss of business income caused by direct physical loss or damage to dependent property at the premises described in the schedule of the endorsement caused by a covered cause of loss, other than loss due solely to loss or damage to electronic data. *Dependent property* is defined to mean property operated by others whom the named insured depends on to (1) supply materials or services to the named uninsured or to others for the named insured's account (contributing locations), or (2) manufactured products for delivery to the named insured's customers under contract of sale (manufacturing locations).

An additional coverage option added with the 2012 revision covers certain secondary dependencies. An example of such as dependency, given by ISO, is where the insured's supplier (a dependent property identified in the schedule) is unable to deliver products or services because of interruption in the business of an entity (a manufacturer) upon which the supplier depends. The insured has no direct business relationship with the manufacturer, and, therefore, the second dependency is not named in the dependent property endorsement. In such a case, the limited coverage for miscellaneous locations would come into play, but the coverage would be limited.

This new option for covering certain secondary dependencies is focused on both contributing and recipient locations. Some of the noteworthy features are the following:

1. Since secondary locations are not identified in the endorsement's schedule, the definitions of *secondary contributing locations*

and *secondary recipient locations* specify that a road, bridge, tunnel, waterway, airfield, pipeline, or other similar area or structure is not a secondary location. This is the same approach taken in the endorsement addressing miscellaneous locations. Also, under the international version of dependent property endorsements, secondary locations are limited to secondary contributing locations since the endorsements do not encompass primary recipient locations.

2.   Coverage for business income losses arising out of physical loss or damage to secondary locations is subject to the same limit of insurance as is applicable to suspension of the insured's operations. In other words, there is no increase in limit for the secondary locations.

3.   As respects miscellaneous locations, a provision was added in 2012 specifying a particular location cannot be both a miscellaneous location and a secondary location.

4.   Another 2012 amendment is that the amount allowable for miscellaneous locations is also part of the limit of insurance and not in addition to it.

5.   The kinds of property not considered to be a secondary contributing location with respect to such services are water supply services, power supply services, and communication supply services relating to Internet access or access to any electronic network. Added with the 2012 changes are wastewater removal services. These are being added to complement a change dealing with utility service endorsements.

The coverage territory condition of the commercial property conditions, which limits coverage to the U.S., its territories, possessions, Puerto Rico, and Canada, does not apply. What international locations are covered is not worldwide. This is the reason this endorsement is for limited international coverage. The locations will depend on what reinsurers permit and underwriting discretion.

The 2012 amendments not only affect the CP 15 01 endorsement, but also the following:

- CP 15 02, Extra Expense From Dependent Properties – Limited International Coverage

- CP 15 08, – Business Income From Dependent Properties – Broad Form

- CP 15 09, Business Income From Dependent Properties – Limited Form

- CP 15 34, Extra Expense From Dependent Properties

Business Income – Landlord As Additional Insured (Rental Value), CP 15 03

If a rental or lease agreement requires the tenant to carry insurance for loss of rental income for the benefit of the landlord in situations where the premises cannot be used for business purposes because of a covered loss, the 2007 commercial property program revision introduced an optional endorsement that provides coverage for loss of rental income for a landlord under a tenant's policy. This option broadens coverage.

Business Personal Property – Limited International Coverage, CP 04 32

The BPP form's coverage territory is limited to the U.S., Canada, and Puerto Rico. Insureds who conduct international business outside of the U.S., Canada, and Puerto Rico can purchase limited international property coverage under this endorsement. Coverage applies to property temporarily in the foreign county indicated in the endorsement, used in the insured's business in that foreign country, and located at the insured's owned or leased business location. Coverage is limited to the dollar amount and time period indicated in the endorsement. This limited, short-term coverage is commonly used when an insured's representative is conducting presentations at foreign trade shows or a similar venue. The endorsement does not cover property that the insured exports to a foreign country, that is held for sale in a foreign country, or property in the care of a carrier or bailee for hire.

Cap on Losses From Certified Acts Of Terrorism, IL 09 52

This endorsement is one of the terrorism provisions created for the commercial property program following the terrorist acts of September 11, 2001.

The endorsement includes the following provision:

A. Cap On Certified Terrorism Losses

"Certified act of terrorism" means an act that is certified by the Secretary of the Treasury, in accordance with the provisions of the federal Terrorism Risk Insurance Act, to be an act pursuant to such Act. The criteria contained in the Terrorism Risk Insurance Act for a "certified act of terrorism" include the following:

1. The act resulted in insured losses in excess of $5 million in the aggregate, attributable to all types of insurance subject to the Terrorism Risk Insurance Act; and

2. The act is a violent act or an act that is dangerous to human life, property or infrastructure and is committed by an individual or individuals as part of an effort to coerce the civilian population of the United States or to influence the policy or affect the conduct of the United States Government by coercion.

If aggregate insured losses attributable to terrorist acts certified under the Terrorism Risk Insurance Act exceed $100 billion in a calendar year and we have met our insurer deductible under the Terrorism Risk Insurance Act, we shall not be liable for the payment of any portion of the amount of such losses that exceeds $100 billion, and in such case insured losses up to that amount are subject to pro rata allocation in accordance with procedures established by the Secretary of the Treasury.

Changes – Electronic Data, CP 01 70

This endorsement reflects the change in treatment of electronic data coverage made in the CP 00 10 04 02 edition. This endorsement is attached to previous editions to reflect the changes.

Via this endorsement, covered property does not include electronic data, except as provided under Limited Coverage – Electronic Data.

The cost to replace or restore the information on valuable papers and records, including those that exist as electronic data, is not covered property. Proprietary information, books of account, deeds, manuscripts, abstracts, drawings, and card index systems are considered valuable papers and records, but this is not an exhaustive list.

The endorsement does provide limited coverage for valuable papers and records, other than those that exist as electronic data, under the Limited Coverage –Valuable Papers and Records (Other Than Electronic Data).

Additionally, the endorsement contains the provisions for the limited coverage for electronic data, valuable papers and records (other than electronic data), and the limited coverage for interruption of computer operations. These policy provisions are discussed in Chapter 2.

Civil Authority Change(s), CP 15 32

Chapter 7 addresses changes made in the 06 07 policy edition to civil authority coverage in the underlying business income policy. The changes include use of a one-mile radius as one of the qualifications to trigger civil authority coverage and a basic coverage period of four weeks. At the same time ISO revised CP 15 32, Civil Authority Change(s), so that the one-mile radius or the four-week coverage period of civil authority coverage can be changed. The endorsement, which previously addressed only the coverage period, was also formerly known as Civil Authority Increased Coverage Period.

No mention was made for the rationale behind changing the civil authority provision, and with the added restriction that the described premises (insured premises) must be within the area immediately surrounding the damaged property but not more than one mile from the damaged property. Presumably, the impetus for this change was based on court cases similar to that of *Assurance Company of America v. BBB Service Co., Inc.* 593 S.E. 2d 7 (Ga. Ct. App 2003).

In September 1999, Brevard County, Florida, issued an order, signed by the chairman of the county commission, declaring a state of emergency "because of the serious threat to the lives and property of residents of that county by Hurricane Floyd." Because of the uncertainty of the path of devastating winds and storm surges, certain persons were ordered to evacuate. Pursuant to this order, the plaintiff, owner of several restaurants in Florida and Georgia, closed its doors and evacuated the area. The plaintiff later submitted a claim to its insurer, stating that it had been unable to do business for two and one-half days, that it had incurred a business loss of $30,000, and that it was entitled to be paid pursuant to its policy's civil authority coverage.

The insurer rejected the claim because the evacuation order was issued due to the threat of damage to the property, not due to actual damage to property, as required by the policy provision. As a result, litigation pursued. The civil authority clause in the insurance policy required two conditions precedent to recover lost business income: (1) that the loss was caused by a civil authority action that prohibited access to the named insured's premises, and (2) that the civil authority action, which prohibited access, was due to the direct physical loss or damage to property, other than the named insured's premises. A number of questions were generated by this case. Why did the named insured not do business for two and one-half days? Did the county or other civil authority prohibit the named insured's access to its restaurants during that entire period? Was the evacuation order in effect for that entire time? At some point after the evacuation order was issued, did property damage in the area or elsewhere become a reason for the county or any other civil authority to prohibit the named insured's access to its premises?

At the bench trial, the parties stipulated that property damage was occurring throughout the effective term of the evacuation order where hurricane winds were making windfall. One member of the group from Brevard County who was authorized to make emergency decisions regarding weather-related problems, stated that the storm had been causing damage in its path, that the forecast indicated the storm was headed to Brevard County, and that it was anticipated to have an impact if it reached the county. These factors, he said, were what led the group to advise the chairman of the county commission to sign the evacuation order.

The court ruled in favor of the insured, thus implicitly finding that a basis for the evacuation order was actual damage to the property, other than the insured's premises. The named insured's policy provision also did not say where the direct physical loss or damage had to take place, as long as it was not at the covered premises. Interestingly, some insurers are using the restriction of one statute mile, which is typically defined as an ordinary mile, as opposed to a nautical or geographical mile. An ordinary or statute mile is 5,280 feet or 1,609 kilometers. A nautical, sea, or geographical mile contains 6,080 feet.

Condominium Commercial Unit-Owners Changes – Standard Property Policy, CP 17 98

The following 2012 revisions that affect the Business and Personal Property Coverage Form, CP 00 10, also affect this endorsement: coverage radius; business personal property in described structures; and newly acquired property. (See Chapter 1.)

Condominium Commercial Unit-Owners Optional Coverages, CP 04 18

The owner of a commercial condominium unit may purchase either of the additional coverages—loss assessment or miscellaneous real property— on this endorsement. In the event of loss to property that all unit-owners hold in common, the association may assess each owner a share of the loss. Such an assessment may include a portion of the master insurance policy's deductible. The association may also assess a portion of the loss itself if there is either no insurance or inadequate insurance. The endorsement covers all assessments, up to the limit of liability. While it limits payment for the insured's share of any deductible to $1,000, provision is made, as a result of a 2012 revision, to provide a means for selecting a higher limitation (sublimit) on an assessment that results from a deductible in the insurance purchased by the condominium association.

Depending on the terms of the association agreement, bylaws, and condominium declaration, the unit-owner may also need to insure some or all of the real property in the condominium. Endorsement CP 04 18 offers miscellaneous real property coverage for such property in the insured's unit only. This coverage is excess over the association coverage on the property, whether the insurance is collectible or not.

The endorsement's schedule was updated in the 2007 revision so that each unit for which coverage applies can be indicated.

Contributing Insurance, CP 99 20

If the insured has coverage with more than one company, the contributing insurance endorsement clarifies the amount for which the insurer is liable.

The endorsement indicates the company's percentage of the total of all contributing insurance. The endorsement also shows the property and coverages to which it applies and the total limits for all contributing insurance.

Debris Removal Additional Insurance, CP 04 15

Debris removal additional insurance provides a way an additional amount of insurance can apply for debris removal expenses incurred due to loss or damage to covered property from a covered cause of loss. Because the basic limit was changed from $10,000 to $25,000 in 2012, the endorsement increases the $25,000 limit that the policy currently provides, as explained in Chapter 2, to the amount shown on the endorsement.

Deductibles By Location, CP 03 29

This endorsement was introduced in 2012. It is designed so that the selected deductibles apply at each location sustained by loss or damage. The endorsement schedule shows separate locations and the deductible for each location. Since the location can be described in terms of a particular site or a particular building, this endorsement is flexible.

Deductible Limitation, CP 03 10

The CP 03 10 endorsement allows the insured to select an annual accumulation amount for the deductible. The insurer agrees not to subtract any more than this amount for all losses the insured has in any one policy year. Losses that are less than 10 percent of the deductible do not count towards this annual figure. After the annual accumulation amount is reached, the insured must notify the insurer of any loss of more than $250. The insurer deducts $250 for such losses. Form CP 03 10 does not apply to any earthquake deductible.

Discharge From Sewer, Drain Or Sump (Not Flood-Related), CP 10 38

This is an optional endorsement that was introduced with the 2012 revisions. Among its features are the following:

- Coverage pertains to physical damage and/or time element loss, indicated in the schedule, caused by the discharge of water or waterborne materials from a sewer, drain, or sump pump at the described premises.

- Coverage is limited to the amounts listed in the schedule of the endorsement, which are sublimits; they do not increase the underlying limit of insurance.

- An annual aggregate limit can be selected.

- The policy deductible applies to this endorsement coverage. There is no separate deductible if an occurrence causes other loss or damage.

- Coverage does not apply to flood or flood-related conditions.

- No coverage applies if a sump pump fails due to power failure unless the policy otherwise covers loss from power failure.

Disclosure Pursuant To Terrorism Risk Insurance Act, IL 09 85

Under provisions of the federal Terrorism Risk Insurance Act (TRIA), insurers are required to provide insureds with a notice disclosing the portion of the premium, if any, attributable to coverage for terrorist acts certified under that Act. The portion of the premium attributable to such coverage is shown in the schedule of this endorsement or in the policy declarations.

B. Disclosure Of Federal Participation In Payment Of Terrorism Losses

The United States Government, Department of the Treasury, will pay a share of terrorism losses insured under the federal program. The federal share equals a percentage (as shown in Part II of the Schedule of this endorsement or in the Policy Declarations) of that portion of the amount of such insured losses that exceeds the applicable insurer retention. However, if aggregate insured losses attributable to terrorist acts certified under the Terrorism Risk Insurance Act exceed $100 billion in a calendar year the Treasury shall not make any payment for any portion of the amount of such losses that exceeds $100 billion.

Discretionary Payroll Expense, CP 15 04

In the 2007 revision of the commercial property program, ISO introduced endorsement CP 15 04, Discretionary Payroll Expense. The business income forms state that the amount of loss is partly based on "the operating expenses, including payroll expenses, necessary to resume 'operations' with the same quality of service that existed just before the direct physical loss or damage." Payroll expense for only certain job classifications or employees is covered as business income loss. However, insureds may want to keep other employees in other job classifications on the payroll. This endorsement was introduced to address such situations.

Under this endorsement, discretionary payroll may be specified in terms of job classification or individual employees. Payroll coverage may be available for the entire period of restoration or limited to a specified maximum number of days; the days do not need to be consecutive. If not identified in the schedule, other job classifications and employees are not affected by the terms of this endorsement.

Distilled Spirits And Wines Market Value, CP 99 05

This endorsement changes the valuation of distilled spirits and wines from actual cash value to market value. Such items may be either the insured's stock or the property of others in the insured's care. The insured schedules on the endorsement the locations to which the endorsement applies.

The endorsement lists five categories of distilled spirits:

1.   Bottled winery products: wine that is either in a bottle or unbottled. If not bottled, it must be irreplaceable and it must be of the kind that the insured would normally bottle or have in his possession.

2.   Bulk wine: anything other than bottled wine.

3.   Irreplaceable bulk distilled spirits: distilled spirits aged in wood, not replaceable, and held by the insured for sale to others.

4.   Older bulk distilled spirits: irreplaceable bulk spirits that have reached a certain age.

5.   Younger bulk distilled spirits: irreplaceable bulk other than older bulk spirits.

Valuation for distilled spirits is essentially market price at the time and place of loss less any discounts and expenses the insured otherwise would have had.

The form divides wines into two categories:

1.   Bottled winery products: valued at the price they would have been sold as case goods; and

2.   Bulk wine: valued at the lesser of:

   a.   the price it could have been sold for; or

   b.   the market price of replaceable bulk wine of like kind and quality.

Values exclude federal taxes, discounts, and expenses the insured otherwise would have had, but include state, county, and local taxes.

Certain insureds covered by the special causes of Loss form, CP 10 30, may want to add endorsement CP 99 10, Alcoholic Beverages Tax Exclusion, when this endorsement is used. For insureds with other types of stock subject to market value, another endorsement, CP 99 31, Market Value – Stock, is available.

Earthquake And Volcanic Eruption Endorsement Form, CP 10 40, and Earthquake And Volcanic Eruption Endorsement (Sub-Limit Form), CP 10 45

Until 1999, endorsement CP 10 40 was known as Causes of Loss – Earthquake Form. The insured may purchase earthquake and volcanic eruption coverage—otherwise specifically excluded—via this endorsement. It covers as one occurrence all shocks or eruption that occur within a 168-hour time period.

The insured may choose specific or blanket earthquake coverage. When choosing specific coverage, the declarations page must indicate the property to which the earthquake coverage applies. Even if the insured chooses blanket earthquake coverage, there may be some buildings it does not wish to cover. In that case, the declarations should, again, reflect the property to which the coverage applies.

Typically, the deductible for earthquake coverage is a percentage of the limit of liability applicable to the covered property. The deductible is calculated separately for and applies separately to the following:

1.   Each building, if two or more buildings sustain loss or damage;

2.   The building and to personal property in that building, if both sustain loss or damage;

3.   Personal property at each building if personal property at two or more buildings sustains loss or damage;

4.   Personal property in the open.

Because a building made of masonry veneer is more likely to sustain heavy damage in an earthquake, the endorsement does not include the value of the veneer when calculating the deductible or applying the coinsurance condition. This limitation does not apply if the building's exterior is less than 10 percent masonry veneer or if the description of the premises specifically includes masonry veneer. The limitation does not apply to stucco.

In both this endorsement and Earthquake and Volcanic Eruption Endorsement (Sub-Limit Form), CP 10 45, the section on deductibles does not mention anything about the application of deductibles involving earthquake sprinkler leakage only coverage. To clarify this, a 2012 revision introduced provision E.2 (Property Damage Deductible) of CP 10 40 and G.2 (Property Damage Deductible) of CP 10 45, which state that the earthquake deductible provisions in these two earthquake endorsements do not apply to the earthquake sprinkler leakage only coverage. It is the fire deductible that applies instead.

Earthquake Inception Extension, CP 10 41

Use of this endorsement avoids a coverage gap when an expiring policy and new policy both include earthquake coverage. The endorsement specifically covers damage that occurs on or after the inception of the new coverage if the damage is caused by earthquake shocks or volcanic eruptions that began within seventy-two hours before the new policy takes effect.

Electrical Apparatus, CP 04 10

This endorsement modifies the electrical apparatus exclusion in the basic, broad, and special causes of loss forms. Those forms exclude damage caused by artificially generated electrical currents. However, an exception allows coverage for any resulting fire damage.

Endorsement CP 04 10 extends this exception to include coverage for damage to electrical equipment or devices from resulting explosions. It also covers damage by electricity after the fire or explosion. In order for such coverage to apply, the fire must continue even after the electrical current is turned off. Unless a higher amount is shown on the declarations, coverage under this endorsement is subject to a $1,000 deductible.

In 2007 ISO updated the artificially generated electrical current exclusion in the causes of loss forms to incorporate various terms reflecting current technology with regard to power sources and associated systems. This endorsement was revised to reflect the changes in the causes of loss forms.

Electronic Commerce (E-Commerce), CP 04 30

This endorsement covers various e-commerce exposures of the insured against data corruption and other electronic exposures. The ISO rules state that electronic commerce, for purposes of this endorsement, is "commerce conducted via the Internet or other computer-based interactive communications network. This includes business-to-business commerce conducted in that manner."

Section 1 of the endorsement covers electronic data that is owned, licensed, or leased by the insured; originates and resides in computers located in the coverage territory; and is used in the e-commerce activity of the insured's business described in the schedule.

The form covers the cost to replace or restore electronic data that has suffered loss or damage by a covered cause of loss. The endorsement states that loss or damage to electronic data means destruction or corruption of electronic data.

Section II provides electronic commerce time element coverage. Coverage is for the actual loss of business income sustained and extra expense incurred due to the necessary suspension (slowdown or cessation) of the e-commerce activity of the business described for the applicable period of time specified. Loss must be caused by a covered loss under section 1 or interruption in normal computer network service or function caused by a covered cause of loss.

If the suspension of e-commerce activity is caused by a loss covered under Section I, the period of coverage begins twenty-four hours after the time of such loss and ends on the earliest of the time when ecommerce activity is resumed, the time when the electronic data is restored, or ninety days after the date of loss.

If the suspension is caused by interruption in normal computer network service or function caused by a covered cause of loss, the period of coverage begins twenty-four hours after the time of the interruption, which is when service to the insured's website is disrupted. The period ends at the earliest of when e-commerce is resumed, service is restored, or two weeks after the interruption began.

The special causes of loss form, modified by provisions of the e-commerce endorsement, provides the covered causes of loss. The utility services exclusion does not apply with respect to power or communications supply services, provided that there is an interruption in utility service caused by a specified cause of loss; the exclusion of artificially generated electrical, magnetic, or electromagnetic energy, does not apply; and the exclusion of mechanical breakdown does not apply with respect to the breakdown of the insured's computers and their related equipment, but this exception is limited to the effect of such mechanical breakdown on electronic data.

The e-commerce endorsement adds eight exclusions:

(1)   A virus, malicious code or similar instruction introduced into or enacted on a computer system (including electronic data) or a network to which it is connected, designed to damage or destroy any part of the system or disrupt its normal operation. But this exclusion does not apply if the insured's e-commerce activity is conducted via a computer system that is equipped with virus-scanning or anti-virus software, or if the Anti-Virus Waiver is indicated as applicable in the Schedule. When this exclusion does not apply, then coverage also extends to shut-down of the computer system if the shut-down is undertaken in response to the detection of a virus or other incident by virus-scanning software, to mitigate or avoid attack, infiltration or infection of the system;

(2)   Unauthorized viewing, copying or use of electronic data (or any proprietary or confidential information or intellectual property in any form) by any person, even if such activity is characterized as theft;

(3)   Errors or omissions in programming or processing electronic data;

(4) Errors or deficiency in design, installation, maintenance, repair or modification of your computer system or any computer system or network to which the insured system is connected or on which the insured system depends (including electronic data);

(5) Manipulation of the insured computer system, including electronic data, by an employee, volunteer worker or contractor, for the purpose of diverting electronic data or causing fraudulent or illegal transfer of any property;

(6) Interruption in normal computer function or network service or function due to insufficient capacity to process transactions or to an overload of activity on the system or network. But this exclusion does not apply if such incident is caused by a virus, malicious code or similar instruction introduced into or enacted on a computer system or network;

(7) Unexplained or indeterminable failure, malfunction or slowdown of a computer system, including electronic data and the inability to access or properly manipulate the electronic data;

(8) Complete or substantial failure, disablement or shut-down of the entire Internet, regardless of the cause.

In 2007 ISO updated the artificially generated electrical current exclusion in the causes of loss forms to incorporate various terms reflecting current technology with regard to power sources and associated systems. This endorsement was revised to reflect the changes in the causes of loss forms.

Equipment Breakdown Cause Of Loss, CP 10 46

This endorsement was introduced with the 2012 revisions and is compatible only with the Causes of Loss – Special Form, CP 10 30.

Equipment breakdown is treated as an additional peril (cause of loss). Thus, coverage for direct damage is subject to the insurance limit applicable to covered equipment as covered property. If the policy includes business income and/or extra expense coverages, the losses are subject to the time element insurance limit applicable to the described premises. It is important to note that equipment breakdown coverage is not subject to an additional limit of insurance. Coverage for ammonia contamination and hazardous substance is limited to 10 percent of the insurance limit or $25,000, whichever is less. Higher limits can be selected on the schedule.

Exclusion Of Loss Due To By-Products Of Production Or Processing Operations (Rental Properties), CP 10 34

This endorsement, introduced with the 2012 revisions, is meant for owners and tenants of rental properties. When business premises are abused, often by tenants, insurers view such physical loss or damage as a business risk and not subject to coverage by the policy. A case cited by ISO to clarify this situation is *Graff v. Allstate Ins. Co.*, 54 P.3d 1266 (Wash. Ct. App. 2002). The named insured (landlord) filed a claim for cleanup expenses after a tenant's methamphetamine laboratory damaged the rental property. The insurer denied the claim, citing the policy's contamination exclusion. The insured therefore filed suit against its insurer. The trial court held in favor of the insured, finding that the policy covered cleanup expenses. The appellate court affirmed the trial court and stated that the operation of this laboratory was vandalism, a covered cause under the policy. This decision, as ISO states, does seem to run counter to a general understanding of what vandalism constitutes.

This endorsement is intended to be issued on property policies issued to owners and tenants of rental property. When issued, the insurer will not pay for loss or damage to the described premises caused by or resulting from "smoke, vapor, gas or any substance released in the course of production operations or processing operations performed at the rental unit(s). This exclusion applies whether such operations are legally permitted or not. This exclusion, however, does not apply to loss or damage by fire or explosion that results from the release of a byproduct of the production or processing operation."

While the case cited by ISO dealt with a dwelling policy, it is not an over-reaction to introduce this kind of exclusion. A review of court cases reveals that as of late 2012, there have been nearly 5,000 cases dealing with meth-related problems, not necessarily dealing with insurance.

Extra Expense From Dependent Properties, CP 15 34

This endorsement pays for the necessary extra expense the named insured incurs due to direct physical loss or damage to property at the premises of a dependent property, as defined, caused by or resulting from a covered cause of loss. This endorsement is changed with the 2012 revisions to include coverage for secondary dependencies—contributing and recipient locations.

Extra Expense From Dependent Properties Limited International Coverage, CP 15 02

This endorsement is similar to Business Income from Dependent Properties Limited International Coverage, CP 15 01, except that it provides extra expense coverage. This endorsement was amended in 2012 to add the same coverage for secondary contributing locations (not named) as in endorsement CP 15 01.

Flood Coverage Endorsement, CP 10 65

The property program allows flood coverage to be endorsed to a policy. In order to provide flood coverage in excess of that on a National Flood Insurance Program (NFIP) policy, this endorsement and the flood coverage schedule, CP DS 65, are added. The CP DS 65 allows for specific or blanket limits. It also shows the limits and deductibles applying at each location. The insured may choose to blanket several items of covered property, several different coverages (such as property and time element), or several different premises.

The rules state that the following are ineligible for this coverage:

1.   Property subject to the builders risk form;

2.   Certain property as defined in the following federal statutes:

     a.   The Coastal Barrier Resources Act; and

     b.   The Coastal Barrier Improvement Act.

The endorsement defines those properties in number 2 as property not covered.

The endorsement defines *flood* as follows:

1.   The overflow of inland or tidal waters;

2.   The unusual or rapid accumulation or runoff of surface waters from any source; or

3.   Mudslides or mudflows which are caused by flooding as defined in C.2. above. For the purpose of this covered cause of loss, a mudslide or mudflow involves a river of liquid and flowing mud on the surface of normally dry land areas as when earth is carried by a current of water and deposited along the path of the current

Many times another peril, such as fire, accompanies a flood. The limits of insurance section specifies that the limit shown on the DS 65 is the most the endorsement will pay and that the limits cannot be stacked.

The endorsement applies as excess over any NFIP coverage. It is also excess of any NFIP coverage that should be in place. If the insured is eligible for NFIP coverage but does not purchase or maintain it, the ISO endorsement pays only in excess of the maximum amount available under the NFIP. For an additional premium, the insured may purchase a waiver of this requirement.

Flood Coverage Schedule, CP DS 65

This schedule is used in conjunction with the Flood Coverage Endorsement, CP 10 65. The schedule indicates the inception date of the Flood Coverage Endorsement, which cannot begin before or within seventy-two hours after the date. The schedule also provides space to enter a description of the premises or locations, personal property in the open (if covered for flood), a flood deductible amount, a box to check to choose a no-coinsurance option, and space to list other flood insurance.

The schedule also contains a box to check for the underlying insurance waiver, space to indicate the annual aggregate limit and single occurrence limits for blanket and separate limits.

Food Contamination (Business Interruption And Extra Expense), CP 15 05

For a number of years, there have been some notable cases involving food contamination. A cheese manufacturer, for example, had a dispute with its insurer over contamination of over 8 million pounds of mozzarella cheese. More recently, another cheese manufacturer had to destroy over 14 million pounds of its cheese. It is not only manufacturers that are caught up in these events. Distributors of food products, such as lettuce tainted with E-coli, have had an adverse effect nationally. Then there are the food caterers who, for one reason or another, have been the alleged causes of food poisoning.

Larger risks are likely to have specialized products contamination insurance or, to the extent contamination is not excluded, some coverage under their property policies. Those smaller risks that are written under ISO forms may be able to obtain some limited coverage. It is these risks that are likely to qualify for the food contamination time element coverage that ISO introduced with its 2012 revisions. The coverage under this endorsement is limited but still undoubtedly welcomed, given that an exposure exists for loss of business income and/or extra expense coverage.

When endorsement CP 15 05 is issued, payment is conditioned on a business described in the schedule that is ordered closed by the Board of Health or any other governmental authority as the result of the discovery or suspicion of "food contamination." This term is defined in the endorsement as meaning "an outbreak of food poisoning or food-related illness of one or more persons arising out of (1) tainted food the named insured distributed or purchased; (2) food improperly processed, stored, handled, or prepared in the course of the named insured's business; or (3) food that has been contaminated by virus or bacteria transmitted through one or more employees, including temporary and leased employees.

The limited coverages applies to the expense of having to clean equipment as required by the Board of Health or other governmental authority; the named insured's cost to replace the food that is or suspected of being contaminated; the named insured's expense to provide necessary medical tests or vaccinations for the named insured's employees who are potentially infected by food contamination—not otherwise covered by workers compensation; loss of business income the named insured sustains due to necessary suspension of its operations as a result of food contamination; and additional advertising expenses the named insured incurs to restore its reputation.

Both food contamination and advertising expense coverages are subject to separate limits of insurance that are annual aggregates.

Functional Building Valuation, CP 04 38

Insureds may add this endorsement to the BPP or the condominium association coverage form to provide an alternate method of valuation for building property. It provides for the replacement of a scheduled building with similar property that performs the same function but is less costly. The endorsement also provides building ordinance coverage at no charge.

The coinsurance condition does not apply. However, the rate for this coverage is 30 percent above the rate charged for buildings subject to the 80 percent coinsurance rule.

If the insured chooses to repair or replace the building, the insurer pays the least of four different amounts. The first choice is the limit of liability. If the building suffers a total loss, the insurer pays the cost to replace the building on the same site with one that is functionally equivalent. If the insured must rebuild on a different site, the endorsement pays to build on that different site.

In the event of a partial loss, payment by the insurer has two components:

a.   the cost to repair or replace the damaged portion in the same architectural style with less costly material (if available); and

b.   the amount the insured spends to demolish the undamaged portion of the building and to clear the site.

The insurer's fourth option is to pay the amount that the insured actually spends to repair or replace the building with less costly material (if available). The insured must contract for the repairs within 180 days of the loss unless the insured and insurer agree otherwise.

If the insured does not select repair or replacement (or does not do so within the 180 day time period), the endorsement pays the smallest of the following:

a.   The limit of liability;

b.   The market value (not including the value of the land) at the time of loss. The endorsement defines *market value* as "the price which the property might be expected to realize if offered for sale in a fair market";

c.   A modified form of actual cash value (the amount to repair or replace on the same site with less costly material and in the same architectural style, less depreciation).

Unlike former endorsement CP 04 35, Functional Replacement Cost, this endorsement and the manual rules do not specifically exclude functional replacement cost coverage for certain fixtures and personal property used to service the premises. The previous form and rules excluded these items because they are subject to rapid depreciation. The current endorsement does not exclude this property. Therefore, items such as awnings or floor coverings; appliances for refrigerating, ventilating, cooking, dishwashing, or laundering; or outdoor equipment or furniture (treated as building property under the property coverage form) can be valued at functional replacement cost. Functional replacement cost coverage may be more favorable for such items than actual cash value.

In the event of other insurance using the same type of valuation, endorsement CP 04 38 responds on a pro rata basis. Coverage is excess when other insurance covering the loss is not subject to the same plan, terms, conditions (such as valuation), and provisions.

Functional Personal Property Valuation (Other Than Stock), CP 04 39

Similar to endorsement CP 04 38, CP 04 39 provides an alternate method of valuation for business personal property. It is used when an item of personal property cannot be replaced with the same type of property (as when the damaged property is technologically obsolete), or when actual cash value would be inappropriate because the item depreciates quickly in value.

Coinsurance does not apply to this endorsement and blanket insurance is not allowed. The rate is 25 percent above that for personal property written with 80 percent coinsurance. Any items scheduled on this endorsement should be excluded from coverage under the Building and Personal Property Coverage Form.

The insured may cover the property for more or less than its actual cash value. For example, a metal stamping plant uses an older piece of machinery with an actual cash value of $50,000. The closest thing available today is one that costs $100,000. Using endorsement CP 04 39, the insured could choose a limit of $100,000 to cover the cost of the new machinery.

The situation is the same when the values are reversed. An insured suffers a fire loss to the central computer. That computer (purchased two years ago) has an actual cash value of $50,000. However, due to advances in technology, the same computer may now be purchased for $30,000. Using endorsement CP 04 39, the insured may cover this computer for $30,000.

The insured must contract for repair or replacement within 180 days of the loss (a time period that may be altered by consent of the insurer and the insured). If the insured does so, the insurer pays the least of the following amounts under functional replacement cost:

1.   The endorsed limit;

2.   The cost to replace, on the same site, with the most equivalent property available; or

3.   The amount the insured spends to repair or replace the property.

If the insured chooses not to repair or replace (or does not do so within the 180 day time period), the insurer pays the smallest of the following:

1.   The limit of liability;

2.   The market value at the time of loss; or

3.   The amount to repair or replace with material of like kind and quality, minus an allowance for physical deterioration and depreciation.

The endorsement defines *market value* as "the price which the property might be expected to realize if offered for sale in a fair market."

Grain Properties – Explosion Limitation, CP 10 51

This endorsement restricts the peril of explosion found in the basic and broad causes of loss forms, CP 10 10 and CP 10 20. It specifies that if a grain elevator or processing plant building or structure ruptures or bursts as a result of a change in temperature, the resulting damage is not covered as part of the explosion peril.

Higher Limits, CP 04 08

This endorsement CP 04 08 is a coverage option that was introduced with the 2012 revisions. Instead of using the declarations to increase certain dollar limits, this endorsement can be used instead. This endorsement, however, does not replace current endorsements used to designate higher limits for certain coverages, such as for debris removal and newly acquired property. The reason is that those and other endorsements also contain certain verbiage regarding coverage and the Higher Limits endorsement does not. It merely shows the higher limits and nothing else. Thus, this endorsement is available only for use when limits are increased and not where something must also be mentioned regarding the scope of coverage.

Household Personal Property Coverage, CP 99 92

This endorsement extends the definition of *covered property* to include household personal property that belongs to the insured, to a member of the insured's family, or to a domestic employee of the insured.

It also covers household personal property for which the insured is legally liable. This includes property purchased through installment plans.

The insured may extend up to 10 percent of the applicable limit to such property away from the premises. According to explanatory information from ISO, this endorsement applies only to owner-occupants of three and four family dwellings.

Increase In Rebuilding Expenses Following Disaster (Additional Expense Coverage On Annual Aggregate Basis), CP 04 09

This coverage option was introduced with the 2012 revisions. It provides additional expenses when the costs of labor and material increase as a result of a disaster and the total cost for repair or replacement exceeds the limit of insurance.

This endorsement is a good idea, given that the costs of labor and material rise following widespread disasters, such as hurricanes and tornadoes. According to ISO, the cost per square foot for housing construction was estimated to have quadrupled in the first six months following hurricanes Rita and Katrina. Among the features of this endorsement are the following:

- Coverage applies only to the buildings identified in the endorsement schedule.

- Coverage applies to damage resulting from an event declared to be a disaster, as well as damage resulting from an event that occurs in close temporal proximity to the disaster—provided all the coverage criteria are met.

- The maximum amount of additional coverage is determined by applying a specified percentage to the limit of insurance for specific insurance, or to the value of the building when blanket insurance is being provided (adjusted for coinsurance),

- A portion of the additional coverage, applying to a building, can be used to cover debris removal and the increased costs of compliance with building codes if the policy includes ordinance or law coverage.

- Coverage is on an annual aggregate basis.

Increased Cost Of Loss And Related Expenses For Green Upgrades, CP 04 02

The schedule for this endorsement was revised with the 2012 revisions to facilitate the identification of personal property when not all personal property is covered for green upgrades and to enable entering different percentage selections for the building and personal property. For purposes of this endorsement, the word *green* is defined as "enhanced energy efficiency or use of environmentally-preferable, sustainable materials, products or methods in design, construction, manufacture or operation, as recognized by a Green Standards-setter."

Leased Property, CP 14 60

The insured may need to insure personal property that he leases. If he chooses not to include such property under the BPP form, this endorsement covers it. The leased property must be specifically described on the schedule. Any property covered by this endorsement should not be included when calculating a value for the insured's personal property or the property of others.

The insured may cover losses under this endorsement for an agreed value. However, unlike the optional agreed value coverage available in the property forms, coinsurance provisions still apply. This endorsement allows the insured to select a valuation other than actual cash value (such as replacement cost) on an item-by-item basis for leased property.

Legal Liability Coverage Schedule, CP DS 05

This endorsement is used in conjunction with form CP 00 40, Legal Liability Coverage Form (see Chapter 7). The form describes the insured's location and occupancy, the property to which coverage applies, and the limits of insurance.

Limitation On Loss Settlement – Blanket Insurance (Margin Clause), CP 12 32

The question of whether a property policy is written to apply on a blanket or specific basis has persisted for years. When insurance is written on a specific insurance basis, a specific amount of insurance applies to the covered property, such as a building or structure, and/or business personal property. When property is written to apply on a blanket basis, the amount of insurance available for any loss is the one amount representing the total values of all covered property.

Blanket insurance generally is employed when a policyholder has one type of property (realty or business personal property, business personal property and personal property of others) contained in one or more buildings. Where one amount is applicable to any loss, a policy holder, assuming it is otherwise in compliance with the coinsurance requirements, could still collect the full amount of its loss even when the value of covered property destroyed is more than the value declared on the statement of values, a document, which is a condition precedent to blanket insurance. To address such issues, ISO introduced a margin clause in 2007 in an optional endorsement for use on blanket policies entitled, Limitation of Loss Settlement – Blanket Insurance (Margin Clause), CP 12 32.

Margin clauses can vary by insurer. In general, however, this clause transforms coverage from a blanket to a specific coverage basis, but the added provision that the maximum amount payable is a certain percentage or margin above the property's value listed on the statement of values.

What may beg the question is why insurers are adding these clauses in the first place. The apparent impetus for these clauses is reinsurance requirements. Following large losses involving hurricanes and other catastrophic events, insurers found that, while many properties were underinsured, insureds were still able to capitalize on recoveries without being penalized. An example is where a policy is written for a blanket limit of $1 million on two buildings, with an agreed value endorsement, and with the statement of values representing that the replacement cost of each building is $500,000. If one of the buildings is destroyed and its costs $1 million to replace it, the insured can collect the $1 million (once it is replaced), even the named insured purchased only $500,000 of insurance on that building. If, on the other hand, a 20 percent margin clause were to be applicable, the most the insured could collect for its loss would be $600,000 (20% times $500,000 for an additional $100,000). If the margin clause were for 50 percent, the amount recoverable would be $750,000.

The fallacy of the reinsurers' argument is that the insured actually paid for $1 million of insurance, so why not give the named insured the coverage it purchased? Another point is that underwriters could avoid this problem by (1) requiring appraisals of real property from qualified professionals every five years or so instead of permitting insurance agents and brokers to calculate estimates based on square footage or other measures, and (2) being more discretionary with issuing the Agreed Value (or formerly known as the Agreed Amount) provision. When the Agreed Value provision is applicable, it, in effect, suspends the coinsurance clause, which otherwise requires an insured to purchase insurance on its property to a certain specified percentage of its full value, ranging from 80 to 100 percent. (When blanket coverage applies, 90 percent is mandatory).

Purchasers of commercial property insurance have come to learn that the Agreed Value provision is a good thing to have so as to maximize the amount of insurance payable in the event of loss. It also avoids having to understand the coinsurance clause, which remains an enigma to many people. In fact, nothing could encourage more policyholders to take advantage of the Agreed Value provision than the approach taken by ISO with its Building and Personal Property Coverage Form, CP 00 10, where agreed value is a coverage option. All that is necessary to activate this provision is to so designated it in the commercial property declarations.

When the margin clause is issued by an insurer, and it is not always done so, it virtually does away with the Agreed Value provision.

Limitations On Coverage For Roof Surfacing, CP 10 36

This endorsement provides a coverage option introduced with the 2012 revisions for roof surfacing, which is susceptible to deterioration over time and must be replaced. It is not unusual for insurers to be required to replace roofs which, prior to a loss, are determined to have been in poor condition. To save on argument and money, the insurer, with the attachment of this endorsement, will pay the actual cash value of such roofing at the time of a covered cause loss, including wind or hail, if covered, instead of replacement cost, to the extent RC applies to a building.

To the extent of any loss or damage by wind and/or hail, to the extent otherwise provided, the insurer agrees not to pay for cosmetic damage to roof surfacing caused by wind or hail.

For purposes of this endorsement, cosmetic damage means that the wind and/or hail caused "marring, pitting or other superficial damage that altered the appearance of the roof surfacing, but such damage does not prevent the roof from continuing to function as a barrier to entrance of the elements to the same extent as it did before the cosmetic damage occurred." Also, for purposes of this endorsement, *roof surfacing* refers to "the shingles, tiles, cladding, metal or synthetic sheeting or similar materials covering the roof and includes all materials used in securing the roof surface and all materials applied to or under the roof surface for moisture protection, as well as roof flashing."

Limitations On Fungus, Wet Rot, Dry Rot And Bacteria, CP 01 71

This endorsement reflects the change in treatment of mold-related damage coverage made in the CP 00 10 04 02 edition. This endorsement is attached to previous editions to reflect the changes. The fungus, wet rot, dry rot, and bacteria exclusion is added and the limited coverage for fungus, wet rot, dry rot, and bacteria is added back by way of additional coverage. See Chapter 2.

Loss Payable Provisions, CP 12 18

When someone other than the named insured has an insurable interest in the covered property, form CP 12 18 protects that interest in one or more of the following ways:

1. Loss payable—this is very similar to loss payable provisions in other policies. Under this provision, any losses payable are payable to the insured and a named loss payee as their interests may appear. Under this provision, the loss payee has no further rights than does the insured.

2. Lender's loss payable—like a mortgage clause, this provision establishes separate rights of the loss payee and insured. Even if the insured breaches any policy condition, the loss payee will still collect on a covered claim. This provision is used when a mortgage holders clause is not applicable. The insured and loss payee may document the loss payee's interest in the property by written instruments such as warehouse receipts; a contract for deed; bills of lading; financing statements; or mortgages, deeds of trust, or security agreements.

3. Contract of sale—this clause protects the duplicate interests of the insured and another party with whom the insured has entered into a contract for the sale of covered property. The endorsement amends the definition of the word *you* to include the loss payee.

4. Building owner—names the building owner as a loss payee and recognizes the owner's interest under a tenant's property damage coverage. Losses for tenants' improvements and betterments will be adjusted with the tenant. The 2007 revision added this clause.

There is no additional premium charge for use of endorsement CP 12 18.

Endorsement CP 12 18 was revised to add an option, building owner loss payable, to identify the building owner and recognize that entity as a loss payee. This endorsement was first introduced in 1985. Its original purpose was to combine in a single document two endorsements previously available: Loss Payable Clause, and Lender's Loss Payable Clause, as well as a Contract of Sale Clause. All that was (and still is) necessary to activate the appropriate clause is to designate it with an X and complete the endorsement schedule, which requests the description of the property and the loss payee's name and address. It should be noted that the 1985 and 1990 editions of the Loss Payable Endorsement described the lender's loss payable provision as covering a creditor (including a mortgage holder or trustee) with whom the named insured has entered into a contract for the sale of coverage property and whose interest in that covered property was established by such written contracts as warehouse receipts, a contract or deed, bills of lading, or financing statement.

Unless a lender specifically requires the issuance of the lender's loss payable provision and confirms that it has been issued, the lender may likely find itself instead in the possession of the loss payable provision, which is more limited in scope. The reason is that to many people, only two forms exist: the mortgagee provision for real estate and the loss payable provision for personal property.

Manufacturers Consequential Loss Assumption, CP 99 02

As with other consequential loss endorsements, this one covers indirect damage. It covers the reduction in value of physically undamaged stock in the process of being manufactured. Such a reduction in value must result from a covered direct loss to other unfinished stock. The rate for this coverage is 25 percent above that for business personal property. When the policy does not break out stock from other personal property, the increase factor is 15 percent.

For coinsurance purposes, the value of stock in process at the insured location includes the additional value that it represents in stock at other locations. The minimum coinsurance amount is 80 percent.

Manufacturer's Selling Price (Finished "Stock" Only), CP 99 30

This endorsement amends the method at which loss to stock is adjusted. It provides for valuation based on selling price less any applicable discounts and expenses for all completed stock. Unlike the BPP form, such adjustment is not limited to finished stock that is sold but not delivered.

Market Value – Stock, CP 99 31

This endorsement amends the method by which loss to certain types of stock is adjusted. It covers stock subject to market value. Such stock is defined as the "kind that is bought and sold at an established market exchange where the market prices are posted and quoted." Stocks of wines and distilled spirits are not eligible for this endorsement (see CP 99 05 earlier in this chapter).

The endorsement agrees to set the value of such stock at the market price less any applicable discounts and expenses.

Molten Material, CP 10 60

The molten material endorsement adds the accidental discharge of molten material from equipment as a covered peril. It also covers damage done by the heat released from the discharged molten material. It applies only to the basic, CP 10 10, or broad, CP 10 20, causes of loss forms because the special form, CP 10 30, contains no exclusion for this cause of loss.

The endorsement excludes the following:

1.   Loss of or damage to the discharged material;

2.   The cost to repair any defect that caused the discharge; or

3.   The cost to remove or recover the discharged material.

Multiple Deductible, CP 03 20

The multiple deductible endorsement allows the insured to schedule different deductible amounts at different locations. It also allows the choice of different deductibles for the perils of wind or hail and theft.

Multiple Location/Premium And Dispersion Credit Application, CP 13 70

Insureds use this endorsement for calculating a provisional premium for use with a reporting form or for determining a multiple location average rate.

Newly Acquired Or Constructed Property – Increased Limit, CP 04 25

The policy automatically provides an extension in the amount of $250,000 for newly acquired or constructed property. This endorsement increases that limit. It must be written for the same causes of loss as the underlying policy and must apply to all policies providing coverage on the same building property.

Off-premises Interruption Of Business – Vehicles And Mobile Equipment, CP 15 06

ISO introduced this endorsement, which carries an 02 14 edition date, to address exposures of companies that have operations wherein mobile equipment and vehicles are used away from the premises. In its explanatory materials, ISO listed the following examples of businesses that may need this coverage: retail stores and manufacturers that provided delivery, repair, or installation services and office risks that operate off-premises services such as document shredding, pet grooming, or mobile medical diagnostics. The form, though, is not designed for businesses with only mobile operations.

The endorsement may be used with the three ISO CP business interruption forms: CP 00 30, CP 00 32, and CP 00 50 (see Chapter 7 for more information on the business income program). Property must be within the policy's coverage territory. The endorsement contains a schedule for vehicles, mobile equipment and machinery or equipment permanently installed on such property, and certain temporary substitute property.

The covered perils and exclusions of the causes of loss form apply, but the endorsement adds a few exclusions and covered causes of loss, such as for loss or damage caused by collision or overturn. Collision can be added as a covered cause of loss in the schedule. Contact with a bird or animal or with falling objects or missiles is covered. Loss or damage caused by using scheduled property in any organized or professional racing or demolition contest is not covered, nor is a suspension of operations due to mechanical or electrical breakdown, malfunction, or failure to operate; wear and tear; or tire blowouts, punctures, or other road damage to tires.

The endorsement does not provide coverage for physical damage to property or for the repair or replacement of damaged property—only loss of income due to a suspension of operations is covered.

Ordinance Or Law Coverage, CP 04 05

The ordinance or law coverage endorsement responds if the enforcement of any building, zoning, or land use law results in added costs that are not covered as direct loss. The insured indicates on the declarations which of three distinct coverages is desired: Coverage A, Loss to the Undamaged Portion of the Building; Coverage B, Demolition Cost Coverage; and Coverage C, Increased Cost of Construction Coverage.

The pre-2000 edition of this endorsement clearly stated that it was only Coverage A where the ordinance or law must have been in force at the time of loss. Reference to when the ordinance or law applied with respect to Coverages B and C was silent. Since the 2000 edition, a new provision, Application of Coverage(s), was added, which clarifies that all coverages are subject to an ordinance or law that was in force at the time of loss. If read literally, this means coverage would not apply if the ordinance or law is enacted or changed as a result of a loss, subject to coverage hereunder. The provision in question reads in part as follows:

> The Coverage(s) provided by this endorsement apply only if both **B.1** and **B.2** are satisfied and are then subject to the qualifications set forth in **B.3**.

1. The ordinance or law:

    a. Regulates the demolition, construction or repair of buildings, or establishes zoning or land use requirements at the described premises; and

    b. Is in force at the time of loss.

1. Coverage A, Loss to the Undamaged Portion of the Building—covers the loss of value to the undamaged portion of the building caused by the enforcement of certain ordinances or laws. Such laws require demolition of a building after it suffers a certain percentage of direct damage. They also regulate construction, repair, zoning, or land use (such as laws that do not allow the same type of land use upon rebuilding as the insured had before the loss). There is no coverage if the insured was required to comply with an ordinance and failed to do so. Coverage A is not an additional amount of insurance but merely an extension of the existing policy limit. Thus, recovery is limited to the lesser of actual cash value or the building coverage limit if replacement cost coverage does not apply. Replacement cost will not apply if an insured chooses not to repair or replace, or if the insured did not buy the coverage.

The insured must purchase coverage for at least 80 percent of the property's replacement cost value if the insured has added Coverage C (see below), or 80 percent of actual cash value if Coverage C is not included. Since coverage C requires that the underlying policy include the replacement cost option, the rules effectively require insurance equal to 80 percent of the property's replacement cost when Coverage C is selected.

2. Coverage B, Demolition Cost Coverage—if the insured must demolish the undamaged portion of the building, this coverage pays the cost of that demolition. It also pays to clear the site of undamaged parts of the property. The CP 04 05 limits the amount of debris removal coverage to the lesser of the amount actually spent to demolish and clear the site or the coverage B limit. Coinsurance does not apply to Coverage B.

3. Coverage C, Increased Cost of Construction—if the insured actually repairs or replaces the building (either at the same or another location), Coverage C pays the increased cost of construction at the same premises or the coverage C limit (whichever is less). The coverage does not require replacement at the same location. It limits payment to the cost to replace *at that location*. If the insured chooses to rebuild elsewhere,

the loss payment is figured on the cost to rebuild at the original location.

However, if the ordinance or law requires relocation, coverage C pays the lesser of the increased cost of construction at the new premises or the applicable limit. The form limits the time to rebuild to two years. However, that limit may be extended by another two years.

The endorsement provides an extensive description of "proportionate loss payment." Many losses involve damage from both covered and uncovered perils. When a building suffers damage from both a flood and a fire, the BPP form covers only the fire damage. The wording on the CP 04 05 emphasizes that any increased costs due to the operation of building laws will be covered on a proportionate basis for damage from the covered perils only.

A statement clarifies that the endorsement responds only to the minimum requirements of that law. It specifically excludes costs of "recommend actions" in excess of what the law actually requires.

Ordinance Or Law – Increased Period Of Restoration, CP 15 31

If property at the described premises sustains loss or damage from a covered cause, coverage is extended to include the amount of actual and necessary loss the named insured sustains during the increased period of suspension of operations caused by or resulting from the reinforcement of any ordinance or law that regulates the construction or repair of any property, requires the tearing down of parts of any property not damaged by a covered cause of loss, and is in force at the time of loss.

In light of the 2012 revisions, the increased period of suspension of operations caused by or resulting from the enforcement of any ordinance or law is replaced with the suspension of operations caused by or resulting from a requirement to comply with any ordinance or law. *Compliance* connotes a broader term than *suspension*.

Outdoor Trees, Shrubs And Plants, CP 14 30

The building and personal property form provides up to $1,000 coverage, subject to a limit of $250, per item for outdoor trees, shrubs, and plants. It covers these items only for the perils of fire, lightning, explosion, riot or civil commotion, or aircraft.

This endorsement increases the coverage on these items and expands it to make them subject to the perils of the policy. The insured may choose to exclude loss caused by vehicles.

Even with open perils coverage, this endorsement still does not cover damage to trees, shrubs, and plants from ice and snow, insects, or animals. The CP 14 30 does not cover outdoor trees, shrubs, and plants for loss from the following:

1. Dampness or dryness of atmosphere;

2. Changes in or extremes of temperature; or

3. Rain, snow, ice, or sleet.

Trees, shrubs, and plants that the insured grows for commercial purposes are not eligible for this coverage, nor is standing timber.

Outdoor Signs, CP 14 40

In the 2007 edition of the commercial property forms, ISO increased the limit of insurance for outdoor signs from $1,000 to $2,500, thus increasing coverage. Coverage was also broadened to include all causes of loss otherwise covered under the applicable causes of loss form.

The Outdoor Signs endorsement, CP 14 40, was revised in accordance with the broadening of coverage on the underlying policies. The endorsement can be used to increase the dollar limit.

The schedule contains information about the covered signs' location, materials from which they are constructed, individual limits, coinsurance percentage, applicable causes of loss form, and additional premium.

The endorsement clarifies that the limit in the basic policy no longer applies. Any unscheduled signs, however, remain subject to the limit of liability and the limited causes of loss in the coverage extension.

Payroll Limitation Or Exclusion, CP 15 10

The term *ordinary payroll* with reference to business income forms means payroll of all employees other than those in the managerial level. In order to facilitate the limitation or exclusion of payroll of all employees, including those in the managerial level, the Ordinary Payroll Limitation or Exclusion Endorsement, CP 15 10, was changed by dropping reference to the word *Ordinary*. This revised endorsement provides a means to limit or exclude the payroll expense of any category of employees.

Peak Season Limit Of Insurance, CP 12 30

Some businesses experience seasonal fluctuations in the value of business personal property. This endorsement addresses that issue by providing increased coverage during designated periods of time.

The insured chooses the property that increases in value, the amount of the increase, and the applicable time period.

Reporting form policies are not eligible for this endorsement. Also, the time periods indicated must not extend beyond the expiration date of the policy (the anniversary date if payable in annual installments).

Pier And Wharf Additional Covered Causes of Loss, CP 10 70

Piers and wharves are specifically eliminated as covered property in the property not covered section of the BPP form. Such items are covered only if added to the policy via endorsement CP 14 10. They face unusual exposure to certain causes of loss not covered by the basic or broad causes of loss forms. This endorsement extends those causes of loss forms to cover loss caused by floating ice or collision of any vessel or floating object.

All pier and wharf structures are eligible for this endorsement except floating structures or equipment not incidental to a fixed pier or wharf. This endorsement is not used with the special causes of loss form, CP 10 30.

Pollutant Cleanup And Removal Additional Aggregate Limit Of Insurance, CP 04 07

CP 04 07 provides an additional annual aggregate limit of insurance applicable exclusively to the costs to remove pollutants from land or water at the insured's premises in excess of the $10,000 additional coverage annual aggregate in the property damage forms.

The unendorsed policy provides an aggregate amount of $10,000 to cover the costs of pollutant cleanup and removal. The BPP form provides coverage if a covered cause of loss causes the discharge, dispersal, seepage, migration, release, or escape of pollutants. This endorsement increases that annual aggregate amount.

The minimum deductible for this endorsement is $1,000, but it should not be less than the largest direct damage deductible for any of the locations shown on the endorsement. This deductible is independent from the direct damage deductible.

Endorsement CP 04 07 does not come into play until both the underlying amount of $10,000 and the scheduled deductible are exceeded. For example, an insured fuel oil distributor suffers an oil spill. This insured purchased CP 04 07 in the amount of $35,000 with a $5,000 deductible. Earlier in the year, he used $7,000 of the policy's coverage to pay for another oil spill.

If the current spill involves cleanup charges of $40,000, payment by the insurer is calculated as follows:

$40,000	Cleanup charges
− 3,000	Amount of coverage remaining under CP policy
− 5,000	Deductible on endorsement CP 04 07
$32,000	Payment by insurer under the CP 04 07

Property In Process Of Manufacturing By Others – Limited International Coverage, CP 04 33

The BPP form's coverage territory is limited to the U.S., Canada, and Puerto Rico. Insureds who conduct international business outside of the U.S., Canada, and Puerto Rico can purchase limited international property coverage under this endorsement. Coverage applies to the insured's property that is being assembled outside of the coverage territory. The manufacturing of the materials and in-process goods must be done at a location that the insured does not own or operate. For example, a U.S.-based insured may have its computer components assembled in China or India rather than have the components assembled in the U.S. The endorsement does not cover the assembled goods for sale or property in the care of a carrier or bailee for hire.

Protective Safeguards, CP 04 11

As a condition of writing a risk, an insurer may require the installation of protective safeguards or the use of some other type of security device. This endorsement identifies the fire protection safeguards that exist on the insured's property. Such devices fall into one of the following five categories, as enumerated on the endorsement:

P-1 Automatic Sprinkler System, including related supervisory services, meaning:

(1) Any automatic fire protective or extinguishing system, including connected:

(a) Sprinklers and discharge nozzles;

(b) Ducts, pipes, valves and fittings;

(c) Tanks, their component parts and supports; and

(d) Pumps and private fire protection mains.

(2) When supplied from an automatic fire protective system:

(a) Non-automatic fire protective systems; and

(b) Hydrants, standpipes and outlets.

P-2 Automatic Fire Alarm, protecting the entire building, that is:

(1) Connected to a central station; or

(2) Reporting to a public or private fire alarm station.

P-3 Security Service, with a recording system or watch clock, making hourly rounds covering the entire building, when the premises are not in actual operation.

P-4 Service Contract with a privately owned fire department providing fire protection service to the described premises.

P-9 The protective system described in the Schedule.

The endorsement also clarifies the insured's duties with respect to the maintenance of such systems. The insured must keep the systems in operation and notify the insurance company if they are not working properly.

If the insured does not notify the insurer, coverage is suspended. If an automatic sprinkler must be shut down due to breakage, leakage, freezing conditions, or the opening of sprinkler heads, the insured has forty-eight hours to restore the systems before they must notify the insurer.

Radio Or Television Antennas, CP 14 50

When this endorsement is issued, covered property is expanded to include radio and television antennas, including satellite dishes, and lead-in wiring, masts, or towers, as described in the schedule of this endorsement.

This endorsement subjects antennas to not only the exclusion of the applicable causes of loss form, but also the three additional exclusions of dampness or dryness of atmosphere; changes in or extremes of temperature; or rain, snow, ice, or sleet.

Radioactive Contamination, CP 10 37

This endorsement extends coverage for loss caused by sudden and accidental radioactive contamination or resultant radiation damage to the described property. Such damage must arise from material used or stored on the described premises.

The endorsement provides two types of radioactive coverage:

1. Limited—the radioactive contamination must be caused by a covered cause of loss.

2. Broad—does not require that the radioactive contamination be caused by a covered cause of loss.

The location and type of property must be scheduled on the endorsement and the type of coverage desired. However, only broad form coverage may be elected if the insured has the special causes of loss form, CP 10 30.

The endorsement describes three instances when coverage does not apply:

1. If the described premises contains a functioning nuclear reactor.

2. If the described premises contains any new or used nuclear fuel intended for or used in such a nuclear reactor.

3. If the radioactive material causing the contamination is not located at the described premises.

Report Of Values, CP 13 60, and Supplemental Report Of Values, CP 13 61

These endorsements are used for submitting reports of property values according to the provisions of the Value Reporting form, CP 13 10. The CP 13 60 no longer refers to itself as an endorsement. ISO says that the word *endorsement* implies a change to the policy and the CP 13 60 makes no changes. Thus, it is called a report.

Specified Business Personal Property Temporarily Away From Premises, CP 04 04

This endorsement, introduced in 2012, is intended to provide coverage for business personal property temporary away from the described premises, in the course of daily business activities, while in the care, custody, or control of the named insured or its employee.

For coverage to apply, the property needs to be described in the schedule either by item or category, along with a limit. This endorsement is not intended to apply to property in the possession of salespersons, except at a fair, trade show, or exhibition, and does not cover stock or products of a business. No coverage applies to personal property in the custody of a common or contract carrier. If the causes of loss form includes theft, business personal property while in a motor vehicle is also covered for theft, provided there is visible signs of such theft.

Spoilage Coverage, CP 04 40

The insured may choose to extend direct coverage for spoilage of perishable stock via this endorsement. ISO lists types of property or occupancy for spoilage coverage, identifying them by class 1, 2, and 3.

Class 1 includes bakery goods, cheese shops, delicatessens, fruits and vegetables, and restaurants. Class 2 includes dairy products (excluding ice cream), grocery stores, meat and poultry markets, pharmaceuticals— non-manufacturing, and supermarkets. Class 3 includes dairy products (including ice cream), florists, greenhouses, and seafood. For other types of property or occupancies not included in any of the three classes, ISO rules say to refer to specific company manuals.

The endorsement offers coverage for loss or damage caused by the following:

    a.   Breakdown or Contamination:

        1.   Change in temperature or humidity resulting from mechanical breakdown or mechanical failure of refrigerating, cooling or humidity control apparatus or equipment, but only while such equipment or apparatus is at the described premises; and

        2.   Contamination by the refrigerant.

    b.   Power outage, meaning change in temperature or humidity resulting from complete or partial interruption of electrical power, either on or off the described premises, due to conditions beyond the insured's control.

If the insured chooses breakdown or contamination coverage, a refrigeration maintenance agreement must be in force. If the insured voluntarily terminates the agreement, the coverage is suspended at that location.

This endorsement has a deductible separate from the rest of the policy. The insured may select to value the property at selling price. In that case the insurer determines the value of the property at selling price less any discounts and expenses.

Sprinkler Leakage – Earthquake Extension, CP 10 39

This endorsement adds sprinkler leakage loss or damage caused by earthquake or volcanic eruption as covered causes of loss. It is not necessary to use the endorsement with the Causes of Loss – Earthquake form, CP 10 40, since that form already includes sprinkler leakage coverage.

Sprinkler Leakage Exclusion, CP 10 56

An insurer or an insured may wish to exclude sprinkler leakage coverage from some items of property. The declarations indicate such property. If a covered cause of loss results, that damage is covered.

This endorsement may be used with any of the causes of loss forms. On the basic and broad forms, sprinkler leakage is excluded unless caused by a covered cause of loss. Also under the broad form, this endorsement deletes sprinkler leakage as a covered cause of collapse.

The endorsement also makes the following changes to the CP 10 30:

1. Eliminates coverage for damage done by liquids, powder, and other listed causes that leak or flow from plumbing, heating, air conditioning equipment, and other listed equipment, unless the insured does his best to maintain heat in the structure or drains the system and shuts off the supply if the heat is not maintained.

2. Agrees to pay for damage to fire extinguishing equipment if the damage was caused by freezing and the insured:

   a. does his/her best to maintain heat in the structure; or

   b. drains the system and shuts off the supply, if the heat is not maintained.

3.   Removes leakage from fire extinguishing equipment from the definition of *specified causes of loss*.

The 2007 revision added a schedule to this endorsement.

Storage Or Repairs Limited Liability, CP 99 42

This endorsement modifies the term *actual cash value* as it relates to personal property of others in the valuation condition. In the event of a covered loss to such property, the insurer pays the lesser of the property's actual cash value or the value shown on the receipt the insured issued to the owner before the loss.

Suspension Or Reinstatement Of Coverage For Loss Caused By Breakdown Of Certain Equipment, CP 10 47

This endorsement was introduced with the 2012 revisions. The purpose of this endorsement is to enable insurers to suspend and reinstate equipment breakdown coverage in accordance with Paragraph E. of CP 10 46. Paragraph E. states that if any covered equipment, as defined, is found to be in, or exposed to, a dangerous condition, the insurer's representative can suspend the coverage by written notice. If there is a breakdown of covered equipment during the period of suspension there, of course, is no coverage. An endorsement must be issued to reinstate coverage.

Tentative Rate, CP 99 93

Used only on specifically rated property, this endorsement states that the premium rates for the commercial property coverage part are tentative and that the insurer will adjust the premium once the rates are determined. If the policy is a renewal, the previous specific rate may need to be changed due to materially changed conditions. The endorsement provides that premium adjustment is effective from the renewal date once the rates are promulgated.

Terrorism Endorsements

Following the September 11, 2001, terrorist attacks and subsequent federal Terrorism Risk Insurance Act (TRIA) ISO developed a series of endorsements to the commercial property program forms related to terrorist acts. A discussion of these endorsements constitute part of Chapter 17.

Theft Exclusion, CP 10 33

If an insurer or insured wishes to exclude theft from a policy subject to the Causes of Loss – Special form, CP 10 30, this endorsement is attached. With this endorsement attached, there is no coverage for theft. However, the following are covered:

1.   Loss or damage due to looting at the time and place of a riot or civil commotion;

2.   Building damage caused by the breaking in or exiting of burglars; or

3.   Any damage caused by a resulting covered cause of loss.

To better facilitate the use of this endorsement when there is more than one location to which this exclusion applies, a 2012 revision introduces a schedule for that purpose.

Theft Of Building Materials And Supplies (Other Than Builders Risk), CP 10 44

This coverage option was introduced with the 2012 revisions. Under the limitations section of the Causes of Loss – Special form, CP 10 30, theft coverage for building materials and supplies that are not part of the building or structure is limited to those that are held for sale by the insured. When this endorsement is attached to the policy it provides coverage for the theft of building materials and supplies that are located on or within 100 feet of the premises when such property is intended to become a permanent part of the building or structure. This endorsement does not apply to the Builders Risk Coverage Form, CP 00 20, Similar coverage can be provided under the builders risk policy by using Builders Risk – Theft of Building Materials, Fixtures, Machinery, Equipment, CP 11 21.

This endorsement is compatible with the Building and Personal Property Coverage Form and the Condominium Association Coverage Form, provided the Causes of Loss – Special form applies without the theft exclusion.

Utility Services – Direct Damage, CP 04 17

This endorsement is necessary to obtain coverage against physical damage to covered property stemming from interruption in utility service on or away from the described premises, in light of the utility services exclusion found in all three of the causes of loss forms, which all read alike. The schedule lists the following exposures available for coverage:

(1) Water Supply. The term *water supply services* is defined to mean pumping stations and water mains supplying water to the described premises.

(2) Communication Supply including overhead transmission lines or not including overhead transmission lines. The term *communication supply services* is defined to mean "property supply communication services, including telephone, radio, microwave or television services to the described premises, such as: a. communication transmission lines, including optic fiber transmission lines; b. coaxial cables; and c. microwave radio relays, except satellites." Overhead transmission lines are not included unless indicated by an X in the schedule.

(3) Power Supply including overhead transmission lines or not including overhead transmission lines. The term *power supply services* is defined to mean "the following types of property supplying electricity, steam or gas to the described premises: a. utility generating plants, b. switching stations; c. substations; d. transformers; and d. transmission lines." Overhead transmission lines are not included unless indicated by an X in the schedule.

Space also is allocated in the endorsement for listing of the covered property and the applicable causes of loss form. Specifically precluded as covered property is electronic data. The meaning of *electronic data* appears in the coverage forms to which this endorsement is attached. These coverage forms are Building and Personal Property, Builders Risk, Condominium Association, Condominium Commercial Unit-Owners, Tobacco Sales Warehouses, and the Standard Property Policy.

Although space is allocated for a utility services limit of insurance, another provision of this endorsement states that the coverage under this endorsement is part of, and not in addition to, the limit of insurance stated in the declarations. Why is a provision made to insert a limit when, in fact, the limit is part of, and not in addition to, the policy limit? The answer is to accommodate those businesses whose properties are scheduled and not all of the properties are exposed to utility services losses. The same rationale applies to businesses with properties written on a blanket basis and not all locations are confronted with the utility services exposure.

Assume, for example, a grocery store purchases this coverage, subject to a broad causes of loss form. If it sustains power supply outage that causes spoilage to foodstuffs because of an act of vandalism at the supplier's premises, coverage would apply, subject to any deductible because the criteria for coverage has been met. Thus, there was loss or damage to the insured's business personal property; there was an interruption of service to the described premises; and the interruption resulted in direct physical damage by vandalism, a covered cause of loss, to the power supply services. It is important to emphasize that all of the criteria must be met. If, for example, the power outage was caused by flood or artificially generated electric currents, neither of which is covered, coverage would not apply for any loss or damage to the insured's covered property.

One of the questions that has persisted is whether coverage should be purchased for overhead transmission lines. To answer that question, one would have to know what overhead transmissions lines are and whether there is any difference between them and overhead power lines. ISO has answered this question with the 2012 revision of this endorsement. A paragraph was added that states, "As used in this endorsement, the term transmission lines includes all lines which serve to transmit communication service or power, including lines which may be identified as distribution lines."

Utility Services – Time Element, CP 15 45

The 2012 revision of this endorsement added a category of utility service: wastewater removal property, which is the utility system for removing wastewater and sewage from the described premises, other than a system designed primarily for draining storm water. The utility property includes sewer mains, pumping stations, and similar equipment for moving the effluent to a holding, treatment, or disposal facility. Coverage, however, does not apply to interruption in waste water removal service caused by a discharge of water or sewage due to heavy rainfall or flooding.

Like Utility Services – Direct Damage endorsement, CP 04 17, this time element endorsement also includes a paragraph D, which clarifies the meaning of *transmission lines*. This 2012 revision states that "the term transmission lines includes all lines which serve to transmit communication services or power, including line which may be identified as distribution lines."

Vacancy Changes, CP 04 60

The BPP form states that a building is vacant when at least 31 percent of its square footage is not rented or being used. This endorsement allows that percentage to be reduced to as low as 10 percent. In its explanatory material, ISO said that this endorsement provides a tool to recognize risks where a lower level of occupancy is sufficient in averting the hazards associated with vacancy.

Endorsements CP 04 50 and CP 04 60 may not be written on the same risk.

Vacancy Permit, CP 04 50

The BPP form covers a vacant building for sixty days. After sixty days of vacancy, there is no coverage for loss from vandalism, sprinkler leakage, building glass breakage, water damage, and theft or attempted theft. Also, after sixty days of vacancy, the policy reduces payment for any other covered claim by 15 percent. If the insured desires coverage for a longer period, this endorsement must be attached.

Coverage for direct physical loss or damage applies only to the locations and for the permit periods scheduled on the form or on the declarations. The insured may also exclude vandalism or sprinkler leakage as covered causes of loss during the vacancy for a reduction in premium.

Endorsements CP 04 50 and CP 04 60 may not be written on the same risk.

Value Reporting Form, CP 13 10

The purpose of the value reporting form is to allow an insured who has property that fluctuates in value to be fully protected at all times and to pay a premium based on the values actually at risk—provided the insured reports values correctly and promptly and maintains a sufficient limit of insurance to cover the highest value at any one time. In other words, if the insured follows the policy requirements, the endorsement provides complete and automatic coverage, avoidance of the dangers of both underinsurance and overinsurance on the property, and no necessity of increasing and decreasing amounts of insurance as values move up and down.

The policy indicates how often reports of value must be made to the insurer: daily, weekly, monthly, quarterly, or by policy year. For daily, weekly, monthly, or quarterly reporting, the first report must be made within sixty days of the end of the first reporting period. Subsequent reports must be made within thirty days of the end of each reporting period. A policy with an annual reporting period requires the report to be made within thirty days of the end of the period. At policy expiration, the insurer charges either an additional premium or tenders a refund, based on the average of the insured's reports of value.

The value reporting form contains a 100 percent coinsurance requirement. The insured must report specific insurance on any items. The insurer then subtracts the specific insurance from the values reported when computing the final premium.

If the insured does not submit the necessary reports, the policy calls for two types of penalty. The first is if the insured does not submit an initial report. In that case, any loss payable is reduced by 25 percent. If the insured fails to submit subsequent reports, any loss is adjusted based on the value last reported.

Vandalism Exclusion, CP 10 55

For a reduction in premium, the insured may choose to exclude vandalism as a covered cause of loss. Also, adding this endorsement may transform an otherwise unacceptable underwriting risk into an acceptable one.

Although the endorsement excludes vandalism, it does cover any resulting loss that is not excluded. The endorsement also deletes vandalism from the list of specified causes of loss.

The 2007 revision added a schedule to this endorsement.

Water Exclusion Endorsement, CP 10 32

Following litigation surrounding the aftermath of 2005's Hurricane Katrina, ISO introduced this 2008 endorsement to replace the water exclusion on the commercial property coverage part or the standard property policy. The purpose of the endorsement is to reinforce the scope of the water exclusion. Also, tsunami and storm surge were added to the list of excluded water. The word *discharged* was added to backup and overflow of sewer, drain, or sump; and *sump pump* and *related equipment* were added as well.

Watercraft Exclusion, CP 10 35

This endorsement excludes damage by watercraft to the following types of property:

1. Retaining walls that are not part of a building;

2. Bulkheads; or

3. Pilings, piers, wharves, or docks.

This endorsement may be used only with the special causes of loss form, CP 10 30.

Windstorm Or Hail Exclusion, CP 10 54

The windstorm or hail exclusion endorsement extends the windstorm or hail exclusion to also apply to indirect losses covered under business income coverage forms, extra expense coverage forms, and leasehold interest form.

The 2007 revision added a schedule to this endorsement.

Windstorm Or Hail Exclusion – Direct Damage, CP 10 53

An insurance company or an insured may desire to exclude certain property, identified in the declarations, from coverage for these perils.

This endorsement modifies the causes of loss forms to eliminate payment for loss caused directly or indirectly by windstorm or hail, regardless of any other cause or event that contributes concurrently or in any sequence to the loss or damage.

It also excludes damage done by rain, snow, or dust resulting from a windstorm. However, any resulting loss that is not excluded is covered.

The endorsement also excludes windstorm or hail damage as a covered cause of collapse and as a specified cause of loss. It also removes windstorm and hail as a covered cause of loss for property in transit.

Windstorm Or Hail Percentage Deductible, CP 03 21

This endorsement allows the insured to choose a deductible for the perils of windstorm or hail, apart from the deductible that applies to all other perils. The available deductibles are 1 percent, 2 percent, or 5 percent of covered property. This deductible is calculated as follows:

A.   Calculation Of The Deductible – All Policies

    1.   A Deductible is calculated separately for, and applies separately to:

        a.   Each building that sustains loss or damage;

        b.   The personal property at each building at which there is loss or damage to personal property;

        c.   Personal property in the open.

        If there is damage to both a building and personal property in that building, separate deductibles apply to the building and to the personal property.

Your Business Personal Property – Separation Of Coverage, CP 19 10

The various categories of business personal property (stock, contents except stock, machinery and equipment, furniture, fixtures, tenant's improvements and betterments) may be assigned individual limits of insurance by using this endorsement. It also functions as a way to exclude certain types of personal property since any categories not listed with an individual limit of insurance are not covered at the specified locations. Care must be taken in specifying a limit on one class of property at a scheduled location (e.g., stock), so that coverage is not inadvertently voided at that location on another category (e.g., all business personal property except stock).

Chapter 14

The Commercial Properties Program of American Association of Insurance Services (AAIS)

Another major insurance services association that provides loss cost services and policy form development is the American Association of Insurance Services (AAIS). AAIS is a national insurance advisory organization that develops policy forms and rating information used by more than 600 property/casualty insurers throughout the United States. Many insurers that do not subscribe to Insurance Services Offices (ISO) services use the resources of AAIS. However, it is not unheard of for some insurers to subscribe to both services

The AAIS program for commercial property exposures is similar to that of ISO, although there are some differences. This chapter highlights those differences.

ISO does not specify what risks are eligible or ineligible for their commercial property program. The AAIS rules manual does contain such a listing. AAIS includes these as eligible risks: habitational, mercantile, nonmanufacturing, and warehousing properties; manufacturers and processors, farm operations, and dwellings are not eligible for the AAIS commercial properties program. AAIS offers other programs for such risks, such as the commercial output program, farm properties program, and dwelling properties program.

In addition to the Building and Personal Property Coverage Part, CP-12, AAIS offers Builders' Risk, CP-14 or CP-15; Condominium Building Coverage Part, CP-19; Condominium Unit Coverage Part, CP-21; Personal Property Coverage Part – Reporting Form, CP-25; Earnings Coverage Part, CP-60; Extra Expense Coverage Part, CP-69; and Income Coverage Part, CP-70. This chapter examines the differences between AAIS and ISO in the primary form, the Building and Personal Property Coverage Part, and in the most often employed causes of loss form, the Special Perils Form, equivalent to ISO's CP 10 30. Having not been revised since its introduction—other than by the development of additional endorsements—the current edition is designated CP-12 Ed. 1.0.

Building and Personal Property Coverage Part

Covered Property

The AAIS form covers essentially the same building property as the ISO form. In addition to the described building, the CP-12 covers the following:

1. Completed additions

2. Fixtures, machinery, and equipment that are a permanent part of the building

3. Outdoor fixtures—ISO separates fixtures from machinery and equipment and does not require that fixtures be permanent. However, use of the word *permanent* may be redundant, as the definition of *fixture* implies permanence.

4. Personal property that the insured owns and uses to maintain or service the building—in addition to fire extinguishing apparatus, floor coverings, and various appliances, AAIS adds air conditioning equipment to the list of examples. Window-unit air conditioners are specifically covered as part of the building.

5. Additions, alterations, and repairs to the building are also covered, as are the materials and supplies used to make the alterations. The policy covers these items only if not covered elsewhere.

AAIS provides simplified coverage for business personal property. Instead of a list of the types of personal property covered, the AAIS policy says that it covers the named insured's business personal property in the buildings and structures described. Like AAIS, the ISO form covers the property within on-hundred feet of the building or structure. But unlike AAIS, ISO also covers property within one-hundred feet of the premises described in the declarations, whichever distance is greater. This ISO language compensates for property located in a high-rise, for example, where the distance to the front entrance is over one-hundred feet. Like ISO, the AAIS form also covers the following:

1. The named insured's interest (labor, material, and services) in the property of others

2. The named insured's use interest in improvements and betterments that is made to a rented building

3. Leased personal property for which the named insured is obligated to provide insurance

The final category of covered property is property belonging to others in the insured's care, custody, or control. As with ISO, the AAIS policy provides $2,500 coverage for property of others as a supplemental coverage when the business personal property supplemental coverage is indicated on the declarations page.

Property Excluded and Limitations

The section is similar to the ISO property not covered section, containing many of the same items. This section of the AAIS form also refers to the section of supplemental coverages where property for items otherwise limited or excluded is found.

The AAIS policy lists the following types of property as either excluded or limited in some fashion:

1. **Animals**—like the ISO form, the policy does not cover animals, unless owned by others that the insured boards or animals belonging to the insured that he holds for sale. Unlike ISO, the AAIS policy does not require animals held for sale to be located in buildings.

2. **Antennas, Awnings, Canopies, Fences, and Signs**—AAIS covers these items under supplemental coverages. This portion is more restrictive than ISO because ISO places no limit on awnings or canopies.

3. **Contraband**—this is the same as the ISO provision.

4. **Foundations, Retaining Walls, Pilings, Piers, Wharves, or Docks**—unlike ISO, AAIS does not include bulkheads as property not covered. Also, AAIS does not further define *foundations* as those of buildings, structures, machinery, or boilers.

5. **Land; Water; Growing Crops or Lawns; Cost of Excavation, Grading, or Filling; Paved Surfaces; or Underground Pipes, Flues, or Drains**—although the meaning of *paved* is fairly clear, ISO shows the following as examples: bridges, roadways, walks, patios. AAIS adds driveways and parking lots, but does not specify patios. ISO also excludes lawns that are a part of a vegetated roof from this category.

6. **Money and Securities**—both provisions are essentially the same.

7. **Property More Specifically Insured**—both provisions are similar and state that while property that is covered under another policy is not covered, any excess over the more specific insurance is covered.

8. **Trees, Shrubs, and Plants**—AAIS covers these items under supplemental coverages but makes an exception for these items the named insured owns and holds for sale. ISO makes an exception for these items, too, that are stock or part of a vegetated roof.

9. **Valuable Papers and Records—Research Cost**—except what AAIS covers under supplemental coverages, the cost to research, replace, or restore information on valuable papers and records, including on electronic or magnetic media, is not covered.

10. **Vehicles, Aircraft, and Watercraf**t—the AAIS policy makes an exception for the following (thus providing coverage):

    a. vehicles the insured manufactures, processes, warehouses, or holds for sale (other than autos held for sale)

    b. rowboats or canoes that are at the described premises and not in the water

The ISO policy excludes personal property while airborne or waterborne. AAIS has no such exclusion.

Additional Coverages

The AAIS Building and Personal Property Coverage Part contains the following additional coverages:

1. **Debris Removal**—the policy covers debris removal for up to 25 percent of the amount spent for the direct damage. This amount is included in the limit of liability. Unlike ISO, AAIS makes no mention of the deductible, thus limiting the insured's coverage for debris removal to 25 percent of the paid loss. The AAIS policy provides an additional $5,000 of debris removal when the total loss exceeds the limit of liability or when the 25 percent is not adequate.

What is not covered under the ISO form for debris removal is listed in five categories. However, the ISO form, unlike the AAIS form, does cover the removal of debris that is not part of the covered property but is on the described premises when the debris is caused by or results from an otherwise covered cause of loss. Also, the ISO form will pay an additional $25,000 (increased from $10,000 in 2012) for debris removal expense of covered property at each location when (1) the expense plus the amount of direct physical loss or damage exceeds the limit of insurance, or (2) the expense exceeds 25 percent of the sum of the deductible and the amount paid for direct physical loss or damage to covered property from a covered cause.

2.   **Emergency Removal**—this is like ISO's preservation of property provision, but AAIS covers the moved personal property for ten days (ISO's policy covers for thirty days).

3.   **Fire Department Service Charges**—$1,000 is available; the ISO form applies to each premises described in the declarations.

4.   **Pollutant Clean Up and Removal**—$10,000 is available, just as in the ISO form.

Supplemental Coverages

AAIS offers several supplemental coverages that are comparable to ISO's coverage extensions. These coverages are available only if a coinsurance percentage of 80 percent or more is shown on the declarations. Unless otherwise indicated, all of these supplemental coverages represent additional amounts of insurance.

The following coverages are available only when a limit is shown for either building or business personal property:

a.   **Antennas, Awnings, Canopies, Fences, and Signs**—$1,000 coverage for loss caused by fire, lightning, aircraft, riot or civil commotion, or explosion. AAIS specifically includes antenna masts, towers, and lead-in wiring. The $1,000 includes direct damage and debris removal.

b.   **Property Off-Premises**—$5,000 for property temporarily off-premises, including stock (merchandise held for sale). ISO provides $10,000. This supplemental coverage does not apply to property in a vehicle, in the care of the insured's salespersons or at a fair or exhibition.

The following coverages are available only when a limit is shown for building property:

a. **Increased Costs - Ordinance or Law**—up to $5,000 for each described premises to cover such costs. ISO's policy contains $10,000 coverage in the basic policy.

b. **Newly Acquired Buildings**—this coverage applies to buildings that are either built or acquired during the policy period. It is broader than ISO's similar provision. Unlike the ISO policy, AAIS does not restrict coverage for buildings being constructed "on the described premises." The limit available under AAIS is an amount equal to 25 percent of the current building limit, with a maximum of $250,000.

c. **Trees, Shrubs, and Plants**—the AAIS policy covers these for $1,000, subject to a maximum of $250 for any one tree, shrub, or plant. It provides coverage for these items for the perils of aircraft, civil commotion, explosion, fire, lightning, or riot. The ISO form provides the same limit against the same named perils but does not include trees, shrubs, or plants that are stock or part of vegetated roofs.

The following coverages are available only when a limit is shown for business personal property:

a. **Condominium Units**—if the described premises is a condo, AAIS provides up to 10 percent of the limit (maximum of $20,000) for fixtures, improvements, and alterations. This amount is included in the limit of liability. ISO has no similar coverage.

b. **Extra Expenses**—$1,000 to cover extra expense incurred in order to continue business after a covered loss. ISO offers this coverage only as part of the business income and extra expense form.

c. **Personal Effects**—$500 for personal effects owned by the named insured or his officers, partners, or employees. The per person limit is $100. ISO offers up to $2,500 per described premises with no per person maximum.

d. **Personal Property - Acquired Locations**—thirty-day coverage for personal property at acquired locations. AAIS provides this coverage in the amount of 10 percent of the business personal property limit, with a maximum of $100,000. This coverage does not apply to property at fairs or exhibitions.

e.   **Personal Property of Others**—$2,500 coverage. Unlike ISO, the AAIS policy also covers this property for the peril of theft.

f.   **Property in Transit**—$1,000 coverage for property in vehicles that the insured owns, leases, or operates. This coverage is available only with the special causes of loss form under the ISO program. The AAIS policy requires visible marks of forced entry.

g.   **Valuable Papers and Records – Research Cost**—$1,000 coverage, compared to ISO's $2,500.

What Must Be Done in Case of Loss

The AAIS policy lists the following loss conditions:

a.   **Notice**—prompt notice must be given to the insurer or the agent. ISO makes no mention of agent, although in general practice it is notice to the agent or broker that triggers notice to the insurer.

b.   **Protect Property**—both forms require that all reasonable steps must be taken to protect property from further loss.

c.   **Proof of Loss**—while ISO merely says that the proof of loss must contain the information that the insurer requests (it does state in a different provision that the insured must submit a description of how, when, and where the loss or damage occurred), AAIS spells out what must be included in the proof:

1.   Time, place, and circumstance of loss

2.   Other policies that might cover the loss

3.   The insured's interest in the damaged property as well as the interests of any others

4.   Changes in the title or occupancy

5.   Detailed estimates for repair or replacement of the covered property

6.   Plans and specifications of buildings or structures

7.   Detailed estimates of income loss and expenses

8.   Inventory of damaged and undamaged property but not if the loss is less than $10,000 or less than 5 percent of the total limit

d.   **Examination under Oath**—like the ISO form, the AAIS form states that if more than one person is examined, the insurer has the right to examine and receive statements separately and not in the presence of others.

e.   **Records**—these must be produced if the insurer requests.

f.   **Damaged Property**—must be available for inspection.

g.   **Volunteer Payments**—the insured must not make any voluntary payments, except at his own expense. This provision does not appear in ISO's policy.

h.   **Abandonment**—the AAIS form states that the insurer does not have to accept any abandonment of property, leaving open the possibility that it could, while the ISO form says that there can be no abandonment of any property to the insurer, leaving no possibility open.

i.   **Cooperation**—the AAIS form requires insured cooperation in performing all acts required by the commercial property coverage, but the ISO form expects insured cooperation specifically in the investigation or settlement of the claim.

Valuation

The AAIS form specifies that if replacement cost is not shown on the declarations page, all losses are adjusted at actual cash value (ACV). This provision describes eight other valuations:

1.   **Limited Replacement Cost**—as with ISO, if the building meets the coinsurance requirement and the loss is less than $2,500, replacement cost applies.

2.   **Glass**—safety glass is used when required by law.

3.   **Merchandise Sold**—at selling price less all discounts and unincurred expenses. ISO refers to this as stock sold but not delivered.

4.   **Valuable Papers and Records**—the cost of blank materials and the labor to transcribe the records.

5.   **Tenant's Improvements**—at ACV if repaired within a reasonable time. If not repaired, the value is based on a portion of the original cost new. This provision is the same as ISO.

6.   **Pair or Set**—the value of a lost or damaged article that is part of a pair or set is based on a reasonable proportion of the value of the entire pair or set but is not considered a total loss of the pair or set. ISO does not contain a similar provision.

7.   **Loss to Parts**—the value of a lost or damaged part of an item that consists of several parts when it is complete is based on the value only of the lost or damaged part or the cost to repair or replace it. ISO does not contain a similar provision.

8.   **Replacement Cost**—with this is option, as with ISO. AAIS specifies that replacement cost does not apply to objects of art, rarity, or antiquity, or to property of others. It also does not apply to paragraphs two through seven. Replacement cost is limited to the cost to repair or replace with similar materials on the same site and used for the same purpose. ISO does not require replacement on the same site, but if a different location is used, replacement cost is limited to the cost that would have been incurred if the building had been rebuilt at the original premises.

How Much We Pay

This section details six things that determine the amount of loss payable.

1.   **Insurable Interest**—AAIS's insurable interest is the same as the ISO policy concept of financial interest.

2.   **Deductible**—unlike ISO, the AAIS form applies the deductible before application of the coinsurance penalty. This formula results in a more favorable result for the insured.

3. **Loss Settlement Terms**—the AAIS policy agrees to pay the lesser of the following:

    a. the value of the property, as described in the valuation provision;

    b. the cost to repair, replace, or rebuild with materials of like kind and quality; or

    c. the applicable limit.

4. **Coinsurance**—the principle is the same as in the ISO form. To figure a loss divide the amount of insurance carried by the amount required and multiply by the amount of the loss. The difference from ISO's form is how the deductible is applied. ISO applies it after application of the coinsurance penalty; AAIS applies it before the coinsurance penalty. AAIS's method is more favorable to the insured, as shown in the following example:

Value of the property: $2,000,000

Coinsurance percentage: 80%

Amount of Insurance Carried: $1,000,000

Deductible: $10,000

Amount of loss: $ 400,000

ISO Method:

Step 1: $2,000,000 \times 80\% = \$1,600,000$ (amount required)

Step 2: $\$1,000,000 \div \$1,600,000 = .625$

Step 3: $\$ 400,000 \times .625 = \$250,000$

Step 4: $ 250,000 – $10,000 = $240,000 (payment by the insurer)

AAIS Method:

Step 1: $2,000,000 × 80% = $1,600,000 (amount required)

Step 2: $1,000,000 ÷ $1,600,000 = .625

Step 3: $ 400,000 – $10,000 = $390,000

Step 4: $ 390,000 × .625 = $243,750 (payment by the insurer)

5. **Insurance Under More Than One Coverage**—the provision is the same as ISO's provision.

6. **Insurance Under More Than One Policy**—the provision is the same as ISO's provision.

Loss Payment

The AAIS policy provides the insurer with the same four options that ISO provides:

1. Pay the value of loss;

2. Pay the cost of repairing or replacing the loss;

3. Rebuild, repair, or replace with property of equivalent kind and quality, to the extent practicable; or

4. Take all or any part of the damaged property at an agreed or appraised value.

The insurer must advise the insured of its intentions within thirty days of receipt of the proof of loss.

Payment for the insured's losses are adjusted with the insured unless another loss payee is named in the policy. A covered loss is payable thirty days after the following:

1.   The insurer receives a satisfactory proof of loss;

2.   The amount of loss has been agreed to in writing; an appraisal award has been filed with the insurer; or

3.   A final judgment has been entered.

Payment for loss to property of others may be adjusted with the insured on behalf of the owner or directly with the owner.

Other Conditions

The AAIS policy is subject to four additional conditions:

1.   **Appraisal**—similar to ISO's condition, but the AAIS policy imposes certain time limits. After the demand for the appraisal each party has twenty days to give the name of its appraiser to the other. The appraisers then have fifteen days to select an umpire, or either party may then submit the umpire choice to a court.

2.   **Mortgage Provisions**—identical to ISO, which calls its provision Mortgageholders.

3.   **Recoveries**—this is called Recovered Property in the ISO form. This condition is similar to ISO's, with one exception. If the insurer's payment for the original loss is less than the agreed loss due to a deductible or other limiting term in the policy, the AAIS policy calls for any recovery to be prorated between the insurer and the insured.

4.   **Vacancy – Unoccupancy**—the AAIS policy imposes one of two penalties on the insured if a building is vacant for more than sixty consecutive days. It also imposes a penalty if the building is unoccupied for the longer of sixty consecutive days or the usual or incidental unoccupancy period for the described premises. The penalties are as follows:

     a.   No payment at all for loss from theft, attempted theft, glass breakage, sprinkler leakage, vandalism, or water damage; and

     b.   Any other loss payable is reduced by 15 percent.

Special Perils Part

The AAIS Special Perils Part, CP-85, is similar to ISO's Causes of Loss – Special Form, CP 10 30.

The AAIS form provides three additional definitions: *sinkhole collapse*, *specified perils*, and *volcanic action*. The definitions of *sinkhole collapse* and *specified perils* are the same as in ISO, but ISO includes *sinkhole collapse* within the definition of specified perils. *Volcanic action* is the same as in ISO, but ISO includes it within the earth movement exclusion, the effect being the same.

The AAIS form covers risks of direct physical loss. The ISO forms had this same wording until 2012. Because reference to "risks of direct physical loss" can connote the chance of, and not an actual physical loss, and in light of some court cases, ISO deleted reference to "risks of direct physical loss." The AAIS coverage is subject to the following exclusions:

1. **Ordinance or Law**—the AAIS form does not cover loss or increased cost caused by enforcement of any code, ordinance, or law regulating the use, construction, or repair of any building or structure or requiring the demolition of any building or structure including the cost of removing its debris. This is similar to the ISO exclusion, which includes not only the enforcement of, but also the compliance with any such ordinances or laws.

2. **Earth Movement or Volcanic Eruption**—loss caused by any earth movement, other than sinkhole collapse, or caused by eruption, explosion, or effusion of a volcano is excluded by the AAIS form. ISO added language to its earth movement exclusion in 2012 to specify that both acts of natures and manmade occurrences are excluded. AAIS does not make this statement.

3. **Civil Authority**—this is called governmental action by ISO. The AAIS form lists confiscation and quarantine of property by civil authority as excluded actions, but the ISO form states that only the seizure or destruction of property by governmental action is excluded.

4. **Nuclear Hazard**—both forms contain similar nuclear hazard exclusions.

5. **Utility Failure**—called utility services by ISO. AAIS also excludes "reduced or increased voltage, low or high pressure, or other interruptions of normal services."

6. **War**—the exclusion is similar to ISO's, but AAIS adds that the discharge of a nuclear weapon, even if accidental, is an act of war.

7. **Water**—AAIS's form contains a few differences from ISO. It does not include mudslide or mudflow as types of water damage; it also does not exclude water that backs up or overflows from a sump. This second difference is a significant benefit to the policyholder, . ISO also excludes waterborne material carried or moved by water referred to in the exclusion. The ISO form states that the exclusion applies whether loss is caused by an act of nature or is otherwise caused. AAIS does not make this statement.

These seven items are excluded regardless of other causes or events that contribute to or aggravate the loss (concurrent causation language).

The following exclusions also apply, but any subsequent loss is covered if not excluded elsewhere:

1. **Animals**—the only subsequent losses that are covered must be caused by a specified peril or glass breakage. The ISO form is more specific is listing nesting, infestation, or discharge or release of waste products or secretions by insects, birds, rodents, or other animals where AAIS excludes loss caused by animals, a broader exclusion.

2. **Collapse**—just as in the ISO form, collapse is excluded except as provided in the additional coverage.

3. **Contamination or Deterioration**—this includes "corrosion, decay, fungus, mildew, mold, rot, rust, or any quality, faulty, or weakness in property that causes it to damage or destroy itself." The ISO form does not exclude loss from contamination. Also, as with ISO, subsequent losses caused by a specified peril or glass breakage are covered.

4. **Criminal, Fraudulent, or Dishonest Acts**—the ISO exclusion has been broadened to keep pace with the AAIS version. Thus, losses caused by such acts of the named insured, partners, members, officers, managers, employees, including temporary and leased ones, trustees, authorized representatives, directors, and anyone to whom the named insured entrusts property are

not covered. AAIS adds the category of "others who have an interest in the property." For instance, such acts committed by the mortgagee might not be covered.

5. **Defects, Errors, and Omissions**—this exclusion applies to such actions in relation to land use, design, construction, and workmanship. Any ensuing loss not excluded is covered.

6. **Electrical Currents**—ISO excludes artificially generated electrical, magnetic, or electromagnetic energy that damages, disturbs, disrupts, or otherwise interferes with any electrical or electronic device, wire, appliance, system, network, or devices, appliances, systems, or networks using cellular or satellite technology. AAIS simply excludes loss caused by arcing or by electrical currents other than lightning.

7. **Explosion**—loss caused by explosion of steam boilers, steam pipes, steam turbines, or steam engines owned or operated by the insured is excluded. ISO's exclusion is similar.

8. **Freezing**—loss caused by water, other liquids, powder, or molten material that leaks or flows from plumbing, heating, or air conditioning systems or appliances as a result of freezing is excluded. ISO's exclusion is similar.

9. **Increased Hazard**—loss occurring while the hazard has been materially increased by any means within the insured's knowledge is excluded. The ISO form does not contain this exclusion.

10. **Loss of Use**—AAIS's exclusion includes loss of use, business interruption, delay, or loss of market. The ISO exclusion does not include business interruption.

11. **Mechanical Breakdown**—both AAIS and ISO exclude mechanical breakdown or rupture or bursting caused by centrifugal force. AAIS covers resulting loss by a specified peril, breakage of building glass, or elevator collision, but ISO covers only resulting damage caused by elevator collision.

12. **Neglect**—both forms exclude the insured's neglect to save covered property at and after the time of a loss; AAIS also excludes the insured's neglect to save and preserve covered property when endangered by a covered peril.

13. **Pollutants**—both forms exclude loss or damage caused by the release, discharge, seepage, migration, dispersal, or escape of pollutants unless caused by a specified peril.

14. **Seepage**—both forms exclude loss or damage caused by the continuous or repeated seepage or leakage of water that occurs over a period of fourteen days or more. AAIS also excludes steam, and ISO also excludes the presence or condensation of humidity, moisture, or vapor.

15. **Settling, Cracking, Shrinking, Bulging, or Expanding**—AAIS adds bulging to this list and states specific property that is excluded: pavements, footings, foundations, walls, ceilings, or roofs.

16. **Smog, Smoke, Vapor, or Gas from Agricultural Smudging or Industrial Operations**—AAIS adds smog to this list; otherwise, both forms are the same.

17. **Temperature/Humidity**—both forms exclude loss or damage to personal property caused by dampness, dryness, or changes in or extremes of temperature.

18. **Voluntary Parting**—loss caused by voluntary parting with property because of fraudulent scheme, trick, or false pretense is excluded by both policies. AAIS specifies that the parting is with title to or possession of any property, while ISO states that the voluntary parting is with any property by the insured or anyone else to whom the insured has entrusted the property. ISO also includes fraudulent device.

19. **Wear and Tear**—AAIS simply excludes loss caused by wear and tear, marring, and scratching. ISO excludes these causes of loss, too, but in the same section provides an extensive list of other excluded causes of loss, including rust or other corrosion, decay, deterioration, hidden or latent defect or any quality in property that causes it to damage or destroy itself. ISO also excludes marring and scratching only with regard to personal property.

20. **Weather**—both forms exclude loss caused by weather conditions if the conditions contribute in any way with a cause or event excluded in paragraph 1 of both forms.

Additional Property Excluded and Limitations

1. **Animals**—animals are not covered unless their death or destruction is caused by a specified peril or glass breakage. ISO covers animals if they are killed or their destruction is made necessary.

2. **Boilers**—neither form covers loss to steam boilers, steam pipes, steam turbines, or steam engines caused by any condition or event inside such equipment except with regards to explosion of gas or fuel in a firebox, combustion chamber, or flue. Loss to hot water boilers or heaters caused by a condition or occurrence within such equipment, other than explosion, is also excluded.

3. **Building Materials**—both forms exclude loss to building materials and supplies not attached to buildings or structures caused by theft, unless held for sale by the insured. The AAIS form covers loss caused by looting or pillaging at the time and place of a riot or civil commotion.

4. **Furs**—both forms provide up to $2,500 per occurrence of theft for fur or fur garments. ISO includes fur-trimmed garments, as well.

5. **Glass Breakage**—$100 per pane, $500 per occurrence. For loss by the specified perils, the policy provides unlimited glass coverage (other than for loss by vandalism). ISO does not contain a provision for glass breakage.

6. **Glassware/Fragile Articles**—AAIS and ISO do not cover breakage of fragile articles. ISO lists statuary, marbles, chinaware, and porcelains as examples, but not glass or containers of property held for sale. AAIS lists glassware, statuary, porcelains, and bric-a-brac as examples, except glass that is part of a building or structure, bottles or other containers held for sale, or lenses of photographic and scientific instruments.

7. **Gutters and Downspouts**—AAIS does not cover gutters or downspouts for loss due to weight of ice, sleet, or snow. ISO does not contain this limitation.

8. **Interior of Buildings**—both forms exclude loss or damage to personal property in a building or structure or to the interior of buildings from rain, snow, sleet, ice, or dust unless the exterior

first suffers damage from a specified peril or the loss is caused by thawing.

9. **Sub-Limits on Certain Types of Property**—theft of jewelry, watches, jewels, pearls, precious stones, and metals is limited to $2,500 per occurrence; theft of patterns, dies, molds, models, and forms is also limited to $2,500 per occurrence; theft of tickets, stamps, or letters of credit is limited to $250 per occurrence.

10. **Machinery, Tools, and Equipment**—both forms exclude builders' machinery, tools, and equipment owned by or entrusted to the insured unless loss or damage is caused by a specified peril or breakage of building glass.

11. **Missing Property**—neither form covers missing property when the only proof of loss is a shortage discovered after taking inventory or other instances where there is no physical evidence to show what happened to the property. AAIS also excludes missing property where the only proof of loss is unexplained or mysterious disappearance.

12. **Personal Property in the Open**—both forms exclude loss to personal property in the open caused by rain, snow, ice, or sleet.

13. **Transferred Property**—neither form covers loss to property that has been transferred to a person or to a place away from the described premises on the basis of unauthorized instructions.

14. **Valuable Papers and Records**—AAIS does not cover loss to valuable papers or records except by specified perils or breakage of building glass. The exclusion applies to the information stored on the records.

Additional Coverages

The AAIS policy contains two additional coverages:

1. **Collapse**—same as ISO for the causes of collapse. However, the AAIS form does not define *collapse* nor does it limit collapse by defining what is not collapse.

2. **Tearing Out and Replacing**—neither form will pay for damage to a system from which water or another substance escapes, but when loss caused by water, other liquids, powder, or molten material is covered, the cost of tearing out and replacing any

part of the building or structure to repair the damaged system or appliance is covered. Also, the cost to repair or replace damaged parts of fire extinguishing equipment that results in discharge of any substance from an automatic fire protection system or is directly caused by freezing is covered.

Other Coverage Parts

In addition to the Building and Personal Property Coverage Part, AAIS offers the following:

1. Builders Risk - Completed Value, CP-14

2. Builders Risk - Reporting Form, CP-15

3. Condominium Building Coverage Part, CP-19

4. Condominium Unit Coverage Part, CP-21

5. Personal Property Coverage Part - Reporting Form, CP-25

6. Earnings Coverage Part, CP-60

7. Extra Expense Coverage Part, CP-69

8. Income Coverage Part, CP-70

9. Basic and Broad Form Perils, CP-82 and CP-83

10. Special Perils, CP-85

11. Earthquake Perils, CP-89

Endorsements

The following endorsements are available under the AAIS commercial property program:

- Alcoholic Beverages Manufacturers – Finished Stock, CP-611

- Alcoholic Beverages Valuation, CP-110

- Antenna Coverage, CP-606

- Automatic Increase, CP-111

- Limited Fungus and Related Perils Coverage, CP 0640

- Loss Payable Options, CP-132

- Manufactured Stock Valuation, CP-133

- Market Price Valuation - Distilled Spirits, CP-135

- Market Price Valuation – Stock, CP-134

- Market Price Valuation – Wines, CP-136

- Market Value, CP-609

- Mine Subsidence Coverage, FO-158

- Non-certified Act of Terrorism Exclusion and War and Military Action Exclusion, CL-0630

- Optional Property Coverage, CP-23

- Ordinance or Law Extension – Increased Cost of Construction, CP-138

- Ordinary Payroll Exclusion, CP-140

- Ordinary Payroll Limitation, CP-141

- Outdoor Signs, CP-605

- Peak Season Increase, CP-144

- Perils Exclusion, CP-145

- Pollutant Clean Up and Removal Coverage, CP-123

- Power, Heat, and Refrigeration Exclusion, CP-153

- Premium Payments, CP-155

- Property Excluded, CP-157

- Protective Device Credit, CP-614

- Radioactive Contamination – Broad Coverage, CP-91

- Radioactive Contamination – Limited Coverage, CP- 90

- Resident Agent Countersignature, CP-162

- Seasonal Leases, CP-73

- Specific Insurance, CP-164

- Spoilage Coverage, CP-601

- Sprinkler Leakage Earthquake Extension, CP-165

- Storage or Repairs Valuation, CP-167

- Terrorism Exclusions, CL 2630

- Theft Exclusion, CP-169

- Trees, Shrubs, and Plants, CP-610

- Tuition Coverage, CP-75

- Utility Interruption – Property Damage, CP-94

- Utility Interruption – Time Element, CP-95

- Vacancy or Unoccupancy Permit, CP-170

- War, Military Action, and Terrorism Exclusions (With Limited Exception), CL 0469

- Water Backup and Overflow Coverage, CP 0607

Chapter 15

The Mutual Service Office Commercial Property Program

General Property Form, MCP 010

Like Insurance Services Office (ISO) and the American Association of Insurance Services (AAIS), the Mutual Service Office, Inc. (MSO) provides custom rates, statistical services, custom forms, and manuals, but for mutual insurers only.

The cornerstone of the MSO commercial property program is a twenty-three-page booklet that, according to MSO, incorporates the provisions of ten separate simplified forms. The booklet includes in a single document all primary property and business interruption coverages, all causes of loss options, and the applicable policy conditions. Commonly used endorsements are preprinted in the body of the policy, thereby eliminating the need for separate attachments; each of these endorsements can be triggered by listing the endorsement number in the declarations. MSO refers to these as endorsements preprinted in the form, but the form itself does not refer to these options as endorsements. State-specific requirements or unusual coverage needs may require additional, separate endorsement(s).

Insuring Agreement

Although many coverages are preprinted in the General Property Form, insurance applies only where a specific limit and premium for that coverage is shown in the declarations, the supplemental declarations, or an attached endorsement.

Insurance applies only to *covered loss*, a term defined at length in the perils section of the form. The term essentially refers to damage or destruction of covered property by a covered peril. If theft is a covered peril, then loss by theft is also a covered loss—even if the property is not damaged or destroyed.

Unless otherwise stated, a covered loss must take place during the policy period. This is substantially different from the wording in ISO's commercial property conditions, which covers loss or damage commencing during the policy period. Suppose a fire starts burning at 11:00 p.m. and the policy period ends at 12:01 a.m., before the fire is extinguished. ISO's commencing language makes it clear that fire damage taking place after 12:01 a.m. is still covered by the expiring policy. A literal interpretation of the MSO language holds that the policy in force when the fire started covers only the direct damage that takes place up until the moment when the policy expires. As regards business income and extra expense, a provision discussed later specifically states that the period of indemnity is not limited by expiration of the policy term.

To be covered, a loss must also take place on the applicable described premises. *Described premises* is not a defined term.

The form also covers loss to personal property that is outdoors or within 100 feet of the described premises. This phrasing could leave a coverage gap in some instances. Consider property on the first-floor loading dock that belongs to a business on the twentieth floor of a high-rise building that lists Suite 2000 as the described premises. The property is not outdoors, and it is not within one-hundred feet of Suite 2000. ISO addressed a similar coverage gap in the 2012 revision of its building and personal property coverage form.

Part I A – Main Property Coverages

Coverage A: Building/Structures

Building coverage includes any buildings or structures (and their completed additions) shown on the declarations page with a limit of insurance. It does not matter whether the additions are in place when the policy is written or if they are added later. Coverage also applies to alterations and repairs in progress.

The provision for coverage of additions is common in forms relating to buildings, but it should not be taken for granted. Though beneficial to the insured by way of automatic coverage for new additions during the term of the policy, it can also lead to difficulty under the terms of the coinsurance clause if the overall amount of insurance is not adjusted to account for the increased values.

The form covers any additions under construction, as well as related building equipment, fixtures, materials, and supplies, on a primary basis if no other insurance exists for the project. If there is other insurance, coverage applies on an excess basis.

The building/structures coverage includes coverage for permanently installed equipment, fixtures, and machinery. Machinery and equipment easily includes drive-on scales, refrigerated lockers, pulleys, and the like.

Coverage disputes occasionally arise over the meaning of *permanently installed*. The phrase is not defined within the form, but *install* commonly means "to set up for use or service" and *permanently* means "continuing or enduring without fundamental or marked change; stable" (*Webster's New Collegiate Dictionary*). Fixtures, under this phrasing, are things that are permanently attached to the building and cannot be removed without affecting either the value or the aesthetics of the structure, and they can include everything from intercoms and public address systems to permanently installed blinds, drapery fittings, or hardware.

An item does not need to become a part of the structure of the building for it to be considered permanently installed. For example, a refrigerated locker is permanently installed if set up for use in the insured's building with the intent that it should remain there without change as long as the insured is in business at that location.

The form also specifically includes outdoor fixtures as building property. While the policy includes a few examples—flag poles, ground lights, and light standards—this is not an exhaustive list. Further examples might include parking stops, mailboxes, and in ground sprinkler systems (underground pipes are excluded, as discussed later).

Coverage B: Business Personal Property

The lead-in language states that coverage for personal property is provided for property located in or on the building described in the declarations. However, the insuring agreement cited previously extends coverage to covered losses that occur outdoors on or within 100 feet of the premises.

Coverage is limited to tangible personal property. This would exclude coverage for intangible property such as data, copyrights and other intellectual property, or goodwill. Property is covered only if it is both owned by a named insured and used in the business/operations described in the declarations. If these conditions are met, coverage would apply to furniture, fixtures, machinery, equipment, stock, and other types of tangible personal property not excluded elsewhere in the form.

Business personal property also contemplates coverage of the labor, materials, and supplies provided by the named insured provided in connection with the tangible personal property of others. If, for example, an insured repairs a computer at a cost of $50 in labor, $75 in materials, and $10 for a special trip to acquire a necessary part, $135 is recoverable under this coverage, less any deductible, if the computer is damaged by an insured peril before it can be returned to the customer.

The form also covers, as personal property, a tenant's remaining use interest in improvements and betterments. Improvements and betterments consist of fixtures, alterations, installations, or additions of a permanent type that have been acquired at some expense by the tenant. They are items of real property such as store fronts, decorations, partitions, or elevators and are not legally removable by a tenant.

This is not the same as coverage on the full value of the improvements and betterments. A loss settlement provision later in the policy clarifies how improvements and betterments losses are to be settled. A tenant's use interest exists as long as any lease is in force. But if the lease contains an option to renew, then the use interest extends to the end of the option period. If the tenant does not promptly repair damage to improvements and betterments, the insurer's obligation is prorated based on the amount of time that has elapsed since the improvement was installed and the amount of time remaining on the lease or any renewal option. If the named insured promptly repairs the damage, it will be settled on the same basis as other covered property.

Improvements and betterments coverage does not apply if the landlord includes the cost of the improvements in the tenant's rent or if the landlord bears the cost of repairing damaged improvements and betterments.

As with any other item or class of covered property, the values of improvements must be taken into account when considering the amount of insurance necessary for compliance with the coinsurance clause.

Coverage C: Personal Property of Others

The third type of direct property loss that can be covered under the building and personal property coverage form is tangible property of others in the insured's care, custody, or control and used in connection with the named insured's business/operations as described in the declarations. Although the wording here appears to limit coverage to personal property in or on the building described in the declarations, the insuring agreement cited earlier extends coverage to covered losses that occur outdoors on or within 100 feet of the premises.

Any loss to property of others is adjusted "solely for the account of the owner" of the property. The insurer has a right to adjust the loss with the property's owners.

Coverage D: Business Income/Extra Expense

Business income and/or extra expense coverage is integrated into the General Property Form as coverage D. Approximately one and a half pages of the form describe this coverage, which applies only if appropriate entries are made in the declarations. The opening paragraphs outline the conditions that must exist for a business income and/or extra expense loss to be covered.

First, the named insured must suffer a loss of business income or incur extra expenses as the result of a direct covered loss. *Direct covered loss* is defined elsewhere in the policy as "fortuitous direct physical loss [by a covered cause of loss] which occurs at described premises occupied by you...which directly results in the subject covered business income loss/ extra expense loss."

In short, the named insured must suffer a business income and/or extra expense loss as the result of fortuitous direct physical damage to, destruction of, or theft of property by a covered cause of loss. The damaged, destroyed, or stolen property need not belong to the named insured.

Second, the direct covered loss must result in a necessary interruption of the named insured's business/operations described in the declarations or the untenantability of the premises. Disputes could conceivably arise in some cases as to whether an interruption was necessary.

Third, the business income and/or extra expense coverage can be triggered by an order of civil authority that prohibits access to the premises described in the declarations because of damage to another party's property at other premises by a covered cause of loss. For example, a tenant's store might not be damaged by a fire in another part of the shopping mall, but authorities might bar access to the entire mall until an investigation is complete and some of the damage has been cleared.

ISO uses three different forms to provide the three basic coverages or coverage combinations available in MSO's General Property Form. Entries in the MSO declarations indicate which coverages apply at each location. For example, if "D.1" is entered in the "coverages" column for Location 1 Building 1, then business income and extra expense coverage applies at that location. Likewise, D.2 means that only business income coverage applies, and "D.3" means that only extra expense coverage applies. If none of these "D" entries appears in the declarations for that location, then none of these coverages applies.

The purpose of business income insurance is to do for the insured during a period of business interruption what the business would have done had no loss occurred. Loss of business earnings, the prime source of money for continuing operating expenses as well as profit (if any) is the subject of this coverage. The form covers loss of net income plus continuing normal operating expenses that businesses would have earned or incurred if no direct damage loss occurred.

A landlord's income is derived from tenants' rents, and a landlord's business income loss involves a loss of rental income. It is not necessary that premises actually be rented at the time of the loss. Damage to property that is customarily held for rental to others but is temporarily vacant at the time of the loss can also result in a loss of rental income. Adjustment of claims of this type will depend upon proof of what is a reasonably anticipated rental income. For example, if the damaged apartment had gone unrented during the entire year prior to the loss, and the insured had no real prospects for its rental, it is not reasonable to anticipate rental income. If, however, the apartment had been rented consistently prior to the loss, and had only recently been vacated, or if the insured has verifiable prospects for a speedy re-rental, then it is appropriate to anticipate rental income.

The rental income coverage also applies to continuing expenses that are normally paid by the tenant but become the landlord's responsibility because of the direct covered loss. For example, a tenant might normally pay the costs of lighting and heating a building. However, if the building cannot be occupied, the landlord must pay these expenses until the premises are repaired and re-rented.

Continuing expenses are not covered if they do not actually continue or need to continue. For example, trash collection services might be discontinued while the business is not operating and is not producing any trash.

The form provides coverage for two categories of extra expense: costs to avoid or minimize the suspension of business at replacement or temporary locations and costs to minimize business suspension if operations cannot continue. Examples of extra expenses of doing business at a temporary or replacement location include costs to set up, rent, and move to the new location and the costs to obtain temporary equipment. If operations cannot be continued, some extra expenses may involve the hiring of additional workers or paying existing employees overtime in order to reopen the business.

Like business income coverage, direct physical damage or loss is required. Only expenses that the business would not otherwise experience except for the direct property loss are covered.

Extra expenses necessary to maintain the "same capability and quality of service as would otherwise exist" are covered. It might be difficult for some businesses to maintain the same level of service while damaged property is being restored. The insured is not required to make do by minimizing its extra expenses. At the same time, however, any extra expenses the insured incurs must be necessary and reasonable.

There is some overlap between this coverage and the extra expense coverage described previously. However, this provision makes it clear that expenses that reduce the covered business income or extra expense loss are covered whether business income and extra expense, business income only, or extra expense only coverage is purchased. If spending $10,000 on overtime pay to get back in operation sooner reduces the business income loss by $20,000, it is obviously in the insurer's best interest to cover the overtime pay. Special costs might also be incurred to expedite the delivery of stock or equipment needed that enables the business to reopen more quickly.

Unlike the extra expense coverage that is aimed at maintaining the same level of service or minimizing the period of interruption, these special costs or increased expenses are covered only to the extent they actually reduce the loss the insurer would otherwise be obligated to pay.

Whether business income and/or extra expense coverage is provided, if a contract is cancelled, lapsed, or suspended because of a covered interruption the insurer will pay for any resulting business income or extra expense loss. The burden of proof is on the insured to demonstrate that the loss would not otherwise have been incurred during the applicable coverage period, as described in the next set of provisions.

The basic period of indemnity begins on the date property is damaged by a covered peril. Here the MSO form differs from ISO's forms, which impose a seventy-two-hour time deductible on its period of restoration. The basic period of indemnity ends on the earlier of two dates.

First, the period ends with "the period required with diligence and ongoing effort" to restore normal operations. Second, even if operations are not restored, the basic period of indemnity ends with the period required to restore the property so it is again ready for operations.

Both provisions refer to the period required. If it takes longer to restore operations or restore the premises because the named insured does not exercise the necessary degree of diligence and effort, the basic indemnity period ends whenever operations or premises could have been restored.

The period of indemnity for covered order of civil authority losses runs for a maximum of fourteen consecutive days.

The period of indemnity lasts a maximum of sixty days if damage to electronic media either causes or contributes to the business income loss.

As mentioned earlier, intangible personal property—such as data or computer programs—is not covered property. Covered here is loss resulting from damage to the media—computer disks or drives—on which data are stored, including the data themselves. In other words, the business income coverage provided here does not apply to data that are accidentally erased or corrupted, but it does apply in the event of physical damage to the tangible media on which data or programming records are stored.

This special period of indemnity can be modified by triggering one of the policy's built-in endorsements.

Endorsement MCP 501 can lengthen or reduce the indemnity period. For example, the sixty-day period can be changed to a ninety-day period of indemnity by entering "MCP 501" along with the number "90" in the declarations.

If endorsement MCP 508 is triggered by an entry in the declarations, the exclusion for computer hacking or computer viruses is eliminated. The effect of MCP 508 is to cover a business income loss to electronic media caused by hacking or viruses.

If required, the extended period of indemnity pays for additional loss of business income after property is actually repaired and operations are resumed, with reasonable speed, until the business generates the business income amount that would have existed had no loss occurred. The basic coverage, as shown in the form, applies for up to thirty consecutive days after the basic period of indemnity ends. A longer extended period of indemnity can be provided by triggering endorsement MCP 502 and inserting a higher number in the declarations. For example, entering "MCP 502" and "90" in the declarations would provide for a ninety-day extended period of indemnity.

Extended business income is designed to enable the insured to recapture its market position following the completion of repairs and the resumption of operations. For example, a retailer that endured a long closure for repairs may not see its customers return right away. The loss of income during this period would be covered by the extended period of indemnity.

Although the direct loss that results in a business income/extra expense loss must take place during the policy term, the period of indemnity may extend past the end of the policy period.

Although extended or special periods of indemnity extend the time period during which business income/extra expense loss is covered, they do not increase the dollar amount of coverage available.

The first special condition applicable to business income and extra expense coverage reiterates an earlier definition of *business/operations*.

Finished stock is defined in the form's glossary as stock that is manufactured by the named insured except for stock held in a covered retail store. A manufacturer's finished stock begins with raw materials. Raw materials gain value as they are converted to finished stock over a period of time that sometimes includes an extended aging or drying process. Direct damage, destruction, or loss of stock—raw materials, goods in the process of manufacture, or finished stock—should be covered under the business personal property coverage.

The business income/extra expense coverages do not cover loss to finished stock, even if damage to the stock is the reason for a business interruption. Likewise, business income coverage does not apply to the manufacturing period; loss to goods in the process of manufacture are reflected in the value of the direct property loss.

The extra expense coverage, however, does apply to the time required to reproduce finished stock. Extra expenses that expedite the manufacturing process—such as working double shifts once the assembly line is restored—can reduce the business income loss or minimize the period of interruption.

Interference at the insured premises by strikers or others is specifically excluded, whether the strike occurs at the described premises or elsewhere.

Losses arising from direct physical loss or damage to radio or television antennas and their lead-in wires, masts, or towers are also not covered. This exclusion may be eliminated by triggering endorsement MCP 503 in the declarations.

Part I B – Supplemental Coverages

The nineteen supplemental coverages printed in this form extend the four main coverages and add additional amounts of insurance as described under each supplement, but they do not otherwise modify the policy.

Some of the supplemental coverages are "keyed to a percentage of the underlying main coverage." For example, coverage on newly acquired business personal property is keyed to 10 percent of the coverage B limit. This percentage is expressed in decimal form as a factor or multiplier; 10 percent is shown as 0.10.

Questions could arise when the form covers multiple items, such as personal property at more than one location. If the supplemental coverage can be keyed to a specific described item then the limit is keyed to the coverage limit for that location. For example, if there is a $100,000 limit on business personal property at Location 2, then the 10 percent limit on newly acquired personal property at Location 2 will be keyed to that limit. However, if the supplemental coverage cannot be keyed to a specific described item, then the greatest limit for that coverage is used. If the insured in the previous example also had a $200,000 business personal property limit at Location 1 and acquired personal property at a third location, there would be $20,000 of newly acquired property coverage available to both locations. The two limits are not added together to come up with $30,000 in coverage.

A similar situation arises when different property items are covered for different causes of loss. Again, coverage is keyed to the perils applicable to a specific described item. When this is not possible, the insurer will use the most relevant causes of loss at the described premises.

Unless otherwise stated, the coinsurance condition does not apply to the supplemental coverages. The insured is not required to meet a coinsurance requirement with respect to one of these coverages, and the dollar amount of any supplemental coverage cannot be used in satisfying a coinsurance requirement.

Accounts Receivable Coverage. Accounts receivable coverage applies when the insured's business personal property is covered. A $3,000 limit is preprinted in the supplementary declarations, but this limit may be changed by entering a different number. A $250 deductible is standard, but this is also subject to change either by showing a different deductible amount in the declarations or by entering "MCP 510" in the declarations. MCP 510 modifies the policy so that the policy's general deductible also applies to accounts receivable coverage.

Loss must be caused by a covered peril that applies to Coverage B. Coverage does not apply to loss caused by accounting, billing, or bookkeeping mistakes or where proof of the loss depends on an audit or inventory computation. Most other limitations and exclusions do not apply to this coverage. However, the intentional loss and wear and tear exclusions do apply.

Automatic Increase/Peak Season Coverages. MSO does not use the inflation guard label, but inflation guard coverage applies if a factor is shown for coverage A and/or coverage B. No suggested factor is preprinted in the supplemental declarations, but entering a factor of 0.06 for coverage A would increase the building limit by 6 percent per year. This increase is prorated across the policy year; if the factor shown is 0.06, the limit has automatically increased by 3 percent after six months.

In other comparable policies, peak season coverage applies during a specific stated time period, presumably the time period when values normally increase. Rather than require specific dates, MSO simply increases coverage "during those periods of time during the year when it is your normal practice to increase the amount of business personal property at the described premises because of customary seasonal or holiday sales."

Inflation guard and peak season increases apply only to Coverages A and B, not to any of the supplemental coverages.

Building Extension Coverages. The effect of these three supplements is to include coverage on building glass, outdoor signs, and certain types of personal property under coverage A.

Depending on the circumstances, glass breakage can be treated as a peril or as the result of another peril. Sometimes glass spontaneously breaks. Often, however, glass damage is the result of another peril such as vandalism or windstorm. The glass extension applies only when a causes of loss option includes glass breakage as a named peril and the glass in question is part of a building. Most glass display cases, for example, do not qualify as part of the building. As discussed later, the glass breakage peril covers damage caused by broken glass, not the broken glass itself, which is the subject of this coverage extension.

The basic limits printed in the supplemental declarations are $1,000, with a sublimit of $100 per item. Other limits may be entered. Vandalism is subject to these limits. Otherwise, these limits do not apply for loss caused by any of the specified causes of loss; instead, the Coverage A limit applies. As defined in Part I C, the *specified causes of loss* include fire; aircraft; explosion; falling objects; lightning; riot or civil commotion; sinkhole collapse; smoke; sprinkler leakage; vandalism; vehicles; volcanic eruption; water damage; weight of ice, sleet, or snow; and windstorm/hail when the applicable peril applies to coverage A.

Outdoor signs are covered for the same perils as the building they are attached to. If the insured has both attached and unattached signs, they are all covered for the same perils. If only unattached signs are involved, they are covered against the basic causes of loss, except for vandalism, which is not covered.

The policy makes no provision for covering signs belonging to a tenant who has not purchased building coverage under coverage A. Therefore, a tenant with a significant outdoor signs exposure should be advised to cover the signs under coverage A.

Personal Property Extension. In ISO's Building and Personal Property Coverage Form, the *building* definition includes personal property used to maintain or service the building. MSO accomplishes essentially the same thing with a personal property extension that lists a nonexhaustive list of examples: "air conditioners; cooking, dishwashing, laundering, refrigeration, and ventilating appliances; fire extinguishers; floor coverings; lawn care and snow removal equipment—including riding mowers and similar items, but not other types of vehicles; outdoor fixtures/furniture."

Debates can develop over what constitutes "similar items." Restriction of eligibility to property that is used "primarily to maintain or service covered buildings" is also potentially confusing. The verb "to service" is virtually synonymous with "maintain," since its definition is "to repair or maintain." Thus, a literal interpretation of the provision eliminates all of the listed items—fire extinguishers, outdoor furniture, floor coverings, appliances—since none are among items generally used to repair or maintain a building or premises.

The supplemental coverage form specifically excludes outdoor fixtures because they are automatically included as building property under coverage A.

Building Code/Law Coverage. This supplemental coverage applies when an ordinance or law regulating the construction or repair of buildings results in increased costs in order for the insured to comply with such ordinance or law. Codes requiring pollutant cleanup are not included. The insurer is not obligated to make any payments under this coverage unless or until the property is repaired as soon as possible.

The amount that the insurer will pay under this supplemental coverage is limited to 10 percent of the building limit unless a different factor is entered in the declarations. This amount is considered additional insurance, that is, not included in the limit of insurance set in the declarations page for covered buildings. There are also restrictions described in this clause as to when the insurer will not pay for demolition and the increased cost of construction: the property must be repaired or rebuilt at the same premises. Endorsement MCP 522, if triggered in the declarations, will permit reconstruction at another premises.

Unless endorsement MCP 506 is triggered by an entry in the declarations, this supplemental coverage applies only to buildings that are covered on a replacement cost basis. If a coinsurance penalty applies to the building coverage, it also applies under this supplemental coverage.

Triggering endorsement MCP 504 extends the business income/extra expense coverage's basic period of indemnity to include the time required to comply with applicable building codes or laws.

Collapse. When broad form or open perils coverage is provided, collapse is covered not as a cause of loss, but as a supplemental coverage. Unlike other supplemental coverages, this is not an additional amount of insurance.

The form's glossary makes it clear that coverage applies only to collapses that are abrupt in nature. The structure must fall down or cave in; sagging or bulging is not considered a collapse. A building or any part of it that is in danger of collapsing does not qualify as a collapse for purposes of this supplemental coverage.

Even when open perils coverage is otherwise provided, the collapse coverage applies on a specified perils basis. Covered causes of loss include the broad causes of loss as well as hidden decay or insect damage that an insured did not know of before the collapse; weight of contents, equipment, animals, or people; weight of rain on a roof; or the use of defective materials.

Coverage is not limited to the collapse of buildings or structures subject to coverage A. However, the damaged property must be covered under the policy, and the damage must be caused by the collapse of some building.

The distinction between buildings and structures must be considered in analyzing this coverage. Both buildings and structures can be insured under coverage A; in fact, coverage A states that "the general term buildings also includes other sorts of structures." However, the collapse supplemental coverage states that various specific types of nonbuilding structures listed in the supplemental coverage are not covered unless their loss directly results from the collapse of a building or a structural part of a building. Specifically excluded—unless resulting from the collapse of a building—is the collapse of antennas; awnings; beach or diving platforms; decks; docks, piers, or wharves; downspouts or gutters; fences; outdoor swimming pools; paved surfaces of any sort; retaining walls; and yard fixtures.

Consequent Loss Coverages (Spoilage). The supplemental coverage for spoilage of covered business personal property, such as food in a freezer, is subject to several limitations and exclusions. However, the limits of this supplemental coverage do not apply to spoilage resulting from damage by a covered peril to covered equipment on the described premises.

Spoilage resulting from an electrical outage or other loss of utility services is covered only when the loss results from damage by a covered peril to the utility's property (not the named insured's property). The basic limit in the supplemental declarations is $1,000, which can be increased by adding another entry, or coverage may be completely eliminated by entering a $0 limit.

Unless another limit is shown or coverage is deleted by entering a $0 limit, spoilage resulting from a mechanical breakdown is limited to $500 during any twelve-month period, provided the cause of loss was not within the insured's control.

Debris Removal Coverage. Because this coverage applies to the removal of debris of a covered loss, it applies to the damage or destruction of covered property by a covered peril. However, coverage is not limited to debris of covered property. It would, therefore, include removing the debris of an airplane that has crashed into a covered building.

The insurer agrees to apply up to 25 percent (the amount preprinted in the supplementary declarations) or another specified percentage of the limit on covered property toward debris removal expenses. This is not additional insurance. However, the insurer will also pay an additional amount of insurance, up to $5,000 (or other specified amount), if the debris removal expense exceeds this amount, or if the value of the direct property damage plus the cost of debris removal exceeds 125 percent (or other percentage) of the limit applicable to the covered property. The costs of removing downed trees, pollutants, or volcanic ash are not covered. Debris removal expenses must be reported to the insurer within 180 days of the covered loss.

Electronic Data Coverage. The policy promises to replace or restore data that has been damaged or corrupted by damage to covered property by a covered cause of loss. Damage done to data by a hacker or a computer virus is covered as long as the virus was not introduced to the system by an employee or any entity hired by the insured to work on the computer system.

The limit for this coverage is an annual aggregate of $3,000 that may be modified in the supplemental declarations. If a loss begins in one policy period and extends into another, only the first policy period's limit applies.

Emergency Removal. The policy covers loss by any direct physical cause to property that has been moved from the insured location because it was in imminent danger of loss or damage by a covered peril. Note that it does not have to be damaged by a covered cause of loss. For example, property is moved because of imminent wildfires. The location where the property is temporarily stored is flooded; this damage is covered. This coverage applies for thirty days. The supplemental declarations do not impose a dollar limit or provide for a modification of the thirty-day coverage period.

Fire Expense Coverages. The insured's contractual obligations to pay service charges assessed by a fire department are paid up to $2,000, but coverage does not apply to false alarms. The cost to recharge used fire extinguishers is covered up to $5,000. These limits are preprinted in the supplemental declarations, and higher limits may be purchased. No deductible applies.

The form includes newly acquired property coverage applicable to coverage A (building), coverage B (business personal property), and coverage D (loss of use). Except as noted, coverage is automatically provided for up to sixty days from the date acquisition or construction begins, but it does not extend past the end of the policy term. An additional premium for the values reported is charged from the date construction begins or the property is acquired.

Newly Acquired Property Coverages. Unless different numbers are shown in the supplemental declarations, newly acquired buildings are covered for 25 percent of the coverage A limit, subject to a maximum of $250,000 at each building. Protection applies to new buildings under construction on the insured's premises and to any buildings at another location that the insured acquires. As to the latter, the new acquisition must be for usage similar to insured buildings or for use as a warehouse.

Business personal property at acquired locations is insured for 10 percent of the coverage B limit, with a maximum of $100,000 at each location. This extension does not encompass personal property at fairs or exhibitions. There is no restriction that the newly acquired business personal property be intended for similar occupancies or purposes.

The full coverage B limit applies if the insured is moving business personal property "from a described premises under this policy to a newly described premises under this policy." The "described" requirement presumably means that this extension applies only after the new location has been added to the policy.

Loss of use, coverage D, applies when a direct covered loss to alterations or additions to described buildings, new buildings, or building materials or supplies associated with a new building delays the start of operations at the described premises. This extension presumably applies to newly acquired buildings only after the new location has been added to and described in the policy. It also applies to business income/extra expense coverages resulting from direct damage to business personal property. Unless different factors or limits are shown, this supplemental coverage is limited to 10 percent of the coverage D limit, subject to a $100,000 maximum; it is not an additional amount of business income/extra expense coverage. The extension is subject to the applicable coinsurance provisions.

Off Premises Coverages. Covered property temporarily at a location not owned, leased, or operated by the insured is insured up to $5,000 unless another amount is entered in the supplemental declarations. This extension specifically excludes property in or on a vehicle; property in the care, custody, or control of salespersons; and stock.

The property in transit coverage applies to covered business personal property (other than property in the custody of salespeople), and coverage is limited to a few causes of loss and to a maximum of $1,000 unless a different limit is shown in the supplemental declarations. Open perils coverage is available as an alternative, and this option is triggered by entering "MCP 505" in the declarations and entering appropriate dollar limits. A separate sublimit, if listed, will apply to theft losses.

Outdoor Property Coverage. The building coverage applies if any of the named perils of fire, lightning, explosion, riot, civil commotion, or aircraft cause damage to outdoor fences, radio antennas, television antennas, satellite dishes, or trees, shrubs, and plants. The policy does not cover the perils to which these types of property are especially susceptible: weather-related perils, vandalism, and vehicle damage.

Up to $1,000 applies to the loss, including debris removal expense (no other debris removal coverage is available for trees). As regards trees, shrubs, and plants, payment is restricted to $250 per item. Different limits may be entered in the supplemental declarations.

Personal Property Coverages: Five extensions modify the types of business personal property to which Coverage B applies but do not add additional amounts of coverage.

Coverage on creatures is limited to creatures held for sale that are inside a described building at the time of the loss and to creatures owned by others that the insured is boarding (as in a dog kennel). Creatures are not covered against injury, but only when they die or need to be killed because of harm by fire; aircraft; explosion; falling objects; lightning; riot or civil commotion; sinkhole collapse; smoke; sprinkler leakage; vandalism; vehicles; volcanic eruption; water damage; weight of ice, sleet, or snow; or windstorm/hail. *Creature* is not a term defined in the policy. Generally, *creature* refers to living things other than plants, a term that would include pets, farm animals, animals found in a zoo, and research specimens of all shapes and sizes.

Unless a different limit is indicated in the supplemental declarations, $3,000 per occurrence is available for loss or damage to personal effects (i.e., items usually worn or carried on the person) owned by the insured or the insured's directors, officers, partners, employees, or volunteer workers.

Personal property of others is a much broader category than personal effects. As discussed earlier, coverage B covers damage to the personal property of others to the extent of the named insured's labor, materials, and supplies. This supplemental coverage automatically extends coverage B to apply $3,000 (or a different limit, if indicated in the supplemental declarations) to property of others in the insured's care, custody, or control that is used in connection with the insured's business or operations. The insurer has a right to adjust the loss with the property's owners. Personal property of others can also be covered under coverage C.

If the named insured has a contractual obligation to insure leased personal property owned by others but in its custody—such as a large photocopy machine—this supplemental coverage also extends coverage B to include the insured's contractual obligations for damage by a covered peril. The full coverage B limit includes this category of nonowned personal property, but this extension does not provide any additional limits of insurance.

Valuable papers coverage applies when business personal property is covered. The $3,000 limit preprinted in the supplementary declarations may be changed. A $250 deductible is standard, but this is also subject to change either by showing a different deductible amount in the declarations or by entering "MCP 511" in the declarations. MCP 511 modifies the policy so that the policy's general deductible also applies to valuable papers coverage. Loss must be caused by a covered peril that applies to coverage B. Most limitations and exclusions do not apply to this coverage, but the intentional loss and wear and tear exclusions do apply.

Coverage B also applies to some vehicles, provided they are customarily kept and operated at the described premises and are not licensed for use on public roads. This category obviously includes riding mowers and snow removal equipment and similar items that can also be covered under the building extension coverages, discussed earlier.

The vehicles category in this context is broad enough to include canoes and rowboats on shore at the described premises, as well as other types of watercraft, aircraft, other types of self-propelled machines, and trailers that the named insured holds for sale, manufactures, processes, or warehouses. Autos held for sale are specifically excluded.

Pollution Clean Up Cost Coverage. An additional coverage—with a separate annual aggregate limit of $10,000 unless the supplemental declarations show a different limit—applies to extract pollutants from land or water on the described premises if the "discharge, dispersal, emission, escape, migration, release or seepage" of pollutants (other than nuclear or radioactive materials) resulted from a covered cause loss.

Covered expenses must be reported to the insurer within 180 days of the date on which the covered loss occurs. The declarations may show a specific deductible for this coverage.

Precious Metals Coverage – Industrial Operations. Another section of the policy excludes coverage for gold and other precious metals used in connection with industrial operations other than manufacturing objects made of precious metals. This supplemental coverage specifically covers such precious metals for up to $3,000 or whatever other amount is shown in the supplemental declarations.

Steam Equipment or Other Fired Vessel Explosion Coverage. It is most important to recognize that this supplemental coverage does not cover explosions that result from steam pressure. It does, however, cover the explosion of fuel or gas used to fire a steam boiler or a hot water heater or the explosion of a hot water heater or boiler. Damage caused by the operation of a boiler's safety valve is covered when open perils coverage applies. This supplemental coverage extends the types of losses that are covered but has no bearing on the applicable amount of insurance.

Water Damage/Related Damage Repair Expense Coverage. As described elsewhere in the policy, coverage under the sprinkler leakage and water damage perils applies to damage to covered property resulting from the abrupt discharge of water. For example, the water might damage a hardwood floor. This supplemental coverage expands coverage to include expenses associated with repairing the leak itself, but it does not provide any additional amount of insurance.

Coverage applies to the cost of tearing out and replacing part of the building or structure to repair damage to the system or appliance. Coverage also applies to the cost to repair or replace the particular defective or damaged part of the appliance, equipment, or system that the water escaped from. Coverage is limited to the leaking or broken joint, pipe, valve, or item; the insurer will not pay under this coverage to repair the entire appliance, equipment, or system. If the pipes in a plumbing system are badly corroded and one suddenly springs a leak, the insurer will repair the leak but will not pay to replace the entire plumbing system.

Weather Related Coverage. This supplementary coverage applies only to buildings and personal property inside a building to which open perils coverage applies. It is directed at losses caused by ice dams and similar situations in which water seeps into a building even though the walls and roof are not otherwise damaged. This supplement clarifies what types of losses are covered, but it does not provide additional limits of coverage. Entering "MCP 515" in the declarations triggers an exclusion for damage to a building's interior elements.

Part I C – Cause of Loss Options

Nearly all of Part IC describes the causes of loss that apply to coverages A, B, and C. Different items of property can be covered against loss by different sets of perils; the causes of loss options listed for each property item in the declarations indicate which perils apply to which property items. In some cases, more than one option may apply to a single property item.

Option 1—Fire Coverage provides the very basic fire coverage of the traditional 165-line standard fire policy, which includes explosion and lightning.

Option 2—Basic Coverage includes the same perils as ISO's basic causes of loss form. These include the packages traditionally known as fire, extended coverage (EC), and vandalism or malicious mischief (VMM), plus sinkhole collapse and volcanic eruption.

Option 3—Broad Coverage in the MSO form likewise parallels ISO's broad causes of loss and adds the perils of falling objects, water damage, and weight of ice, sleet, or snow. It also adds glass breakage as a peril. As defined, this peril does not apply to the glass itself but rather to property damaged by broken glass. For example, merchandise inside a store's display window may be damaged if the glass breaks.

Option 4—Sprinkler Leakage Coverage, may be added to options 1, 2, or 3 when coverage applies to a building with an automatic sprinkler system. If sprinkler leakage is covered, the declarations entry for a sprinklered building with broad form coverage would then show both option 3 and option 4 for that building.

Option 5—Expanded Coverage provides open perils coverage. The expanded terminology nicely evades troublesome all-risk or risk-of-loss wording while having the same effect. This option specifically includes broad form coverage and sprinkler leakage coverage. Other open perils policies are invariably intended to be at least as broad as broad form policies with respect to the basic and broad forms' specified perils, but failure to be explicit on that point occasionally creates unintended coverage gaps. MSO's expanded coverage specifically includes broad form perils and sprinkler leakage, as well as "direct physical loss to or theft of covered property not otherwise excluded." However, coverage for falling objects and sinkhole collapse is still no broader than that of the broad coverage option.

Option 6—Provides earthquake coverage, as described in a separate endorsement that is not incorporated within the policy. A common exclusion precludes coverage for earthquake under all causes of loss options, so unless option 6 is activated, earthquake coverage is excluded.

Options A, B, C, and D—Can be used to eliminate theft, vandalism, water damage, and windstorm/hail as covered perils. Mechanically, this is accomplished by adding one or more letters after the option number. So, if the intent is to provide coverage for a specific building against the basic causes of loss other than vandalism, the declarations would show Option 2B as the causes of loss option applicable to that item.

Fire is not defined here, but the peril itself is listed as "Fire (hostile fire)." The courts have long interpreted the standard fire policy as covering only hostile fire, which is a fire that is out of bounds. For example, personal property that is burned in a trash fire would not typically be considered covered for the fire damage to it. However, when the fire escapes its normal boundaries—such as when flames jump from a campfire to a forest or buildings—it is transformed into a hostile fire and resulting damage to covered property typically is covered.

Although *explosion* is also not defined, the coverage for damage caused by explosion is narrowed through the explosion of steam equipment exclusion, discussed later.

Description of Listed Causes of Loss

In addition to physical contact with an aircraft or vehicle, including a spacecraft or self-propelled missile, the aircraft cause of loss applies specifically to objects falling from aircraft.

Loss or damage caused by falling objects to personal property outdoors is not covered. Another exception to the falling objects cause of loss precludes coverage for personal property within a structure or the interior of the structure itself unless the roof or an outside wall is first damaged by a falling object. Under this exception, there would be no coverage for damage to personal property located within a manufacturing plant if, for example, a piece of steel being lifted by an indoor crane were dropped and crushed the personal property. In that instance, even though the piece of steel can be considered a falling object, the steel did not pierce a hole in the roof or an outside wall on its way down.

The glass breakage coverage applies to property other than the glass that is damaged by broken building glass.

Acts of striking employees occupying the described premises are covered under the riot or civil commotion cause of loss, as is looting at the time and place of a riot or civil commotion.

The form clarifies that sinkhole collapse coverage does not include those instances where the ground sinks or collapses into manmade cavities in the earth. This exposure is more appropriately the subject of mine subsidence coverage. The cost of filling sinkholes is not covered.

Abrupt, accidental direct physical loss to covered property by smoke is covered. To clarify this and other uses of the term, the form states that *abrupt* makes it clear that an abrupt event is instantaneous—"not gradual, ongoing, or repeated over time." Other property policies make it a point to exclude smoke damage from agricultural smudging or industrial operations. The MSO form accomplishes the same effect in a separate exclusion discussed later.

When applicable, sprinkler leakage coverage is for damage caused by the leakage or discharge from an automatic sprinkler system, including the collapse of the system's tank if there is one. *Automatic sprinkler system* is defined in the form's glossary. It refers to an "automatic fire protection or extinguishing system" and includes sprinklers, nozzles, ducts, pipes, valves, fittings, tanks, pumps, and private fire protection mains. It also includes nonautomatic systems, hydrants, standpipes, and outlets supplied from an automatic system.

Vandalism is generally a covered peril, but as mentioned earlier, it can be excluded with cause of loss option B. Vandalism involves willful and malicious damage to or destruction of the insured property. Building damage caused by the break-in or exit of burglars is covered, but breakage of building glass and other loss caused by or resulting from theft is excluded under this peril.

Damage caused by direct physical contact with a vehicle is covered, but loss caused by vehicles owned by the named insured or by vehicles operated in the course of the named insured's business is excluded. Because of this exception, damage caused to an insured's building when a customer backs into the loading dock would be covered. However, if an employee driving a company-owned delivery van has the same accident, neither the basic nor the broad causes of loss forms would pay for the damage to the building.

The volcanic action peril includes damage from the above-ground effects of a volcanic eruption—airborne blast and shock waves, ash, dust, particulate matter, and lava flow. It does not include the seismic effects of a volcanic eruption, as detailed in one of the form's common exclusions.

All volcanic eruptions occurring within a seven-day period (168 hours) are considered a single occurrence. No provision is made for modifying this time period.

Coverage under the water damage peril applies to damage to covered property resulting from the abrupt discharge of water—including steam. For example, the water might damage a hardwood floor. A supplemental coverage discussed earlier expands coverage to include expenses associated with repairing the leak itself.

Specified Causes of Loss

A definition clarifies which perils are included in the specified causes of loss that apply to some of the form's supplemental coverages. The perils are merely named in this definition, but the preceding descriptions or definitions provide any necessary elaboration.

The specified causes of loss are fire; aircraft; explosion; falling objects; lightning; riot or civil commotion; sinkhole collapse; smoke; sprinkler leakage; vandalism; vehicles; volcanic eruption; water damage; weight of ice, sleet, or snow; and windstorm/hail.

Covered Loss

The preceding causes of loss options involved direct damage to buildings, structures, and personal property covered under coverages A, B, and C. As described elsewhere, coverage D provides indirect loss coverage when a business income and/or extra expense loss results as the consequence of a direct covered loss.

Part I D – Property Exclusions/Limitations

Some types of property or losses excluded in this section of the policy are not covered at all. Others are excluded from the policy's full coverage because one of the form's supplemental coverages provides more limited or focused coverage. The first section of exclusions applies to all coverages, A, B, C, and D.

Building glass is not covered property except to the extent it is covered under the glass extension, discussed earlier, where it is subject to a sublimit except for damage by one of the specified causes of loss other than vandalism.

Crops, even harvested crops, are not covered at all. It seems questions could arise, in some circumstances, as to whether a bin full of wheat or a storeroom full of apples contains an excluded crop or covered stock.

Land and water are not covered property. Neither is generally susceptible to the causes of loss that a property insurance policy is designed to cover.

Other policy provisions attempt to limit coverage to described buildings, premises, locations, or operations or to covered property. An exclusion underscores this intent by specifically stating that coverage does not apply to property that is not described in the policy.

There is no coverage at all for personal property that is also the subject of other, more specific, insurance. However, the building coverage (coverage A) applies as excess over other more specific insurance. For example, an expensive piece of specialized machinery is insured with the building if permanently installed. If the insured has purchased other insurance identifying the machine and insuring it separately, then the machine is more specifically covered by the other contract. This form will pick up the difference, if any, between the insured's loss and the recovery under the other contract.

Certain types of outdoor property are covered by supplemental coverage 13, where coverage is subject to sublimits and coverage is limited to certain perils. Outdoor signs, likewise, are addressed under supplemental coverage 3.B.

Vehicles and their equipment should generally be covered under an auto, watercraft, aircraft, or inland marine policy such as a contractors equipment floater. However, supplemental coverage 14.E. extends coverage B to apply to certain types of vehicles.

Certain types of property that might qualify as buildings or structures are excluded from coverage because they are not especially susceptible to damage by most of the perils that the policy covers. Because these items are not covered property, they also are not included in any coinsurance computations.

Another set of excluded property and losses applies to business personal property of the insured and personal property of others. Creatures, money and securities, electronic data, precious metals, and valuable papers are not covered under coverages A and B, but they are covered to a limited extent by supplemental coverages.

Precious metals are not covered under coverages A and B. However, precious metals used in industrial operations are covered, subject to a sublimit, by supplemental coverage 16. Precious metals used in jewelry or used to make jewelry are covered—but only for loss by theft and even then only when open perils coverage is provided. A standard $100 per item, $3,000 per loss limit applies (unless it is modified in the supplemental declarations). In short, the only coverage available on precious metals used in jewelry applies to theft (not fire or other perils) of items worth more than $100 (or other indicated sublimit) and then only up to $3,000 (or other indicated aggregate limit). Other jewelry-type property is covered subject to coverage B limits except that loss by theft is limited to $3,000 per loss or $100 per item, and individual items with a retail value of less than the per-item limit (e.g., $100) are not covered at all.

Theft of furs is subject to a $3,000 per occurrence limit unless a different amount is indicated. The word *aggregate* is not used here in its usual sense. The form characterizes the $3,000 (unless modified) limits on jewelry and furs as "aggregate limits for all described property per occurrence." In other words, these are per-occurrence limits, not annual aggregate limits.

Item D. of this exclusion states that personal property is not covered at all under coverages A and B while it is airborne or waterborne. Coverages A and B apply to on-premises property. Although it is not mentioned at this point in the form, the off-premises supplemental coverage does apply to property in transit on a motor vehicle that the named insured leases, operates, or owns. *Motor vehicle* is not defined, but supplemental coverage 14.E. suggests that aircraft and watercraft, as well as cars and trucks, are vehicles. In summary, personal property is not covered if it is airborne (in a tethered balloon?) or waterborne on the premises, but it could arguably be covered—subject to limitations or restrictions—away from the premises.

Part I E – Property Loss Limitations

This set of provisions does not apply to the accounts receivable or valuable papers supplemental coverages.

The title of this set of provisions contains the phrase "loss limitations"; the "exclusions and limitations" in this provision are not a list of excluded perils or a list of types of property that are not covered. Rather, they are characterized as provisions that apply in connection with certain property to the extent the loss and property are otherwise covered. In other words, these exclusions and limitations apply to losses that would otherwise be covered.

These provisions are not limited to any particular property coverage(s), so they apply not only to direct damage to buildings and personal property but also to loss of use and to the form's supplemental coverages. Most of the exclusions or limitations here relate to losses that can be minimized or mitigated with the use of sound loss control.

Builders/Building Items. Direct damage or loss of use to builders' equipment, machinery, and tools away from the premises are excluded. These items are highly susceptible to loss, and they can more specifically be addressed with a contractors equipment floater.

Building materials that are not yet incorporated in the building are attractive to thieves, and the theft exposure is best addressed through loss control measures rather than insurance. This exclusion also impacts the loss of use coverage, since theft of critical building materials can seriously delay completion of a construction project.

Disappearance of Property and Unauthorized/Voluntary Transfer of Property. Insurance practitioners commonly use the term *mysterious disappearance* to apply to property that has disappeared when theft is suspected, but it cannot be proven. The disappearance of property limitation makes it clear that disappearance is not a covered cause of loss. Voluntary parting with or transfer of property likewise is not covered, even if theft is involved.

Fragile Items. Fragile items by definition are easily broken, and such breakage is excluded unless the breakage is caused by one of the specified causes of loss as defined: fire; aircraft; explosion; falling objects; lightning; riot or civil commotion; sinkhole collapse; smoke; sprinkler leakage; vandalism; vehicles; volcanic eruption; water damage; weight of ice, sleet, or snow; windstorm/hail. Including falling objects in this list seems like a loophole until one looks at the description of falling objects and realizes that coverage applies to property damaged by the falling object, not to the fallen object itself.

Hot Water/Steam Equipment. Damage caused by internal conditions to hot water or steam boilers is covered only to the extent that supplemental coverage 17 applies.

Part I F – Losses Not Insured

Except for the intentional loss and wear-and-tear exclusions, this set of provisions does not apply to the accounts receivable or valuable papers supplemental coverages.

The lead-in language to this set of provisions closely resembles the lead-in to the property loss limitations. One difference is that this section does not refer to "damage or loss" but only to "loss." Also, it omits the sentence that says the provisions apply "to the extent that the subject loss and property are otherwise covered." Taken together, these differences indicate that the exclusions in this set of provisions describe losses that are not insured at all. However, that is not necessarily the case. Some of these exclusions do not apply to certain supplemental coverages, some relate to losses that are covered in some manner by a supplemental coverage, and others provide coverage for ensuing losses.

Computer Hacking and Computer Virus Exclusion. This exclusion deals with defined terms whose definitions contain no surprises. What is noteworthy is that this exclusion does not apply to the supplemental electronic data coverage. The exclusion can also be deleted with respect to the electronic media—special period of indemnity provision that applies to business income/extra expense coverage.

Delay or Loss of Market/Loss of Use Exclusions. Delay of market and other consequential losses are not covered unless and to the extent business income/extra expense and the spoilage supplemental coverage apply. Same here.

Dishonesty Exclusion. As is customary with property insurance policies, this one excludes employee dishonesty. That exposure is best covered under a fidelity bond or crime insurance specifically designed to cover theft by employees.

Electrical Damage Exclusion. Virtually all property insurance policies—including option 1 under this policy—cover loss by lightning, a form of naturally generated electrical current. Loss by short circuits, brownouts, or electrical or electronic malfunction is not covered unless it leads to an ensuing fire.

Explosion of Steam Equipment Exclusion. In conjunction with supplemental coverage 17, this policy excludes explosions caused by steam pressure but covers combustion explosions.

Flood/Flooding Exclusion and Water Damage Exclusion. These exclusions are best understood when read together. These provisions are designed to preclude coverage for flooding loss caused by surface waters and for underground, subsurface water or pressure it might cause, while preserving loss for ensuing fire, explosion, or theft (when the policy covers theft). The water damage exclusion also precludes coverage for sewer backups, but this exclusion can be eliminated by triggering endorsement MCP 507 with an entry in the declarations. Sprinkler leakage ensuing from subsurface water or sewer backups is covered.

Freezing of Appliances or Other Equipment Exclusion. Freezing resulting from the insured's negligence is excluded, as are losses intentionally caused by any insured (including insureds that are not a named insured).

Intentional Loss Exclusion. This exclusion applies for acts committed by—or at the direction of—any insured. There must be an intent to cause a loss.

Law or Ordinance/Governmental Directive Exclusions and Power, Heating, or Cooling Failure Exclusion. These are excluded unless the designated Supplemental Coverage provides coverage.

Wear, Tear, and Other Specified Loss/Cause of Loss Exclusions. Property insurance policies generally include a group of exclusions typically referred to as wear-and-tear or maintenance exclusions. MSO's wear-and-tear exclusion is unusual in that pollution and mold exclusions are buried within the long list that begins with "wear and tear." Pollution cleanup costs are available in a supplemental coverage.

An earth movement exclusion is separately enumerated with a cross-reference to the common exclusion for earthquake/earth movement/ volcanic action.

The *smoke peril* definition, which applies to abrupt losses, is supplemented by a provision that specifically precludes coverage for smoke—and for smog or vapor—from agricultural or industrial activities.

Weather/Related Exclusions. The weather-related exclusions restrict—or further define—coverage for certain perils. However, the restrictions vary depending on the applicable causes of loss option.

With options 2 and 3 (basic and broad form perils), windstorm/hail losses are covered without further definition or description. The weather-related exclusion restricts the hail cover by making it clear that cold, frost, ice, sleet, and snow—with or without wind—still are not covered under the windstorm/hail peril. Neither is damage caused by the weight of hail, ice, sleet, or snow to personal property outdoors.

With basic, broad, or open perils (options 2, 3, and 5), weather-related damage to interior property is limited to instances in which the building's roof or walls have first been breached. However, a supplemental coverage covers damage from thawing caused by ice dams and similar situations when option 5 (the open perils approach) applies to the damaged property. Unless an otherwise covered ensuing loss occurs (such as a fire), even open perils option 5 does not cover loss of certain enumerated weather-related types.

Part I G – Special Part I Conditions

Duties When Loss/Danger of Loss Occurs

This form imposes the usual duties on parties who have suffered a property loss. These duties are not to be taken lightly, which is why this set of provisions concludes by stating in bold face print that failure to comply with these conditions can alter or void the insurer's obligations.

The lead-in sentence makes it clear that these duties apply not only to the named insured but also to other insureds and other coverage beneficiaries. The latter category would apply primarily to personal property of others. Recall that the insurer has a right to settle such losses directly with the property owner.

How Losses Are Settled

Most building and personal property losses are valued on an actual cash value basis. Replacement cost coverage can be substituted for actual cash value coverage by entering "MCP 520" in the declarations for each item to be valued on a replacement cost basis. Actual cash value and replacement cost are described in more detail later in this section of the form.

Limit of Liability per Loss Occurrence and Special Conditions. The insurer will not pay more than the reasonable cost of repairing, restoring, or replacing damaged property. If the insured pays more than that reasonable cost or adds an upgrade, the insurer is not obligated to pay the extra amount. On the other hand, if the insured completes repairs for a lesser amount, the insurer will not pay more than the amount that is actually paid. The insurer (not the insured) is entitled to benefit from any negotiations that reduce the actual repair cost.

Of course, the insurer will not pay more than the amount of insurance applicable to the damaged property, nor will the insurer pay any amount that exceeds the extent of the named insured's insurable interest in the property unless another party with an insurable interest in the property is also named in the form.

Special valuation provisions apply to some types of property, even though they may be components of the building or tangible personal property.

A unique characteristic of glass is that ordinances may require that glass in certain locations, such as doors or shower stalls, must be replaced with safety glass even if the original glass was not safety glass. The insurer will pay the extra cost to replace broken ordinary glass with safety glass if necessary. However, glass coverage is still subject to the sublimits shown in the supplemental declarations.

U. S. money, if it is covered at all, is valued at its face value. The value of foreign currency and securities fluctuates, so to eliminate disputes, foreign money (if covered) is valued at its exchange rate, and securities (if covered) on their market value at the close of business on the date the loss is reported to the insurer.

A selling price clause (not labeled as such in this form) values sold-but-not-delivered stock at its net selling price.

The valuation of tenants' improvements and betterments was discussed earlier in connection with coverage B.

Valuable papers and records not subject to the supplemental coverage are valued on the cost of blank materials and the cost of copying any duplicates of the damaged records. In most cases the cost of blank materials is nominal compared to the value of the intellectual property contained in those records, and the cost of downloading backup data or photocopying duplicate paper records is also nominal.

Limit of Liability per Loss Occurrence for Business Income and Extra Expense. In the Coverage D insuring agreement, the insurer may agree to cover a loss of business income. The provisions here include a nonexhaustive list of factors the insurer will consider when determining the maximum amount of the business income loss for which the insurer is liable, including those associated with the insured's post-loss duties. The insurer's liability is reduced to the extent the named insured can resume normal operations in whole or in part. The word *can* indicates that the insurer's obligations are reduced even if the insured fails to resume partial operations when it is possible to do so.

If the insurer provides extra expense coverage in coverage D, the loss adjustment takes into account whatever extraordinary expenses are incurred to maintain operations. If business income coverage is provided, the insurer also takes into account any expenses incurred to reduce the business income loss.

Extra expenses often involve acquiring equipment or other tangible property for use during the period of interruption. This is not a license to acquire property at the insurer's expense. If the property has any value after it has served its purpose, the insurer is entitled to reduce its obligations by that amount—referred to here as the property's salvage value. In this context, the salvage might be nearly new property, not scrap. The form does not say the insurer takes ownership of the salvage, merely that the insurer's liability is reduced by the value of the salvage.

The insurer's obligations are also reduced by any recovery from other type of insurance. If another party caused the insured's property loss, this might include recoveries from a third party's liability insurance. As with business income coverage, the insurer's obligations are reduced to the extent normal operations can be resumed.

The insurer's obligations do not exceed the dollar limits for business income and/or extra expense coverage at each location, as shown in the declarations.

Bases of Loss Settlement. Unless otherwise specified, buildings and business personal property of the named insured are valued on an actual cash value basis. As defined in the form's glossary, the insurer may consider the following factors in determining an item's actual cash value: "age; condition; cost to repair, replace, or restore the property, subject to deduction for depreciation; deterioration; economic value; market value; obsolescence (both structural and functional); original cost; use; utility; or other circumstances that may reasonably affect value."

As is commonly done in forms that cover buildings, the form also specifies that smaller losses to building property (with some exceptions) are to be settled on a replacement cost basis. In this case, the cut-off point for smaller losses is the replacement threshold limit stated in the supplemental declarations. The standard replacement threshold limit is $3,000, but this is subject to modification. Replacement cost coverage does not apply to these building items that tend to depreciate rapidly: awnings; cooking, dishwashing, laundering, refrigerating, or ventilating appliances; fire extinguishers; floor coverings; lawn care and snow removal equipment; or outdoor fixtures/furniture.

Replacement cost coverage replaces the standard actual cash value coverage for items for which MCP 520 is listed in the declarations. A statement in the declarations may also indicate that replacement cost coverage is applicable. Even when replacement cost coverage applies, certain hard-to-value or irreplaceable items are valued on an actual cash value basis: manuscripts, property of others, and antiques or works of art.

Stock is also valued at actual cash value unless the selling price option (MCP 521) applies to stock that has been sold but not delivered.

Replacement cost coverage applies only when the property is actually repaired, replaced, or restored. An insured has the option of settling on an actual cash value basis and then 180 days to submit a claim for the difference between the actual cash value and the replacement cost of repairs that have actually been completed. As discussed earlier, the same limitation applies to additional ordinance or law costs incurred under supplemental coverage 4. The policy is silent as to what happens if repairs take longer than 180 days. In contrast, the ISO Building and Personal Property Coverage Form provides 180 days for the insured to notify the insurer of its intent to make a replacement cost claim once restoration is completed, but it does not limit payment to work that is completed within 180 days.

Repair, replacement, or restoration of the damaged property must be made at the same location unless the declarations include MCP 522 with respect to the property.

Appraisal. The described appraisal process may be used in settling disputes over the amount of any loss under either the main coverages or the supplemental coverages. The appraisal condition provides that if either the insurance company or the insured submits a written demand for an appraisal after a property loss, each has thirty days to choose an appraiser and the two appraisers, in turn, have fifteen days in which to select an umpire. In the event the appraisers fail to agree on both the value of the property and the amount of loss, the issue is given to the umpire (previously selected by the two appraisers or appointed by a judge from any court having jurisdiction). When an agreement is reached by any two of these parties (among the appraisers and umpire), the decision stands. Any expenses beyond the cost of each party's appraiser are divided equally between the insurance company and the insured. It is stated within the appraisal provision that the insurance company may still deny a claim even if an appraisal has been agreed to. The purpose of the statement is to avoid a legal argument that the insurer's participation in the appraisal process carries an implied agreement to pay that prevents subsequent denial.

Coinsurance Requirements. As respects buildings and personal property, MSO's two-part coinsurance provision is laudably concise and clear. A coinsurance factor (typically 0.80, 0.90, or 1.00) is shown in the declarations for each building or personal property item. Full liability—meaning no coinsurance penalty—is applied if the amount of insurance equals or exceeds the coinsurance factor times the insurable value of the damaged, destroyed, or lost property at the time of the loss. Reduced liability—application of a coinsurance penalty—applies when the amount of insurance does not meet this standard. With reduced liability, the insurer's obligation is prorated in proportion to the ratio of the insurance limit to the amount of insurance that should have been carried to meet the coinsurance requirement.

Unless otherwise stated, the coinsurance condition applies only to coverages A, B, and C; it does not apply to this form's supplemental coverages.

As respects business income coverage, MSO's two-part coinsurance condition parallels the approach taken with respect to buildings and personal property. However, it can be more difficult to establish business income values than it is to determine the insurable value of tangible property.

Calculations begin by determining the net income and operating expenses that would have been earned during the current twelve-month policy period if no direct covered loss had occurred at some point during the policy period. This amount, referred to as "a," is then multiplied by the coinsurance factor specified in the policy, referred to as "b." If the amount of business income insurance equals or exceeds the product of a times b, the insurer has full liability and will pay the business income loss in full, subject to policy terms and conditions.

Reduced liability applies when the amount of insurance is less than the amount previously determined, in which case the amount of the loss is prorated in proportion to the amount of insurance that should have been carried.

The coinsurance condition is waived (that is, no coinsurance penalty applies) for smaller business income losses. The supplemental declarations include a dollar limit ($10,000 is standard but can be modified) and a factor (0.05 is standard but can be modified) that apply in determining which losses this applies to. The coinsurance penalty is waived for losses that meet both of two conditions. First, the amount of the covered business income loss must be less than the dollar limit (e.g., $10,000), and second it must be less than the factor (e.g., 0.05) times the applicable amount of insurance.

Deductible. The deductibles discussed here apply only to building and personal property coverage; no dollar deductible applies to business income or extra expense coverage. The applicable deductible amount appears in the declarations. The insurer has no obligation with respect to any loss that is less than the deductible, and the deductible is subtracted from larger losses.

When coinsurance and deductibles are involved, questions arise as to where in the sequence the deductible is applied. When a coinsurance penalty (reduced liability) is involved, the deductible in this form is to be subtracted from the amount of the loss, not the amount of the recovery.

MCP 512 offers a disappearing deductible option. Disappearing deductibles are attractive—in theory—but they have all but disappeared in practice. Property insurance deductibles are intended to encourage loss prevention by ensuring that the insured has some skin in the game and to eliminate the disproportionately high cost of settling small claims that are more efficiently handled outside the insurance mechanism. These objectives are most relevant to small losses. Disappearing deductibles apply to small losses but gradually become smaller, and eventually disappear, as the size of the loss increases. Disappearing deductibles are theoretically appealing because they meet the objectives of a deductible with respect to small losses without penalizing the insured who suffers a larger loss. Unfortunately, they are difficult to explain and often misunderstood by insureds.

Loss to a Portion of a Pair or Set of Articles. Loss to one item that is part of a pair or set of related items (for example, the second volume of a three-volume book set) often disproportionately affects the value of the remaining items. This form's pair or set clause makes it clear that loss of one component does not automatically create a total loss but, if the insurer agrees to pay for a total loss, the insurer is entitled to take possession of the remaining parts.

Insurer's Options for Settling Losses. Following a covered loss, the insurance company has four options. First—and most commonly—the insurer will simply provide money to pay the loss. Second, the insurer may repair or replace the property. For example, the insurer might arrange to have a glass contractor, with whom it does business, to replace damaged glass. Third, the company may take the property and pay the insured an agreed or appraised price. The insurer promises to notify the insured within thirty days of receipt of the sworn statement of loss if it intends to pursue this option. Finally, the company may settle the claim with the named insured, any named loss payee, or any other party legally entitled to payment—such as the owner of personal property of others.

Claims involving a loss payee or personal property of others in the insured's custody occasionally give rise to a legal action against the insured. When this happens, the insurer has a right to conduct and control a defense, at the insurer's expense, but defense costs are within applicable limits.

Recovery of Covered Property. This condition provides a method for loss readjustment in case damaged or stolen property is recovered after the insurer has paid a claim. The insured has the option to return the amount of any claim payment in return for the original item, in which case the insurer is to be compensated. Alternatively, the insured may keep the claims payment, but the recovered property then belongs to the insurer.

When Loss Becomes Payable/Payment to Others. The insurer must pay the claim within thirty days after reaching an agreement with the involved parties. The insurer has a right to decide whether the claim draft is payable to the insured, or it may be payable jointly to all interested parties. This is normally done by naming the various parties and adding "as their interests may appear." The insured may assign claims proceeds to another party, but the insurer will not pay the other party without the insured's consent. The insurer may settle a claim with a trustee who represents other interested parties.

The policy's limits are not aggregate limits, so payment of any claim does not reduce the amount that is still available to pay future claims.

Other Special Part I Conditions

Abandonment of Property. The insured may not simply abandon damaged property to the insurance company.

Increase in Hazard. An increase in hazard condition was a standard fixture in the 1943 Standard Fire Policy that once served as the foundation document for commercial property insurance. However, insurers have found it difficult to enforce this condition. Today, few policies include an increase in hazard condition per se.

Vacancy and unoccupancy represent an increase in hazard. A vacant building does not contain the contents that are customary to its occupancy, but a building under construction is not considered vacant. Coverage is suspended completely when a building is vacant or unoccupied for more than sixty consecutive days. However, this condition does not apply to a seasonal building that is normally closed during part of a year.

Because it completely suspends coverage, this condition is harsher than the vacancy condition in the ISO Building and Personal Property Coverage Form, which eliminates coverage for certain perils and reduces the amount of recovery for loss by other perils when a building is vacant for more than sixty days.

Mortgagee Agreement. This condition spells out the rights and duties of any mortgagees or trustees (here referred to as mortgageholders) that are named on the declarations and comply with certain conditions.

The mortgageholder is required to notify the insurance company of any known change in ownership or occupancy, as well as any foreclosure proceeding or increase of hazard. On the insurer's demand, the mortgageholder is also required to pay any required premium that the insured has not paid and to furnish a proof of loss, within sixty days, if the insured has not.

If claim payment is made to a mortgageholder, the insurance company inherits the mortgageholder's rights of recovery against a third party who may be responsible for the loss, but the mortgageholder still retains a right to recover the full amount of the claim.

At the insurance company's option, the mortgageholder may be paid the full payment of the principal and interest on the mortgage in exchange for transfer of the mortgage to the insurance company. The insured continues mortgage payments, but to the insurance company instead of the original mortgageholder.

If payment for a claim is denied to an insured (due to the insured's actions or lack of compliance with the terms for coverage) a mortgage holder is still entitled to loss payment as long as any obligations concerning premium or proof of loss due to the company are taken care of by the mortgageholder.

No Benefit to Bailee. Like many other property insurance forms, this policy will not cover the liability of a bailee for property that is in the bailee's possession.

Part I H – Glossary

Italicized terms and phrases elsewhere in the form have the meanings defined in this glossary. If a liability form is Part II of this policy, these definitions apply only to Part I—the property coverages.

Many of the defined terms are discussed elsewhere in this analysis. Others, though they are important, contain no surprises and require no elaboration.

Part I – Common Conditions

These Common Conditions Apply in Addition to Part I G.

Action or Suit Against Us. If the insured wishes to sue the insurer, the insured must comply with conditions expressed elsewhere in the policy or in a state-specific endorsement. Typically, the insured must first be in full compliance with the terms of the policy, and the action must be brought within a specified time period, such as one or two years, following the loss or damage.

Assignment of Your Interest. The insurer's written consent is required for any transfer to another person of the insured's rights and duties under the policy. The single exception to this requirement of written consent is transfer to a legal representative upon the death of an individual named insured. In such cases, the legal representative exercises the deceased insured's rights and duties while acting as legal representative. Until a legal representative is appointed, rights and duties of the deceased insured with respect to the deceased insured's property pass to anyone having proper temporary custody of that property.

Cancellation/Termination. Either the insurer or the insured may cancel the policy. Dealings between insurer and insured with respect to cancellation are to be carried out by "the first Named Insured shown in the Declarations" when more than one insured is named in the policy. It is the first named insured—not any insured—who must mail or deliver notice of cancellation to the insurer. Premium refund is also made to the first named insured.

The policy automatically terminates if the named insured purchases a replacement policy from another insurer and does not pay the premium on this policy when it becomes due. If the business or premises are sold, coverage automatically terminates at the time title is transferred unless the named insured retains an insurable interest in the property.

Whether the insured or the insurer cancels the policy, return premium is calculated on a pro rata basis, but the insurer may retain a minimum earned premium.

Insurers' cancellation, termination, and nonrenewal rights vary by state. Unless otherwise described in this policy, the insurer's rights are described in a state-specific endorsement.

Concealment/Misrepresentation/Fraud. This provision voids coverage should the named insured commit a fraudulent act or if the named insured or any other insured commits fraud or intentionally conceals or misrepresents a material fact about the coverage, the covered property, a claim, the named insured's interest in the property, or any other aspect of this insurance. Note that the concealment, misrepresentation, or fraud condition works to void coverage whether the fraud, concealment, or misrepresentation occurs before or after a loss.

The language does not state that the act of any other insured voids the policy only as to that individual. Conceivably, therefore, the act of any insured could void the policy as to all other insureds, including the named insured. However, the insurer may choose to honor the contract with respect to insureds other than the one who was personally guilty of concealment, misrepresentation, or fraud. In some jurisdictions or situations, the insurer may be required to provide coverage for a battered spouse or other innocent coinsured.

Conformity with Statute. Provisions in the policy are amended to conform to all applicable statutory requirements.

Coverage Territory. To be covered under the commercial property policy, loss or damage must occur within the coverage territory: the fifty United States (including its territories and possessions), Washington D.C., Canada, and Puerto Rico. The U.S. Government lists the following territories and possessions: the Northern Mariana Islands, Guam, American Samoa, Federated States of Micronesia, U.S. Virgin Islands, Midway Islands, Republic of the Marshall Islands, and Republic of Palau.

Examination/Changes. This provision underscores the point that one should not assume an insurance provision's contents based on its title. Based on experience with other insurance policies' changes provisions, one might expect from the title of this provision that it explains that policy changes may be made only by the insurer and then only in writing. Not so; that issue is addressed in another condition. This condition deals with the insurer's right to conduct inspections and to examine the insured's books and records.

This condition gives the insurer the right (but does not impose any obligation) to conduct inspections, to make surveys, and to make recommendations. The nature of these recommendations is not specified, but recommendations made to the insured typically deal with safety or compliance issues. This condition does not place the insurer (or any rating, advisory, or similar organization making inspections under the policy) in the position of warranting that conditions connected with the insured's operations are safe or healthful or that the insured is in compliance with legal requirements that may pertain to those operations.

This condition also gives the insurer the right to audit the insured's books and records relating to the policy. The examination or audit may be made during the policy period or any time within three years after the policy period ends. The insurer may make premium adjustments based on the inspection and audit. This condition is linked to the premiums condition that appears later in the form's alphabetical sequence. The premiums condition allows the insurer to charge a provisional premium if MCP 550 is listed in the declarations, with a final premium, retroactive to policy inception, based on a rating inspection or investigation of the insured premises.

MSO conducts detailed property inspections on every nonresidential risk to develop specific rates for the building and its contents. The specific fire rate reflects the unique circumstances surrounding the individual risk, including building construction, operational hazards, and distance to the fire department and hydrants. In addition to the schedule rate, MSO develops an idealized rate that would apply if all correctable hazards were eliminated. For insureds that may not want or are not able to address all recommendations, MSO will develop tentative rates that show what the rate will be if some of the recommendations are complied with.

Insurance under More Than One Coverage. This anti-stacking provision prevents the insured from duplicate coverage.

Liberalization. Insurers periodically introduce new policy editions that contain some changes. Any broadening of coverage produced by a revision of the coverage form that is introduced during the policy period or in the forty-five days preceding its inception will immediately apply to the insured's unrevised policy. However, the liberalization clause does not apply if the revision that broadens coverage also includes coverage restrictions or requires any extra premium. This provision is standard in many insurance forms.

Other Insurance. The condition does not state that the insured cannot have other insurance. Rather, many insureds with commercial property to insure will carry more than one policy or more than one insurance company will insure a specific risk. The other insurance condition recognizes this but reduces all situations in which other insurance might apply to two: (1) the existence of other insurance written on any other basis than this policy, in which case the policy responds as excess insurance; and (2) the existence of other insurance written with the same provisions as this policy, in which case the policy and others are primary insurers. When two or more other primary insurers provide for contributions by equal shares, this policy contributes on that basis. Otherwise, this policy responds pro rata by limits.

If this policy covers loss by a peril that another policy would also cover except that the other policy does not cover that peril, then the loss will be apportioned the same as though the other policy did cover that cause of loss.

Premiums. The first named insured is responsible for making all premium payments and receiving any return premiums. The rest of this provision was previously analyzed in connection with the examination/ changes provision.

Recovery from Others. The most important point here is that, if the insured waives it rights of recovery against a third party after a loss has occurred, the insurer may not be obligated to pay a claim that might otherwise be covered.

This condition defines the insurer's subrogation rights under the policy, which arise when the insurer makes a payment to or for "any insured (or others)." The reference to others preserves the insurer's subrogation rights with respect to third parties who might recover for a loss under the policy—a mortgagee or bailor, for instance. It clarifies that the insurer takes over the subrogation rights of not only the named insured, but also of any third-party claimant but only to the extent of any payment the insurer has made to that third party.

The insured's right to waive possible recovery against third parties is retained if the waiver is made before a loss. The insured is also permitted to waive its rights of recovery after a loss when the waiver is given to another insured or to a business owned or controlled by the insured or one owning or controlling the insured.

Time of Inception and Coverage Period. Coverage basically begins at midnight, but insurers refer instead to 12:01 A.M. This might seem like an unusual time for a policy period to begin, but it avoids ambiguity. 12:00 A.M. might arguably be interpreted to mean either noon or midnight, and midnight is ambiguous as to whether it is the moment in time that begins or ends a particular calendar date.

This policy covers losses that take place during the policy period, typically one year, between 12:01 A.M. on the policy's inception date and its expiration date unless otherwise specifically provided. For example, the coverage D policy term extension provision specifically states that the described periods of indemnity are not limited by expiration of the policy term.

Waiver or Change of Provisions. This condition stipulates that any changes in the terms of the policy can be made only by endorsement issued by the insurer. Requests for changes on the insured's part must be made by the first named insured.

Part I – Common Exclusions

Like virtually all insurance policies, this one broadly excludes all coverage for war and for nuclear incidents, but it preserves coverage for direct fire damage that ensues from a nuclear incident. Whether it is war-related, damage or destruction of property that is ordered by civil authorities is also excluded; however, damage intentionally ordered to prevent the spread of fire (such as setting a backfire or clearing an open area) is covered.

Earth movement, including earthquakes and volcanic activity, are also broadly excluded. With respect to this peril, ensuing fire, explosion, or theft (if theft is a covered peril) is, however, covered. Volcanic eruption (including damage by shock waves, ash, or lava flow) is not excluded; it is a covered peril in most policies, as discussed earlier in connection with the form's cause of loss options.

Endorsements Preprinted in the MSO General Property Form

MCP 501 extends the sixty-day day electronic media period of indemnity under coverage D to the number of days shown in the declarations.

MCP 502 extends the thirty-day extended period of indemnity under coverage D to the number of days shown in the declarations.

MCP 503 deletes the antenna exclusion under coverage D.

MCP 504 extends coverage D to the increased period of time needed to comply with the subject building code or law.

MCP 505 extends cause of loss option 5 to property in transit.

MCP 506 permits building code/law coverage although property is not covered on replacement basis.

MCP 507 modifies the water damage exclusion to cover backup of sewers and drains.

MCP 508 extends business income coverage to cover computer hacking or viruses.

MCP 510 applies a general policy deductible (instead of a standard $250 deductible) to accounts receivable supplemental coverage.

MCP 511 applies a general policy deductible (instead of a standard $250 deductible) to valuable papers and records coverage.

MCP 512 provides a disappearing deductible.

MCP 515 deletes certain coverage for loss to the interior under the weather related supplemental coverage.

MCP 520 provides replacement coverage in connection with coverages A and B.

MCP 521 extends replacement coverage to stock.

MCP 522 permits replacement under replacement coverage at another premises.

MCP 550 permits the use of provisional rates.

Chapter 16

E-Issues under the Building and Personal Property Coverage Form

Cyberspace—What Is It?

From a layperson's perspective, the term *cyberspace* refers to that vast area of virtual space occupied by the Internet, World Wide Web, web pages, websites, electronic mail, discussion groups, public and private online seminars, and other means of communicating via computers. It is a communications medium seemingly without physical walls or boundaries outside the means of communicating through it.

The term *cyberspace* was said to have been coined in 1984 by science fiction writer William Gibson, who wrote the following in *Neuromancer 51* (as cited by M. Ethan Katsh, "Is Cyberspace Lawyer-Friendly? [*Trial Magazine*, p. 35, Dec. 1995]):

> Cyberspace. A consensual Hallucination experienced daily by billions of legitimate operators in every nation ... A graphic representation of data abstracted from the banks of every computer in the human system. Unthinkable complexity. Lines of light ranged in the nonspace of the mind, clusters and constellations of data. Like city light, receding ....

The cyberspace medium, also referred to as the Internet, is used for a variety of purposes by lawyers, doctors, researchers, businesses, business partners, and others to advertise, solicit clients, locate experts, and for other purposes, some of which are unlawful or result in an actionable offense.

As with all technological advances, the use of cyberspace generates all kinds of issues and abuses arising from its use. Lawyers, risk managers, consultants, agents, brokers, claims personnel, and other insurance professionals not only should learn the insurance implications involved with this medium but should also strive to keep pace with it, if possible. Those who wait will soon find themselves far behind.

Intangible Property

"We are heading at blinding speed into a completely new world built on a foundation of information and communication technology. Change—driven by technology and put in motion across society—will be the biggest risk of all to manage." That provocative prediction was penned in 1998 by Scott K. Lange, former risk manager for Microsoft, for *E-Risk, Liabilities in a Wired World*, published by the National Underwriter Company, when the issues of electronic and intangible property were under development.

Today a business's only property may be intangible—its customer records, services, accounts, trademarks, brands, patents, and copyrights. Such assets are often of far greater importance than the traditional tangible assets disclosed on balance sheets. Intangible property is the fuel of e-commerce. The National Underwriter Company book *Cyber Liability and Insurance: Managing the Risks of Intangible Assets* contains what is referred to as a "Substantially Incomplete List of Intangible Assets" that shows how broad the area of intangible assets has grown in the modern era. Borrowed from there and reproduced here, intangible assets nonexclusively include the following:

1. Marketing Assets

   - Trademarks and service marks

   - Trade names and brand names

   - Logotypes

   - Colors

2. Technology Assets

   - Patents and patent applications

   - Technical documentation (e.g., laboratory notebooks, technical know-how)

3. Artistic Assets

   - Maps

   - Literary works and copyrights

   - Musical compositions

   - Photographs

4. Data Processing Assets

    • Software and software copyrights

    • Databases

5. Engineering Assets

    • Industrial designs

    • Engineering drawings, schematics, and blue prints

    • Technical know-how and trade secrets

6. Customer-Related Assets

    • Customer relationships, contracts, and lists

    • Open purchase orders

7. Contractual Assets

    • License and franchise agreements

    • Operating license

8. Human Capital Assets

    • Trained workforce and wages

    • Union and other employment contracts

9. Location-Related Assets

    • Easements and mineral exploitation rights

    • Water and air rights

10. Online-Related Assets

    • Domain names and website design

    • Linkages

The Building and Personal Property form was developed and evolved as a vehicle by which tangible property—buildings and structures, business personal property, property of others on the insured's premises—is protected.

Thus, there have been some conflicts in scope of coverage, resulting in the revamping of standard policies to address and provide some limit of coverage to intangible property. For example, the BPP form has been revised to affirmatively cover electronic data (a type of intangible property) that is integrated in a building's operating systems under the building's property limit. A separate $2,500 limit for electronic data is also applicable under its additional coverages. These coverages are reviewed in Chapters 1 and 2.

Because of the growing importance of intangible assets and the challenges of cyber-security, protecting this type of property has become a major challenge facing agents, insurers, and risk managers. The traditional insurance mechanism for protecting tangible property must be reevaluated in light of the e-business world.

Insuring Intangible Assets

This country's founding fathers recognized the right of individuals and companies to protect their intellectual property. Article I, Section 8 of the Constitution states: "Congress shall have power to promote the progress of science and useful arts, by securing for limited times to authors and inventors the exclusive right to their respective writings and discoveries."

In order to properly protect these assets, they must be adequately and fully described for the insurer. Insurers have developed specialized applications for e-property.

One problem faced by insurers is how to value such assets. Traditional property can be appraised and a value set. Such property and the things that happen to it usually can be seen. But in cyber-liability instead of physically appraising a building, insurers must grapple with the following questions:

- What is the value of a concept?

- What is the value of research and development?

- What is the value of a name?

- What is the value of customer service?

- What is the value of advertising?

- What is the value of speed to market?

- What is the value of a reputation?

A simple example will suffice. What happens when an employee's laptop computer is stolen, as has happened at banks, universities, and even within the federal government? The company did not lose just the value of the physical laptop. Of much more value is the data stored on the laptop. And how is it quantified? Is it the cost to recreate the data or the cost of the physical components? The BPP form has been revised in various ways, and although limited property coverage for electronic data is provided under the BPP, it is generally inadequate for most business operations.

While computer tapes and disks are undoubtedly tangible property, a question that has persisted for many years has been whether the information they contain likewise falls into the category of tangible property. (While the subject of this book is property insurance, the mention of cases dealing with property damage liability is still germane since both property damage and physical loss or damage are similar in many respects).

In *Retail Systems, Inc. v. CNA Ins. Companies*, 469 N.W.2d 735 (Minn. App. 1991), the court ruled that the disappearance and loss of a computer tape containing stored information, while in possession of an insured, was considered to be physical injury to tangible property. The court's rationale was that the information on the tape was of permanent value and was integrated completely with the physical property of the tape. The court explained that, like a motion picture film, where the information and the film medium are integrated, so too were the tape and data integrated when the tape was lost. The policy's care, custody, or control exclusion also did not apply because it was replaced by broad form property damage coverage, and nothing within that coverage precluded protection. In addition, even if that exclusion had been applicable, the court noted that coverage would still have been applicable under Section I of the package policy offering coverage on loss or damage to property.

Some courts have decided that in view of the language in current policies, damage to data is not damage to tangible property and, thus, not covered. In *Seagate Technology, Inc., v. St. Paul Fire & Marine Ins. Co.*, 11 F. Supp.2d 1150 (N.D. Cal. 1998), a manufacturer of hardware lost the battle in court when trying to prove that defective hard drives had caused ensuing damage to tangible property. The basic holding is that the typical property insurance policy responds only to actual physical damage to a company's hardware or equipment. The forms have been clarified with this intent, as is discussed in the property not covered portion of Chapter 1 and the coverage extensions and additional coverage material in Chapter 2.

The Meaning of *Property*

The Building and Personal Property Coverage Form promises to pay for "direct physical loss or damage to covered property at the premises described in the Declarations caused by or resulting from any Covered Cause of Loss." In the traditional sense, *property* has always meant tangible property. However, the interpretation of the word *property* was challenged in court as the importance of electronic data rose. The interpretation of the word *property* has implications both for direct damage policies and business income policies. A business income policy requires damage to property at the described premises before coverage applies. If data is not property there is no insured business income loss.

A question that also needs to be pondered is this: at what point does tangible property come into being? A great deal of commentary on this point focuses on whether the data can be touched or has some other physical property. This, however, is a primitive measure of tangible property in relation to current technology and the data stored on computer disks. Current definitions and measures of what constitutes tangible property have evolved over the years based on technology that required there be a hard copy (hand written or typed) before the work product on the hard copy could be used or accessed. These approaches, however, have no use in the computer era where data are stored and continually added until printed.

From the perspective of insureds (or laypeople) and the application of property and/or liability coverage, once data can be viewed on a computer screen, edited and printed, they are tangible property. Whether the material has actually been printed does not alter the nature of the data and their tangible properties once removed from the computer to paper.

Intangible property such as copyrights or goodwill have no tangible property characteristics even if printed, except for the value of the property they are printed on. The reason is that goodwill and copyrights are concepts in the law that have value only as the concept itself. This is in stark contrast to computer data, which have inherent value as databases, reports, or other forms, once they make the transition from thought process to paper or computer storage medium. That value derives not from the law applying the idea or concept, but from the data themselves, which are used for business purposes whether printed or on the computer screen. Computer data then do have tangible property characteristics from the moment of their conception, whether printed or left on the computer storage medium.

From the perspective of insureds, damage to data created by the insured are physical damage to tangible property; an entity, for example, that loses a large report in progress on its computer hard drive essential to its operations. There would be little argument that such data are tangible property once printed. Why, therefore, is data not tangible property while waiting to be printed or edited? Once information goes from the thought process to written form capable of being printed, it becomes tangible property for purposes of property or liability coverage.

Prior to the advent of computers, as they are known today, there were at least two schools of thought dealing with the transition of data to tangible property, and the insurability thereof. The first school of thought was that when reports and data had to be typed or handwritten, the information, from the thought process of the author to paper, became tangible property because it was in hard copy form. It had value because the cost to reproduce it could be substantial. Why then should this result be circumvented simply because technology allows the data to be stored and edited prior to being printed on paper?

The second school of thought was not whether data had been converted to print on paper. It was actually more basic than that. Since data represent ideas (plans, solutions, formulas), they are by insurers not to be insurable because property policies do not insure ideas. For example, valuable papers coverage will pay to recreate the valuable papers but not the ideas. While the courts have produced mixed results on whether data is tangible property, the insurers are firmly of the opinion that data is not tangible property. It is these kinds of questions that led to both property and liability coverage forms being revised in recent years to define *electronic data* and to add exclusions where necessary. The BPP form, for example, defines *electronic data*, excludes it, but adds some limited coverage back.

In one case, *American Guarantee & Liability Ins. Co. v. Ingram Micro, Inc.*, No. 99–185 TUC ACM, 2000 WL 726789 (D. Ariz. April 18, 2000), the judge termed such use of the word property as archaic. In that case, Ingram Micro lost data when its computers were shut down due to a power outage. Because the data were the only property damaged, the insurer denied payment for any direct loss and for any business interruption loss. In addition to his description of the policy interpretation as archaic, the judge also said, "At a time when computer technology dominates our professional as well as personal lives, the Court must side with Ingram's broader definition of physical damage."

The problem is that the standard property policy protects against a range of standard perils. In this new world, insureds face not only direct damage to their property, but interruption of their services and possible reputational damage. Such losses may involve a hacker getting into a company's records or website. Email may be stolen; access to the website may be severely limited. Recent notable examples of these exposures include the security breaches of customers' personal data at retailers such as Target and Home Depot, and the damage suffered by the Sony Corporation after its servers were hacked, confidential information disclosed, and threats forced the postponement of a film's release.

All of this costs the insured money, but these are not the exposures contemplated in the historical actuarial evolution of property rates. The answer has been to revise commercial property forms to limit electronic data and the cost to restore or recreate it, but the industry has also responded with a number of specialty and nonstandard coverage forms.

E-Property Policies

As a response to the issues surrounding e-property, insurers have developed policies to protect it. Generally, these policies fall into one of the following three categories:

1. Third-party liability

2. Prosecution or abatement

3. First-party liability/loss

Because it is not within the purview of this book to examine third-party issues, this discussion is limited to the first-party issues surrounding e-property (see *Cyber Liability and Insurance: Managing the Risks of Intangible Assets*, published by The National Underwriter Company, for more information). Specialty coverage is available, but it is usually menu-based, meaning that one must select the coverages just as one does with named perils coverage. Sometimes, it is like trying to fit a square peg into a round hole. ISO, for example, has offered an Internet Liability and Network Protection Policy, EC 00 10, that is menu-based, since it offers five coverages (three liability and two property) that can purchased individually or altogether. The two property coverages are Insuring Agreement C – Replacement or Restoration of Electronic Data and Insuring Agreement E – Business Income and Extra Expense.

When Insuring Agreement C is purchased, coverage applies for the costs of replacing or restoring electronic data stored within the insured's computer system, which is lost or rendered inaccessible as the direct result of an e-commerce incident. The term *e-commerce incident* is defined in the policy as "a virus, malicious instruction; or denial of service attack introduced into the insured's computer system." The term *electronic data* also is defined. An important point about that definition is the specific statement that electronic data does not include the insured's electronic data if licensed, leased, rented, or loaned to others.

When Insuring Agreement E is purchased, coverage applies for loss of business income or extra expense incurred as the direct result of an e-commerce incident or from an extortion threat (another coverage agreement).

Coverage C is subject to a monetary deductible, whereas Coverage E is subject to both a monetary deductible and a waiting period. What can complicate matters is exclusions. This particular policy has twenty-eight exclusions. Unfortunately, there is no allocation among the insuring agreements and exclusions so all of the exclusions can be cited for one or more coverages.

This policy was introduced by ISO in 2005 to address the coverage needs of entities using and maintaining a website to conduct business. The form is designed for both commercial enterprises and not-for profit organizations. The second phase of this policy, introduced in 2008, was intended for financial institutions. In fact, the name of the policy is very telling on that score: Financial Institutions Information Security Protection Policy, EC 00 11. This policy has eight insuring agreements with three of them considered to be first-party coverages. These are Insuring Agreement 4., Replacement or Restoration of Electronic Data; Insuring Agreement 6., Business Income and Extra Expense; and Insuring Agreement 7., Public Relations Expense. This policy has twenty-six exclusions.

The standard BPP form has been revised to exclude electronic data under the property not covered section but provides a limited additional coverage for electronic data loss, including viruses and hacker attacks.

There are also a growing number of excess and surplus lines carriers that write first-party coverage for e-assets. These policies protect against damage from the following:

1.   Unauthorized access to a company's website

2.   Insertion of unauthorized code (a virus) into a company's system

3.   Denial of service (for example, the flooding of a site with thousands of email messages, making it difficult or impossible for the company to use the site)

4.   Denial of access (in this scenario, the wrongdoer redirects traffic away from the insured's website, thus causing the loss of business)

In order to collect, the policies typically say that the act must be malicious. If the attacker cannot be caught, malice cannot be shown.

Additionally, many losses involving data are simply caused by mistakes in programming with no malice, or from unknown incompatibilities between programs. Some of these simply will not work together.

The last issue to examine is valuation. What these policies protect is the insured's revenue stream from operations. As with business income policies, they settle based on actual loss sustained. Under these forms, the insured estimates business income losses and insures accordingly. The problem is in the adjustment of claims. The insured will not realize what the settlement is until the claim has been adjusted.

In many businesses, the website and other e-operations do not earn a profit. In that case, the net loss on the website operation may offset any potential recovery under a business income form. Because there are no physical items to rebuild after a website attack, the typical site is down for only a few hours or days. Thus, the amount of income lost may appear small.

A careful review of policy language is needed when selecting coverage and a carrier to provide that coverage. Most producers will likely choose two or, perhaps, three carriers to use, so the initial choice is critical. Despite the fact that many carriers were initially reluctant to formally design products for this market, the insurers that offer coverage tend to change their forms frequently. Additional coverage to address a special exposure may be available by endorsement or through manuscript wording.

Chapter 17

Miscellaneous Commercial Property Coverage Issues

Since the introduction of the first edition of this work some commercial property coverage areas have arisen that were not the issues they have become. Primarily are the development of various terrorism endorsements following the terrorist attacks of September 11, 2001, and the subsequently enacted federal Terrorism Risk Insurance Act of 2002 (TRIA) and the Terrorism Risk Insurance Program Reauthorization Act of 2007, which extended the Terrorism Risk Insurance Act through December 31, 2014. The Terrorism Risk Insurance Program Reauthorization Act of 2015 extends the program through December 31, 2020.

The hurricane seasons of 2004, 2005, and 2012 with their attendant coverage questions and disputes following hurricane, flooding, and windstorm damage and conventional insurance policies' response have also made an impact on the industry.

ISO Interline Terrorism Endorsements

Following the property losses due to the terrorist attacks of September 11, 2001, there was a need to clarify the insurance industry role in coverage for catastrophic damage caused by terrorist acts and the responsibility of the government. In compliance with the Terrorism Risk Insurance Extension Act (TRIA), Insurance Services Office (ISO) issued a number of endorsements for use with the commercial property program that exclude or provide limited coverage for terrorist acts. TRIA was originally enacted in 2002. The Terrorism Risk Insurance Extension Act was enacted in 2005, followed by the Terrorism Risk Insurance Program Reauthorization Act of 2007.

The 2005 extension revised the 2002 act's definition of *insurer deductible* to include provisions for the years 2006 and 2007. The extension also excluded commercial auto, burglary and theft, surety, and farm owners multiperil insurance from its definition of *property and casualty insurance*. A new program trigger was also added, stating that for any certified act occurring after March 31, 2006, federal compensation will be paid only if resulting aggregate industry losses exceed $50 million in 2006 and $100 million in 2007.

The federal share of compensation was 90 percent of the insured losses exceeding the insurer deductible in 2006; 85 percent in 2007. The insurance marketplace aggregate retention amount for purposes of recouping the federal share was $25 billion for 2006 and $27.5 billion for 2007.

The 2007 extension changed the definition of *certified act of terrorism* to include acts executed by domestic terrorists. The deductible was fixed at 20 percent multiplied by the direct earned premium for the preceding calendar year. The federal share was also fixed at 85 percent.

The introduction to the Terrorism supplement to the ISO Commercial Lines Manual (CLM) explains the federal Terrorism Risk Insurance Act of 2002 and its effect on and coverage response from the insurance industry:

> The Terrorism Risk Insurance Act (TRIA) establishes a program within the Department of the Treasury in which the Federal Government will share the risk of loss from terrorist attacks with the insurance industry. Federal participation will be triggered when the Secretary of the Treasury certifies an act of terrorism, in concurrence with the Secretary of State and the Attorney General of the United States, to be an act of terrorism committed by an individual(s) acting on behalf of any foreign interest, provided the terrorist act results in aggregate losses in excess of an amount stated in the Act. With respect to insured losses resulting from a certified act of terrorism, the Federal Government will reimburse individual insurers for a percentage of losses (as stated in the Act) in excess of the insurer's retention, which is based on a specified percentage of the insurer's earned premium for the year preceding the loss. Insured losses covered by the program are capped at $100 billion per year unless subsequent action of Congress changes that amount; this provision serves to limit insurers' liability for losses. All insurers providing commercial property insurance are required to participate in the program to the extent of offering and making available coverage for certified acts of terrorism in accordance with the terms and conditions of coverage which apply to other perils.
>
> For all new and renewal business, an insurer must make available to insureds coverage for losses caused by certified acts of terrorism. The insurer must disclose to the policyholder the premium for losses covered and the federal share of compensation for such losses under the program at the time of offer, purchase and renewal of the policy.

To accomplish this, Insurance Services Office (ISO) has developed a number of interline endorsements (meaning they apply across various lines of coverage). These endorsements are used with up to a dozen coverage parts, including the following:

- Commercial Crime Coverage Form

- Commercial Crime Policy

- Commercial Inland Marine

- Commercial Property Coverage Part

- Employee Theft and Forgery Policy

- Equipment Breakdown

- Farm Coverage Part

- Government Crime Coverage Form

- Government Crime Policy

- Kidnap/ransom and extortion coverage form

- Kidnap/Ransom and Extortion Policy

- Standard Property Policy

With the passage of the 2002 TRIA and its extensions in 2005 and 2007, ISO developed and filed many terrorism-related endorsements. Some of the endorsements exclude or limit terrorism coverage, some provide disclosures as required by TRIA, and some are conditional on TRIA being terminated or replaced with provisions that do not require insurers to make terrorism coverage available (with certain conditions).

The Terrorism Risk Insurance Program Reauthorization Act of 2015 was signed into law on January 12, 2015. The act extends the program through December 31, 2020. The amount of the federal share is set to decrease by 1 percent starting on January 1, 2016, and will decrease by one percentage point per calendar year until it is equal to 80 percent.

The federal compensation will be paid only if resulting aggregate industry losses exceed $100 million in 2015, $120 million in 2016, $140 million in 2017, $160 million in 2018, $180 million in 2019, and $200 million in 2020 and beyond. The mandatory recoupment increases from $27.5 billion to $37.5 billion over five years.

The following endorsements were introduced after the Terrorism Risk Insurance Program Reauthorization Act of 2015 became effective:

- IL 09 52 01 15, Cap On Losses From Certified Acts Of Terrorism

- IL 09 53 01 15, Exclusion Of Certified Acts Of Terrorism

- IL 09 85 01 15, Disclosure Pursuant To Terrorism Risk Insurance Act

- IL 09 86 01 15, Exclusion Of Certified Acts Of Terrorism Involving Nuclear, Biological, Chemical Or Radiological Terrorism; Cap On Covered Certified Acts Losses

- IL 09 87 01 15, Limitation Of Coverage For Certified Acts Of Terrorism (Sub-Limit On Annual Aggregate Basis)

- IL 09 98 01 15, Disclosure Of Premium Through End Of Year For Certified Acts Of Terrorism Coverage (Pursuant To Terrorism Risk Insurance Act)

- IL 09 99 01 15, Disclosure Of Premium And Estimated Premium For Certified Acts Of Terrorism Coverage (Pursuant To Terrorism Risk Insurance Act)

Catastrophic Weather Loss Claims Issues

Windstorm can be handled efficiently by private for-profit insurance companies. When windstorm causes damage, not all exposed units covered by an insurer are damaged or damaged to a total extent. Flood, on the other hand, affects all exposed units in the afflicted area to total or almost total loss. This has not been the province of private insurers. Actuarially there is no way to insure the flood exposure and remain profitable or solvent. The federal National Flood Insurance Program was developed to respond to catastrophic flood exposures in recognition that flood insurance is more in the manner of a social insurance program and not a private enterprise coverage area. Details about flood coverage and access to the NFIP forms are contained in *FC&S*, published by The National Underwriter Company.

The hurricane season of 2004 struck Florida with no fewer than four major-class storms, and the 2005 season with its triple-whammy of hurricanes Katrina, Rita, and Wilma, caused unprecedented storm and flooding damage throughout huge areas of the Gulf Coast, including massive damage in New Orleans. Superstorm Sandy, which hit parts of the East Coast in 2012, also wreaked havoc and resulted in unprecedented damages.

These storms posed coverage issues previously not raised, or certainly not so widely and prominently. Many of these questions reached the *FC&S* staff. Several of these issues are presented in this section.

Wind, Water, and Wind-Driven Water

The issue that created the most controversy following Hurricane Katrina and the subsequent breeching of the levy system allowing much of New Orleans to flood is the interplay of the windstorm peril (covered) and the water peril (excluded). The water damage exclusion is frequently referred to as the flood exclusion. The questions are: does the windstorm peril include coverage for subsequent flooding and is the water damage exclusion validly applied to water damage that occurs subsequent to a windstorm?

The CP 10 30's water exclusion reads as follows:

1. We will not pay for loss or damage caused directly or indirectly by any of the following. Such loss or damage is excluded regardless of any other cause or event that contributes concurrently or in any sequence to the loss.

    G. Water

        (1) Flood, surface water, waves (including tidal wave and tsunami), tides, tidal water, overflow of any body of water, or spray from any of these, all whether driven by wind or not (including storm surge);

        (2) Mudslide or mudflow;

        (3) Water that backs up or overflows or is otherwise discharged from a sewer, drain, sump, sump pump or related equipment;

        (4) Water under the ground surface pressing on, or flowing or seeping through:

            (a) Foundations, walls, floors or paved surfaces;

            (b) Basements, whether paved or not;

            (c) Doors, windows or other openings; or

        (5) Waterborne material carried or otherwise moved by any of the water referred to in Paragraph (1), (3) or (4) or material carried or otherwise moved by mudslide or mudflow.

    This exclusion applies regardless of whether any of the above, in Paragraphs (1) through (5), is caused by an act of nature or is otherwise caused. An example of a situation to which this exclusion applies is the situation where a dam, levee, seawall or other boundary or containment system fails in whole or in part, for any reason, to contain the water.

But if any of the above, in Paragraphs (1) through (5), results in fire, explosion or sprinkler leakage, we will pay for the loss or damage caused by that fire, explosion or sprinkler leakage (if sprinkler leakage is a Covered Cause of Loss).

The Water Exclusion endorsement, CP 10 32 08 08, added tsunamis and storm surge to G. (1) and added "or is otherwise discharged from" before "sewer, drain or sump" in G. (2). "Sump pump or related equipment" were also inserted at the end of that section. The endorsement contains an additional category: "Waterborne material carried or otherwise moved by any of the water referred to in Paragraph 1., 3., or 4., or material carried or otherwise moved by mudslide or mudflow." These changes were incorporated into the 2012 revised forms.

The 2008 endorsement, and subsequently the 2012 forms, also added phrasing that specifically addresses the failure of dams, levees, seawalls, or other boundaries or containment systems in whole or in part. However, this wording was not on the ISO forms in place during the 2004 and 2005 hurricane seasons.

The exclusion is broad reaching based on the actuarial recognition that flood and certain other types of water damage are beyond reach of traditional private insurance; this is why the National Flood Insurance Program (NFIP) exists. But, it can be expensive and its need undervalued. Many people do not purchase flood coverage.

The argument of proponents for invalidating the water exclusion in cases arising from the 2004 and 2005 storms was both political and an issue of proximate cause. According to one theory, the wind caused the New Orleans levy system to become overextended, and, without the hurricane, there would have been no damage. Even though the stakes are much higher, the issue is the same as other consequential damage (spoilage following power outage) discussed in Chapter 1. Where there is direct wind damage, of course, that part of any loss is covered.

The first part of the pre-2008 exclusion seemingly encompassed all of the proximate causation issues that litigation around the windstorm versus flood damage disputes involve—tides, waves, overflows, spray, "all whether driven by wind or not." To get at specifically catastrophic (and really uninsurable) losses, ISO inserted this phrase at the end of the exclusions section: "Exclusions B.1.a. through B.1.h. apply whether or not the loss event results in widespread damage or affects a substantial area."

Although complex litigation was initiated, some Katrina homeowners cases indicated that the water exclusion would be held valid as long as insurers carefully assess what is covered wind damage and what is excluded as legitimate flood loss.

In *Buente v. Allstate Ins. Co.*, No. 1:05 CV 712 LTS JMR, 2006 WL 980784 (S.D. Miss. April 12, 2006), a home was seriously damaged during Hurricane Katrina and the subsequent flooding. The homeowners claimed damage by windstorm, wind-driven rain, and rising waters caused by wind and wind-driven rain. The insurer denied coverage, saying that all damage was excluded—flood includes surface water, driven by wind or not, on ground regardless of source. The insured's argument was that the water exclusion is ambiguous, as storm surge was not addressed.

The trial court upheld the exclusion; the water doing the damage was tidal water and therefore fit the policy flood definition. In a subsequent action with the same insureds on the same facts, Allstate moved to dismiss. The court ruled that the exclusions of water and flood would not necessarily bar recovery for storm surges. Damage from wind and rain is covered regardless of later water causing additional damage that is excluded. However, again the court found that the exclusions for water damage and flood are valid. The importance of the decision is that the water or flood exclusion in property damage policies is valid, but coverage forensics is necessary to determine what part of the loss is appropriately covered as windstorm damage and which part is legitimately excluded as flood.

Wind Percentage Deductible

The Windstorm or Hail Percentage Deductible endorsement, CP 03 21, is often used in underwriting commercial property risks in windstorm prone areas. It provides a 1, 2, or 5 percent deductible for covered damage by windstorm or hail. During the hurricane seasons of 2004 and 2005, it created some coverage confusion and disputes. The form was updated in 2007 and in 2012, so policy language varies from the forms that were in place when the damage in these scenarios took place. The following scenarios illustrate this provision and its application.

Windstorm Deductible—How Applied?

The insured has a 2 percent windstorm deductible. If a hurricane struck and caused a tree to fall on the insured building, would the resulting damage to the building be subject to the 2 percent windstorm deductible or the regular policy deductible?

The 2 percent deductible would apply, although there is nothing specifically in the policy or in the windstorm percentage deductible endorsement stating this. The reasoning is that the efficient proximate cause of the tree's falling on the building is the force of the wind. The insured could point to the named peril of falling objects, but in this instance all the provisions should be given their full meaning; that is, the coverage for windstorm, the coverage for falling objects, and the deductible.

In *Roach-Strayhan-Holland Post No. 20 American Legion Club v. Continental Ins. Co.*, 112 So. 2d 680, (La. 1959), the court said, "In the absence of a definition or limitation on the subject, a 'windstorm' must be taken to be a wind of sufficient violence to be capable of damaging insured property either by impact of its own force or by projecting some object against the property, and in order to recover on a windstorm insurance policy, not otherwise limited or defined, it is sufficient to show that wind was the proximate or efficient cause of loss or damage notwithstanding other factors that contributed to loss." If this is true, in order to collect on a windstorm policy, then by inference it is logical to apply the deductible to all loss proximately caused by the storm. This makes sense. Otherwise insureds could find themselves subject to two deductibles—one for the loss caused by the falling object (the tree), and another to loss caused by the force of the wind ripping off siding and part of the roof.

The following coverage scenario provides an illustration of how the percentage wind deductible is applied in a situation where the insured has premises in different locations covered under a blanket limit, all damaged by the same hurricane or windstorm.

Percent Deductible Application under Building and Personal Property Coverage Form

The insured property was a strip mall consisting of several buildings in Florida. In 2004, both Hurricanes Charley and Frances damaged three of the buildings. The insured had a blanket limit on the policy for buildings. There was a 2 percent wind deductible and the company adjuster took a separate deductible on each building. The adjuster added that the deductible should be 2 percent of the total amount of insurance. On the other hand, the insured's broker believes it should be 2 percent of the amount of the damage. How many deductibles should apply, and is the percentage deductible calculated based on the total amount of the loss or the total value of the buildings?

The ISO Windstorm or Hail Percent Deductible endorsement, CP 03 21 06 95, states that "a deductible is calculated separately for, and applies separately to…each building, if two or more buildings sustain loss or damage." (The 2007 and 2012 forms state, "Each building that sustains loss or damage.") Thus, in this instance, a separate deductible should be taken for each building. To further complicate matters, Charley and Frances would be viewed as separate events, and new deductibles would apply for damage caused by Frances, the second hurricane to strike.

The endorsement also provides instructions for calculating the percentage deductible. For blanket insurance, an amount equal to 2 percent (or whatever percentage is selected) of the value of the property, as reported on the most recent Statement or Report of Values, that has sustained loss or damage is deducted.

The endorsement provides an example of two buildings, each with a value of $500,000, that sustain losses. The first building sustains $40,000 in damage; the second sustains $20,000 in damage. Two percent of the first building's value of $500,000 ($10,000) is subtracted from the amount of the loss—the amount payable for the first building is $30,000. Another deductible equal to 2 percent of the second building's value of $500,000 is applied to its damage—$10,000 is subtracted from the $20,000 loss to yield an amount payable of $10,000. The most the insurer will pay is $40,000 after the application of the 2 percent wind deductible to those losses.

Under the standard ISO endorsement, it is clear that a deductible applies to each building damaged and is calculated based on the value of the building, not on the amount of the damage. This point was also made in *General Star Indem. Co. v. West Florida Village Inn, Inc.*, 874 So.2d 26 (Fla. App. 2004), where the court stated that the deductible of 2 percent meant 2 percent of the policy limit.

Application of Blanket Condo Policy with Wind Deductible

Situation: Blanket condo policy with wind deductible of 3 percent per building. Loss figures are as follows:

Wind damage to building	$809,282
Code upgrade	$78,495
Total loss	$887,777
Dollar amount of 3 percent deductible	$43,263

There is a $10,000 sublimit for code upgrade, so $68,495 of the code loss would not be insured damage. There is no other question of coverage and no coinsurance problem.

> The property is insured under CP 00 17 04 02. The Windstorm or Hail Percentage Deductible endorsement, CP 03 21 06 95, is attached.
>
> The endorsement states in the deductible application section that the insurer will deduct an amount equal to the percentage deductible of the limit(s) of insurance applicable *to the property that has sustained loss or damage* (not covered loss or damage). However, the endorsement also states that the insurer will pay the amount of loss or damage in excess of the deductible.
>
> The $10,000 of code upgrade is additional insurance. The policy excludes code upgrade but reintroduces coverage subject to the sublimit as an additional insurance.
>
> Should the amount of uninsured code upgrade ($68,495) be applied to reduce the amount of the applicable deductible?
>
> The insured cannot recover more than the limit that is insured for code upgrade. Therefore, the loss should be adjusted and the deductible applied to the $809,282 property damage for a settlement of $765,999 ($809,282 − $43,263 = $765,999). The $10,000 sublimit for code upgrade is then paid in addition to the property damage settlement for a total amount paid of $775,999.

Named Windstorms Deductible Endorsements

Both ISO and AAIS provide named storm deductibles. ISO's endorsement is the Named Storm Percentage Deductible, CP 03 25. ISO also provides state-specific endorsements; for example, North Carolina – Named Storm Percentage Deductible, CP 03 28. These endorsements are available with the following ISO coverage forms: Builders' Risk Coverage Form, Building and Personal Property Coverage Form, Condominium Association Coverage Form, Condominium Commercial Unit-Owners Coverage Form, Tobacco Sales Warehouses Coverage Form, and the Standard Property Policy.

AAIS also provides state-specific endorsements, such as South Carolina – Named Storm Windstorm or Hail Deductible, CP 04 90.

The schedule for the ISO endorsement CP 03 25 requires specific identification of the premises, building number, if more than one building exists, and the deductible to apply—1, 2, or 5 percent. A *named storm* is defined under this endorsement as "a storm system that has been identified as a tropical storm or hurricane and assigned a name by the National Hurricane Center or the Central Pacific Hurricane Center of the National Weather Service (hereinafter referred to as NHC and CPHC)."

A named storm begins at the time a "Watch or Warning is issued by the NHC or CPHC for the area in which the affected premises are located, and ends 72 hours after the termination of the last Watch or Warning issued for that area by the NHC or CPHC."

This endorsement explains how the deductible is calculated for (1) all policies, (2) specific insurance other than builders' risk, with property not subject to value reporting or subject to value reporting forms, (3) blanket insurance other than builders' risk, not subject to value report or subject to value reporting, and (4) builders' risk.

The following are the steps to follow for the calculation of the named windstorm deductible applicable to all policies:

1.　A Deductible is calculated separately for, and applies separately to:

　　a.　Each building that sustains loss or damage;

　　b.　The personal property at each building at which there is loss or damage to personal property;

　　c.　Personal property in the open.

　　If there is damage to both a building and personal property in that building, separate deductibles apply to the building and to the personal property.

2.　We will not pay for loss or damage until the amount of loss or damage exceeds the applicable Deductible. We then pay the amount of loss or damage in excess of that Deductible, up to the applicable Limit of Insurance, after any reduction required by any of the following: Coinsurance Condition; Agreed Value Optional Coverage; Additional Condition – Need for Adequate Insurance or Additional Condition – Need For Full Reports.

3.　When property is covered under the Coverage Extension for Newly Acquired or Constructed Property: In determining the amount, if any, that we will pay for loss or damage, we will deduct an amount equal to a percentage of the value(s) of the property at the time of loss. The applicable percentage for Newly Acquired or Constructed Property is the highest percentage shown in the Schedule for any described premises.

The following is the example of the deductible calculation when the property is written on a blanket basis without value reporting:

　　The sum of the values of Building 1 ($500,000), Building 2 ($500,000) and Building 3 ($1,000,000), as shown in the most recent Statement of Values on file with us is $2,000,000.

The Coinsurance percentage shown in the Declarations is 90%; the minimum Blanket Limit of Insurance needed to meet the coinsurance requirement is $1,800,000 (90% of $2,000,000).

The actual Blanket Limit of Insurance covering Buildings 1, 2, and 3, shown in the Declarations, is $1,800,000 (therefore no Coinsurance penalty).

Buildings 1 and 2 have sustained damage; the amounts of loss to these buildings are $40,000 (Building 1) and $20,000 (Building 2).

The Deductible is 2%.

Building 1

Step (1): $500,000 × 2% = $10,000

Step (2): $40,000 – $10,000 = $30,000

Building 2

Step (1): $500,000 × 2% = $10,000

Step (2): $20,000 – $ 10,000 = $10,000

The most we will pay is $40,000. The portion of the total loss that is not covered due to application of the Deductible is $20,000.

Disputed Deductible Issues

Despite how clear policies may be with regard to deductible provisions, disputes still arise. One non-ISO windstorm deductible provision that was the center of dispute is discussed in *SEACOR Holdings, Inc. v. Commonwealth Ins. Co*, 635 F.3d 675 (5th Cir. 2011). Commonwealth, a Canadian corporation, issued SEACOR an all-risk property policy for the 2005 calendar year. This policy included a provision denoting various deductibles depending on the nature of the damage. Each occurrence resulting in a claim for loss was to be adjusted separately, and the insurer's liability was limited to that amount by which the loss exceeded the deductible amounts up to the limit of liability.

The deductible provision stated the following:

(c)   In respect of loss caused directly by the peril of windstorm, as defined: $25,000, except

(d) In respect of loss caused directly by the peril of a "Named Windstorm," as defined, 3% of the total insurable values ... subject to a minimum of $50,000 per occurrence.

(e) In respect of loss caused directly by the peril of Flood, as defined: 425,000; except Flood Zones A and V, excess maximum National Flood Insurance Program (NFIP) limits available.

Both SEACOR and its insurer disagreed as to whether the damages from Hurricanes Katrina and Rita should have been covered using only the named windstorm deductible or using both the named windstorm and flood deductibles. The parties also disputed application of the policy's limit of liability provision, which read: "The Company's liability for the cumulative total of adjusted net claims resulting from any one loss, casualty, disaster or occurrence (including all costs, fees, charges and expenses) shall not exceed $10,000,000."

Without increasing the policy limit, the insurer agreed that loss caused by the peril of flood, as defined, was subject to an annual aggregate limit of $5 million.

While the parties promptly resolved the loss values and settled all contractual issues, the only remaining dispute was over the application of its deductibles. SEACOR filed a declaratory judgment action with regard to whether the loss or damage it suffered was caused by windstorm, named windstorm, or flood, as defined in the policy. SEACOR maintained that all of its losses resulted from a named windstorm. In contrast, the insurer argued that Hurricane Katrina was a multiperil occurrence that required the use of deductibles and liability limits for both flood and named windstorm.

The policy defined *named windstorm* as "any Windstorm...or any atmospheric disturbance which have [sic] been declared to be a tropical storm and/or hurricane by the National Weather Service or National Hurricane Center." Notably, this definition included atmospheric disturbances declared to be hurricanes, regardless of whether those disturbances met the policy's definitional requirements of a windstorm. For windstorm, the policy's definition section stated, "Windstorm shall constitute a single claim hereunder, provided, if more than windstorm shall occur within any period of seventy-two (72) hours during the term of this Policy, such windstorm shall be deemed to be a single windstorm within the meaning thereof."

Flood was defined as "waves, tide or tidal water, inundation, rainfall and/or resultant runoff, and the rising (including overflowing or breakage of boundaries) of lakes, ponds, reservoirs, rivers, harbors, streams, or similar bodies of water whether wind-driven or not." No separate provision in the policy denoted whether multiple deductibles could apply.

The district court concluded that only the named windstorm deductible applied and that the flood liability limit did not apply because the named windstorm's percentage-based deductible structure included a possibility of greater damages and a correspondingly higher deductible when compared to the flood's flat-rate deductible. In light of this decision, the insurer appealed.

On appeal, one of the questions was whether, in the absence of a specific provision allowing multiple deductibles, the policy required SEACOR to pay both the flood and named windstorm deductibles, or whether the single named windstorm deductible encompassed Katrina's wind and water damage. Turning to the policy's definition of *named windstorm*, the court stated that the definition incorporated the *windstorm* definition but that latter definition, itself, was inadequate. The policy, the court said, never described what event or conditions qualified as a windstorm but merely stated that multiple windstorms within a seventy-two hour period would be deemed as one windstorm. Given this deficiency, the court stated that a windstorm must be taken as a wind of sufficient violence to be capable of damaging the insured property either by impact of its own force or by projecting some object against the property.

The court added that the policy's *named windstorm* definition did not rely on the *windstorm* definition alone. Instead, a named windstorm also included "any atmospheric disturbance" that the National Weather Service declared to be a hurricane or a tropical storm. The National Weather Service, the court said, declared Katrina and Rita to be hurricanes. These events, therefore, and the damage they caused, fell within the *named windstorm* definition and required use of the named windstorm deductible.

The insurer asserted that water damage could not be covered under the named windstorm deductible because the definition of *named windstorm* did not include flooding. The court did not find this argument to be persuasive. Referring to the *American Heritage Dictionary*, the court pointed to the definition of *hurricane* as a "severe tropical cyclone ... usually involving heavy rains." Applying ordinary definitions, the court said, losses caused by a named windstorm could include losses by heavy rains.

Most insurance policies specifically exclude coverage for water-related events that often accompany windstorms. SEACOR's was one of the exceptions. It did not contain such an exclusion, but rather contained separate deductibles for the perils of named windstorm and flood, without indicating when, if ever, multiple deductibles applied. The provision simply stated that the named windstorm deductible applied to "loss caused directly by the peril of a Named Windstorm."

The court therefore concluded that if the damage caused by rain and flood was caused directly by Katrina, then it may be covered under the named windstorm deductible. Because the policy did not define "loss caused directly by," the court added that, in relying on Louisiana law, equated "direct loss" to "proximate or efficient cause." In affirming the district court, the court of appeals stated that it agreed with SEACOR's policy interpretation that the named windstorm deductible encompassed both wind and water damage caused by Hurricanes Katrina and Rita and with its holding that the flood liability limit did not apply.

While court cases can be informative and helpful as precedent, they do not necessarily have to be followed by the courts and can be overruled. Still, cases can be helpful, particularly in complex areas, such as deductible provisions involving a combination of wind and water.

Expense to Restore or Repair Undamaged Condo Units

In the wake of Hurricane Katrina and subsequent flooding, damage to condo units raised some interesting coverage questions, such as in the following scenario.

Is Condominium Gutting Excluded as an Act or Decision?

Several customers of an insurance company were insured on standard condominium unit-owners policies and resided in a large condominium complex. The condo building suffered hurricane damage; however, not all units sustained physical damage. Because some of the damaged units were found to contain mold, the condo association made the decision to gut all units to prevent any further spread. The insureds looked to their carrier to cover these costs.

Assuming that the units in question did not sustain direct physical damage from wind or water, the standard condominium policy does not provide coverage in the situation described.

The policy excludes loss to property caused by *acts or decisions of any organization*. The condo association is the *organization*; the *decision* was to gut the property and the *act* was the actual gutting. Therefore, there is no coverage.

However, in the course of the gutting, if an ensuing loss occurred—such as collapse because of faulty methods in renovation or fire from an improperly disconnected gas line—that loss would be covered unless otherwise excluded.

Chinese Drywall

It was the aftermath of Hurricanes Rita and Katrina in the southern states between 2005 and 2008 that, in part, brought about the high demand for building material. Another attribute to this demand was the growth of the housing market in general. A large part of this demand for building materials was filled by manufacturers of wall board (also referred to as drywall) imported from China. After this wall board was installed in both newly-constructed and renovated properties, the occupants began noticing unusual odors, blackening and corrosion of metallic items, and health issues.

Tests of some Chinese drywall had shown that it gave off a rotten egg odor from volatile sulfur compounds when exposed to heat and moisture. In the presence of moisture these vapors created a corrosive environment. The average humidity in Florida is over 50 percent year round, which could account for why Florida was the leader in drywall complaints. The Gypsum Association stated that 300 million square feet of Chinese drywall was imported in 2006-07. A construction consultant estimated that between 2006 and the first two months of 2007 enough drywall was imported to produce at least 50,000 homes of 2,000 square feet each.

In light of these conditions, property owners began filing suits in both federal and state courts against those involved in this wall board, including the installers, builders, suppliers, importers, exporters, manufacturers, and their insurers. Since this wall board produced similar results to a large part of the population in the affected areas, much of the litigation was combined into class actions directed at both property and liability claims.

Property Loss Issue

A representation of a typical property loss suit, which was brought by one homeowner instead of a class, is *TravCo Ins. Co. v. Ward*, No. 120347, 2012 WL 5358705 (Va. Nov. 1, 2012). The question before the court was, for purposes of interpreting an all risk homeowners insurance policy, whether any damage resulting from the drywall was unambiguously excluded from coverage because loss was caused by the following:

(a) mechanical breakdown, latent defect, inherent vice, or any quality in property that causes it to damage itself;

(b) faulty, inadequate, or defective materials;

(c) rust or other corrosion; or

(d) pollutants, where *pollutant* was defined as any solid, liquid, gaseous or thermal irritant or contaminant, including smoke, vapor, soot, fumes, acids, alkalis, chemicals and waste.

The homeowner sought coverage under his homeowners policy issued by TravCo Insurance Company for damages allegedly caused by sheets of drywall manufactured in China that were installed in his home during its construction. The named insured alleged that the drywall emitted various sulfide gases and/or toxic chemicals through "off-gassing" that created noxious odors and caused health issues, damage, and corrosion. In light of this situation, the named insured filed a complaint against the developer, builder, and drywall contractor. The insurer denied the claim and brought a declaratory judgment action in the U.S. district court for the eastern district of Virginia, seeking a declaratory judgment that its policy did not provide coverage.

Latent Defect Exclusion

Addressing the latent defect exclusion first, the named insured argued that this exclusion was susceptible to multiple meanings. He also argued that use of the terms *latent defect* and *inherent vice* in the exclusion caused ambiguity because *latent defect* was ordinarily defined as undiscoverable by proper inspection or known tests, while *inherent vice* referred to a loss from internal decomposition. Additionally, the named insured asserted that testing would have revealed the problems with Chinese drywall and the defect, therefore, was not latent.

The insurer, on the other hand, responded that the latent defect exclusion was valid and operated to preclude coverage. The insurer also asserted that the drywall contained a latent defect because the defect was hidden or concealed for two years before the named insured discovered a problem. The insurer also maintained that the named insured's proposed construction of the exclusion violated basic rules of grammar and insurance contract construction.

Although, as the named insured argued, the sulfuric content of the drywall was potentially discoverable through testing after the product was manufactured, the actual defect was the release of sulfuric gases by the drywall. The future release of gas by the drywall was not discoverable, said the court, and the defect was "hidden or concealed, and not visible or apparent."

Faulty, Inadequate, or Defective Materials Exclusion

The named insured argued that the faulty or defective materials exclusion did not apply because these terms were not defined and did not apply as the drywall maintained its form and performed its function.

The insurer disagreed, stating that the exclusion applied because the drywall released sulfuric gas.

The court agreed with the insurer. The drywall, it said, was defective. It also explained that it was only necessary that the drywall meet but one of the terms—*faulty* or *defective*—to apply.

Loss Caused by Smog, Rust, Corrosion, Mold, Fungi, or Wet or Dry Rot

The named insured maintained that the rust or other corrosion exclusion did not apply because those terms were not defined in the policy, and the damage to his home was not caused by corrosion but was the corrosion itself. The named insured also asserted that a reasonable insured would believe the corrosion exclusion was inapplicable because the named insured's loss was not caused by corrosion and *rust* was ambiguous and in this context connotes damage gradually resulting from moisture. The insurer, though, claimed that the plain language of this exclusion did not make a distinction between naturally occurring corrosion and other corrosion, and the named insured's attempt to limit the definition of *corrosion* to a gradual, natural process was ineffective. The insurer also stated that the corrosion of metals in the named insured's house was in fact a gradual process, occurring over two years.

The court agreed with the insurer. In doing so, the court stated that the definitions and the logical, common understanding of the term *corrosion* did not draw a distinction between naturally occurring and other corrosion. Their similarly was not basis, the court added, for reading a temporal element into this exclusion. (However, a footnote reference in this case was *Webster's International Dictionary* at page 512, which stated that *corrosion* is defined to mean "a gradual wearing away.")

The Pollution Exclusion

The pollution exclusion in the homeowner's policy stated that the insurer did not insure loss caused by "[d]ischarge, dispersal, seepage, migration, release or escape of pollutants unless the discharge, dispersal, seepage, migration, release or escape is itself caused by a peril insured against under Coverage C. 'Pollutants' means any solid, liquid, gaseous or thermal irritant or contaminant, including smoke, vapor, soot, fumes, acids, alkalis, chemicals or waste. Waste includes materials to be recycled, reconditioned or claimed."

The named insured asserted that the policy's pollution exclusion was "ambiguous, overbroad, unreasonable," and inapplicable to his loss.

He claimed that the process by which elemental sulfur escaped the drywall, off-gassing, was not a discharge of pollutants as contemplated by the exclusion or as a reasonable person would understand.

The insurer argued that the pollution exclusion applied because the sulfuric gas emanating from the drywall was an irritant or contaminant under the plain language of the policy. The insurer also explained that the sulfur gas in the named insured's house was a contaminant because it was not supposed to be in the house and it caused harm. The sulfuric gas was likewise an irritant, the insurer said, because it caused the named insured and his family to suffer nosebleeds and other problems. The sulfuric gas, it added, moved from the drywall to the air in the house by way of "discharge, dispersal, seepage, migration, release or escape."

The court concluded that the pollution exclusion applied. It stated that it was beyond dispute that the sulfuric substance emanating from the drywall was gaseous. In the named insured's answer to the complaint, he asserted the presence of "odorous fumes in the residence," described the gas as "toxic," and alleged that it caused skin rashes, lesion, sinus congestion, and nosebleeds. These properties, the court said, place the sulfuric gas from the residence within the definition of *irritant or contaminant* contemplated by the policy and commonly understood.

The court also pointed to relevant state and federal regulations that described sulfuric gas as a pollutant. Finally, the court stated that the sulfuric gases at issue were pollutants within the purview of the exclusion, thereby precluding coverage. All of the exclusions therefore were held to be applicable under the named insured's homeowner's policy.

From a liability standpoint, a case worth mentioning is *Great American Fidelity Ins. Co. v. JWR Const. Services, Inc.*, No. 10–61423–CIV, 2012 WL 1193848 (S.D. Fla. Nov. 2, 2012). The insurers sought a declaration under two similar environmental liability policies issued to JWR, a general contractor that they had no duty to defend or indemnify. Gulf Reflections, owners of condominium units where JWR and subcontractors were working, maintained that the policies provided coverage to JWR for the claims set forth in the underlying action. While the issue of defense was said to be ripe for adjudication, the duty to indemnify depended on the outcome of the underlying state court action, which was then ongoing.

In June 2009, the general contractor began to suspect a problem with the Chinese drywall in the condominium units. Consequently, the general contractor notified its insurance agent of an occurrence twice in writing. In January 2010 the condo unit owners filed a class action complaint against the general contractor and others. The allegations of the condo unit owners were that a latent defect caused monetary damages, including (1) the need to replace the drywall; (2) damage to other property, including ceiling materials, electrical systems, air conditioning, insulation, certain copper and brass plumbing components, and studs; (3) damage to personal property, including electrical devices, computers, appliances, jewelry, plumbing fixtures, and silverware; and (4) loss of use and enjoyment of the unit as well as additional living expenses while forced to live away from the unit and loss of market value of the unit.

Under the negligence count against the general contractor, it was alleged that the general contractor breached its duty of reasonable care when it failed to reasonably inspect and warn of a product that was inherently dangerous and breached its duty of reasonable care when it installed defective Chinese drywall, despite the fact that it knew, or should have known, of the defective nature of this product—the smell and abnormal elemental makeup of this product.

The unit owners also alleged that the general contractor breached its duty of reasonable care because it failed to investigate and test drywall that it knew or should have known had an abnormal smell and had for the very first time been imported from a foreign country with no proven track record in the U.S.

The court did not identify the kind of liability policies that were the subject of dispute here, but from the description of the insuring agreement and numerous other terms and provisions, they appeared to be on the order of contractors' general and pollution liability coverage. In any case, the insurers denied defense and indemnity on the faulty workmanship and own work exclusion and the products liability exclusion.

The first of two exclusions relied on by the insurer to deny coverage was the faulty workmanship/own work exclusion. In pertinent part, it read as follows:

> This Insurance does not apply to any **LOSS, CLEAN-UP COSTS, LEGAL EXPENSE** or other coverage afforded under the Policy... *based upon or arising out of the cost to repair or replace faulty workmanship, construction, fabrication, installation,* assembly or remediation if such faulty workmanship, construction, fabrication, installation, assembly or remediation was *performed in whole in part by an INSURED*. (emphasis added)

With regard to this exclusion, the insurer acknowledged that it had no basis to believe that the general contractor had installed the drywall. In fact, the insurer indicated that it was a subcontractor who performed that installation. According to the court, this meant that the insurer knew that this exclusion would apply only to preclude coverage if faulty construction or workmanship by the general contractor was found on account of negligence assuming that a failure to inspect and warn that a product was inherently dangerous or a failure to investigate and test the drywall was considered faulty work (rather than a failure to perform work). Thus, said the court, since liability for noncompliant construction under the implied warranty count had no *mens rea* (no wrongful purpose) and did not depend on fault, under the negligence count, suggested that the general contractor could have liability covered by the policy and not precluded by the exclusion in question.

The second exclusion relied on by the insurer to deny coverage and defense was the products liability exclusion, which read in pertinent part as follows:

> This Insurance does not apply to any LOSS, CLEAN-UP COSTS, LEGAL EXPENSE or other coverage afforded under this Policy, *based upon or arising out of goods or products* manufactured, *sold handled* or distributed, altered or repaired *by the INSURED* or by (sic) other trading under the INSURED's name, including any container thereof, any failure to warn, or any reliance upon a representation or warranty made at any time with respect thereto. This exclusion does not apply to such goods or products while they remain within the legal boundaries of a COVERED LOCATION. (emphasis added)

On the subject of the products exclusion, the insurer contended that a cursory review of the verbs, adjectives, and gerunds underscored in the policy provisions revealed that the allegations fell squarely within the products liability exclusion.

The general contractor argued that the products exclusion did not apply because building construction was not a product under New York law. In essence, this would mean that any allegation treating the condominium units themselves, as opposed to only the drywall, as the defective product would fall outside the products liability exclusion. The general contractor did not argue that the drywall, prior to incorporation into the units of real estate, was not a product. He also argued, in essence, and the insurer did not demonstrate otherwise, that if the drywall were considered to be a product, the general contractor did not sell, distribute, or handle the drywall, because he did not trade or deal in drywall.

From the court's perspective, there were no facts to suggest that the general contractor sold or distributed drywall. In fact, it was stated that the insurer conceded that the units were sold by a developer and the drywall was sold and distributed by others. Thus, the court held that the general contractor was in the business, which entailed the performance of a service and not the sale of a product.

Commentary

If these contractors' general and pollution liability policies had the same territorial restrictions as the standard CGL policy, it would have meant that the occurrence giving rise to claim would have to happen in the U.S., its territories, possessions, Canada, or Puerto Rico.

Instead of simply raising the two exclusions as the insurer did in this case, another alternative might have been for the insurer to maintain that the defect in the Chinese drywall took place in China. This, of course, is not a slam-dunk argument because some courts have held that the time of the occurrence is at the time of injury or damage. Considering that insurers list as many reasons for denying coverage means either than the insurer (1) overlooked this possibility, (2) considered it as a possibility but decided against it, or (3) the policy did not specify where the occurrence had to happen.

In any event, the two cases discussed demonstrate the kind of arguments that must be raised by the parties involved in this kind of litigation. What must be remembered, too, is whether the argument will be won or lost hinges on many variables, including the fact pattern, the policy language, how the respective parties prepare and argue their motions, and existing common law that the courts also must consider in making their decisions.

Green Building Coverage Issues

Green building is a rapidly developing concept dealing with design and construction of new buildings, along with those that need to be renovated or retrofitted, which not only may increase the overall efficiency of their operation through energy and water conservation but also the use of materials that are recyclable and therefore produce less waste. The end result may also enhance the health aspects of the occupants through environmentally-friendly technology and construction and even increase the building's marketability. Some of the buzz words used in relation to green building are *building sustainability, energy-efficient, reduction of material waste, reduction of life cycle costs, renewable materials*, and *waste reduction*.

To cut heating or cooling costs, for example, solar panels can be used, and reliance on glass panels can shed more natural light than what might otherwise require considerable costs for electrical power. Also, vegetative roofs may be used on buildings for cooling purposes.

To cut costs on the use of water, it may be possible to recycle water as, for example, relying on rain water and melting snow or water from sinks and water fountains to be used for toilets and to water lawns.

Although the green building movement has been embraced by many environmentally conscience insureds, it does not come without its associated costs and risks. For example, if a building owner is contemplating the installation of solar panels to reduce electricity costs, does the installation make sense from a business perspective? Similarly, will the installation of solar panels or other green technologies increase a building's susceptibility to loss? These and other factors are reviewed in the following section.

Green Building Requirements

At the core of the green building concept is compliance with certain standards that regulate the methods of attaining them. Many governmental organizations are required by law to follow green standards with regard to the construction of buildings. However, it is with nongovernmental entities where the green building concept has most of its potential. The question is, however, what incentives would encourage privately-owned property owners in undertaking these projects? Certainly increasing the marketability of a project is an incentive and so, too, is the reduction in operating costs. However, there usually needs to be more than those aspects to convince entities to go through the trouble of following special codes to meet green standards. What may be the convincing factors are the possibility of tax incentives and grants.

It is not the purpose here to explain in detail what project owners and developers confront in having to meet green certification. It is necessary to explain briefly what has to be done to meet the goal of green sustainability.

First of all, certain so-called standards are available, with a corresponding sponsor, that have eligibility requirements and the nature of the kind of construction attributes to be implemented. If a project owner or developer is interested in pursuing the green building concept, it must consider what it wants to attain in terms of green standards, such as site development or an all-around energy efficient structure. It must then determine under what standard it is eligible.

One of the more recognized standards, or at least commonly mentioned with reference to the green concept, is the Leadership in Energy and Environmental Design (LEED) green building rating system introduced in 1998 and sponsored by the U.S. Green Building Council. This rating system can be applied to any kind of construction, such as commercial, residential, new, and renovations. Depending on what the objectives are, the

LEED system grants points used to meet the level of certification sought: Certified, Silver, Gold, or Platinum. The higher the certification, the better the rewards, such as tax credits, but more rigorous the requirements to be attained.

It is not an easy task to meet the standards and certification levels. Under the LEED program, for example, a lengthy application must be completed at the outset, followed by interim reports during the construction process completed by qualified professionals. It may also take as long as two years after construction before the certified level is finally determined. LEED is not limited to one program. It has several, and as time progresses, there are likely to be more such programs. Other sponsoring organizations in addition to those of the U.S. Green Building Council and their standard are Green Buildings Initiative (Green Globes), National Association of Home Builders (National Green Building Program), and U.S. Environmental Protection Agency (Energy Star).

As one might expect, failing to meet the goal of a certain, selected certification level may lead to dispute and litigation, In fact, the purported first legal dispute is *Southern Builders v. Shaw Development*, No. 19-C-07-011405, Circuit Court, Somerset Co., Md. (2008). This was a dispute between the developer of a condominium and a general contractor. The work required the general contractor to build an environmentally sound green building in conformance with a Silver certification level according to the LEED rating system. The developer alleged damages in the amount of a $635,000 tax credit, among other damages. While this case was settled out of court, it indicates that a lot is at stake when a project owner or developer aims at a certain rating level and fails to attain it because a contractor drops the ball.

Another case that involved a green building project is *Control Air Conditioning Corp. v. WSP Flack & Kurtz, Inc.*, G04550, 2012 WL 1899794 (Cal. Ct. App. 4th Dist., Div. 3, May 25, 2012), an unpublished, noncitable opinion. The owner decided to build a new building to house its campus in Santa Monica. The owner wanted a green building with operable windows and an under floor air distribution system, subject to LEED standards. The owner hired both an architectural firm and a general contractor. The architectural firm, in turn, subcontracted with an engineering firm, whereas the general contractor subcontracted with another entity to supply and install the necessary heating, ventilation, and air conditioning units. The owner ultimately concluded that the air conditioners did not supply the required cooling capacity or energy efficiency and requested that they be removed. When the general contractor did not pay the HVAC subcontractor, numerous suits were filed. This case was remanded for further proceedings. While this kind of case could exist even without a green building project, it goes to show that the green building concept also is a fertile area for litigation.

The burgeoning interest in environmentally friendly and green construction and technology presents issues for the insurance industry. Forms need to be changed in order to provide proper coverage for green construction. Debris may need to be disposed of in a specific way, and construction or repair may be more costly than standard construction. Traditional policy language may leave gaps in coverage.

Many insurers currently provide policies and endorsements to their commercial property and builders risk policies to accommodate green building exposures. In one such endorsement that was introduced when LEED and Green Globes were the only two rating systems, the insurer agreed, when its policy covered business real property or tenants improvements and betterments, to repair or replace defined building materials with environmental quality alternative materials and products of otherwise equivalent quality or function. A condition of this agreement was that there first be direct physical loss or damage due to a covered cause of loss. If there were no equivalent material or product acceptable under the LEED Green Building Rating System or the Green Globes Assessment and Rating System, the upgrade coverage did not apply. From the standpoint of debris removal, the insurer agreed to pay for increased costs that the named insured incurred to divert debris caused by or resulting from a covered cause of loss from the named insured's covered building to recycling facilities, rather than landfills, if such debris could otherwise be recycled.

Prior to the introduction of the green building concept, policies did not discuss plants as part of the roof structure. Plants have generally been considered as part of the landscape and coverage for them has been limited. However, that limited amount did not provide coverage for the plants on the roof. The question then became whether plants on the roof were considered building materials or just plants. It made a tremendous difference in coverage for the insured.

Importantly, one of the standard ISO commercial property changes for 2012 dealt with vegetative roofs, which are representative of the green trend in building construction. Currently, the property not covered section of the BPP precludes coverage for trees, shrubs, plants (other than stock), and lawns, with the exception of limited coverage (limited perils and a sublimit) for trees, shrubs, and plants under the outdoor property coverage extension. In light of the 2012 revisions, ISO revised the property not covered section to make an exception for lawns, trees, shrubs, and plants that are part of a vegetative roof, thereby treating such property as an insured part of the building (subject to all applicable covered perils and the full limit of insurance on the building) so that an existing vegetative roof can be replaced with like kind in the event of loss to the extent coverage applies. This change, however, made it necessary to revise the outdoor property coverage extension to remove reference to the foregoing property, since the broader coverage replaces the coverage provided by the extension.

As a consequence of extending insured property status to the vegetation that is part of a vegetative roof, certain limitations are also necessary. Thus, the vegetation is not covered for loss caused by dampness or dryness of atmosphere or soil, changes in temperature, disease, frost, hail, rain, snow, ice, or sleet. Similar limitations also apply to personal property, especially in the open. Also, the policy's additional coverage for mold does not apply to vegetation that is part of a vegetative roof. Other vegetation that is not part of a vegetative roof is not covered because such other vegetation is not property not covered and is given limited coverage under the outdoor property coverage extension. ISO stated that none of the limitations affect the roof structure. If a roof beam or support were to be damaged and mold developed, the mold would be covered under the terms of the additional coverage for mold.

Another coverage issue is workmanship of new technology. A contractor who has just started working with solar panels may have an increase in faulty workmanship or construction defect claims due to the learning curve of working with a new material. In such situations, whether the contractor has a professional green certification becomes important if the granting of various certifications accurately indicates the contractor's level of expertise.

While proponents may say that the technology provides sturdier, energy efficient, and environmentally friendly structures, the inherent underwriting risks have changed substantially. Time required to rebuild a structure may be significantly increased, and supplies and experienced labor may be even harder to obtain after a natural disaster than regular supplies, and therefore, even more expensive. As with any new technology, unanticipated issues may arise later as green materials age. Those unexpected issues may become substantial coverage gaps.

Underinsurance is another concern. If the property owner replaces or upgrades equipment with green materials that cost more to replace, the property is at risk of being underinsured unless steps are taken to ensure the property is insured to value.

The green building concept brings about some improvements in the health, safety, and efficiency of various forms of construction, a number of different insurance coverage forms, and another avenue for litigation.

Marijuana Manufacturing/Distribution

Over the years a number of states have legalized the use of medical marijuana. Most recently, Colorado and Washington have also legalized its use for recreational purposes. These changes have created a dilemma for both manufacturers and distributors of marijuana as business owners in securing insurance coverage as well as for insurers in underwriting the associated risks. To understand the dilemma faced by marijuana manufacturers and distributors, and their prospective insurers, it is important to understand the legal status of marijuana as property as well as how it is categorized under the BPP form from an insurance perspective.

Marijuana is classified by the Food and Drug Administration (FDA) as a Schedule 1 substance. Its possession or use is illegal under federal law although two states (Colorado and Washington) permit recreational use while twenty-three other states and the District of Columbia permit medical use. Although federal law has jurisdiction over states, the U.S. Justice Department has indicated that it will not enforce the law in states where marijuana is legal (either for recreational or medicinal use). To further complicate matters, the BPP form does not cover contraband, which by definition is "unlawful property." This legal dysfunction and ambiguity accompanied by the BPP's language of not covering contraband begs the question: how does a marijuana manufacturer or distributor insure its product?

At present, standard insurers have chosen not to insure these types of operations. From their perspective, marijuana is considered contraband and not covered under the BPP. In addition, most standard insurers consider the marijuana manufacturer and/or distributor to have greater exposures to loss than similar standard-type operations (greenhouse, nursery, retail store, pharmacy). For example, a marijuana manufacturer is generally growing plants in a uniquely controlled indoor environment with unique fire and explosion risks. Moreover, the marijuana distributor/retailer generally conducts business on a "cash only" basis since the banking/credit card industry is reluctant to partner with such establishments. These unique exposures and its legal ambiguity cause these types of businesses to be placed in the surplus lines market.

Income Disruption Insurance

Business income insurance replaces a business's loss of income when its operations are interrupted by damage to property caused by a covered cause of loss. Classic examples include loss of business income due to an extensive fire or windstorm loss. Most businesses cover this exposure through the purchase of standard business income insurance. However, a major coverage gap in most business's risk management and insurance program is the business income loss caused by noncovered causes of loss.

To illustrate this exposure, assume a region sustains an extreme snow storm resulting in a wide range of road closures causing a precipitous drop in sales. If the business purchased business income insurance and sustains a covered direct physical loss—collapse of the building, for example—coverage would apply to its loss of business income. If, however, the business had no direct physical loss or damage, its business income insurance would not apply. Income disruption insurance meets this need when there is an income disruption with no physical loss or damage to the insured's business property. This scenario played out in the Buffalo, New York, area in the fall of 2014 when it was struck by a massive snow storm. Similar examples occurred after Superstorm Sandy in the fall of 2012 in the New York/New Jersey area. More recently, coverage would have also applied to businesses that boarded up their properties to minimize possible property damage due to civil unrest, as in the aftermath of the Ferguson, Missouri, riots.

The following are other examples of claims where income disruption insurance may be triggered:

- Weather events such as an extreme snow storm, hurricane, tornado, or superstorm

- Threat of communicable disease such as Ebola, SARS, and Legionnaires

- Threat of riot and civil commotion triggered by civil unrest

Income disruption insurance would apply in each of these examples even though no physical loss or damage occurred to the insured property.

Income disruption insurance is a relatively new coverage presently offered in the surplus lines market.

Specimen Forms

COMMERCIAL PROPERTY
CP 00 10 10 12

BUILDING AND PERSONAL PROPERTY COVERAGE FORM

Various provisions in this policy restrict coverage. Read the entire policy carefully to determine rights, duties and what is and is not covered.

Throughout this policy, the words "you" and "your" refer to the Named Insured shown in the Declarations. The words "we", "us" and "our" refer to the company providing this insurance.

Other words and phrases that appear in quotation marks have special meaning. Refer to Section **H.** Definitions.

A. Coverage

We will pay for direct physical loss of or damage to Covered Property at the premises described in the Declarations caused by or resulting from any Covered Cause of Loss.

1. Covered Property

Covered Property, as used in this Coverage Part, means the type of property described in this section, **A.1.**, and limited in **A.2.** Property Not Covered, if a Limit Of Insurance is shown in the Declarations for that type of property.

a. **Building,** meaning the building or structure described in the Declarations, including:

(1) Completed additions;

(2) Fixtures, including outdoor fixtures;

(3) Permanently installed:

  (a) Machinery; and

  (b) Equipment;

(4) Personal property owned by you that is used to maintain or service the building or structure or its premises, including:

  (a) Fire-extinguishing equipment;

  (b) Outdoor furniture;

  (c) Floor coverings; and

  (d) Appliances used for refrigerating, ventilating, cooking, dishwashing or laundering;

(5) If not covered by other insurance:

  (a) Additions under construction, alterations and repairs to the building or structure;

  (b) Materials, equipment, supplies and temporary structures, on or within 100 feet of the described premises, used for making additions, alterations or repairs to the building or structure.

b. **Your Business Personal Property** consists of the following property located in or on the building or structure described in the Declarations or in the open (or in a vehicle) within 100 feet of the building or structure or within 100 feet of the premises described in the Declarations, whichever distance is greater:

(1) Furniture and fixtures;

(2) Machinery and equipment;

(3) "Stock";

(4) All other personal property owned by you and used in your business;

(5) Labor, materials or services furnished or arranged by you on personal property of others;

(6) Your use interest as tenant in improvements and betterments. Improvements and betterments are fixtures, alterations, installations or additions:

  (a) Made a part of the building or structure you occupy but do not own; and

  (b) You acquired or made at your expense but cannot legally remove;

(7) Leased personal property for which you have a contractual responsibility to insure, unless otherwise provided for under Personal Property Of Others.

c. **Personal Property Of Others** that is:

(1) In your care, custody or control; and

(2) Located in or on the building or structure described in the Declarations or in the open (or in a vehicle) within 100 feet of the building or structure or within 100 feet of the premises described in the Declarations, whichever distance is greater.

However, our payment for loss of or damage to personal property of others will only be for the account of the owner of the property.

2. **Property Not Covered**

Covered Property does not include:

a. Accounts, bills, currency, food stamps or other evidences of debt, money, notes or securities. Lottery tickets held for sale are not securities;

b. Animals, unless owned by others and boarded by you, or if owned by you, only as "stock" while inside of buildings;

c. Automobiles held for sale;

d. Bridges, roadways, walks, patios or other paved surfaces;

e. Contraband, or property in the course of illegal transportation or trade;

f. The cost of excavations, grading, backfilling or filling;

g. Foundations of buildings, structures, machinery or boilers if their foundations are below:

   (1) The lowest basement floor; or

   (2) The surface of the ground, if there is no basement;

h. Land (including land on which the property is located), water, growing crops or lawns (other than lawns which are part of a vegetated roof);

i. Personal property while airborne or waterborne;

j. Bulkheads, pilings, piers, wharves or docks;

k. Property that is covered under another coverage form of this or any other policy in which it is more specifically described, except for the excess of the amount due (whether you can collect on it or not) from that other insurance;

l. Retaining walls that are not part of a building;

m. Underground pipes, flues or drains;

n. Electronic data, except as provided under the Additional Coverage, Electronic Data. Electronic data means information, facts or computer programs stored as or on, created or used on, or transmitted to or from computer software (including systems and applications software), on hard or floppy disks, CD-ROMs, tapes, drives, cells, data processing devices or any other repositories of computer software which are used with electronically controlled equipment. The term computer programs, referred to in the foregoing description of electronic data, means a set of related electronic instructions which direct the operations and functions of a computer or device connected to it, which enable the computer or device to receive, process, store, retrieve or send data. This paragraph, **n.**, does not apply to your "stock" of prepackaged software, or to electronic data which is integrated in and operates or controls the building's elevator, lighting, heating, ventilation, air conditioning or security system;

o. The cost to replace or restore the information on valuable papers and records, including those which exist as electronic data. Valuable papers and records include but are not limited to proprietary information, books of account, deeds, manuscripts, abstracts, drawings and card index systems. Refer to the Coverage Extension for Valuable Papers And Records (Other Than Electronic Data) for limited coverage for valuable papers and records other than those which exist as electronic data;

p. Vehicles or self-propelled machines (including aircraft or watercraft) that:

   (1) Are licensed for use on public roads; or

   (2) Are operated principally away from the described premises.

This paragraph does not apply to:

   (a) Vehicles or self-propelled machines or autos you manufacture, process or warehouse;

 CP 00 10 10 12

(b) Vehicles or self-propelled machines, other than autos, you hold for sale;

(c) Rowboats or canoes out of water at the described premises; or

(d) Trailers, but only to the extent provided for in the Coverage Extension for Non-owned Detached Trailers; or

q. The following property while outside of buildings:

(1) Grain, hay, straw or other crops;

(2) Fences, radio or television antennas (including satellite dishes) and their lead-in wiring, masts or towers, trees, shrubs or plants (other than trees, shrubs or plants which are "stock" or are part of a vegetated roof), all except as provided in the Coverage Extensions.

3. Covered Causes Of Loss

See applicable Causes Of Loss form as shown in the Declarations.

4. Additional Coverages

a. Debris Removal

(1) Subject to Paragraphs **(2)**, **(3)** and **(4)**, we will pay your expense to remove debris of Covered Property and other debris that is on the described premises, when such debris is caused by or results from a Covered Cause of Loss that occurs during the policy period. The expenses will be paid only if they are reported to us in writing within 180 days of the date of direct physical loss or damage.

(2) Debris Removal does not apply to costs to:

(a) Remove debris of property of yours that is not insured under this policy, or property in your possession that is not Covered Property;

(b) Remove debris of property owned by or leased to the landlord of the building where your described premises are located, unless you have a contractual responsibility to insure such property and it is insured under this policy;

(c) Remove any property that is Property Not Covered, including property addressed under the Outdoor Property Coverage Extension;

(d) Remove property of others of a type that would not be Covered Property under this Coverage Form;

(e) Remove deposits of mud or earth from the grounds of the described premises;

(f) Extract "pollutants" from land or water; or

(g) Remove, restore or replace polluted land or water.

(3) Subject to the exceptions in Paragraph **(4)**, the following provisions apply:

(a) The most we will pay for the total of direct physical loss or damage plus debris removal expense is the Limit of Insurance applicable to the Covered Property that has sustained loss or damage.

(b) Subject to **(a)** above, the amount we will pay for debris removal expense is limited to 25% of the sum of the deductible plus the amount that we pay for direct physical loss or damage to the Covered Property that has sustained loss or damage. However, if no Covered Property has sustained direct physical loss or damage, the most we will pay for removal of debris of other property (if such removal is covered under this Additional Coverage) is $5,000 at each location.

(4) We will pay up to an additional $25,000 for debris removal expense, for each location, in any one occurrence of physical loss or damage to Covered Property, if one or both of the following circumstances apply:

(a) The total of the actual debris removal expense plus the amount we pay for direct physical loss or damage exceeds the Limit of Insurance on the Covered Property that has sustained loss or damage.

(b) The actual debris removal expense exceeds 25% of the sum of the deductible plus the amount that we pay for direct physical loss or damage to the Covered Property that has sustained loss or damage.

Therefore, if **(4)(a)** and/or **(4)(b)** applies, our total payment for direct physical loss or damage and debris removal expense may reach but will never exceed the Limit of Insurance on the Covered Property that has sustained loss or damage, plus $25,000.

(5) Examples

The following examples assume that there is no Coinsurance penalty.

Example 1

Limit of Insurance:	$ 90,000
Amount of Deductible:	$ 500
Amount of Loss:	$ 50,000
Amount of Loss Payable:	$ 49,500
	($50,000 – $500)
Debris Removal Expense:	$ 10,000
Debris Removal Expense Payable:	$ 10,000

($10,000 is 20% of $50,000.)

The debris removal expense is less than 25% of the sum of the loss payable plus the deductible. The sum of the loss payable and the debris removal expense ($49,500 + $10,000 = $59,500) is less than the Limit of Insurance. Therefore, the full amount of debris removal expense is payable in accordance with the terms of Paragraph **(3)**.

Example 2

Limit of Insurance:	$ 90,000
Amount of Deductible:	$ 500
Amount of Loss:	$ 80,000
Amount of Loss Payable:	$ 79,500
	($80,000 – $500)
Debris Removal Expense:	$ 40,000
Debris Removal Expense Payable	
Basic Amount:	$ 10,500
Additional Amount:	$ 25,000

The basic amount payable for debris removal expense under the terms of Paragraph **(3)** is calculated as follows: $80,000 ($79,500 + $500) x .25 = $20,000, capped at $10,500. The cap applies because the sum of the loss payable ($79,500) and the basic amount payable for debris removal expense ($10,500) cannot exceed the Limit of Insurance ($90,000).

The additional amount payable for debris removal expense is provided in accordance with the terms of Paragraph **(4)**, because the debris removal expense ($40,000) exceeds 25% of the loss payable plus the deductible ($40,000 is 50% of $80,000), and because the sum of the loss payable and debris removal expense ($79,500 + $40,000 = $119,500) would exceed the Limit of Insurance ($90,000). The additional amount of covered debris removal expense is $25,000, the maximum payable under Paragraph **(4)**. Thus, the total payable for debris removal expense in this example is $35,500; $4,500 of the debris removal expense is not covered.

b. Preservation Of Property

If it is necessary to move Covered Property from the described premises to preserve it from loss or damage by a Covered Cause of Loss, we will pay for any direct physical loss or damage to that property:

(1) While it is being moved or while temporarily stored at another location; and

(2) Only if the loss or damage occurs within 30 days after the property is first moved.

c. Fire Department Service Charge

When the fire department is called to save or protect Covered Property from a Covered Cause of Loss, we will pay up to $1,000 for service at each premises described in the Declarations, unless a higher limit is shown in the Declarations. Such limit is the most we will pay regardless of the number of responding fire departments or fire units, and regardless of the number or type of services performed.

This Additional Coverage applies to your liability for fire department service charges:

(1) Assumed by contract or agreement prior to loss; or

(2) Required by local ordinance.

No Deductible applies to this Additional Coverage.

d. Pollutant Clean-up And Removal

We will pay your expense to extract "pollutants" from land or water at the described premises if the discharge, dispersal, seepage, migration, release or escape of the "pollutants" is caused by or results from a Covered Cause of Loss that occurs during the policy period. The expenses will be paid only if they are reported to us in writing within 180 days of the date on which the Covered Cause of Loss occurs.

This Additional Coverage does not apply to costs to test for, monitor or assess the existence, concentration or effects of "pollutants". But we will pay for testing which is performed in the course of extracting the "pollutants" from the land or water.

The most we will pay under this Additional Coverage for each described premises is $10,000 for the sum of all covered expenses arising out of Covered Causes of Loss occurring during each separate 12-month period of this policy.

e. Increased Cost Of Construction

(1) This Additional Coverage applies only to buildings to which the Replacement Cost Optional Coverage applies.

(2) In the event of damage by a Covered Cause of Loss to a building that is Covered Property, we will pay the increased costs incurred to comply with the minimum standards of an ordinance or law in the course of repair, rebuilding or replacement of damaged parts of that property, subject to the limitations stated in **e.(3)** through **e.(9)** of this Additional Coverage.

(3) The ordinance or law referred to in **e.(2)** of this Additional Coverage is an ordinance or law that regulates the construction or repair of buildings or establishes zoning or land use requirements at the described premises and is in force at the time of loss.

(4) Under this Additional Coverage, we will not pay any costs due to an ordinance or law that:

(a) You were required to comply with before the loss, even when the building was undamaged; and

(b) You failed to comply with.

(5) Under this Additional Coverage, we will not pay for:

(a) The enforcement of or compliance with any ordinance or law which requires demolition, repair, replacement, reconstruction, remodeling or remediation of property due to contamination by "pollutants" or due to the presence, growth, proliferation, spread or any activity of "fungus", wet or dry rot or bacteria; or

(b) Any costs associated with the enforcement of or compliance with an ordinance or law which requires any insured or others to test for, monitor, clean up, remove, contain, treat, detoxify or neutralize, or in any way respond to, or assess the effects of "pollutants", "fungus", wet or dry rot or bacteria.

(6) The most we will pay under this Additional Coverage, for each described building insured under this Coverage Form, is $10,000 or 5% of the Limit of Insurance applicable to that building, whichever is less. If a damaged building is covered under a blanket Limit of Insurance which applies to more than one building or item of property, then the most we will pay under this Additional Coverage, for that damaged building, is the lesser of $10,000 or 5% times the value of the damaged building as of the time of loss times the applicable Coinsurance percentage.

The amount payable under this Additional Coverage is additional insurance.

(7) With respect to this Additional Coverage:

(a) We will not pay for the Increased Cost of Construction:

(i) Until the property is actually repaired or replaced at the same or another premises; and

(ii) Unless the repair or replacement is made as soon as reasonably possible after the loss or damage, not to exceed two years. We may extend this period in writing during the two years.

(b) If the building is repaired or replaced at the same premises, or if you elect to rebuild at another premises, the most we will pay for the Increased Cost of Construction, subject to the provisions of **e.(6)** of this Additional Coverage, is the increased cost of construction at the same premises.

(c) If the ordinance or law requires relocation to another premises, the most we will pay for the Increased Cost of Construction, subject to the provisions of **e.(6)** of this Additional Coverage, is the increased cost of construction at the new premises.

(8) This Additional Coverage is not subject to the terms of the Ordinance Or Law Exclusion to the extent that such Exclusion would conflict with the provisions of this Additional Coverage.

(9) The costs addressed in the Loss Payment and Valuation Conditions and the Replacement Cost Optional Coverage, in this Coverage Form, do not include the increased cost attributable to enforcement of or compliance with an ordinance or law. The amount payable under this Additional Coverage, as stated in **e.(6)** of this Additional Coverage, is not subject to such limitation.

f. Electronic Data

(1) Under this Additional Coverage, electronic data has the meaning described under Property Not Covered, Electronic Data. This Additional Coverage does not apply to your "stock" of prepackaged software, or to electronic data which is integrated in and operates or controls the building's elevator, lighting, heating, ventilation, air conditioning or security system.

(2) Subject to the provisions of this Additional Coverage, we will pay for the cost to replace or restore electronic data which has been destroyed or corrupted by a Covered Cause of Loss. To the extent that electronic data is not replaced or restored, the loss will be valued at the cost of replacement of the media on which the electronic data was stored, with blank media of substantially identical type.

(3) The Covered Causes of Loss applicable to Your Business Personal Property apply to this Additional Coverage, Electronic Data, subject to the following:

(a) If the Causes Of Loss – Special Form applies, coverage under this Additional Coverage, Electronic Data, is limited to the "specified causes of loss" as defined in that form and Collapse as set forth in that form.

(b) If the Causes Of Loss – Broad Form applies, coverage under this Additional Coverage, Electronic Data, includes Collapse as set forth in that form.

(c) If the Causes Of Loss form is endorsed to add a Covered Cause of Loss, the additional Covered Cause of Loss does not apply to the coverage provided under this Additional Coverage, Electronic Data.

(d) The Covered Causes of Loss include a virus, harmful code or similar instruction introduced into or enacted on a computer system (including electronic data) or a network to which it is connected, designed to damage or destroy any part of the system or disrupt its normal operation. But there is no coverage for loss or damage caused by or resulting from manipulation of a computer system (including electronic data) by any employee, including a temporary or leased employee, or by an entity retained by you or for you to inspect, design, install, modify, maintain, repair or replace that system.

         CP 00 10 10 12

(4) The most we will pay under this Additional Coverage, Electronic Data, is $2,500 (unless a higher limit is shown in the Declarations) for all loss or damage sustained in any one policy year, regardless of the number of occurrences of loss or damage or the number of premises, locations or computer systems involved. If loss payment on the first occurrence does not exhaust this amount, then the balance is available for subsequent loss or damage sustained in but not after that policy year. With respect to an occurrence which begins in one policy year and continues or results in additional loss or damage in a subsequent policy year(s), all loss or damage is deemed to be sustained in the policy year in which the occurrence began.

5. Coverage Extensions

Except as otherwise provided, the following Extensions apply to property located in or on the building described in the Declarations or in the open (or in a vehicle) within 100 feet of the described premises.

If a Coinsurance percentage of 80% or more, or a Value Reporting period symbol, is shown in the Declarations, you may extend the insurance provided by this Coverage Part as follows:

a. Newly Acquired Or Constructed Property

(1) Buildings

If this policy covers Building, you may extend that insurance to apply to:

(a) Your new buildings while being built on the described premises; and

(b) Buildings you acquire at locations, other than the described premises, intended for:

(i) Similar use as the building described in the Declarations; or

(ii) Use as a warehouse.

The most we will pay for loss or damage under this Extension is $250,000 at each building.

(2) Your Business Personal Property

(a) If this policy covers Your Business Personal Property, you may extend that insurance to apply to:

(i) Business personal property, including such property that you newly acquire, at any location you acquire other than at fairs, trade shows or exhibitions; or

(ii) Business personal property, including such property that you newly acquire, located at your newly constructed or acquired buildings at the location described in the Declarations.

The most we will pay for loss or damage under this Extension is $100,000 at each building.

(b) This Extension does not apply to:

(i) Personal property of others that is temporarily in your possession in the course of installing or performing work on such property; or

(ii) Personal property of others that is temporarily in your possession in the course of your manufacturing or wholesaling activities.

(3) Period Of Coverage

With respect to insurance provided under this Coverage Extension for Newly Acquired Or Constructed Property, coverage will end when any of the following first occurs:

(a) This policy expires;

(b) 30 days expire after you acquire the property or begin construction of that part of the building that would qualify as covered property; or

(c) You report values to us.

We will charge you additional premium for values reported from the date you acquire the property or begin construction of that part of the building that would qualify as covered property.

b. Personal Effects And Property Of Others

You may extend the insurance that applies to Your Business Personal Property to apply to:

(1) Personal effects owned by you, your officers, your partners or members, your managers or your employees. This Extension does not apply to loss or damage by theft.

(2) Personal property of others in your care, custody or control.

The most we will pay for loss or damage under this Extension is $2,500 at each described premises. Our payment for loss of or damage to personal property of others will only be for the account of the owner of the property.

c. Valuable Papers And Records (Other Than Electronic Data)

(1) You may extend the insurance that applies to Your Business Personal Property to apply to the cost to replace or restore the lost information on valuable papers and records for which duplicates do not exist. But this Extension does not apply to valuable papers and records which exist as electronic data. Electronic data has the meaning described under Property Not Covered, Electronic Data.

(2) If the Causes Of Loss – Special Form applies, coverage under this Extension is limited to the "specified causes of loss" as defined in that form and Collapse as set forth in that form.

(3) If the Causes Of Loss – Broad Form applies, coverage under this Extension includes Collapse as set forth in that form.

(4) Under this Extension, the most we will pay to replace or restore the lost information is $2,500 at each described premises, unless a higher limit is shown in the Declarations. Such amount is additional insurance. We will also pay for the cost of blank material for reproducing the records (whether or not duplicates exist) and (when there is a duplicate) for the cost of labor to transcribe or copy the records. The costs of blank material and labor are subject to the applicable Limit of Insurance on Your Business Personal Property and, therefore, coverage of such costs is not additional insurance.

d. Property Off-premises

(1) You may extend the insurance provided by this Coverage Form to apply to your Covered Property while it is away from the described premises, if it is:

(a) Temporarily at a location you do not own, lease or operate;

(b) In storage at a location you lease, provided the lease was executed after the beginning of the current policy term; or

(c) At any fair, trade show or exhibition.

(2) This Extension does not apply to property:

(a) In or on a vehicle; or

(b) In the care, custody or control of your salespersons, unless the property is in such care, custody or control at a fair, trade show or exhibition.

(3) The most we will pay for loss or damage under this Extension is $10,000.

e. Outdoor Property

You may extend the insurance provided by this Coverage Form to apply to your outdoor fences, radio and television antennas (including satellite dishes), trees, shrubs and plants (other than trees, shrubs or plants which are "stock" or are part of a vegetated roof), including debris removal expense, caused by or resulting from any of the following causes of loss if they are Covered Causes of Loss:

(1) Fire;

(2) Lightning;

(3) Explosion;

(4) Riot or Civil Commotion; or

(5) Aircraft.

The most we will pay for loss or damage under this Extension is $1,000, but not more than $250 for any one tree, shrub or plant. These limits apply to any one occurrence, regardless of the types or number of items lost or damaged in that occurrence.

Subject to all aforementioned terms and limitations of coverage, this Coverage Extension includes the expense of removing from the described premises the debris of trees, shrubs and plants which are the property of others, except in the situation in which you are a tenant and such property is owned by the landlord of the described premises.

f. Non-owned Detached Trailers

(1) You may extend the insurance that applies to Your Business Personal Property to apply to loss or damage to trailers that you do not own, provided that:

(a) The trailer is used in your business;

(b) The trailer is in your care, custody or control at the premises described in the Declarations; and

(c) You have a contractual responsibility to pay for loss or damage to the trailer.

(2) We will not pay for any loss or damage that occurs:

(a) While the trailer is attached to any motor vehicle or motorized conveyance, whether or not the motor vehicle or motorized conveyance is in motion;

(b) During hitching or unhitching operations, or when a trailer becomes accidentally unhitched from a motor vehicle or motorized conveyance.

(3) The most we will pay for loss or damage under this Extension is $5,000, unless a higher limit is shown in the Declarations.

(4) This insurance is excess over the amount due (whether you can collect on it or not) from any other insurance covering such property.

g. Business Personal Property Temporarily In Portable Storage Units

(1) You may extend the insurance that applies to Your Business Personal Property to apply to such property while temporarily stored in a portable storage unit (including a detached trailer) located within 100 feet of the building or structure described in the Declarations or within 100 feet of the premises described in the Declarations, whichever distance is greater.

(2) If the applicable Covered Causes of Loss form or endorsement contains a limitation or exclusion concerning loss or damage from sand, dust, sleet, snow, ice or rain to property in a structure, such limitation or exclusion also applies to property in a portable storage unit.

(3) Coverage under this Extension:

(a) Will end 90 days after the business personal property has been placed in the storage unit;

(b) Does not apply if the storage unit itself has been in use at the described premises for more than 90 consecutive days, even if the business personal property has been stored there for 90 or fewer days as of the time of loss or damage.

(4) Under this Extension, the most we will pay for the total of all loss or damage to business personal property is $10,000 (unless a higher limit is indicated in the Declarations for such Extension) regardless of the number of storage units. Such limit is part of, not in addition to, the applicable Limit of Insurance on Your Business Personal Property. Therefore, payment under this Extension will not increase the applicable Limit of Insurance on Your Business Personal Property.

(5) This Extension does not apply to loss or damage otherwise covered under this Coverage Form or any endorsement to this Coverage Form or policy, and does not apply to loss or damage to the storage unit itself.

Each of these Extensions is additional insurance unless otherwise indicated. The Additional Condition, Coinsurance, does not apply to these Extensions.

B. Exclusions And Limitations

See applicable Causes Of Loss form as shown in the Declarations.

C. Limits Of Insurance

The most we will pay for loss or damage in any one occurrence is the applicable Limit Of Insurance shown in the Declarations.

The most we will pay for loss or damage to outdoor signs, whether or not the sign is attached to a building, is $2,500 per sign in any one occurrence.

The amounts of insurance stated in the following Additional Coverages apply in accordance with the terms of such coverages and are separate from the Limit(s) Of Insurance shown in the Declarations for any other coverage:

1. Fire Department Service Charge;

2. Pollutant Clean-up And Removal;

3. Increased Cost Of Construction; and

4. Electronic Data.

Payments under the Preservation Of Property Additional Coverage will not increase the applicable Limit of Insurance.

D. Deductible

In any one occurrence of loss or damage (hereinafter referred to as loss), we will first reduce the amount of loss if required by the Coinsurance Condition or the Agreed Value Optional Coverage. If the adjusted amount of loss is less than or equal to the Deductible, we will not pay for that loss. If the adjusted amount of loss exceeds the Deductible, we will then subtract the Deductible from the adjusted amount of loss and will pay the resulting amount or the Limit of Insurance, whichever is less.

When the occurrence involves loss to more than one item of Covered Property and separate Limits of Insurance apply, the losses will not be combined in determining application of the Deductible. But the Deductible will be applied only once per occurrence.

Example 1

(This example assumes there is no Coinsurance penalty.)

Deductible:	$ 250
Limit of Insurance – Building 1:	$ 60,000
Limit of Insurance – Building 2:	$ 80,000
Loss to Building 1:	$ 60,100
Loss to Building 2:	$ 90,000

The amount of loss to Building 1 ($60,100) is less than the sum ($60,250) of the Limit of Insurance applicable to Building 1 plus the Deductible.

The Deductible will be subtracted from the amount of loss in calculating the loss payable for Building 1:

$ 60,100
– 250
$ 59,850 Loss Payable – Building 1

The Deductible applies once per occurrence and therefore is not subtracted in determining the amount of loss payable for Building 2. Loss payable for Building 2 is the Limit of Insurance of $80,000.

Total amount of loss payable:

$59,850 + $80,000 = $139,850

Example 2

(This example, too, assumes there is no Coinsurance penalty.)

The Deductible and Limits of Insurance are the same as those in Example 1.

Loss to Building 1:	$ 70,000
(Exceeds Limit of Insurance plus Deductible)	
Loss to Building 2:	$ 90,000
(Exceeds Limit of Insurance plus Deductible)	
Loss Payable – Building 1:	$ 60,000
(Limit of Insurance)	
Loss Payable – Building 2:	$ 80,000
(Limit of Insurance)	
Total amount of loss payable:	$ 140,000

E. Loss Conditions

The following conditions apply in addition to the Common Policy Conditions and the Commercial Property Conditions:

1. Abandonment

There can be no abandonment of any property to us.

2. Appraisal

If we and you disagree on the value of the property or the amount of loss, either may make written demand for an appraisal of the loss. In this event, each party will select a competent and impartial appraiser. The two appraisers will select an umpire. If they cannot agree, either may request that selection be made by a judge of a court having jurisdiction. The appraisers will state separately the value of the property and amount of loss. If they fail to agree, they will submit their differences to the umpire. A decision agreed to by any two will be binding. Each party will:

a. Pay its chosen appraiser; and

b. Bear the other expenses of the appraisal and umpire equally.

If there is an appraisal, we will still retain our right to deny the claim.

3. Duties In The Event Of Loss Or Damage

a. You must see that the following are done in the event of loss or damage to Covered Property:

(1) Notify the police if a law may have been broken.

(2) Give us prompt notice of the loss or damage. Include a description of the property involved.

(3) As soon as possible, give us a description of how, when and where the loss or damage occurred.

(4) Take all reasonable steps to protect the Covered Property from further damage, and keep a record of your expenses necessary to protect the Covered Property, for consideration in the settlement of the claim. This will not increase the Limit of Insurance. However, we will not pay for any subsequent loss or damage resulting from a cause of loss that is not a Covered Cause of Loss. Also, if feasible, set the damaged property aside and in the best possible order for examination.

(5) At our request, give us complete inventories of the damaged and undamaged property. Include quantities, costs, values and amount of loss claimed.

(6) As often as may be reasonably required, permit us to inspect the property proving the loss or damage and examine your books and records.

Also, permit us to take samples of damaged and undamaged property for inspection, testing and analysis, and permit us to make copies from your books and records.

(7) Send us a signed, sworn proof of loss containing the information we request to investigate the claim. You must do this within 60 days after our request. We will supply you with the necessary forms.

(8) Cooperate with us in the investigation or settlement of the claim.

b. We may examine any insured under oath, while not in the presence of any other insured and at such times as may be reasonably required, about any matter relating to this insurance or the claim, including an insured's books and records. In the event of an examination, an insured's answers must be signed.

4. **Loss Payment**

a. In the event of loss or damage covered by this Coverage Form, at our option, we will either:

(1) Pay the value of lost or damaged property;

(2) Pay the cost of repairing or replacing the lost or damaged property, subject to **b.** below;

(3) Take all or any part of the property at an agreed or appraised value; or

(4) Repair, rebuild or replace the property with other property of like kind and quality, subject to **b.** below.

We will determine the value of lost or damaged property, or the cost of its repair or replacement, in accordance with the applicable terms of the Valuation Condition in this Coverage Form or any applicable provision which amends or supersedes the Valuation Condition.

b. The cost to repair, rebuild or replace does not include the increased cost attributable to enforcement of or compliance with any ordinance or law regulating the construction, use or repair of any property.

c. We will give notice of our intentions within 30 days after we receive the sworn proof of loss.

d. We will not pay you more than your financial interest in the Covered Property.

e. We may adjust losses with the owners of lost or damaged property if other than you. If we pay the owners, such payments will satisfy your claims against us for the owners' property. We will not pay the owners more than their financial interest in the Covered Property.

f. We may elect to defend you against suits arising from claims of owners of property. We will do this at our expense.

g. We will pay for covered loss or damage within 30 days after we receive the sworn proof of loss, if you have complied with all of the terms of this Coverage Part, and:

(1) We have reached agreement with you on the amount of loss; or

(2) An appraisal award has been made.

h. A party wall is a wall that separates and is common to adjoining buildings that are owned by different parties. In settling covered losses involving a party wall, we will pay a proportion of the loss to the party wall based on your interest in the wall in proportion to the interest of the owner of the adjoining building. However, if you elect to repair or replace your building and the owner of the adjoining building elects not to repair or replace that building, we will pay you the full value of the loss to the party wall, subject to all applicable policy provisions including Limits of Insurance, the Valuation and Coinsurance Conditions and all other provisions of this Loss Payment Condition. Our payment under the provisions of this paragraph does not alter any right of subrogation we may have against any entity, including the owner or insurer of the adjoining building, and does not alter the terms of the Transfer Of Rights Of Recovery Against Others To Us Condition in this policy.

5. Recovered Property

If either you or we recover any property after loss settlement, that party must give the other prompt notice. At your option, the property will be returned to you. You must then return to us the amount we paid to you for the property. We will pay recovery expenses and the expenses to repair the recovered property, subject to the Limit of Insurance.

6. Vacancy

a. Description Of Terms

(1) As used in this Vacancy Condition, the term building and the term vacant have the meanings set forth in **(1)(a)** and **(1)(b)** below:

(a) When this policy is issued to a tenant, and with respect to that tenant's interest in Covered Property, building means the unit or suite rented or leased to the tenant. Such building is vacant when it does not contain enough business personal property to conduct customary operations.

(b) When this policy is issued to the owner or general lessee of a building, building means the entire building. Such building is vacant unless at least 31% of its total square footage is:

(i) Rented to a lessee or sublessee and used by the lessee or sublessee to conduct its customary operations; and/or

(ii) Used by the building owner to conduct customary operations.

(2) Buildings under construction or renovation are not considered vacant.

b. Vacancy Provisions

If the building where loss or damage occurs has been vacant for more than 60 consecutive days before that loss or damage occurs:

(1) We will not pay for any loss or damage caused by any of the following, even if they are Covered Causes of Loss:

(a) Vandalism;

(b) Sprinkler leakage, unless you have protected the system against freezing;

(c) Building glass breakage;

(d) Water damage;

(e) Theft; or

(f) Attempted theft.

(2) With respect to Covered Causes of Loss other than those listed in **b.(1)(a)** through **b.(1)(f)** above, we will reduce the amount we would otherwise pay for the loss or damage by 15%.

7. Valuation

We will determine the value of Covered Property in the event of loss or damage as follows:

a. At actual cash value as of the time of loss or damage, except as provided in **b., c., d.** and **e.** below.

b. If the Limit of Insurance for Building satisfies the Additional Condition, Coinsurance, and the cost to repair or replace the damaged building property is $2,500 or less, we will pay the cost of building repairs or replacement.

The cost of building repairs or replacement does not include the increased cost attributable to enforcement of or compliance with any ordinance or law regulating the construction, use or repair of any property.

However, the following property will be valued at the actual cash value, even when attached to the building:

(1) Awnings or floor coverings;

(2) Appliances for refrigerating, ventilating, cooking, dishwashing or laundering; or

(3) Outdoor equipment or furniture.

c. "Stock" you have sold but not delivered at the selling price less discounts and expenses you otherwise would have had.

d. Glass at the cost of replacement with safety-glazing material if required by law.

e. Tenants' Improvements and Betterments at:

(1) Actual cash value of the lost or damaged property if you make repairs promptly.

(2) A proportion of your original cost if you do not make repairs promptly. We will determine the proportionate value as follows:

(a) Multiply the original cost by the number of days from the loss or damage to the expiration of the lease; and

(b) Divide the amount determined in **(a)** above by the number of days from the installation of improvements to the expiration of the lease.

If your lease contains a renewal option, the expiration of the renewal option period will replace the expiration of the lease in this procedure.

(3) Nothing if others pay for repairs or replacement.

F. Additional Conditions

The following conditions apply in addition to the Common Policy Conditions and the Commercial Property Conditions:

1. Coinsurance

If a Coinsurance percentage is shown in the Declarations, the following condition applies:

a. We will not pay the full amount of any loss if the value of Covered Property at the time of loss times the Coinsurance percentage shown for it in the Declarations is greater than the Limit of Insurance for the property.

Instead, we will determine the most we will pay using the following steps:

(1) Multiply the value of Covered Property at the time of loss by the Coinsurance percentage;

(2) Divide the Limit of Insurance of the property by the figure determined in Step **(1)**;

(3) Multiply the total amount of loss, before the application of any deductible, by the figure determined in Step **(2)**; and

(4) Subtract the deductible from the figure determined in Step **(3)**.

We will pay the amount determined in Step **(4)** or the Limit of Insurance, whichever is less. For the remainder, you will either have to rely on other insurance or absorb the loss yourself.

Example 1 (Underinsurance)

When:	The value of the property is:	$ 250,000
	The Coinsurance percentage for it is:	80%
	The Limit of Insurance for it is:	$ 100,000
	The Deductible is:	$ 250
	The amount of loss is:	$ 40,000

Step (1): $250,000 \times 80\% = \$200,000$

(the minimum amount of insurance to meet your Coinsurance requirements)

Step (2): $100,000 \div \$200,000 = .50$

Step (3): $40,000 \times .50 = \$20,000$

Step (4): $20,000 - \$250 = \$19,750$

We will pay no more than $19,750. The remaining $20,250 is not covered.

Example 2 (Adequate Insurance)

When:	The value of the property is:	$ 250,000
	The Coinsurance percentage for it is:	80%
	The Limit of Insurance for it is:	$ 200,000
	The Deductible is:	$ 250
	The amount of loss is:	$ 40,000

The minimum amount of insurance to meet your Coinsurance requirement is $200,000 ($250,000 x 80%). Therefore, the Limit of Insurance in this example is adequate, and no penalty applies. We will pay no more than $39,750 ($40,000 amount of loss minus the deductible of $250).

b. If one Limit of Insurance applies to two or more separate items, this condition will apply to the total of all property to which the limit applies.

Example 3

When: The value of the property is:

Building at Location 1:	$ 75,000
Building at Location 2:	$ 100,000
Personal Property at Location 2:	$ 75,000
	$ 250,000

The Coinsurance percentage for it is: 90%

The Limit of Insurance for Buildings and Personal Property at Locations 1 and 2 is:	$ 180,000
The Deductible is:	$ 1,000

The amount of loss is:

Building at Location 2:	$ 30,000
Personal Property at Location 2:	$ 20,000
	$ 50,000

Step (1): $250,000 x 90% = $225,000

(the minimum amount of insurance to meet your Coinsurance requirements and to avoid the penalty shown below)

Step (2): $180,000 ÷ $225,000 = .80

Step (3): $50,000 x .80 = $40,000

Step (4): $40,000 – $1,000 = $39,000

We will pay no more than $39,000. The remaining $11,000 is not covered.

2. Mortgageholders

a. The term mortgageholder includes trustee.

b. We will pay for covered loss of or damage to buildings or structures to each mortgageholder shown in the Declarations in their order of precedence, as interests may appear.

c. The mortgageholder has the right to receive loss payment even if the mortgageholder has started foreclosure or similar action on the building or structure.

d. If we deny your claim because of your acts or because you have failed to comply with the terms of this Coverage Part, the mortgageholder will still have the right to receive loss payment if the mortgageholder:

(1) Pays any premium due under this Coverage Part at our request if you have failed to do so;

(2) Submits a signed, sworn proof of loss within 60 days after receiving notice from us of your failure to do so; and

(3) Has notified us of any change in ownership, occupancy or substantial change in risk known to the mortgageholder.

All of the terms of this Coverage Part will then apply directly to the mortgageholder.

e. If we pay the mortgageholder for any loss or damage and deny payment to you because of your acts or because you have failed to comply with the terms of this Coverage Part:

(1) The mortgageholder's rights under the mortgage will be transferred to us to the extent of the amount we pay; and

(2) The mortgageholder's right to recover the full amount of the mortgageholder's claim will not be impaired.

At our option, we may pay to the mortgageholder the whole principal on the mortgage plus any accrued interest. In this event, your mortgage and note will be transferred to us and you will pay your remaining mortgage debt to us.

f. If we cancel this policy, we will give written notice to the mortgageholder at least:

(1) 10 days before the effective date of cancellation if we cancel for your nonpayment of premium; or

(2) 30 days before the effective date of cancellation if we cancel for any other reason.

g. If we elect not to renew this policy, we will give written notice to the mortgageholder at least 10 days before the expiration date of this policy.

G. Optional Coverages

If shown as applicable in the Declarations, the following Optional Coverages apply separately to each item:

1. Agreed Value

a. The Additional Condition, Coinsurance, does not apply to Covered Property to which this Optional Coverage applies. We will pay no more for loss of or damage to that property than the proportion that the Limit of Insurance under this Coverage Part for the property bears to the Agreed Value shown for it in the Declarations.

b. If the expiration date for this Optional Coverage shown in the Declarations is not extended, the Additional Condition, Coinsurance, is reinstated and this Optional Coverage expires.

c. The terms of this Optional Coverage apply only to loss or damage that occurs:

(1) On or after the effective date of this Optional Coverage; and

(2) Before the Agreed Value expiration date shown in the Declarations or the policy expiration date, whichever occurs first.

2. Inflation Guard

a. The Limit of Insurance for property to which this Optional Coverage applies will automatically increase by the annual percentage shown in the Declarations.

b. The amount of increase will be:

(1) The Limit of Insurance that applied on the most recent of the policy inception date, the policy anniversary date, or any other policy change amending the Limit of Insurance, times

(2) The percentage of annual increase shown in the Declarations, expressed as a decimal (example: 8% is .08), times

(3) The number of days since the beginning of the current policy year or the effective date of the most recent policy change amending the Limit of Insurance, divided by 365.

Example

If: The applicable Limit of Insurance is: $ 100,000

The annual percentage increase is: 8%

The number of days since the beginning of the policy year (or last policy change) is: 146

The amount of increase is: $100,000 x .08 x 146 ÷ 365 = $ 3,200

3. Replacement Cost

a. Replacement Cost (without deduction for depreciation) replaces Actual Cash Value in the Valuation Loss Condition of this Coverage Form.

b. This Optional Coverage does not apply to:

(1) Personal property of others;

(2) Contents of a residence;

(3) Works of art, antiques or rare articles, including etchings, pictures, statuary, marbles, bronzes, porcelains and bric-a-brac; or

(4) "Stock", unless the Including "Stock" option is shown in the Declarations.

Under the terms of this Replacement Cost Optional Coverage, tenants' improvements and betterments are not considered to be the personal property of others.

c. You may make a claim for loss or damage covered by this insurance on an actual cash value basis instead of on a replacement cost basis. In the event you elect to have loss or damage settled on an actual cash value basis, you may still make a claim for the additional coverage this Optional Coverage provides if you notify us of your intent to do so within 180 days after the loss or damage.

d. We will not pay on a replacement cost basis for any loss or damage:

(1) Until the lost or damaged property is actually repaired or replaced; and

(2) Unless the repair or replacement is made as soon as reasonably possible after the loss or damage.

With respect to tenants' improvements and betterments, the following also apply:

(3) If the conditions in **d.(1)** and **d.(2)** above are not met, the value of tenants' improvements and betterments will be determined as a proportion of your original cost, as set forth in the Valuation Loss Condition of this Coverage Form; and

(4) We will not pay for loss or damage to tenants' improvements and betterments if others pay for repairs or replacement.

e. We will not pay more for loss or damage on a replacement cost basis than the least of **(1)**, **(2)** or **(3)**, subject to **f.** below:

(1) The Limit of Insurance applicable to the lost or damaged property;

(2) The cost to replace the lost or damaged property with other property:

(a) Of comparable material and quality; and

(b) Used for the same purpose; or

(3) The amount actually spent that is necessary to repair or replace the lost or damaged property.

If a building is rebuilt at a new premises, the cost described in **e.(2)** above is limited to the cost which would have been incurred if the building had been rebuilt at the original premises.

f. The cost of repair or replacement does not include the increased cost attributable to enforcement of or compliance with any ordinance or law regulating the construction, use or repair of any property.

4. Extension Of Replacement Cost To Personal Property Of Others

a. If the Replacement Cost Optional Coverage is shown as applicable in the Declarations, then this Extension may also be shown as applicable. If the Declarations show this Extension as applicable, then Paragraph **3.b.(1)** of the Replacement Cost Optional Coverage is deleted and all other provisions of the Replacement Cost Optional Coverage apply to replacement cost on personal property of others.

b. With respect to replacement cost on the personal property of others, the following limitation applies:

If an item(s) of personal property of others is subject to a written contract which governs your liability for loss or damage to that item(s), then valuation of that item(s) will be based on the amount for which you are liable under such contract, but not to exceed the lesser of the replacement cost of the property or the applicable Limit of Insurance.

H. Definitions

1. "Fungus" means any type or form of fungus, including mold or mildew, and any mycotoxins, spores, scents or by-products produced or released by fungi.

2. "Pollutants" means any solid, liquid, gaseous or thermal irritant or contaminant, including smoke, vapor, soot, fumes, acids, alkalis, chemicals and waste. Waste includes materials to be recycled, reconditioned or reclaimed.

3. "Stock" means merchandise held in storage or for sale, raw materials and in-process or finished goods, including supplies used in their packing or shipping.

© Insurance Services Office, Inc., 2011 **CP 00 10 10 12**

COMMERCIAL PROPERTY
CP 00 17 10 12

CONDOMINIUM ASSOCIATION COVERAGE FORM

Various provisions in this policy restrict coverage. Read the entire policy carefully to determine rights, duties and what is and is not covered.

Throughout this policy, the words "you" and "your" refer to the Named Insured shown in the Declarations. The words "we", "us" and "our" refer to the company providing this insurance.

Other words and phrases that appear in quotation marks have special meaning. Refer to Section **H.** Definitions.

A. Coverage

We will pay for direct physical loss of or damage to Covered Property at the premises described in the Declarations caused by or resulting from any Covered Cause of Loss.

1. Covered Property

Covered Property, as used in this Coverage Part, means the type of property described in this section, **A.1.,** and limited in **A.2.** Property Not Covered, if a Limit Of Insurance is shown in the Declarations for that type of property.

a. Building, meaning the building or structure described in the Declarations, including:

(1) Completed additions;

(2) Fixtures, outside of individual units, including outdoor fixtures;

(3) Permanently installed:

(a) Machinery; and

(b) Equipment;

(4) Personal property owned by you that is used to maintain or service the building or structure or its premises, including:

(a) Fire-extinguishing equipment;

(b) Outdoor furniture;

(c) Floor coverings; and

(d) Appliances used for refrigerating, ventilating, cooking, dishwashing or laundering that are not contained within individual units;

(5) If not covered by other insurance:

(a) Additions under construction, alterations and repairs to the building or structure;

(b) Materials, equipment, supplies, and temporary structures, on or within 100 feet of the described premises, used for making additions, alterations or repairs to the building or structure; and

(6) Any of the following types of property contained within a unit, regardless of ownership, if your Condominium Association Agreement requires you to insure it:

(a) Fixtures, improvements and alterations that are a part of the building or structure; and

(b) Appliances, such as those used for refrigerating, ventilating, cooking, dishwashing, laundering, security or housekeeping.

But Building does not include personal property owned by, used by or in the care, custody or control of a unit-owner except for personal property listed in Paragraph **A.1.a.(6)** above.

b. Your Business Personal Property located in or on the building or structure described in the Declarations or in the open (or in a vehicle) within 100 feet of the described premises, consisting of the following:

(1) Personal property owned by you or owned indivisibly by all unit-owners;

(2) Your interest in the labor, materials or services furnished or arranged by you on personal property of others; and

(3) Leased personal property for which you have a contractual responsibility to insure, unless otherwise provided for under Personal Property Of Others.

But Your Business Personal Property does not include personal property owned only by a unit-owner.

c. Personal Property Of Others that is:

(1) In your care, custody or control; and

(2) Located in or on the building or structure described in the Declarations or in the open (or in a vehicle) within 100 feet of the described premises.

However, our payment for loss of or damage to personal property of others will only be for the account of the owner of the property.

2. Property Not Covered

Covered Property does not include:

a. Accounts, bills, currency, food stamps or other evidences of debt, money, notes or securities. Lottery tickets held for sale are not securities;

b. Animals, unless owned by others and boarded by you;

c. Automobiles held for sale;

d. Bridges, roadways, walks, patios or other paved surfaces;

e. Contraband, or property in the course of illegal transportation or trade;

f. The cost of excavations, grading, backfilling or filling;

g. Foundations of buildings, structures, machinery or boilers if their foundations are below:

(1) The lowest basement floor; or

(2) The surface of the ground if there is no basement;

h. Land (including land on which the property is located), water, growing crops or lawns (other than lawns which are part of a vegetated roof);

i. Personal property while airborne or waterborne;

j. Bulkheads, pilings, piers, wharves or docks;

k. Property that is covered under this or any other policy in which it is more specifically described, except for the excess of the amount due (whether you can collect on it or not) from that other insurance;

l. Retaining walls that are not part of a building;

m. Underground pipes, flues or drains;

n. Electronic data, except as provided under the Additional Coverage, Electronic Data. Electronic data means information, facts or computer programs stored as or on, created or used on, or transmitted to or from computer software (including systems and applications software), on hard or floppy disks, CD-ROMs, tapes, drives, cells, data processing devices or any other repositories of computer software which are used with electronically controlled equipment. The term computer programs, referred to in the foregoing description of electronic data, means a set of related electronic instructions which direct the operations and functions of a computer or device connected to it, which enable the computer or device to receive, process, store, retrieve or send data. This paragraph, **n.,** does not apply to electronic data which is integrated in and operates or controls the building's elevator, lighting, heating, ventilation, air conditioning or security system;

o. The cost to replace or restore the information on valuable papers and records, including those which exist as electronic data. Valuable papers and records include but are not limited to proprietary information, books of account, deeds, manuscripts, abstracts, drawings and card index systems. Refer to the Coverage Extension for Valuable Papers And Records (Other Than Electronic Data) for limited coverage for valuable papers and records other than those which exist as electronic data;

p. Vehicles or self-propelled machines (including aircraft or watercraft) that:

(1) Are licensed for use on public roads; or

(2) Are operated principally away from the described premises.

This paragraph does not apply to:

(a) Vehicles or self-propelled machines or autos you manufacture or warehouse;

(b) Vehicles or self-propelled machines, other than autos, you hold for sale;

(c) Rowboats or canoes out of water at the described premises; or

(d) Trailers, but only to the extent provided for in the Coverage Extension for Non-owned Detached Trailers; or

© Insurance Services Office, Inc., 2011

q. The following property while outside of buildings:

(1) Grain, hay, straw or other crops; or

(2) Fences, radio or television antennas (including satellite dishes) and their lead-in wiring, masts or towers, trees, shrubs or plants (other than trees, shrubs or plants which are "stock" or are part of a vegetated roof), all except as provided in the Coverage Extensions.

3. **Covered Causes Of Loss**

See applicable Causes Of Loss form as shown in the Declarations.

4. **Additional Coverages**

a. **Debris Removal**

(1) Subject to Paragraphs **(2)**, **(3)** and **(4)**, we will pay your expense to remove debris of Covered Property and other debris that is on the described premises, when such debris is caused by or results from a Covered Cause of Loss that occurs during the policy period. The expenses will be paid only if they are reported to us in writing within 180 days of the date of direct physical loss or damage.

(2) Debris Removal does not apply to costs to:

(a) Remove debris of property of yours that is not insured under this policy, or property in your possession that is not Covered Property;

(b) Remove any property that is Property Not Covered, including property addressed under the Outdoor Property Coverage Extension;

(c) Remove property of others of a type that would not be Covered Property under this Coverage Form;

(d) Remove deposits of mud or earth from the grounds of the described premises;

(e) Extract "pollutants" from land or water; or

(f) Remove, restore or replace polluted land or water.

(3) Subject to the exceptions in Paragraph **(4)**, the following provisions apply:

(a) The most we will pay for the total of direct physical loss or damage plus debris removal expense is the Limit of Insurance applicable to the Covered Property that has sustained loss or damage.

(b) Subject to **(a)** above, the amount we will pay for debris removal expense is limited to 25% of the sum of the deductible plus the amount that we pay for direct physical loss or damage to the Covered Property that has sustained loss or damage. However, if no Covered Property has sustained direct physical loss or damage, the most we will pay for removal of debris of other property (if such removal is covered under this Additional Coverage) is $5,000 at each location.

(4) We will pay up to an additional $25,000 for debris removal expense, for each location, in any one occurrence of physical loss or damage to Covered Property, if one or both of the following circumstances apply:

(a) The total of the actual debris removal expense plus the amount we pay for direct physical loss or damage exceeds the Limit of Insurance on the Covered Property that has sustained loss or damage.

(b) The actual debris removal expense exceeds 25% of the sum of the deductible plus the amount that we pay for direct physical loss or damage to the Covered Property that has sustained loss or damage.

Therefore, if **(4)(a)** and/or **(4)(b)** applies, our total payment for direct physical loss or damage and debris removal expense may reach but will never exceed the Limit of Insurance on the Covered Property that has sustained loss or damage, plus $25,000.

(5) **Examples**

The following examples assume that there is no Coinsurance penalty.

Example 1

Limit of Insurance:	$ 90,000
Amount of Deductible:	$ 500
Amount of Loss:	$ 50,000
Amount of Loss Payable:	$ 49,500
	($50,000 – $500)
Debris Removal Expense:	$ 10,000
Debris Removal Expense Payable:	$ 10,000

($10,000 is 20% of $50,000.)

The debris removal expense is less than 25% of the sum of the loss payable plus the deductible. The sum of the loss payable and the debris removal expense ($49,500 + $10,000 = $59,500) is less than the Limit of Insurance. Therefore, the full amount of debris removal expense is payable in accordance with the terms of Paragraph **(3)**.

Example 2

Limit of Insurance:	$ 90,000
Amount of Deductible:	$ 500
Amount of Loss:	$ 80,000
Amount of Loss Payable:	$ 79,500
	($80,000 – $500)
Debris Removal Expense:	$ 40,000
Debris Removal Expense Payable	
Basic Amount:	$ 10,500
Additional Amount:	$ 25,000

The basic amount payable for debris removal expense under the terms of Paragraph **(3)** is calculated as follows: $80,000 ($79,500 + $500) x .25 = $20,000, capped at $10,500. The cap applies because the sum of the loss payable ($79,500) and the basic amount payable for debris removal expense ($10,500) cannot exceed the Limit of Insurance ($90,000).

The additional amount payable for debris removal expense is provided in accordance with the terms of Paragraph **(4)**, because the debris removal expense ($40,000) exceeds 25% of the loss payable plus the deductible ($40,000 = 50% of $80,000), and because the sum of the loss payable and debris removal expense ($79,500 + $40,000 = $119,500) would exceed the Limit of Insurance ($90,000). The additional amount of covered debris removal expense is $25,000, the maximum payable under Paragraph **(4)**. Thus, the total payable for debris removal expense in this example is $35,500; $4,500 of the debris removal expense is not covered.

b. Preservation Of Property

If it is necessary for you to move Covered Property from the described premises to preserve it from loss or damage by a Covered Cause of Loss, we will pay for any direct physical loss or damage to that property:

(1) While it is being moved or while temporarily stored at another location; and

(2) Only if the loss or damage occurs within 30 days after the property is first moved.

c. Fire Department Service Charge

When the fire department is called to save or protect Covered Property from a Covered Cause of Loss, we will pay up to $1,000 for service at each premises described in the Declarations unless a higher limit is shown in the Declarations. Such limit is the most we will pay regardless of the number of responding fire departments or fire units, and regardless of the number or type of services performed.

This Additional Coverage applies to your liability for fire department service charges:

(1) Assumed by contract or agreement prior to loss; or

(2) Required by local ordinance.

No Deductible applies to this Additional Coverage.

d. Pollutant Clean-up And Removal

We will pay your expense to extract "pollutants" from land or water at the described premises if the discharge, dispersal, seepage, migration, release or escape of the "pollutants" is caused by or results from a Covered Cause of Loss that occurs during the policy period. The expenses will be paid only if they are reported to us in writing within 180 days of the date on which the Covered Cause of Loss occurs.

This Additional Coverage does not apply to costs to test for, monitor or assess the existence, concentration or effects of "pollutants". But we will pay for testing which is performed in the course of extracting the "pollutants" from the land or water.

The most we will pay under this Additional Coverage for each described premises is $10,000 for the sum of all covered expenses arising out of Covered Causes of Loss occurring during each separate 12-month period of this policy.

e. **Increased Cost Of Construction**

(1) This Additional Coverage applies only to buildings to which the Replacement Cost Optional Coverage applies.

(2) In the event of damage by a Covered Cause of Loss to a building that is Covered Property, we will pay the increased costs incurred to comply with the minimum standards of an ordinance or law in the course of repair, rebuilding or replacement of damaged parts of that property, subject to the limitations stated in **e.(3)** through **e.(9)** of this Additional Coverage.

(3) The ordinance or law referred to in **e.(2)** of this Additional Coverage is an ordinance or law that regulates the construction or repair of buildings or establishes zoning or land use requirements at the described premises and is in force at the time of loss.

(4) Under this Additional Coverage, we will not pay any costs due to an ordinance or law that:

(a) You were required to comply with before the loss, even when the building was undamaged; and

(b) You failed to comply with.

(5) Under this Additional Coverage, we will not pay for:

(a) The enforcement of or compliance with any ordinance or law which requires demolition, repair, replacement, reconstruction, remodeling or remediation of property due to contamination by "pollutants" or due to the presence, growth, proliferation, spread or any activity of "fungus", wet or dry rot or bacteria; or

(b) Any costs associated with the enforcement of or compliance with an ordinance or law which requires any insured or others to test for, monitor, clean up, remove, contain, treat, detoxify or neutralize, or in any way respond to, or assess the effects of "pollutants", "fungus", wet or dry rot or bacteria.

(6) The most we will pay under this Additional Coverage, for each described building insured under this Coverage Form, is $10,000 or 5% of the Limit of Insurance applicable to that building, whichever is less. If a damaged building is covered under a blanket Limit of Insurance which applies to more than one building or item of property, then the most we will pay under this Additional Coverage, for that damaged building, is the lesser of $10,000 or 5% times the value of the damaged building as of the time of loss times the applicable Coinsurance percentage.

The amount payable under this Additional Coverage is additional insurance.

(7) With respect to this Additional Coverage:

(a) We will not pay for the Increased Cost of Construction:

(i) Until the property is actually repaired or replaced, at the same or another premises; and

(ii) Unless the repair or replacement is made as soon as reasonably possible after the loss or damage, not to exceed two years. We may extend this period in writing during the two years.

(b) If the building is repaired or replaced at the same premises, or if you elect to rebuild at another premises, the most we will pay for the Increased Cost of Construction, subject to the provisions of **e.(6)** of this Additional Coverage, is the increased cost of construction at the same premises.

(c) If the ordinance or law requires relocation to another premises, the most we will pay for the Increased Cost of Construction, subject to the provisions of **e.(6)** of this Additional Coverage, is the increased cost of construction at the new premises.

(8) This Additional Coverage is not subject to the terms of the Ordinance Or Law Exclusion to the extent that such Exclusion would conflict with the provisions of this Additional Coverage.

(9) The costs addressed in the Loss Payment and Valuation Conditions and the Replacement Cost Optional Coverage, in this Coverage Form, do not include the increased cost attributable to enforcement of or compliance with an ordinance or law. The amount payable under this Additional Coverage, as stated in **e.(6)** of this Additional Coverage, is not subject to such limitation.

f. Electronic Data

(1) Under this Additional Coverage, electronic data has the meaning described under Property Not Covered, Electronic Data. This Additional Coverage does not apply to electronic data which is integrated in and operates or controls the building's elevator, lighting, heating, ventilation, air conditioning or security system.

(2) Subject to the provisions of this Additional Coverage, we will pay for the cost to replace or restore electronic data which has been destroyed or corrupted by a Covered Cause of Loss. To the extent that electronic data is not replaced or restored, the loss will be valued at the cost of replacement of the media on which the electronic data was stored, with blank media of substantially identical type.

(3) The Covered Causes of Loss applicable to Your Business Personal Property apply to this Additional Coverage, Electronic Data, subject to the following:

(a) If the Causes Of Loss – Special Form applies, coverage under this Additional Coverage, Electronic Data, is limited to the "specified causes of loss" as defined in that form and Collapse as set forth in that form.

(b) If the Causes Of Loss – Broad Form applies, coverage under this Additional Coverage, Electronic Data, includes Collapse as set forth in that form.

(c) If the Causes Of Loss form is endorsed to add a Covered Cause of Loss, the additional Covered Cause of Loss does not apply to the coverage provided under this Additional Coverage, Electronic Data.

(d) The Covered Causes of Loss include a virus, harmful code or similar instruction introduced into or enacted on a computer system (including electronic data) or a network to which it is connected, designed to damage or destroy any part of the system or disrupt its normal operation. But there is no coverage for loss or damage caused by or resulting from manipulation of a computer system (including electronic data) by any employee, including a temporary or leased employee, or by an entity retained by you or for you to inspect, design, install, modify, maintain, repair or replace that system.

(4) The most we will pay under this Additional Coverage, Electronic Data, is $2,500 (unless a higher limit is shown in the Declarations) for all loss or damage sustained in any one policy year, regardless of the number of occurrences of loss or damage or the number of premises, locations or computer systems involved. If loss payment on the first occurrence does not exhaust this amount, then the balance is available for subsequent loss or damage sustained in but not after that policy year. With respect to an occurrence which begins in one policy year and continues or results in additional loss or damage in a subsequent policy year(s), all loss or damage is deemed to be sustained in the policy year in which the occurrence began.

5. Coverage Extensions

Except as otherwise provided, the following Extensions apply to property located in or on the building described in the Declarations or in the open (or in a vehicle) within 100 feet of the described premises.

If a Coinsurance percentage of 80% or more is shown in the Declarations, you may extend the insurance provided by this Coverage Part as follows:

a. Newly Acquired Or Constructed Property

(1) Buildings

You may extend the insurance that applies to Building to apply to:

(a) Your new buildings while being built on the described premises; and

(b) Buildings you acquire at locations, other than the described premises, intended for:

(i) Similar use as the building described in the Declarations; or

(ii) Use as a warehouse.

The most we will pay for loss or damage under this Extension is $250,000 at each building.

(2) Your Business Personal Property

(a) If this policy covers Your Business Personal Property, you may extend that insurance to apply to:

(i) Business personal property, including such property that you newly acquire, at any location you acquire other than at fairs, trade shows or exhibitions; or

(ii) Business personal property, including such property that you newly acquire, located at your newly constructed or acquired buildings at the location described in the Declarations.

The most we will pay for loss or damage under this Extension is $100,000 at each building.

(b) This Extension does not apply to:

(i) Personal property of others that is temporarily in your possession in the course of installing or performing work on such property; or

(ii) Personal property of others that is temporarily in your possession in the course of your manufacturing or wholesaling activities.

(3) Period Of Coverage

With respect to insurance provided under this Coverage Extension for Newly Acquired Or Constructed Property, coverage will end when any of the following first occurs:

(a) This policy expires;

(b) 30 days expire after you acquire the property or begin construction of that part of the building that would qualify as covered property; or

(c) You report values to us.

We will charge you additional premium for values reported from the date you acquire the property or begin construction of that part of the building that would qualify as covered property.

b. Personal Effects And Property Of Others

You may extend the insurance that applies to Your Business Personal Property to apply to:

(1) Personal effects owned by you, your officers, your partners or members, your managers or your employees. This Extension does not apply to loss or damage by theft.

(2) Personal property of others in your care, custody or control.

The most we will pay for loss or damage under this Extension is $2,500 at each described premises. Our payment for loss of or damage to personal property of others will only be for the account of the owner of the property.

c. Valuable Papers And Records (Other Than Electronic Data)

(1) You may extend the insurance that applies to Your Business Personal Property to apply to the cost to replace or restore the lost information on valuable papers and records for which duplicates do not exist. But this Extension does not apply to valuable papers and records which exist as electronic data. Electronic data has the meaning described under Property Not Covered, Electronic Data.

(2) If the Causes Of Loss – Special Form applies, coverage under this Extension is limited to the "specified causes of loss" as defined in that form and Collapse as set forth in that form.

(3) If the Causes Of Loss – Broad Form applies, coverage under this Extension includes Collapse as set forth in that form.

(4) Under this Extension, the most we will pay to replace or restore the lost information is $2,500 at each described premises, unless a higher limit is shown in the Declarations. Such amount is additional insurance. We will also pay for the cost of blank material for reproducing the records (whether or not duplicates exist) and (when there is a duplicate) for the cost of labor to transcribe or copy the records. The costs of blank material and labor are subject to the applicable Limit of Insurance on Your Business Personal Property and, therefore, coverage of such costs is not additional insurance.

d. Property Off-premises

(1) You may extend the insurance provided by this Coverage Form to apply to your Covered Property while it is away from the described premises, if it is:

(a) Temporarily at a location you do not own, lease or operate;

(b) In storage at a location you lease, provided the lease was executed after the beginning of the current policy term; or

(c) At any fair, trade show or exhibition.

(2) This Extension does not apply to property:

(a) In or on a vehicle; or

(b) In the care, custody or control of your salespersons, unless the property is in such care, custody or control at a fair, trade show or exhibition.

(3) The most we will pay for loss or damage under this Extension is $10,000.

e. Outdoor Property

You may extend the insurance provided by this Coverage Form to apply to your outdoor fences, radio and television antennas (including satellite dishes), trees, shrubs and plants (other than trees, shrubs or plants which are "stock" or are part of a vegetated roof), including debris removal expense, caused by or resulting from any of the following causes of loss if they are Covered Causes of Loss:

(1) Fire;

(2) Lightning;

(3) Explosion;

(4) Riot or Civil Commotion; or

(5) Aircraft.

The most we will pay for loss or damage under this Extension is $1,000, but not more than $250 for any one tree, shrub or plant. These limits apply to any one occurrence, regardless of the types or number of items lost or damaged in that occurrence.

Subject to all aforementioned terms and limitations of coverage, this Coverage Extension includes the expense of removing from the described premises the debris of trees, shrubs and plants which are the property of others.

f. Non-owned Detached Trailers

(1) You may extend the insurance that applies to Your Business Personal Property to apply to loss or damage to trailers that you do not own, provided that:

(a) The trailer is used in your business;

(b) The trailer is in your care, custody or control at the premises described in the Declarations; and

(c) You have a contractual responsibility to pay for loss or damage to the trailer.

(2) We will not pay for any loss or damage that occurs:

(a) While the trailer is attached to any motor vehicle or motorized conveyance, whether or not the motor vehicle or motorized conveyance is in motion;

(b) During hitching or unhitching operations, or when a trailer becomes accidentally unhitched from a motor vehicle or motorized conveyance.

(3) The most we will pay for loss or damage under this Extension is $5,000, unless a higher limit is shown in the Declarations.

(4) This insurance is excess over the amount due (whether you can collect on it or not) from any other insurance covering such property.

g. Business Personal Property Temporarily In Portable Storage Units

(1) You may extend the insurance that applies to Your Business Personal Property to apply to such property while temporarily stored in a portable storage unit (including a detached trailer) located within 100 feet of the described premises.

(2) If the applicable Covered Causes of Loss form or endorsement contains a limitation or exclusion concerning loss or damage from sand, dust, sleet, snow, ice or rain to property in a structure, such limitation or exclusion also applies to property in a portable storage unit.

(3) Coverage under this Extension:

(a) Will end 90 days after the business personal property has been placed in the storage unit;

(b) Does not apply if the storage unit itself has been in use at the described premises for more than 90 consecutive days, even if the business personal property has been stored there for 90 or fewer days as of the time of loss or damage.

(4) Under this Extension, the most we will pay for the total of all loss or damage to business personal property is $10,000 (unless a higher limit is indicated in the Declarations for such Extension) regardless of the number of storage units. Such limit is part of, not in addition to, the applicable Limit of Insurance on Your Business Personal Property. Therefore, payment under this Extension will not increase the applicable Limit of Insurance on Your Business Personal Property.

(5) This Extension does not apply to loss or damage otherwise covered under this Coverage Form or any endorsement to this Coverage Form or policy, and does not apply to loss or damage to the storage unit itself.

Each of these Extensions is additional insurance unless otherwise indicated. The Additional Condition, Coinsurance, does not apply to these Extensions.

B. Exclusions And Limitations

See applicable Causes Of Loss form as shown in the Declarations.

C. Limits Of Insurance

The most we will pay for loss or damage in any one occurrence is the applicable Limit Of Insurance shown in the Declarations.

The most we will pay for loss or damage to outdoor signs, whether or not the sign is attached to a building, is $2,500 per sign in any one occurrence.

The amounts of insurance stated in the following Additional Coverages apply in accordance with the terms of such coverages and are separate from the Limit(s) Of Insurance shown in the Declarations for any other coverage:

1. Fire Department Service Charge;

2. Pollutant Clean-up And Removal;

3. Increased Cost Of Construction; and

4. Electronic Data.

Payments under the Preservation Of Property Additional Coverage will not increase the applicable Limit of Insurance.

D. Deductible

In any one occurrence of loss or damage (hereinafter referred to as loss), we will first reduce the amount of loss if required by the Coinsurance Condition or the Agreed Value Optional Coverage. If the adjusted amount of loss is less than or equal to the Deductible, we will not pay for that loss. If the adjusted amount of loss exceeds the Deductible, we will then subtract the Deductible from the adjusted amount of loss and will pay the resulting amount or the Limit of Insurance, whichever is less.

When the occurrence involves loss to more than one item of Covered Property and separate Limits of Insurance apply, the losses will not be combined in determining application of the Deductible. But the Deductible will be applied only once per occurrence.

Example 1

(This example assumes there is no Coinsurance penalty.)

Deductible:	$ 250
Limit of Insurance – Building 1:	$ 60,000
Limit of Insurance – Building 2:	$ 80,000
Loss to Building 1:	$ 60,100
Loss to Building 2:	$ 90,000

The amount of loss to Building 1 ($60,100) is less than the sum ($60,250) of the Limit of Insurance applicable to Building 1 plus the Deductible.

The Deductible will be subtracted from the amount of loss in calculating the loss payable for Building 1:

$$\begin{array}{r} \$ \ 60,100 \\ - \quad 250 \\ \hline \$ \ 59,850 \end{array} \text{ Loss Payable – Building 1}$$

The Deductible applies once per occurrence and therefore is not subtracted in determining the amount of loss payable for Building 2. Loss payable for Building 2 is the Limit of Insurance of $80,000.

Total amount of loss payable:

$59,850 + $80,000 = $139,850

Example 2

(This example, too, assumes there is no Coinsurance penalty.)

The Deductible and Limits of Insurance are the same as those in Example 1.

Loss to Building 1:	$ 70,000
(Exceeds Limit of Insurance plus Deductible)	
Loss to Building 2:	$ 90,000
(Exceeds Limit of Insurance plus Deductible)	
Loss Payable – Building 1:	$ 60,000
(Limit of Insurance)	
Loss Payable – Building 2:	$ 80,000
(Limit of Insurance)	
Total amount of loss payable:	$ 140,000

E. Loss Conditions

The following conditions apply in addition to the Common Policy Conditions and the Commercial Property Conditions:

1. Abandonment

There can be no abandonment of any property to us.

2. Appraisal

If we and you disagree on the value of the property or the amount of loss, either may make written demand for an appraisal of the loss. In this event, each party will select a competent and impartial appraiser. The two appraisers will select an umpire. If they cannot agree, either may request that selection be made by a judge of a court having jurisdiction. The appraisers will state separately the value of the property and amount of loss. If they fail to agree, they will submit their differences to the umpire. A decision agreed to by any two will be binding. Each party will:

a. Pay its chosen appraiser; and

b. Bear the other expenses of the appraisal and umpire equally.

If there is an appraisal, we will still retain our right to deny the claim.

3. Duties In The Event Of Loss Or Damage

a. You must see that the following are done in the event of loss or damage to Covered Property:

(1) Notify the police if a law may have been broken.

(2) Give us prompt notice of the loss or damage. Include a description of the property involved.

(3) As soon as possible, give us a description of how, when and where the loss or damage occurred.

(4) Take all reasonable steps to protect the Covered Property from further damage, and keep a record of your expenses necessary to protect the Covered Property, for consideration in the settlement of the claim. This will not increase the Limit of Insurance. However, we will not pay for any subsequent loss or damage resulting from a cause of loss that is not a Covered Cause of Loss. Also, if feasible, set the damaged property aside and in the best possible order for examination.

(5) At our request, give us complete inventories of the damaged and undamaged property. Include quantities, costs, values and amount of loss claimed.

(6) As often as may be reasonably required, permit us to inspect the property proving the loss or damage and examine your books and records.

Also, permit us to take samples of damaged and undamaged property for inspection, testing and analysis, and permit us to make copies from your books and records.

(7) Send us a signed, sworn proof of loss containing the information we request to investigate the claim. You must do this within 60 days after our request. We will supply you with the necessary forms.

(8) Cooperate with us in the investigation or settlement of the claim.

 CP 00 17 10 12

b. We may examine any insured under oath, while not in the presence of any other insured and at such times as may be reasonably required, about any matter relating to this insurance or the claim, including an insured's books and records. In the event of an examination, an insured's answers must be signed.

4. Loss Payment

a. In the event of loss or damage covered by this Coverage Form, at our option, we will either:

   (1) Pay the value of lost or damaged property;

   (2) Pay the cost of repairing or replacing the lost or damaged property, subject to **b.** below;

   (3) Take all or any part of the property at an agreed or appraised value; or

   (4) Repair, rebuild or replace the property with other property of like kind and quality, subject to **b.** below.

   We will determine the value of lost or damaged property, or the cost of its repair or replacement, in accordance with the applicable terms of the Valuation Condition in this Coverage Form or any applicable provision which amends or supersedes the Valuation Condition.

b. The cost to repair, rebuild or replace does not include the increased cost attributable to enforcement of or compliance with any ordinance or law regulating the construction, use or repair of any property.

c. We will give notice of our intentions within 30 days after we receive the sworn proof of loss.

d. We will not pay you more than your financial interest in the Covered Property.

e. We may adjust losses with the owners of lost or damaged property if other than you. If we pay the owners, such payments will satisfy your claims against us for the owners' property. We will not pay the owners more than their financial interest in the Covered Property.

f. We may elect to defend you against suits arising from claims of owners of property. We will do this at our expense.

g. We will pay for covered loss or damage to Covered Property within 30 days after we receive the sworn proof of loss, if you have complied with all of the terms of this Coverage Part, and:

   (1) We have reached agreement with you on the amount of loss; or

   (2) An appraisal award has been made.

   If you name an insurance trustee, we will adjust losses with you, but we will pay the insurance trustee. If we pay the trustee, the payments will satisfy your claims against us.

h. A party wall is a wall that separates and is common to adjoining buildings that are owned by different parties. In settling covered losses involving a party wall, we will pay a proportion of the loss to the party wall based on your interest in the wall in proportion to the interest of the owner of the adjoining building. However, if you elect to repair or replace your building and the owner of the adjoining building elects not to repair or replace that building, we will pay you the full value of the loss to the party wall, subject to all applicable policy provisions including Limits of Insurance, the Valuation and Coinsurance Conditions and all other provisions of this Loss Payment Condition. Our payment under the provisions of this paragraph does not alter any right of subrogation we may have against any entity, including the owner or insurer of the adjoining building, and does not alter the terms of the Transfer Of Rights Of Recovery Against Others To Us Condition in this policy.

5. Recovered Property

If either you or we recover any property after loss settlement, that party must give the other prompt notice. At your option, the property will be returned to you. You must then return to us the amount we paid to you for the property. We will pay recovery expenses and the expenses to repair the recovered property, subject to the Limit of Insurance.

6. Unit-owner's Insurance

A unit-owner may have other insurance covering the same property as this insurance. This insurance is intended to be primary and not to contribute with such other insurance.

7. **Vacancy**

   a. **Description Of Terms**

      (1) As used in this Vacancy Condition, the term building and the term vacant have the meanings set forth in **(1)(a)** and **(1)(b)** below:

         (a) When this policy is issued to a tenant, and with respect to that tenant's interest in Covered Property, building means the unit or suite rented or leased to the tenant. Such building is vacant when it does not contain enough business personal property to conduct customary operations.

         (b) When this policy is issued to the owner or general lessee of a building, building means the entire building. Such building is vacant unless at least 31% of its total square footage is:

            (i) Rented to a lessee or sublessee and used by the lessee or sublessee to conduct its customary operations; and/or

            (ii) Used by the building owner to conduct customary operations.

      (2) Buildings under construction or renovation are not considered vacant.

   b. **Vacancy Provisions**

      If the building where loss or damage occurs has been vacant for more than 60 consecutive days before that loss or damage occurs:

      (1) We will not pay for any loss or damage caused by any of the following even if they are Covered Causes of Loss:

         (a) Vandalism;

         (b) Sprinkler leakage, unless you have protected the system against freezing;

         (c) Building glass breakage;

         (d) Water damage;

         (e) Theft; or

         (f) Attempted theft.

      (2) With respect to Covered Causes of Loss other than those listed in **b.(1)(a)** through **b.(1)(f)** above, we will reduce the amount we would otherwise pay for the loss or damage by 15%.

8. **Valuation**

   We will determine the value of Covered Property in the event of loss or damage as follows:

   a. At actual cash value as of the time of loss or damage, except as provided in **b.** and **c.** below.

   b. If the Limit of Insurance for Building satisfies the Additional Condition, Coinsurance, and the cost to repair or replace the damaged building property is $2,500 or less, we will pay the cost of building repairs or replacement.

      The cost of building repairs or replacement does not include the increased cost attributable to enforcement of or compliance with any ordinance or law regulating the construction, use or repair of any property. However, the following property will be valued at the actual cash value, even when attached to the building:

      (1) Awnings or floor coverings;

      (2) Appliances for refrigerating, ventilating, cooking, dishwashing or laundering; or

      (3) Outdoor equipment or furniture.

   c. Glass at the cost of replacement with safety-glazing material if required by law.

9. **Waiver Of Rights Of Recovery**

   We waive our rights to recover payment from any unit-owner of the condominium that is shown in the Declarations.

F. **Additional Conditions**

   The following conditions apply in addition to the Common Policy Conditions and the Commercial Property Conditions:

   1. **Coinsurance**

      If a Coinsurance percentage is shown in the Declarations, the following condition applies:

      a. We will not pay the full amount of any loss if the value of Covered Property at the time of loss times the Coinsurance percentage shown for it in the Declarations is greater than the Limit of Insurance for the property.

         Instead, we will determine the most we will pay using the following steps:

         (1) Multiply the value of Covered Property at the time of loss by the Coinsurance percentage;

         (2) Divide the Limit of Insurance of the property by the figure determined in Step **(1)**;

(3) Multiply the total amount of loss, before the application of any deductible, by the figure determined in Step **(2)**; and

(4) Subtract the deductible from the figure determined in Step **(3)**.

We will pay the amount determined in Step **(4)** or the Limit of Insurance, whichever is less. For the remainder, you will either have to rely on other insurance or absorb the loss yourself.

Example 1 (Underinsurance)

When: The value of the property is: $ 250,000

The Coinsurance percentage for it is: 80%

The Limit of Insurance for it is: $ 100,000

The Deductible is: $ 250

The amount of loss is: $ 40,000

Step **(1)**: $250,000 x 80% = $200,000

(the minimum amount of insurance to meet your Coinsurance requirements)

Step **(2)**: $100,000 ÷ $200,000 = .50

Step **(3)**: $40,000 x .50 = $20,000

Step **(4)**: $20,000 – $250 = $19,750

We will pay no more than $19,750. The remaining $20,250 is not covered.

Example 2 (Adequate Insurance)

When: The value of the property is: $ 250,000

The Coinsurance percentage for it is: 80%

The Limit of Insurance for it is: $ 200,000

The Deductible is: $ 250

The amount of loss is: $ 40,000

The minimum amount of insurance to meet your Coinsurance requirement is $200,000 ($250,000 x 80%). Therefore, the Limit of Insurance in this example is adequate and no penalty applies. We will pay no more than $39,750 ($40,000 amount of loss minus the deductible of $250).

b. If one Limit of Insurance applies to two or more separate items, this condition will apply to the total of all property to which the limit applies.

Example 3

When: The value of the property is:

Building at Location 1: $ 75,000

Building at Location 2: $ 100,000

Personal Property at Location 2: $ 75,000

$ 250,000

The Coinsurance percentage for it is: 90%

The Limit of Insurance for Buildings and Personal Property at Locations 1 and 2 is: $ 180,000

The Deductible is: $ 1,000

The amount of loss is:

Building at Location 2: $ 30,000

Personal Property at Location 2: $ 20,000

$ 50,000

Step **(1)**: $250,000 x 90% = $225,000

(the minimum amount of insurance to meet your Coinsurance requirements and to avoid the penalty shown below)

Step **(2)**: $180,000 ÷ $225,000 = .80

Step **(3)**: $50,000 x .80 = $40,000

Step **(4)**: $40,000 – $1,000 = $39,000

We will pay no more than $39,000. The remaining $11,000 is not covered.

2. Mortgageholders

a. The term mortgageholder includes trustee.

b. We will pay for covered loss of or damage to buildings or structures to each mortgageholder shown in the Declarations in their order of precedence, as interests may appear.

c. The mortgageholder has the right to receive loss payment even if the mortgageholder has started foreclosure or similar action on the building or structure.

d. If we deny your claim because of your acts or because you have failed to comply with the terms of this Coverage Part, the mortgageholder will still have the right to receive loss payment if the mortgageholder:

(1) Pays any premium due under this Coverage Part at our request if you have failed to do so;

(2) Submits a signed, sworn proof of loss within 60 days after receiving notice from us of your failure to do so; and

(3) Has notified us of any change in ownership, occupancy or substantial change in risk known to the mortgageholder.

All of the terms of this Coverage Part will then apply directly to the mortgageholder.

e. If we pay the mortgageholder for any loss or damage and deny payment to you because of your acts or because you have failed to comply with the terms of this Coverage Part:

(1) The mortgageholder's rights under the mortgage will be transferred to us to the extent of the amount we pay; and

(2) The mortgageholder's right to recover the full amount of the mortgageholder's claim will not be impaired.

At our option, we may pay to the mortgageholder the whole principal on the mortgage plus any accrued interest. In this event, your mortgage and note will be transferred to us and you will pay your remaining mortgage debt to us.

f. If we cancel this policy, we will give written notice to the mortgageholder at least:

(1) 10 days before the effective date of cancellation if we cancel for your nonpayment of premium; or

(2) 30 days before the effective date of cancellation if we cancel for any other reason.

g. If we elect not to renew this policy, we will give written notice to the mortgageholder at least 10 days before the expiration date of this policy.

G. Optional Coverages

If shown as applicable in the Declarations, the following Optional Coverages apply separately to each item:

1. Agreed Value

a. The Additional Condition, Coinsurance, does not apply to Covered Property to which this Optional Coverage applies. We will pay no more for loss of or damage to that property than the proportion that the Limit of Insurance under this Coverage Part for the property bears to the Agreed Value shown for it in the Declarations.

b. If the expiration date for this Optional Coverage shown in the Declarations is not extended, the Additional Condition, Coinsurance, is reinstated and this Optional Coverage expires.

c. The terms of this Optional Coverage apply only to loss or damage that occurs:

(1) On or after the effective date of this Optional Coverage; and

(2) Before the Agreed Value expiration date shown in the Declarations or the policy expiration date, whichever occurs first.

2. Inflation Guard

a. The Limit of Insurance for property to which this Optional Coverage applies will automatically increase by the annual percentage shown in the Declarations.

b. The amount of increase will be:

(1) The Limit of Insurance that applied on the most recent of the policy inception date, the policy anniversary date, or any other policy change amending the Limit of Insurance, times

(2) The percentage of annual increase shown in the Declarations, expressed as a decimal (example: 8% is .08), times

(3) The number of days since the beginning of the current policy year or the effective date of the most recent policy change amending the Limit of Insurance, divided by 365.

Example

If:	The applicable Limit of Insurance is:	$ 100,000
	The annual percentage increase is:	8%
	The number of days since the beginning of the policy year (or last policy change) is:	146
	The amount of increase is: $100,000 x .08 x 146 ÷ 365 =	$ 3,200

3. Replacement Cost

a. Replacement Cost (without deduction for depreciation) replaces Actual Cash Value in the Loss Condition, Valuation, of this Coverage Form.

b. This Optional Coverage does not apply to:

(1) Personal property of others;

(2) Contents of a residence; or

(3) Works of art, antiques or rare articles, including etchings, pictures, statuary, marbles, bronzes, porcelains and bric-a-brac.

Under the terms of this Replacement Cost Optional Coverage, personal property owned indivisibly by all unit-owners, and the property covered under Paragraph **A.1.a.(6)** of this Coverage Form, are not considered to be the personal property of others.

c. You may make a claim for loss or damage covered by this insurance on an actual cash value basis instead of on a replacement cost basis. In the event you elect to have loss or damage settled on an actual cash value basis, you may still make a claim for the additional coverage this Optional Coverage provides if you notify us of your intent to do so within 180 days after the loss or damage.

d. We will not pay on a replacement cost basis for any loss or damage:

(1) Until the lost or damaged property is actually repaired or replaced; and

(2) Unless the repair or replacement is made as soon as reasonably possible after the loss or damage.

e. We will not pay more for loss or damage on a replacement cost basis than the least of (1), (2) or (3), subject to f. below:

(1) The Limit of Insurance applicable to the lost or damaged property;

(2) The cost to replace the lost or damaged property with other property:

(a) Of comparable material and quality; and

(b) Used for the same purpose; or

(3) The amount actually spent that is necessary to repair or replace the lost or damaged property.

If a building is rebuilt at a new premises, the cost described in **e.(2)** above is limited to the cost which would have been incurred if the building had been rebuilt at the original premises.

f. The cost of repair or replacement does not include the increased cost attributable to enforcement of or compliance with any ordinance or law regulating the construction, use or repair of any property.

4. **Extension Of Replacement Cost To Personal Property Of Others**

a. If the Replacement Cost Optional Coverage is shown as applicable in the Declarations, then this Extension may also be shown as applicable. If the Declarations show this Extension as applicable, then Paragraph **3.b.(1)** of the Replacement Cost Optional Coverage is deleted and all other provisions of the Replacement Cost Optional Coverage apply to replacement cost on personal property of others.

b. With respect to replacement cost on the personal property of others, the following limitation applies:

If an item(s) of personal property of others is subject to a written contract which governs your liability for loss or damage to that item(s), then valuation of that item(s) will be based on the amount for which you are liable under such contract, but not to exceed the lesser of the replacement cost of the property or the applicable Limit of Insurance.

H. **Definitions**

1. "Fungus" means any type or form of fungus, including mold or mildew, and any mycotoxins, spores, scents or by-products produced or released by fungi.

2. "Pollutants" means any solid, liquid, gaseous or thermal irritant or contaminant, including smoke, vapor, soot, fumes, acids, alkalis, chemicals and waste. Waste includes materials to be recycled, reconditioned or reclaimed.

3. "Stock" means merchandise held in storage or for sale, raw materials and in-process or finished goods, including supplies used in their packing or shipping.

COMMERCIAL PROPERTY
CP 00 18 10 12

CONDOMINIUM COMMERCIAL UNIT-OWNERS COVERAGE FORM

Various provisions in this policy restrict coverage. Read the entire policy carefully to determine rights, duties and what is and is not covered.

Throughout this policy, the words "you" and "your" refer to the Named Insured shown in the Declarations. The words "we", "us" and "our" refer to the company providing this insurance.

Other words and phrases that appear in quotation marks have special meaning. Refer to Section **H.** Definitions.

A. Coverage

We will pay for direct physical loss of or damage to Covered Property at the premises described in the Declarations caused by or resulting from any Covered Cause of Loss.

1. Covered Property

Covered Property, as used in this Coverage Part, means the type of property described in this section, **A.1.**, and limited in **A.2.** Property Not Covered, if a Limit Of Insurance is shown in the Declarations for that type of property.

a. Your Business Personal Property consists of the following property located in or on the building or structure described in the Declarations or in the open (or in a vehicle) within 100 feet of the building or structure or within 100 feet of the premises described in the Declarations, whichever distance is greater:

(1) Furniture;

(2) Fixtures, improvements and alterations making up part of the building and owned by you;

(3) Machinery and equipment;

(4) "Stock";

(5) All other personal property owned by you and used in your business;

(6) Labor, materials or services furnished or arranged by you on personal property of others;

(7) Leased personal property for which you have a contractual responsibility to insure, unless otherwise provided for under Personal Property Of Others.

b. Personal Property Of Others that is:

(1) In your care, custody or control; and

(2) Located in or on the building or structure described in the Declarations or in the open (or in a vehicle) within 100 feet of the building or structure or within 100 feet of the premises described in the Declarations, whichever distance is greater.

However, our payment for loss of or damage to personal property of others will only be for the account of the owner of the property.

2. Property Not Covered

Covered Property does not include:

a. Accounts, bills, currency, food stamps or other evidences of debt, money, notes or securities. Lottery tickets held for sale are not securities;

b. Animals, unless owned by others and boarded by you, or if owned by you, only as "stock" while inside of buildings;

c. Automobiles held for sale;

d. Contraband, or property in the course of illegal transportation or trade;

e. Water, growing crops or lawns;

f. Personal property while airborne or waterborne;

g. Property that is covered under another Coverage Form of this or any other policy in which it is more specifically described, except for the excess of the amount due (whether you can collect on it or not) from that other insurance;

h. Electronic data, except as provided under the Additional Coverage, Electronic Data. Electronic data means information, facts or computer programs stored as or on, created or used on, or transmitted to or from computer software (including systems and applications software), on hard or floppy disks, CD-ROMs, tapes, drives, cells, data processing devices or any other repositories of computer software which are used with electronically controlled equipment. The term computer programs, referred to in the foregoing description of electronic data, means a set of related electronic instructions which direct the operations and functions of a computer or device connected to it, which enable the computer or device to receive, process, store, retrieve or send data. This paragraph, **h.**, does not apply to your "stock" of prepackaged software, or to electronic data which is integrated in and operates or controls the building's elevator, lighting, heating, ventilation, air conditioning or security system;

i. The cost to replace or restore the information on valuable papers and records, including those which exist as electronic data. Valuable papers and records include but are not limited to proprietary information, books of account, deeds, manuscripts, abstracts, drawings and card index systems. Refer to the Coverage Extension for Valuable Papers And Records (Other Than Electronic Data) for limited coverage for valuable papers and records other than those which exist as electronic data;

j. Vehicles or self-propelled machines (including aircraft or watercraft) that:

(1) Are licensed for use on public roads; or

(2) Are operated principally away from the described premises.

This paragraph does not apply to:

(a) Vehicles or self-propelled machines or autos you manufacture, process or warehouse;

(b) Vehicles or self-propelled machines, other than autos, you hold for sale;

(c) Rowboats or canoes out of water at the described premises; or

(d) Trailers, but only to the extent provided for in the Coverage Extension for Non-owned Detached Trailers;

k. The following property while outside of buildings:

(1) Grain, hay, straw or other crops; or

(2) Fences, radio or television antennas (including satellite dishes) and their lead-in wiring, masts or towers, trees, shrubs or plants (other than "stock" of trees, shrubs or plants), all except as provided in the Coverage Extensions;

l. Any of the following types of property contained within a unit, regardless of ownership, if your Condominium Association Agreement requires the Association to insure it:

(1) Fixtures, improvements and alterations that are a part of the building; and

(2) Appliances, such as those used for refrigerating, ventilating, cooking, dishwashing, laundering, security or housekeeping.

3. Covered Causes Of Loss

See applicable Causes Of Loss form as shown in the Declarations.

4. Additional Coverages

a. Debris Removal

(1) Subject to Paragraphs **(2)**, **(3)** and **(4)**, we will pay your expense to remove debris of Covered Property and other debris that is on the described premises, when such debris is caused by or results from a Covered Cause of Loss that occurs during the policy period. The expenses will be paid only if they are reported to us in writing within 180 days of the date of direct physical loss or damage.

(2) Debris Removal does not apply to costs to:

(a) Remove debris of property of yours that is not insured under this policy, or property in your possession that is not Covered Property;

(b) Remove any property that is Property Not Covered, including property addressed under the Outdoor Property Coverage Extension;

© Insurance Services Office, Inc., 2011

(c) Remove property of others of a type that would not be Covered Property under this Coverage Form;

(d) Remove deposits of mud or earth from the grounds of the described premises;

(e) Extract "pollutants" from land or water; or

(f) Remove, restore or replace polluted land or water.

(3) Subject to the exceptions in Paragraph (4), the following provisions apply:

(a) The most we will pay for the total of direct physical loss or damage plus debris removal expense is the Limit of Insurance applicable to the Covered Property that has sustained loss or damage.

(b) Subject to (a) above, the amount we will pay for debris removal expense is limited to 25% of the sum of the deductible plus the amount that we pay for direct physical loss or damage to the Covered Property that has sustained loss or damage. However, if no Covered Property has sustained direct physical loss or damage, the most we will pay for removal of debris of other property (if such removal is covered under this Additional Coverage) is $5,000 at each location.

(4) We will pay up to an additional $25,000 for debris removal expense, for each location, in any one occurrence of physical loss or damage to Covered Property, if one or both of the following circumstances apply:

(a) The total of the actual debris removal expense plus the amount we pay for direct physical loss or damage exceeds the Limit of Insurance on the Covered Property that has sustained loss or damage.

(b) The actual debris removal expense exceeds 25% of the sum of the deductible plus the amount that we pay for direct physical loss or damage to the Covered Property that has sustained loss or damage.

Therefore, if (4)(a) and/or (4)(b) applies, our total payment for direct physical loss or damage and debris removal expense may reach but will never exceed the Limit of Insurance on the Covered Property that has sustained loss or damage, plus $25,000.

(5) **Examples**

The following examples assume that there is no Coinsurance penalty.

Example 1

Limit of Insurance:	$ 90,000
Amount of Deductible:	$ 500
Amount of Loss:	$ 50,000
Amount of Loss Payable:	$ 49,500
	($50,000 – $500)
Debris Removal Expense:	$ 10,000
Debris Removal Expense Payable:	$ 10,000

($10,000 is 20% of $50,000.)

The debris removal expense is less than 25% of the sum of the loss payable plus the deductible. The sum of the loss payable and the debris removal expense ($49,500 + $10,000 = $59,500) is less than the Limit of Insurance. Therefore the full amount of debris removal expense is payable in accordance with the terms of Paragraph (3).

Example 2

Limit of Insurance:	$ 90,000
Amount of Deductible:	$ 500
Amount of Loss:	$ 80,000
Amount of Loss Payable:	$ 79,500
	($80,000 – $500)
Debris Removal Expense:	$ 40,000
Debris Removal Expense Payable:	
Basic Amount:	$ 10,500
Additional Amount:	$ 25,000

The basic amount payable for debris removal expense under the terms of Paragraph (3) is calculated as follows: $80,000 ($79,500 + $500) x .25 = $20,000; capped at $10,500. The cap applies because the sum of the loss payable ($79,500) and the basic amount payable for debris removal expense ($10,500) cannot exceed the Limit of Insurance ($90,000).

The additional amount payable for debris removal expense is provided in accordance with the terms of Paragraph **(4)**, because the debris removal expense ($40,000) exceeds 25% of the loss payable plus the deductible ($40,000 is 50% of $80,000), and because the sum of the loss payable and debris removal expense ($79,500 + $40,000 = $119,500) would exceed the Limit of Insurance ($90,000). The additional amount of covered debris removal expense is $25,000, the maximum payable under Paragraph **(4)**. Thus, the total payable for debris removal expense in this example is $35,500; $4,500 of the debris removal expense is not covered.

b. Preservation Of Property

If it is necessary to move Covered Property from the described premises to preserve it from loss or damage by a Covered Cause of Loss, we will pay for any direct physical loss or damage to that property:

(1) While it is being moved or while temporarily stored at another location; and

(2) Only if the loss or damage occurs within 30 days after the property is first moved.

c. Fire Department Service Charge

When the fire department is called to save or protect Covered Property from a Covered Cause of Loss, we will pay up to $1,000 for service at each premises described in the Declarations, unless a higher limit is shown in the Declarations. Such limit is the most we will pay regardless of the number of responding fire departments or fire units, and regardless of the number or type of services performed.

This Additional Coverage applies to your liability for fire department service charges:

(1) Assumed by contract or agreement prior to loss; or

(2) Required by local ordinance.

No Deductible applies to this Additional Coverage.

d. Pollutant Clean-up And Removal

We will pay your expense to extract "pollutants" from land or water at the described premises if the discharge, dispersal, seepage, migration, release or escape of the "pollutants" is caused by or results from a Covered Cause of Loss that occurs during the policy period. The expenses will be paid only if they are reported to us in writing within 180 days of the date on which the Covered Cause of Loss occurs.

This Additional Coverage does not apply to costs to test for, monitor or assess the existence, concentration or effects of "pollutants". But we will pay for testing which is performed in the course of extracting the "pollutants" from the land or water.

The most we will pay under this Additional Coverage for each described premises is $10,000 for the sum of all covered expenses arising out of Covered Causes of Loss occurring during each separate 12-month period of this policy.

e. Electronic Data

(1) Under this Additional Coverage, electronic data has the meaning described under Property Not Covered, Electronic Data. This Additional Coverage does not apply to your "stock" of prepackaged software, or to electronic data which is integrated in and operates or controls the building's elevator, lighting, heating, ventilation, air conditioning or security system.

(2) Subject to the provisions of this Additional Coverage, we will pay for the cost to replace or restore electronic data which has been destroyed or corrupted by a Covered Cause of Loss. To the extent that electronic data is not replaced or restored, the loss will be valued at the cost of replacement of the media on which the electronic data was stored, with blank media of substantially identical type.

(3) The Covered Causes of Loss applicable to Your Business Personal Property apply to this Additional Coverage, Electronic Data, subject to the following:

(a) If the Causes Of Loss – Special Form applies, coverage under this Additional Coverage, Electronic Data, is limited to the "specified causes of loss" as defined in that form and Collapse as set forth in that form.

(b) If the Causes Of Loss – Broad Form applies, coverage under this Additional Coverage, Electronic Data, includes Collapse as set forth in that form.

© Insurance Services Office, Inc., 2011 CP 00 18 10 12

(c) If the Causes Of Loss form is endorsed to add a Covered Cause of Loss, the additional Covered Cause of Loss does not apply to the coverage provided under this Additional Coverage, Electronic Data.

(d) The Covered Causes of Loss include a virus, harmful code or similar instruction introduced into or enacted on a computer system (including electronic data) or a network to which it is connected, designed to damage or destroy any part of the system or disrupt its normal operation. But there is no coverage for loss or damage caused by or resulting from manipulation of a computer system (including electronic data) by any employee, including a temporary or leased employee, or by an entity retained by you or for you to inspect, design, install, modify, maintain, repair or replace that system.

(4) The most we will pay under this Additional Coverage, Electronic Data, is $2,500 (unless a higher limit is shown in the Declarations) for all loss or damage sustained in any one policy year, regardless of the number of occurrences of loss or damage or the number of premises, locations or computer systems involved. If loss payment on the first occurrence does not exhaust this amount, then the balance is available for subsequent loss or damage sustained in but not after that policy year. With respect to an occurrence which begins in one policy year and continues or results in additional loss or damage in a subsequent policy year(s), all loss or damage is deemed to be sustained in the policy year in which the occurrence began.

5. Coverage Extensions

Except as otherwise provided, the following Extensions apply to property located in or on the building described in the Declarations or in the open (or in a vehicle) within 100 feet of the described premises.

If a Coinsurance percentage of 80% or more, or a Value Reporting period symbol, is shown in the Declarations, you may extend the insurance provided by this Coverage Part as follows:

a. Newly Acquired Property

(1) You may extend the insurance that applies to Your Business Personal Property to apply to:

(a) Business personal property, including such property that you newly acquire, at any location you acquire other than at fairs, trade shows or exhibitions; or

(b) Business personal property, including such property that you newly acquire, located at your newly constructed or acquired buildings at the location described in the Declarations.

The most we will pay for loss or damage under this Extension is $100,000 at each building.

(2) This Extension does not apply to:

(a) Personal property of others that is temporarily in your possession in the course of installing or performing work on such property; or

(b) Personal property of others that is temporarily in your possession in the course of your manufacturing or wholesaling activities.

(3) Insurance under this Coverage Extension for Newly Acquired Property will end when any of the following first occurs:

(a) This policy expires;

(b) 30 days expire after you acquire the property; or

(c) You report values to us.

We will charge you additional premium for values reported from the date you acquire the property.

b. Personal Effects And Property Of Others

You may extend the insurance that applies to Your Business Personal Property to apply to:

(1) Personal effects owned by you, your officers, your partners or members, your managers or your employees. This Extension does not apply to loss or damage by theft.

(2) Personal property of others in your care, custody or control.

The most we will pay for loss or damage under this Extension is $2,500 at each described premises. Our payment for loss of or damage to personal property of others will only be for the account of the owner of the property.

c. Valuable Papers And Records (Other Than Electronic Data)

(1) You may extend the insurance that applies to Your Business Personal Property to apply to the cost to replace or restore the lost information on valuable papers and records for which duplicates do not exist. But this Extension does not apply to valuable papers and records which exist as electronic data. Electronic data has the meaning described under Property Not Covered, Electronic Data.

(2) If the Causes Of Loss – Special Form applies, coverage under this Extension is limited to the "specified causes of loss" as defined in that form and Collapse as set forth in that form.

(3) If the Causes Of Loss – Broad Form applies, coverage under this Extension includes Collapse as set forth in that form.

(4) Under this Extension, the most we will pay to replace or restore the lost information is $2,500 at each described premises, unless a higher limit is shown in the Declarations. Such amount is additional insurance. We will also pay for the cost of blank material for reproducing the records (whether or not duplicates exist) and (when there is a duplicate) for the cost of labor to transcribe or copy the records. The costs of blank material and labor are subject to the applicable Limit of Insurance on Your Business Personal Property and, therefore, coverage of such costs is not additional insurance.

d. Property Off-premises

(1) You may extend the insurance that applies to Your Business Personal Property to apply to your business personal property while it is away from the described premises, if it is:

(a) Temporarily at a location you do not own, lease or operate;

(b) In storage at a location you lease, provided the lease was executed after the beginning of the current policy term; or

(c) At any fair, trade show or exhibition.

(2) This Extension does not apply to property:

(a) In or on a vehicle; or

(b) In the care, custody or control of your salespersons, unless the property is in such care, custody or control at a fair, trade show or exhibition.

(3) The most we will pay for loss or damage under this Extension is $10,000.

e. Outdoor Property

You may extend the insurance that applies to Your Business Personal Property to apply to your outdoor fences, radio and television antennas (including satellite dishes), trees, shrubs and plants (other than "stock" of trees, shrubs or plants), including debris removal expense, caused by or resulting from any of the following causes of loss if they are Covered Causes of Loss:

(1) Fire;

(2) Lightning;

(3) Explosion;

(4) Riot or Civil Commotion; or

(5) Aircraft.

The most we will pay for loss or damage under this Extension is $1,000, but not more than $250 for any one tree, shrub or plant. These limits apply to any one occurrence, regardless of the types or number of items lost or damaged in that occurrence.

Subject to all aforementioned terms and limitations of coverage, this Coverage Extension includes the expense of removing from the described premises the debris of trees, shrubs and plants which are the property of others.

f. Non-owned Detached Trailers

(1) You may extend the insurance that applies to Your Business Personal Property to apply to loss or damage to trailers that you do not own, provided that:

  (a) The trailer is used in your business;

  (b) The trailer is in your care, custody or control at the premises described in the Declarations; and

  (c) You have a contractual responsibility to pay for loss or damage to the trailer.

(2) We will not pay for any loss or damage that occurs:

  (a) While the trailer is attached to any motor vehicle or motorized conveyance, whether or not the motor vehicle or motorized conveyance is in motion;

  (b) During hitching or unhitching operations, or when a trailer becomes accidentally unhitched from a motor vehicle or motorized conveyance.

(3) The most we will pay for loss or damage under this Extension is $5,000, unless a higher limit is shown in the Declarations.

(4) This insurance is excess over the amount due (whether you can collect on it or not) from any other insurance covering such property.

g. Business Personal Property Temporarily In Portable Storage Units

(1) You may extend the insurance that applies to Your Business Personal Property to apply to such property while temporarily stored in a portable storage unit (including a detached trailer) located within 100 feet of the building or structure described in the Declarations or within 100 feet of the premises described in the Declarations, whichever distance is greater.

(2) If the applicable Covered Causes of Loss form or endorsement contains a limitation or exclusion concerning loss or damage from sand, dust, sleet, snow, ice or rain to property in a structure, such limitation or exclusion also applies to property in a portable storage unit.

(3) Coverage under this Extension:

  (a) Will end 90 days after the business personal property has been placed in the storage unit;

  (b) Does not apply if the storage unit itself has been in use at the described premises for more than 90 consecutive days, even if the business personal property has been stored there for 90 or fewer days as of the time of loss or damage.

(4) Under this Extension, the most we will pay for the total of all loss or damage to business personal property is $10,000 (unless a higher limit is indicated in the Declarations for such Extension) regardless of the number of storage units. Such limit is part of, not in addition to, the applicable Limit of Insurance on Your Business Personal Property. Therefore, payment under this Extension will not increase the applicable Limit of Insurance on Your Business Personal Property.

(5) This Extension does not apply to loss or damage otherwise covered under this Coverage Form or any endorsement to this Coverage Form or policy, and does not apply to loss or damage to the storage unit itself.

Each of these Extensions is additional insurance unless otherwise indicated. The Additional Condition, Coinsurance, does not apply to these Extensions.

B. Exclusions And Limitations

See applicable Causes Of Loss form as shown in the Declarations.

C. Limits Of Insurance

The most we will pay for loss or damage in any one occurrence is the applicable Limit Of Insurance shown in the Declarations.

The most we will pay for loss or damage to outdoor signs, whether or not the sign is attached to a building, is $2,500 per sign in any one occurrence.

The amounts of insurance stated in the following Additional Coverages apply in accordance with the terms of such coverages and are separate from the Limit(s) Of Insurance shown in the Declarations for any other coverage:

1. Fire Department Service Charge;

2. Pollutant Clean-up And Removal; and

3. Electronic Data.

Payments under the Preservation Of Property Additional Coverage will not increase the applicable Limit of Insurance.

D. Deductible

In any one occurrence of loss or damage (hereinafter referred to as loss), we will first reduce the amount of loss if required by the Coinsurance Condition or the Agreed Value Optional Coverage. If the adjusted amount of loss is less than or equal to the Deductible, we will not pay for that loss. If the adjusted amount of loss exceeds the Deductible, we will then subtract the Deductible from the adjusted amount of loss and will pay the resulting amount or the Limit of Insurance, whichever is less.

When the occurrence involves loss to more than one item of Covered Property and separate Limits of Insurance apply, the losses will not be combined in determining application of the Deductible. But the Deductible will be applied only once per occurrence.

Example 1

(This example assumes there is no Coinsurance penalty.)

Deductible:	$ 250
Limit of Insurance – Building 1:	$ 60,000
Limit of Insurance – Building 2:	$ 80,000
Loss to Building 1:	$ 60,100
Loss to Building 2:	$ 90,000

The amount of loss to Building 1 ($60,100) is less than the sum ($60,250) of the Limit of Insurance applicable to Building 1 plus the Deductible.

The Deductible will be subtracted from the amount of loss in calculating the loss payable for Building 1:

$ 60,100
– 250
$ 59,850   Loss Payable – Building 1

The Deductible applies once per occurrence and therefore is not subtracted in determining the amount of loss payable for Building 2. Loss payable for Building 2 is the Limit of Insurance of $80,000.

Total amount of loss payable:

$59,850 + $80,000 = $139,850

Example 2

(This example, too, assumes there is no Coinsurance penalty.)

The Deductible and Limits of Insurance are the same as those in Example 1.

Loss to Building 1:	$ 70,000
(Exceeds Limit of Insurance plus Deductible)	
Loss to Building 2:	$ 90,000
(Exceeds Limit of Insurance plus Deductible)	
Loss Payable – Building 1:	$ 60,000
(Limit of Insurance)	
Loss Payable – Building 2:	$ 80,000
(Limit of Insurance)	
Total amount of loss payable:	$ 140,000

E. Loss Conditions

The following conditions apply in addition to the Common Policy Conditions and the Commercial Property Conditions:

1. **Abandonment**

There can be no abandonment of any property to us.

2. **Appraisal**

If we and you disagree on the value of the property or the amount of loss, either may make written demand for an appraisal of the loss. In this event, each party will select a competent and impartial appraiser. The two appraisers will select an umpire. If they cannot agree, either may request that selection be made by a judge of a court having jurisdiction. The appraisers will state separately the value of the property and amount of loss. If they fail to agree, they will submit their differences to the umpire. A decision agreed to by any two will be binding. Each party will:

a. Pay its chosen appraiser; and

b. Bear the other expenses of the appraisal and umpire equally.

If there is an appraisal, we will still retain our right to deny the claim.

3. **Condominium Association Insurance**

The Condominium Association may have other insurance covering the same property as this insurance. This insurance is intended to be excess, and not to contribute with that other insurance.

© Insurance Services Office, Inc., 2011   CP 00 18 10 12

4. Duties In The Event Of Loss Or Damage

a. You must see that the following are done in the event of loss or damage to Covered Property:

(1) Notify the police if a law may have been broken.

(2) Give us prompt notice of the loss or damage. Include a description of the property involved.

(3) As soon as possible, give us a description of how, when and where the loss or damage occurred.

(4) Take all reasonable steps to protect the Covered Property from further damage, and keep a record of your expenses necessary to protect the Covered Property, for consideration in the settlement of the claim. This will not increase the Limit of Insurance. However, we will not pay for any subsequent loss or damage resulting from a cause of loss that is not a Covered Cause of Loss. Also, if feasible, set the damaged property aside and in the best possible order for examination.

(5) At our request, give us complete inventories of the damaged and undamaged property. Include quantities, costs, values and amount of loss claimed.

(6) As often as may be reasonably required, permit us to inspect the property proving the loss or damage and examine your books and records.

Also permit us to take samples of damaged and undamaged property for inspection, testing and analysis, and permit us to make copies from your books and records.

(7) Send us a signed, sworn proof of loss containing the information we request to investigate the claim. You must do this within 60 days after our request. We will supply you with the necessary forms.

(8) Cooperate with us in the investigation or settlement of the claim.

b. We may examine any insured under oath, while not in the presence of any other insured and at such times as may be reasonably required, about any matter relating to this insurance or the claim, including an insured's books and records. In the event of an examination, an insured's answers must be signed.

5. Loss Payment

a. In the event of loss or damage covered by this Coverage Form, at our option, we will either:

(1) Pay the value of lost or damaged property;

(2) Pay the cost of repairing or replacing the lost or damaged property, subject to **b.** below;

(3) Take all or any part of the property at an agreed or appraised value; or

(4) Repair, rebuild or replace the property with other property of like kind and quality, subject to **b.** below.

We will determine the value of lost or damaged property, or the cost of its repair or replacement, in accordance with the applicable terms of the Valuation Condition in this Coverage Form or any applicable provision which amends or supersedes the Valuation Condition.

b. The cost to repair, rebuild or replace does not include the increased cost attributable to enforcement of or compliance with any ordinance or law regulating the construction, use or repair of any property.

c. We will give notice of our intentions within 30 days after we receive the sworn proof of loss.

d. We will not pay you more than your financial interest in the Covered Property.

e. We may adjust losses with the owners of lost or damaged property if other than you. If we pay the owners, such payments will satisfy your claims against us for the owners' property. We will not pay the owners more than their financial interest in the Covered Property.

f. We may elect to defend you against suits arising from claims of owners of property. We will do this at our expense.

g. We will pay for covered loss or damage within 30 days after we receive the sworn proof of loss, if you have complied with all of the terms of this Coverage Part, and:

(1) We have reached agreement with you on the amount of loss; or

(2) An appraisal award has been made.

6. **Recovered Property**

If either you or we recover any property after loss settlement, that party must give the other prompt notice. At your option, the property will be returned to you. You must then return to us the amount we paid to you for the property. We will pay recovery expenses to repair the recovered property, subject to the Limit of Insurance.

7. **Vacancy**

   a. **Description Of Terms**

      (1) As used in this Vacancy Condition, the term building and the term vacant have the meanings set forth in **(1)(a)** and **(1)(b)** below:

         (a) When this policy is issued to a tenant, and with respect to that tenant's interest in Covered Property, building means the unit or suite rented or leased to the tenant. Such building is vacant when it does not contain enough business personal property to conduct customary operations.

         (b) When this policy is issued to the owner or general lessee of a building, building means the entire building. Such building is vacant unless at least 31% of its total square footage is:

            (i) Rented to a lessee or sublessee and used by the lessee or sublessee to conduct its customary operations; and/or

            (ii) Used by the building owner to conduct customary operations.

      (2) Buildings under construction or renovation are not considered vacant.

   b. **Vacancy Provisions**

      If the building where loss or damage occurs has been vacant for more than 60 consecutive days before that loss or damage occurs:

      (1) We will not pay for any loss or damage caused by any of the following, even if they are Covered Causes of Loss:

         (a) Vandalism;

         (b) Sprinkler leakage, unless you have protected the system against freezing;

         (c) Building glass breakage;

         (d) Water damage;

         (e) Theft; or

         (f) Attempted theft.

      (2) With respect to Covered Causes of Loss other than those listed in **b.(1)(a)** through **b.(1)(f)** above, we will reduce the amount we would otherwise pay for the loss or damage by 15%.

8. **Valuation**

   We will determine the value of Covered Property in the event of loss or damage as follows:

   a. At actual cash value as of the time of loss or damage, except as provided in **b.** and **c.** below.

   b. "Stock" you have sold but not delivered at the selling price less discounts and expenses you otherwise would have had.

   c. Glass at the cost of replacement with safety-glazing material if required by law.

F. **Additional Condition**

   COINSURANCE

   If a Coinsurance percentage is shown in the Declarations, the following condition applies in addition to the Common Policy Conditions and the Commercial Property Conditions:

   a. We will not pay the full amount of any loss if the value of Covered Property at the time of loss times the Coinsurance percentage shown for it in the Declarations is greater than the Limit of Insurance for the property.

   Instead, we will determine the most we will pay using the following steps:

      (1) Multiply the value of Covered Property at the time of loss by the Coinsurance percentage;

      (2) Divide the Limit of Insurance of the property by the figure determined in Step **(1)**;

      (3) Multiply the total amount of loss, before the application of any deductible, by the figure determined in Step **(2)**; and

      (4) Subtract the deductible from the figure determined in Step **(3)**.

   We will pay the amount determined in Step **(4)** or the Limit of Insurance, whichever is less. For the remainder, you will either have to rely on other insurance or absorb the loss yourself.

Example 1 (Underinsurance)

When:	The value of the property is:	$ 250,000
	The Coinsurance percentage for it is:	80%
	The Limit of Insurance for it is:	$ 100,000
	The Deductible is:	$ 250
	The amount of loss is:	$ 40,000

Step **(1)**: $250,000 x 80% = $200,000

(the minimum amount of insurance to meet your Coinsurance requirements)

Step **(2)**: $100,000 ÷ $200,000 = .50

Step **(3)**: $40,000 x .50 = $20,000

Step **(4)**: $20,000 – $250 = $19,750

We will pay no more than $19,750. The remaining $20,250 is not covered.

Example 2 (Adequate Insurance)

When:	The value of the property is:	$ 250,000
	The Coinsurance percentage for it is:	80%
	The Limit of Insurance for it is:	$ 200,000
	The Deductible is:	$ 250
	The amount of loss is:	$ 40,000

The minimum amount of insurance to meet your Coinsurance requirement is $200,000 ($250,000 x 80%). Therefore, the Limit of Insurance in this example is adequate and no penalty applies. We will pay no more than $39,750 ($40,000 amount of loss minus the deductible of $250).

   b. If one Limit of Insurance applies to two or more separate items, this condition will apply to the total of all property to which the limit applies.

Example 3

When:	The value of the property is:	
	Personal Property at Location 1:	$ 175,000
	Personal Property at Location 2:	$ 75,000
		$ 250,000
	The Coinsurance percentage for it is:	90%
	The Limit of Insurance for Personal Property at Locations 1 and 2 is:	$ 180,000
	The Deductible is:	$ 1,000
	The amount of loss is:	
	Personal Property at Location 1:	$ 30,000
	Personal Property at Location 2:	$ 20,000
		$ 50,000

Step **(1)**: $250,000 x 90% = $225,000

(the minimum amount of insurance to meet your Coinsurance requirements and to avoid the penalty shown below)

Step **(2)**: $180,000 ÷ $225,000 = .80

Step **(3)**: $50,000 x .80 = $40,000

Step **(4)**: $40,000 – $1,000 = $39,000

We will pay no more than $39,000. The remaining $11,000 is not covered.

G. Optional Coverages

If shown as applicable in the Declarations, the following Optional Coverages apply separately to each item:

   1. Agreed Value

      a. The Additional Condition, Coinsurance, does not apply to Covered Property to which this Optional Coverage applies. We will pay no more for loss of or damage to that property than the proportion that the Limit of Insurance under this Coverage Part for the property bears to the Agreed Value shown for it in the Declarations.

b. If the expiration date for this Optional Coverage shown in the Declarations is not extended, the Additional Condition, Coinsurance, is reinstated and this Optional Coverage expires.

c. The terms of this Optional Coverage apply only to loss or damage that occurs:

(1) On or after the effective date of this Optional Coverage; and

(2) Before the Agreed Value expiration date shown in the Declarations or the policy expiration date, whichever occurs first.

2. Inflation Guard

a. The Limit of Insurance for property to which this Optional Coverage applies will automatically increase by the annual percentage shown in the Declarations.

b. The amount of increase will be:

(1) The Limit of Insurance that applied on the most recent of the policy inception date, the policy anniversary date, or any other policy change amending the Limit of Insurance, times

(2) The percentage of annual increase shown in the Declarations, expressed as a decimal (example: 8% is .08), times

(3) The number of days since the beginning of the current policy year or the effective date of the most recent policy change amending the Limit of Insurance, divided by 365.

Example

If:	The applicable Limit of Insurance is:	$ 100,000
	The annual percentage increase is:	8%
	The number of days since the beginning of the policy year (or last policy change) is:	146
	The amount of increase is: $100,000 x .08 x 146 ÷ 365 =	$ 3,200

3. Replacement Cost

a. Replacement Cost (without deduction for depreciation) replaces Actual Cash Value in the Loss Condition, Valuation, of this Coverage Form.

b. This Optional Coverage does not apply to:

(1) Personal property of others;

(2) Contents of a residence;

(3) Works of art, antiques or rare articles, including etchings, pictures, statuary, marbles, bronzes, porcelains and bric-a-brac; or

(4) "Stock", unless the Including "Stock" option is shown in the Declarations.

c. You may make a claim for loss or damage covered by this insurance on an actual cash value basis instead of on a replacement cost basis. In the event you elect to have loss or damage settled on an actual cash value basis, you may still make a claim for the additional coverage this Optional Coverage provides if you notify us of your intent to do so within 180 days after the loss or damage.

d. We will not pay on a replacement cost basis for any loss or damage:

(1) Until the lost or damaged property is actually repaired or replaced; and

(2) Unless the repairs or replacement are made as soon as reasonably possible after the loss or damage.

e. We will not pay more for loss or damage on a replacement cost basis than the least of **(1)**, **(2)** or **(3)**, subject to **f.** below:

(1) The Limit of Insurance applicable to the lost or damaged property;

(2) The cost to replace the lost or damaged property with other property:

(a) Of comparable material and quality; and

(b) Used for the same purpose; or

(3) The amount actually spent that is necessary to repair or replace the lost or damaged property.

If a building is rebuilt at a new premises, the cost described in **e.(2)** above is limited to the cost which would have been incurred if the building had been rebuilt at the original premises.

f. The cost of repair or replacement does not include the increased cost attributable to enforcement of or compliance with any ordinance or law regulating the construction, use or repair of any property.

4. Extension Of Replacement Cost To Personal Property Of Others

a. If the Replacement Cost Optional Coverage is shown as applicable in the Declarations, then this Extension may also be shown as applicable. If the Declarations show this Extension as applicable, then Paragraph **3.b.(1)** of the Replacement Cost Optional Coverage is deleted and all other provisions of the Replacement Cost Optional Coverage apply to replacement cost on personal property of others.

b. With respect to replacement cost on the personal property of others, the following limitation applies:

If an item(s) of personal property of others is subject to a written contract which governs your liability for loss or damage to that item(s), then valuation of that item(s) will be based on the amount for which you are liable under such contract, but not to exceed the lesser of the replacement cost of the property or the applicable Limit of Insurance.

H. Definitions

1. "Pollutants" means any solid, liquid, gaseous or thermal irritant or contaminant, including smoke, vapor, soot, fumes, acids, alkalis, chemicals and waste. Waste includes materials to be recycled, reconditioned or reclaimed.

2. "Stock" means merchandise held in storage or for sale, raw materials and in-process or finished goods, including supplies used in their packing or shipping.

COMMERCIAL PROPERTY
CP 00 20 10 12

BUILDERS RISK COVERAGE FORM

Various provisions in this policy restrict coverage. Read the entire policy carefully to determine rights, duties and what is and is not covered.

Throughout this policy, the words "you" and "your" refer to the Named Insured shown in the Declarations. The words "we", "us" and "our" refer to the company providing this insurance.

Other words and phrases that appear in quotation marks have special meaning. Refer to Section **G.** Definitions.

A. Coverage

We will pay for direct physical loss of or damage to Covered Property at the premises described in the Declarations caused by or resulting from any Covered Cause of Loss.

1. Covered Property

Covered Property, as used in this Coverage Part, means the type of property described in this section, **A.1.**, and limited in **A.2.** Property Not Covered, if a Limit Of Insurance is shown in the Declarations for that type of property.

Building Under Construction, meaning the building or structure described in the Declarations while in the course of construction, including:

a. Foundations;

b. The following property:

(1) Fixtures and machinery;

(2) Equipment used to service the building; and

(3) Your building materials and supplies used for construction;

provided such property is intended to be permanently located in or on the building or structure described in the Declarations or within 100 feet of its premises;

c. If not covered by other insurance, temporary structures built or assembled on site, including cribbing, scaffolding and construction forms.

2. Property Not Covered

Covered Property does not include:

a. Land (including land on which the property is located) or water;

b. The following property when outside of buildings:

(1) Lawns, trees, shrubs or plants (other than lawns, trees, shrubs or plants which are part of a vegetated roof);

(2) Radio or television antennas (including satellite dishes) and their lead-in wiring, masts or towers; or

(3) Signs (other than signs attached to buildings).

3. Covered Causes Of Loss

See applicable Causes Of Loss Form as shown in the Declarations.

4. Additional Coverages

a. Debris Removal

(1) Subject to Paragraphs **(2)**, **(3)** and **(4)**, we will pay your expense to remove debris of Covered Property and other debris that is on the described premises, when such debris is caused by or results from a Covered Cause of Loss that occurs during the policy period. The expenses will be paid only if they are reported to us in writing within 180 days of the date of direct physical loss or damage.

(2) Debris Removal does not apply to costs to:

(a) Remove debris of property of yours that is not insured under this policy, or property in your possession that is not Covered Property;

(b) Remove debris of property owned by or leased to the landlord of the building where your described premises are located, unless you have a contractual responsibility to insure such property and it is insured under this policy;

(c) Remove any property that is Property Not Covered, including property addressed under the Sod, Trees, Shrubs And Plants Coverage Extension;

(d) Remove property of others of a type that would not be Covered Property under this Coverage Form;

© Insurance Services Office, Inc., 2011

(e) Remove deposits of mud or earth from the grounds of the described premises;

(f) Extract "pollutants" from land or water; or

(g) Remove, restore or replace polluted land or water.

(3) Subject to the exceptions in Paragraph (4), the following provisions apply:

(a) The most we will pay for the total of direct physical loss or damage plus debris removal expense is the Limit of Insurance applicable to the Covered Property that has sustained loss or damage.

(b) Subject to (a) above, the amount we will pay for debris removal expense is limited to 25% of the sum of the deductible plus the amount that we pay for direct physical loss or damage to the Covered Property that has sustained loss or damage. However, if no Covered Property has sustained direct physical loss or damage, the most we will pay for removal of debris of other property (if such removal is covered under this Additional Coverage) is $5,000 at each location.

(4) We will pay up to an additional $25,000 for debris removal expense, for each location, in any one occurrence of physical loss or damage to Covered Property, if one or both of the following circumstances apply:

(a) The total of the actual debris removal expense plus the amount we pay for direct physical loss or damage exceeds the Limit of Insurance on the Covered Property that has sustained loss or damage.

(b) The actual debris removal expense exceeds 25% of the sum of the deductible plus the amount that we pay for direct physical loss or damage to the Covered Property that has sustained loss or damage.

Therefore, if (4)(a) and/or (4)(b) applies, our total payment for direct physical loss or damage and debris removal expense may reach but will never exceed the Limit of Insurance on the Covered Property that has sustained loss or damage, plus $25,000.

(5) **Examples**

The following examples assume that there is no Coinsurance penalty.

Example 1

Limit of Insurance:	$ 90,000
Amount of Deductible:	$ 500
Amount of Loss:	$ 50,000
Amount of Loss Payable:	$ 49,500
	($50,000 – $500)
Debris Removal Expense:	$ 10,000
Debris Removal Expense Payable:	$ 10,000

($10,000 is 20% of $50,000.)

The debris removal expense is less than 25% of the sum of the loss payable plus the deductible. The sum of the loss payable and the debris removal expense ($49,500 + $10,000 = $59,500) is less than the Limit of Insurance. Therefore, the full amount of debris removal expense is payable in accordance with the terms of Paragraph (3).

Example 2

Limit of Insurance:	$ 90,000
Amount of Deductible:	$ 500
Amount of Loss:	$ 80,000
Amount of Loss Payable:	$ 79,500
	($80,000 – $500)
Debris Removal Expense:	$ 40,000
Debris Removal Expense Payable	
Basic Amount:	$ 10,500
Additional Amount:	$ 25,000

The basic amount payable for debris removal expense under the terms of Paragraph (3) is calculated as follows: $80,000 ($79,500 + $500) x .25 = $20,000, capped at $10,500. The cap applies because the sum of the loss payable ($79,500) and the basic amount payable for debris removal expense ($10,500) cannot exceed the Limit of Insurance ($90,000).

       CP 00 20 10 12

The additional amount payable for debris removal expense is provided in accordance with the terms of Paragraph **(4),** because the debris removal expense ($40,000) exceeds 25% of the loss payable plus the deductible ($40,000 is 50% of $80,000), and because the sum of the loss payable and debris removal expense ($79,500 + $40,000 = $119,500) would exceed the Limit of Insurance ($90,000). The additional amount of covered debris removal expense is $25,000, the maximum payable under Paragraph **(4).** Thus the total payable for debris removal expense in this example is $35,500; $4,500 of the debris removal expense is not covered.

b. Preservation Of Property

If it is necessary to move Covered Property from the described premises to preserve it from loss or damage by a Covered Cause of Loss, we will pay for any direct physical loss or damage to that property:

(1) While it is being moved or while temporarily stored at another location; and

(2) Only if the loss or damage occurs within 30 days after the property is first moved.

c. Fire Department Service Charge

When the fire department is called to save or protect Covered Property from a Covered Cause of Loss, we will pay up to $1,000 for service at each premises described in the Declarations, unless a higher limit is shown in the Declarations. Such limit is the most we will pay regardless of the number of responding fire departments or fire units, and regardless of the number or type of services performed.

This Additional Coverage applies to your liability for fire department service charges:

(1) Assumed by contract or agreement prior to loss; or

(2) Required by local ordinance.

No Deductible applies to this Additional Coverage.

d. Pollutant Clean-up And Removal

We will pay your expense to extract "pollutants" from land or water at the described premises if the discharge, dispersal, seepage, migration, release or escape of the "pollutants" is caused by or results from a Covered Cause of Loss that occurs during the policy period. The expenses will be paid only if they are reported to us in writing within 180 days of the date on which the Covered Cause of Loss occurs.

This Additional Coverage does not apply to costs to test for, monitor or assess the existence, concentration or effects of "pollutants". But we will pay for testing which is performed in the course of extracting the "pollutants" from the land or water.

The most we will pay under this Additional Coverage for each described premises is $10,000 for the sum of all covered expenses arising out of Covered Causes of Loss occurring during each separate 12-month period of this policy.

5. Coverage Extensions

a. Building Materials And Supplies Of Others

(1) You may extend the insurance provided by this Coverage Form to apply to building materials and supplies that are:

(a) Owned by others;

(b) In your care, custody or control;

(c) Located in or on the building described in the Declarations, or within 100 feet of its premises; and

(d) Intended to become a permanent part of the building.

(2) The most we will pay for loss or damage under this Extension is $5,000 at each described premises, unless a higher Limit of Insurance is specified in the Declarations. Our payment for loss of or damage to property of others will only be for the account of the owner of the property.

b. Sod, Trees, Shrubs And Plants

You may extend the insurance provided by this Coverage Form to apply to loss or damage to sod, trees, shrubs and plants outside of buildings on the described premises, if the loss or damage is caused by or results from any of the following causes of loss:

(1) Fire;

(2) Lightning;

(3) Explosion;

(4) Riot or Civil Commotion; or

(5) Aircraft.

The most we will pay for loss or damage under this Extension is $1,000, but not more than $250 for any one tree, shrub or plant. These limits apply to any one occurrence, regardless of the types or number of items lost or damaged in that occurrence.

Subject to all aforementioned terms and limitations of coverage, this Coverage Extension includes the expense of removing from the described premises the debris of trees, shrubs and plants which are the property of others, except in the situation in which you are a tenant and such property is owned by the landlord of the described premises.

B. Exclusions And Limitations

See applicable Causes Of Loss form as shown in the Declarations.

C. Limits Of Insurance

The most we will pay for loss or damage in any one occurrence is the applicable Limit Of Insurance shown in the Declarations.

The most we will pay for loss or damage to outdoor signs attached to buildings is $2,500 per sign in any one occurrence.

The limits applicable to the Coverage Extensions and the Fire Department Service Charge and Pollutant Clean-up And Removal Additional Coverages are in addition to the Limits of Insurance.

Payments under the Preservation Of Property Additional Coverage will not increase the applicable Limit of Insurance.

D. Deductible

In any one occurrence of loss or damage (hereinafter referred to as loss), we will first reduce the amount of loss if required by the Additional Condition, Need For Adequate Insurance. If the adjusted amount of loss is less than or equal to the Deductible, we will not pay for that loss. If the adjusted amount of loss exceeds the Deductible, we will then subtract the Deductible from the adjusted amount of loss and will pay the resulting amount or the Limit of Insurance, whichever is less.

When the occurrence involves loss to more than one item of Covered Property and separate Limits of Insurance apply, the losses will not be combined in determining application of the Deductible. But the Deductible will be applied only once per occurrence.

Example 1

(This example assumes there is no penalty for underinsurance.)

Deductible:	$ 1,000
Limit of Insurance – Building 1:	$ 60,000
Limit of Insurance – Building 2:	$ 80,000
Loss to Building 1:	$ 60,100
Loss to Building 2:	$ 90,000

The amount of loss to Building 1 ($60,100) is less than the sum ($61,000) of the Limit of Insurance applicable to Building 1 plus the Deductible.

The Deductible will be subtracted from the amount of loss in calculating the loss payable for Building 1:

$ 60,100
– 1,000
$ 59,100   Loss Payable – Building 1

The Deductible applies once per occurrence and therefore is not subtracted in determining the amount of loss payable for Building 2. Loss payable for Building 2 is the Limit of Insurance of $80,000.

Total amount of loss payable: $59,100 + $80,000 = $139,100.

Example 2

(This example, too, assumes there is no penalty for underinsurance.)

The Deductible and Limits of Insurance are the same as those in Example 1.

Loss to Building 1:	$ 70,000
(Exceeds Limit of Insurance plus Deductible)	
Loss to Building 2:	$ 90,000
(Exceeds Limit of Insurance plus Deductible)	
Loss Payable – Building 1:	$ 60,000
(Limit of Insurance)	
Loss Payable – Building 2:	$ 80,000
(Limit of Insurance)	
Total amount of loss payable:	$ 140,000

E. Loss Conditions

The following conditions apply in addition to the Common Policy Conditions and the Commercial Property Conditions.

1. Abandonment

There can be no abandonment of any property to us.

© Insurance Services Office, Inc., 2011   **CP 00 20 10 12**

2. **Appraisal**

If we and you disagree on the value of the property or the amount of loss, either may make written demand for an appraisal of the loss. In this event, each party will select a competent and impartial appraiser. The two appraisers will select an umpire. If they cannot agree, either may request that selection be made by a judge of a court having jurisdiction. The appraisers will state separately the value of the property and amount of loss. If they fail to agree, they will submit their differences to the umpire. A decision agreed to by any two will be binding. Each party will:

a. Pay its chosen appraiser; and

b. Bear the other expenses of the appraisal and umpire equally.

If there is an appraisal, we will still retain our right to deny the claim.

3. **Duties In The Event Of Loss Or Damage**

a. You must see that the following are done in the event of loss or damage to Covered Property:

(1) Notify the police if a law may have been broken.

(2) Give us prompt notice of the loss or damage. Include a description of the property involved.

(3) As soon as possible, give us a description of how, when and where the loss or damage occurred.

(4) Take all reasonable steps to protect the Covered Property from further damage, and keep a record of your expenses necessary to protect the Covered Property, for consideration in the settlement of the claim. This will not increase the Limit of Insurance. However, we will not pay for any subsequent loss or damage resulting from a cause of loss that is not a Covered Cause of Loss. Also, if feasible, set the damaged property aside and in the best possible order for examination.

(5) At our request, give us complete inventories of the damaged and undamaged property. Include quantities, costs, values and amount of loss claimed.

(6) As often as may be reasonably required, permit us to inspect the property proving the loss or damage and examine your books and records.

Also permit us to take samples of damaged and undamaged property for inspection, testing and analysis, and permit us to make copies from your books and records.

(7) Send us a signed, sworn proof of loss containing the information we request to investigate the claim. You must do this within 60 days after our request. We will supply you with the necessary forms.

(8) Cooperate with us in the investigation or settlement of the claim.

b. We may examine any insured under oath, while not in the presence of any other insured and at such times as may be reasonably required, about any matter relating to this insurance or the claim, including an insured's books and records. In the event of an examination, an insured's answers must be signed.

4. **Loss Payment**

a. In the event of loss or damage covered by this Coverage Form, at our option, we will either:

(1) Pay the value of lost or damaged property;

(2) Pay the cost of repairing or replacing the lost or damaged property, subject to **b.** below;

(3) Take all or any part of the property at an agreed or appraised value; or

(4) Repair, rebuild or replace the property with other property of like kind and quality, subject to **b.** below.

We will determine the value of lost or damaged property, or the cost of its repair or replacement, in accordance with the applicable terms of the Valuation Condition in this Coverage Form or any applicable provision which amends or supersedes the Valuation Condition.

b. The cost to repair, rebuild or replace does not include the increased cost attributable to enforcement of or compliance with any ordinance or law regulating the construction, use or repair of any property.

c. We will give notice of our intentions within 30 days after we receive the sworn proof of loss.

d. We will not pay you more than your financial interest in the Covered Property.

e. We may adjust losses with the owners of lost or damaged property if other than you. If we pay the owners, such payments will satisfy your claims against us for the owners' property. We will not pay the owners more than their financial interest in the Covered Property.

f. We may elect to defend you against suits arising from claims of owners of property. We will do this at our expense.

g. We will pay for covered loss or damage within 30 days after we receive the sworn proof of loss, if you have complied with all of the terms of this Coverage Part, and:

(1) We have reached agreement with you on the amount of loss; or

(2) An appraisal award has been made.

h. A party wall is a wall that separates and is common to adjoining buildings that are owned by different parties. In settling covered losses involving a party wall, we will pay a proportion of the loss to the party wall based on your interest in the wall in proportion to the interest of the owner of the adjoining building. However, if you elect to repair or replace your building and the owner of the adjoining building elects not to repair or replace that building, we will pay you the full value of the loss to the party wall, subject to all applicable policy provisions including Limits of Insurance, the Valuation and Coinsurance Conditions and all other provisions of this Loss Payment Condition. Our payment under the provisions of this paragraph does not alter any right of subrogation we may have against any entity, including the owner or insurer of the adjoining building, and does not alter the terms of the Transfer Of Rights Of Recovery Against Others To Us Condition in this policy.

5. Recovered Property

If either you or we recover any property after loss settlement, that party must give the other prompt notice. At your option, the property will be returned to you. You must then return to us the amount we paid to you for the property. We will pay recovery expenses and the expenses to repair the recovered property, subject to the Limit of Insurance.

6. Valuation

We will determine the value of Covered Property at actual cash value as of the time of loss or damage.

F. Additional Conditions

The following conditions apply in addition to the Common Policy Conditions and the Commercial Property Conditions:

1. Mortgageholders

a. The term mortgageholder includes trustee.

b. We will pay for covered loss of or damage to buildings or structures to each mortgageholder shown in the Declarations in their order of precedence, as interests may appear.

c. The mortgageholder has the right to receive loss payment even if the mortgageholder has started foreclosure or similar action on the building or structure.

d. If we deny your claim because of your acts or because you have failed to comply with the terms of this Coverage Part, the mortgageholder will still have the right to receive loss payment if the mortgageholder:

(1) Pays any premium due under this Coverage Part at our request if you have failed to do so;

(2) Submits a signed, sworn proof of loss within 60 days after receiving notice from us of your failure to do so; and

(3) Has notified us of any change in ownership, occupancy or substantial change in risk known to the mortgageholder.

All of the terms of this Coverage Part will then apply directly to the mortgageholder.

e. If we pay the mortgageholder for any loss or damage and deny payment to you because of your acts or because you have failed to comply with the terms of this Coverage Part:

(1) The mortgageholder's rights under the mortgage will be transferred to us to the extent of the amount we pay; and

(2) The mortgageholder's right to recover the full amount of the mortgageholder's claim will not be impaired.

At our option, we may pay to the mortgageholder the whole principal on the mortgage plus any accrued interest. In this event, your mortgage and note will be transferred to us and you will pay your remaining mortgage debt to us.

       CP 00 20 10 12

f. If we cancel this policy, we will give written notice to the mortgageholder at least:

   (1) 10 days before the effective date of cancellation if we cancel for your nonpayment of premium; or

   (2) 30 days before the effective date of cancellation if we cancel for any other reason.

g. If we elect not to renew this policy, we will give written notice to the mortgageholder at least 10 days before the expiration date of this policy.

2. Need For Adequate Insurance

We will not pay a greater share of any loss than the proportion that the Limit of Insurance bears to the value on the date of completion of the building described in the Declarations.

Example 1 (Underinsurance)

When:

The value of the building on the date of completion is:	$ 200,000
The Limit of Insurance for it is:	$ 100,000
The Deductible is:	$ 500
The amount of loss is:	$ 80,000

Step **(1)**: $100,000 ÷ $200,000 = .50

Step **(2)**: $ 80,000 x .50 = $40,000

Step **(3)**: $ 40,000 – $500 = $39,500

We will pay no more than $39,500. The remaining $40,500 is not covered.

Example 2 (Adequate Insurance)

When:

The value of the building on the date of completion is:	$ 200,000
The Limit of Insurance for it is:	$ 200,000
The Deductible is:	$ 1,000
The amount of loss is:	$ 80,000

The Limit of Insurance in this example is adequate and therefore no penalty applies. We will pay no more than $79,000 ($80,000 amount of loss minus the Deductible of $1,000).

3. Restriction Of Additional Coverage – Collapse

If the Causes Of Loss – Broad Form is applicable to this Coverage Form, Paragraph **C.2.f.** of the Additional Coverage, Collapse, does not apply to this Coverage Form.

If the Causes Of Loss – Special Form is applicable to this Coverage Form, Paragraphs **D.2.c.** and **D.2.d.** of the Additional Coverage, Collapse, do not apply to this Coverage Form.

4. When Coverage Ceases

The insurance provided by this Coverage Form will end when one of the following first occurs:

a. This policy expires or is cancelled;

b. The property is accepted by the purchaser;

c. Your interest in the property ceases;

d. You abandon the construction with no intention to complete it;

e. Unless we specify otherwise in writing:

   (1) 90 days after construction is complete; or

   (2) 60 days after any building described in the Declarations is:

      (a) Occupied in whole or in part; or

      (b) Put to its intended use.

G. Definitions

"Pollutants" means any solid, liquid, gaseous or thermal irritant or contaminant, including smoke, vapor, soot, fumes, acids, alkalis, chemicals and waste. Waste includes materials to be recycled, reconditioned or reclaimed.

COMMERCIAL PROPERTY
CP 00 30 10 12

BUSINESS INCOME (AND EXTRA EXPENSE) COVERAGE FORM

Various provisions in this policy restrict coverage. Read the entire policy carefully to determine rights, duties and what is and is not covered.

Throughout this policy, the words "you" and "your" refer to the Named Insured shown in the Declarations. The words "we", "us" and "our" refer to the company providing this insurance.

Other words and phrases that appear in quotation marks have special meaning. Refer to Section **F.** Definitions.

A. Coverage

1. Business Income

Business Income means the:

a. Net Income (Net Profit or Loss before income taxes) that would have been earned or incurred; and

b. Continuing normal operating expenses incurred, including payroll.

For manufacturing risks, Net Income includes the net sales value of production.

Coverage is provided as described and limited below for one or more of the following options for which a Limit Of Insurance is shown in the Declarations:

(1) Business Income Including "Rental Value".

(2) Business Income Other Than "Rental Value".

(3) "Rental Value".

If option **(1)** above is selected, the term Business Income will include "Rental Value". If option **(3)** above is selected, the term Business Income will mean "Rental Value" only.

If Limits of Insurance are shown under more than one of the above options, the provisions of this Coverage Part apply separately to each.

We will pay for the actual loss of Business Income you sustain due to the necessary "suspension" of your "operations" during the "period of restoration". The "suspension" must be caused by direct physical loss of or damage to property at premises which are described in the Declarations and for which a Business Income Limit Of Insurance is shown in the Declarations. The loss or damage must be caused by or result from a Covered Cause of Loss. With respect to loss of or damage to personal property in the open or personal property in a vehicle, the described premises include the area within 100 feet of such premises.

With respect to the requirements set forth in the preceding paragraph, if you occupy only part of a building, your premises means:

(a) The portion of the building which you rent, lease or occupy;

(b) The area within 100 feet of the building or within 100 feet of the premises described in the Declarations, whichever distance is greater (with respect to loss of or damage to personal property in the open or personal property in a vehicle); and

(c) Any area within the building or at the described premises, if that area services, or is used to gain access to, the portion of the building which you rent, lease or occupy.

2. Extra Expense

a. Extra Expense Coverage is provided at the premises described in the Declarations only if the Declarations show that Business Income Coverage applies at that premises.

b. Extra Expense means necessary expenses you incur during the "period of restoration" that you would not have incurred if there had been no direct physical loss or damage to property caused by or resulting from a Covered Cause of Loss.

We will pay Extra Expense (other than the expense to repair or replace property) to:

(1) Avoid or minimize the "suspension" of business and to continue operations at the described premises or at replacement premises or temporary locations, including relocation expenses and costs to equip and operate the replacement location or temporary location.

(2) Minimize the "suspension" of business if you cannot continue "operations".

We will also pay Extra Expense to repair or replace property, but only to the extent it reduces the amount of loss that otherwise would have been payable under this Coverage Form.

3. Covered Causes Of Loss, Exclusions And Limitations

See applicable Causes Of Loss form as shown in the Declarations.

4. Additional Limitation – Interruption Of Computer Operations

a. Coverage for Business Income does not apply when a "suspension" of "operations" is caused by destruction or corruption of electronic data, or any loss or damage to electronic data, except as provided under the Additional Coverage, Interruption Of Computer Operations.

b. Coverage for Extra Expense does not apply when action is taken to avoid or minimize a "suspension" of "operations" caused by destruction or corruption of electronic data, or any loss or damage to electronic data, except as provided under the Additional Coverage, Interruption Of Computer Operations.

c. Electronic data means information, facts or computer programs stored as or on, created or used on, or transmitted to or from computer software (including systems and applications software), on hard or floppy disks, CD-ROMs, tapes, drives, cells, data processing devices or any other repositories of computer software which are used with electronically controlled equipment. The term computer programs, referred to in the foregoing description of electronic data, means a set of related electronic instructions which direct the operations and functions of a computer or device connected to it, which enable the computer or device to receive, process, store, retrieve or send data.

d. This Additional Limitation does not apply when loss or damage to electronic data involves only electronic data which is integrated in and operates or controls a building's elevator, lighting, heating, ventilation, air conditioning or security system.

5. Additional Coverages

a. **Civil Authority**

In this Additional Coverage, Civil Authority, the described premises are premises to which this Coverage Form applies, as shown in the Declarations.

When a Covered Cause of Loss causes damage to property other than property at the described premises, we will pay for the actual loss of Business Income you sustain and necessary Extra Expense caused by action of civil authority that prohibits access to the described premises, provided that both of the following apply:

(1) Access to the area immediately surrounding the damaged property is prohibited by civil authority as a result of the damage, and the described premises are within that area but are not more than one mile from the damaged property; and

(2) The action of civil authority is taken in response to dangerous physical conditions resulting from the damage or continuation of the Covered Cause of Loss that caused the damage, or the action is taken to enable a civil authority to have unimpeded access to the damaged property.

Civil Authority Coverage for Business Income will begin 72 hours after the time of the first action of civil authority that prohibits access to the described premises and will apply for a period of up to four consecutive weeks from the date on which such coverage began.

Civil Authority Coverage for Extra Expense will begin immediately after the time of the first action of civil authority that prohibits access to the described premises and will end:

(1) Four consecutive weeks after the date of that action; or

(2) When your Civil Authority Coverage for Business Income ends;

whichever is later.

       CP 00 30 10 12

b. Alterations And New Buildings

We will pay for the actual loss of Business Income you sustain and necessary Extra Expense you incur due to direct physical loss or damage at the described premises caused by or resulting from any Covered Cause of Loss to:

(1) New buildings or structures, whether complete or under construction;

(2) Alterations or additions to existing buildings or structures; and

(3) Machinery, equipment, supplies or building materials located on or within 100 feet of the described premises and:

(a) Used in the construction, alterations or additions; or

(b) Incidental to the occupancy of new buildings.

If such direct physical loss or damage delays the start of "operations", the "period of restoration" for Business Income Coverage will begin on the date "operations" would have begun if the direct physical loss or damage had not occurred.

c. Extended Business Income

(1) Business Income Other Than "Rental Value"

If the necessary "suspension" of your "operations" produces a Business Income loss payable under this policy, we will pay for the actual loss of Business Income you incur during the period that:

(a) Begins on the date property (except "finished stock") is actually repaired, rebuilt or replaced and "operations" are resumed; and

(b) Ends on the earlier of:

(i) The date you could restore your "operations", with reasonable speed, to the level which would generate the business income amount that would have existed if no direct physical loss or damage had occurred; or

(ii) 60 consecutive days after the date determined in **(1)(a)** above.

However, Extended Business Income does not apply to loss of Business Income incurred as a result of unfavorable business conditions caused by the impact of the Covered Cause of Loss in the area where the described premises are located.

Loss of Business Income must be caused by direct physical loss or damage at the described premises caused by or resulting from any Covered Cause of Loss.

(2) "Rental Value"

If the necessary "suspension" of your "operations" produces a "Rental Value" loss payable under this policy, we will pay for the actual loss of "Rental Value" you incur during the period that:

(a) Begins on the date property is actually repaired, rebuilt or replaced and tenantability is restored; and

(b) Ends on the earlier of:

(i) The date you could restore tenant occupancy, with reasonable speed, to the level which would generate the "Rental Value" that would have existed if no direct physical loss or damage had occurred; or

(ii) 60 consecutive days after the date determined in **(2)(a)** above.

However, Extended Business Income does not apply to loss of "Rental Value" incurred as a result of unfavorable business conditions caused by the impact of the Covered Cause of Loss in the area where the described premises are located.

Loss of "Rental Value" must be caused by direct physical loss or damage at the described premises caused by or resulting from any Covered Cause of Loss.

d. Interruption Of Computer Operations

(1) Under this Additional Coverage, electronic data has the meaning described under Additional Limitation – Interruption Of Computer Operations.

(2) Subject to all provisions of this Additional Coverage, you may extend the insurance that applies to Business Income and Extra Expense to apply to a "suspension" of "operations" caused by an interruption in computer operations due to destruction or corruption of electronic data due to a Covered Cause of Loss. However, we will not provide coverage under this Additional Coverage when the Additional Limitation – Interruption Of Computer Operations does not apply based on Paragraph **A.4.d.** therein.

(3) With respect to the coverage provided under this Additional Coverage, the Covered Causes of Loss are subject to the following:

(a) If the Causes Of Loss – Special Form applies, coverage under this Additional Coverage, Interruption Of Computer Operations, is limited to the "specified causes of loss" as defined in that form and Collapse as set forth in that form.

(b) If the Causes Of Loss – Broad Form applies, coverage under this Additional Coverage, Interruption Of Computer Operations, includes Collapse as set forth in that form.

(c) If the Causes Of Loss form is endorsed to add a Covered Cause of Loss, the additional Covered Cause of Loss does not apply to the coverage provided under this Additional Coverage, Interruption Of Computer Operations.

(d) The Covered Causes of Loss include a virus, harmful code or similar instruction introduced into or enacted on a computer system (including electronic data) or a network to which it is connected, designed to damage or destroy any part of the system or disrupt its normal operation. But there is no coverage for an interruption related to manipulation of a computer system (including electronic data) by any employee, including a temporary or leased employee, or by an entity retained by you or for you to inspect, design, install, maintain, repair or replace that system.

(4) The most we will pay under this Additional Coverage, Interruption Of Computer Operations, is $2,500 (unless a higher limit is shown in the Declarations) for all loss sustained and expense incurred in any one policy year, regardless of the number of interruptions or the number of premises, locations or computer systems involved. If loss payment relating to the first interruption does not exhaust this amount, then the balance is available for loss or expense sustained or incurred as a result of subsequent interruptions in that policy year. A balance remaining at the end of a policy year does not increase the amount of insurance in the next policy year. With respect to any interruption which begins in one policy year and continues or results in additional loss or expense in a subsequent policy year(s), all loss and expense is deemed to be sustained or incurred in the policy year in which the interruption began.

(5) This Additional Coverage, Interruption Of Computer Operations, does not apply to loss sustained or expense incurred after the end of the "period of restoration", even if the amount of insurance stated in **(4)** above has not been exhausted.

6. Coverage Extension

If a Coinsurance percentage of 50% or more is shown in the Declarations, you may extend the insurance provided by this Coverage Part as follows:

Newly Acquired Locations

a. You may extend your Business Income and Extra Expense Coverages to apply to property at any location you acquire other than fairs or exhibitions.

b. The most we will pay under this Extension, for the sum of Business Income loss and Extra Expense incurred, is $100,000 at each location, unless a higher limit is shown in the Declarations.

c. Insurance under this Extension for each newly acquired location will end when any of the following first occurs:

(1) This policy expires;

© Insurance Services Office, Inc., 2011

(2) 30 days expire after you acquire or begin to construct the property; or

(3) You report values to us.

We will charge you additional premium for values reported from the date you acquire the property.

The Additional Condition, Coinsurance, does not apply to this Extension.

B. Limits Of Insurance

The most we will pay for loss in any one occurrence is the applicable Limit Of Insurance shown in the Declarations.

Payments under the following coverages will not increase the applicable Limit of Insurance:

1. Alterations And New Buildings;

2. Civil Authority;

3. Extra Expense; or

4. Extended Business Income.

The amounts of insurance stated in the Interruption Of Computer Operations Additional Coverage and the Newly Acquired Locations Coverage Extension apply in accordance with the terms of those coverages and are separate from the Limit(s) Of Insurance shown in the Declarations for any other coverage.

C. Loss Conditions

The following conditions apply in addition to the Common Policy Conditions and the Commercial Property Conditions:

1. Appraisal

If we and you disagree on the amount of Net Income and operating expense or the amount of loss, either may make written demand for an appraisal of the loss. In this event, each party will select a competent and impartial appraiser.

The two appraisers will select an umpire. If they cannot agree, either may request that selection be made by a judge of a court having jurisdiction. The appraisers will state separately the amount of Net Income and operating expense or amount of loss. If they fail to agree, they will submit their differences to the umpire. A decision agreed to by any two will be binding. Each party will:

a. Pay its chosen appraiser; and

b. Bear the other expenses of the appraisal and umpire equally.

If there is an appraisal, we will still retain our right to deny the claim.

2. Duties In The Event Of Loss

a. You must see that the following are done in the event of loss:

(1) Notify the police if a law may have been broken.

(2) Give us prompt notice of the direct physical loss or damage. Include a description of the property involved.

(3) As soon as possible, give us a description of how, when and where the direct physical loss or damage occurred.

(4) Take all reasonable steps to protect the Covered Property from further damage, and keep a record of your expenses necessary to protect the Covered Property, for consideration in the settlement of the claim. This will not increase the Limit of Insurance. However, we will not pay for any subsequent loss or damage resulting from a cause of loss that is not a Covered Cause of Loss. Also, if feasible, set the damaged property aside and in the best possible order for examination.

(5) As often as may be reasonably required, permit us to inspect the property proving the loss or damage and examine your books and records.

Also permit us to take samples of damaged and undamaged property for inspection, testing and analysis, and permit us to make copies from your books and records.

(6) Send us a signed, sworn proof of loss containing the information we request to investigate the claim. You must do this within 60 days after our request. We will supply you with the necessary forms.

(7) Cooperate with us in the investigation or settlement of the claim.

(8) If you intend to continue your business, you must resume all or part of your "operations" as quickly as possible.

b. We may examine any insured under oath, while not in the presence of any other insured and at such times as may be reasonably required, about any matter relating to this insurance or the claim, including an insured's books and records. In the event of an examination, an insured's answers must be signed.

3. **Loss Determination**

   a. The amount of Business Income loss will be determined based on:

   (1) The Net Income of the business before the direct physical loss or damage occurred;

   (2) The likely Net Income of the business if no physical loss or damage had occurred, but not including any Net Income that would likely have been earned as a result of an increase in the volume of business due to favorable business conditions caused by the impact of the Covered Cause of Loss on customers or on other businesses;

   (3) The operating expenses, including payroll expenses, necessary to resume "operations" with the same quality of service that existed just before the direct physical loss or damage; and

   (4) Other relevant sources of information, including:

   (a) Your financial records and accounting procedures;

   (b) Bills, invoices and other vouchers; and

   (c) Deeds, liens or contracts.

   b. The amount of Extra Expense will be determined based on:

   (1) All expenses that exceed the normal operating expenses that would have been incurred by "operations" during the "period of restoration" if no direct physical loss or damage had occurred. We will deduct from the total of such expenses:

   (a) The salvage value that remains of any property bought for temporary use during the "period of restoration", once "operations" are resumed; and

   (b) Any Extra Expense that is paid for by other insurance, except for insurance that is written subject to the same plan, terms, conditions and provisions as this insurance; and

   (2) Necessary expenses that reduce the Business Income loss that otherwise would have been incurred.

   c. **Resumption Of Operations**

   We will reduce the amount of your:

   (1) Business Income loss, other than Extra Expense, to the extent you can resume your "operations", in whole or in part, by using damaged or undamaged property (including merchandise or stock) at the described premises or elsewhere.

   (2) Extra Expense loss to the extent you can return "operations" to normal and discontinue such Extra Expense.

   d. If you do not resume "operations", or do not resume "operations" as quickly as possible, we will pay based on the length of time it would have taken to resume "operations" as quickly as possible.

4. **Loss Payment**

   We will pay for covered loss within 30 days after we receive the sworn proof of loss, if you have complied with all of the terms of this Coverage Part, and:

   a. We have reached agreement with you on the amount of loss; or

   b. An appraisal award has been made.

D. **Additional Condition**

COINSURANCE

If a Coinsurance percentage is shown in the Declarations, the following condition applies in addition to the Common Policy Conditions and the Commercial Property Conditions.

We will not pay the full amount of any Business Income loss if the Limit of Insurance for Business Income is less than:

1. The Coinsurance percentage shown for Business Income in the Declarations; times

2. The sum of:

   a. The Net Income (Net Profit or Loss before income taxes), and

   b. Operating expenses, including payroll expenses,

   that would have been earned or incurred (had no loss occurred) by your "operations" at the described premises for the 12 months following the inception, or last previous anniversary date, of this policy (whichever is later).

       CP 00 30 10 12

Instead, we will determine the most we will pay using the following steps:

Step **(1):** Multiply the Net Income and operating expense for the 12 months following the inception, or last previous anniversary date, of this policy by the Coinsurance percentage;

Step **(2):** Divide the Limit of Insurance for the described premises by the figure determined in Step **(1);** and

Step **(3):** Multiply the total amount of loss by the figure determined in Step **(2).**

We will pay the amount determined in Step **(3)** or the limit of insurance, whichever is less. For the remainder, you will either have to rely on other insurance or absorb the loss yourself.

In determining operating expenses for the purpose of applying the Coinsurance condition, the following expenses, if applicable, shall be deducted from the total of all operating expenses:

    (1) Prepaid freight – outgoing;

    (2) Returns and allowances;

    (3) Discounts;

    (4) Bad debts;

    (5) Collection expenses;

    (6) Cost of raw stock and factory supplies consumed (including transportation charges);

    (7) Cost of merchandise sold (including transportation charges);

    (8) Cost of other supplies consumed (including transportation charges);

    (9) Cost of services purchased from outsiders (not employees) to resell, that do not continue under contract;

    (10) Power, heat and refrigeration expenses that do not continue under contract (if Form **CP 15 11** is attached);

    (11) All payroll expenses or the amount of payroll expense excluded (if Form **CP 15 10** is attached); and

    (12) Special deductions for mining properties (royalties unless specifically included in coverage; actual depletion commonly known as unit or cost depletion – not percentage depletion; welfare and retirement fund charges based on tonnage; hired trucks).

Example 1 (Underinsurance)

When: The Net Income and operating expenses for the 12 months following the inception, or last previous anniversary date, of this policy at the described premises would have been: $ 400,000

    The Coinsurance percentage is: 50%

    The Limit of Insurance is: $ 150,000

    The amount of loss is: $ 80,000

Step **(1):** $400,000 x 50% = $200,000

    (the minimum amount of insurance to meet your Coinsurance requirements)

Step **(2):** $150,000 ÷ $200,000 = .75

Step **(3):** $80,000 x .75 = $60,000

We will pay no more than $60,000. The remaining $20,000 is not covered.

Example 2 (Adequate Insurance)

When: The Net Income and operating expenses for the 12 months following the inception, or last previous anniversary date, of this policy at the described premises would have been: $ 400,000

    The Coinsurance percentage is: 50%

    The Limit of Insurance is: $ 200,000

    The amount of loss is: $ 80,000

The minimum amount of insurance to meet your Coinsurance requirement is $200,000 ($400,000 x 50%). Therefore, the Limit of Insurance in this example is adequate and no penalty applies. We will pay no more than $80,000 (amount of loss).

This condition does not apply to Extra Expense Coverage.

E. Optional Coverages

    If shown as applicable in the Declarations, the following Optional Coverages apply separately to each item.

    1. Maximum Period Of Indemnity

        a. The Additional Condition, Coinsurance, does not apply to this Coverage Form at the described premises to which this Optional Coverage applies.

b. The most we will pay for the total of Business Income loss and Extra Expense is the lesser of:

(1) The amount of loss sustained and expenses incurred during the 120 days immediately following the beginning of the "period of restoration"; or

(2) The Limit Of Insurance shown in the Declarations.

2. Monthly Limit Of Indemnity

a. The Additional Condition, Coinsurance, does not apply to this Coverage Form at the described premises to which this Optional Coverage applies.

b. The most we will pay for loss of Business Income in each period of 30 consecutive days after the beginning of the "period of restoration" is:

(1) The Limit of Insurance, multiplied by

(2) The fraction shown in the Declarations for this Optional Coverage.

Example

When:	The Limit of Insurance is:	$ 120,000
	The fraction shown in the Declarations for this Optional Coverage is:	1/4
	The most we will pay for loss in each period of 30 consecutive days is:	$ 30,000

($120,000 x 1/4 = $30,000)

If, in this example, the actual amount of loss is:

Days 1–30:	$ 40,000
Days 31–60:	$ 20,000
Days 61–90:	$ 30,000
	$ 90,000

We will pay:

Days 1–30:	$ 30,000
Days 31–60:	$ 20,000
Days 61–90:	$ 30,000
	$ 80,000

The remaining $10,000 is not covered.

3. Business Income Agreed Value

a. To activate this Optional Coverage:

(1) A Business Income Report/Work Sheet must be submitted to us and must show financial data for your "operations":

(a) During the 12 months prior to the date of the Work Sheet; and

(b) Estimated for the 12 months immediately following the inception of this Optional Coverage.

(2) The Declarations must indicate that the Business Income Agreed Value Optional Coverage applies, and an Agreed Value must be shown in the Declarations. The Agreed Value should be at least equal to:

(a) The Coinsurance percentage shown in the Declarations; multiplied by

(b) The amount of Net Income and operating expenses for the following 12 months you report on the Work Sheet.

b. The Additional Condition, Coinsurance, is suspended until:

(1) 12 months after the effective date of this Optional Coverage; or

(2) The expiration date of this policy;

whichever occurs first.

c. We will reinstate the Additional Condition, Coinsurance, automatically if you do not submit a new Work Sheet and Agreed Value:

(1) Within 12 months of the effective date of this Optional Coverage; or

(2) When you request a change in your Business Income Limit of Insurance.

d. If the Business Income Limit of Insurance is less than the Agreed Value, we will not pay more of any loss than the amount of loss multiplied by:

(1) The Business Income Limit of Insurance; divided by

(2) The Agreed Value.

Example

When:	The Limit of Insurance is:	$ 100,000
	The Agreed Value is:	$ 200,000
	The amount of loss is:	$ 80,000

Step (1): $100,000 ÷ $200,000 = .50

Step (2): .50 x $80,000 = $40,000

We will pay $40,000. The remaining $40,000 is not covered.

4. Extended Period Of Indemnity

Under Paragraph **A.5.c., Extended Business Income**, the number 60 in Subparagraphs **(1)(b)** and **(2)(b)** is replaced by the number shown in the Declarations for this Optional Coverage.

F. Definitions

1. "Finished stock" means stock you have manufactured.

   "Finished stock" also includes whiskey and alcoholic products being aged, unless there is a Coinsurance percentage shown for Business Income in the Declarations.

   "Finished stock" does not include stock you have manufactured that is held for sale on the premises of any retail outlet insured under this Coverage Part.

2. "Operations" means:

   a. Your business activities occurring at the described premises; and

   b. The tenantability of the described premises, if coverage for Business Income Including "Rental Value" or "Rental Value" applies.

3. "Period of restoration" means the period of time that:

   a. Begins:

      (1) 72 hours after the time of direct physical loss or damage for Business Income Coverage; or

      (2) Immediately after the time of direct physical loss or damage for Extra Expense Coverage;

      caused by or resulting from any Covered Cause of Loss at the described premises; and

   b. Ends on the earlier of:

      (1) The date when the property at the described premises should be repaired, rebuilt or replaced with reasonable speed and similar quality; or

      (2) The date when business is resumed at a new permanent location.

   "Period of restoration" does not include any increased period required due to the enforcement of or compliance with any ordinance or law that:

      (1) Regulates the construction, use or repair, or requires the tearing down, of any property; or

      (2) Requires any insured or others to test for, monitor, clean up, remove, contain, treat, detoxify or neutralize, or in any way respond to, or assess the effects of "pollutants".

   The expiration date of this policy will not cut short the "period of restoration".

4. "Pollutants" means any solid, liquid, gaseous or thermal irritant or contaminant, including smoke, vapor, soot, fumes, acids, alkalis, chemicals and waste. Waste includes materials to be recycled, reconditioned or reclaimed.

5. "Rental Value" means Business Income that consists of:

   a. Net Income (Net Profit or Loss before income taxes) that would have been earned or incurred as rental income from tenant occupancy of the premises described in the Declarations as furnished and equipped by you, including fair rental value of any portion of the described premises which is occupied by you; and

   b. Continuing normal operating expenses incurred in connection with that premises, including:

      (1) Payroll; and

      (2) The amount of charges which are the legal obligation of the tenant(s) but would otherwise be your obligations.

6. "Suspension" means:

   a. The slowdown or cessation of your business activities; or

   b. That a part or all of the described premises is rendered untenantable, if coverage for Business Income Including "Rental Value" or "Rental Value" applies.

COMMERCIAL PROPERTY
CP 00 40 10 12

LEGAL LIABILITY COVERAGE FORM

Various provisions in this policy restrict coverage. Read the entire policy carefully to determine rights, duties and what is and is not covered.

Throughout this policy, the words "you" and "your" refer to the Named Insured shown in the Declarations. The words "we", "us" and "our" refer to the company providing this insurance.

Other words and phrases that appear in quotation marks have special meaning. Refer to Section **F.** Definitions.

A. Coverage

We will pay those sums that you become legally obligated to pay as damages because of direct physical loss or damage, including loss of use, to Covered Property caused by accident and arising out of any Covered Cause of Loss. We will have the right and duty to defend any "suit" seeking those damages. However, we have no duty to defend you against a "suit" seeking damages for direct physical loss or damage to which this insurance does not apply. We may investigate and settle any claim or "suit" at our discretion. But:

(1) The amount we will pay for damages is limited as described in Section **C.** Limits Of Insurance; and

(2) Our right and duty to defend end when we have used up the Limit of Insurance in the payment of judgments or settlements.

1. Covered Property And Limitations

Covered Property, as used in this Coverage Form, means tangible property of others in your care, custody or control that is described in the Declarations or on the Legal Liability Coverage Schedule.

Covered Property does not include electronic data. Electronic data means information, facts or computer programs stored as or on, created or used on, or transmitted to or from computer software (including systems and applications software), on hard or floppy disks, CD-ROMs, tapes, drives, cells, data processing devices or any other repositories of computer software which are used with electronically controlled equipment. The term computer programs, referred to in the foregoing description of electronic data, means a set of related electronic instructions which direct the operations and functions of a computer or device connected to it, which enable the computer or device to receive, process, store, retrieve or send data. This paragraph does not apply to electronic data which is integrated in and operates or controls the building's elevator, lighting, heating, ventilation, air conditioning or security system.

2. Covered Causes Of Loss

See applicable Causes of Loss form as shown in the Declarations.

3. **Additional Coverage**

SUPPLEMENTARY PAYMENTS

We will pay, with respect to any claim or any "suit" against you we defend:

a. All expenses we incur.

b. The cost of bonds to release attachments, but only for bond amounts within our Limit of Insurance. We do not have to furnish these bonds.

c. All reasonable expenses incurred by you at our request, including actual loss of earnings up to $250 a day because of time off from work.

d. All costs taxed against you in the "suit".

e. Prejudgment interest awarded against you on that part of the judgment we pay. If we make an offer to pay the Limit of Insurance, we will not pay any prejudgment interest based on that period of time after the offer.

f. All interest on the full amount of any judgment that accrues after entry of the judgment and before we have paid, offered to pay, or deposited in court the part of the judgment that is within our Limit of Insurance.

These payments will not reduce the applicable Limit of Insurance.

4. **Coverage Extensions**

a. **Additional Insureds**

If the Named Insured shown in the Declarations is a partnership, limited liability company or corporation, throughout this Coverage Form the words "you" and "your" include:

(1) Partners, members, executive officers, trustees, directors and stockholders of such partnership, limited liability company or corporation, but only with respect to their duties as such; and

(2) Managers of a limited liability company, but only with respect to their duties as such.

b. **Newly Acquired Organizations**

Throughout this Coverage Form, the words "you" and "your" also include any organization (other than a partnership, joint venture or limited liability company) you newly acquire or form and over which you maintain ownership or majority interest if there is no other similar insurance available to that organization.

This Coverage Extension ends:

(1) 90 days after you acquire or form the organization; or

(2) At the end of the policy period shown in the Declarations;

whichever is earlier.

This Extension does not apply to direct physical loss or damage that occurred before you acquired or formed the organization.

c. **Newly Acquired Property**

(1) You may extend the insurance that applies to Covered Property, as used in this Coverage Form, to apply to your liability for tangible property of others that comes under your care, custody or control after the beginning of the current policy period. This Extension is subject to the following:

(a) All terms and Conditions of this Coverage Form.

(b) Buildings must be intended for:

(i) Similar use as the building described in the Declarations or on the Legal Liability Coverage Schedule; or

(ii) Use as a warehouse.

The most we will pay as the result of any one accident for loss or damage to buildings covered under this Extension is $250,000 at each building.

(c) Personal property must be at a location:

(i) That you own; or

(ii) That is or comes under your care, custody or control;

other than at fairs or exhibitions.

The most we will pay as the result of any one accident for loss or damage to personal property covered under this Extension is $100,000 at each building.

(2) Insurance under this Extension for each item of property of others will end when any of the following first occurs:

(a) This policy expires;

(b) 30 days expire after the property has come under your care, custody or control; or

(c) You report values to us.

© Insurance Services Office, Inc., 2011   CP 00 40 10 12

We will charge you additional premium for values reported from the date the property comes under your care, custody or control.

This Extension does not apply to direct physical loss or damage that occurred before the property came under your care, custody or control.

B. Exclusions And Limitations

See applicable Causes of Loss form as shown in the Declarations.

C. Limits Of Insurance

The most we will pay in damages as the result of any one accident is the applicable Limit Of Insurance shown on the Legal Liability Coverage Schedule, or in the Declarations.

Payments under the Additional Coverage and the Newly Acquired Property Coverage Extension are in addition to the Limits of Insurance.

The existence of one or more:

1. Additional Insureds; or

2. Newly Acquired Organizations,

does not increase the Limit of Insurance.

D. Loss Conditions

The following conditions apply in addition to the Commercial Property Conditions:

1. **Duties In The Event Of Accident, Claim Or Suit**

   a. You must see to it that we are notified promptly of any accident that may result in a claim. Notice should include:

      (1) How, when and where the accident took place; and

      (2) The names and addresses of any witnesses.

      Notice of an accident is not notice of a claim.

   b. If a claim is made or "suit" is brought against you, you must see to it that we receive prompt written notice of the claim or "suit".

   c. You must:

      (1) Immediately send us copies of any demands, notices, summonses or legal papers received in connection with the claim or "suit";

      (2) Authorize us to obtain records and other information;

      (3) Cooperate with us in the investigation, settlement or defense of the claim or "suit"; and

      (4) Assist us, upon our request, in the enforcement of any right against any person or organization that may be liable to you because of damage to which this insurance may also apply.

   d. You will not, except at your own cost, voluntarily make a payment, assume any obligation, or incur any expense without our consent.

2. **Legal Action Against Us**

   No person or organization has a right under this Coverage Form:

   a. To join us as a party or otherwise bring us into a "suit" asking for damages from you; or

   b. To sue us on this Coverage Form unless all of its terms have been fully complied with.

   A person or organization may sue us to recover on an agreed settlement or on a final judgment against you obtained after an actual trial; but we will not be liable for damages that are not payable under the terms of this Coverage Form or that are in excess of the Limit of Insurance. An agreed settlement means a settlement and release of liability signed by us, you and the claimant or the claimant's legal representative.

3. **Other Insurance**

   You may have other insurance covering the same loss as the insurance under this Coverage Form. If you do, we will pay our share of the covered loss. Our share is the proportion that the Limit of Insurance under this Coverage Form covering such loss bears to the Limits of Insurance of all insurance covering the loss.

4. **Transfer Of Rights Of Recovery Against Others To Us**

   If you have rights to recover all or part of any payment we have made under this Coverage Form, those rights are transferred to us. You must do nothing after loss to impair them. At our request, you will bring "suit" or transfer those rights to us and help us enforce them.

E. Additional Conditions

The following conditions apply in addition to the Common Policy Conditions:

1. **Amendment Of Commercial Property Conditions**

   None of the Commercial Property Conditions apply to this Coverage Form, except:

   a. Condition A. Concealment, Misrepresentation Or Fraud;

b. Condition **C.** Insurance Under Two Or More Coverages; and

c. Condition **E.** Liberalization.

2. Bankruptcy

Bankruptcy or insolvency of you or your estate will not relieve us of our obligations under this Coverage Form.

3. Policy Period, Coverage Territory

Under this Coverage Form:

a. We will pay for loss or damage caused by an accident that occurs:

(1) During the Policy Period shown in the Declarations; and

(2) Within the coverage territory.

b. The coverage territory is:

(1) The United States of America;

(2) Puerto Rico; and

(3) Canada.

4. Separation Of Insureds

The insurance under this Coverage Form applies separately to you and each additional insured, except with respect to the Limits of Insurance.

F. Definitions

"Suit" includes an arbitration proceeding to which you must submit or submit with our consent.

COMMERCIAL PROPERTY
CP 00 60 06 95

LEASEHOLD INTEREST COVERAGE FORM

Throughout this policy the words "you" and "your" refer to the Named Insured shown in the Declarations. The words "we", "us" and "our" refer to the Company providing this insurance.

Other words and phrases that appear in quotation marks have special meaning. Refer to SECTION **F. – DEFINITIONS**.

A. COVERAGE

We will pay for loss of Covered Leasehold Interest you sustain due to the cancellation of your lease. The cancellation must result from direct physical loss of or damage to property at the premises described in the Declarations caused by or resulting from any Covered Cause of Loss.

1. Covered Leasehold Interest

Covered Leasehold Interest means the following for which an amount of "net leasehold interest" at inception is shown in the Leasehold Interest Coverage Schedule:

a. Tenants' Lease Interest, meaning the difference between the:

(1) Rent you pay at the described premises; and

(2) Rental value of the described premises that you lease.

b. Bonus Payments, meaning the unamortized portion of a cash bonus that will not be refunded to you. A cash bonus is money you paid to acquire your lease. It does not include:

(1) Rent, whether or not prepaid; or

(2) Security.

c. Improvements and Betterments, meaning the unamortized portion of payments made by you for improvements and betterments. It does not include the value of improvements and betterments recoverable under any other insurance, but only to the extent of such other insurance.

Improvements and betterments are fixtures, alterations, installations or additions:

(1) Made a part of the building or structure you occupy but do not own; and

(2) You acquired or made at your expense but cannot legally remove.

d. Prepaid Rent, meaning the unamortized portion of any amount of advance rent you paid that will not be refunded to you. This does not include the customary rent due at:

(1) The beginning of each month; or

(2) Any other rental period.

2. Covered Causes Of Loss

See applicable Causes of Loss Form as shown in the Declarations.

B. EXCLUSIONS AND LIMITATIONS

See applicable Causes of Loss Form as shown in the Declarations.

C. LIMITS OF INSURANCE

1. Applicable to Tenants' Lease Interest

a. The most we will pay for loss because of the cancellation of any one lease is your "net leasehold interest" at the time of loss.

But, if your lease is cancelled and your landlord lets you continue to use your premises under a new lease or other arrangement, the most we will pay for loss because of the cancellation of any one lease is the lesser of:

(1) The difference between the rent you now pay and the rent you will pay under the new lease or other arrangement; or

(2) Your "net leasehold interest" at the time of loss.

b. Your "net leasehold interest" decreases automatically each month. The amount of "net leasehold interest" at any time is your "gross leasehold interest" times the leasehold interest factor for the remaining months of your lease. A proportionate share applies for any period of time less than a month.

Refer to the end of this form for a table of leasehold interest factors.

2. Applicable to Bonus Payments, Improvements and Betterments and Prepaid Rent

a. The most we will pay for loss because of the cancellation of any one lease is your "net leasehold interest" at the time of loss.

But, if your lease is cancelled and your landlord lets you continue to use your premises under a new lease or other arrangement, the most we will pay for loss because of the cancellation of any one lease is the lesser of:

(1) The loss sustained by you; or

(2) Your "net leasehold interest" at the time of loss.

b. Your "net leasehold interest" decreases automatically each month. The amount of each decrease is your "monthly leasehold interest". A proportionate share applies for any period of time less than a month.

D. LOSS CONDITIONS

The following conditions apply in addition to the Common Policy Conditions and the Commercial Property Conditions.

1. Appraisal

If we and you disagree on the amount of loss, either may make written demand for an appraisal. In this event, each party will select a competent and impartial appraiser. The two appraisers will select an umpire. If they cannot agree, either may request that selection be made by a judge of a court having jurisdiction. The appraisers will state the amount of loss. If they fail to agree, they will submit their differences to the umpire. A decision agreed to by any two will be binding. Each party will:

a. Pay its chosen appraiser; and

b. Bear the other expenses of the appraisal and umpire equally.

If there is an appraisal, we will still retain our right to deny the claim.

2. Duties In The Event Of Loss Of Covered Leasehold Interest

a. You must see that the following are done in the event of loss of Covered Leasehold Interest:

(1) Notify the police if a law may have been broken.

(2) Give us prompt notice of the direct physical loss or damage. Include a description of the property involved.

(3) As soon as possible, give us a description of how, when and where the direct physical loss or damage occurred.

(4) Take all reasonable steps to protect the property at the described premises from further damage by a Covered Cause of Loss. However, we will not pay for any subsequent loss or damage resulting from a cause of loss that is not a Covered Cause of Loss. Also, if feasible, set the damaged property aside and in the best possible order for examination.

(5) As often as may be reasonably required, permit us to inspect the property proving the loss or damage and examine your books and records.

Also permit us to take samples of damaged and undamaged property for inspection, testing and analysis, and permit us to make copies from your books and records.

(6) Send us a signed, sworn proof of loss containing the information we request to investigate the claim. You must do this within 60 days after our request. We will supply you with the necessary forms.

(7) Cooperate with us in the investigation or settlement of the claim.

b. We may examine any insured under oath, while not in the presence of any other insured and at such times as may be reasonably required, about any matter relating to this insurance or the claim, including an insured's books and records. In the event of an examination, an insured's answers must be signed.

3. Loss Payment

We will pay for covered loss within 30 days after we receive the sworn proof of loss, if:

a. You have complied with all of the terms of this Coverage Part; and

b.(1) We have reached agreement with you on the amount of loss; or

(2) An appraisal award has been made.

4. Vacancy

a. Description of Terms

(1) As used in this Vacancy Condition, with respect to the tenant's interest in Covered Property, building means the unit or suite rented or leased to the tenant. Such building is vacant when it does not contain enough business personal property to conduct customary operations.

(2) Buildings under construction or renovation are not considered vacant.

b. Vacancy Provisions – Subleased Premises

The following provisions apply if the building where direct physical loss or damage occurs has been vacant for more than 60 consecutive days before that loss or damage occurs, provided you have entered into an agreement to sublease the described premises as of the time of loss or damage:

(1) We will not pay for any loss or damage caused by any of the following even if they are Covered Causes of Loss:

(a) Vandalism;

(b) Sprinkler leakage, unless you have protected the system against freezing;

(c) Building glass breakage;

(d) Water damage;

(e) Theft; or

(f) Attempted theft.

(2) With respect to a Covered Cause of Loss not listed in **(1)(a)** through **(1)(f)** above, we will reduce the amount we would otherwise pay for the loss or damage by 15%.

c. If you have not entered into an agreement to sublease the described premises as of the time of loss or damage, we will not pay for any loss of Covered Leasehold Interest.

E. ADDITIONAL CONDITION

The following condition replaces the Cancellation Common Policy Condition:

CANCELLATION

1. The first Named Insured shown in the Declarations may cancel this policy by mailing or delivering to us advance notice of cancellation.

2. We may cancel this policy by mailing or delivering to the first Named Insured written notice of cancellation at least:

a. 10 days before the effective date of cancellation if we cancel for nonpayment of premium; or

b. 30 days before the effective date of cancellation if we cancel for any other reason.

3. We will mail or deliver our notice to the first Named Insured's last mailing address known to us.

4. Notice of cancellation will state the effective date of cancellation. The policy will end on that date.

5. If this policy is cancelled, we will send the first Named Insured any premium refund due. The cancellation will be effective even if we have not made or offered a refund.

6. If this coverage is cancelled, we will calculate the earned premium by:

a. Computing the average of the "net leasehold interest" at the:

(1) Inception date, and

(2) Cancellation date,

of this coverage.

b. Multiplying the rate for the period of coverage by the average "net leasehold interest".

c. If we cancel, we will send you a premium refund based on the difference between the:

(1) Premium you originally paid us; and

(2) Proportion of the premium calculated by multiplying the amount in paragraph **a.** times the rate for the period of coverage for the expired term of the policy.

d. If you cancel, your refund may be less than the refund calculated in paragraph **c.**

7. If notice is mailed, proof of mailing will be sufficient proof of notice.

F. DEFINITIONS

1. **"Gross Leasehold Interest"** means the difference between the:

   a. Monthly rental value of the premises you lease; and

   b. Actual monthly rent you pay including taxes, insurance, janitorial or other service that you pay for as part of the rent.

   This amount is not changed:

   (1) Whether you occupy all or part of the premises; or

   (2) If you sublet the premises.

   Example:

Rental value of your leased premises	$5,000
Monthly rent including taxes, insurance, janitorial or other service that you pay for as part of the rent	−4,000
"Gross Leasehold Interest"	$1,000

2. **"Monthly Leasehold Interest"** means the monthly portion of covered Bonus Payments, Improvements and Betterments and Prepaid Rent. To find your "monthly leasehold interest", divide your original costs of Bonus Payments, Improvements and Betterments or Prepaid Rent by the number of months left in your lease at the time of the expenditure.

   Example:

Original cost of Bonus Payment	$12,000
With 24 months left in the lease at time of Bonus Payment	÷ 24
"Monthly Leasehold Interest"	$500

3. **"Net Leasehold Interest":**

   a. Applicable to Tenants' Lease Interest.

      "Net Leasehold Interest" means the present value of your "gross leasehold interest" for each remaining month of the term of the lease at the rate of interest shown in the Leasehold Interest Coverage Schedule.

      The "net leasehold interest" is the amount that, placed at the rate of interest shown in the Leasehold Interest Coverage Schedule, would be equivalent to your receiving the "Gross Leasehold Interest" for each separate month of the unexpired term of the lease.

      To find your "net leasehold interest" at any time, multiply your "gross leasehold interest" by the leasehold interest factor found in the table of leasehold interest factors attached to this form.

      Example:

      (20 months left in lease, 10% effective annual rate of interest)

"Gross Leasehold Interest"	$ 1,000
Leasehold Interest Factor	× 18.419
"Net Leasehold Interest"	$18,419

   b. Applicable to Bonus Payments, Improvements and Betterments or Prepaid Rent.

      "Net Leasehold Interest" means the unamortized amount shown in the Schedule. Your "net leasehold interest" at any time is your "monthly leasehold interest" times the number of months left in your lease.

      Example:

"Monthly Leasehold Interest"	$ 500
With 10 months left in lease	× 10
"Net Leasehold Interest"	$5,000

     CP 00 60 06 95   □

COMMERCIAL PROPERTY
CP 00 70 10 12

MORTGAGEHOLDERS ERRORS AND OMISSIONS COVERAGE FORM

Various provisions in this policy restrict coverage. Read the entire policy carefully to determine rights, duties and what is and is not covered.

Throughout this policy, the words "you" and "your" refer to the Named Insured shown in the Declarations. The words "we", "us" and "our" refer to the company providing this insurance.

Other words and phrases that appear in quotation marks have special meaning. Refer to Section **G.** Definitions.

A. Coverage

1. Coverage A – Mortgageholder's Interest

We will pay for loss to your "mortgageholder's interest" in Covered Property due to error or accidental omission, by you or your representative, in the operation of your customary procedure in requiring, procuring and maintaining "valid insurance" payable to you as mortgageholder against the Covered Causes of Loss.

a. Covered Property

Covered Property means:

(1) Real property; and

(2) Personal property secured in connection with that real property.

It includes such property:

(a) During and after your foreclosure; and

(b) Sold under an agreement in which you retain title, such as a conditional sales agreement.

b. Property Not Covered

Covered Property does not include:

(1) Accounts, bills, currency, deeds, food stamps or other evidences of debt, money, notes or securities. Lottery tickets held for sale are not securities;

(2) Land (including land on which the property is located), water, growing crops or lawns (other than lawns which are part of a vegetated roof); or

(3) Electronic data, meaning information, facts or computer programs stored as or on, created or used on, or transmitted to or from computer software (including systems and applications software), on hard or floppy disks, CD-ROMs, tapes, drives, cells, data processing devices or any other repositories of computer software which are used with electronically controlled equipment. The term computer programs, referred to in the foregoing description of electronic data, means a set of related electronic instructions which direct the operations and functions of a computer or device connected to it, which enable the computer or device to receive, process, store, retrieve or send data. This paragraph, **(3)**, does not apply to electronic data which is integrated in and operates or controls the building's elevator, lighting, heating, ventilation, air conditioning or security system.

c. Covered Causes Of Loss

The Covered Causes of Loss are those causes of loss against which you customarily require mortgagors to provide insurance policies that protect your "mortgageholder's interest". They do not include:

(1) Causes of Loss excluded under Section **B.** Exclusions; or

(2) Losses insured under mortgage guarantee insurance policies or programs, or title, life, health or accident insurance policies.

d. Coverage Extension – Mortgages Serviced For Others

We will cover loss arising from mortgages owned by others and serviced by you as if you owned the "mortgageholder's interest" in them. All such mortgages must be serviced under a written contract. We will make loss payment payable jointly to you and the mortgage owner.

2. Coverage B – Property Owned Or Held In Trust

We will pay for direct physical loss of or damage to Covered Property caused by or resulting from any Covered Cause of Loss; provided the loss is not otherwise insured due to error or accidental omission, by you or your representative, in the operation of your customary procedure in procuring and maintaining "valid insurance" payable to you as owner or trustee of the Covered Property.

a. Covered Property

Covered Property means real and personal property:

(1) You own; or

(2) In which you have a fiduciary interest as trustee or otherwise.

b. Property Not Covered

Covered Property does not include:

(1) Accounts, bills, currency, deeds, food stamps or other evidences of debt, money, notes or securities. Lottery tickets held for sale are not securities;

(2) Land (including land on which the property is located), water, growing crops or lawns (other than lawns which are part of a vegetated roof); or

(3) Electronic data, meaning information, facts or computer programs stored as or on, created or used on, or transmitted to or from computer software (including systems and applications software), on hard or floppy disks, CD-ROMs, tapes, drives, cells, data processing devices or any other repositories of computer software which are used with electronically controlled equipment. The term computer programs, referred to in the foregoing description of electronic data, means a set of related electronic instructions which direct the operations and functions of a computer or device connected to it, which enable the computer or device to receive, process, store, retrieve or send data. This paragraph, **(3),** does not apply to electronic data which is integrated in and operates or controls the building's elevator, lighting, heating, ventilation, air conditioning or security system.

c. Covered Causes Of Loss

The Covered Causes of Loss are:

(1) Fire.

(2) Lightning.

(3) Explosion, including the explosion of gases or fuel within the furnace of any fired vessel or within the flues or passages through which the gases of combustion pass. This cause of loss does not include loss or damage by:

(a) Rupture, bursting or operation of pressure-relief devices; or

(b) Rupture or bursting due to expansion or swelling of the contents of any building or structure, caused by or resulting from water.

(4) Windstorm or Hail, but not including:

(a) Frost or cold weather;

(b) Ice (other than hail), snow or sleet, whether driven by wind or not;

(c) Loss or damage to the interior of any building or structure, or the property inside the building or structure, caused by rain, snow, sand or dust, whether driven by wind or not, unless the building or structure first sustains wind or hail damage to its roof or walls through which the rain, snow, sand or dust enters; or

(d) Loss or damage by hail to lawns, trees, shrubs or plants which are part of a vegetated roof.

               CP 00 70 10 12

(5) Smoke causing sudden and accidental loss or damage. This cause of loss does not include smoke from agricultural smudging or industrial operations.

(6) Aircraft or Vehicles, meaning only physical contact of an aircraft, a spacecraft, a self-propelled missile, a vehicle or an object thrown up by a vehicle with the property or with the building or structure containing the property. This cause of loss includes loss or damage by objects falling from aircraft.

We will not pay for loss or damage caused by or resulting from vehicles you own or operate.

(7) Riot or Civil Commotion, including:

(a) Acts of striking employees while occupying the premises; and

(b) Looting occurring at the time and place of a riot or civil commotion.

(8) Sinkhole Collapse, meaning loss or damage caused by the sudden sinking or collapse of land into underground empty spaces created by the action of water on limestone or dolomite. This cause of loss does not include:

(a) The cost of filling sinkholes; or

(b) Sinking or collapse of land into man-made underground cavities.

(9) Volcanic Action, meaning direct loss or damage resulting from the eruption of a volcano when the loss or damage is caused by:

(a) Airborne volcanic blast or airborne shock waves;

(b) Ash, dust or particulate matter; or

(c) Lava flow.

With respect to coverage for Volcanic Action as set forth in **(9)(a)**, **(9)(b)** and **(9)(c)**, all volcanic eruptions that occur within any 168-hour period will constitute a single occurrence.

This cause of loss does not include the cost to remove ash, dust or particulate matter that does not cause direct physical loss or damage to the property.

3. Coverage C – Mortgageholder's Liability

We will pay those sums that you become legally obligated to pay as damages due to error or accidental omission in the operation of your customary procedure in processing and maintaining "valid insurance" against the Covered Causes of Loss for the benefit of the mortgagor in amounts, and under conditions, customarily accepted by the mortgagor. We will have the right and duty to defend any "suit" seeking those damages. However, we have no duty to defend you against a "suit" seeking damages to which this insurance does not apply. We may investigate and settle any claim or "suit" at our discretion. But:

(1) The amount we will pay for damages is limited as described in Section **C.** Limits Of Insurance; and

(2) Our right and duty to defend end when we have used up the Limit of Insurance in the payment of judgments or settlements.

The damages payable under this Coverage Form must arise out of your capacity as a mortgageholder, mortgage fiduciary or mortgage servicing agency.

a. Covered Causes Of Loss

The Covered Causes of Loss are those causes of loss against which the mortgagor customarily obtains insurance policies.

They do not include:

(1) Causes of loss excluded under Section **B.** Exclusions; or

(2) Losses insured under mortgage guarantee insurance policies or programs, or title, life, health or accident insurance policies.

b. Additional Coverage – Supplementary Payments

We will pay, with respect to any claim or any "suit" against you we defend:

(1) All expenses we incur.

(2) The cost of bonds to release attachments, but only for bond amounts within our Limit of Insurance. We do not have to furnish these bonds.

(3) All reasonable expenses incurred by you at our request, including actual loss of earnings up to $250 a day because of time off from work.

(4) All costs taxed against you in the "suit".

(5) Prejudgment interest awarded against you on that part of the judgment we pay. If we make an offer to pay the Limit of Insurance, we will not pay any prejudgment interest based on that period of time after the offer.

(6) All interest on the full amount of any judgment that accrues after entry of the judgment and before we have paid, offered to pay, or deposited in court the part of the judgment that is within our Limit of Insurance.

These payments will not reduce the applicable Limit of Insurance.

c. Coverage Extensions

(1) Additional Insureds

If the Named Insured shown in the Declarations is a partnership, limited liability company or corporation, under Coverage **C** – Mortgageholder's Liability, the words "you" and "your" are extended to include:

(a) Your partners, members, executive officers, trustees, directors and stockholders of such partnership, limited liability company or corporation, but only with respect to their duties as such; and

(b) Managers of a limited liability company, but only with respect to their duties as such.

The existence of one or more Additional Insureds does not increase the Limit of Insurance.

(2) Newly Acquired Organizations

Under Coverage **C** – Mortgageholder's Liability, the words "you" and "your" also include any organization (other than a partnership, joint venture or limited liability company) that you acquire or form and over which you maintain ownership or majority interest if there is no other similar insurance available to that organization.

This Coverage Extension ends:

(a) 90 days after you acquire or form the organization; or

(b) At the end of the policy period shown in the Declarations;

whichever is earlier.

This Extension does not apply to errors or accidental omissions that occurred before you acquired or formed the organization.

4. Coverage D – Real Estate Tax Liability

We will pay for damages for which you are legally liable due to error or accidental omission in paying real estate taxes, as agreed, on behalf of the mortgagor.

B. Exclusions

The following exclusions apply to Coverages **A, B, C** and **D**.

1. We will not pay for loss or damage caused directly or indirectly by any of the following. Such loss or damage is excluded regardless of any other cause or event that contributes concurrently or in any sequence to the loss:

a. Ordinance Or Law

The enforcement of or compliance with any ordinance or law:

(1) Regulating the construction, use or repair of any property; or

(2) Requiring the tearing down of any property, including the cost of removing its debris.

This exclusion, Ordinance Or Law, applies whether the loss results from:

(a) An ordinance or law that is enforced even if the property has not been damaged; or

(b) The increased costs incurred to comply with an ordinance or law in the course of construction, repair, renovation, remodeling or demolition of property, or removal of its debris, following a physical loss to that property.

b. Earth Movement

(1) Earthquake, including tremors and aftershocks and any earth sinking, rising or shifting related to such event;

(2) Landslide, including any earth sinking, rising or shifting related to such event;

(3) Mine subsidence, meaning subsidence of a man-made mine, whether or not mining activity has ceased;

© Insurance Services Office, Inc., 2011

(4) Earth sinking (other than sinkhole collapse), rising or shifting including soil conditions which cause settling, cracking or other disarrangement of foundations or other parts of realty. Soil conditions include contraction, expansion, freezing, thawing, erosion, improperly compacted soil and the action of water under the ground surface.

But if Earth Movement, as described in **b.(1)** through **b.(4)** above, results in fire or explosion, we will pay for the loss or damage caused by that fire or explosion.

(5) Volcanic eruption, explosion or effusion. But if volcanic eruption, explosion or effusion results in fire or Volcanic Action, we will pay for the loss or damage caused by that fire or Volcanic Action.

This exclusion applies regardless of whether any of the above, in Paragraphs **(1)** through **(5)**, is caused by an act of nature or is otherwise caused.

c. Governmental Action

Seizure or destruction of property by order of governmental authority.

But we will pay for loss or damage caused by or resulting from acts of destruction ordered by governmental authority and taken at the time of a fire to prevent its spread, if the fire would be covered by this Coverage Part.

d. Nuclear Hazard

Nuclear reaction or radiation, or radioactive contamination, however caused.

But if nuclear reaction or radiation, or radioactive contamination, results in fire, we will pay for the loss or damage caused by that fire.

e. Utility Services

The failure of power, communication, water or other utility service supplied to the described premises, however caused, if the failure:

(1) Originates away from the described premises; or

(2) Originates at the described premises, but only if such failure involves equipment used to supply the utility service to the described premises from a source away from the described premises.

Failure of any utility service includes lack of sufficient capacity and reduction in supply.

Loss or damage caused by a surge of power is also excluded, if the surge would not have occurred but for an event causing a failure of power.

But if the failure or surge of power, or the failure of communication, water or other utility service, results in a Covered Cause of Loss, we will pay for the loss or damage caused by that Covered Cause of Loss.

Communication services include, but are not limited to, service relating to Internet access or access to any electronic, cellular or satellite network.

f. War And Military Action

(1) War, including undeclared or civil war;

(2) Warlike action by a military force, including action in hindering or defending against an actual or expected attack, by any government, sovereign or other authority using military personnel or other agents; or

(3) Insurrection, rebellion, revolution, usurped power, or action taken by governmental authority in hindering or defending against any of these.

g. Water

(1) Flood, surface water, waves (including tidal wave and tsunami), tides, tidal water, overflow of any body of water, or spray from any of these, all whether or not driven by wind (including storm surge);

(2) Mudslide or mudflow;

(3) Water that backs up or overflows or is otherwise discharged from a sewer, drain, sump, sump pump or related equipment;

(4) Water under the ground surface pressing on, or flowing or seeping through:

(a) Foundations, walls, floors or paved surfaces;

(b) Basements, whether paved or not; or

(c) Doors, windows or other openings; or

(5) Waterborne material carried or otherwise moved by any of the water referred to in Paragraph **(1)**, **(3)** or **(4)**, or material carried or otherwise moved by mudslide or mudflow.

This exclusion applies regardless of whether any of the above, in Paragraphs **(1)** through **(5)**, is caused by an act of nature or is otherwise caused. An example of a situation to which this exclusion applies is the situation where a dam, levee, seawall or other boundary or containment system fails in whole or in part, for any reason, to contain the water.

But if any of the above, in Paragraphs **(1)** through **(5)**, results in fire, explosion or sprinkler leakage, we will pay for the loss or damage caused by that fire, explosion or sprinkler leakage (if sprinkler leakage is a Covered Cause of Loss).

h. **"Fungus", Wet Rot, Dry Rot And Bacteria**

Presence, growth, proliferation, spread or any activity of "fungus", wet or dry rot or bacteria.

But if "fungus", wet or dry rot or bacteria result in a "specified cause of loss", we will pay for the loss or damage caused by that "specified cause of loss".

This exclusion does not apply:

(1) When "fungus", wet or dry rot or bacteria result from fire or lightning; or

(2) To the extent that coverage is provided in the Additional Coverage, Limited Coverage For "Fungus", Wet Rot, Dry Rot And Bacteria, with respect to loss or damage by a cause of loss other than fire or lightning.

Exclusions **B.1.a.** through **B.1.h.** apply whether or not the loss event results in widespread damage or affects a substantial area.

2. We will not pay for loss or damage caused by or resulting from:

a. Discharge, dispersal, seepage, migration, release or escape of "pollutants". If you customarily require mortgagors to provide insurance against causes of loss on a special form basis (covering any cause of loss not excluded or limited in the policy), this exclusion does not apply if the discharge, dispersal, seepage, migration, release or escape is itself caused by any of the "specified causes of loss".

If the discharge, dispersal, seepage, migration, release or escape of "pollutants" results in a "specified cause of loss", we will pay for the loss or damage caused by that "specified cause of loss".

b. Artificially generated electrical, magnetic or electromagnetic energy that damages, disturbs, disrupts or otherwise interferes with any:

(1) Electrical or electronic wire, device, appliance, system or network; or

(2) Device, appliance, system or network utilizing cellular or satellite technology;

For the purpose of this exclusion, electrical, magnetic or electromagnetic energy includes but is not limited to:

(a) Electrical current, including arcing;

(b) Electrical charge produced or conducted by a magnetic or electromagnetic field;

(c) Pulse of electromagnetic energy; or

(d) Electromagnetic waves or microwaves.

But if fire results, we will pay for the loss or damage caused by that fire.

c. We will not pay for loss of or damage to lawns, trees, shrubs or plants which are part of a vegetated roof, caused by or resulting from:

(1) Dampness or dryness of atmosphere or of soil supporting the vegetation;

(2) Changes in or extremes of temperature;

(3) Disease;

(4) Frost or hail; or

(5) Rain, snow, ice or sleet.

d. Any event that occurs more than 30 days after you know that an error or accidental omission may have occurred.

e. Your failure to obtain, maintain or properly handle the following types of insurance policies or programs:

(1) Title;

(2) Mortgage guarantee;

(3) Life; or

(4) Health or accident.

f. Neglect of an insured to use all reasonable means to save and preserve property from further damage at and after the time of loss.

3. We will not pay for loss or damage caused by or resulting from any of the following, **3.a.** through **3.d.** But if an excluded cause of loss that is listed in **3.a.** through **3.d.** results in a Covered Cause of Loss, we will pay for the loss or damage caused by that Covered Cause of Loss.

 CP 00 70 10 12

a. Collapse, including any of the following conditions of property or any part of the property:

  (1) An abrupt falling down or caving in;

  (2) Loss of structural integrity, including separation of parts of the property or property in danger of falling down or caving in; or

  (3) Any cracking, bulging, sagging, bending, leaning, settling, shrinkage or expansion, as such condition relates to **(1)** or **(2)** above.

  This exclusion, **a.**, does not apply:

  (a) To the extent that coverage is provided under the Additional Coverage – Collapse; or

  (b) To collapse caused by one or more of the following:

    (i) The "specified causes of loss";

    (ii) Breakage of building glass;

    (iii) Weight of rain that collects on a roof; or

    (iv) Weight of people or personal property.

b. Weather conditions, if weather conditions contribute in any way with a cause or event excluded in Paragraph **1.** above to produce the loss or damage.

c. Acts or decisions, including the failure to act or decide, of any person, group, organization or governmental body.

d. Faulty, inadequate or defective:

  (1) Planning, zoning, development, surveying, siting;

  (2) Design, specifications, workmanship, repair, construction, renovation, remodeling, grading, compaction;

  (3) Materials used in repair, construction, renovation or remodeling; or

  (4) Maintenance;

  of part or all of any property on or off the described premises.

4. Additional Exclusion

The following provisions apply only to the specified property:

Loss Or Damage To Products

We will not pay for loss or damage to any merchandise, goods or other product caused by or resulting from error or omission by any person or entity (including those having possession under an arrangement where work or a portion of the work is outsourced) in any stage of the development, production or use of the product, including planning, testing, processing, packaging, installation, maintenance or repair. This exclusion applies to any effect that compromises the form, substance or quality of the product. But if such error or omission results in a Covered Cause of Loss, we will pay for the loss or damage caused by that Covered Cause of Loss.

C. Limits Of Insurance

The most we will pay under this Coverage Form for all loss arising from one error or accidental omission is the applicable Limit Of Insurance shown in the Declarations, subject to the following additional limitations:

1. Under Coverage **A** – Mortgageholder's Interest, or Coverage **B** – Property Owned Or Held In Trust, we will not pay more than the least of:

  a. The amount of direct physical loss or damage determined in accordance with the insurance policies that would have covered the loss or damage if no error or accidental omission occurred, less the amount of any other insurance recovery payable to you on the Covered Property;

  b. The amount that would have been paid to you under insurance policies you would customarily have procured and maintained if the error or accidental omission had not occurred; or

  c. The amount of your "mortgageholder's interest" under Coverage **A.**

2. Under Coverage **D** – Real Estate Tax Liability, we will not pay more than 15% of the Limit Of Insurance shown in the Declarations as applicable to this Coverage Form, for damages due to error or accidental omission in paying real estate taxes in connection with any single mortgage.

D. Additional Coverage – Collapse

The coverage provided under this Additional Coverage, Collapse, applies only to an abrupt collapse as described and limited in **D.1.** through **D.6.**

1. For the purpose of this Additional Coverage, Collapse, abrupt collapse means an abrupt falling down or caving in of a building or any part of a building with the result that the building or part of the building cannot be occupied for its intended purpose.

2. We will pay for direct physical loss or damage to Covered Property, caused by abrupt collapse of a building or any part of a building that is insured under this Coverage Form or that contains Covered Property insured under this Coverage Form, if such collapse is caused by one or more of the following:

   a. Building decay that is hidden from view, unless the presence of such decay is known to a mortgagor prior to collapse;

   b. Insect or vermin damage that is hidden from view, unless the presence of such damage is known to a mortgagor prior to collapse;

   c. Use of defective material or methods in construction, remodeling or renovation if the abrupt collapse occurs during the course of the construction, remodeling or renovation; or

   d. Use of defective material or methods in construction, remodeling or renovation if the abrupt collapse occurs after the construction, remodeling or renovation is complete, but only if the collapse is caused in part by:

      (1) A cause of loss listed in **2.a.** or **2.b.**;

      (2) One or more of the "specified causes of loss";

      (3) Breakage of building glass;

      (4) Weight of people or personal property; or

      (5) Weight of rain that collects on a roof.

3. This Additional Coverage, Collapse, does **not** apply to:

   a. A building or any part of a building that is in danger of falling down or caving in;

   b. A part of a building that is standing, even if it has separated from another part of the building; or

   c. A building that is standing or any part of a building that is standing, even if it shows evidence of cracking, bulging, sagging, bending, leaning, settling, shrinkage or expansion.

4. If personal property abruptly falls down or caves in and such collapse is **not** the result of abrupt collapse of a building, we will pay for loss or damage to Covered Property caused by such collapse of personal property only if:

   a. The collapse of personal property was caused by a cause of loss listed in **2.a.** through **2.d.**; and

   b. The personal property which collapses is inside a building.

   The coverage stated in this paragraph, **4.**, does not apply to personal property if marring and/or scratching is the only damage to that personal property caused by the collapse.

5. This Additional Coverage, Collapse, does not apply to personal property that has not abruptly fallen down or caved in, even if the personal property shows evidence of cracking, bulging, sagging, bending, leaning, settling, shrinkage or expansion.

6. This Additional Coverage, Collapse, will not increase the Limits of Insurance provided in this Coverage Part.

7. The term Covered Cause of Loss includes the Additional Coverage, Collapse, as described and limited in **D.1.** through **D.6.**

E. Additional Coverage – Limited Coverage For "Fungus", Wet Rot, Dry Rot And Bacteria

1. The coverage described in **E.2.** only applies when the "fungus", wet or dry rot or bacteria are the result of one or more of the following causes that occur during the policy period and only if all reasonable means were used to save and preserve the property from further damage at the time of and after that occurrence:

   a. A "specified cause of loss" other than fire or lightning; or

   b. Flood, if the Flood Coverage Endorsement applies to the affected premises.

   This Additional Coverage does not apply to lawns, trees, shrubs or plants which are part of a vegetated roof.

 CP 00 70 10 12

2. We will pay for loss or damage by "fungus", wet or dry rot or bacteria. As used in this Limited Coverage, the term loss or damage means:

   a. Direct physical loss or damage to Covered Property caused by "fungus", wet or dry rot or bacteria, including the cost of removal of the "fungus", wet or dry rot or bacteria;

   b. The cost to tear out and replace any part of the building or other property as needed to gain access to the "fungus", wet or dry rot or bacteria; and

   c. The cost of testing performed after removal, repair, replacement or restoration of the damaged property is completed, provided there is a reason to believe that "fungus", wet or dry rot or bacteria are present.

3. The coverage described under **E.2.** of this Limited Coverage is limited to $15,000. Regardless of the number of claims, this limit is the most we will pay for the total of all loss or damage arising out of all occurrences of "specified causes of loss" (other than fire or lightning) and Flood which take place in a 12-month period (starting with the beginning of the present annual policy period). With respect to a particular occurrence of loss which results in "fungus", wet or dry rot or bacteria, we will not pay more than a total of $15,000 even if the "fungus", wet or dry rot or bacteria continue to be present or active, or recur, in a later policy period.

4. The coverage provided under this Limited Coverage does not increase the applicable Limit of Insurance on any Covered Property. If a particular occurrence results in loss or damage by "fungus", wet or dry rot or bacteria, and other loss or damage, we will not pay more, for the total of all loss or damage, than the applicable Limit of Insurance on the affected Covered Property.

   If there is covered loss or damage to Covered Property, not caused by "fungus", wet or dry rot or bacteria, loss payment will not be limited by the terms of this Limited Coverage, except to the extent that "fungus", wet or dry rot or bacteria cause an increase in the loss. Any such increase in the loss will be subject to the terms of this Limited Coverage.

5. The terms of this Limited Coverage do not increase or reduce the coverage provided under the Additional Coverage, Collapse.

F. Additional Conditions

The following conditions apply in addition to the Common Policy Conditions:

1. **Condition Applicable To Coverage A – Mortgageholder's Interest**

   Transfer Of Mortgage – Coverage A

   We and all other insurance companies covering a loss, if in agreement, may pay you an amount equal to the outstanding balance on the mortgage, even if that amount is greater than the amount of loss. If so, we and the other insurance companies may demand and receive a full assignment of the mortgage, including all securities held as collateral for the debt, as interests may appear.

2. **Conditions Applicable To Coverage B – Property Owned Or Held In Trust**

   a. **Our Options – Coverage B**

      In the event of loss or damage covered under Coverage **B,** at our option, we will either:

      (1) Pay the value of lost or damaged property;

      (2) Pay the cost of repairing or replacing the lost or damaged property;

      (3) Take all or any part of the property at an agreed or appraised value; or

      (4) Repair, rebuild or replace the property with other property of like kind and quality.

      We will give notice of our intentions within 30 days after we receive the sworn statement of loss.

      We will not pay you more than your financial interest in the Covered Property.

   b. **Recovered Property – Coverage B**

      If either you or we recover any property after loss settlement, that party must give the other prompt notice. At your option, the property will be returned to you. You must then return to us the amount we paid to you for the property. We will pay recovery expenses and the expenses to repair the recovered property, subject to the Limit of Insurance.

   c. **Time Period – Coverage B**

      Coverage on each item of Covered Property applies only during the period of time that:

      (1) Begins on the day you acquire the property or your fiduciary interest in it begins; and

(2) Ends on the earlier of:

(a) 90 days after the date in Paragraph **(1)** above; or

(b) The day other insurance on the property is obtained.

d. Valuation – Coverage B

We will determine the value of Covered Property in the event of loss or damage at actual cash value as of the time of loss or damage.

3. Conditions Applicable To Coverage C – Mortgageholder's Liability And Coverage D – Real Estate Tax Liability

a. Bankruptcy – Coverages C And D

Bankruptcy or insolvency of you or your estate will not relieve us of our obligations under Coverages **C** and **D**.

b. Separation Of Insureds – Coverages C And D

The insurance under Coverages **C** and **D** applies separately to you and each additional insured, except with respect to the Limits of Insurance.

4. Conditions Applicable To All Coverages

a. Abandonment

There can be no abandonment of any property to us.

b. Appraisal – Coverages A And B Only

If we and you disagree on the amount of loss, either may make written demand for an appraisal of the loss. In this event, each party will select a competent and impartial appraiser. The two appraisers will select an umpire. If they cannot agree, either may request that selection be made by a judge of a court having jurisdiction. The appraisers will state separately the amount of loss. If they fail to agree, they will submit their differences to the umpire. A decision agreed to by any two will be binding. Each party will:

(1) Pay its chosen appraiser; and

(2) Bear the other expenses of the appraisal and umpire equally.

If there is an appraisal, we will still retain our right to deny the claim.

c. Duties In The Event Of Loss

(1) Under Coverages **A** and **B**:

(a) You must see that the following are done in the event of loss or damage to Covered Property:

(i) Notify the police if a law may have been broken.

(ii) Give us prompt notice of the loss or damage once you are aware of it. Include a description of the property involved.

(iii) Take all reasonable steps to protect the Covered Property from further damage, and keep a record of your expenses necessary to protect the Covered Property, for consideration in the settlement of the claim. This will not increase the Limit of Insurance. However, we will not pay for any subsequent loss or damage resulting from a cause of loss that is not a Covered Cause of Loss. Also, if feasible, set the damaged property aside and in the best possible order for examination.

(iv) At our request, give us complete inventories of the damaged and undamaged property. Include quantities, costs, values and amount of loss claimed.

(v) As often as may be reasonably required, permit us to inspect the property proving the loss or damage and examine your books and records.

Also, permit us to take samples of damaged and undamaged property for inspection, testing and analysis, and permit us to make copies from your books and records.

(vi) Send us a signed, sworn proof of loss containing the information we request to investigate the claim. You must do this within 60 days after our request. We will supply you with the necessary forms.

       CP 00 70 10 12

(vii) Cooperate with us in the investigation or settlement of the claim.

(b) We may examine any insured under oath, while not in the presence of any other insured and at such times as may be reasonably required, about any matter relating to this insurance or the claim, including an insured's books and records. In the event of an examination, an insured's answers must be signed.

(2) Under Coverages **C** and **D**:

(a) If a claim is made or "suit" is brought against you, you must see to it that we receive prompt written notice of the claim or "suit".

(b) You must:

(i) Immediately send us copies of any demands, notices, summonses or legal papers received in connection with the claim or "suit";

(ii) Authorize us to obtain records and other information;

(iii) Cooperate with us in the investigation, settlement or defense of the claim or "suit";

(iv) Assist us, upon our request, in the enforcement of any right against any person or organization that may be liable to you because of damage to which this insurance may also apply; and

(v) If requested, give us a signed statement of facts containing the information we request to determine our rights and duties under this insurance.

(c) You will not, except at your own cost, voluntarily make a payment, assume any obligation, or incur any expense without our consent.

d. Insurance Under Two Or More Coverages

If two or more of this policy's coverages apply to the same loss or damage, we will not pay more than the actual amount of the loss or damage.

e. Legal Action Against Us

(1) No one may bring a legal action against us under Coverages **A** and **B** unless:

(a) There has been full compliance with all of the terms of Coverages **A** and **B**; and

(b) The action is brought within two years after you discover the error or accidental omission.

(2) No person or organization has a right under Coverages **C** and **D**:

(a) To join us as a party or otherwise bring us into a "suit" asking for damages from you; or

(b) To sue us on this Coverage Form unless all of its terms have been fully complied with.

A person or organization may sue us to recover on an agreed settlement or on a final judgment against you obtained after an actual trial; but we will not be liable for damages that are not payable under the terms of this Coverage Form or that are in excess of the Limit of Insurance. An agreed settlement means a settlement and release of liability signed by us, you and the claimant or the claimant's legal representative.

f. Liberalization

If we adopt any revision that would broaden the coverage under this Coverage Part without additional premium within 45 days prior to or during the policy period, the broadened coverage will immediately apply to this Coverage Part.

g. Loss Payment

We will pay for covered loss or damage to Covered Property within 30 days after we receive the sworn proof of loss, if you have complied with all of the terms of this Coverage Part and:

(1) We have reached agreement with you on the amount of loss; or

(2) An appraisal award has been made.

h. Other Insurance

(1) You may have other insurance subject to the same plan, terms, conditions and provisions as the insurance under this Coverage Part. If you do, we will pay our share of the covered loss or damage. Our share is the proportion that the applicable Limit of Insurance under this Coverage Part bears to the Limits of Insurance of all insurance covering on the same basis.

(2) If there is other insurance covering the same loss or damage, other than that described in **(1)** above, we will pay only for the amount of covered loss or damage in excess of the amount due from that other insurance, whether you can collect on it or not. But we will not pay more than the applicable Limit of Insurance.

i. Policy Period, Coverage Territory

Under this Coverage Form:

(1) These coverages only apply to:

(a) Loss or damage; or

(b) Claims or "suits" arising from an event;

that occurs during the policy period shown in the Declarations. The date of error or accidental omission does not have to be within the policy period.

(2) We will pay for loss arising from errors or accidental omissions in connection with insurance policies or real estate tax payments on property located in:

(a) The United States of America (including its territories and possessions); and

(b) Puerto Rico.

j. Transfer Of Rights Of Recovery Against Others To Us

(1) Under Coverages **A** and **B**, if any person or organization to or for whom we make payment under this Coverage Form has rights to recover damages from another, those rights are transferred to us to the extent of our payment. That person or organization must do everything necessary to secure our rights and must do nothing after loss to impair them. But you may waive your rights against another party in writing:

(a) Prior to a loss to your Covered Property.

(b) After a loss to your Covered Property only if, at time of loss, that party is one of the following:

(i) Someone insured by this insurance;

(ii) A business firm:

i. Owned or controlled by you; or

ii. That owns or controls you; or

(iii) Your tenant.

This will not restrict your insurance.

(2) Under Coverages **C** and **D,** if you have rights to recover all or part of any payment we have made under this Coverage Form, those rights are transferred to us. You must do nothing after loss to impair them. At our request, you will bring "suit" or transfer those rights to us and help us enforce them.

k. Vacancy

We will not pay for any loss or damage if the building where loss or damage occurs, or out of which a claim or "suit" arises, has been vacant for more than 60 days before that loss or damage, or the event that gives rise to the claim or "suit".

A building is vacant unless at least 31% of its total square footage is:

(1) Rented to a lessee or sublessee and used by the lessee or sublessee to conduct its customary operations; and/or

(2) Used by the building owner to conduct customary operations.

l. Your Duties

You must make every reasonable effort, with respect to:

(1) Coverage **A** – Mortgageholder's Interest, to require, procure and maintain "valid insurance", payable to you as mortgageholder, against the Covered Causes of Loss.

(2) Coverage **B** – Property Owned Or Held In Trust, to procure and maintain "valid insurance" against the Covered Causes of Loss in amounts, and under conditions, you customarily require to protect your interest as owner, fiduciary or trustee of the Covered Property.

© Insurance Services Office, Inc., 2011

(3) Coverage **C** – Mortgageholder's Liability, to maintain "valid insurance" against the Covered Causes of Loss in amounts, and under conditions, customarily accepted by the mortgagor, as agreed.

(4) Coverage **D** – Real Estate Tax Liability, to promptly pay real estate taxes, if agreed to, on behalf of the mortgagor.

G. Definitions

1. "Fungus" means any type or form of fungus, including mold or mildew, and any mycotoxins, spores, scents or by-products produced or released by fungi.

2. "Mortgageholder's interest" means your interest, as mortgageholder, in real or personal property, including your interest in any legal fiduciary capacity.

3. "Pollutants" means any solid, liquid, gaseous or thermal irritant or contaminant, including smoke, vapor, soot, fumes, acids, alkalis, chemicals and waste. Waste includes materials to be recycled, reconditioned or reclaimed.

4. "Specified causes of loss" means the following: fire; lightning; explosion; windstorm or hail; smoke; aircraft or vehicles; riot or civil commotion; vandalism; leakage from fire-extinguishing equipment; sinkhole collapse; volcanic action; falling objects; weight of snow, ice or sleet; water damage. Water damage means accidental discharge or leakage of water or steam as the direct result of the breaking apart or cracking of any part of a system or appliance (other than a sump system including its related equipment and parts) containing water or steam.

5. "Suit" includes an arbitration proceeding to which you must submit or submit with our consent.

6. "Valid insurance" means a valid policy, or other evidence, of insurance.

COMMERCIAL PROPERTY
CP 00 80 10 12

TOBACCO SALES WAREHOUSES COVERAGE FORM

Various provisions in this policy restrict coverage. Read the entire policy carefully to determine rights, duties and what is and is not covered.

Throughout this policy, the words "you" and "your" refer to the Named Insured shown in the Declarations. The words "we", "us" and "our" refer to the company providing this insurance.

Other words and phrases that appear in quotation marks have special meaning. Refer to Section **G.** Definitions.

A. Coverage

We will pay for direct physical loss of or damage to Covered Property at the premises described in the Declarations caused by or resulting from any Covered Cause of Loss.

1. Covered Property

Covered Property, as used in this Coverage Part, means the following type of property for which a Limit Of Insurance is shown in the Declarations:

Tobacco in Sales Warehouses, meaning leaf, loose, scrap and stem tobacco located in the building or structure described in the Declarations:

a. That belongs to others and is in your care, custody or control for auction; or

b. On your leaf account for resale.

Coverage for Tobacco in Sales Warehouses applies only between:

(1) 12:01 AM of the 15th day before the opening of the regular auction season at the described premises; and

(2) 12:01 AM of the 15th day following the official closing date of the regular auction season at the described premises.

2. Property Not Covered

Covered Property does not include:

a. Growing crops or water;

b. Tobacco that is insured under this or any other policy in which it is more specifically described, except for the excess of the amount due (whether you can collect on it or not) from that other insurance;

c. Tobacco while outside buildings or structures;

d. Tobacco while waterborne; and

e. Contraband, or property in the course of illegal transportation or trade.

3. Covered Causes Of Loss

See applicable Causes Of Loss form as shown in the Declarations.

4. Additional Coverages

a. Debris Removal

(1) Subject to Paragraphs **(3)** and **(4)**, we will pay your expense to remove debris of Covered Property caused by or resulting from a Covered Cause of Loss that occurs during the policy period. The expenses will be paid only if they are reported to us in writing within 180 days of the date of direct physical loss or damage.

(2) Debris Removal does not apply to costs to:

(a) Extract "pollutants" from land or water; or

(b) Remove, restore, or replace polluted land or water.

(3) Subject to the exceptions in Paragraph **(4)**, the following provisions apply:

(a) The most we will pay for the total of direct physical loss or damage plus debris removal expense is the Limit of Insurance applicable to the Covered Property that has sustained loss or damage.

(b) Subject to **(a)** above, the amount we will pay for debris removal expense is limited to 25% of the sum of the deductible plus the amount that we pay for direct physical loss or damage to the Covered Property that has sustained loss or damage.

(4) We will pay up to an additional $25,000 for debris removal expense, for each location, in any one occurrence of physical loss or damage to Covered Property, if one or both of the following circumstances apply:

   (a) The total of the actual debris removal expense plus the amount we pay for direct physical loss or damage exceeds the Limit of Insurance on the Covered Property that has sustained loss or damage.

   (b) The actual debris removal expense exceeds 25% of the sum of the deductible plus the amount that we pay for direct physical loss or damage to the Covered Property that has sustained loss or damage.

   Therefore, if **(4)(a)** and/or **(4)(b)** applies, our total payment for direct physical loss or damage and debris removal expense may reach but will never exceed the Limit of Insurance on the Covered Property that has sustained loss or damage, plus $25,000.

(5) Examples

   The following examples assume that there is no Coinsurance penalty.

Example 1

Limit of Insurance:	$ 90,000
Amount of Deductible:	$ 500
Amount of Loss:	$ 50,000
Amount of Loss Payable:	$ 49,500
	($50,000 – $500)
Debris Removal Expense:	$ 10,000
Debris Removal Expense Payable:	$ 10,000

($10,000 is 20% of $50,000.)

The debris removal expense is less than 25% of the sum of the loss payable plus the deductible. The sum of the loss payable and the debris removal expense ($49,500 + $10,000 = $59,500) is less than the Limit of Insurance. Therefore, the full amount of debris removal expense is payable in accordance with the terms of Paragraph **(3)**.

Example 2

Limit of Insurance:	$ 90,000
Amount of Deductible:	$ 500
Amount of Loss:	$ 80,000
Amount of Loss Payable:	$ 79,500
	($80,000 – $500)
Debris Removal Expense:	$ 40,000
Debris Removal Expense Payable:	
Basic Amount:	$ 10,500
Additional Amount:	$ 25,000

The basic amount payable for debris removal expense under the terms of Paragraph **(3)** is calculated as follows: $80,000 ($79,500 + $500) x .25 = $20,000; capped at $10,500. The cap applies because the sum of the loss payable ($79,500) and the basic amount payable for debris removal expense ($10,500) cannot exceed the Limit of Insurance ($90,000).

The additional amount payable for debris removal expense is provided in accordance with the terms of Paragraph **(4)**, because the debris removal expense ($40,000) exceeds 25% of the loss payable plus the deductible ($40,000 is 50% of $80,000), and because the sum of the loss payable and debris removal expense ($79,500 + $40,000 = $119,500) would exceed the Limit of Insurance ($90,000). The additional amount of covered debris removal expense is $25,000, the maximum payable under Paragraph **(4)**. Thus, the total payable for debris removal expense in this example is $35,500; $4,500 of the debris removal expense is not covered.

b. Preservation Of Property

   If it is necessary to move Covered Property from the described premises to preserve it from loss or damage by a Covered Cause of Loss, we will pay for any direct physical loss or damage to that property:

   (1) While it is being moved or while temporarily stored at another location; and

   (2) Only if the loss or damage occurs within 30 days after the property is first moved.

   CP 00 80 10 12

c. Fire Department Service Charge

When the fire department is called to save or protect Covered Property from a Covered Cause of Loss, we will pay up to $1,000 for service at each premises described in the Declarations, unless a higher limit is shown in the Declarations. Such limit is the most we will pay regardless of the number of responding fire departments or fire units, and regardless of the number or type of services performed.

This Additional Coverage applies to your liability for fire department service charges:

(1) Assumed by contract or agreement prior to loss; or

(2) Required by local ordinance.

No deductible applies to this Additional Coverage.

d. Pollutant Clean-up And Removal

We will pay your expense to extract "pollutants" from land or water at the described premises if the discharge, dispersal, seepage, migration, release or escape of the "pollutants" is caused by or results from a Covered Cause of Loss that occurs during the policy period. The expenses will be paid only if they are reported to us in writing within 180 days of the date on which the Covered Cause of Loss occurs.

This Additional Coverage does not apply to costs to test for, monitor or assess the existence, concentration or effects of "pollutants". But we will pay for testing which is performed in the course of extracting the "pollutants" from the land or water.

The most we will pay under this Additional Coverage for each described premises is $10,000 for the sum of all covered expenses arising out of Covered Causes of Loss occurring during each separate 12-month period of this policy.

5. Coverage Extension

PROPERTY OFF-PREMISES

You may extend the insurance provided by this Coverage Form to apply to Covered Property that is temporarily located in a building or structure you do not own, lease or operate. This Extension does not apply to Covered Property:

a. In a vehicle;

b. In the care, custody or control of your salespersons; or

c. At any fair or exhibition.

The most we will pay for loss or damage under this Extension is $10,000.

This Extension is additional insurance. The Additional Condition, Need For Full Reports, does not apply to this Extension.

B. Exclusions And Limitations

See applicable Causes Of Loss form as shown in the Declarations.

C. Limits Of Insurance

The most we will pay for loss or damage in any one occurrence is the applicable Limit Of Insurance shown in the Declarations.

The limits applicable to the Coverage Extension and the Fire Department Service Charge and Pollutant Clean-up And Removal Additional Coverages are in addition to the Limits of Insurance.

Payments under the Preservation Of Property Additional Coverage will not increase the applicable Limit of Insurance.

D. Deductible

In any one occurrence of loss or damage (hereinafter referred to as loss), we will first reduce the amount of loss if required by the Additional Condition, Need For Full Reports. If the adjusted amount of loss is less than or equal to the Deductible, we will not pay for that loss. If the adjusted amount of loss exceeds the Deductible, we will then subtract the Deductible from the adjusted amount of loss, and will pay the resulting amount or the Limit of Insurance, whichever is less.

E. Loss Conditions

The following conditions apply in addition to the Common Policy Conditions and the Commercial Property Conditions:

1. Abandonment

There can be no abandonment of any property to us.

2. Appraisal

If we and you disagree on the value of the property or the amount of loss, either may make written demand for an appraisal of the loss. In this event, each party will select a competent and impartial appraiser. The two appraisers will select an umpire. If they cannot agree, either may request that selection be made by a judge of a court having jurisdiction. The appraisers will state separately the value of the property and amount of loss. If they fail to agree, they will submit their differences to the umpire. A decision agreed to by any two will be binding. Each party will:

a. Pay its chosen appraiser; and

b. Bear the other expenses of the appraisal and umpire equally.

If there is an appraisal, we will still retain our right to deny the claim.

3. Duties In The Event Of Loss Or Damage

a. You must see that the following are done in the event of loss or damage to Covered Property:

(1) Notify the police if a law may have been broken.

(2) Give us prompt notice of the loss or damage. Include a description of the property involved.

(3) As soon as possible, give us a description of how, when and where the loss or damage occurred.

(4) Take all reasonable steps to protect the Covered Property from further damage, and keep a record of your expenses necessary to protect the Covered Property, for consideration in the settlement of the claim. This will not increase the Limit of Insurance. However, we will not pay for any subsequent loss or damage resulting from a cause of loss that is not a Covered Cause of Loss. Also, if feasible, set the damaged property aside and in the best possible order for examination.

(5) At our request, give us complete inventories of the damaged and undamaged property. Include quantities, costs, values and amount of loss claimed.

(6) As often as may be reasonably required, permit us to inspect the property proving the loss or damage and examine your books and records.

Also permit us to take samples of damaged and undamaged property for inspection, testing and analysis, and permit us to make copies from your books and records.

(7) Send us a signed, sworn proof of loss containing the information we request to investigate the claim. You must do this within 60 days after our request. We will supply you with the necessary forms.

(8) Cooperate with us in the investigation or settlement of the claim.

b. We may examine any insured under oath, while not in the presence of any other insured and at such times as may be reasonably required, about any matter relating to this insurance or the claim, including an insured's books and records. In the event of an examination, an insured's answers must be signed.

4. Loss Payment

a. In the event of loss or damage covered by this Coverage Form, at our option, we will either:

(1) Pay the value of lost or damaged property;

(2) Pay the cost of repairing or replacing the lost or damaged property, subject to **b.** below;

(3) Take all or any part of the property at an agreed or appraised value; or

(4) Repair, rebuild or replace the property with other property of like kind and quality, subject to **b.** below.

We will determine the value of lost or damaged property, or the cost of its repair or replacement, in accordance with the applicable terms of the Valuation Condition in this Coverage Form or any applicable provision which amends or supersedes the Valuation Condition.

b. The cost to repair, rebuild or replace does not include the increased cost attributable to enforcement of or compliance with any ordinance or law regulating the construction, use or repair of any property.

c. We will give notice of our intentions within 30 days after we receive the sworn proof of loss.

d. We will not pay you more than your financial interest in the Covered Property.

e. We may adjust losses with the owners of lost or damaged property if other than you. If we pay the owners, such payments will satisfy your claims against us for the owners' property. We will not pay the owners more than their financial interest in the Covered Property.

f. We may elect to defend you against suits arising from claims of owners of property. We will do this at our expense.

g. We will pay for covered loss or damage within 30 days after we receive the sworn proof of loss, if you have complied with all of the terms of this Coverage Part, and:

   (1) We have reached agreement with you on the amount of loss; or

   (2) An appraisal award has been made.

5. Recovered Property

If either you or we recover any property after loss settlement, that party must give the other prompt notice. At your option, the property will be returned to you.

You must then return to us the amount we paid to you for the property. We will pay recovery expenses and the expenses to repair the recovered property, subject to the Limit of Insurance.

6. Valuation

a. We will determine the value of Tobacco in Sales Warehouses in the event of loss or damage at the average price on sales of tobacco of like grades and types:

   (1) On the day loss occurs;

   (2) On the two sales days immediately prior to the day loss occurs; and

   (3) On the two sales days immediately following the day loss occurs.

b. Prices will be based on sales at the tobacco sales warehouse nearest the premises where loss or damage occurs. We will determine the average price as follows:

   (1) Divide the total sales by the total number of pounds; and

   (2) Deduct any unearned warehouse charges, unearned auction fees and unpaid government taxes at the time of the loss.

F. Additional Conditions

The following conditions apply in addition to the Common Policy Conditions and the Commercial Property Conditions:

1. Need For Full Reports

a. We will not pay a greater proportion of loss than:

   (1) The values you reported, divided by

   (2) The value of the Covered Property during the last auction season,

   if your last report of values before loss or damage at any location shows less than the full value of the Covered Property at that location during the last auction season.

b. For locations you acquire after the last report of values, we will not pay a greater proportion of loss than:

   (1) The values you reported for all locations, divided by

   (2) The value of the Covered Property at all locations during the last auction season.

2. Premium Adjustment

a. The premium charged at the inception of each policy year is an advance premium. We will determine the final premium for this insurance after the policy year or expiration, based on your reports of value.

b. Based on the difference between the advance premium and the final premium, for each policy year, we will:

   (1) Charge additional premium; or

   (2) Return excess premium.

3. Reports Of Value

You must file with us a report, within 30 days of the official closing of the sales auction season, showing separately for each location listed in the Declarations:

a. The total number of pounds of tobacco sold and resold during the last sales auction season; and

b. The total price paid per pound.

G. Definitions

"Pollutants" means any solid, liquid, gaseous or thermal irritant or contaminant, including smoke, vapor, soot, fumes, acids, alkalis, chemicals and waste. Waste includes materials to be recycled, reconditioned or reclaimed.

COMMERCIAL PROPERTY CONDITIONS

This Coverage Part is subject to the following conditions, the Common Policy Conditions and applicable Loss Conditions and Additional Conditions in Commercial Property Coverage Forms.

A. CONCEALMENT, MISREPRESENTATION OR FRAUD

This Coverage Part is void in any case of fraud by you as it relates to this Coverage Part at any time. It is also void if you or any other insured, at any time, intentionally conceal or misrepresent a material fact concerning:

1. This Coverage Part;
2. The Covered Property;
3. Your interest in the Covered Property; or
4. A claim under this Coverage Part.

B. CONTROL OF PROPERTY

Any act or neglect of any person other than you beyond your direction or control will not affect this insurance.

The breach of any condition of this Coverage Part at any one or more locations will not affect coverage at any location where, at the time of loss or damage, the breach of condition does not exist.

C. INSURANCE UNDER TWO OR MORE COVERAGES

If two or more of this policy's coverages apply to the same loss or damage, we will not pay more than the actual amount of the loss or damage.

D. LEGAL ACTION AGAINST US

No one may bring a legal action against us under this Coverage Part unless:

1. There has been full compliance with all of the terms of this Coverage Part; and
2. The action is brought within 2 years after the date on which the direct physical loss or damage occurred.

E. LIBERALIZATION

If we adopt any revision that would broaden the coverage under this Coverage Part without additional premium within 45 days prior to or during the policy period, the broadened coverage will immediately apply to this Coverage Part.

F. NO BENEFIT TO BAILEE

No person or organization, other than you, having custody of Covered Property will benefit from this insurance.

G. OTHER INSURANCE

1. You may have other insurance subject to the same plan, terms, conditions and provisions as the insurance under this Coverage Part. If you do, we will pay our share of the covered loss or damage. Our share is the proportion that the applicable Limit of Insurance under this Coverage Part bears to the Limits of Insurance of all insurance covering on the same basis.

2. If there is other insurance covering the same loss or damage, other than that described in 1. above, we will pay only for the amount of covered loss or damage in excess of the amount due from that other insurance, whether you can collect on it or not. But we will not pay more than the applicable Limit of Insurance.

H. POLICY PERIOD, COVERAGE TERRITORY

Under this Coverage Part:

1. We cover loss or damage commencing:

   a. During the policy period shown in the Declarations; and
   b. Within the coverage territory.

2. The coverage territory is:

   a. The United States of America (including its territories and possessions);
   b. Puerto Rico; and
   c. Canada.

I. TRANSFER OF RIGHTS OF RECOVERY AGAINST OTHERS TO US

If any person or organization to or for whom we make payment under this Coverage Part has rights to recover damages from another, those rights are transferred to us to the extent of our payment. That person or organization must do everything necessary to secure our rights and must do nothing after loss to impair them. But you may waive your rights against another party in writing:

1. Prior to a loss to your Covered Property or Covered Income.

2. After a loss to your Covered Property or Covered Income only if, at time of loss, that party is one of the following:

  a. Someone insured by this insurance;

  b. A business firm:

    (1) Owned or controlled by you; or

    (2) That owns or controls you; or

  c. Your tenant.

This will not restrict your insurance.

COMMERCIAL PROPERTY
CP 10 10 10 12

CAUSES OF LOSS – BASIC FORM

Words and phrases that appear in quotation marks have special meaning. Refer to Section **E.** Definitions.

A. Covered Causes Of Loss

When Basic is shown in the Declarations, Covered Causes of Loss means the following:

1. Fire.

2. Lightning.

3. Explosion, including the explosion of gases or fuel within the furnace of any fired vessel or within the flues or passages through which the gases of combustion pass. This cause of loss does not include loss or damage by:

    a. Rupture, bursting or operation of pressure-relief devices; or

    b. Rupture or bursting due to expansion or swelling of the contents of any building or structure, caused by or resulting from water.

4. Windstorm or Hail, but not including:

    a. Frost or cold weather;

    b. Ice (other than hail), snow or sleet, whether driven by wind or not;

    c. Loss or damage to the interior of any building or structure, or the property inside the building or structure, caused by rain, snow, sand or dust, whether driven by wind or not, unless the building or structure first sustains wind or hail damage to its roof or walls through which the rain, snow, sand or dust enters; or

    d. Loss or damage by hail to lawns, trees, shrubs or plants which are part of a vegetated roof.

5. Smoke causing sudden and accidental loss or damage. This cause of loss does not include smoke from agricultural smudging or industrial operations.

6. Aircraft or Vehicles, meaning only physical contact of an aircraft, a spacecraft, a self-propelled missile, a vehicle or an object thrown up by a vehicle with the described property or with the building or structure containing the described property. This cause of loss includes loss or damage by objects falling from aircraft.

    We will not pay for loss or damage caused by or resulting from vehicles you own or which are operated in the course of your business.

7. Riot or Civil Commotion, including:

    a. Acts of striking employees while occupying the described premises; and

    b. Looting occurring at the time and place of a riot or civil commotion.

8. Vandalism, meaning willful and malicious damage to, or destruction of, the described property.

    We will not pay for loss or damage caused by or resulting from theft, except for building damage caused by the breaking in or exiting of burglars.

9. Sprinkler Leakage, meaning leakage or discharge of any substance from an Automatic Sprinkler System, including collapse of a tank that is part of the system.

    If the building or structure containing the Automatic Sprinkler System is Covered Property, we will also pay the cost to:

    a. Repair or replace damaged parts of the Automatic Sprinkler System if the damage:

        (1) Results in sprinkler leakage; or

        (2) Is directly caused by freezing.

    b. Tear out and replace any part of the building or structure to repair damage to the Automatic Sprinkler System that has resulted in sprinkler leakage.

    Automatic Sprinkler System means:

    (1) Any automatic fire-protective or extinguishing system, including connected:

        (a) Sprinklers and discharge nozzles;

        (b) Ducts, pipes, valves and fittings;

        (c) Tanks, their component parts and supports; and

        (d) Pumps and private fire protection mains.

    (2) When supplied from an automatic fire-protective system:

        (a) Non-automatic fire-protective systems; and

        (b) Hydrants, standpipes and outlets.

10. Sinkhole Collapse, meaning loss or damage caused by the sudden sinking or collapse of land into underground empty spaces created by the action of water on limestone or dolomite. This cause of loss does not include:

   a. The cost of filling sinkholes; or

   b. Sinking or collapse of land into man-made underground cavities.

11. Volcanic Action, meaning direct loss or damage resulting from the eruption of a volcano when the loss or damage is caused by:

   a. Airborne volcanic blast or airborne shock waves;

   b. Ash, dust or particulate matter; or

   c. Lava flow.

   With respect to coverage for Volcanic Action as set forth in 11.a., 11.b. and 11.c., all volcanic eruptions that occur within any 168-hour period will constitute a single occurrence.

   This cause of loss does not include the cost to remove ash, dust or particulate matter that does not cause direct physical loss or damage to the described property.

B. Exclusions

1. We will not pay for loss or damage caused directly or indirectly by any of the following. Such loss or damage is excluded regardless of any other cause or event that contributes concurrently or in any sequence to the loss.

   a. Ordinance Or Law

      The enforcement of or compliance with any ordinance or law:

      (1) Regulating the construction, use or repair of any property; or

      (2) Requiring the tearing down of any property, including the cost of removing its debris.

      This exclusion, Ordinance Or Law, applies whether the loss results from:

      (a) An ordinance or law that is enforced even if the property has not been damaged; or

      (b) The increased costs incurred to comply with an ordinance or law in the course of construction, repair, renovation, remodeling or demolition of property, or removal of its debris, following a physical loss to that property.

   b. Earth Movement

      (1) Earthquake, including tremors and aftershocks and any earth sinking, rising or shifting related to such event;

      (2) Landslide, including any earth sinking, rising or shifting related to such event;

      (3) Mine subsidence, meaning subsidence of a man-made mine, whether or not mining activity has ceased;

      (4) Earth sinking (other than sinkhole collapse), rising or shifting including soil conditions which cause settling, cracking or other disarrangement of foundations or other parts of realty. Soil conditions include contraction, expansion, freezing, thawing, erosion, improperly compacted soil and the action of water under the ground surface.

      But if Earth Movement, as described in b.(1) through (4) above, results in fire or explosion, we will pay for the loss or damage caused by that fire or explosion.

      (5) Volcanic eruption, explosion or effusion. But if volcanic eruption, explosion or effusion results in fire or Volcanic Action, we will pay for the loss or damage caused by that fire or Volcanic Action.

      This exclusion applies regardless of whether any of the above, in Paragraphs (1) through (5), is caused by an act of nature or is otherwise caused.

   c. Governmental Action

      Seizure or destruction of property by order of governmental authority.

      But we will pay for loss or damage caused by or resulting from acts of destruction ordered by governmental authority and taken at the time of a fire to prevent its spread, if the fire would be covered under this Coverage Part.

   d. Nuclear Hazard

      Nuclear reaction or radiation, or radioactive contamination, however caused.

      But if nuclear reaction or radiation, or radioactive contamination, results in fire, we will pay for the loss or damage caused by that fire.

e. Utility Services

The failure of power, communication, water or other utility service supplied to the described premises, however caused, if the failure:

(1) Originates away from the described premises; or

(2) Originates at the described premises, but only if such failure involves equipment used to supply the utility service to the described premises from a source away from the described premises.

Failure of any utility service includes lack of sufficient capacity and reduction in supply.

Loss or damage caused by a surge of power is also excluded, if the surge would not have occurred but for an event causing a failure of power.

But if the failure or surge of power, or the failure of communication, water or other utility service, results in a Covered Cause of Loss, we will pay for the loss or damage caused by that Covered Cause of Loss.

Communication services include but are not limited to service relating to Internet access or access to any electronic, cellular or satellite network.

f. War And Military Action

(1) War, including undeclared or civil war;

(2) Warlike action by a military force, including action in hindering or defending against an actual or expected attack, by any government, sovereign or other authority using military personnel or other agents; or

(3) Insurrection, rebellion, revolution, usurped power, or action taken by governmental authority in hindering or defending against any of these.

g. Water

(1) Flood, surface water, waves (including tidal wave and tsunami), tides, tidal water, overflow of any body of water, or spray from any of these, all whether or not driven by wind (including storm surge);

(2) Mudslide or mudflow;

(3) Water that backs up or overflows or is otherwise discharged from a sewer, drain, sump, sump pump or related equipment;

(4) Water under the ground surface pressing on, or flowing or seeping through:

(a) Foundations, walls, floors or paved surfaces;

(b) Basements, whether paved or not; or

(c) Doors, windows or other openings; or

(5) Waterborne material carried or otherwise moved by any of the water referred to in Paragraph **(1)**, **(3)** or **(4)**, or material carried or otherwise moved by mudslide or mudflow.

This exclusion applies regardless of whether any of the above, in Paragraphs **(1)** through **(5)**, is caused by an act of nature or is otherwise caused. An example of a situation to which this exclusion applies is the situation where a dam, levee, seawall or other boundary or containment system fails in whole or in part, for any reason, to contain the water.

But if any of the above, in Paragraphs **(1)** through **(5)**, results in fire, explosion or sprinkler leakage, we will pay for the loss or damage caused by that fire, explosion or sprinkler leakage (if sprinkler leakage is a Covered Cause of Loss).

h. "Fungus", Wet Rot, Dry Rot And Bacteria

Presence, growth, proliferation, spread or any activity of "fungus", wet or dry rot or bacteria.

But if "fungus", wet or dry rot or bacteria result in a Covered Cause of Loss, we will pay for the loss or damage caused by that Covered Cause of Loss.

This exclusion does not apply:

(1) When "fungus", wet or dry rot or bacteria result from fire or lightning; or

(2) To the extent that coverage is provided in the Additional Coverage, Limited Coverage For "Fungus", Wet Rot, Dry Rot And Bacteria, with respect to loss or damage by a cause of loss other than fire or lightning.

Exclusions **B.1.a.** through **B.1.h.** apply whether or not the loss event results in widespread damage or affects a substantial area.

2. We will not pay for loss or damage caused by or resulting from:

a. Artificially generated electrical, magnetic or electromagnetic energy that damages, disturbs, disrupts or otherwise interferes with any:

(1) Electrical or electronic wire, device, appliance, system or network; or

(2) Device, appliance, system or network utilizing cellular or satellite technology.

For the purpose of this exclusion, electrical, magnetic or electromagnetic energy includes but is not limited to:

(a) Electrical current, including arcing;

(b) Electrical charge produced or conducted by a magnetic or electromagnetic field;

(c) Pulse of electromagnetic energy; or

(d) Electromagnetic waves or microwaves.

But if fire results, we will pay for the loss or damage caused by that fire.

b. Rupture or bursting of water pipes (other than Automatic Sprinkler Systems) unless caused by a Covered Cause of Loss.

c. Leakage or discharge of water or steam from any part of a system or appliance containing water or steam (other than an Automatic Sprinkler System), unless the leakage or discharge occurs because the system or appliance was damaged by a Covered Cause of Loss. But we will not pay for loss or damage caused by or resulting from continuous or repeated seepage or leakage of water, or the presence or condensation of humidity, moisture or vapor, that occurs over a period of 14 days or more.

d. Explosion of steam boilers, steam pipes, steam engines or steam turbines owned or leased by you, or operated under your control.

But if explosion of steam boilers, steam pipes, steam engines or steam turbines results in fire or combustion explosion, we will pay for the loss or damage caused by that fire or combustion explosion.

e. Mechanical breakdown, including rupture or bursting caused by centrifugal force.

But if mechanical breakdown results in a Covered Cause of Loss, we will pay for the loss or damage caused by that Covered Cause of Loss.

f. Neglect of an insured to use all reasonable means to save and preserve property from further damage at and after the time of loss.

3. Special Exclusions

The following provisions apply only to the specified Coverage Forms:

a. Business Income (And Extra Expense) Coverage Form, Business Income (Without Extra Expense) Coverage Form, Or Extra Expense Coverage Form

We will not pay for:

(1) Any loss caused by or resulting from:

(a) Damage or destruction of "finished stock"; or

(b) The time required to reproduce "finished stock".

This exclusion does not apply to Extra Expense.

(2) Any loss caused by or resulting from direct physical loss or damage to radio or television antennas (including satellite dishes) and their lead-in wiring, masts or towers.

(3) Any increase of loss caused by or resulting from:

(a) Delay in rebuilding, repairing or replacing the property or resuming "operations", due to interference at the location of the rebuilding, repair or replacement by strikers or other persons; or

(b) Suspension, lapse or cancellation of any license, lease or contract. But if the suspension, lapse or cancellation is directly caused by the "suspension" of "operations", we will cover such loss that affects your Business Income during the "period of restoration" and any extension of the "period of restoration" in accordance with the terms of the Extended Business Income Additional Coverage and the Extended Period Of Indemnity Optional Coverage or any variation of these.

(4) Any Extra Expense caused by or resulting from suspension, lapse or cancellation of any license, lease or contract beyond the "period of restoration".

(5) Any other consequential loss.

© Insurance Services Office, Inc., 2011   **CP 10 10 10 12**

b. **Leasehold Interest Coverage Form**

(1) Paragraph **B.1.a.**, Ordinance Or Law, does not apply to insurance under this Coverage Form.

(2) We will not pay for any loss caused by:

(a) Your cancelling the lease;

(b) The suspension, lapse or cancellation of any license; or

(c) Any other consequential loss.

c. **Legal Liability Coverage Form**

(1) The following exclusions do not apply to insurance under this Coverage Form:

(a) Paragraph **B.1.a.** Ordinance Or Law;

(b) Paragraph **B.1.c.** Governmental Action;

(c) Paragraph **B.1.d.** Nuclear Hazard;

(d) Paragraph **B.1.e.** Utility Services; and

(e) Paragraph **B.1.f.** War And Military Action.

(2) The following additional exclusions apply to insurance under this Coverage Form:

(a) **Contractual Liability**

We will not defend any claim or "suit", or pay damages that you are legally liable to pay, solely by reason of your assumption of liability in a contract or agreement. But this exclusion does not apply to a written lease agreement in which you have assumed liability for building damage resulting from an actual or attempted burglary or robbery, provided that:

(i) Your assumption of liability was executed prior to the accident; and

(ii) The building is Covered Property under this Coverage Form.

(b) **Nuclear Hazard**

We will not defend any claim or "suit", or pay any damages, loss, expense or obligation, resulting from nuclear reaction or radiation, or radioactive contamination, however caused.

C. **Additional Coverage – Limited Coverage For "Fungus", Wet Rot, Dry Rot And Bacteria**

1. The coverage described in **C.2.** and **C.6.** only applies when the "fungus", wet or dry rot or bacteria are the result of one or more of the following causes that occur during the policy period and only if all reasonable means were used to save and preserve the property from further damage at the time of and after that occurrence:

a. A Covered Cause of Loss other than fire or lightning; or

b. Flood, if the Flood Coverage Endorsement applies to the affected premises.

This Additional Coverage does not apply to lawns, trees, shrubs or plants which are part of a vegetated roof.

2. We will pay for loss or damage by "fungus", wet or dry rot or bacteria. As used in this Limited Coverage, the term loss or damage means:

a. Direct physical loss or damage to Covered Property caused by "fungus", wet or dry rot or bacteria, including the cost of removal of the "fungus", wet or dry rot or bacteria;

b. The cost to tear out and replace any part of the building or other property as needed to gain access to the "fungus", wet or dry rot or bacteria; and

c. The cost of testing performed after removal, repair, replacement or restoration of the damaged property is completed, provided there is a reason to believe that "fungus", wet or dry rot or bacteria are present.

3. The coverage described under **C.2.** of this Limited Coverage is limited to $15,000. Regardless of the number of claims, this limit is the most we will pay for the total of all loss or damage arising out of all occurrences of Covered Causes of Loss (other than fire or lightning) and Flood which take place in a 12-month period (starting with the beginning of the present annual policy period). With respect to a particular occurrence of loss which results in "fungus", wet or dry rot or bacteria, we will not pay more than a total of $15,000 even if the "fungus", wet or dry rot or bacteria continue to be present or active, or recur, in a later policy period.

4. The coverage provided under this Limited Coverage does not increase the applicable Limit of Insurance on any Covered Property. If a particular occurrence results in loss or damage by "fungus", wet or dry rot or bacteria, and other loss or damage, we will not pay more, for the total of all loss or damage, than the applicable Limit of Insurance on the affected Covered Property.

If there is covered loss or damage to Covered Property, not caused by "fungus", wet or dry rot or bacteria, loss payment will not be limited by the terms of this Limited Coverage, except to the extent that "fungus", wet or dry rot or bacteria cause an increase in the loss. Any such increase in the loss will be subject to the terms of this Limited Coverage.

5. The terms of this Limited Coverage do not increase or reduce the coverage provided under Paragraph **b.** of Covered Causes Of Loss **9.** Sprinkler Leakage.

6. The following, **6.a.** or **6.b.**, applies only if Business Income and/or Extra Expense Coverage applies to the described premises and only if the "suspension" of "operations" satisfies all terms and conditions of the applicable Business Income and/or Extra Expense Coverage Form:

a. If the loss which resulted in "fungus", wet or dry rot or bacteria does not in itself necessitate a "suspension" of "operations", but such "suspension" is necessary due to loss or damage to property caused by "fungus", wet or dry rot or bacteria, then our payment under Business Income and/or Extra Expense is limited to the amount of loss and/or expense sustained in a period of not more than 30 days. The days need not be consecutive.

b. If a covered "suspension" of "operations" was caused by loss or damage other than "fungus", wet or dry rot or bacteria but remediation of "fungus", wet or dry rot or bacteria prolongs the "period of restoration", we will pay for loss and/or expense sustained during the delay (regardless of when such a delay occurs during the "period of restoration"), but such coverage is limited to 30 days. The days need not be consecutive.

D. Limitation

We will pay for loss of animals only if they are killed or their destruction is made necessary.

E. Definitions

"Fungus" means any type or form of fungus, including mold or mildew, and any mycotoxins, spores, scents or by-products produced or released by fungi.

COMMERCIAL PROPERTY
CP 10 20 10 12

CAUSES OF LOSS – BROAD FORM

Words and phrases that appear in quotation marks have special meaning. Refer to Section **F.** Definitions.

A. Covered Causes Of Loss

When Broad is shown in the Declarations, Covered Causes of Loss means the following:

1. Fire.

2. Lightning.

3. Explosion, including the explosion of gases or fuel within the furnace of any fired vessel or within the flues or passages through which the gases of combustion pass. This cause of loss does not include loss or damage by:

   a. Rupture, bursting or operation of pressure-relief devices; or

   b. Rupture or bursting due to expansion or swelling of the contents of any building or structure, caused by or resulting from water.

4. Windstorm or Hail, but not including:

   a. Frost or cold weather;

   b. Ice (other than hail), snow or sleet, whether driven by wind or not;

   c. Loss or damage to the interior of any building or structure, or the property inside the building or structure, caused by rain, snow, sand or dust, whether driven by wind or not, unless the building or structure first sustains wind or hail damage to its roof or walls through which the rain, snow, sand or dust enters; or

   d. Loss or damage by hail to lawns, trees, shrubs or plants which are part of a vegetated roof.

5. Smoke causing sudden and accidental loss or damage. This cause of loss does not include smoke from agricultural smudging or industrial operations.

6. Aircraft or Vehicles, meaning only physical contact of an aircraft, a spacecraft, a self-propelled missile, a vehicle or an object thrown up by a vehicle with the described property or with the building or structure containing the described property. This cause of loss includes loss or damage by objects falling from aircraft.

   We will not pay for loss or damage caused by or resulting from vehicles you own or which are operated in the course of your business.

7. Riot or Civil Commotion, including:

   a. Acts of striking employees while occupying the described premises; and

   b. Looting occurring at the time and place of a riot or civil commotion.

8. Vandalism, meaning willful and malicious damage to, or destruction of, the described property.

   We will not pay for loss or damage caused by or resulting from theft, except for building damage caused by the breaking in or exiting of burglars.

9. Sprinkler Leakage, meaning leakage or discharge of any substance from an Automatic Sprinkler System, including collapse of a tank that is part of the system.

   If the building or structure containing the Automatic Sprinkler System is Covered Property, we will also pay the cost to:

   a. Repair or replace damaged parts of the Automatic Sprinkler System if the damage:

      (1) Results in sprinkler leakage; or

      (2) Is directly caused by freezing.

   b. Tear out and replace any part of the building or structure to repair damage to the Automatic Sprinkler System that has resulted in sprinkler leakage.

   Automatic Sprinkler System means:

   (1) Any automatic fire-protective or extinguishing system, including connected:

      (a) Sprinklers and discharge nozzles;

      (b) Ducts, pipes, valves and fittings;

      (c) Tanks, their component parts and supports; and

      (d) Pumps and private fire protection mains.

   (2) When supplied from an automatic fire-protective system:

      (a) Non-automatic fire-protective systems; and

      (b) Hydrants, standpipes and outlets.

10. Sinkhole Collapse, meaning loss or damage caused by the sudden sinking or collapse of land into underground empty spaces created by the action of water on limestone or dolomite. This cause of loss does not include:

   a. The cost of filling sinkholes; or

   b. Sinking or collapse of land into man-made underground cavities.

11. Volcanic Action, meaning direct loss or damage resulting from the eruption of a volcano when the loss or damage is caused by:

   a. Airborne volcanic blast or airborne shock waves;

   b. Ash, dust or particulate matter; or

   c. Lava flow.

   With respect to coverage for Volcanic Action as set forth in **11.a.**, **11.b.** and **11.c.**, all volcanic eruptions that occur within any 168-hour period will constitute a single occurrence.

   This cause of loss does not include the cost to remove ash, dust or particulate matter that does not cause direct physical loss or damage to the described property.

12. **Falling Objects**

   But we will not pay for loss or damage to:

   a. Personal property in the open; or

   b. The interior of a building or structure, or property inside a building or structure, unless the roof or an outside wall of the building or structure is first damaged by a falling object.

13. **Weight Of Snow, Ice Or Sleet**

   But we will not pay for loss or damage to personal property outside of buildings or structures, or for loss or damage to lawns, trees, shrubs or plants which are part of a vegetated roof.

14. **Water Damage**

   a. Water Damage, meaning accidental discharge or leakage of water or steam as the direct result of the breaking apart or cracking of a plumbing, heating, air conditioning or other system or appliance, that is located on the described premises and contains water or steam.

   However, Water Damage does not include:

   (1) Discharge or leakage from:

      (a) An Automatic Sprinkler System;

      (b) A sump or related equipment and parts, including overflow due to sump pump failure or excessive volume of water; or

      (c) Roof drains, gutters, downspouts or similar fixtures or equipment;

   (2) The cost to repair any defect that caused the loss or damage;

   (3) Loss or damage caused by or resulting from continuous or repeated seepage or leakage of water, or the presence or condensation of humidity, moisture or vapor, that occurs over a period of 14 days or more; or

   (4) Loss or damage caused by or resulting from freezing, unless:

      (a) You do your best to maintain heat in the building or structure; or

      (b) You drain the equipment and shut off the water supply if the heat is not maintained.

   b. If coverage applies subject to **a.** above, and the building or structure containing the system or appliance is Covered Property, we will also pay the cost to tear out and replace any part of the building or structure to repair damage to the system or appliance from which the water or steam escapes. But we will not pay the cost to repair any defect that caused the loss or damage.

B. **Exclusions**

1. We will not pay for loss or damage caused directly or indirectly by any of the following. Such loss or damage is excluded regardless of any other cause or event that contributes concurrently or in any sequence to the loss.

   a. **Ordinance Or Law**

      The enforcement of or compliance with any ordinance or law:

      (1) Regulating the construction, use or repair of any property; or

      (2) Requiring the tearing down of any property including the cost of removing its debris.

      This exclusion, Ordinance Or Law, applies whether the loss results from:

      (a) An ordinance or law that is enforced even if the property has not been damaged; or

(b) The increased costs incurred to comply with an ordinance or law in the course of construction, repair, renovation, remodeling or demolition of property, or removal of its debris, following a physical loss to that property.

b. Earth Movement

(1) Earthquake, including tremors and aftershocks and any earth sinking, rising or shifting related to such event;

(2) Landslide, including any earth sinking, rising or shifting related to such event;

(3) Mine subsidence, meaning subsidence of a man-made mine, whether or not mining activity has ceased;

(4) Earth sinking (other than sinkhole collapse), rising or shifting including soil conditions which cause settling, cracking or other disarrangement of foundations or other parts of realty. Soil conditions include contraction, expansion, freezing, thawing, erosion, improperly compacted soil and the action of water under the ground surface.

But if Earth Movement, as described in **b.(1)** through **(4)** above, results in fire or explosion, we will pay for the loss or damage caused by that fire or explosion.

(5) Volcanic eruption, explosion or effusion. But if volcanic eruption, explosion or effusion results in fire, building glass breakage or Volcanic Action, we will pay for the loss or damage caused by that fire, building glass breakage or Volcanic Action.

This exclusion applies regardless of whether any of the above, in Paragraphs **(1)** through **(5)**, is caused by an act of nature or is otherwise caused.

c. Governmental Action

Seizure or destruction of property by order of governmental authority.

But we will pay for loss or damage caused by or resulting from acts of destruction ordered by governmental authority and taken at the time of a fire to prevent its spread, if the fire would be covered under this Coverage Part.

d. Nuclear Hazard

Nuclear reaction or radiation, or radioactive contamination, however caused.

But if nuclear reaction or radiation, or radioactive contamination, results in fire, we will pay for the loss or damage caused by that fire.

e. Utility Services

The failure of power, communication, water or other utility service supplied to the described premises, however caused, if the failure:

(1) Originates away from the described premises; or

(2) Originates at the described premises, but only if such failure involves equipment used to supply the utility service to the described premises from a source away from the described premises.

Failure of any utility service includes lack of sufficient capacity and reduction in supply.

Loss or damage caused by a surge of power is also excluded, if the surge would not have occurred but for an event causing a failure of power.

But if the failure or surge of power, or the failure of communication, water or other utility service, results in a Covered Cause of Loss, we will pay for the loss or damage caused by that Covered Cause of Loss.

Communication services include but are not limited to service relating to Internet access or access to any electronic, cellular or satellite network.

f. War And Military Action

(1) War, including undeclared or civil war;

(2) Warlike action by a military force, including action in hindering or defending against an actual or expected attack, by any government, sovereign or other authority using military personnel or other agents; or

(3) Insurrection, rebellion, revolution, usurped power, or action taken by governmental authority in hindering or defending against any of these.

g. Water

(1) Flood, surface water, waves (including tidal wave and tsunami), tides, tidal water, overflow of any body of water, or spray from any of these, all whether or not driven by wind (including storm surge);

(2) Mudslide or mudflow;

(3) Water that backs up or overflows or is otherwise discharged from a sewer, drain, sump, sump pump or related equipment;

(4) Water under the ground surface pressing on, or flowing or seeping through:

(a) Foundations, walls, floors or paved surfaces;

(b) Basements, whether paved or not; or

(c) Doors, windows or other openings; or

(5) Waterborne material carried or otherwise moved by any of the water referred to in Paragraph (1), (3) or (4), or material carried or otherwise moved by mudslide or mudflow.

This exclusion applies regardless of whether any of the above, in Paragraphs (1) through (5), is caused by an act of nature or is otherwise caused. An example of a situation to which this exclusion applies is the situation where a dam, levee, seawall or other boundary or containment system fails in whole or in part, for any reason, to contain the water.

But if any of the above, in Paragraphs (1) through (5), results in fire, explosion or sprinkler leakage, we will pay for the loss or damage caused by that fire, explosion or sprinkler leakage (if sprinkler leakage is a Covered Cause of Loss).

h. **"Fungus", Wet Rot, Dry Rot And Bacteria**

Presence, growth, proliferation, spread or any activity of "fungus", wet or dry rot or bacteria.

But if "fungus", wet or dry rot or bacteria result in a Covered Cause of Loss, we will pay for the loss or damage caused by that Covered Cause of Loss.

This exclusion does not apply:

(1) When "fungus", wet or dry rot or bacteria result from fire or lightning; or

(2) To the extent that coverage is provided in the Additional Coverage, Limited Coverage For "Fungus", Wet Rot, Dry Rot And Bacteria, with respect to loss or damage by a cause of loss other than fire or lightning.

Exclusions **B.1.a.** through **B.1.h.** apply whether or not the loss event results in widespread damage or affects a substantial area.

2. We will not pay for loss or damage caused by or resulting from:

a. Artificially generated electrical, magnetic or electromagnetic energy that damages, disturbs, disrupts or otherwise interferes with any:

(1) Electrical or electronic wire, device, appliance, system or network; or

(2) Device, appliance, system or network utilizing cellular or satellite technology.

For the purpose of this exclusion, electrical, magnetic or electromagnetic energy includes but is not limited to:

(a) Electrical current, including arcing;

(b) Electrical charge produced or conducted by a magnetic or electromagnetic field;

(c) Pulse of electromagnetic energy; or

(d) Electromagnetic waves or microwaves.

But if fire results, we will pay for the loss or damage caused by that fire.

b. Explosion of steam boilers, steam pipes, steam engines or steam turbines owned or leased by you, or operated under your control.

But if explosion of steam boilers, steam pipes, steam engines or steam turbines results in fire or combustion explosion, we will pay for the loss or damage caused by that fire or combustion explosion.

c. Mechanical breakdown, including rupture or bursting caused by centrifugal force.

But if mechanical breakdown results in a Covered Cause of Loss, we will pay for the loss or damage caused by that Covered Cause of Loss.

d. Neglect of an insured to use all reasonable means to save and preserve property from further damage at and after the time of loss.

3. **Special Exclusions**

The following provisions apply only to the specified Coverage Forms:

a. **Business Income (And Extra Expense) Coverage Form, Business Income (Without Extra Expense) Coverage Form, Or Extra Expense Coverage Form**

We will not pay for:

(1) Any loss caused by or resulting from:

(a) Damage or destruction of "finished stock"; or

CP 10 20 10 12

(b) The time required to reproduce "finished stock".

This exclusion does not apply to Extra Expense.

(2) Any loss caused by or resulting from direct physical loss or damage to radio or television satellite antennas (including satellite dishes) and their lead-in wiring, masts or towers.

(3) Any increase of loss caused by or resulting from:

(a) Delay in rebuilding, repairing or replacing the property or resuming "operations", due to interference at the location of the rebuilding, repair or replacement by strikers or other persons; or

(b) Suspension, lapse or cancellation of any license, lease or contract. But if the suspension, lapse or cancellation is directly caused by the "suspension" of "operations", we will cover such loss that affects your Business Income during the "period of restoration" and any extension of the "period of restoration" in accordance with the terms of the Extended Business Income Additional Coverage and the Extended Period Of Indemnity Optional Coverage or any variation of these.

(4) Any Extra Expense caused by or resulting from suspension, lapse or cancellation of any license, lease or contract beyond the "period of restoration".

(5) Any other consequential loss.

b. Leasehold Interest Coverage Form

(1) Paragraph **B.1.a.,** Ordinance Or Law, does not apply to insurance under this Coverage Form.

(2) We will not pay for any loss caused by:

(a) Your cancelling the lease;

(b) The suspension, lapse or cancellation of any license; or

(c) Any other consequential loss.

c. Legal Liability Coverage Form

(1) The following exclusions do not apply to insurance under this Coverage Form:

(a) Paragraph **B.1.a.** Ordinance Or Law;

(b) Paragraph **B.1.c.** Governmental Action;

(c) Paragraph **B.1.d.** Nuclear Hazard;

(d) Paragraph **B.1.e.** Utility Services; and

(e) Paragraph **B.1.f.** War And Military Action.

(2) The following additional exclusions apply to insurance under this Coverage Form:

(a) Contractual Liability

We will not defend any claim or "suit", or pay damages that you are legally liable to pay, solely by reason of your assumption of liability in a contract or agreement. But this exclusion does not apply to a written lease agreement in which you have assumed liability for building damage resulting from an actual or attempted burglary or robbery, provided that:

(i) Your assumption of liability was executed prior to the accident; and

(ii) The building is Covered Property under this Coverage Form.

(b) Nuclear Hazard

We will not defend any claim or "suit", or pay any damages, loss, expense or obligation, resulting from nuclear reaction or radiation, or radioactive contamination, however caused.

C. Additional Coverage – Collapse

The coverage provided under this Additional Coverage, Collapse, applies only to an abrupt collapse as described and limited in **C.1.** through **C.7.**

1. For the purpose of this Additional Coverage, Collapse, abrupt collapse means an abrupt falling down or caving in of a building or any part of a building with the result that the building or part of the building cannot be occupied for its intended purpose.

2. We will pay for direct physical loss or damage to Covered Property, caused by abrupt collapse of a building or any part of a building that is insured under this Coverage Form or that contains Covered Property insured under this Coverage Form, if such collapse is caused by one or more of the following:

   a. Fire; lightning; explosion; windstorm or hail; smoke; aircraft or vehicles; riot or civil commotion; vandalism; leakage from fire-extinguishing equipment; sinkhole collapse; volcanic action; breakage of building glass; falling objects; weight of snow, ice or sleet; water damage, meaning accidental discharge or leakage of water or steam as the direct result of the breaking apart or cracking of a plumbing, heating, air conditioning or other system or appliance (other than a sump system including its related equipment and parts), that is located on the described premises and contains water or steam; all only as insured against in this Coverage Part;

   b. Building decay that is hidden from view, unless the presence of such decay is known to an insured prior to collapse;

   c. Insect or vermin damage that is hidden from view, unless the presence of such damage is known to an insured prior to collapse;

   d. Weight of people or personal property;

   e. Weight of rain that collects on a roof;

   f. Use of defective material or methods in construction, remodeling or renovation if the abrupt collapse occurs during the course of the construction, remodeling or renovation. However, if such collapse occurs after construction, remodeling or renovation is complete and is caused in part by a cause of loss listed in **2.a.** through **2.e.**, we will pay for the loss or damage even if use of defective material or methods, in construction, remodeling or renovation, contributes to the collapse.

This Additional Coverage, Collapse, does not limit the coverage otherwise provided under this Causes Of Loss form for the causes of loss listed in **2.a.**

3. This **Additional Coverage – Collapse** does **not** apply to:

   a. A building or any part of a building that is in danger of falling down or caving in;

   b. A part of a building that is standing, even if it has separated from another part of the building; or

c. A building that is standing or any part of a building that is standing, even if it shows evidence of cracking, bulging, sagging, bending, leaning, settling, shrinkage or expansion.

4. With respect to the following property:

   a. Outdoor radio or television antennas (including satellite dishes) and their lead-in wiring, masts or towers;

   b. Awnings, gutters and downspouts;

   c. Yard fixtures;

   d. Outdoor swimming pools;

   e. Fences;

   f. Piers, wharves and docks;

   g. Beach or diving platforms or appurtenances;

   h. Retaining walls; and

   i. Walks, roadways and other paved surfaces;

   if an abrupt collapse is caused by a cause of loss listed in **2.b.** through **2.f.** we will pay for loss or damage to that property only if:

   (1) Such loss or damage is a direct result of the abrupt collapse of a building insured under this Coverage Form; and

   (2) The property is Covered Property under this Coverage Form.

5. If personal property abruptly falls down or caves in and such collapse is **not** the result of abrupt collapse of a building, we will pay for loss or damage to Covered Property caused by such collapse of personal property only if:

   a. The collapse of personal property was caused by a cause of loss listed in **2.a.** through **2.f.** above;

   b. The personal property which collapses is inside a building; and

   c. The property which collapses is not of a kind listed in **4.**, regardless of whether that kind of property is considered to be personal property or real property.

The coverage stated in this Paragraph **5.** does not apply to personal property if marring and/or scratching is the only damage to that personal property caused by the collapse.

6. This Additional Coverage, Collapse, does not apply to personal property that has not abruptly fallen down or caved in, even if the personal property shows evidence of cracking, bulging, sagging, bending, leaning, settling, shrinkage or expansion.

       CP 10 20 10 12

7. This Additional Coverage, Collapse, will not increase the Limits of Insurance provided in this Coverage Part.

8. The term Covered Cause of Loss includes the Additional Coverage, Collapse, as described and limited in **C.1.** through **C.7.**

D. Additional Coverage – Limited Coverage For "Fungus", Wet Rot, Dry Rot And Bacteria

1. The coverage described in **D.2.** and **D.6.** only applies when the "fungus", wet or dry rot or bacteria are the result of one or more of the following causes that occur during the policy period and only if all reasonable means were used to save and preserve the property from further damage at the time of and after that occurrence:

a. A Covered Cause of Loss other than fire or lightning; or

b. Flood, if the Flood Coverage Endorsement applies to the affected premises.

This Additional Coverage does not apply to lawns, trees, shrubs or plants which are part of a vegetated roof.

2. We will pay for loss or damage by "fungus", wet or dry rot or bacteria. As used in this Limited Coverage, the term loss or damage means:

a. Direct physical loss or damage to Covered Property caused by "fungus", wet or dry rot or bacteria, including the cost of removal of the "fungus", wet or dry rot or bacteria;

b. The cost to tear out and replace any part of the building or other property as needed to gain access to the "fungus", wet or dry rot or bacteria; and

c. The cost of testing performed after removal, repair, replacement or restoration of the damaged property is completed, provided there is a reason to believe that "fungus", wet or dry rot or bacteria are present.

3. The coverage described under **D.2.** of this Limited Coverage is limited to $15,000. Regardless of the number of claims, this limit is the most we will pay for the total of all loss or damage arising out of all occurrences of Covered Causes of Loss (other than fire or lightning) and Flood which take place in a 12-month period (starting with the beginning of the present annual policy period). With respect to a particular occurrence of loss which results in "fungus", wet or dry rot or bacteria, we will not pay more than a total of $15,000 even if the "fungus", wet or dry rot or bacteria continue to be present or active, or recur, in a later policy period.

4. The coverage provided under this Limited Coverage does not increase the applicable Limit of Insurance on any Covered Property. If a particular occurrence results in loss or damage by "fungus", wet or dry rot or bacteria, and other loss or damage, we will not pay more, for the total of all loss or damage, than the applicable Limit of Insurance on the affected Covered Property.

If there is covered loss or damage to Covered Property, not caused by "fungus", wet or dry rot or bacteria, loss payment will not be limited by the terms of this Limited Coverage, except to the extent that "fungus", wet or dry rot or bacteria cause an increase in the loss. Any such increase in the loss will be subject to the terms of this Limited Coverage.

5. The terms of this Limited Coverage do not increase or reduce the coverage provided under Paragraph **b.** of Covered Cause Of Loss **9.** Sprinkler Leakage, or Paragraph **b.** of Covered Causes Of Loss **14.** Water Damage, or under the Additional Coverage, Collapse.

6. The following, **6.a.** or **6.b.**, applies only if Business Income and/or Extra Expense Coverage applies to the described premises and only if the "suspension" of "operations" satisfies all terms and conditions of the applicable Business Income and/or Extra Expense Coverage Form:

a. If the loss which resulted in "fungus", wet or dry rot or bacteria does not in itself necessitate a "suspension" of "operations", but such "suspension" is necessary due to loss or damage to property caused by "fungus", wet or dry rot or bacteria, then our payment under Business Income and/or Extra Expense is limited to the amount of loss and/or expense sustained in a period of not more than 30 days. The days need not be consecutive.

b. If a covered "suspension" of "operations" was caused by loss or damage other than "fungus", wet or dry rot or bacteria but remediation of "fungus", wet or dry rot or bacteria prolongs the "period of restoration", we will pay for loss and/or expense sustained during the delay (regardless of when such a delay occurs during the "period of restoration"), but such coverage is limited to 30 days. The days need not be consecutive.

E. Limitation

We will pay for loss of animals only if they are killed or their destruction is made necessary.

F. Definitions

"Fungus" means any type or form of fungus, including mold or mildew, and any mycotoxins, spores, scents or by-products produced or released by fungi.

COMMERCIAL PROPERTY
CP 10 30 10 12

CAUSES OF LOSS – SPECIAL FORM

Words and phrases that appear in quotation marks have special meaning. Refer to Section **G.** Definitions.

A. Covered Causes Of Loss

When Special is shown in the Declarations, Covered Causes of Loss means direct physical loss unless the loss is excluded or limited in this policy.

B. Exclusions

1. We will not pay for loss or damage caused directly or indirectly by any of the following. Such loss or damage is excluded regardless of any other cause or event that contributes concurrently or in any sequence to the loss.

   a. Ordinance Or Law

   The enforcement of or compliance with any ordinance or law:

   (1) Regulating the construction, use or repair of any property; or

   (2) Requiring the tearing down of any property, including the cost of removing its debris.

   This exclusion, Ordinance Or Law, applies whether the loss results from:

   (a) An ordinance or law that is enforced even if the property has not been damaged; or

   (b) The increased costs incurred to comply with an ordinance or law in the course of construction, repair, renovation, remodeling or demolition of property, or removal of its debris, following a physical loss to that property.

   b. Earth Movement

   (1) Earthquake, including tremors and aftershocks and any earth sinking, rising or shifting related to such event;

   (2) Landslide, including any earth sinking, rising or shifting related to such event;

   (3) Mine subsidence, meaning subsidence of a man-made mine, whether or not mining activity has ceased;

   (4) Earth sinking (other than sinkhole collapse), rising or shifting including soil conditions which cause settling, cracking or other disarrangement of foundations or other parts of realty. Soil conditions include contraction, expansion, freezing, thawing, erosion, improperly compacted soil and the action of water under the ground surface.

   But if Earth Movement, as described in **b.(1)** through **(4)** above, results in fire or explosion, we will pay for the loss or damage caused by that fire or explosion.

   (5) Volcanic eruption, explosion or effusion. But if volcanic eruption, explosion or effusion results in fire, building glass breakage or Volcanic Action, we will pay for the loss or damage caused by that fire, building glass breakage or Volcanic Action.

   Volcanic Action means direct loss or damage resulting from the eruption of a volcano when the loss or damage is caused by:

   (a) Airborne volcanic blast or airborne shock waves;

   (b) Ash, dust or particulate matter; or

   (c) Lava flow.

   With respect to coverage for Volcanic Action as set forth in **(5)(a)**, **(5)(b)** and **(5)(c)**, all volcanic eruptions that occur within any 168-hour period will constitute a single occurrence.

   Volcanic Action does not include the cost to remove ash, dust or particulate matter that does not cause direct physical loss or damage to the described property.

   This exclusion applies regardless of whether any of the above, in Paragraphs **(1)** through **(5)**, is caused by an act of nature or is otherwise caused.

c. Governmental Action

Seizure or destruction of property by order of governmental authority.

But we will pay for loss or damage caused by or resulting from acts of destruction ordered by governmental authority and taken at the time of a fire to prevent its spread, if the fire would be covered under this Coverage Part.

d. Nuclear Hazard

Nuclear reaction or radiation, or radioactive contamination, however caused.

But if nuclear reaction or radiation, or radioactive contamination, results in fire, we will pay for the loss or damage caused by that fire.

e. Utility Services

The failure of power, communication, water or other utility service supplied to the described premises, however caused, if the failure:

(1) Originates away from the described premises; or

(2) Originates at the described premises, but only if such failure involves equipment used to supply the utility service to the described premises from a source away from the described premises.

Failure of any utility service includes lack of sufficient capacity and reduction in supply.

Loss or damage caused by a surge of power is also excluded, if the surge would not have occurred but for an event causing a failure of power.

But if the failure or surge of power, or the failure of communication, water or other utility service, results in a Covered Cause of Loss, we will pay for the loss or damage caused by that Covered Cause of Loss.

Communication services include but are not limited to service relating to Internet access or access to any electronic, cellular or satellite network.

f. War And Military Action

(1) War, including undeclared or civil war;

(2) Warlike action by a military force, including action in hindering or defending against an actual or expected attack, by any government, sovereign or other authority using military personnel or other agents; or

(3) Insurrection, rebellion, revolution, usurped power, or action taken by governmental authority in hindering or defending against any of these.

g. Water

(1) Flood, surface water, waves (including tidal wave and tsunami), tides, tidal water, overflow of any body of water, or spray from any of these, all whether or not driven by wind (including storm surge);

(2) Mudslide or mudflow;

(3) Water that backs up or overflows or is otherwise discharged from a sewer, drain, sump, sump pump or related equipment;

(4) Water under the ground surface pressing on, or flowing or seeping through:

(a) Foundations, walls, floors or paved surfaces;

(b) Basements, whether paved or not; or

(c) Doors, windows or other openings; or

(5) Waterborne material carried or otherwise moved by any of the water referred to in Paragraph (1), (3) or (4), or material carried or otherwise moved by mudslide or mudflow.

This exclusion applies regardless of whether any of the above, in Paragraphs (1) through (5), is caused by an act of nature or is otherwise caused. An example of a situation to which this exclusion applies is the situation where a dam, levee, seawall or other boundary or containment system fails in whole or in part, for any reason, to contain the water.

But if any of the above, in Paragraphs (1) through (5), results in fire, explosion or sprinkler leakage, we will pay for the loss or damage caused by that fire, explosion or sprinkler leakage (if sprinkler leakage is a Covered Cause of Loss).

h. "Fungus", Wet Rot, Dry Rot And Bacteria

Presence, growth, proliferation, spread or any activity of "fungus", wet or dry rot or bacteria.

But if "fungus", wet or dry rot or bacteria result in a "specified cause of loss", we will pay for the loss or damage caused by that "specified cause of loss".

       CP 10 30 10 12

This exclusion does not apply:

(1) When "fungus", wet or dry rot or bacteria result from fire or lightning; or

(2) To the extent that coverage is provided in the Additional Coverage, Limited Coverage For "Fungus", Wet Rot, Dry Rot And Bacteria, with respect to loss or damage by a cause of loss other than fire or lightning.

Exclusions **B.1.a.** through **B.1.h.** apply whether or not the loss event results in widespread damage or affects a substantial area.

2. We will not pay for loss or damage caused by or resulting from any of the following:

a. Artificially generated electrical, magnetic or electromagnetic energy that damages, disturbs, disrupts or otherwise interferes with any:

   (1) Electrical or electronic wire, device, appliance, system or network; or

   (2) Device, appliance, system or network utilizing cellular or satellite technology.

   For the purpose of this exclusion, electrical, magnetic or electromagnetic energy includes but is not limited to:

   (a) Electrical current, including arcing;

   (b) Electrical charge produced or conducted by a magnetic or electromagnetic field;

   (c) Pulse of electromagnetic energy; or

   (d) Electromagnetic waves or microwaves.

   But if fire results, we will pay for the loss or damage caused by that fire.

b. Delay, loss of use or loss of market.

c. Smoke, vapor or gas from agricultural smudging or industrial operations.

d.(1) Wear and tear;

   (2) Rust or other corrosion, decay, deterioration, hidden or latent defect or any quality in property that causes it to damage or destroy itself;

   (3) Smog;

   (4) Settling, cracking, shrinking or expansion;

(5) Nesting or infestation, or discharge or release of waste products or secretions, by insects, birds, rodents or other animals.

(6) Mechanical breakdown, including rupture or bursting caused by centrifugal force. But if mechanical breakdown results in elevator collision, we will pay for the loss or damage caused by that elevator collision.

(7) The following causes of loss to personal property:

   (a) Dampness or dryness of atmosphere;

   (b) Changes in or extremes of temperature; or

   (c) Marring or scratching.

But if an excluded cause of loss that is listed in **2.d.(1)** through **(7)** results in a "specified cause of loss" or building glass breakage, we will pay for the loss or damage caused by that "specified cause of loss" or building glass breakage.

e. Explosion of steam boilers, steam pipes, steam engines or steam turbines owned or leased by you, or operated under your control. But if explosion of steam boilers, steam pipes, steam engines or steam turbines results in fire or combustion explosion, we will pay for the loss or damage caused by that fire or combustion explosion. We will also pay for loss or damage caused by or resulting from the explosion of gases or fuel within the furnace of any fired vessel or within the flues or passages through which the gases of combustion pass.

f. Continuous or repeated seepage or leakage of water, or the presence or condensation of humidity, moisture or vapor, that occurs over a period of 14 days or more.

g. Water, other liquids, powder or molten material that leaks or flows from plumbing, heating, air conditioning or other equipment (except fire protective systems) caused by or resulting from freezing, unless:

   (1) You do your best to maintain heat in the building or structure; or

(2) You drain the equipment and shut off the supply if the heat is not maintained.

h. Dishonest or criminal act (including theft) by you, any of your partners, members, officers, managers, employees (including temporary employees and leased workers), directors, trustees or authorized representatives, whether acting alone or in collusion with each other or in collusion with any other party; or theft by any person to whom you entrust the property for any purpose, whether acting alone or in collusion with any other party.

This exclusion:

(1) Applies whether or not an act occurs during your normal hours of operation;

(2) Does not apply to acts of destruction by your employees (including temporary employees and leased workers) or authorized representatives; but theft by your employees (including temporary employees and leased workers) or authorized representatives is not covered.

i. Voluntary parting with any property by you or anyone else to whom you have entrusted the property if induced to do so by any fraudulent scheme, trick, device or false pretense.

j. Rain, snow, ice or sleet to personal property in the open.

k. Collapse, including any of the following conditions of property or any part of the property:

(1) An abrupt falling down or caving in;

(2) Loss of structural integrity, including separation of parts of the property or property in danger of falling down or caving in; or

(3) Any cracking, bulging, sagging, bending, leaning, settling, shrinkage or expansion as such condition relates to **(1)** or **(2)** above.

But if collapse results in a Covered Cause of Loss at the described premises, we will pay for the loss or damage caused by that Covered Cause of Loss.

This exclusion, **k.,** does not apply:

(a) To the extent that coverage is provided under the Additional Coverage, Collapse; or

(b) To collapse caused by one or more of the following:

(i) The "specified causes of loss";

(ii) Breakage of building glass;

(iii) Weight of rain that collects on a roof; or

(iv) Weight of people or personal property.

l. Discharge, dispersal, seepage, migration, release or escape of "pollutants" unless the discharge, dispersal, seepage, migration, release or escape is itself caused by any of the "specified causes of loss". But if the discharge, dispersal, seepage, migration, release or escape of "pollutants" results in a "specified cause of loss", we will pay for the loss or damage caused by that "specified cause of loss".

This exclusion, **l.,** does not apply to damage to glass caused by chemicals applied to the glass.

m. Neglect of an insured to use all reasonable means to save and preserve property from further damage at and after the time of loss.

3. We will not pay for loss or damage caused by or resulting from any of the following, **3.a.** through **3.c.** But if an excluded cause of loss that is listed in **3.a.** through **3.c.** results in a Covered Cause of Loss, we will pay for the loss or damage caused by that Covered Cause of Loss.

a. Weather conditions. But this exclusion only applies if weather conditions contribute in any way with a cause or event excluded in Paragraph **1.** above to produce the loss or damage.

b. Acts or decisions, including the failure to act or decide, of any person, group, organization or governmental body.

c. Faulty, inadequate or defective:

(1) Planning, zoning, development, surveying, siting;

(2) Design, specifications, workmanship, repair, construction, renovation, remodeling, grading, compaction;

(3) Materials used in repair, construction, renovation or remodeling; or

(4) Maintenance;

of part or all of any property on or off the described premises.

     CP 10 30 10 12

4. **Special Exclusions**

The following provisions apply only to the specified Coverage Forms:

a. **Business Income (And Extra Expense) Coverage Form, Business Income (Without Extra Expense) Coverage Form, Or Extra Expense Coverage Form**

We will not pay for:

(1) Any loss caused by or resulting from:

(a) Damage or destruction of "finished stock"; or

(b) The time required to reproduce "finished stock".

This exclusion does not apply to Extra Expense.

(2) Any loss caused by or resulting from direct physical loss or damage to radio or television antennas (including satellite dishes) and their lead-in wiring, masts or towers.

(3) Any increase of loss caused by or resulting from:

(a) Delay in rebuilding, repairing or replacing the property or resuming "operations", due to interference at the location of the rebuilding, repair or replacement by strikers or other persons; or

(b) Suspension, lapse or cancellation of any license, lease or contract. But if the suspension, lapse or cancellation is directly caused by the "suspension" of "operations", we will cover such loss that affects your Business Income during the "period of restoration" and any extension of the "period of restoration" in accordance with the terms of the Extended Business Income Additional Coverage and the Extended Period Of Indemnity Optional Coverage or any variation of these.

(4) Any Extra Expense caused by or resulting from suspension, lapse or cancellation of any license, lease or contract beyond the "period of restoration".

(5) Any other consequential loss.

b. **Leasehold Interest Coverage Form**

(1) Paragraph **B.1.a.**, Ordinance Or Law, does not apply to insurance under this Coverage Form.

(2) We will not pay for any loss caused by:

(a) Your cancelling the lease;

(b) The suspension, lapse or cancellation of any license; or

(c) Any other consequential loss.

c. **Legal Liability Coverage Form**

(1) The following exclusions do not apply to insurance under this Coverage Form:

(a) Paragraph **B.1.a.** Ordinance Or Law;

(b) Paragraph **B.1.c.** Governmental Action;

(c) Paragraph **B.1.d.** Nuclear Hazard;

(d) Paragraph **B.1.e.** Utility Services; and

(e) Paragraph **B.1.f.** War And Military Action.

(2) The following additional exclusions apply to insurance under this Coverage Form:

(a) **Contractual Liability**

We will not defend any claim or "suit", or pay damages that you are legally liable to pay, solely by reason of your assumption of liability in a contract or agreement. But this exclusion does not apply to a written lease agreement in which you have assumed liability for building damage resulting from an actual or attempted burglary or robbery, provided that:

(i) Your assumption of liability was executed prior to the accident; and

(ii) The building is Covered Property under this Coverage Form.

(b) **Nuclear Hazard**

We will not defend any claim or "suit", or pay any damages, loss, expense or obligation, resulting from nuclear reaction or radiation, or radioactive contamination, however caused.

5. Additional Exclusion

The following provisions apply only to the specified property:

Loss Or Damage To Products

We will not pay for loss or damage to any merchandise, goods or other product caused by or resulting from error or omission by any person or entity (including those having possession under an arrangement where work or a portion of the work is outsourced) in any stage of the development, production or use of the product, including planning, testing, processing, packaging, installation, maintenance or repair. This exclusion applies to any effect that compromises the form, substance or quality of the product. But if such error or omission results in a Covered Cause of Loss, we will pay for the loss or damage caused by that Covered Cause of Loss.

C. Limitations

The following limitations apply to all policy forms and endorsements, unless otherwise stated:

1. We will not pay for loss of or damage to property, as described and limited in this section. In addition, we will not pay for any loss that is a consequence of loss or damage as described and limited in this section.

   a. Steam boilers, steam pipes, steam engines or steam turbines caused by or resulting from any condition or event inside such equipment. But we will pay for loss of or damage to such equipment caused by or resulting from an explosion of gases or fuel within the furnace of any fired vessel or within the flues or passages through which the gases of combustion pass.

   b. Hot water boilers or other water heating equipment caused by or resulting from any condition or event inside such boilers or equipment, other than an explosion.

   c. The interior of any building or structure, or to personal property in the building or structure, caused by or resulting from rain, snow, sleet, ice, sand or dust, whether driven by wind or not, unless:

      (1) The building or structure first sustains damage by a Covered Cause of Loss to its roof or walls through which the rain, snow, sleet, ice, sand or dust enters; or

      (2) The loss or damage is caused by or results from thawing of snow, sleet or ice on the building or structure.

   d. Building materials and supplies not attached as part of the building or structure, caused by or resulting from theft.

      However, this limitation does not apply to:

      (1) Building materials and supplies held for sale by you, unless they are insured under the Builders Risk Coverage Form; or

      (2) Business Income Coverage or Extra Expense Coverage.

   e. Property that is missing, where the only evidence of the loss or damage is a shortage disclosed on taking inventory, or other instances where there is no physical evidence to show what happened to the property.

   f. Property that has been transferred to a person or to a place outside the described premises on the basis of unauthorized instructions.

   g. Lawns, trees, shrubs or plants which are part of a vegetated roof, caused by or resulting from:

      (1) Dampness or dryness of atmosphere or of soil supporting the vegetation;

      (2) Changes in or extremes of temperature;

      (3) Disease;

      (4) Frost or hail; or

      (5) Rain, snow, ice or sleet.

2. We will not pay for loss of or damage to the following types of property unless caused by the "specified causes of loss" or building glass breakage:

   a. Animals, and then only if they are killed or their destruction is made necessary.

   b. Fragile articles such as statuary, marbles, chinaware and porcelains, if broken. This restriction does not apply to:

      (1) Glass; or

      (2) Containers of property held for sale.

   c. Builders' machinery, tools and equipment owned by you or entrusted to you, provided such property is Covered Property.

      However, this limitation does not apply:

      (1) If the property is located on or within 100 feet of the described premises, unless the premises is insured under the Builders Risk Coverage Form; or

      (2) To Business Income Coverage or to Extra Expense Coverage.

© Insurance Services Office, Inc., 2011   **CP 10 30 10 12**

3. The special limit shown for each category, **a.** through **d.,** is the total limit for loss of or damage to all property in that category. The special limit applies to any one occurrence of theft, regardless of the types or number of articles that are lost or damaged in that occurrence. The special limits are (unless a higher limit is shown in the Declarations):

a. $2,500 for furs, fur garments and garments trimmed with fur.

b. $2,500 for jewelry, watches, watch movements, jewels, pearls, precious and semiprecious stones, bullion, gold, silver, platinum and other precious alloys or metals. This limit does not apply to jewelry and watches worth $100 or less per item.

c. $2,500 for patterns, dies, molds and forms.

d. $250 for stamps, tickets, including lottery tickets held for sale, and letters of credit.

These special limits are part of, not in addition to, the Limit of Insurance applicable to the Covered Property.

This limitation, **C.3.,** does not apply to Business Income Coverage or to Extra Expense Coverage.

4. We will not pay the cost to repair any defect to a system or appliance from which water, other liquid, powder or molten material escapes. But we will pay the cost to repair or replace damaged parts of fire-extinguishing equipment if the damage:

a. Results in discharge of any substance from an automatic fire protection system; or

b. Is directly caused by freezing.

However, this limitation does not apply to Business Income Coverage or to Extra Expense Coverage.

D. Additional Coverage – Collapse

The coverage provided under this Additional Coverage, Collapse, applies only to an abrupt collapse as described and limited in **D.1.** through **D.7.**

1. For the purpose of this Additional Coverage, Collapse, abrupt collapse means an abrupt falling down or caving in of a building or any part of a building with the result that the building or part of the building cannot be occupied for its intended purpose.

2. We will pay for direct physical loss or damage to Covered Property, caused by abrupt collapse of a building or any part of a building that is insured under this Coverage Form or that contains Covered Property insured under this Coverage Form, if such collapse is caused by one or more of the following:

a. Building decay that is hidden from view, unless the presence of such decay is known to an insured prior to collapse;

b. Insect or vermin damage that is hidden from view, unless the presence of such damage is known to an insured prior to collapse;

c. Use of defective material or methods in construction, remodeling or renovation if the abrupt collapse occurs during the course of the construction, remodeling or renovation.

d. Use of defective material or methods in construction, remodeling or renovation if the abrupt collapse occurs after the construction, remodeling or renovation is complete, but only if the collapse is caused in part by:

(1) A cause of loss listed in **2.a.** or **2.b.;**

(2) One or more of the "specified causes of loss";

(3) Breakage of building glass;

(4) Weight of people or personal property; or

(5) Weight of rain that collects on a roof.

3. This **Additional Coverage – Collapse** does **not** apply to:

a. A building or any part of a building that is in danger of falling down or caving in;

b. A part of a building that is standing, even if it has separated from another part of the building; or

c. A building that is standing or any part of a building that is standing, even if it shows evidence of cracking, bulging, sagging, bending, leaning, settling, shrinkage or expansion.

4. With respect to the following property:

a. Outdoor radio or television antennas (including satellite dishes) and their lead-in wiring, masts or towers;

b. Awnings, gutters and downspouts;

c. Yard fixtures;

d. Outdoor swimming pools;

e. Fences;

f. Piers, wharves and docks;

g. Beach or diving platforms or appurtenances;

h. Retaining walls; and

i. Walks, roadways and other paved surfaces;

if an abrupt collapse is caused by a cause of loss listed in **2.a.** through **2.d.**, we will pay for loss or damage to that property only if:

    (1) Such loss or damage is a direct result of the abrupt collapse of a building insured under this Coverage Form; and

    (2) The property is Covered Property under this Coverage Form.

5. If personal property abruptly falls down or caves in and such collapse is **not** the result of abrupt collapse of a building, we will pay for loss or damage to Covered Property caused by such collapse of personal property only if:

a. The collapse of personal property was caused by a cause of loss listed in **2.a.** through **2.d.;**

b. The personal property which collapses is inside a building; and

c. The property which collapses is not of a kind listed in **4.**, regardless of whether that kind of property is considered to be personal property or real property.

The coverage stated in this Paragraph **5.** does not apply to personal property if marring and/or scratching is the only damage to that personal property caused by the collapse.

6. This Additional Coverage, Collapse, does not apply to personal property that has not abruptly fallen down or caved in, even if the personal property shows evidence of cracking, bulging, sagging, bending, leaning, settling, shrinkage or expansion.

7. This Additional Coverage, Collapse, will not increase the Limits of Insurance provided in this Coverage Part.

8. The term Covered Cause of Loss includes the Additional Coverage, Collapse, as described and limited in **D.1.** through **D.7.**

E. Additional Coverage – Limited Coverage For "Fungus", Wet Rot, Dry Rot And Bacteria

1. The coverage described in **E.2.** and **E.6.** only applies when the "fungus", wet or dry rot or bacteria are the result of one or more of the following causes that occur during the policy period and only if all reasonable means were used to save and preserve the property from further damage at the time of and after that occurrence:

a. A "specified cause of loss" other than fire or lightning; or

b. Flood, if the Flood Coverage Endorsement applies to the affected premises.

This Additional Coverage does not apply to lawns, trees, shrubs or plants which are part of a vegetated roof.

2. We will pay for loss or damage by "fungus", wet or dry rot or bacteria. As used in this Limited Coverage, the term loss or damage means:

a. Direct physical loss or damage to Covered Property caused by "fungus", wet or dry rot or bacteria, including the cost of removal of the "fungus", wet or dry rot or bacteria;

b. The cost to tear out and replace any part of the building or other property as needed to gain access to the "fungus", wet or dry rot or bacteria; and

c. The cost of testing performed after removal, repair, replacement or restoration of the damaged property is completed, provided there is a reason to believe that "fungus", wet or dry rot or bacteria are present.

3. The coverage described under **E.2.** of this Limited Coverage is limited to $15,000. Regardless of the number of claims, this limit is the most we will pay for the total of all loss or damage arising out of all occurrences of "specified causes of loss" (other than fire or lightning) and Flood which take place in a 12-month period (starting with the beginning of the present annual policy period). With respect to a particular occurrence of loss which results in "fungus", wet or dry rot or bacteria, we will not pay more than a total of $15,000 even if the "fungus", wet or dry rot or bacteria continue to be present or active, or recur, in a later policy period.

       CP 10 30 10 12

4. The coverage provided under this Limited Coverage does not increase the applicable Limit of Insurance on any Covered Property. If a particular occurrence results in loss or damage by "fungus", wet or dry rot or bacteria, and other loss or damage, we will not pay more, for the total of all loss or damage, than the applicable Limit of Insurance on the affected Covered Property.

If there is covered loss or damage to Covered Property, not caused by "fungus", wet or dry rot or bacteria, loss payment will not be limited by the terms of this Limited Coverage, except to the extent that "fungus", wet or dry rot or bacteria cause an increase in the loss. Any such increase in the loss will be subject to the terms of this Limited Coverage.

5. The terms of this Limited Coverage do not increase or reduce the coverage provided under Paragraph **F.2.** (Water Damage, Other Liquids, Powder Or Molten Material Damage) of this Causes Of Loss form or under the Additional Coverage, Collapse.

6. The following, **6.a.** or **6.b.**, applies only if Business Income and/or Extra Expense Coverage applies to the described premises and only if the "suspension" of "operations" satisfies all terms and conditions of the applicable Business Income and/or Extra Expense Coverage Form:

   a. If the loss which resulted in "fungus", wet or dry rot or bacteria does not in itself necessitate a "suspension" of "operations", but such "suspension" is necessary due to loss or damage to property caused by "fungus", wet or dry rot or bacteria, then our payment under Business Income and/or Extra Expense is limited to the amount of loss and/or expense sustained in a period of not more than 30 days. The days need not be consecutive.

   b. If a covered "suspension" of "operations" was caused by loss or damage other than "fungus", wet or dry rot or bacteria but remediation of "fungus", wet or dry rot or bacteria prolongs the "period of restoration", we will pay for loss and/or expense sustained during the delay (regardless of when such a delay occurs during the "period of restoration"), but such coverage is limited to 30 days. The days need not be consecutive.

F. **Additional Coverage Extensions**

1. **Property In Transit**

   This Extension applies only to your personal property to which this form applies.

   a. You may extend the insurance provided by this Coverage Part to apply to your personal property (other than property in the care, custody or control of your salespersons) in transit more than 100 feet from the described premises. Property must be in or on a motor vehicle you own, lease or operate while between points in the coverage territory.

   b. Loss or damage must be caused by or result from one of the following causes of loss:

      (1) Fire, lightning, explosion, windstorm or hail, riot or civil commotion, or vandalism.

      (2) Vehicle collision, upset or overturn. Collision means accidental contact of your vehicle with another vehicle or object. It does not mean your vehicle's contact with the roadbed.

      (3) Theft of an entire bale, case or package by forced entry into a securely locked body or compartment of the vehicle. There must be visible marks of the forced entry.

   c. The most we will pay for loss or damage under this Extension is $5,000.

   This Coverage Extension is additional insurance. The Additional Condition, Coinsurance, does not apply to this Extension.

2. **Water Damage, Other Liquids, Powder Or Molten Material Damage**

   If loss or damage caused by or resulting from covered water or other liquid, powder or molten material damage loss occurs, we will also pay the cost to tear out and replace any part of the building or structure to repair damage to the system or appliance from which the water or other substance escapes. This Coverage Extension does not increase the Limit of Insurance.

3. **Glass**

   a. We will pay for expenses incurred to put up temporary plates or board up openings if repair or replacement of damaged glass is delayed.

b. We will pay for expenses incurred to remove or replace obstructions when repairing or replacing glass that is part of a building. This does not include removing or replacing window displays.

This Coverage Extension **F.3.** does not increase the Limit of Insurance.

G. Definitions

1. "Fungus" means any type or form of fungus, including mold or mildew, and any mycotoxins, spores, scents or by-products produced or released by fungi.

2. "Specified causes of loss" means the following: fire; lightning; explosion; windstorm or hail; smoke; aircraft or vehicles; riot or civil commotion; vandalism; leakage from fire-extinguishing equipment; sinkhole collapse; volcanic action; falling objects; weight of snow, ice or sleet; water damage.

   a. Sinkhole collapse means the sudden sinking or collapse of land into underground empty spaces created by the action of water on limestone or dolomite. This cause of loss does not include:

      (1) The cost of filling sinkholes; or

      (2) Sinking or collapse of land into man-made underground cavities.

   b. Falling objects does not include loss or damage to:

      (1) Personal property in the open; or

      (2) The interior of a building or structure, or property inside a building or structure, unless the roof or an outside wall of the building or structure is first damaged by a falling object.

c. Water damage means:

   (1) Accidental discharge or leakage of water or steam as the direct result of the breaking apart or cracking of a plumbing, heating, air conditioning or other system or appliance (other than a sump system including its related equipment and parts), that is located on the described premises and contains water or steam; and

   (2) Accidental discharge or leakage of water or waterborne material as the direct result of the breaking apart or cracking of a water or sewer pipe that is located off the described premises and is part of a municipal potable water supply system or municipal sanitary sewer system, if the breakage or cracking is caused by wear and tear.

But water damage does not include loss or damage otherwise excluded under the terms of the Water Exclusion. Therefore, for example, there is no coverage under this policy in the situation in which discharge or leakage of water results from the breaking apart or cracking of a pipe which was caused by or related to weather-induced flooding, even if wear and tear contributed to the breakage or cracking. As another example, and also in accordance with the terms of the Water Exclusion, there is no coverage for loss or damage caused by or related to weather-induced flooding which follows or is exacerbated by pipe breakage or cracking attributable to wear and tear.

To the extent that accidental discharge or leakage of water falls within the criteria set forth in **c.(1)** or **c.(2)** of this definition of "specified causes of loss," such water is not subject to the provisions of the Water Exclusion which preclude coverage for surface water or water under the surface of the ground.

 CP 10 30 10 12

IL 00 17 11 98

COMMON POLICY CONDITIONS

All Coverage Parts included in this policy are subject to the following conditions.

A. Cancellation

1. The first Named Insured shown in the Declarations may cancel this policy by mailing or delivering to us advance written notice of cancellation.

2. We may cancel this policy by mailing or delivering to the first Named Insured written notice of cancellation at least:

   a. 10 days before the effective date of cancellation if we cancel for nonpayment of premium; or

   b. 30 days before the effective date of cancellation if we cancel for any other reason.

3. We will mail or deliver our notice to the first Named Insured's last mailing address known to us.

4. Notice of cancellation will state the effective date of cancellation. The policy period will end on that date.

5. If this policy is cancelled, we will send the first Named Insured any premium refund due. If we cancel, the refund will be pro rata. If the first Named Insured cancels, the refund may be less than pro rata. The cancellation will be effective even if we have not made or offered a refund.

6. If notice is mailed, proof of mailing will be sufficient proof of notice.

B. Changes

This policy contains all the agreements between you and us concerning the insurance afforded. The first Named Insured shown in the Declarations is authorized to make changes in the terms of this policy with our consent. This policy's terms can be amended or waived only by endorsement issued by us and made a part of this policy.

C. Examination Of Your Books And Records

We may examine and audit your books and records as they relate to this policy at any time during the policy period and up to three years afterward.

D. Inspections And Surveys

1. We have the right to:

   a. Make inspections and surveys at any time;

   b. Give you reports on the conditions we find; and

   c. Recommend changes.

2. We are not obligated to make any inspections, surveys, reports or recommendations and any such actions we do undertake relate only to insurability and the premiums to be charged. We do not make safety inspections. We do not undertake to perform the duty of any person or organization to provide for the health or safety of workers or the public. And we do not warrant that conditions:

   a. Are safe or healthful; or

   b. Comply with laws, regulations, codes or standards.

3. Paragraphs 1. and 2. of this condition apply not only to us, but also to any rating, advisory, rate service or similar organization which makes insurance inspections, surveys, reports or recommendations.

4. Paragraph 2. of this condition does not apply to any inspections, surveys, reports or recommendations we may make relative to certification, under state or municipal statutes, ordinances or regulations, of boilers, pressure vessels or elevators.

E. Premiums

The first Named Insured shown in the Declarations:

1. Is responsible for the payment of all premiums; and

2. Will be the payee for any return premiums we pay.

F. Transfer Of Your Rights And Duties Under This Policy

Your rights and duties under this policy may not be transferred without our written consent except in the case of death of an individual named insured.

If you die, your rights and duties will be transferred to your legal representative but only while acting within the scope of duties as your legal representative. Until your legal representative is appointed, anyone having proper temporary custody of your property will have your rights and duties but only with respect to that property.

AAIS

CP-12
Ed 1.0

BUILDING AND PERSONAL PROPERTY COVERAGE PART

We cover direct physical loss to covered property at the premises described on the **declarations** caused by a covered peril.

PROPERTY COVERED

We cover the following types of property for which a **limit** is shown on the **declarations**.

BUILDING PROPERTY

This means buildings and structures described on the **declarations**, including:

1. completed additions;

2. fixtures, machinery, and equipment which are a permanent part of the described building or structure;

3. outdoor fixtures;

4. personal property owned by **you** and used to maintain or service the described building or structure or its premises, including air-conditioning equipment; fire extinguishing apparatus; floor coverings; and appliances for refrigerating, cooking, dish washing, and laundering;

5. if not covered by other insurance;

   a. additions under construction, alterations, and repairs to the building or structure; and

   b. materials, equipment, supplies, and temporary structures, on or within 100 feet of the described premises, used for making additions, alterations, or repairs to the building or structure.

BUSINESS PERSONAL PROPERTY

This means **your** business personal property in the buildings and structures described on the **declarations** or in the open (or in vehicles) on or within 100 feet of the described premises. Unless otherwise specified on the **declarations**, this includes:

1. **your** interest in personal property of others to the extent of **your** labor, material, and services;

2. **your** use interest as tenant in improvements to the described building or structure. Improvements are fixtures, alterations, installations, or additions:

   a. to a building or structure **you** occupy but do not own; and

   b. made or acquired at **your** expense and which cannot be legally removed by **you**; and

3. leased personal property which **you** have a contractual responsibility to insure, unless otherwise insured by the Commercial Property Coverage under Personal Property of Others.

PERSONAL PROPERTY OF OTHERS

This means personal property of others:

1. that is in **your** care, custody, or control; and

2. located in the buildings and structures described on the **declarations** or in the open (or in vehicles) on or within 100 feet of the described premises.

However, **our** payment for loss to personal property of others is only for the benefit of the owners of the personal property.

PROPERTY EXCLUDED AND LIMITATIONS

1. **Animals** -- **We** do not cover animals, including birds and fish, unless owned by others and boarded by **you**. **We** do cover animals **you** own and hold for sale.

2. **Antennas, Awnings, Canopies, Fences, and Signs** -- Except as provided under Supplemental Coverages, **we** do not cover outdoor:

   a. radio, television, satellite, dish-type, or other antennas including their masts, towers, and lead-in wiring;

   b. awnings or canopies of fabric or slat construction or their supports;

   c. fences; or

   d. signs, other than signs attached to buildings.

3. **Contraband -- We** do not cover contraband or property in the course of illegal transportation or trade.

4. **Foundations, Retaining Walls, Piling, Piers, Wharves, or Docks -- We** do not cover foundations which are below the lowest basement floor or below ground level if there is no basement; retaining walls that are not part of buildings or structures; or pilings, piers, wharves, or docks.

5. **Land; Water; Growing Crops or Lawns; Cost of Excavation, Grading, or Filling; Paved Surfaces; or Underground Pipes, Flues, or Drains -- We** do not cover:

   a. land, including land on which the property is located;

   b. underground or surface water;

   c. growing crops or lawns;

   d. cost of excavations, grading, or filling;

   e. paved outdoor surfaces, including driveways, parking lots, roads, bridges, and walks; or

   f. underground pipes, flues, and drains.

6. **Money and Securities -- We** do not cover accounts, bills, currency, food stamps, or other evidences of debt, lottery tickets not held for sale, money, notes, or securities.

7. **Property More Specifically Insured -- We** do not cover property which is more specifically insured in whole or in part by any other insurance. **We** do cover the amount in excess of the amount due from the more specific insurance.

8. **Trees, Shrubs, and Plants --** Except as provided under Supplemental Coverages, **we** do not cover trees; shrubs; plants; and grain, hay, straw, or other crops, when outdoors. However, **we** do cover trees, shrubs, and plants **you** own and hold for sale.

9. **Valuable Papers and Records -- Research Cost--** Except as provided under Supplemental Coverages, **we** do not cover the cost to research, replace, or restore the information on valuable papers and records, including those which exist on electronic or magnetic media.

10. **Vehicles, Aircraft, and Watercraft -- We** do not cover vehicles or self-propelled machines (including aircraft or watercraft and their motors, equipment, and accessories) that are:

   a. required to be licensed for use on public roads; or

   b. operated principally away from the described premises.

   We do cover vehicles or self-propelled machines **you** manufacture, process, warehouse, or hold for sale. However, this does not include autos **you** hold for sale. **We** also cover rowboats or canoes out of water at the described premises.

ADDITIONAL COVERAGES

1. **Debris Removal -- We** cover the cost to remove the debris of covered property that is caused by a covered peril. This coverage does not include costs to:

   a. extract **pollutants** from land or water; or

   b. remove, restore, or replace polluted land or water.

   We do not pay any more under this coverage than 25 percent of the amount **we** pay for the direct physical loss. **We** do not pay more for loss to property and debris removal combined than the **limit** for the damaged property.

   However, **we** pay an additional amount of debris removal expense up to $5,000 when the debris removal expense exceeds 25 percent of the amount **we** pay for direct physical loss or when the loss to property and debris removal combined exceeds the **limit** for the damaged property.

   We do not pay any expenses unless they are reported to **us** in writing within 180 days from the date of direct physical loss to covered property.

2. **Emergency Removal -- We** cover loss to covered property while moved or being moved from the described premises for preservation from loss caused by a covered peril. **We** pay for any direct physical loss to that property. This coverage applies for up to 10 days after the property is first moved. This does not increase the **limit**.

3. **Fire Department Service Charges -- We** pay up to $1,000 to cover **your** liability, assumed by contract or agreement prior to the loss, for fire department service charges.

This coverage is limited to charges incurred when the fire department is called to save or protect covered property from a covered peril.

No deductible applies.

This is an additional **limit**.

4. **Pollutant Clean Up and Removal -- We** pay **your** expense to extract **pollutants** from land or water at the described premises if the discharge, dispersal, seepage, migration, release, or escape of the **pollutants** is caused by a covered peril that occurs during the policy period.

We pay the cost of testing, evaluating, observing, or recording the existence, level, or effects of **pollutants** only when the expense of extracting the **pollutants** is covered by this Additional Coverage.

The most **we** pay for each described premises is $10,000 for the sum of all such expenses arising out of a covered peril occurring during each separate 12 month period of this policy. The expenses are paid only if they are reported to **us** in writing within 180 days from the date the covered peril occurs.

This is an additional **limit**.

PERILS COVERED

See the applicable Perils Part shown on the **declarations**.

SUPPLEMENTAL COVERAGES

If a Coinsurance percentage of 80% or more is shown on the **declarations**, **we** provide the following supplemental coverages.

Unless otherwise stated, each supplemental coverage:

a. applies for loss caused by a covered peril;

b. applies to property in or on buildings or structures described on the **declarations** or in the open (or in vehicles) within 100 feet of the described premises;

c. is an additional amount of coverage; and

d. is not subject to and not considered in applying coinsurance.

1. The following supplemental coverages apply when a **limit** is shown on the **declarations** for either Building Property or Business Personal Property.

a. **Antennas, Awnings, Canopies, Fences, and Signs -- We** pay up to $1,000 for **your** outdoor:

1) radio, television, satellite, dish-type, or other antennas including their masts, towers, and lead-in wiring;
2) awnings or canopies of fabric or slat construction or their supports;
3) fences; or
4) signs.

We only cover direct physical loss caused by aircraft, civil commotion, explosion, fire, lightning, or riot, including debris removal expense.

b. **Property Off Premises -- We** pay up to $5,000 for covered property while temporarily at a location that **you** do not own, control, rent, or lease.

This coverage does not include property:

1) in or on a vehicle;
2) in the care, custody, or control of **your** salesperson; or
3) at any fair or exhibition.

2. The following supplemental coverages apply only when a **limit** is shown on the **declarations** for Building Property.

a. **Increased Costs -- Ordinance or Law -- We** pay up to $5,000 for each described premises to cover the increased costs of a covered loss, including debris removal expense, resulting from the enforcement of any ordinance, law, or decree that regulates or requires:

1) the construction, use, or repair of any property; or
2) the demolition of any property, in part or in whole, not damaged by a covered peril.

The ordinance, law, or decree must be in force at the time of loss.

Under Perils Excluded, Ordinance or Law does not apply to this Supplemental Coverage.

b. **Newly Acquired Buildings -- We** cover **your** buildings or structures being built or that **you** acquire during the policy period.

This coverage applies for 30 days after construction is started or for 30 days from the date **you** acquire the building or structure; or until **you** report the newly acquired property to **us**; whichever occurs first. This coverage does not extend beyond the end of the policy period.

You must pay any additional premium due from the date construction is started or the date **you** acquire the property.

We pay up to 25 percent of the **limit** shown on the **declarations** for Building Property but not exceeding $250,000 for each building or structure.

c. **Trees, Shrubs, and Plants -- We** pay up to $1,000 for **your** outdoor trees, shrubs, and plants not held for sale. **We** only cover loss caused by aircraft, civil commotion, explosion, fire, lightning, or riot. This coverage is limited to $250 on any one tree, shrub, or plant, including debris removal.

3. The following supplemental coverages apply only when a **limit** is shown on the **declarations** for Business Personal Property.

a. **Condominium Units --** If the described premises is a condominium unit that **you** own, **we** cover the fixtures, improvements, and alterations within **your** unit.

We pay up to 10 percent of the **limit** shown on the **declarations** for Business Personal Property but not exceeding $20,000 for each building or structure.

This is not an additional amount of coverage.

b. **Extra Expenses -- We** pay up to $1,000 for the necessary extra expenses that **you** incur in order to continue as nearly as practical **your** normal business following loss by a covered peril. This applies when the damage is to property in the described buildings or structures or in the open (or in vehicles) on or within 100 feet of the described premises.

We cover **your** extra expenses for the time it should reasonably take to resume **your** normal business, but not longer than the time it should reasonably take to rebuild, repair, or replace the property that has incurred the loss.

We do not cover the normal cost of repair, replacement, or restoration of property. **We** cover expenses in excess of normal that **you** necessarily incur to reduce loss, but only to the extent they reduce the loss under this coverage.

We do not cover the cost of research or other extra expense necessary to reproduce, replace, or restore lost information on lost or damaged valuable papers and records, including those which exist on electronic or magnetic media.

We cover expenses in excess of normal that **you** necessarily incur to reduce loss, but only to the extent that they reduce the loss under this coverage.

c. **Personal Effects -- We** pay up to $500, at each described premises, for personal effects owned by **you, your** officers, **your** partners, or **your** employees. This coverage is limited to $100 on property owned by any one person.

d. **Personal Property -- Acquired Locations -- We** cover **your** business personal property at locations that **you** acquire, other than fairs or exhibitions.

This coverage applies for 30 days from the date **you** acquire the location or until **you** report the acquired location to **us**, whichever occurs first. This coverage does not extend beyond the end of the policy period.

You must pay any additional premium due from that date **you** acquire the location.

We pay up to 10 percent of the **limit** shown on the **declarations** for Business Personal Property but not exceeding $100,000 for each location.

e. **Personal Property of Others -- We** pay up to $2,500, at each described premises, for personal property of others in **your** care, custody, or control. This coverage is only for the benefit of the owners of the personal property.

f. **Property in Transit -- We** pay up to $1,000 for covered business personal property (other than property in the care, custody, or control of **your** salesperson) in transit more than 100 feet from the described premises in vehicles **you** own, lease, or operate.

We only cover direct physical loss caused by civil commotion; collision with another vehicle or object, other than the road bed; explosion, fire; hail; lightning; overturn or upset of the vehicle; riot; vandalism; or windstorm.

This coverage also includes loss of an entire package, case, or bale from within a locked part of **your** vehicle caused by theft. Theft must be proven by visible marks of forced entry.

g. **Valuable Papers and Records -- Research Cost -- We** pay up to $1,000 for the cost of research or other expenses necessary to reproduce, replace, or restore lost information on lost or damaged valuable papers and records, including those which exist on electronic or magnetic media, for which duplicates do not exist.

WHAT MUST BE DONE IN CASE OF LOSS

1. **Notice** -- In case of a loss, **you** must:

   a. give **us** or **our** agent prompt notice including a description of the property involved (**we** may request written notice);

   b. give notice to the police when the act that causes the loss is a crime; and

   c. give notice to the credit card company if the loss involves a credit card.

2. **Protect Property -- You** must take all reasonable steps to protect covered property at and after an insured loss to avoid further loss. **We** pay the reasonable costs incurred by **you** for necessary repairs or emergency measures performed solely to protect covered property from further damage by a covered peril if a covered peril has already caused a loss to covered property. However, **we** do not pay for such repairs or emergency measures performed on property which has not been damaged by a covered peril. This does not increase **our limit**.

3. **Proof of Loss -- You** must send **us**, within 60 days after **our** request, a signed, sworn proof of loss. This must include the following information:

   a. the time, place, and circumstances of the loss;

   b. other policies of insurance that may cover the loss;

   c. **your** interest and the interests of all others in the property involved, including all mortgages and liens;

d. changes in title or occupancy of the covered property during the policy period;

e. detailed estimates for repair or replacement of covered property;

f. available plans and specifications of buildings or structures;

g. detailed estimates of any covered loss of income and expenses; and

h. an inventory of damaged and undamaged covered personal property showing in detail the quantity, description, cost, actual cash value, and amount of the loss. **You** must attach to the inventory copies of all bills, receipts, and related documents that substantiate the inventory. An inventory of undamaged personal property is not required if the total claim for a loss is less than $10,000 and less than five percent of the total **limit**.

4. **Examination Under Oath -- You** must submit to examination under oath in matters connected with the loss as often as **we** reasonably request and give **us** sworn statements of the answers. If more than one person is examined, **we** have the right to examine and receive statements separately and not in the presence of the others.

5. **Records -- You** must produce records, including tax returns and bank microfilms of all cancelled checks, relating to value, loss, and expense and permit copies and extracts to be made of them as often as **we** reasonably request.

6. **Damaged Property -- You** must exhibit the damaged and undamaged property as often as **we** reasonably request and allow **us** to inspect or take samples of the property.

7. **Volunteer Payments -- You** must not, except at **your** own expense, voluntarily make any payments, assume any obligations, pay or offer any rewards, or incur any other expenses except as respects protecting property from further damage.

8. **Abandonment -- We** do not have to accept any abandonment of property.

9. **Cooperation -- You** must cooperate in performing all acts required by the Commercial Property Coverage.

VALUATION

1. **Actual Cash Value** -- When replacement cost is not shown on the **declarations** for covered property, the value is based on the actual cash value at the time of the loss (with a deduction for depreciation), except as provided in paragraphs 2. through 9. below.

2. **Limited Replacement Cost** -- When the **limit** for Building Property satisfies the coinsurance requirement, **we** pay up to $2,500 to cover the cost to repair or replace **your** buildings or structures. This applies only when the total loss does not exceed $2,500. This provision does not apply to awnings; canopies; floor coverings; appliances for refrigerating, ventilating, cooking, dishwashing, or laundering; or outdoor equipment or furniture.

3. **Glass** -- The value of glass is based on the cost of safety glazing material where required by code, ordinance, or law.

4. **Merchandise Sold** -- The value of merchandise that **you** have sold but not delivered is based on the selling price less all discounts and unincurred expenses.

5. **Valuable Papers and Records** -- The value of valuable papers and records, including those which exist on electronic or magnetic media (other than prepackaged software programs) is based on the cost of blank materials, and the labor to transcribe or copy the records when there is a duplicate.

6. **Tenant's Improvements** -- The value of tenant's improvements losses is based on the actual cash value if repaired or replaced at **your** expense within a reasonable time.

   The value of tenant's improvements losses is based on a portion of **your** original cost if not repaired or replaced within a reasonable time. This portion is determined as follows:

   a. Divide the number of days from the date of the loss to the expiration date of the lease by the number of days from the date of installation to the expiration date of the lease; and

   b. Multiply the figure determined in 6.a. above by the original cost.

   If **your** lease contains a renewal option, the expiration of the lease in this procedure is replaced by the expiration of the renewal option period.

Tenant's improvements losses are not covered if repaired or replaced at another's expense.

7. **Pair or Set** -- The value of a lost or damaged article which is part of a pair or set is based on a reasonable proportion of the value of the entire pair or set. The loss is not considered a total loss of the pair or set.

8. **Loss to Parts** -- The value of a lost or damaged part of an item that consists of several parts when it is complete is based on the value of only the lost or damaged part or the cost to repair or replace it.

9. **Replacement Cost** -- When replacement cost is shown on the **declarations** for covered property, the value is based on replacement cost without any deduction for depreciation.

   This replacement cost provision does not apply to objects of art, rarity, or antiquity; property of others; or paragraphs 3. through 8. above.

   The replacement cost is limited to the cost of repair or replacement with similar materials on the same site and used for the same purpose. The payment shall not exceed the amount **you** spend to repair or replace the damaged or destroyed property.

   Except as provided under Limited Replacement Cost, replacement cost valuation does not apply until the damaged or destroyed property is repaired or replaced. **You** may make a claim for actual cash value before repair or replacement takes place, and later for the replacement cost if **you** notify **us** of **your** intent within 180 days after the loss.

HOW MUCH WE PAY

1. **Insurable Interest** -- **We** do not cover more than **your** insurable interest in any property.

2. **Deductible** -- **We** pay only that part of **your** loss over the deductible amount stated on the **declarations** in any one occurrence. The deductible applies to the loss before application of any coinsurance or reporting provision.

3. **Loss Settlement Terms** -- Subject to paragraphs 1., 2., 4., 5., and 6. under How Much We Pay, **we** pay the lesser of:

   a. the amount determined under Valuation;

   b. the cost to repair, replace, or rebuild the property with material of like kind and quality to the extent practicable; or

   c. the **limit** that applies to covered property.

4. **Coinsurance** -- When a coinsurance percentage is shown on the **declarations**, **we** only pay a part of the loss if the **limit** is less than the value of the covered property at the time of the loss multiplied by the coinsurance percentage shown for it on the **declarations**. **Our** part of the loss is determined using the following steps:

a. Multiply the value of the covered property at the time of the loss by the coinsurance percentage;

b. Divide the **limit** for covered property by the figure determined in 4.a. above; and

c. Multiply the total amount of loss, after the application of any deductible, by the figure determined in 4.b. above.

The most **we** pay is the amount determined in 4.c. above or the **limit**, whichever is less. **We** do not pay any remaining part of the loss.

If there is more than one **limit** shown on the **declarations** for this Coverage Part, this procedure applies separately to each **limit**.

If there is only one **limit** shown on the **declarations** for this Coverage Part, this procedure applies to the total of all covered property to which the **limit** applies.

Example -- Underinsurance

Value of covered property	$100,000
Coinsurance	80%
Limit	$60,000
Loss	$21,000
Deductible	$1,000

Step a.: $100,000 x 80% = $80,000 (minimum **limit** needed to meet coinsurance requirements)

Step b.: $60,000 ÷ $80,000 = .75

Step c.: $21,000 - $1,000 = $20,000
$20,000 x .75 = $15,000

We pay no more than $15,000. **We** do not pay the remaining $6,000.

Example -- Sufficient Insurance

Value of covered property	$100,000
Coinsurance	80%
Limit	$80,000
Loss	$21,000
Deductible	$1,000

Step a.: $100,000 x 80% = $80,000 (minimum **limit** needed to meet coinsurance requirements)

Step b.: $80,000 ÷ $80,000 = 1.00

Step c.: $21,000 - $1,000 = $20,000
$20,000 x 1.00 = $20,000

We pay no more than $20,000 in excess of the deductible. No penalty applies.

Example -- Blanket Limit

Value of covered property	
Building at Location 1.	$75,000
Building at Location 2.	$75,000
Personal Property at Location 2.	$50,000
Total Value of covered property	$200,000
Coinsurance	80%
Limit	$128,000
Loss	
Building at Location 2.	$20,000
Personal Property at Location 2.	$11,000
Total Loss	$31,000
Deductible	$1,000

Step a.: $200,000 x 80% = $160,000 (minimum **limit** needed to meet coinsurance requirements)

Step b.: $128,000 ÷ $160,000 = .80

Step c.: $31,000 - $1,000 = $30,000
$30,000 x .80 = $24,000

We pay no more than $24,000. **We** do not pay the remaining $7,000.

5. **Insurance Under More Than One Coverage** -- If more than one coverage of this policy insures the same loss, **we** pay no more than the actual claim or loss sustained.

6. **Insurance Under More Than One Policy** -- **You** may have another policy subject to the same plan, **terms**, conditions, and provisions as this policy. If **you** do, **we** pay **our** share of the covered loss. **Our** share is the proportion that the applicable **limit** under this policy bears to the **limit** of all policies covering on the same basis.

If there is another policy covering the same loss, other than that described above, **we** pay only for the amount of covered loss in excess of the amount due from that other policy, whether **you** can collect on it or not. But **we** do not pay more than the applicable **limit**.

LOSS PAYMENT

1. **Our Options -- We** may:

   a. pay the value of the loss;

   b. pay the cost of repairing or replacing the loss;

   c. rebuild, repair, or replace with property of equivalent kind and quality, to the extent practicable; or

   d. take all or any part of the damaged property at the agreed or appraised value.

   We must give **you** notice of **our** intentions within 30 days after we have received a satisfactory proof of loss.

2. **Your Losses -- We** adjust all losses with **you.** Payment is made to **you** unless another loss payee is named in the policy. A covered loss is payable 30 days after a satisfactory proof of loss is received, and:

   a. the amount of the loss has been agreed to in writing;

   b. an appraisal award has been filed with **us**; or

   c. a final judgment has been entered.

3. **Property of Others --** Losses to property of others may be adjusted with and paid to:

   a. **you** on behalf of the owner; or

   b. the owner.

   If **we** pay the owner, **we** do not have to pay **you**. **We** may also choose to defend any suits arising from the owners at **our** expense.

OTHER CONDITIONS

In addition to the policy **terms** which are contained in other sections of the Commercial Property Coverage, the following conditions apply.

1. **Appraisal --** If **you** and **we** do not agree on the amount of the loss or the actual cash value of covered property, either party may demand that these amounts be determined by appraisal.

If either makes a written demand for appraisal, each selects a competent, independent appraiser and notifies the other of the appraiser's identity within 20 days of receipt of the written demand. The two appraisers then select a competent, impartial umpire. If the two appraisers are unable to agree upon an umpire within 15 days, **you** or **we** can ask a judge of a court of record in the state where the property is located to select an umpire.

The appraisers then determine and state separately the amount of each loss.

The appraisers also determine the actual cash value of covered property items at the time of the loss, if requested.

A written agreement is binding on all parties. If the appraisers fail to agree within a reasonable time, they submit only their differences to the umpire. Written agreement so itemized and signed by any two of these three is binding on all parties.

Each appraiser is paid by the party selecting that appraiser. Other expenses of the appraisal and the compensation of the umpire is paid equally by **you** and **us**.

If there is an appraisal, **we** retain **our** right to deny the claim.

2. **Mortgage Provisions --** If a mortgagee (mortgage holder) is named in this policy, loss to Building Property shall be paid to the mortgagee and **you** as their interest appears. If more than one mortgagee is named, they shall be paid in order of precedence.

The insurance for the mortgagee continues in effect even when **your** insurance may be void because of **your** acts, neglect, or failure to comply with the coverage **terms.** The insurance for the mortgagee does not continue in effect if the mortgagee is aware of changes in ownership or substantial increase in risk and does not notify **us**.

If **we** cancel this policy, **we** notify the mortgagee at least 10 days before the effective date of cancellation if **we** cancel for **your** nonpayment of premium, or 30 days before the effective date of cancellation if **we** cancel for any other reason.

We may request payment of the premium from the mortgagee, if **you** fail to pay the premium.

If **we** pay the mortgagee for a loss where **your** insurance may be void, the mortgagee's right to collect that portion of the mortgage debt from **you** then belongs to **us.** This does not affect the mortgagee's right to collect the remainder of the mortgage debt from **you.** As an alternative, **we** may pay the mortgagee the remaining principal and accrued interest in return for a full assignment of the mortgagee's interest and any instruments given as security for the mortgage debt.

If **we** choose not to renew this policy, **we** give written notice to the mortgagee at least 10 days before the expiration date of this policy.

3. **Recoveries --** If **we** pay **you** for the loss and lost or damaged property is recovered, or payment is made by those responsible for the loss, the following provisions apply:

   a. **You** must notify **us** promptly if **you** recover property or receive payment.

   b. **We** must notify **you** promptly if **we** recover property, or receive payment.

   c. Any recovery expenses incurred by either are reimbursed first.

   d. **You** may keep the recovered property but **you** must refund to **us** the amount of the claim paid, or any lesser amount to which **we** agree.

   e. If the claim paid is less than the agreed loss due to a deductible or other limiting **term** of this

policy any recovery is pro rated between **you** and **us** based on **our** respective interest in the loss.

4. **Vacancy -- Unoccupancy -- We** do not pay for loss caused by attempted theft, breakage of building glass, sprinkler leakage (unless **you** have protected the system against freezing), theft, vandalism, or water damage occurring while the building or structure has been:

   a. vacant for more than 60 consecutive days; or

   b. unoccupied for more than

      1) 60 consecutive days; or
      2) the usual or incidental unoccupancy period for the described premises

   whichever is longer.

The amount **we** pay for any loss that is not otherwise excluded is reduced by 15%.

Unoccupied means that the customary activities or operations of the described occupancy are suspended, but business personal property has not been removed. The building or structure shall be considered vacant and not unoccupied when the occupants have moved, leaving the building or structure empty or containing only limited business personal property. Buildings or structures under construction are not considered vacant or unoccupied.

GENERAL PROPERTY FORM – MCP 010 06 12

YOUR POLICY INCLUDES:

- The Declarations / Supplemental Declarations, Including Information About –
  - *You* and *Your* Business
  - The Locations and Property Items Covered
  - The Applicable Coverages
  - The Applicable General Limits and Deductible
  - The Applicable Special Limits and Factors
  - Who *We* are, and *Your* Insurance Representative

- This General Property Form – MCP 010.

- Additional Endorsements, if Applicable.

THIS INSURANCE FORM INCLUDES:

DEFINITIONS AND WORD MEANINGS

Words shown in *italics* are defined for the purposes of this insurance in Glossaries: See the Glossary and Part I C.

The word "provisions" refers to all or part of the text of this insurance contract – including agreements, conditions, exclusions, limits, limitations, and all other terms. The term "described buildings" means buildings described in the Declarations. The term "premises / locations" means the premises / locations described in the Declarations. The term "business / operations" means the business/operations described in the Declarations.

The meaning of other words / phrases not specifically defined in the Glossaries are to be found in their relevant conventional definition based on consideration of the context in which they are used in this policy.

COVERAGE PARTS

Part I – this coverage part – includes provisions relating to General Property Insurance for *your* buildings and / or business personal property. If included in this insurance contract, Part II relates to General Liability Insurance for covered operations and premises.

© 2012 MSO®, Inc.

PART I A • MAIN COVERAGES

INSURING AGREEMENT

A. *We* provide insurance for those of the following coverages for which a specific limit of liability and related premium charge is shown in the Declarations (the term "Declarations" also includes a Supplemental Declarations or any other similar form), subject to all applicable provisions. If a series of Declarations or Change Endorsements are issued, then this term means the current Declarations or Change Endorsement.

B. Unless otherwise specifically provided in this policy, this insurance applies only to *covered loss* that takes place during the current policy term on the applicable described premises.

C. With respect to personal property covered by this policy (including any covered within the definition of or by Extension of Coverage A), coverage is extended to *covered loss* that also takes place outdoors (meaning not in a building) on, or within 100 feet of, the described premises.

D. **Insuring Agreement Qualification**
The Coverages in this policy are subject to certain Exclusions and Limitations, including Part I Common Exclusions and Parts I D, E, and F.

COVERAGE A • BUILDINGS / STRUCTURES

We cover described buildings (the general term buildings also includes other sorts of structures). Coverage A also includes the following property to the extent that such is part of, or incidental to the use of, described buildings:

1. Additions under construction.*

2. Alterations or repairs.

3. Building equipment, fixtures, materials, and supplies, intended for use in alteration, construction, or repair of described buildings.*

4. Completed additions.

5. Equipment, fixtures, and machinery permanently installed as part of described buildings.

6. Outdoor fixtures. For example, flag poles, ground lights, light standards.

* Such property is covered by this policy only on an excess basis, if covered by other insurance.

COVERAGE B • BUSINESS PERSONAL PROPERTY

We cover the following property located in or on described buildings:

1. Tangible personal property (including equipment, fixtures, and machines not subject to Coverage A) owned by *you* and used in *your* described business / operations.

2. Tangible personal property of others – but only to the extent of the value of the labor, materials, and supplies provided by *you* in connection with such property.

3. Tenant's improvements and betterments. This means *your* remaining use interest in additions, alterations, fixtures, and installations, not legally removable by *you*, that are both: made part of a building that *you* occupy (but do not own) and

acquired or made at *your* expense.

This coverage applies only if the cost of such property is not included in *your* rent and repair or replacement is at *your* expense.

COVERAGE C • PERSONAL PROPERTY OF OTHERS

We cover tangible personal property of others, located in or on described buildings, in *your* care, control, or custody in connection with *your* described business / operations.

Our payment under this coverage is solely for the account of the owner of such tangible personal property. Such beneficiary must comply with all relevant loss settlement and other conditions.

COVERAGE D • LOSS OF USE RESULTING FROM DIRECT COVERED LOSS

A. *We* cover *your* loss of Business Income / Extra Expense, as described in the following paragraphs, that is the direct result of a *direct covered loss* that results in either:

1. The necessary interruption of *your* described business / operations; or

2. The described premises being made incapable of being occupied.

We also cover such loss if access to the described premises is prohibited by order of any civil authority. This order must result from fortuitous direct physical loss to property at a premises other than the described premises (provided such other premises / property is not occupied or owned by *you*) caused by an applicable cause of loss covered under this policy.

B. **Coverage Description**

1. **The following coverages apply as described in the Declarations:**

   a. If Coverage D: Business Income (D.1) and Extra Expense (D.2).

   b. If Coverage D.1: Business Income (Only).

   c. If Coverage D.2: Extra Expense (Only).

2. **Coverage D. 1 – Business Income**
   We cover *your* following loss of Business Income, as described, to the extent that such would otherwise be earned or incurred by *your* business / operations had the *direct covered loss* not occurred.

   a. **Net Income**
   Your loss of net income (net profit or loss before income taxes) plus continuing necessary normal operating expenses to the extent that such would exist had the *direct covered loss* not occurred.

   b. **Rental Income**
   Your loss of rents from tenant occupancies (that *you* rent or customarily hold for rental to others under written leases) plus continuing expenses that are the obligation of tenants, under such leases, but which become *your* obligation because of the *direct covered loss*.

– 2 –

Coverage D. 1 does not extend to any expenses that do not continue, or need not continue, during the applicable coverage period.

3. Coverage D. 2 – Extra Expense

a. *We* cover any sort of necessary reasonable expenses that *you* incur in order:

1. To continue, to the extent feasible, *your* normal business / operations at the same capability and quality of service as would otherwise exist had the *direct covered loss* not occurred – whether continued at the described premises or elsewhere (a replacement or temporary location); or

2. To minimize the period of interruption if *you* cannot continue *your* normal business / operations at the same capability and quality of service as would otherwise exist had the *direct covered loss* not occurred.

b. Extra expense means those increased expenses, incurred as described in the preceding Paragraphs a.1 and 2, that *you* would not otherwise incur in *your* normal business / operations had the *direct covered loss* not occurred – including the expenses to relocate at or equip and operate a replacement or temporary location.

4. Special Costs or Expenses

We also cover any sort of special costs or increased expenses that *you* incur specifically to minimize or reduce *covered loss:* but not for an amount more than such costs or expenses reduce the amount *we* would be otherwise obligated to pay had *you* not incurred such costs or expenses.

5. Cancellation of Contract

If the subject interruption or unoccupancy directly causes the cancellation, lapse, or suspension of a written agreement, contract, or lease, *we* also cover *your* loss of Business Income and / or Extra Expense directly arising out of such, provided that *you* can demonstrate that *you* otherwise would have been able to satisfy and meet all the requirements of the agreement, contract, or lease had the *direct covered loss* not occurred.

This does not apply to any loss of Business Income and / or Extra Expense that may continue beyond the applicable coverage period.

C. Coverage Period(s)

1. Basic Period of Indemnity

Our obligation begins on the date of the *direct covered loss* and ends on the date that (a) or (b) ends, whichever is the shorter period:

a. The period required with diligence and ongoing effort to restore *your* covered business / operations to substantially the same capability and quality of service that existed immediately prior to the *direct covered loss;* or

b. The period required with diligence and ongoing effort to repair, replace, or restore the damaged property for the same purpose and occupancy.

But, if *you* occupy a premises owned by others and do not have control of its repair or restoration then: *we* provide coverage (if required) beyond this period for the additional time required to effect such repair, replacement, or restoration or 90 days, whichever one is the shorter period.

2. Civil Authority – Special Period of Indemnity

Our obligation for *covered loss* caused by order of any civil authority begins on the date of the order prohibiting access and runs for 14 consecutive days or the end of the period that access is denied, whichever one is the shorter period.

3. Electronic Media – Special Period of Indemnity

a. *We* cover *your* loss of Business Income, up to a period not exceeding 60 consecutive days (subject to the preceding Paragraph 1), if *direct covered loss* to electronic media causes or contributes to such loss: any additional loss beyond such period caused by the failure to replace or restore electronic media is not covered by *us*.

b. Electronic media are: (1) any sort of electronic data processing, recording, or storage media, including the data stored on such media; (2) programming records used for electronic data processing or electronically controlled equipment.

c. If MCP 501 along with a number is listed in the Declarations, the number "60" in the preceding Paragraph 3.a, is replaced by the number shown for the subject described premises.

d. If MCP 508 is listed in the Declarations, Exclusion 1 in Part I F does not apply.

4. Extended Period of Indemnity

a. To assist *you* in *your* recovery after the end of the basic period, *we* extend coverage (if required) for up to an additional 30 consecutive days beyond the basic period described in the preceding Paragraph 1.

b. If MCP 502 along with a number is listed in the Declarations, the number "30" in the preceding Paragraph 4.a, is replaced by the number shown for the subject described premises.

5. Policy Term Extension

The described periods are not limited by expiration of the policy term.

6. Special / Extended Periods of Indemnity and Coverage D Limit

The described extended / special periods do not increase the applicable limit.

D. Special Conditions

1. *Your* business / operations, as referred to in this policy, means those activities and the associated expenses and income that are normal to *your* described business / operations at the described premises.

2. *You* are required to resume, in whole or in part, *your* normal business / operations as soon as possible and to

the maximum extent feasible.

E.   Special Exclusions / Limitations
We do not cover expense or loss caused by or resulting from the following:
1. **Cancellation**
The cancellation or suspension of any agreement, contract, lease, or license, other than as provided for in Part I A, Coverage D, Item B.5.

2. *Finished stock*
Loss to *finished stock* or the time required to reproduce

finished stock: this does not apply to Extra Expense.

3. **Interference**
Delay caused by strikers (or others) with rebuilding, repairing, or replacing property or resuming *your* business / operations at the described premises, whether such delay arises at the described premises or elsewhere.

4. **Antennas and Satellite Dishes**
Loss to antennas and satellite dishes (including their lead-in wiring, masts, and towers): this is deleted if MCP 503 is listed in the Declarations.

PART I B • SUPPLEMENTAL COVERAGES

SUPPLEMENTAL COVERAGES – ADDITIONAL CONDITIONS
We provide the following Supplemental Coverages as extensions of the main coverages (but only when, and then to the extent that, such main coverages apply under this policy) subject to the following:

A. These Supplemental Coverages do not modify or waive any provisions in this policy except to the extent specifically described: such are subject to all underlying provisions applicable in this policy, except to the extent specifically modified in Part I B.

B. The limits shown for the following Supplemental Coverages are additional amounts of insurance unless otherwise indicated. However, these special limits are not increased or added together because *we* provide multiple coverages or cover multiple locations in one or more policies.

C. If the Supplemental Coverage is keyed to a percentage of the underlying main coverage and such coverage is provided on multiple items at different limits, then:
1. If the Supplemental Coverage can be keyed to a specific described item, *we* use the coverage limit for that item as the basis limit.
2. If the Supplemental Coverage cannot be keyed to a specific described item, *we* use the single greatest limit provided in this policy for that coverage as the basis limit.

D. If the Supplemental Coverage is keyed to property subject to different causes of loss, then:
1. If the Supplemental Coverage can be keyed to a specific described item, *we* use the causes of loss for that item.
2. If the Supplemental Coverage cannot be keyed to a specific described item, *we* use the most relevant causes of loss at the described premises for the subject property: if at a newly acquired location, *we* use the most relevant causes of loss at the described premises for the subject property.

E. The Coinsurance Condition is not applicable to these Supplemental Coverages, except where specifically stated. However, any additional amounts of insurance applicable to the Supplemental Coverages may not be used to satisfy the Coinsurance Condition requirements for the underlying main coverage.

1. **ACCOUNTS RECEIVABLE COVERAGE**
A. *We* cover, up to the applicable limit shown in the Supplemental Declarations, loss arising out of *your* inability to collect on accounts receivable / credit card billings because of *covered loss* to records of such accounts. This covers all sums due *you* from customers which are uncollectible because of such loss. This also includes *your* increased collection expenses as well as other reasonable necessary expenses incurred by *you* to replace or restore these records.

Parts I E and I F (other than 8 and 12.A) do not apply.

Coverage does not apply to loss:
1. Due to accounting, billing, or bookkeeping error or omission; or
2. Where proof is dependent upon an audit, or inventory computation. But such audit can be used in support of a claim which *you* prove through other sources.

B. **Deductible**
1. A $250 deductible applies to this coverage unless MCP 510 is listed in the Declarations: if MCP 510 is applicable, the general deductible amount shown in the Declarations applies to this coverage.
2. If a specific separate deductible amount is specified for this coverage in the Declarations, such specific deductible applies (the preceding paragraph does not apply in such cases).

C. This Supplemental Coverage applies only in connection with Coverage B.

2. **AUTOMATIC INCREASE / PEAK SEASON COVERAGES**
A. **Automatic Increase**
The current limit of liability shown for Coverage A or Coverage B is increased on an annual pro rata basis by the factor shown in the Supplemental Declarations.

If no factor is shown in the Supplemental Declarations, then no automatic increase is applicable.

B. **Peak Season**
The current limit of liability shown for Coverage B is increased by the factor shown in the Supplemental Declarations during those periods of time during the year

when it is *your* normal practice to increase the amount of business personal property at the described premises because of customary seasonal or holiday sales.

If no factor is shown in the Supplemental Declarations, then no peak season increase is applicable.

C. These increases do not apply to any Supplemental Coverages and are not applicable in determining the basis limit for the Supplemental Coverages.

3. **BUILDING EXTENSION COVERAGES**

A. **Glass Extension (Cause of Loss Options 3 and 5 Only)**
We cover, up to the applicable limits shown in the Supplemental Declarations, loss to glass (other than signs) that is part of a building. The "per item" limit applies separately to each pane, panel, plate (or multiple plate) and similar discrete item or unit.

If the loss is caused by any of the *specified causes of loss* (other than vandalism), or the building is constructed of glass curtain walls, the special limits do not apply.

This Supplemental Coverage does not provide an additional amount of insurance.

B. **Outdoor Signs Extension**
Coverage A is extended to cover, up to the applicable limits shown in the Supplemental Declarations:
1. Outdoor signs (including sign posts and poles) not attached to buildings. The applicable causes of loss are those applicable to outdoor signs attached to buildings: if there are no outdoor signs attached to buildings, cause of loss Option 2. B applies.

2. Outdoor signs (including sign posts and poles) attached to buildings for the causes of loss applicable to the subject building.

C. **Personal Property Extension**
Coverage A is extended to cover the following property when both owned by *you* and used primarily to maintain or service covered buildings / described premises: air conditioners; cooking, dishwashing, laundering, refrigeration, and ventilating appliances; fire extinguishers; floor coverings; lawn care and snow removal equipment – including riding mowers and similar items, but not other types of vehicles; outdoor fixtures / furniture.

This Supplemental Coverage does not provide an additional amount of insurance.

4. **BUILDING CODE / LAW COVERAGE**

A. Coverage A is extended to cover the following losses or expenses that ensue as a direct consequence of *covered loss* at the described premises. *We* cover such for an amount determined by applying the applicable factor shown in the Supplemental Declarations to the Coverage A limit for the subject property: the product is the specified limit for this Supplemental Coverage (Items 1, 2, and 3 combined). The losses or expenses covered are:
1. The loss caused by enforcement of any building, land use, or zoning code / law in force the date of the

covered loss, that:
a. Requires the demolition of parts of the same property not damaged by a covered cause of loss.

b. Regulates the construction or repair of buildings, or establishes building, land use or zoning requirements at the described premises.

2. The increased expense *you* incur to construct, rebuild, or repair the property caused by enforcement of building, land use, or zoning code / law in force on the date of the *covered loss:* the property must be intended for the same use / occupancy as the current property unless otherwise prohibited by such code / law.

3. The expense *you* incur to demolish undamaged parts of property and clear the site of such parts caused by enforcement of building, land use, or zoning code / law in force on the date of the *covered loss.*

If MCP 504 is listed in the Declarations, then Coverage D is extended, as to Condition C. 1 under Part I A, to the increased period of time required to comply with the conditions described in the preceding Paragraph 1.

B. *We* are not liable for payment under this Supplemental Coverage:
1. Until the property is repaired or replaced by *you* or by *us* (at the same premises or elsewhere if permitted or required by this policy); and

Unless the repair or replacement is made as soon as possible after the loss, but no later than the period described in Part I G, Condition 2.C. 2.b.

2. For any loss or expense arising out of the enforcement of any code, directive, law, ordinance, or regulation requiring any *insured* or others to clean up, contain, detoxify, monitor, neutralize, remove, test for, or treat any *pollutants,* asbestos, *fungi,* mold or lead contamination.

C. *Our* maximum liability under this Supplemental Coverage (A.1, 2 and 3 combined), subject to (1), the specified limit and (2), the applicable limits and limitations on *our* liability described in Part I G, Condition 2.A, is the sum of the following:
1. The cost to demolish the property and clear the site. And,

2. The cost to reconstruct / replace the property on the described premises.

D. If a Coinsurance Condition reduction applies to the underlying *covered loss* (See Part I G), then the same amount of reduction applies to this Supplemental Coverage.

E. **This Supplemental Coverage applies only to buildings covered on a replacement basis (See Part I G, Condition 2) – unless MCP 506 is listed in the Declarations.**

5. *COLLAPSE – CAUSE OF LOSS OPTIONS 3 AND 5 ONLY*

   A. Coverage is extended to cover the *collapse* of a building or any structural part of a building that ensues only as a consequence of the following:

      1. Any cause of loss provided for in Cause of Loss Option 3. Under this coverage, these causes of loss apply to both covered buildings and business personal property.

      2. Hidden decay, unless such decay is known to an *insured* prior to *collapse.*

      3. Hidden insect or vermin damage, unless such damage is known to an *insured* prior to *collapse.*

      4. Weight of contents, equipment, animals, or people.

      5. Weight of rain that collects on a roof.

      6. Use of defective material or methods in construction, remodeling, renovation or repair.

   B. For the preceding Items A.2 through A.6, *we* do not cover the following unless the loss is a direct result of the *collapse* of a building or a structural part of a building: antennas, including their lead-in wires, masts, or towers; awnings; beach or diving platforms and related equipment or structures; decks; docks, piers or wharves; downspouts or gutters; fences; outdoor swimming pools; paved surfaces of any sort (including but not limited to, bridges, driveways, parking lots, patios, pavements, roads, walks); retaining walls; yard fixtures.

   C. **This Supplemental Coverage applies only to property covered in this policy by Cause of Loss Options 3 or 5.**

   This Supplemental Coverage does not provide an additional amount of insurance.

6. **CONSEQUENT LOSS COVERAGES (SPOILAGE)**

   A. *We* cover, up to the applicable limits shown in the Supplemental Declarations, loss to covered business personal property spoiled as a consequence of the disruption of cooling, electrical, heating, or refrigeration services on the described premises resulting from the following:

      1. **Loss of Utility Services**

         The loss of utility services to the described premises arising out of fortuitous direct physical loss to property of the utility caused by a cause of loss that would be covered by this policy if it were *your* property.

      2. **Mechanical Breakdown**

         The abrupt accidental mechanical breakdown or faulty operation (including refrigerant leakage) of equipment providing cooling, electrical, heating, or refrigeration services: the limit shown for this Extension is *our* total aggregate limit for all such loss during any annual (12 month) policy term.

         This coverage does not include any loss arising out of conditions within *your* control. For example: failure to repair a defect or to repair or replace defective

equipment or parts if the defect is known to *you, your* employees, or those acting on *your* behalf; insufficient fuel, inadequate or improper maintenance; disconnection of or failure to connect units to power source; failure to turn on power or units; failure to set proper temperature.

   If a $0 (zero) limit is specified, then the subject coverage is not applicable under this policy.

   B. Spoilage that results from *covered loss* to covered cooling, electrical, heating, or refrigeration equipment on the described premises is not subject to the special limits.

7. **DEBRIS REMOVAL COVERAGE – COVERAGES A, B, C**

   A. *We* cover, subject to the limits specified in the following Paragraphs B and C, the necessary reasonable expenses incurred to remove the debris of a *covered loss.*

   B. *We* pay such debris removal expense that *you* incur – but only up to an amount not exceeding that equal to the product of the amount otherwise payable by *us* for the *covered loss* times the factor shown in the Supplemental Declarations. This amount is not additional insurance and does not increase *our* maximum limit of liability on the loss.

   C. *We* also pay such debris removal expense, up to the applicable limit shown in the Supplemental Declarations, if either:

      1. The debris removal expense incurred exceeds the amount available for debris removal expense calculated in the preceding Paragraph B; or

      2. The sum of the debris removal expense incurred and the amount otherwise payable by *us* for the *covered loss* exceeds *our* maximum limit of liability on the loss.

   We pay up to the shortfall or the special limit, whichever is the lesser amount.

   D. This Supplemental Coverage does not apply to any of the following expenses:

      1. To remove the debris of trees.

      2. To extract *pollutants* (whether or not covered property) from land or water.*

      3. To remove, replace, or restore land or water that is polluted or is a *pollutant.* *

      4. To remove volcanic ash, dust, or particulate matter that does not cause loss.

      * This also excludes the expense to safely dispose of such as required by any code, directive, law, ordinance, or regulation.

   E. This Supplemental Coverage applies only to such covered expenses reported to *us* in writing within 180 days from the date of the *covered loss.*

   F. Other than Extension C, these Extensions do not provide additional amounts of insurance.

8. **ELECTRONIC DATA COVERAGE**

   A. Coverage is extended to cover, up to the applicable limit shown in the Declarations Supplement, *your* expenses to replace or restore electronic data corrupted or destroyed by direct physical loss covered by this policy.

   B. Exclusion 1 in Part I F does not apply to this Supplemental Coverage. However, *we* do not cover any loss or damage caused by or resulting from manipulation of a computer or computer system, including its electronic data, by any of *your* employees or any entity retained, by or for *you,* to design, inspect, install, maintain, modify, repair or replace such computer or computer system.

   C. The special limit specified for this Supplemental Coverage is *our* total liability for all such expenses for each annual (12 month) term of the policy – regardless of the number of occurrences or total expenses incurred.

   The limit is not cumulative from year to year even if the occurrence takes place over a period of years. If an occurrence begins in one policy term and continues into another policy term, all loss or damage is considered to have been sustained in the policy term in which the occurrence began. Coverage for that occurrence will not apply under the subsequent policy term.

9. **EMERGENCY REMOVAL**

   We cover fortuitous direct physical loss to covered property when removed from the described premises because of imminent danger of loss by a covered cause of loss.

   This Supplemental Coverage applies for 30 consecutive days from the first day of removal.

10. **FIRE EXPENSE COVERAGES**

    A. **Fire Department Service Charges**

    We cover, up to the applicable limit shown in the Supplemental Declarations, *your* written contractual obligation to pay service charges when a fire department is called to protect or save property from imminent loss by an applicable covered cause of loss. The deductible does not apply.

    This Supplemental Coverage does not cover service charges:

    1. Incurred prior to assumption of *your* contractual obligation;

    2. Arising in connection with a false alarm.

    B. **Fire Extinguisher Recharge Expense**

    We cover, up to the applicable limit shown in the Supplemental Declarations, the cost to recharge fire extinguishers / related equipment discharged in pursuit of extinguishing a fire at the described premises. The deductible does not apply.

11. **NEWLY ACQUIRED PROPERTY COVERAGES**

    A. *We* cover property newly acquired or constructed by *you,* as well as Loss of Use (if covered by this policy) resulting from fortuitous direct physical loss to such property, as follows:

    1. **Coverage A**

       We cover, up to the applicable limits shown in the

Supplemental Declarations, the following:

a. New buildings while being built on described premises.

   We also cover temporary structures erected to assist in construction of new buildings or of additions / alterations to described buildings while such construction is taking place: but such are covered by this policy only on an excess basis if covered by any other insurance.

b. Buildings at a location newly acquired by *you* if such buildings are intended for use either similar to that of described buildings or as a warehouse.

2. **Coverage B**

   We cover, up to the applicable limits shown in the Supplemental Declarations business personal property owned by *you* at a location newly acquired by *you,* other than exhibitions and fairs. However, when *you* are moving covered property from a described premises under this policy to a newly described premises under this policy, then the applicable Coverage B limit applies for all such premises for 10 days after moving begins.

3. **Coverage D**

   We cover the subject loss arising out of *direct covered loss* to the following property:

   a. **Alterations or New Buildings at Described Premises**

      1. Alterations or additions to described buildings.

      2. New buildings, whether under construction or completed.

      3. Building materials or supplies and equipment or machinery which are used in alteration or construction at described premises or incidental to *your* occupancy of the new building.

      If the subject *direct covered loss* delays the start of *your* covered business / operations at the described premises, then this Extension begins on the projected start up date (had the *direct covered loss* not occurred).

      This Extension is subject to the Coverage D limit and Coinsurance Condition. This Extension does not provide an additional amount of insurance.

   b. **Newly Acquired Locations**

      Property owned by *you* at any location that *you* newly acquire, other than exhibitions or fairs: *we* cover such up to the applicable limits shown in the Supplemental Declarations.

4. **Special Limits**

   The special limits referred in the preceding paragraphs are developed by multiplying the subject coverage limit (Coverage A, B, or D) by the applicable factor shown in the Supplemental

Declarations: The product is the amount available for *covered loss* to new buildings (Coverage A) or *covered loss* at new locations (Coverages B and D) – all subject to the specified maximum limit per building or per location.

B. Coverage Period

This Supplemental Coverage applies for up to a period of 60 consecutive days from the beginning date of the subject acquisition or construction: but, in no case, beyond the end of the policy term or the date on which *you* report the values to *us*, whichever date is earlier.

This coverage period does not apply to the Extension in the preceding Paragraph A.3.a.

C. Additional Premium

Additional premium is applicable for the values *you* report to *us* based on the date of acquisition or the date that *you* first begin construction.

12. OFF PREMISES COVERAGES

A. Property at Other Locations

We cover, up to the applicable limit shown in the Supplemental Declarations, loss to covered property temporarily at locations that *you* do not lease, operate, or own.

This Extension does not apply to property: at exhibitions or fairs; in or on any vehicle; in the care, control, or custody of *your* sales people; that is *stock*.

B. Property in Transit – Cause of Loss Option 5 Extension

1. *We* cover, up to the applicable limit shown in the Supplemental Declarations, *your* business personal property covered by this policy (other than property in the care, control, or custody of *your* sales people) while in course of transit away from the described premises. Such property is covered for fortuitous direct physical loss (as described in the following Paragraph 2) while in or on a motor vehicle leased, operated, or owned by *you*.

2. The direct physical losses *we* cover under this Extension are:
    a. Collision, overturn, or upset of *your* vehicle.
    b. Fire (hostile fire) or lightning, explosion, riot or civil commotion, vandalism, windstorm / hail.
    c. Theft of an entire bale, case or package by forced entry (there must be marks of forced entry) into a securely locked body or compartment of the vehicle.

3. If MCP 505 is listed in the Declarations, *we* cover, subject to the applicable limit shown in the Supplemental Declarations *(we* may show a separate sub-limit for loss by theft), *your* property while in the course of transit away from the described premises for all loss covered by Cause of Loss Option 5. The coverage described in the preceding Paragraph B.1, is deleted and replaced by that of MCP 505 and the limitations of coverage described in the preceding

Paragraphs 1 and 2 do not apply to loss covered by MCP 505.

4. This Extension and Option MCP 505:
    a. Apply only to property covered by Loss Option 5 at the described premises from which the property is in transit.
    b. Do not apply to property within 100 feet of any described premises.

C. The limits under this Supplemental Coverage do not apply to property moved pursuant to Supplemental Coverage 9 – Emergency Removal.

13. OUTDOOR PROPERTY COVERAGE

Coverage A is extended to cover, up to the applicable limit shown in the Supplemental Declarations, *your* outdoor: antennas, satellite dishes (including lead-in wiring, masts, and towers); fences; decorative plants, shrubs and trees (including any debris removal expense. Loss to any one plant, shrub, or tree is also subject to the applicable limit per item shown in the Supplemental Declarations.

Such property is covered for fortuitous direct physical loss caused by fire (hostile fire), aircraft, explosion, lightning, or riot or civil commotion, to the extent such are covered causes of loss.

14. PERSONAL PROPERTY COVERAGES

A. Creatures

Coverage B is extended to cover the following creatures:
1. Held for sale: but only if inside the building at the described premises at the time of loss.
2. Owned by others: but only if being boarded by *you* at the time of loss.

This Extension applies only to creatures destroyed by, or where their destruction is made necessary because of harm by, a *specified cause of loss*.

This Extension does not provide an additional amount of insurance.

B. Personal Effects

Coverage B is extended to cover, up to the applicable limit shown in the Supplemental Declarations, personal effects owned by *you*, or *your* directors, employees, officers, partners, or volunteer workers, while on the described premises.

C. Personal Property of Others

1. Coverage B is extended to cover, up to the applicable limit shown in the Supplemental Declarations, personal property of others in *your* care, control, or custody in connection with *your* covered business / operations (but see the Extension in the following Paragraph 2, as to leased property). *Our* payment under this coverage is solely for the account of the owner of such property, and such beneficiary must comply with all relevant loss settlement and other conditions.

This Extension is in addition to Coverage B. 2 under Part I A.

MCP 010 06 12

2. Coverage B is extended to cover leased property in *your* care, custody, or control for which *you* are contractually obligated to provide property insurance. This Extension: (a) applies for the causes of loss for which *you* are contractually responsible to the extent such causes of loss are otherwise applicable to *your* property; (b) is not subject to the Extension in the preceding Paragraph 1 or Coverage B.2 under Part I A.

This Extension does not provide an additional amount of insurance.

D. *Valuable Papers and Records*

1. Coverage B is extended to cover, up to the applicable limit shown in the Supplemental Declarations, *your* expenses, including the cost of research, incurred to replace or restore the information contained in *your* *valuable papers and records* (including electronic or magnetic media) for which duplicates do not exist because of *covered loss* to such property.

Parts I E and I F (other than 8 and 12. A) do not apply.

2. The full Coverage B limit applies to the cost of replacement of *valuable papers and records* in blank form.

3. Deductible

a. A $250 deductible applies to this coverage unless MCP 511 is listed in the Declarations: if MCP 511 is applicable, the general deductible amount shown in the Declarations applies to this coverage.

b. If a specific separate deductible amount is specified for this coverage in the Declarations, such specific deductible applies (the preceding paragraph does not apply in such case).

E. Vehicles

1. Coverage B is extended to cover the following property owned by *you:*

a. Aircraft, self-propelled machines, semi-trailers and trailers, watercraft, or other vehicles which *you:* hold for sale (other than automobiles), manufacture, process, or warehouse.

b. Canoes and rowboats while ashore at the described premises.

c. Vehicles principally operated at the described premises specifically to service the described premises or *your* described business / operations.

2. This Extension does not apply to vehicles: licensed for use on public roads; not customarily kept and operated at the described premises.

3. This Extension does not provide an additional amount of insurance.

15. POLLUTION CLEAN UP COST COVERAGE – COVERAGES A, B, C

A. *We* cover, up to the applicable limit shown in the Supplemental Declarations, the necessary reasonable expenses that *you* incur to extract *pollutants* from land or water at the described premises: but only if the discharge, dispersal, emission, escape, migration, release or seepage of *pollutants* is a consequence of a *covered loss.*

The special limit specified for this Supplemental Coverage is *our* total liability for all such expense for each annual (12 month) term of the policy – regardless of the number of occurrences or total expenses incurred.

This Supplemental Coverage applies only to such expenses reported to *us* in writing within 180 days from the date of the subject *covered loss.*

B. This Supplemental Coverage does not apply to the extraction of any sort of nuclear or radioactive materials – whether such is natural or human made.

C. If a specific deductible is shown for this Supplemental Coverage, such deductible applies in lieu of any other deductible otherwise shown as applicable in this policy.

16. PRECIOUS METALS COVERAGE – INDUSTRIAL OPERATIONS

We cover, up to the applicable limit shown in the Supplemental Declarations, *your* gold, silver, or other precious metals that are used by *you* for manufacturing purposes in connection with *your* industrial operations covered in this policy. This does not apply to the manufacturing of gold, silver, or other precious metal products.

17. STEAM EQUIPMENT OR OTHER FIRED VESSEL EXPLOSION COVERAGE

A. *We* cover loss by explosion of fuel or gas within the furnace of a fired vessel or flues or passages through which the gases of combustion pass – including such explosion loss to steam boilers, engines, pipes or turbines.

B. *We* cover loss by explosion to hot water boilers or other equipment for heating water.

C. Unless Cause of Loss Option 5 applies, explosion does not include bursting, operation, or rupture of a pressure relief device.

This Supplemental Coverage does not provide an additional amount of insurance.

18. WATER DAMAGE / RELATED DAMAGE REPAIR EXPENSE COVERAGE

A. *We* cover the following additional expenses incurred in connection with an otherwise covered sprinkler leakage loss or water damage loss (including freezing), as described under Part I C, Cause of Loss Options, when the building containing the appliance, equipment, or system is covered property under this policy:

1. The expense to repair damage to the building that occurs because of necessary reasonable efforts to get at and repair damage to the appliance, equipment, or system from which the "water" escapes.

2. The concurrently incurred expense to repair or replace that particular defective / damaged part (joint, piece of pipe, valve, or similar specific item) of the appliance, equipment, or system from which the "water" escapes.

B. This Supplemental Coverage does not apply:

1. To the expense to repair or replace the subject appliances, equipment, or systems, other than the particular defective / damaged part as provided for in the preceding Paragraph A.2.

2. If others are responsible by contract or law for payment of such expenses.

This Supplemental Coverage does not provide an additional amount of insurance.

19. WEATHER RELATED COVERAGE – CAUSE OF LOSS OPTION 5

We cover the following loss to the interior of a covered building or covered personal property within a building by hail, ice, rain, sleet, or snow:

A. Loss arising out of the thawing of hail, ice, sleet, or snow on the building.

B. Loss by any such elements to the interior of the building although the exterior walls or roof are not first damaged by a covered Cause of Loss allowing these elements to enter into the interior: but, if MCP 515 is listed in the Declarations, this Extension is deleted.

C. Loss by such elements to personal property within a building.

This Supplemental Coverage applies only to property covered by Cause of Loss Option 5.

This Supplemental Coverage does not provide an additional amount of insurance.

PART I C • CAUSE OF LOSS OPTIONS

GENERAL CAUSE OF LOSS CONDITIONS – COVERAGES A, B, C

A. Subject to all applicable provisions in this policy, property covered under this policy is insured for that coverage option (see descriptions) which is designated in the Declarations as applicable to the specific item. Accordingly, the same sort of property – buildings, for example – can be insured for differing causes of loss based upon the option selected to apply to the specific item.

B. The various described causes of loss cover fortuitous direct physical loss not otherwise excluded or limited. *Loss covered loss* – means: **fortuitous direct physical damage to or destruction of covered property by a covered cause of loss, and if covered under Cause of Loss Option 5 the term "damage" includes the taking of the subject covered property by theft (including damage arising in the course of such theft).** Covered cause of loss means a cause of loss contemplated by the following coverage options to the extent that such are described as applicable to the subject covered property.

Direct physical loss does not include or mean any sort of consequent loss, loss of use, or loss of utility. But such loss may otherwise be specifically provided for in this policy: for example, see Coverage D or Supplemental Coverage 6

C. CAUSES OF LOSS COVERAGE OPTIONS

The following are subject to all applicable Exclusions and Limitations described in this policy:

1. OPTION 1 – FIRE COVERAGE

Option 1 includes the following:
- **Fire** (hostile fire)
- **Explosion**
- **Lightning**

2. OPTION 2 – BASIC COVERAGE

Option 2 includes the following:
- **Fire** (hostile fire)
- **Aircraft***
- **Explosion**
- **Lightning**
- **Riot or Civil Commotion***
- **Sinkhole Collapse***
- **Smoke***
- **Vandalism***
- **Vehicles***
- **Volcanic Eruption***
- **Windstorm / Hail**
- *   **See following cause of loss descriptions.**

3. OPTION 3 – BROAD COVERAGE

Option 3 includes the following:
- **Fire** (hostile fire)
- **Aircraft***
- **Explosion**
- **Falling Objects***
- **Glass Breakage***
- **Lightning**
- **Riot or Civil Commotion***
- **Sinkhole Collapse***
- **Smoke***
- **Vandalism***

- **Vehicles***
- **Volcanic Eruption***
- **Water Damage***
- **Weight of Ice, Sleet, or Snow**
- **Windstorm / Hail**
- *** See following cause of loss descriptions.**

4. **OPTION 4 – SPRINKLER LEAKAGE COVERAGE**
Option 4 adds **Sprinkler Leakage** to Options 1, 2, or 3.

5. **OPTION 5 – EXPANDED COVERAGE**
Option 5 includes Options 3 and 4, plus other fortuitous direct physical loss to or theft of covered property not otherwise excluded or limited in this policy. The losses and costs excluded in the following descriptions of the listed causes of loss in the following paragraphs with regard to Falling Objects and Sinkhole Collapse also apply to Option 5.

6. **OPTION 6 – EARTHQUAKE**
Option 6 is **Earthquake:** Option 6 is described in Endorsement MCP 119.

7. **EXCLUSION OPTION A – THEFT**
When Exclusion Option A is designated as applicable with Option 5, the covered causes of loss do not include theft (theft also includes burglary / robbery).

8. **EXCLUSION OPTION B – VANDALISM**
When Exclusion Option B is designated as applicable along with any other option (for example, Option 2 B), the covered causes of loss do not include vandalism.

9. **EXCLUSION OPTION C – WATER DAMAGE**
When Exclusion Option C is designated as applicable along with any other option (for example, Option 3 C), the covered causes of loss do not include water damage – other than that caused by covered freezing of an appliance or system.

10. **EXCLUSION OPTION D – WINDSTORM / HAIL**
When Exclusion Option D is designated as applicable along with any other option (for example, Option 5 D), the covered causes of loss do not include windstorm / hail.

11. **DESCRIPTION OF LISTED CAUSES OF LOSS**
The following definitions apply to and limit the scope of the listed causes of loss:

a. **Aircraft:** This means direct physical contact of aircraft with covered property. Aircraft includes objects that fall from aircraft, spacecraft, or self-propelled missiles.

b. **Falling Objects:** This means damage to other property caused by the falling object.
This does not include:
1. Loss to personal property outdoors (not in buildings).
2. Loss to the interior of a building, or any property within a building, unless the falling object first penetrates the roof or exterior walls of the building.

c. **Glass Breakage:** This means damage to other property caused by breakage of glass that is part of buildings.

d. **Riot or Civil Commotion:** This includes, but is not limited to:
1. Acts of striking employees while occupying the described premises;
2. Looting occurring at the time and place of riot or civil commotion.

e. **Sinkhole Collapse:** This means abrupt collapsing or sinking of land causing loss to covered property: such collapsing or sinking must be into an underground empty space created by the action of water on limestone or similar rock.
This does not include: the cost of filling sinkholes; collapsing or sinking into man-made cavities.

f. **Smoke:** This means smoke causing abrupt accidental direct physical loss.

g. **Sprinkler Leakage:** This means accidental discharge or leakage from an *automatic sprinkler system* and the collapsing of a tank that is part of such system.

h. **Vandalism:** This means willful malicious damage to property, and includes such damage done to a building by burglars while breaking into or out of such building.
This does not include: breakage of building glass; loss by theft.

i. **Vehicles:** This means direct physical contact of a vehicle, or an object thrown up by a vehicle, with covered property.
This does not include: loss caused by vehicles *you* own or which are operated in the course of *your* business.

j. **Volcanic Eruption:** This means only:
1. Airborne blast or shock waves;
2. Ash, dust, or particulate matter other than that which can be swept or washed away without leaving physical damage; and
3. Lava flow;
caused by eruption of a volcano: but see Part I, Common Exclusion 1.

All volcanic eruptions that take place within a continuous 168 hour period are considered a single occurrence and constitute a single loss.

k. **Water Damage:** This means abrupt accidental discharge of water as a direct result of the breaking or cracking of any part of an appliance, equipment, or system containing water: but see Sprinkler Leakage for an *automatic sprinkler system*. Water includes steam and, as to Cause of Loss Option 5, includes such discharge of other liquids or materials.

– 11 –

NOTE: The term "abrupt" refers to an event instantaneous in time – not gradual, ongoing, or repeated over time.

D. *SPECIFIED CAUSES OF LOSS*

Where the term *specified causes of loss* is used, the term means the following: fire; aircraft; explosion; falling objects; lightning; riot or civil commotion; sinkhole collapse; smoke; sprinkler leakage; vandalism; vehicles; volcanic eruption; water damage; weight of ice, sleet, or snow; windstorm / hail. However, these apply only to the extent that the subject property is otherwise insured for such causes of loss.

E. *COVERED LOSS*

1. **Coverages A, B, C**

   Covered loss is described in Part I C, General Cause of Loss Condition B.

2. **Coverage D**

   Relevant to the context in which it is used:

   a. *Direct covered loss* means: fortuitous direct physical loss as described in Part I C, General Cause of Loss Condition B which occurs at described premises occupied by *you* (occupancy is not a condition for Rental Income loss), which directly results in the subject covered Business Income Loss / Extra Expense.

   b. *Covered loss* means: the subject covered Business Income loss / Extra Expense which results as a direct consequence of such described *direct covered loss*.

PART I D • PROPERTY EXCLUSIONS / LIMITATIONS

We do not cover the following property or loss except to the extent otherwise specifically provided for in this policy.

1. **ALL PROPERTY COVERAGES**

   A. Building Glass: but see Supplemental Coverage 3. A.

   B. Crops of any sort, whether growing, harvested, or in any way held.

   C. Land, including land on which covered property is located. Water.

   D. Property not described in this policy.

   E. Property that is more specifically described and insured under another coverage form in this policy or by any other insurance: but as to Coverage A, this insurance applies excess.

   F. Outdoor property, as follows (but see Supplemental Coverage 13):

   1. Antennas and satellite dishes, including their lead-in wiring, masts, and towers.

   2. Fences.

   3. Lawns.

   4. Plants, shrubs, or trees.

   G. Signs (outdoor signs): but see Supplemental Coverage 3.B.

   H. Vehicles, as follows: aircraft, motorized land vehicles, self-propelled machines, or watercraft – including their accessories, equipment, motor, parts, tires, or trailers. This also includes: devices designed to be powered through their electrical systems, radar detectors, recorded discs and tapes in such vehicles for use in the vehicle.

   But see Supplemental Coverage 14.E.

2. **COVERAGE A**

   A. Cost of backfilling or filling, excavations or grading.

   B. Docks, piers, pilings, or wharves.

   C. Foundations of buildings, boilers, or machinery that are below the lowest basement floor or, if no basement, below ground level.

   D. Paved surfaces of any sort, including – but not limited to – bridges, driveways, parking lots, patios, roads, or walks.

   E. Retaining walls that are not part of described buildings.

   F. Underground drains, flues, or pipes.

3. **COVERAGES B AND C**

   A. Creatures of any sort: but see Supplemental Coverage 14.A.

   B. *Money.* Gold, silver, and other precious alloys or metals other than as provided for in the following Paragraph 4: but also see Supplemental Coverage 16.

   C. Electronic Data. But see Supplemental Coverage 8

   D. Property while airborne or waterborne.

   E. *Securities.*

   F. *Valuable papers and records* as well as the cost to replace, research, or restore the information on *valuable papers and records:* but see Supplemental Coverage 14.D.

4. **COVERAGES B AND C (CAUSE OF LOSS OPTION 5)** Loss by theft to the following property is covered only up to the applicable limits shown in the Supplemental Declarations (these limits are aggregate limits for all described property per occurrence).

   A. Furs (this also includes both fur and fur trimmed garments).

   B. Jewelry-type property meaning: (1) jewels, jewelry, pearls, precious and semi-precious stones, watches and watch movements; (2) gold, silver, platinum and other precious alloys or metals used to make jewelry.

   This does not apply to items of jewelry-type property worth, at *your* regular retail price, less than the applicable limit per item shown in the Supplemental Declarations.

PART I E • PROPERTY LOSS LIMITATIONS

We do not provide insurance under Part I for any sort of damage or loss directly or indirectly, wholly or partially, aggravated by, consisting of, or resulting from the following – even if loss otherwise covered contributes to such concurrently or in any sequence. The following exclusions and limitations of loss in connection with certain property apply to the extent that the subject loss and property are otherwise covered under this policy.

1. **BUILDERS / BUILDING ITEMS**
   A. **Builders' Equipment**
      Loss to builders' equipment, machinery, or tools either owned by *you* or in *your* care, custody, or control while away from the described premises.

   B. **Building Property**
      Loss by theft of building materials or supplies – unless attached to and forming an integral part of the building under alteration, construction, or repair at the time of loss, other than such property held for sale by *you*.

2. **DISAPPEARANCE OF PROPERTY**
   Loss, otherwise covered by this policy, in connection with covered property that is missing where there exists no physical evidence to show what happened to the property. Loss discovered or inferred upon taking inventory. Acts of appropriation, pilferage or shoplifting.

3. **FRAGILE ITEMS**
   Breakage of any sort of fragile items (including, but not limited to, chinaware, glassware, marbles, porcelains, or statuary). This does not apply to: loss caused by a *specified cause of loss;* building glass; containers of property held for sale by *you;* lenses of photographic or scientific instruments.

4. **HOT WATER / STEAM EQUIPMENT**
   A. **Hot Water Boilers**
      Loss to hot water boilers or other water heating equipment by any condition or event inside such boilers or equipment.

   B. **Steam Equipment**
      Loss to steam boilers, engines, pipes, or turbines by any condition or event inside such equipment.

      But see Supplemental Coverage 17.

5. **UNAUTHORIZED / VOLUNTARY TRANSFER OF PROPERTY**
   A. **Unauthorized Transfer**
      Loss in connection with property that is given or transferred to any persons or transferred to any place (not the described premises) on the basis of false / unauthorized instructions – however such are given or transmitted.

   B. **Voluntary Transfer**
      Loss in connection with property that *you* (or others to whom *you* have entrusted the property) voluntarily give or transfer to anyone on the basis of being induced to do so by false pretense or fraudulent device, scheme, or trick.

PART I F • LOSSES NOT INSURED

We do not provide insurance under Part I for any sort of loss directly or indirectly, wholly or partially, aggravated by, consisting of, or resulting from the following – even if loss otherwise covered contributes to such concurrently or in any sequence.

1. ***COMPUTER HACKING* AND *COMPUTER VIRUS* EXCLUSION**
   Computer hacking or *computer viruses.*

2. **DELAY OR LOSS OF MARKET / LOSS OF USE EXCLUSIONS**
   Delay or loss of market or sale. Loss of occupancy. Because property cannot be occupied or used. Consequent loss. But see Coverage D and Supplemental Coverage 6 for certain described coverage.

3. **DISHONESTY EXCLUSION**
   Criminal or dishonest acts by *you,* by any of *your* employees, officers, partners, representatives, trustees, volunteer workers, or by any other person to whom *you* entrust property.

   This applies whether any such persons act alone or in collusion with others or such acts take place within or outside of working hours.

   This Exclusion does not pertain to acts of physical damage by *your* employees.

4. **ELECTRICAL DAMAGE EXCLUSION**
   Loss, however caused, by artificially generated electrical currents to electrical or electronic appliances, devices or wiring.

   If loss resulting from fire ensues, *we* insure such resulting loss.

5. **EXPLOSION OF STEAM EQUIPMENT EXCLUSION**
   Explosion of steam boilers, engines, pipes, or turbines which are leased to *you,* owned by *you,* or operated under *your* control: but see Supplemental Coverage 17.

   If loss resulting from fire or combustion explosion ensues, *we* insure such resulting loss.

6. **FLOOD / FLOODING EXCLUSION**
   Flood, flooding, surface water, waves, storm surge, tidal water or tidal waves, overflow of streams or other bodies of water, or their spray, aggravated by or resulting from any natural or human made causes: all, whether or not caused by, or a consequence of, rain, snow, wind or other condition of the weather, or an otherwise covered cause of loss.

MCP 010 06 12

If loss resulting from fire, explosion, or theft (to the extent insured by this policy) ensues, *we* insure such resulting loss.

7. FREEZING OF APPLIANCES OR OTHER EQUIPMENT EXCLUSION

Leakage or overflow of any liquids or any other materials from air conditioning, heating, plumbing, or other appliances or equipment (other than fire protection systems), or damage to such appliances or equipment, caused by freezing.

If *you* (and others *you* designate to care for the premises) exercise ongoing care to maintain adequate heat in the building, or such appliances or equipment are drained and kept dry, this exclusion is waived to the extent that such loss is otherwise insured by this policy.

8. INTENTIONAL LOSS EXCLUSION

Acts committed by, or at the direction of, any *insured* with the intent to cause a loss.

9. LAW OR ORDINANCE / GOVERNMENTAL DIRECTIVE EXCLUSIONS

Enforcement of any code, law, ordinance, or regulation, including those pertaining to construction, repair, or use of property or demolition of property (including debris removal). Any governmental directive. But see Supplemental Coverage 4.

10. POWER, HEATING, OR COOLING FAILURE EXCLUSION

Power, heating, or cooling failure or loss of utility services that takes place off the described premises. If loss by a covered cause of loss ensues, *we* insure such resulting loss.

But see Supplemental Coverage 6.

11. WATER DAMAGE EXCLUSION

A. Underground, surface or subsurface water that exerts pressure on or flows, seeps or leaks through: basements; doors, windows, or other openings; driveways, floors; foundations; paved surfaces; sidewalks; swimming pools; walls. See also mudflow or mudslide under Exclusion 12.E.

B. Water or sewage that backs up through sewers or drains or overflows from a sump; or the discharge of sewers or water mains originating off the described premises. If MCP 507 is listed in the Declarations, this Paragraph (B) is deleted with regard to water or sewage that backs up through sewers or drains or overflows from a sump originating on the described premises.

If loss resulting from fire, explosion, or sprinkler leakage (to the extent insured by this policy) ensues, *we* insure such resulting loss.

12. WEAR, TEAR, AND OTHER SPECIFIED LOSS / CAUSE OF LOSS EXCLUSIONS

A. Wear and tear; birds, domestic animals, insects, raccoons, rodents, or vermin; contamination or pollution including, but not limited to: (1) the discharge, dispersal, emission, escape, migration, release, or seepage of *pollutants*; (2) the costs associated with enforcement of any governmental directive, law or ordinance which requires *you* or any others to cleanup, contain, detoxify, monitor,

neutralize, remove, test for, or in any way respond to *pollutants*, asbestos, *fungi*, mold or lead contamination or assess the effects of *pollutants*, asbestos, *fungi*, mold or lead contamination: but see Supplemental Coverage 15 for certain coverage; corrosion; decay or deterioration; deficiency, error, or omission in design, materials, plans, or workmanship; disease; dry or wet rot; *fungi*, mold, spores, mildew, bacterium, or other natural growth; inherent vice (a customary characteristic of the property); latent defect (an original condition or fault leading to loss); mechanical breakdown; rust.

B. Buckling, bulging, contracting, cracking, expansion, settling, shrinkage, or sinking.

C. Contamination by any virus or other pathological agent that causes disease or illness in humans, animals, birds, or other creatures, or the costs associated with enforcement of any governmental directive, law or ordinance which requires *you* or any others to clean up, contain, detoxify, monitor, neutralize, remove, test for, or in any way respond to any virus or other pathological agent.

D. Continuous or repeated leakage or seepage from any part of an appliance or system which contains water or other liquids resulting from a condition which *you* fail to repair.

E. Earth / ground / land movement on or below the surface of the earth aggravated by or resulting from any natural or human made causes including, but not limited to: earth / ground / land collapsing (other than sinkhole collapse), pressure, rising, shifting, sinking, sliding, or subsidence; landslide; mine subsidence; mudflow; mudslide; rockslides or rock falls. See also Part I, Common Exclusion 1 as to catastrophic earth movement.

F. Marring or scratching: but these apply solely to personal property.

G. Smog, smoke, or vapor from agricultural or industrial activities.

If loss by a covered *specified cause of loss* ensues *we* insure such resulting loss.

13. WEATHER / RELATED EXCLUSIONS

A. Cause of Loss Options 2 and 3

1. As to Windstorm / Hail: cold or frost; ice (other than hail), sleet or snow, whether or not wind driven.

2. Weight of hail, ice, sleet or snow: but these apply only to personal property while outdoors at the time of loss.

B. Cause of Loss Options 2, 3, and 5

1. Building Interior

Loss by dust, hail, ice, rain, sand, sleet, or snow, whether or not wind driven, to: (a) the interior of a building; or (b) property within a building: but see Supplemental Coverage 19. But, if the building first sustains loss by any covered cause of loss to the exterior roof or walls, which then allows these elements to enter the building, *we* insure the resulting loss by such elements.

2. Downspouts or Gutters
Loss by weight of hail, ice, sleet, or snow to downspouts or gutters.

C. Cause of Loss Option 5
1. Drought.

2. Freezing, hail, ice, rain, sleet, or snow: but these only apply to personal property while outdoors at the time of loss;

3. Changes or extremes of temperature or dampness or dryness of the atmosphere: but these only apply to personal property; and

4. Any other weather conditions: but this only applies if weather conditions contribute with a cause, condition, or event, otherwise excluded by this policy, to produce the loss.

If loss otherwise covered by this policy ensues, *we* insure such resulting loss.

PART I G • SPECIAL PART I CONDITIONS

1. DUTIES WHEN LOSS / DANGER OF LOSS OCCURS
You, other *insureds*, and other coverage beneficiaries must do all of the following things:

A. Report the Loss
Give immediate written notice to *us* of any loss. Also, immediately notify the police in case of theft, vandalism, or other violation of law. As soon as possible, give *us* a description of how, when, and where the loss occurred.

B. Protect Property
Protect property if in imminent danger from a covered cause of loss or, if loss has occurred, from further loss. For example, by taking exposed property indoors, by covering openings or windows, or by making temporary repairs. *We* cover the reasonable necessary expenses that *you* incur for such immediate temporary repairs or safeguards.

However, it is *your* ongoing obligation, at *your* expense, to – as soon as feasible after *you, your* employees, or those *you* authorize to act on *your* behalf become aware of any condition under *your* control which could lead to loss while this policy is in force – undertake all reasonable construction, maintenance, or repair necessary to protect property from such *covered loss.* Listing of all such conditions is not feasible, but examples include: if a roof is leaking, to repair such; if a flooring support is collapsing / deteriorating, to repair such; if new supports or retaining walls become required, to construct such.

Any additional or subsequent loss resulting from *your* neglect of these duties is not covered under this policy, and *you* must either rely on other insurance or absorb such loss *yourself.*

C. Cooperation on the Loss
As often as *we* may reasonably request / require:
1. Immediately exhibit all that remains of the damaged and undamaged property, and allow *us* to take samples of such property for examination and inspection.

2. Produce for examination and copying: the inventory described in the following Paragraph D; all relevant accounting procedures, affidavits, books of account, bills, contracts, deeds, documents, evidence, financial records, invoices, liens, leases, receipts, records, tax returns, vouchers, or other sources of information, or facsimiles acceptable to *us.*

3. Submit to examination and provide statements under oath and sign and swear to such. If more than one person is examined, *we* reserve the right to make such examination of each person out of the presence of the others. *We* also reserve the right to video record any examinations.

4. Otherwise cooperate with *us* in the investigation / settlement of the claim.

D. Inventory
At *our* request, prepare and sign an inventory of all damaged and undamaged property, showing in detail: age; description; quantity; *actual cash value* and, if so covered, replacement cost; source; amount of loss claimed. To the extent possible, set the damaged property aside and put such in best possible order for *our* examination.

E. Statement of Loss / Proof of Loss
Submit to *us* a statement about the loss that includes all information reasonably required by *us* (including, but not limited to, that described in the preceding Paragraphs C.2 and D) to determine: coverage; *our* liability for the loss and the amount and scope of loss; specifications of any damaged buildings. The statement is also to include detailed repair estimates.

And if required: submit to *us* within 60 days after *our* request a signed, sworn proof of loss. This is to include the information described in the preceding paragraphs and any other information reasonably required by *us,* including all knowledge available to *you,* and others about:
1. The time and cause of loss.

2. *Your* interest and that of all others in the property involved (including a description of all encumbrances on such property).

3. All other insurance policies which may apply to the loss.

4. Any changes in occupancy, title, or use of the property during the policy term.

Failure to comply with these (or other Conditions) can alter or void *our* obligations under this policy.

MCP 010 06 12

2. HOW LOSSES ARE SETTLED

A. Limit of Liability per Loss Occurrence – Coverages A, B, C

Our **maximum liability is that amount which is the least one of all the following:**

1. The *actual cash value* or the replacement value (if MCP 520 is listed in the Declarations – see Condition 2.C.2) of the damaged portions of subject property at the time of loss. But, in no event, exceeding the lesser of Paragraph a or Paragraph b:

   a. The lesser cost reasonably required, with diligence and ongoing effort, to:

      1. Repair or restore the damaged property with like materials of comparable quality used for the same purpose / same occupancy, bringing such to the same general condition as existed immediately prior to the loss; or,

      2. Replace the damaged property, at the same described premises, with like property of comparable quality used for the same purpose / same occupancy;

   b. The necessary reasonable expense paid to repair, replace, or restore the damaged property.

2. Any factors, limits, special limits, or other recovery limitations described or specified in this policy as applicable to the subject loss and property, whether shown in the Declarations, any endorsements, or elsewhere in this policy.

   The inclusion of any sort of recovery limitations or special limits or the inclusion of more than one item within any provision in this policy do not increase or otherwise modify any of the general limits shown in this policy – unless specifically stated to be additional insurance.

3. The insurable interest of the *insured* (or other named interests) at the time of loss.

And, in all cases subject to the following special conditions:

4. **Glass**

   Loss to glass is settled on the basis of the cost of replacement with safety glazing material when such replacement is required by law or ordinance.

   Loss to glass is subject to the applicable limits shown in the Supplemental Declarations; the "per item" limit applies to each individual pane or panel or similar item.

5. *Money* (If covered under this policy)

   At face value: if foreign money, at its exchange rate (in dollars) on the date that the loss is reported to *us* by *you*.

6. *Securities* (If covered under this policy)

   At their value at the close of business on the date that the loss is reported to *us* by *you*.

7. *Stock*

   Loss to *stock* that *you* have sold but not delivered at the selling price, less discounts and expenses that *you* would otherwise have.

8. **Tenant's Improvements and Betterments**

   a. If *you* make repairs as soon as feasible, loss is settled as described in the preceding paragraphs.

   b. If *you* do not make repairs as soon as feasible, *our* obligation is limited to a proportion of *your* original cost for the improvements, determined as follows:

      1. Divide the number of days from the date of loss to the expiration date of the lease by the number of days from the date of installation (of the improvement) to the expiration date of the lease, then

      2. Multiply the original cost by the figure resulting from this division.

      Note: If *your* lease contains a renewal option, *we* use the expiration date of the renewal option in lieu of the expiration date of the current lease.

9. *Valuable Papers and Records*

   Loss to *valuable papers and records* (other than prepackaged software programs) not subject to Supplemental Coverage 14.D is settled on the basis of the cost of blank materials for reproducing such records plus the cost of labor to copy such records when duplicates of such exist.

B. Limit of Liability per Loss Occurrence – Coverage D

Our **maximum liability is determined based on consideration of all the following:**

1. **Coverage D.1 – Business Income**

   a. The net income / rental income of the business / operations before the date the *direct covered loss* occurred.

   b. The likely net income / rental income of the business / operations had the *direct covered loss* not occurred.

   c. The operating expenses, including payroll expenses, necessary to resume *your* normal business / operations at the same capability and quality of service as existed immediately prior to the date the *direct covered loss* occurred.

   d. Any other relevant sources of information, including all information described under Part I G, Condition 1 – "Duties."

   e. Any liability *we* otherwise have, as determined in the preceding Paragraphs, is reduced to the extent that *you* can resume *your* normal business / operations, in whole or in part, including by using any property (including damaged property) at the described premises or elsewhere: See Part I A, Coverage D, Condition D.2.

2. **Coverage D. 2 – Extra Expense**

  a. All expenses that exceed the normal operating expenses that *you* would otherwise incur in *your* business / operations during the coverage period of indemnity had the *direct covered loss* not occurred.

  b. All necessary expenses that reduce the Business Income loss that would otherwise be incurred: but this applies only if Coverage D.1 applies under this policy.

  c. Any liability *we* otherwise have for Extra Expense, as determined in the preceding Paragraph 2.a. is reduced by the following:

    1. The remaining salvage value of any property bought for temporary use during the coverage period of indemnity once *your* business / operations are resumed.

    2. Any Extra Expense that is paid for by other insurance that is not subject to the same provisions that apply under this policy.

    3. To the extent that *you* can resume normal business / operations.

3. **Coverage D.1 and D.2**

  Conditions 1 and 2 apply to each described premises at which *direct covered loss* occurs, and *our* maximum liability for such loss does not exceed the limits or other recovery limitations otherwise shown in this policy applicable to the subject *covered loss*.

C. **Bases of Loss Settlement – Coverages A, B, C**

1. ***Actual Cash Value* Basis**

  Loss settlement under Coverages A, B, and C is on an *actual cash value* basis.

  However, if the cost to repair a damaged building is less than the replacement threshold limit specified in the Supplemental Declarations, then loss settlement is on a replacement basis (pursuant to the provisions of the following Condition C.2) other than loss to the following property: awnings; cooking, dishwashing, laundering, refrigerating, or ventilating appliances; fire extinguishers; floor coverings; lawn care and snow removal equipment; outdoor fixtures / furniture.

2. **Replacement Cost Coverage Option – Coverages A / B**

  a. If MCP 520 is listed in the Declarations (or the replacement cost option is otherwise designated as applicable in this policy) then the expense of replacement applies in lieu of *actual cash value* as the basis for loss settlement on those buildings and that personal property designated in this policy as subject to this Option. However, in any case, loss to the following property remains on an *actual cash value* basis:

    1. Manuscripts.

    2. Property of others.

3. *Stock* – Unless MCP 521 is listed in the Declarations.

4. Works of art, antiques, or rare articles, including – but not limited to – bronzes, bric-a-brac, etchings, marble, pictures, porcelains.

  b. *We* are not liable for payment on a replacement basis until *you* complete repair, replacement, or restoration of the subject property.

  You may submit a claim on an *actual cash value* basis and then, no later than 180 days following settlement on an *actual cash value* basis (or *our* offer of such if *you* decline settlement), make further claim in writing on repair, replacement, or restoration which *you* have completed at the time *you* make such claim.

3. Unless MCP 522 is listed in the Declarations as applicable to the subject property, *you* must make repair, replacement, or restoration at the same described premises. But see Supplemental Coverage 4, if such is prohibited by law or ordinance.

D. **Appraisal**

1. If *you* and *we* do not agree on the amount of the loss or values or on the amount of Business Income or operating expenses, either one can require that the items in dispute be set by appraisal. Within 30 days of receipt of a written demand for appraisal, each is to select a competent and disinterested appraiser. Each party is to then notify the other of the appraiser selected.

2. The two appraisers are to select a competent and disinterested umpire. If the appraisers are unable to agree upon an umpire within fifteen days, *you* or *we* may petition a judge of a Court of Record to select an umpire.

3. The appraisers are to reach a mutual agreement on the items in dispute. If the appraisers fail to agree within a reasonable time, they are to submit their differences to the umpire. Written agreement signed by any two of these three persons constitutes settlement on the items in dispute.

4. Each appraiser is paid by the party selecting the appraiser. All other expenses of the appraisal are paid equally by *you* and *us*.

5. If *we* agree to appraisal, *we* specifically retain *our* right to deny the claim.

E. **Coinsurance Requirements – Coverages A, B, C**
  When the Declarations show a Coinsurance factor, the following Conditions apply:

1. **Full Liability**

  We pay the full amount of *our* obligation on the loss, as otherwise determined and limited in this policy, if the product of "a" times "b" is an amount equal to or less than the applicable limit for the property shown in the Declarations, where:

a. "**a**" is 100% of the applicable value of the property at the time of loss (if two or more items are covered by one limit, use the sum of their separate values).

b. "**b**" is the applicable Coinsurance factor specified in this policy.

But if this figure exceeds the applicable limit, *our* maximum obligation on the loss is reduced, as determined in Condition E.2. (But see the following Special Condition).

2. Reduced Liability

If the figure in the preceding Paragraph E.1 (that is, "a" x "b") exceeds the applicable limit for the property, *our* obligation, subject to all other provisions, is as follows:

a. Divide the applicable limit by the figure determined in Paragraph E.1; then

b. Multiply the amount of loss (less deductible) by the figure determined in Paragraph E.2.a: *Our* maximum obligation is this reduced amount (the product of [b]).

F. Coinsurance Requirements – Coverage D.1
When the Declarations show a Coinsurance factor, the following Conditions apply:
1. Full Liability

We pay the full amount of *our* obligation on the loss, as otherwise determined and limited in this policy, if the product of "a" times "b" is an amount equal to or less than the applicable limit for such loss shown in the Declarations, where:

a. "**a**" is the sum of the net income (net profit or loss prior to income tax) plus all operating expenses (including payroll).

b. "**b**" is the applicable Coinsurance factor specified in this policy.

But if this figure exceeds the applicable limit, *our* maximum obligation on the loss is reduced, as determined in Condition F. 2 (But see the following Special Condition).

The net income and operating expenses used are those that would have been earned (had the *direct covered loss* not occurred) by *your* business / operations at the described premises for the 12 months following the latest one of the following dates, as applicable to the policy: the inception date, if a new policy; the renewal date, if a renewal policy; the last applicable anniversary date, if a term policy.

2. Reduced Liability

If the figure in the preceding Paragraph F.1 (that is, "a" x "b") exceeds the applicable limit for the loss, *our* obligation, subject to all other provisions, is as follows:

a. Divide the applicable limit by the figure determined in Paragraph F.1; then

b. Multiply the amount of loss by the figure determined in Paragraph F.2.a: *Our* maximum obligation is this reduced amount (the product of [b]).

Special Condition – Waiver of Conditions E and F.

When the amount of *covered loss* is less than both: the Special Condition limit specified in the Supplemental Declarations and the product of the amount of insurance (applicable to the *covered loss)* times the Special Condition factor specified in the Supplemental Declarations – the Coinsurance Condition is waived on such loss.

G. Deductible – Coverages A, B, C

1. *We* are liable for *covered loss* in any occurrence only when the loss is in excess of the deductible amount shown in the Declarations, and then only on the amount of loss less the deductible amount.

2. However, if MCP 512 is listed in the Declarations as applicable to the subject property loss and if the loss is 5 (five) times or more the deductible amount, then: reduce the applicable deductible by 2% (.02) of the amount of loss up to a maximum reduction of 100% of such deductible amount. For example, if the loss is $20,000 and the deductible is $1,000 the net deductible is $600 (.02 x $20,000 = $400; $1,000 - $400 = $600).

H. Loss to a Portion of a Pair or Set of Articles – Coverages B / C

1. Loss to some portion of a pair or set of articles or to property consisting of two or more parts (when complete) is not considered a total loss unless: because of such loss, the remainder is of no use and repair or replacement is not feasible.

2. In case *we* agree to pay for total loss, *you* are required to give *us* the remainder of such property, at *our* request, prior to such payment.

I. *Our* Liability and Satisfaction of *Your* Loss

If the maximum liability payable by *us* on *covered loss,* as determined under this policy, does not fully satisfy *your* loss, then *you* must either seek insurance that may be provided by others for the difference or otherwise absorb the unsatisfied portion of the loss *yourself.*

J. *Our* Options in Settling Losses – Coverages A, B, C

1. *We* may pay for the loss in money.

2. *We* may repair or replace all or any part of the property as provided for in this policy, or take all or any part of such property at a mutually agreed, or appraised, value. *We* may give notice of *our* intent to do so at any time up to 30 days after *our* acceptance of *our* liability for the loss (i.e., proof of loss).

3. *We* may settle the claim with *you,* any loss payee named in this policy, or others legally entitled to receive payment. If the claim applies to property of others, *we* have the right to adjust the loss with the owners of the property: satisfaction of their claim is also satisfaction of *your* claim as to such property.

If legal action is taken in a claim against *you, we* have the right to conduct and control a defense at *our* expense (but without increasing *our* liability under this policy).

K.   Recovery of Covered Property

In the event *we* make a payment for loss and a subsequent recovery is made of any of the property, *you* may choose to keep the property *you* have recovered or receive the property that *we* have recovered. If *you* choose this option, *our* liability is reduced accordingly: payment is adjusted for the amount which *you* received for the loss to such property, and *you* must compensate *us* for the amount *we* previously paid.

If *you* do not choose this option, the recovered property becomes *our* property: if *you* have such property, *you* are required to give *us* those items *we* request.

L.   When Loss Becomes Payable / Payment to Others

1. Loss becomes payable 30 days after completion and acceptance by *us* of a written agreement between the parties, or after an award is filed with *us* as provided in this policy. *Our* payment does not reduce the amount of insurance provided under this policy.

2. With respect to any mortgagee or secured party named in this policy; governmental entity; or others with contractual, legal, or statutory rights in loss payable under this policy: *we* may make payment jointly to all interested parties at *our* option. But *we* need not pay any loss assignee, unless they receive a full assignment of the loss from *you.*

3. If an insurance trustee is named in this policy, *we* may negotiate the loss and make payment solely to such trustee – to the extent that the trustee represents those with an interest under this policy.

3.   OTHER SPECIAL PART I CONDITIONS

A.   Abandonment of Property

Abandonment of any property to *us* is prohibited.

B.   Increase in Hazard / Related Conditions

1. **Increased Hazards**

    a. This insurance is suspended while the hazards *we* initially undertook to insure are increased by means within *your* control or control of those *you* designate to act for *you:* loss, otherwise covered, is not insured during such suspension of this insurance. Lawful building alteration, construction, maintenance or repair, unless changing the use of premises, is not an increase in hazard.

    b. An increase in hazard at one described premises does not affect this insurance at another described premises when no increase in hazard exists at such other described premises.

    c. Increase in hazard includes changes which affect one or more of the following: use of the premises; the rates for this insurance; the acceptability of the hazard / risk to *us,* including breach of conditions which were the basis of *our*

acceptance of such; the underwriting conditions and changes in physical conditions required by *us* for such hazard / risk; ongoing continuous effectiveness and use of any protective safeguards, required by *us* for which we have given premium consideration; circumstances which would affect the scope of coverage, covered causes of loss, or amounts of insurance otherwise acceptable to *us* for such hazard / risk.

2. **Vacancy**

This insurance is suspended when a covered building becomes vacant beyond a period of 60 consecutive days. Vacant means not containing the contents customary to occupancy of the building. A building in the course of lawful alteration, construction, or repair is not considered vacant.

3. **Unoccupancy**

This insurance is suspended when a covered building becomes unoccupied beyond a period of 60 consecutive days.

This Condition does not apply to unoccupancy during that part of the year when it is *your* normal previous custom to close because of seasonal use.

C.   Mortgagee Agreement

Mortgagees named in this policy are covered for loss to the extent of their interest and in order of precedence of the mortgages. This Condition applies to those mortgagees (this term includes trustees) named in this policy who comply with the following Conditions.

Provided that the mortgagee will:

1. Without delay, notify *us* of any change in ownership or occupancy, foreclosure proceeding, or increased hazard known to the mortgagee.

2. Pay, on *our* demand, any required premium because the *insured* fails to do so.

3. Furnish proof of loss within 60 days after *our* request if the *insured* fails to do so.

4. Give *us* the mortgagee's rights of recovery against anyone liable for the loss. This does not impair the mortgagee's right to recover the full amount of the claim.

5. Permit *us,* after a loss, to satisfy the mortgage requirements and receive a full assignment of the mortgage and all collateral securities to the debt.

We agree to provide this insurance to protect the mortgagee's interest in covered property even if *we* deny *your* claim.

See elsewhere in this policy for Conditions relating to Cancellation by *us.*

D.   No Benefit to Bailee

This insurance does not apply to the benefit of any others having custody of covered property. Any assignment to such persons or organizations has no standing under this policy.

E. Special Factors, Limits, or Limitations

This Part includes references in certain provisions to factors, limits or special limits, and other limitations described or specified in this policy: these are shown in the Declarations and Supplemental Declarations (or other similar attachments) to this contract.

PART I H • GLOSSARY

The following words shown in italics are defined for the purposes of insurance under Part I to mean the following.

Actual Cash Value

Consideration may be given by *us* in *our* determination of *actual cash value* to: age; condition; cost to repair, replace, or restore the property, subject to deduction for depreciation; deterioration; economic value; market value; obsolescence (both structural and functional); original cost; use; utility; or other circumstances that may reasonably affect value.

Automatic Sprinkler System

Automatic sprinkler system means:

A. Any automatic fire protection or extinguishing system, including any of the following connected parts:

1. Ducts, fittings, pipes, or valves.

2. Pumps and private fire protection mains.

3. Sprinklers and other discharge nozzles.

4. Tanks, including their component parts and supports.

B. When supplied by an automatic fire protection or extinguishing system:

1. Hydrants, outlets, or stand pipes.

2. Non-automatic fire protection or extinguishing systems.

Collapse

Collapse means an abrupt falling down or caving in of a building or structural parts of a building.

Collapse does not include a building or part of a building that is:

1. In danger of falling down or caving in; or

2. Standing, even if it has separated from another part of the building.

Collapse does not include bulging, cracking, expanding, settling or shrinking.

Computer Hacking

Computer hacking means unauthorized intrusion into a computer network, hardware, software or website including entry of a computer worm or Trojan Horse, spyware or adware, that results in:

1. Alteration, contamination, corruption, degradation, destruction or modification of the integrity, quality or performance of computer media, data, prepackaged programs, hardware or software;

2. Copying, observation or scanning of data records, programs and applications and proprietary programs;

3. Corruption, damage, degradation, destruction, inadequacy or malfunction of any hardware or media used with hardware;

4. Deletion, destruction, generation or modification of software; or

5. Denial of access to or denial of service from *your* computer network, hardware or website.

Computer Virus

Computer virus means the introduction into hardware, software or a website of any malicious self-replicating electronic data processing code or other code that is intended to result in, but is not limited to:

1. Alteration, contamination, corruption, degradation, destruction or modification of the integrity, quality or performance of computer media, data, prepackaged programs, hardware or software;

2. Corruption, damage, degradation, destruction, inadequacy or malfunction of any hardware or media used with hardware;

3. Deletion, destruction, generation or modification of software; or

4. Denial of access to or denial of service from *your* computer network, hardware or website.

Covered Loss

Covered loss: See Part I C – Cause of Loss Options.

Direct Covered Loss

Direct covered loss: See Part I C – Cause of Loss Options.

Finished Stock

Finished stock means – stock manufactured by *you:* but does not include such stock that is held for sale on the premises of a covered retail outlet.

Fungi

Fungi means any type or form of fungus, mold, mildew spores, algae, smut, protists, rusts or *rot and decay organisms,* and any similar or related organisms and any mycotoxin, substance, compounds, chemicals, mist or vapor produced by any *fungi* in any form, or any byproducts or waste produced by *fungi,* but does not include any *fungi* intended to be edible.

Insured

Insured means the person or entity designated as *insured* in the Declarations or otherwise named as an *insured* in this policy.

Money / Securities

Money means bank notes, bearer bonds, bullion, coins, currency, lottery tickets, money orders, prepaid phone cards, registered checks, stored value cards, and travelers checks held for sale to the public.

Securities means negotiable and non-negotiable contracts or instruments that represent obligations to pay *money* or pay other property and that are collectible at the time of loss: examples of such include – but are not limited to – accounts, bills, deeds, evidence of debt, notes, revenue and other stamps, tickets (not *money),* or tokens now in use.

Pollutants

Pollutants are any gaseous, liquid, solid, or thermal contaminant or irritant, including acids, alkalis, chemicals, fumes, smoke, soot, vapors, and waste (including materials to be reclaimed, reconditioned, or recycled).

Rot and Decay Organisms

Rot and decay organisms means any living organism that causes decomposition of physical property.

Stock

Stock means: merchandise held in storage or for sale; in-process or finished goods; raw materials; supplies used in packing or shipping of such goods, merchandise, or materials.

Valuable Papers and Records

Valuable papers and records includes: abstracts, books of account, card index systems, drawings, manuscripts, microfilm, microfiche; as well as cell, disk, drum, film, tape, or other data processing, recording, or storage media.

We / Us / Our

We, us, and *our* refer to the Insurance Company named in this policy.

You / Your / Yourself

You, your and *yourself* refer to the *named insureds* who are the *insureds* named in the Declarations. *First named insured* is the *insured* named first in the Declarations.

PART I • COMMON CONDITIONS
These Common Conditions Apply in Addition to Part I G.

1. ACTION OR SUIT AGAINST *US*
The conditions for bringing an action or suit against *us* are described elsewhere in this policy in the state mandatory endorsement.

2. ASSIGNMENT OF YOUR INTEREST
No assignment of an interest in this policy is binding on *us* without *our* written consent. However, if *you* are an individual and die this insurance applies:

   A. To *your* legal representative, while acting within the scope of the representative's duties.

   B. To those with custody of *your* property prior to appointment of a legal representative.

3. CANCELLATION / TERMINATION
   A. General
   You may cancel this policy by: surrendering the policy to *us* or *our* agent or by mailing *us* or *our* agent notice stating a subsequent cancellation date for the policy. Such request made by the *first named insured* applies for all *insureds* / interests named under this policy. All cancellations are pro rata, but a minimum earned premium may apply. Any return premium is payable to the *first named insured* – within 30 days after the cancellation date.

   If *you* secure insurance with another insurer to replace *our* policy and do not pay the premium, or installment payment, for this policy when due: this policy terminates at the time such other insurance becomes effective. If *you* sell the described business or premises to others, coverage under this policy terminates at the time title is transferred to others with respect to such business or premises – unless *you* retain an insurable interest.

   B. *Our* Right to Cancel or Terminate
   Our rights to cancel or terminate this insurance are described elsewhere in this policy in the state mandatory endorsement.

4. CONCEALMENT / MISREPRESENTATION / FRAUD
This policy is void if, either before or after a loss, any *insured* misrepresents or knowingly conceals any material fact or circumstance, commits fraud, or swears falsely relating to any aspect of this insurance (including the information *we* relied upon in issuing this contract). However, if *we* specifically choose not to declare this policy void, *we* do not provide insurance under this policy to, or for the benefit of, any such *insureds.*

5. CONFORMITY WITH STATUTE
It is agreed by *us* that the provisions in this policy are amended to conform to all applicable statutory requirements.

6. COVERAGE TERRITORY
We cover damage or loss only within the fifty states of the United States of America (including its possessions and territories), the District of Columbia, Puerto Rico and Canada.

7. EXAMINATION / CHANGES
We may, at *our* option, inspect *your* property and operations at any time, make surveys, and make recommendations. However, *our* reports or recommendations or those of any inspection bureau or rating bureau do not constitute a determination or representation that any premises or operations are in compliance with law or regulation, healthful, or safe.

We may inspect and audit *your* books and records at any time (including up to 3 years after termination of this insurance contract) to the extent such pertains to the subject of this insurance or payment of premium. The *first named insured* is required to keep all records necessary for such and send complete accurate copies to *us* at *our* request.

We may make premium adjustments based on the findings of *our* inspection and audit, or because of the application of MCP 550 (See Part I, Common Condition 11).

8. INSURANCE UNDER MORE THAN ONE COVERAGE
In the event that more than one coverage under this policy covers the same loss, *we* are liable only for the amount of *our* obligation, up to *our* limit of liability, not exceeding the amount of loss.

9. LIBERALIZATION
This policy is automatically extended to include provisions approved during the policy period or within 45 days prior to its inception, which would broaden coverage under this policy, if such are not subject to additional premium or concurrent with coverage restrictions.

MCP 010 06 12

10. OTHER INSURANCE

A. This insurance is excess insurance over other insurance *you* may have applicable to the loss (whether *you* can collect on it or not) that is not subject to the same provisions contained in this policy.

B. When this insurance is excess over other insurance: *We* pay only *our* share of the remaining loss that exceeds the sum of both:

    1. The total amount payable by all such insurance, as described, in the absence of this insurance, plus

    2. The total of any deductibles or self-insured amounts under all such insurance.

Furthermore, any remaining loss is then shared by *us* with any other insurance remaining on the loss in accordance with the provisions described in the following Paragraph C.

C. With regard to other insurance subject to the same provisions contained in this policy or where *we* otherwise are a primary insurer (among others) *we* pay in one of the following ways:

    1. If all such other insurers provide for contributions by equal shares: *we* and all other insurers contribute equal amounts until the amount of obligation is paid or the insurer's applicable limit of liability is used up, whichever comes first.

    2. If any other insurer does not provide for equal shares: *we* pay no greater proportion of the total amount of loss than *our* obligation on the applicable limit of liability of this policy bears to the total amount of insurance of all insurers covering the loss.

However, if *you* have any other insurance applicable to property covered by this policy – but not covering a cause of loss covered under this policy, then: any loss payable under this policy in connection with such cause of loss is apportioned and payable by *us* in the same way as if such other insurance covered the loss.

11. PREMIUMS

The *first named insured* is responsible for the payment of all premiums, and will be the sole payee of any premiums *we* return.

MCP 550 – Provisional Rates and Premiums

If MCP 550 is listed in the Declarations, the rates for the subject items are interim provisional rates and the subject premiums are tentative premiums. When the final specific rates (based on rating inspection / investigation of the subject premises) are promulgated such rates are applicable from inception of the current policy term.

The applicable tentative premiums are then recalculated using the final rates, and either a return premium or additional premium is applicable for the current policy term.

12. RECOVERY FROM OTHERS

If any *insured* (or others) to whom, or for whom, *we* make payment has any rights of recovery on the loss from another, those rights are transferred to *us* to the extent of *our* payment under this policy. *Insureds* (or such others) must do whatever *we* require to secure these rights. *You* may waive such rights in writing prior to a *covered loss*. *You* may also waive such rights after a loss, but only if the waiver is given to either:

A. Another *insured* under this policy; or

B. A business either controlled or owned by *you* or that controls or runs *your* business.

But *we* have no obligation to pay under this policy on the loss if these rights are otherwise waived.

13. TIME OF INCEPTION AND COVERAGE PERIOD

The time of inception and expiration is 12:01 A.M. Standard Time at the described premises. Unless otherwise specifically provided for under this policy, this insurance applies only to *covered loss* that takes place during the policy term.

14. WAIVER OR CHANGE OF PROVISIONS

Only the *first named insured* may request changes in this policy. The terms in this policy may not be waived or changed except in writing, signed by our agent and attached to this policy. The exercise of our rights under this policy is not an act of waiver. This policy contains all related agreements between *you* and us.

NOTE: **Similar Common Conditions are included in Part II (if made part of this Contract).**

PART I • COMMON EXCLUSIONS

We **provide no insurance for any sort of damages, expenses, liability, or loss directly or indirectly, wholly or partially, aggravated by, consisting of, or resulting from the following – even if loss otherwise covered contributes to such concurrently or in any sequence.**

These Common Exclusions Apply in Addition to Parts I D, E, and F.

1. EARTH MOVEMENT / EARTHQUAKE / VOLCANIC ACTIVITY

Earthquake; volcanic activity (including volcanic effusion, eruption or explosion) other than that specifically described as included in volcanic eruption under Part I C, Cause of Loss Options; or other catastrophic earth movement. But if loss resulting from fire or explosion, or theft (to the extent otherwise insured by this policy) ensues, *we* insure such resulting loss.

2. GOVERNMENTAL / LEGAL / WAR

A. Any act or condition of: war (declared or not), civil war, invasion, insurrection, rebellion, revolution, or seizure of power, including acts done to defend against any such act or condition, whether actual or expected.

B. Knowing violation of penal law or ordinance committed by, or with the consent of, an *insured.* Statutory fines or liability. Exemplary or punitive damages.

C. Confiscation, loss, or seizure under customs, drug enforcement, or quarantine legislation or regulations. Loss to property that is contraband or in the course of illegal transportation or trade.

D. Damage or destruction of property ordered by civil authority, other than immediate acts of destruction ordered by authorized civil authorities for the purpose of preventing the spread of fire – provided the fire originates from a cause of loss covered in this policy.

3. NUCLEAR / RADIOACTIVE LOSS

A. Any nuclear event, occurrence, or operation, including nuclear explosion, nuclear reaction, nuclear radiation, or radioactive contamination. These are not fire, explosion, smoke or any other covered cause of loss. However, if these result in fire *we* insure such resulting direct fire loss, but not any other direct physical loss which may ensue.

B. The explosive, radioactive, toxic, or other injurious properties of nuclear or radioactive materials – whether such materials are natural or manufactured.

NOTE: Similar Common Exclusions are included in Part II (if made part of this Contract).

MCP 010 06 12

Index